business solutions

VBA and Macros
for
Microsoft® Excel

Bill Jelen, Mr. Excel

Tracy Syrstad

800 East 96th Street
Indianapolis, Indiana 46240

VBA and Macros for Microsoft Excel

International Standard Book Number: 0-7897-3129-0

Library of Congress Catalog Card Number: 2004102247

Printed in the United States of America

First Printing: April 2004
Reprinted with Corrections: October 2004

06   05   04   4   3

Trademarks

All terms mentioned in this book that are known to be trademarks or service marks have been appropriately capitalized. Sams Publishing cannot attest to the accuracy of this information. Use of a term in this book should not be regarded as affecting the validity of any trademark or service mark.

Warning and Disclaimer

Every effort has been made to make this book as complete and as accurate as possible, but no warranty or fitness is implied. The information provided is on an "as is" basis. The authors and the publisher shall have neither liability nor responsibility to any person or entity with respect to any loss or damages arising from the information contained in this book.

Bulk Sales

Sams Publishing offers excellent discounts on this book when ordered in quantity for bulk purchases or special sales. For more information, please contact

U.S. Corporate and Government Sales
1-800-382-3419
corpsales@pearsontechgroup.com

For sales outside of the U.S., please contact

International Sales
1-317-428-3341
international@pearsoned.com

Associate Publisher
Michael Stephens

Acquisitions Editor
Loretta Yates

Development Editor
Sean Dixon

Managing Editor
Charlotte Clapp

Project Editor
Andy Beaster

Copy Editor
Margo Catts

Indexer
Erika Millen

Proofreader
Kathy Bidwell

Technical Editor
Tom Urtis

Publishing Coordinator
Cindy Teeters

Book Designer
Anne Jones

Page Layout
Bronkella Publishing
Kelly Maish
Michelle Mitchell

Contents

I FIRST STEPS UP THE VBA LEARNING CURVE

II AUTOMATING EXCEL POWER IN VBA

About the Authors

Bill Jelen, "Mr. Excel," is an accomplished Excel author and the principal behind the leading Excel Web site, MrExcel.com. As an Excel consultant, he has written Excel VBA solutions for hundreds of clients around the English-speaking world. His Web site hosts more than 10 million page views annually. Prior to founding MrExcel.com, Jelen spent 12 years in the trenches—working as a financial analyst for finance, marketing, accounting, and operations departments of a $500 million public company. He lives near Akron, Ohio, with his wife Mary Ellen and sons Josh and Zeke.

Tracy Syrstad works as a programmer and consultant for the MrExcel Consulting team. She remembers the painful trek up the VBA learning curve while developing applications for co-workers at a former job. She is co-editor of *Holy Macro! It's 1,900 Excel VBA Examples* CD and editor of *Dreamboat On Word*. She lives on an arboreous acreage in eastern South Dakota with her husband John and dog General.

Dedications

Dedicated to Mary Ellen Jelen

—*Bill*

Dedicated to John Syrstad, whose confidence in me gave me strength to take this path

—*Tracy*

Acknowledgments

Thank you to Mala Singh of XLSoft Consulting for expertise with Chapter 10. Tom Urtis for technical editing. Jerry Kohl for many of the ideas in this book. Jeanette Garcia, Barb Jelen, and Doug and Stacy Jefferies for technical assistance. Zeke, Josh, and Mary Ellen Jelen for their patience. Tom Macioszek for peer review. Chad Rothschiller at Microsoft for teaching me everything there is to know about Excel XML. Dave Gainer, Steve Zaske, Eric Patterson, and Joe Chirilov at Microsoft. Loretta Yates, Sean Dixon, Margo Catts, Andy Beaster, Greg Wiegand, Amy Sorokas, Kim Spilker, Erika Millen, Kathy Bidwell, Cindy Teeters, Michelle Mitchell, and Gary Adair at Pearson. Ivana Taylor for her marketing brilliance. All the MrExcel.com readers and MVPs and clients. Dan Bricklin, Bob Frankston, and Mitch Kapor for being spreadsheet pioneers. William Brown at Waterside. Pam Gensel for macro lesson number 1. Robert F. Jelen for being my first programming fan. Robert K. Jelen for inspiration. Bonnie Hilliard for P.R. Laurelle Riippa at PW. Leo LaPorte and Fawn Luu at TechTV. Dan Poynter. Craig Crossman at Computer America. Walter Mossberg at the *Wall Street Journal*.

—Bill

Thank you to Cort Chilldon-Hoff for offering support and being a sounding board when I was stumped. Juan Pablo González Ruiz for offering his expertise, especially with the functions found in Chapter 4. Daniel Klann, Dennis Wallentin, Ivan F. Moala, Juan Pablo González, Masaru Kaji, Nathan P. Oliver, Richie Sills, Russell Hauf, Suat Mehmet Ozgur, Tom Urtis, Tommy Miles, Wei Jiang for their contributions to Chapter 13. Chris Lemair for introducing me to Excel and the power of its macros. Anne Troy who introduced Bill and I in the first place. The Computer America chat room for distracting me when I was supposed to be working on the book.

—Tracy

We Want to Hear from You!

As the reader of this book, *you* are our most important critic and commentator. We value your opinion and want to know what we're doing right, what we could do better, what areas you'd like to see us publish in, and any other words of wisdom you're willing to pass our way.

As an associate publisher for Sams, I welcome your comments. You can email or write me directly to let me know what you did or didn't like about this book—as well as what we can do to make our books better.

Please note that I cannot help you with technical problems related to the topic of this book. We do have a User Services group, however, where I will forward specific technical questions related to the book.

When you write, please be sure to include this book's title and author as well as your name, email address, and phone number. I will carefully review your comments and share them with the authors and editors who worked on the book.

Email: feedback@samspublishing.com

Mail: Michael Stephens
           Associate Publisher
           Sams Publishing
           800 East 96th Street
           Indianapolis, IN 46240 USA

For more information about this book or another Sams title, visit our Web site at www.samspublishing.com. Type the ISBN (0789731290) or the title of a book in the Search field to find the page you're looking for.

Introduction

Getting Results with VBA

As the macro language for Microsoft Excel, Visual Basic for Applications enables you to achieve tremendous efficiencies in your day-to-day use of Excel.

As corporate IT departments have found themselves with long backlogs of requests, Excel users have found that they can produce the reports needed to run their business themselves. This is both a good and bad thing. On the good side, without waiting for resources from IT, you've probably been able to figure out how to import data and produce reports in Excel. On the bad side, you are now stuck importing data and producing reports in Excel.

Case Study: Monthly Accounting Reports

This is a true story. Valerie is a business analyst in the accounting department of a medium-size corporation. Her company recently installed an over-budget $16 million ERP system. As the project ground to a close, there were no resources left in the IT budget to produce the monthly report that this corporation used to summarize each department.

Valerie, however, had been close enough to the implementation process to think of a way to produce the report herself. She understood that she could export General Ledger data from the ERP system to a text file with comma-separated values. Using Excel, Valerie was able to import the G/L data from the ERP system into Excel.

Creating the report was not easy. Like many companies, there were exceptions in the data. Valerie knew that certain accounts in one particular cost center needed to be reclassed as an expense. She knew that other accounts needed to be excluded from the report entirely. Working carefully in Excel, Valerie made these adjustments. She created one pivot table to produce the first summary section of the report. She cut the pivot table results and pasted them into a blank worksheet. Then she created a new pivot table report for the second section of the summary. After about three hours, she had imported the data, produced five pivot tables, arranged them in a summary, and had neatly formatted the report in color.

Becoming the Hero

Valerie handed this report to her manager. The manager had just heard from the IT department that it would be months before they could get around to producing "that convoluted report." Valerie walked in, handed the Excel report over, and became the instant hero of the day. In three hours, Valerie had managed to do the impossible. Valerie was on cloud nine after a well-deserved "atta-girl."

More Cheers

The next day, this manager attended the monthly department meeting. When the department managers started complaining that they couldn't get the report from the ERP system, this manager pulled out his department report and placed it on the table. The other managers were amazed. How was he able to produce this report? Everyone was greatly relieved to hear that someone had cracked the code. The company president asked Valerie's manager if he could have the report produced for each department.

The Cheers Turn to Dread

You can certainly see this coming. This particular company had 46 departments. That means 46 one-page summaries had to be produced once a month. Each required importing data from the ERP system, backing out certain accounts, producing five pivot tables, and then formatting in color. It had taken Valerie three hours to produce the first report. She found that after she got into the swing of things, she was able to produce the 46 reports in 40 hours. This is horrible. Valerie had a job to do before she won the responsibility of spending 40 hours a month producing these reports in Excel.

VBA to the Rescue

Valerie found my company, MrExcel Consulting, and explained her situation. In the course of about a week, I was able to produce a series of macros in Visual Basic that did all the mundane tasks. It imported the data. It backed out certain accounts. It did five pivot tables and applied the color formatting. From start to finish, the entire 40-hour manual process was reduced to two button clicks and about four minutes.

Right now, either you or someone in your company is probably stuck doing manual tasks in Excel that can be automated with VBA. I am confident that I can walk into any company with 20 or more Excel users and find a case as amazing as Valerie's.

What Is in This Book

You've taken the right step by purchasing this book. I can help you get up the learning curve so you can write your own VBA macros and put an end to the burden of generating reports manually.

Getting Up the Learning Curve

This introduction provides a brief history of spreadsheets. Chapter 1 introduces the tools and confirms what you probably already know: The macro recorder does not work. Chapter 2 helps you understand the crazy syntax of VBA. Chapter 3 breaks the code on how to efficiently work with ranges and cells.

By the time you get to Chapter 4, you will know enough to put to immediate use the 25 sample user-defined functions in that chapter.

Chapter 5 covers the power of looping using VBA. In Valerie's case study, after we wrote the program to produce the first department report, it took only another minute to wrap that report routine in a loop that produced all 46 reports.

Chapters 6 and 7 cover R1C1 style formulas and names. Chapter 8 has some great tricks that use event programming. Chapter 9 introduces custom dialog boxes that you can use to collect information from the human using Excel.

Excel VBA Power

Chapters 10–12 provide an in-depth look at charting, Advanced Filter, and pivot tables. Any report automation tool is going to rely heavily on these concepts.

Chapter 13 includes another 25 code samples designed to exhibit the power of Excel VBA.

Chapters 14–16 handle Web queries, XML, and automating another Office program such as Word.

The Techie Stuff Needed to Produce Applications for Others

Chapter 17 shows you how to use arrays to build fast applications. Chapters 18 and 19 handle reading and writing to text files and Access databases. The techniques for using Access databases enable you to build an application with the multi-user features of Access yet keep the friendly front-end of Excel.

Chapter 20 covers VBA from the point of view of a Visual Basic programmer. It teaches you about classes and collections. Chapter 21 discusses advanced userform topics. Chapter 22 teaches you some tricky ways to achieve tasks using the Windows Application Programming Interface. Chapters 23–25 deal with error handling, custom menus, and add-ins. Chapter 26 closes with a case study of a full-blown VBA application.

Will This Book Teach Excel?

At the Microsoft Office 2003 launch event, Microsoft revealed that they think the average Office user touches only 10% of the features in Office. I realize everyone reading this book is above average. I think that I have a pretty smart audience at MrExcel.com. A poll of 2000 MrExcel.com readers shows that only 42% of smarter-than-average users are using any one of the top 10 power features in Excel. I regularly do an Excel seminar for accountants. These are hard-core Excelers who use Excel 30–40 hours every week. Again, two things come out in every seminar. First, half the audience gasps when they see how quickly you can do tasks with a particular feature (such as automatic subtotals or pivot tables). Second, I am routinely trumped by someone in the audience. Someone will ask a question, I will answer, and someone in the second row will raise a hand and give a better answer. The point? You and I both really know a lot about Excel. However, I will assume that in any given chapter, maybe 58% of the people haven't used pivot tables before and maybe even less have used the "Top 10 Autoshow" feature of pivot tables. Before I show you how to automate something in VBA, I will briefly cover how to do the same task in the Excel interface. This book does not teach you how to do pivot tables, but it does alert you that you might want to go explore something and learn it elsewhere.

A Brief History of Spreadsheets and Macros

Up through 1978, any accountant could tell you that a spreadsheet comprised green ledger paper, a mechanical pencil, and an eraser. Daily sales were recorded in pencil and a running total was kept with an adding machine. If you discovered on the 30th of the month that the sales figure for the 5th of the month was wrong, you had a lot of erasing and recalculating to do.

Two guys changed everything in 1979. They produced what they called a "visual calculator" to run on the Apple II computer. Dan Bricklin and Bob Frankston's VisiCalc was the first spreadsheet program. It was eventually ported to several platforms, including the first IBM PC. In 1981, they released an extended version of VisiCalc for the Apple III that supported command-line macros. Legal wrangling hurt VisiCalc and the company was dead by 1985.

Bob Frankston and Dan Bricklin invented VisiCalc, the first spreadsheet, in 1979. Two years later, extended VisiCalc offered the first spreadsheet macros.

Mitch Kapor designed Lotus 1-2-3 in 1983. It ran in DOS, but it ran circles around VisiCalc. Sales in the first year were an astounding $53 million. Lotus 1-2-3 dominated the spreadsheet market throughout the 80s and early 90s. There were other minor players—Quattro, Multiplan, and others—but Lotus 1-2-3 was the de facto standard in accounting departments everywhere.

In 1985, Lotus release 2 offered an unprecedented 8,192 rows and 256 columns—more than 2 million cells. You could easily record simple macros. In 1990, I would have been 100% convinced that Lotus 1-2-3 would absolutely own the spreadsheet market for always and eternity.

However, in the early 90s, Lotus bet the farm by producing a version of Lotus for the CP/M operating system. At the same time, Microsoft was improving their spreadsheet product, now named Excel. Excel version 3.0 in 1990 wasn't as good as Lotus 1-2-3. But every 1–2 years, Microsoft improved. Excel 4 in 1992 started to become popular and offered a macro language called XLM. In 1993, Excel 5 introduced multiple worksheets in a workbook and offered the first support for VBA macros. Microsoft offered a Lotus 1-2-3 transition mode and their sales force began making serious inroads. The mid-90s were the glory years in Excel development. Excel 95 and Excel 97 were loaded with new features such as pivot tables, autofilter, and automatic subtotals. The new VBA development environment was introduced in Excel 97. Microsoft was brilliant in their ability to chip away at Lotus 1-2-3's dominance. They have put together a winning combination of Excel and VBA that sits on 400 million desktops around the world. Today, I am 100% convinced that Excel will absolutely own the spreadsheet market for always and eternity. Of course, I was wrong before.

The Future of VBA and Excel

Star Office is not as good as Excel, but with every release, they get closer. For someone who doesn't need every feature of Excel, Star Office is good enough. The problem, as I see it, is that Star Office does not offer VBA or any real macro language. To me, a spreadsheet without a macro language is useless and therefore Star Office is not a credible threat to Excel.

Perhaps you've heard the rumblings from inside Microsoft that someday VBA may go away. On one hand, this doesn't seem possible. Microsoft is still supporting XLM macros (the old Excel version 4 macro language) 11 years after VBA was introduced. Microsoft is on the record that VBA will be supported in Excel 2005. Given that most people tend to upgrade every second version of Office, that means that Excel VBA will be running on a majority of desktops until at least 2009. Is this a reason for us to be concerned that our VBA knowledge will be useless?

No rational person would believe that Microsoft would remove support for the most important feature that differentiates Excel from Star Office: VBA.

Security has moved to the forefront for Microsoft. In October 2003, Microsoft announced new security initiatives that make it clear that security is job 1 at Microsoft. This is relevant because the infamous Melissa virus spread rapidly by using VBA in Word. The press and powers that be took this situation and moved VBA over to the endangered species list. If Microsoft continues to take more heat for security, then the company may indeed be forced into removing VBA from Office.

Office 2003 now offers Visual Basic .NET Office System Tools. Visual Basic 6 offered the ability to automate Excel XP tasks from Visual Basic. With the release of Office 2003, we now have major new features that can only be automated from .NET. If you want to program a smart document or publish content for the research pane, you cannot do so if you are using VBA.

So, Microsoft has to do something to combat the security issues in VBA. The .NET team at Microsoft is certainly making a pitch that .NET Tools for Office could be the replacement. However, I think this would be an incredible mistake. Right now, all the 400 million Office users could buy this book and within a week start developing VBA solutions in Excel. White collar productivity would skyrocket and our reliance on the MIS department would diminish. If Microsoft would switch over to .NET, then VBA and the ability to write macro code is removed from the inside of Excel. At that point, there is less of a compelling reason to buy Excel over Star Office, who will certainly have a macro language by 2007. These concerns over security could be the distraction that causes Microsoft to lose their hold on the spreadsheet market.

However, in the meantime, feel safe in knowing that VBA is with us for the rest of this decade. Also, the knowledge that you gain in Excel VBA is directly portable to the .NET framework. Code in .NET looks remarkably like code in VBA.

Special Elements and Typographical Conventions

The following typographical conventions are used in this book:

- *Italic*. Indicates new terms when they are defined, special emphasis, non-English words or phrases, and letters or words used as words.
- `Monospace`. Indicates parts of VBA code, such as object or method names, and filenames.
- `Italic Monospace`. Indicates placeholder text in code syntax.
- **`Bold Monospace`**. Indicates user input.

In addition to these text conventions, there are also several special elements. Each chapter has at least one Case Study, which shows you real-world solutions to common problems and practical applications of topics discussed in the text. In addition to these case studies, you will also see Notes, Tips, and Cautions.

NOTE

Notes provide additional information outside the main thread of the chapter discussion that might still be useful for you to know.

TIP

Tips provide you with quick workarounds and timesaving techniques to help you do your work more efficiently.

CAUTION

Cautions warn you about potential pitfalls you might encounter. Pay attention to these, because they could alert you to problems that otherwise could cause you hours of frustration.

Versions Covered

At the time of writing, Excel 2003 is the current version of Excel. Other than the concepts in Chaapter 15 which will only work in Excel 2003 or newer, most of the code in this book is compatible with Excel 2002 and Excel 2000. For readers who are using Excel 97, none of the examples in Chapter 12 will work except for the case study on page 288. See page 479 for a discussion of other version-specific issues.

Code Files

As a thank-you for buying this book, the authors have put together a set of 50 Excel workbooks demonstrating the concepts in this book. This set of files incluides all of the code from the book, sample data, additional notes from the authors, plus 25 bonus macros. To download the code files, visit `http://www.mrexcel.com/getcode.html`.

Next Steps

Chapter 1 introduces the editing tools of the Visual Basic environment and shows you why using the macro recorder is not a good way to learn Excel VBA.

First Steps up the VBA Learning Curve

IN THIS PART

Unleash the Power of Excel with VBA!

The Power of Excel

Visual Basic for Applications combined with Microsoft Excel is probably the most powerful tool available to you. This tool is sitting on the desktops of 400 million users of Microsoft Office and most have never figured out how to harness the power of VBA in Excel. Using VBA, you can speed the production of any task in Excel. If you regularly use Excel to produce a series of monthly charts, you can have VBA do the same task for you in a matter of seconds.

Barriers to Entry

There are two barriers to learning successful VBA programming. First, Excel's macro recorder is flawed and does not produce workable code for you to use as a model. Second, for many who learned a programming language such as BASIC, the syntax of VBA is horribly frustrating.

The Macro Recorder Doesn't Work!

Microsoft began to dominate the spreadsheet market in the mid-90s. Although they were wildly successful in building a powerful spreadsheet program toward which any Lotus 1-2-3 user could easily transition, the macro language was just too different. Anyone proficient in recording Lotus 1-2-3 macros who tried recording a few macros in Excel most likely failed. Although the Microsoft VBA programming language is far more powerful than the Lotus 1-2-3 macro language, the one fundamental flaw is that the macro recorder does not work.

With Lotus 1-2-3, you could record a macro today, play it back tomorrow, and it would faithfully work. When you attempt the same feat in Microsoft Excel, the macro might work today but not tomorrow. I was horribly frustrated in 1995 when I tried to record my first Excel macro.

Visual Basic Is Not Like BASIC

The code generated by the macro was unlike anything that I had ever seen. It said this was "Visual Basic." I had the pleasure of learning half of dozen programming languages at various times; this bizarre-looking language was horribly unintuitive and did not at all resemble the BASIC language that I had learned in high school.

To make matters worse, even in 1995, I was the spreadsheet wizard in my office. My company had just forced everyone to convert from Lotus 1-2-3 to Excel. I was now faced with a macro recorder that didn't work and a language that I could not understand. This was not a good combination of events.

My assumption in writing this book is that you are pretty talented with a spreadsheet. You probably know more than 90% of the people in your office. I will assume that you are not a programmer, but that you might have taken a class in BASIC in high school. This isn't a requirement—it actually is a barrier to entry into the ranks of being a successful VBA programmer. There is a pretty good chance that you've recorded a macro in Excel and a similar chance that you were not happy with the results.

The Good News—It Is Easy to Climb the Learning Curve

Even if you've been frustrated with the macro recorder before, it is really just a small speed bump on your road to writing powerful programs in Excel. This book will teach you why the macro recorder fails, but also will show how to easily change the recorded code into something useful. For all the former BASIC programmers in the audience, I will decode this bizarre-looking language so that you can easily pick through recorded macro code and understand what is going on.

The Great News—Excel with VBA Is Worth the Effort

Although you've probably been frustrated with Microsoft over your inability to record macros in Excel, the great news is that Excel VBA is powerful. Absolutely anything that you can do in the Excel interface can be duplicated with stunning speed in Excel VBA. If you find yourself routinely creating the same reports manually day after day or week after week, Excel VBA will greatly streamline those tasks.

The authors work for MrExcel Consulting. In this role, we get to help automate reports for hundreds of clients. The stories are often similar: The M.I.S. department has a several-month backlog of requests. Someone in accounting or engineering discovers that he or she can import some data into Excel and get the reports necessary to run the business. This is a liberating event—you no longer need to wait months for the I.T. department to write a program. However, the problem is that after you import the data into Excel and win accolades from your manager for producing the report, you then find yourself producing the same report every month or every week. This becomes very tedious.

Again, the great news is that with a few hours of VBA programming, you can automate the reporting process and turn it into a few button clicks. The reward is great. Hang with me as we cover a few of the basics.

This chapter is going to expose why the macro recorder does not work. I will walk through a simple example of recorded code and demonstrate why it will work today but fail tomorrow. You will be seeing code here, and I realize that this code may not be familiar to you yet. That's OK. The point of this chapter is to demonstrate the fundamental problem with the macro recorder. We'll also cover the fundamentals of the Visual Basic Environment.

Knowing Your Tools—The Visual Basic Toolbar

We'll start with a basic overview of the tools needed to get around with VBA. In Excel, select View, Toolbars, Visual Basic to display the Visual Basic toolbar (see Figure 1.1).

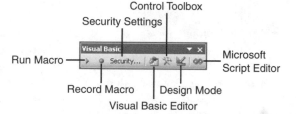

Figure 1.1
The Visual Basic toolbar provides an interface for running and recording macros.

Excel's Visual Basic toolbar provides these seven actions:

- **Run Macro**—Displays a list of available macros.
- **Record Macro**—Begins the process of recording a macro and displays the Stop Recording toolbar as shown in Figure 1.2.

Figure 1.2
The Stop Recording toolbar is one of the smallest toolbars in Excel, yet the relative reference button on the right is one of the most important in getting your recorded macros close to working.

- **Visual Basic Editor**—Opens up the Visual Basic Editor.
- **Control Toolbox**—Displays the controls that can be added to a worksheet.

- **Design Mode**—Turns on the design mode, enabling the user to edit controls on the worksheet. If you attempt to edit a control before you are in design mode, you will cause the action associated with that control to be performed.

- **Microsoft Script Editor**—Opens the Script Editor, useful for creating scripts for Web sites. This isn't related to VBA, so we won't be discussing it.

When you click the Record button, the Stop Recording toolbar appears. As shown in Figure 1.2, it provides these two actions:

  • **Stop Recording**—Ends the current recording session.

  • **Relative Reference**—Tells Excel to record with relative reference rather than the absolute reference.

Macro Security

After VBA macros were used as the delivery method for some high-profile viruses, Microsoft changed the default security settings to prevent macros from running. Thus, before we can begin discussing the recording of a macro, we need to show you how to adjust the default settings.

The macro security settings can be found under Tools, Macro, Security. There are four levels of security: Very High, High, Medium, and Low. By default, Excel sets the security to High (see Figure 1.3). This setting will prevent all unsigned macros from running or even being edited. You need to adjust this setting to Medium to begin writing code.

Figure 1.3
Excel macro security settings are set to High by default.

Very High Security

This is the first option of using Microsoft's "Sandbox" paradigm for security. The paradigm says that your network administrator can set up a highly protected network directory and define it as a trusted location. This area is called the *Sandbox*. You are allowed to play any macros located in the Sandbox. Anything that is installed outside the Sandbox is off limits. The theory is that viruses will not be able to locate themselves into the secured trusted area.

High Security

The High security setting allows only trusted macros to run. A macro is trusted when it has been digitally signed and you choose to trust the source. Because macro signing requires that you buy a digital certificate from an agency such as VeriSign, this setting effectively disallows all macros that you write yourself. If a workbook contains an unsigned macro, the workbook opens but the macros are automatically disabled—no prompt appears informing you of this.

Medium Security

With Medium security, you get to choose whether you want to Enable or Disable macros each time that you open each workbook. This is the setting I recommend. On the one hand, it is annoying to be asked constantly to enable the macro every time you open a workbook. However, this question is the last line of defense when someone has sent you a workbook with malicious virus code, and being able to disable macros when you did not expect code to be in a received workbook is the safest setting.

Low Security

With Low security, all macros enable automatically. This can be dangerous if you ever receive a workbook with a malicious macro. I do not recommend this setting.

If you are considering this setting because you're tired of enabling your personal macros, then look into adding a digital signature to your macros.

Overview of Recording, Storing, and Running a Macro

Recording a macro is very useful when you do not have enough experience in writing lines of code in a macro. As you gain more knowledge and experience, you will begin to record lines of code less and less frequently.

To begin recording a macro, select Tools, Macro, Record New Macro, or press the Record Macro button on the VBA toolbar. Before recording begins, Excel displays the Record Macro dialog box, as shown in Figure 1.4.

Filling Out the Record Macro Dialog

In the Macro Name field, type a name for the macro. Be sure to type continuous characters; for example, type `Macro1` and not `Macro 1` (with a space). Assuming you will soon be creating many macros, use a meaningful name for the macro. A name such as "FormatReport" is more useful than "Macro1."

Figure 1.4
Use the Record Macro dialog box to assign a name and a shortcut key to the soon-to-be-recorded macro.

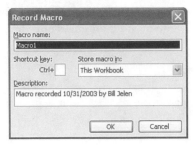

The second field in the Record Macro dialog box is a shortcut key. If you type **j** in this field, then pressing Ctrl+j causes this macro to run.

In the Record Macro dialog box, you can choose where you want to save a macro when you record it: Personal Macro Workbook, New Workbook, This Workbook. I recommend storing macros related to a particular workbook in This Workbook.

The Personal Macro Workbook (`Personal.xls`) is not an open workbook; it is created if you choose to save the recording in the Personal Macro Workbook. This workbook is used to save a macro in a workbook that will open automatically when you start Excel, thereby enabling you to use the macro. After Excel is started, the workbook is hidden. If you want to display it, select Unhide from the Window menu.

It is not recommended you use the personal workbook for every macro you save. Save only those macros that will assist you in general tasks—not in tasks that are performed in a specific sheet or workbook.

After you select the location where you want to store the macro, click OK. Record your macro. When you are finished recording the macro, click the Stop button on the Stop Recording dialog box.

Running a Macro

If you assigned a shortcut key to your macro, you can play it by pressing the key combination. Macros can also be assigned to toolbar buttons, forms controls, or you can run them from the Visual Basic toolbar.

Creating a Macro Button

If you want to create a macro to assist in your Excel work, store the macro in a personal workbook and attach it to a toolbar button:

1. Right-click on a toolbar and select Customize.
2. Select the Commands tab (see Figure 1.5).

Figure 1.5
Use Customize to insert a Macro button into a toolbar.

3. From Categories, select Macros.

4. Select the Custom button (with the yellow smiley face) and drag it onto a toolbar.

5. Right-click on the icon (do not close the Customize dialog box).

6. Select Assign Macro, select the macro, and click OK.

7. Close the Customize dialog box.

Assigning a Macro to a Form Control

If you want to create a macro specific to a workbook, store the macro to the workbook and attach it to a form control on the sheet, as shown in Figure 1.6.

Figure 1.6
Assigning a macro to a form control is appropriate for macros stored in the same workbook as the control.

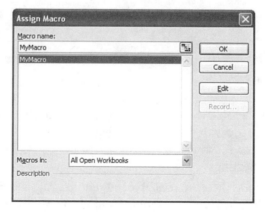

Follow these steps to attach a macro to a form control on the sheet:

1. Display the Forms toolbar by selecting View, Toolbars, Forms.

2. Click the Button image.

3. Draw a button on the sheet by clicking and holding the left mouse button while drawing a box shape. Release the button when you are finished.

4. Select a macro from the Assign Macro dialog box and click OK.

5. Click the button to run the macro.

Understanding the Visual Basic Editor (VBE)

Figure 1.7 shows an example of the typical VBE screen. You can see three windows: Project Explorer, the Properties window, and the Programming window. Don't worry if your window doesn't look exactly like this; as we review the editor, I'll show you how to display the windows you'll need.

Figure 1.7
The VBE window.

VBE Settings

Several settings in the VBE enable you to customize it as you want. I'm going to go over only the ones that can help you with your programming.

Customizing VBE Options Settings

Under Tools, Options, Editor, there are several useful settings. All settings except for one are set correctly by default. The remaining setting requires some consideration on your part. This setting is Require Variable Declaration. By default, Excel doesn't require you to declare variables. Bill prefers this setting. It can save you time in creating a program. Tracy prefers changing this setting to require variable declaration. This forces the compiler to stop if it finds a variable that it does not recognize. This cuts down on misspelled variable names. It is a matter of your personal preference if you turn this on or keep it off.

Enabling Digital Signatures

If you're like me, you write a lot of personal macros. After a while, it gets tiresome having to approve the enabling of macros you wrote. That's where digital signatures come in.

The Project Explorer

The Project Explorer lists any open workbooks and add-ins that are loaded. If you click the + icon next to the VBA Project, you will see that there is a folder with Microsoft Excel Objects. There can also be folders for Forms, Class Modules, and (standard) Modules. Each folder includes one or more individual components.

Right-clicking on a component and selecting View Code, or just double-clicking on the components, brings up any code in the Programming Window (except for UserForms, where double-clicking displays the UserForm in Design View).

 To display this window, select View, Project Explorer from the menu, press Ctrl+R, or click the Project Explorer icon on the toolbar.

The Project Explorer pane is shown in Figure 1.8. This pane can show Microsoft Excel Objects, Userforms, Modules, and/or Class Modules.

Figure 1.8
The Project Explorer, displaying different types of modules.

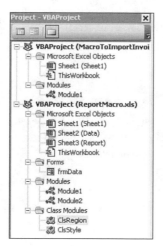

To insert a module, right-click your project, select Insert, and then select the type of module you want.

Microsoft Excel Objects

By default, a project consists of sheet modules for each sheet in the workbook and a single ThisWorkbook module. Code specific to a sheet, such as controls or sheet events, is placed on the corresponding sheet. Workbook events are placed in the ThisWorkbook module. We'll learn more about events in Chapter 8, "Event Programming."

Forms

Excel allows you to design your own forms to interact with the user. We'll learn more about these forms in Chapter 9, "UserForms—An Introduction."

Modules

When you record a macro, Excel automatically creates a module to place the code. It is in these types of modules that most of your code will reside.

Class Modules

Class modules are Excel's way of letting you create your own objects. Also, class modules allow pieces of code to be shared among programmers without the programmer needing to understand how it works. We'll learn more about class modules in Chapter 20, "Creating Classes, Records, and Collections."

The Properties Window

The Properties Window enables you to edit the properties of various components—sheets, workbooks, modules, or form controls. Its property list varies according to what component is selected.

 To display this window, select View, Properties Window from the menu, press F4, or click the Project Properties icon on the toolbar.

CASE STUDY

Let's say you work in an accounting department. Each day you receive a text file from the company system showing all the invoices produced the prior day. This text file has commas separating each field. The columns in the file are `InvoiceDate`, `InvoiceNumber`, `SalesRepNumber`, `CustomerNumber`, `ProductRevenue`, `ServiceRevenue`, and `ProductCost` (see Figure 1.9).

Figure 1.9
`Invoice.txt` file.

```
Invoice.txt - Notepad
File  Edit  Format  View  Help
InvoiceDate,InvoiceNumber,SalesRepNumber,CustomerNumber,ProductRevenue,ServiceRevenue,ProductCost
06/05/2004,123801,S82,C8754,639600,12000,325438
06/05/2004,123802,S93,C7874,964600,0,435587
06/05/2004,123803,S43,C4844,988900,0,587630
06/05/2004,123804,S54,C4940,673800,15000,346164
06/05/2004,123805,S43,C7969,513500,0,233842
06/05/2004,123806,S93,C8468,760600,0,355305
06/05/2004,123807,S82,C1620,894100,0,457577
06/05/2004,123808,S17,C3238,316200,45000,161877
06/05/2004,123809,S32,C5214,111500,0,62956
06/05/2004,123810,S45,C3717,747600,0,444162
06/05/2004,123811,S87,C7492,857400,0,410493
06/05/2004,123812,S43,C7780,200700,0,97937
```

As you arrive at work each morning, you manually import this file into Excel. You add a total row to the data, bold the headings, and then print the report for distribution to a few managers.

Preparing to Record the Macro

This is a task that is perfect for a macro. Before you record any macro, you should think about the steps that you will use before you begin. In our case, these steps are as follows:

1. From the menu, select File, Open.
2. Navigate to the proper folder.
3. Choose All Files(*.*) from the Files of Type: dropdown list.
4. Select `Invoice.txt`.
5. Click Open.
6. In the Text Import Wizard—Step 1 of 3, select Delimited from the Original data type section.
7. Click Next.
8. In the Text Import Wizard—Step 2 of 3, uncheck the Tab key and check Comma in the Delimiters section.
9. Click Next.
10. In the Text Import Wizard—Step 3 of 3, select General in the Column data format section and change it to Date: MDY.
11. Click Finish to import the file.
12. Press the End key followed by the down arrow to move to the last row of data.
13. Press the down arrow one more time to move to the total row.
14. Type the word `Total`.
15. Press the right arrow key four times to move to column E of the total row.
16. Click the Autosum button and press Ctrl+Enter to add a total to the Product Revenue column while remaining in that cell.
17. Grab the Autofill handle and drag from Column E over to Column G to copy the total formula over to Columns F and G.
18. Highlight Row 1 and click the Bold icon to set the headings in bold.
19. Highlight the Total row and click the Bold icon to set the totals in bold.
20. Press Ctrl+A to select all cells.
21. From the menu, select Format, Column, Autofit Selection.

After you've rehearsed these steps in your head, you are ready to record your first macro. Open a blank workbook and save it with a name like `MacroToImportInvoices.xls`. Click the Record button or select Tools, Macro, Record New Macro.

In the Record Macro dialog, the default macro name is `Macro1`. Change this to something descriptive like `ImportInvoice`. Make sure that the macros will be stored in This Workbook. You might want an easy way to run this macro later, so enter the letter **i** in the Shortcut Key field. In the Description field, you will, by default, have your name and date. Add a little descriptive text to tell what the macro is doing (see Figure 1.10). When you are ready, click OK.

Figure 1.10
Before recording your
macro, complete the
Record Macro dialog
box.

Recording the Macro

Don't be nervous, but the Macro Recorder is now recording your every move. You want to try to perform your steps in exact order without extraneous actions. If you accidentally move to column F and then back to E to enter the first total, the recorded macro blindly makes that same mistake day after day after day. Recorded macros move fast, but this is nothing like having to watch your same mistakes played out by the macro recorder again and again.

> **CAUTION**
>
> Resist the temptation to hide the Stop Recording toolbar. If the floating toolbar gets in the way, grab the blue title bar to move it to an out-of-the-way place. (The action of moving the Stop Recording Toolbar is not recorded.) If you do happen to hide the toolbar with the "X," then you will have to use the hard-to-find Tools, Macro, Stop Recording option on the menu.

Carefully, execute all the actions necessary to produce the report. After you have performed the final step, click the Stop button on the Stop Recording toolbar. The toolbar disappears.

> **CAUTION**
>
> Again, resist the temptation to close the toolbar. This does not stop the recording. If you do accidentally close the toolbar, you can stop recording by choosing Tools, Macro, Stop Recording from the main menu.

It is time to take a look at your code. Switch to the Visual Basic Editor by choosing Tools, Macro, Visual Basic Editor or pressing Alt+F11.

Examining Code in the Programming Window

Let's take a look at the code you just recorded from the case study; don't worry if it doesn't make sense yet.

To open the Visual Basic Editor press Alt+F11. In our VBA Project (`MacroToImportInvoices.xls`), find the component `Module1`, right-click on it, and select View Code. Notice that some lines start with an apostrophe—these are comments and are ignored by the program. The macro recorder starts your macros with a few comments, using the description that you entered in the Record Macro dialog. The comment for the Keyboard Shortcut is there to remind you of the shortcut.

> **CAUTION**
>
> The comment does *not* assign the shortcut. If you change the comment to be Ctrl+j, it does not change the shortcut. This has to be done in the Macro dialog box from Excel.

Recorded macro code is usually pretty neat (see Figure 1.11). Each non-comment line of code is indented four characters. If a line is longer than 100 characters, the recorder breaks it into multiple lines and indents the lines an additional four characters. To continue a line of code, you type a space and an underscore at the end of the line. Note that the physical limitations of this book do not allow 100 characters on a single line. I will break the lines at 80 characters so that they fit on this page. Your recorded macro might look slightly different than the ones that appear here.

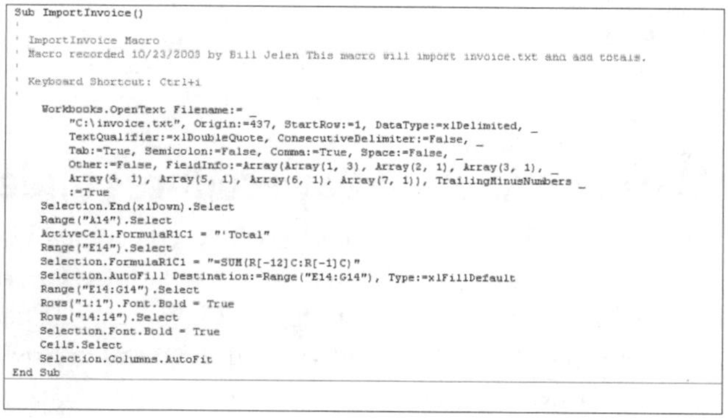

Figure 1.11
The recorded macro is neat looking and nicely indented.

```
Sub ImportInvoice()

' ImportInvoice Macro
' Macro recorded 10/23/2003 by Bill Jelen This macro will import invoice.txt and add totals.

' Keyboard Shortcut: Ctrl+i

    Workbooks.OpenText Filename:= _
        "C:\invoice.txt", Origin:=437, StartRow:=1, DataType:=xlDelimited, _
        TextQualifier:=xlDoubleQuote, ConsecutiveDelimiter:=False, _
        Tab:=True, Semicolon:=False, Comma:=True, Space:=False, _
        Other:=False, FieldInfo:=Array(Array(1, 3), Array(2, 1), Array(3, 1), _
        Array(4, 1), Array(5, 1), Array(6, 1), Array(7, 1)), TrailingMinusNumbers _
        :=True
    Selection.End(xlDown).Select
    Range("A14").Select
    ActiveCell.FormulaR1C1 = "'Total"
    Range("E14").Select
    Selection.FormulaR1C1 = "=SUM(R[-12]C:R[-1]C)"
    Selection.AutoFill Destination:=Range("E14:G14"), Type:=xlFillDefault
    Range("E14:G14").Select
    Rows("1:1").Font.Bold = True
    Rows("14:14").Select
    Selection.Font.Bold = True
    Cells.Select
    Selection.Columns.AutoFit
End Sub
```

Consider that the following seven lines of recorded code is actually only one line of code that has been broken down into seven lines for readability:

```
Workbooks.OpenText Filename:= _
    "C:\invoice.txt", Origin:=437, StartRow:=1, DataType:=xlDelimited, _
    TextQualifier:=xlDoubleQuote, ConsecutiveDelimiter:=False, _
    Tab:=True, Semicolon:=False, Comma:=True, Space:=False, _
    Other:=False, FieldInfo:=Array(Array(1, 3), Array(2, 1), Array(3, 1), _
    Array(4, 1), Array(5, 1), Array(6, 1), Array(7, 1)), _
    TrailingMinusNumbers:=True
```

Counting the above as one line, the macro recorder was able to record our 21-step process in 14 lines of code, which is pretty impressive.

> **TIP**
>
> Each action that you perform in the Excel user interface may equate to one or more lines of recorded code. Some actions might generate a dozen lines of code.

It is always a good idea to test out your macro. Return to the regular Excel interface, using Alt+F11. Close `Invoice.txt` without saving any changes. You still have `MacroToImportInvoices.xls` open.

Press Ctrl+i to run the recorded macro. It works beautifully! The data is imported, totals are added, bold formatting is applied, and the columns are made wider. This seems like a perfect solution (see Figure 1.12).

Figure 1.12
The macro formats the data in the sheet beautifully.

	A	B	C	D	E	F	G
1	InvoiceDate	InvoiceNumber	SalesRepNumber	CustomerNumber	ProductRevenue	ServiceRevenue	ProductCost
2	6/5/2004	123801	S82	C8754	639600	12000	325438
3	6/5/2004	123802	S93	C7874	964600	0	435587
4	6/5/2004	123803	S43	C4844	988900	0	587630
5	6/5/2004	123804	S54	C4940	673800	15000	346164
6	6/5/2004	123805	S43	C7969	513500	0	233842
7	6/5/2004	123806	S93	C8468	760600	0	355305
8	6/5/2004	123807	S82	C1620	894100	0	457577
9	6/5/2004	123808	S17	C3238	316200	45000	161877
10	6/5/2004	123809	S32	C5214	111500	0	62956
11	6/5/2004	123810	S45	C3717	747600	0	444162
12	6/5/2004	123811	S87	C7492	857400	0	410493
13	6/5/2004	123812	S43	C7780	200700	0	97937
14	Total				7668500	72000	3918968
15							

Running the Macro on Another Day Produces Undesired Results

So, you would have saved your macro file. The next day, you come to work and you have a new `invoice.txt` file from the system. You open the macro, press Ctrl+i to run it, and disaster strikes. The data for June 5th happened to have 12 invoices. The data for the 6th had 16 invoices. However, the recorded macro blindly added the totals in Row 14, because this was where we put the totals when the macro was recorded (see Figure 1.13).

Figure 1.13
On another day, the macro fails horribly. The intent of the recorded macro was to add a total at the end of the data, but the recorder made a macro to always add totals at Row 14.

	A	B	C	D	E	F	G
1	InvoiceDate	InvoiceNumber	SalesRepNumber	CustomerNumber	ProductRevenue	ServiceRevenue	ProductCost
2	6/6/2004	123813	S82	C8754	716100	12000	423986
3	6/6/2004	123814		C4894	224200	0	131243
4	6/6/2004	123815	S43	C7278	277000	0	139208
5	6/6/2004	123816	S54	C6425	746100	15000	350683
6	6/6/2004	123817	S43	C6291	928300	0	488988
7	6/6/2004	123818	S43	C1000	723200	0	383069
8	6/6/2004	123819	S82	C6025	982600	0	544025
9	6/6/2004	123820	S17	C8026	490100	45000	243808
10	6/6/2004	123821	S43	C4244	615800	0	300579
11	6/6/2004	123822	S45	C1007	271300	0	153253
12	6/6/2004	123823	S87	C1878	338100	0	165666
13	6/6/2004	123824	S43	C3068	567900	0	265775
14	Total	123825	S87	C4913	6880700	72000	3590283
15	6/6/2004	123826	S55	C7181	37900	0	19811
16	6/6/2004	123827	S43	C7570	582700	0	292000
17	6/6/2004	123828	S87	C5302	495000	0	241504
18							

A Possible Solution: Using Relative References when Recording

By default, the macro recorder records all actions as *absolute* actions. If you navigate to Row 14 when you record the macro on Monday, then the macro will always go to Row 14 when the macro is run. When dealing with variable numbers of rows of data, this is rarely appropriate.

There is an option to use relative references when recording.

Absolute reference means that the actual address of the cell is used, for example "A1." Relative reference means that the location of the cell is based off of another cell. For example, R[16],C[-1] refers to a cell 16 rows down and 1 column to the left of the active cell.

CASE STUDY

Let's try to record the macro again, using relative references. Close `Invoice.txt` without saving changes. In the workbook `MacroToImportInvoices.xls`, record a new macro by choosing Tools, Macro, Record New Macro. Give the new macro a name of `ImportInvoicesRelative` and assign it a different shortcut key, such as Ctrl+j (Figure 1.14).

Figure 1.14
Getting ready to record a second try.

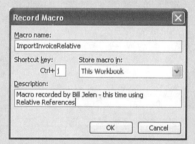

As you start to record the macro, go through the process of opening the `invoice.txt` file. Before navigating to the last row of data (using End+Down), click the Relative Reference button on the Stop Recording toolbar (refer to Figure 1.2).

Continue through the actions in the script from the case study:

1. Press the End key followed by the Down arrow to move to the last row of data.

2. Press the Down arrow one more time to move to the total row.

3. Type the word `Total`.

4. Press the Right arrow key four times to move to column E of the total row.

5. Press the Autosum button and then press Ctrl+Enter to add a total to the Product Revenue column while remaining in that cell.

6. Grab the Autofill handle and drag from Column E over to Column G to copy the total formula over to Columns F and G.

7. Use Shift+Spacebar to select the entire row and apply bold formatting to it.

At this point, you need to move to Cell A1 to apply bold to the headings. You do not want the macro recorder to record the movement from Row 18 to Row 1—it would record this as moving 17 rows up, which may not be correct tomorrow. Before moving to A1, toggle the Relative Recording button off, then continue recording the rest of the macro.

8. Highlight Row 1 and hit the Bold icon to set the headings in bold.

9. Press Ctrl+A to select all cells.

10. From the menu, select Format, Column, Autofit.

11. Stop recording.

Press Alt+F11 to go to the VB Editor to review your code. The new macro appears in Module1 below the previous macro.

> **CAUTION**
>
> If you close Excel between recording the first and second macro, Excel inserts a new module, called "Module2," for the newly recorded macro.

I've edited the code in Figure 1.15 with two comments to show where I remember turning the relative recording on and then off.

Figure 1.15
Macro recorded with Relative References on during part of the recording process.

```
Sub ImportInvoicesRelative()
'
' ImportInvoicesRelative Macro
' Macro recorded by Bill Jelen this time with relative recording turned on.
'
' Keyboard Shortcut: Ctrl+j
'
    Workbooks.OpenText Filename:=" _
        "C:\invoice.txt", Origin _
        :=437, StartRow:=1, DataType:=xlDelimited, TextQualifier:=xlDoubleQuote _
        , ConsecutiveDelimiter:=False, Tab:=True, Semicolon:=False, Comma:=True _
        , Space:=False, Other:=False, FieldInfo:=Array(Array(1, 3), Array(2, 1), _
        Array(3, 1), Array(4, 1), Array(5, 1), Array(6, 1), Array(7, 1)), TrailingMinusNumbers _
        :=True
' Turned on relative recording here
    Selection.End(xlDown).Select
    ActiveCell.Offset(1, 0).Range("A1").Select
    ActiveCell.FormulaR1C1 = "'Total"
    ActiveCell.Offset(0, 4).Range("A1").Select
    Selection.FormulaR1C1 = "=SUM(R[-16]C:R[-1]C)"
    Selection.AutoFill Destination:=ActiveCell.Range("A1:C1"), Type:= _
        xlFillDefault
' Turned off relative recording here
    ActiveCell.Range("A1:C1").Select
    ActiveCell.Rows("1:1").EntireRow.Select
    ActiveCell.Activate
    Selection.Font.Bold = True
    Rows("1:1").Select
    Selection.Font.Bold = True
    Cells.Select
    Selection.Columns.AutoFit
End Sub
```

To test the macro, close `Invoice.txt` without saving, then run the macro with Ctrl+j. Everything looks good—I get the same results.

The next test is to see whether the program works on the next day when you might have more rows. Figure 1.16 shows the data for June 7th.

Figure 1.16
Will the macro with Relative References work with this data?

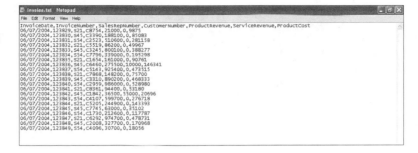

I open `MacroToImportInvoices.xls` and run the new macro with Ctrl+J. This time, everything looks pretty good. The totals are where they are supposed to be. Look at Figure 1.17—see anything out of the ordinary?

Figure 1.17
The result of running the Relative macro.

If you aren't careful, you might just print these off for your manager. You would be in trouble. Look in Cell E23. Luckily, Excel has a green triangle there telling you to look at the cell. If you would have happened to try this back in Excel 95 or Excel 97 before we had smart tags, there would have been no indicator that anything was wrong.

Move the cellpointer to E23. An alert indicator pops up near the cell. The indicator tells you that the formula fails to include adjacent cells. If you look in the formula bar, you can see that the macro totaled only from Row 7 to Row 22. Neither the relative recording nor the non-relative recording is smart enough to replicate the logic of the AutoSum button.

At this point, any sane person would give up. But imagine that you might have had fewer invoice records on this particular day. Excel would have rewarded you with the illogical formula of =SUM(E10:E65531) and a circular reference as shown in Figure 1.18.

Figure 1.18
The result of running the
Relative Macro with
fewer invoice records.

	A	B	C	D	E	F	G
	E11		▼	fx =SUM(E10:E65531)			
1	InvoiceDate	InvoiceNumber	SalesRepNumber	CustomerNumber	ProductRevenue	ServiceRevenue	ProductCost
2	6/7/2004	123829	S21	C8754	538400	0	299897
3	6/7/2004	123830	S45	C4056	588600	0	307563
4	6/7/2004	123831	S54	C8323	882200	0	521726
5	6/7/2004	123832	S21	C6026	830900	0	494831
6	6/7/2004	123833	S45	C3025	673600	0	374953
7	6/7/2004	123834	S54	C8663	966300	0	528575
8	6/7/2004	123835	S21	C1508	467100	0	257942
9	6/7/2004	123836	S45	C7366	658500	10000	308719
10	6/7/2004	123837	S54	C4533	191700	0	109534
11	Total				0	0	0
12							
13							
14				Circular Reference ▼ ×			
15				$E$11			
16							
17							

Frustration

If you are like me, you are cursing Microsoft. We've wasted a good deal of time over a couple of days and neither macro will work. What makes it worse is that this sort of procedure would have been handled perfectly by the old Lotus 1-2-3 macro recorder introduced in 1983. Mitch Kapor solved this problem 21 years ago and Microsoft still can't get it right.

Did you know that up through Excel 97, Microsoft Excel secretly would run Lotus command line macros? I didn't either, but I found out right after Microsoft quit supporting Excel 97. A number of companies then upgraded to Excel XP, which no longer supported the Lotus 1-2-3 macros. Many of these companies hired us to convert the old Lotus 1-2-3 macros to Excel VBA. It is interesting that from Excel 5, Excel 95, and Excel 97, Microsoft offered an interpreter that could handle the Lotus macros that solved this problem correctly, yet their own macro recorder couldn't (and still can't!) solve the problem.

Next Steps: Learning VBA Is the Solution

The only solution is to dive in and figure out Visual Basic. The recorded macro gets us close. With some added human intelligence, you can produce awesome macros to speed up your daily work. In Chapter 2, "This Sounds Like BASIC, So Why Doesn't It Look Familiar?" we'll take a look at these two macros we recorded in an effort to make some sense out of them. After you know how to decode the VBA code, it will feel natural to either correct the recorded code or simply write code from scratch. Hang on through one more chapter and you will be writing useful code that works consistently.

This Sounds Like BASIC, So Why Doesn't It Look Familiar?

I Can't Understand This Code

As I mentioned before, if you've taken a class in a procedural language such as BASIC or COBOL, then you might be really confused when you look at VBA code. Yes, VBA stands for "Visual Basic for Applications," but it is an *object-oriented* version of BASIC. Here is a bit of VBA code:

```
Selection.End(xlDown).Select
Range("A14").Select
ActiveCell.FormulaR1C1 = "'Total"
Range("E14").Select
Selection.FormulaR1C1 = "=SUM(R[-12]C:R[-1]C)"
Selection.AutoFill Destination:=Range(_
    "E14:G14"), Type:=xlFillDefault
```

This code will likely make no sense to anyone who knows only procedural languages, and unfortunately, your first introduction to programming in school (assuming you are over 20 years old) would have been a procedural language.

Here is a section of code written in BASIC:

```
For x = 1 to 10
    Print Rpt$(" ",x);
    Print "*"
Next x
```

If you run this code, you get a pyramid of asterisks on your screen:

```
*
 *
  *
   *
    *
     *
      *
       *
        *
         *
```

If you've ever been in a procedural programming class, you can probably look at the code and figure out what is going on. I think that a procedural language is more English-like than object-oriented languages. The statement `Print "Hello World"` follows the verb-object format and is how you would generally talk. Let's step away from programming for a second and think about a concrete example.

Understanding the Parts of VBA "Speech"

If you were going to play soccer using BASIC, the instruction to kick a ball would look something like

> "Kick the Ball"

Hey—this is how we talk! It makes sense. You have a verb (kick) and then a noun (the ball). In the BASIC code in the preceding section, you have a verb (print) and a noun (an asterisk). Life is good.

Here is the problem. VBA doesn't work like this. No object-oriented language works like this. In an object-oriented language, the objects (the nouns) are most important (hence, the name—object-oriented). If you are going to play soccer with VBA, the basic structure would be

> Ball.Kick

You have a noun—the Ball. It comes first. In VBA this is an *object*. Then you have the verb—to kick. It comes next. In VBA, this is a *method*.

The basic structure of VBA is a bunch of lines of code where you have

> *Object.Method*

Sorry, this is not English. If you took a romance language in high school, you will remember that they used a "noun adjective" construct, but I don't know anyone who speaks in "noun verb" when telling someone to do something. Do you talk like this:

```
Water.Drink
Food.Eat
Girl.Kiss
```

Of course not. That is why VBA is so confusing to someone who once stepped foot in a procedural programming class.

Let's carry the analogy on a bit. Imagine you walk onto a grassy field and there are five balls in front of you. There is a soccer ball, a basketball, a baseball, a bowling ball, and a tennis ball. You want to instruct the kid on your soccer team to

> Kick the soccer ball

If you tell him kick the ball (or `ball.kick`), you really aren't sure which one he will kick. Maybe he will kick the one closest to him. This could be a real problem if he is standing in front of the bowling ball.

For almost any noun, or object, in VBA, there is a collection of that object. Think about Excel. If you can have a row, you can have a bunch of rows. If you can have a cell, you can have a bunch of cells. If you can have a worksheet, you can have a bunch of worksheets. The only difference between an object and a collection is that you will add an "s" to the name of the object:

Row becomes Rows

Cell becomes Cells

Ball becomes Balls

When you refer to something that is a collection, you have to tell the programming language to which item you are referring. There are a couple of ways to do this. You can refer to an item by using a number:

```
Balls(2).Kick
```

This will work fine, but it seems a dangerous way to program. It might work on Tuesday, but if you get to the field on Wednesday and someone has rearranged the balls, then `Balls(2).Kick` might be a painful exercise.

The other way is to use a name for the object. To me, this is a far safer way to go. You can say:

```
Balls("Soccer").Kick
```

With this method, you always know that it will be the soccer ball that it being kicked.

So far, so good. You know you can kick a ball and you know that it will be the soccer ball. For most of the verbs, or methods, in Excel VBA, there are parameters that tell *how* to do the action. These act as adverbs. You might want the soccer ball to be kicked to the left and with a hard force. Most methods have a number of parameters that tell how the program should perform the method.

```
Balls("Soccer").Kick Direction:=Left, Force:=Hard
```

As you are looking at VBA code, when you see the colon-equals combination, you know that you are looking at parameters of how the verb should be performed.

Sometimes, a method will have a list of 10 parameters. Some may be optional. Perhaps the `.Kick` method has an `Elevation` parameter. You might have this line of code:

```
Balls("Soccer").Kick Direction:=Left, Force:=Hard, Elevation:=High
```

Here is the radically confusing part. Every method has a default order for its parameters. If you are not a conscientious programmer and you happen to know the order of the parameters, you can leave off the parameter names. The following code is equivalent to the previous line of code:

```
Balls("Soccer").Kick Left, Hard, High
```

This throws a monkey wrench into our understanding. Without the colon-equals, it is not obvious that we have parameters. Unless you know the parameter order, you might not understand what is being said. It is pretty easy with Left, Hard, and High, but when you have parameters like the following:

```
WordArt.Add Left:=10, Top:=20, Width:=100, Height:=200
```

It gets really confusing to see:

```
WordArt.Add 10, 20, 100, 200
```

The preceding is valid code, but unless you know that the default order of the parameters for this Add method is Left, Top, Width, Height, this code will not make sense. The default order for any particular method is the order of the parameters as shown in the help topic for that method.

To make life more confusing, you are allowed to start specifying parameters in their default order without naming them, and then all of a sudden switch to naming parameters when you hit one that does not match the default order. If you wanted to kick the ball to the left and high, but do not care about the force (you were willing to accept the default force), then the following two statements are equivalent:

```
Balls("Soccer").Kick Direction:=Left, Elevation:=High
```

```
Balls("Soccer").Kick Left, Elevation:=High
```

As soon as you start naming parameters, then they have to be named for the remainder of that line of code.

Some methods simply act on their own. To simulate pressing the F9 key, you would use this code:

```
Application.Calculate
```

Other methods perform an action and create something. For example, you can add a worksheet with

```
Worksheets.Add Before:=Worksheets(1)
```

However, because Worksheets.Add actually creates a new object, you can assign the results of this method to a variable. In this case, you must surround the parameters with parentheses:

```
Set MyWorksheet = Worksheets.Add(Before:=Worksheets(1))
```

One final bit of grammar is necessary. Adjectives. Adjectives describe a noun. Properties describe an object. We are all Excel fans here, so I am going to switch from the soccer analogy to an Excel analogy midstream. There is an object to describe the active cell. Luckily for us, it has the very intuitive name of

```
ActiveCell
```

Let's say that we want to change the color of the active cell to yellow. There is a property called Interior.ColorIndex for a cell. It uses a complex series of codes, but you can turn a cell to yellow by using this code:

```
ActiveCell.Interior.ColorIndex = 6
```

Did I lose you? Can you see how this is so confusing? Again there's the Noun-dot-Something construct, but this time it is `Object.Property` rather than `Object.Method`. How do you tell them apart? Well, it is really subtle. There is no colon before the equal sign. A property is almost always being set equal to something, or perhaps the value of a property is being assigned to something else.

To make this cell color the same as Cell A1, you might say

```
ActiveCell.Interior.ColorIndex = Range("A1").Interior.ColorIndex
```

`Interior.ColorIndex` is a property. By changing the value of a property, you can make things look different. It is kind of bizarre—change an adjective and you are actually doing something to the cell. Humans would say "Color the cell yellow." VBA would say:

```
ActiveCell.Interior.ColorIndex = 30
```

Table 2.1 summarizes the VBA "parts of speech."

Table 2.1	The Parts of the VBA Programming Language	
VBA Component	**Analogous to**	**Notes**
Object	Noun	
Collection	Plural Noun	Usually specifies which object: `Worksheets(1)`
Method	Verb	`Object.Method`
Parameter	Adverb	Lists parameters after the method. Separate the parameter name from its value with `:=`
Property	Adjective	You can set a property `activecell.height = 10` or query the value of a property `x = activecell.height`

Is VBA Really This Hard? No!

Knowing whether you are dealing with properties or methods will help you to set up the correct syntax for your code. Don't worry if it all seems confusing right now. When you are writing VBA code from scratch, it is tough to know whether the process of changing a cell to yellow requires a verb or simply an adjective. Is it a method or a property?

This is where the beauty of the macro recorder comes in. When you don't know how to code something, you record a short little macro, look at the recorded code, and figure out what is going on.

VBA Help Files—Using F1 to Find Anything

This is a radically cool feature, but I might make you jump through hoops first. If you are going to write VBA macros, you absolutely *must* have the VBA help installed. The problem: the VBA Help file is not installed in the default Office install. Here is how to see whether you have it.

1. Open Excel and switch to the VBA editor, using Alt+F11. From the menu, select Insert, Module (see Figure 2.1).

Figure 2.1
Insert a new module in the blank workbook.

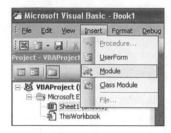

2. Type the three lines of code shown in Figure 2.2. Click inside the word MsgBox.

Figure 2.2
Click inside the word MsgBox and hit F1.

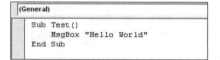

3. With the cursor in the word MsgBox, press the F1 key on the keyboard. If VBA Help is installed, you will see the help topic shown in Figure 2.3.

Figure 2.3
If VBA Help has been installed, you will get this screen.

If instead you get a message saying that VBA Help is not installed, you have to find the original CDs (or get your network administrator to grant rights to the installation folder) so that you can install the VBA Help file. Go through the process of doing a reinstall. During reinstall, select the custom install and be sure to select the VBA help files.

Using Help Topics

If you request help on a function or method, the help walks you through the various arguments available to you. On line 2 of each topic are three possible hyperlinks: See Also, Example, and Specifics. The Example hyperlink is a great resource. Click on Example and you are taken to a help window with a code sample (see Figure 2.4).

Figure 2.4
Most help topics have an example.

It is possible to select the code, copy it to the clipboard with Ctrl+C (see Figure 2.5), then paste it into your module using Ctrl+V.

Figure 2.5
Highlight code in the help file and copy with Ctrl+C.

```
MsgBox Function Example

This example uses the MsgBox function to display a critical-error message in a dialog box
with Yes and No buttons. The No button is specified as the default response. The value
returned by the MsgBox function depends on the button chosen by the user. This
example assumes that DEMO.HLP is a Help file that contains a topic with a Help context
number equal to 1000.

Dim Msg, Style, Title, Help, Ctxt, Response, MyString
Msg = "Do you want to continue ?"    ' Define message.
Style = vbYesNo + vbCritical + vbDefaultButton2    ' Define button
Title = "MsgBox Demonstration"    ' Define title.
Help = "DEMO.HLP"    ' Define Help file.
Ctxt = 1000    ' Define topic
        ' context.
        ' Display message.
Response = MsgBox(Msg, Style, Title, Help, Ctxt)
If Response = vbYes Then    ' User chose Yes.
    MyString = "Yes"    ' Perform some action.
Else    ' User chose No.
    MyString = "No"    ' Perform some action.
End If
```

After you record a macro, undoubtedly there will be objects or methods that you are not sure of. Insert the cursor in any keyword and press F1 to get help on that topic.

Examining Recorded Macro Code—Using the VB Editor and Help

Let's take a look at the code that was recorded in Chapter 1, "Unleash the Power of Excel with VBA!" to see whether it makes more sense now in the context of objects, properties, and methods. You can also see whether it's possible to correct the errors brought about by the macro recorder.

Here is the first code that Excel recorded in Chapter 1 (see Figure 2.6).

Figure 2.6
Recorded code.

Now that you understand the concept of Noun.Verb or Object.Method, look at the first line of code. It says `Workbooks.OpenText`. In this case, `Workbooks` is an object. `OpenText` is a method. Click your cursor inside the word `OpenText` and press F1 for an explanation of the `OpenText` method (see Figure 2.7).

Figure 2.7
Help topic for the
OpenText Method.
Methods usually have an
Applies To link on the
second line, which helps
to identify when you can
use a particular method.

The help file confirms that `OpenText` is a method or an action word. In the grey box is the default order for all the arguments that can be used with `OpenText`. Notice that only one argument is required—`FileName`. All the other arguments are listed as optional.

Optional Parameters

What happens if you skip an optional parameter? The help file can tell you. For `StartRow`, the help file indicates that the default value is 1. If you leave out the `StartRow` parameter, Excel starts importing at Row 1. This is fairly safe. Look at the help file note about `Origin`. If this argument is omitted, then you inherit whatever value was used for `Origin` the last time someone used this feature in Excel on this computer. That is certainly a recipe for disaster—your code may work 98% of the time, but immediately after someone imports an Arabic file, Excel will remember the setting for Arabic and assume this is what your macro wants if you don't explicitly code this parameter.

Defined Constants

Look at the help file entry for `DataType` in Figure 2.8. The help file says that it can be one of these constants: `xlDelimited` or `xlFixedWidth`. The help file says that these are the valid `xlTextParsingType` constants. These constants are pre-defined in Excel VBA. In the VB Editor, hit Ctrl+G to bring up the Immediate pane. In the Immediate pane, type this line and press Enter:

```
Print xlFixedWidth
```

The answer appears in the Immediate pane. `xlFixedWidth` is the equivalent of saying "2" (see Figure 2.8). Ask the Immediate pane to `Print xlDelimited`. This is really the same as typing 1. Microsoft correctly assumes that it is easier for someone to read code that uses the somewhat English-like term `xlDelimited` instead of 1.

Figure 2.8
In the Immediate pane of the VB Editor, query to see the true value of constants such as `xlFixedWidth`.

```
Immediate
    print xlFixedWidth
     2
    print xlDelimited
     1
```

If you were an evil programmer, you could certainly memorize all these constants and write code using the numeric equivalents of the constants. However, the programming gods (as well as the next person who has to look at your code) will curse you for this.

In most cases, the help file either specifically calls out the valid values of the constants, or offers a blue hyperlink that causes the help file to expand and show you the valid values for the constants (see Figure 2.9).

Figure 2.9
Click the blue hyperlink to see all of the possible constant values. Here, the 10 possible `xlColumnDataType` constants are revealed in the middle of the help topic.

My one complaint with this excellent help system is that it does not identify which parameters may be new to a given version. In this particular case, `TrailingMinusNumbers` was introduced in Excel 2002. If you attempt to give this program to someone who is still using Excel 2000, the code does not run because it does not understand the `TrailingMinusNumbers` parameter. This is a frustrating problem, and the only way to learn to handle it is through trial and error.

If you read the help topic on `OpenText`, you can surmise that it is basically the equivalent of opening a file using the Text Import Wizard. In the first step of the Wizard, you normally choose either Delimited or Fixed Width. You also specify the File Origin and at which row to start (see Figure 2.10). This first step of the Wizard is handled by these parameters of the `OpenText` method:

```
Origin:=437
StartRow:=1
DataType:=xlDelimited
```

Figure 2.10
The first step of the Text Import Wizard in Excel is covered by three parameters of the `OpenText` method.

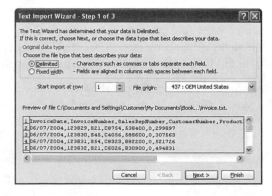

Step 2 of the Text to Columns Wizard enables you to specify that your fields are delimited by a comma. We don't want to treat two commas as a single comma, so Treat Consecutive Delimiters As One is unchecked. Sometimes, a field may contain a comma—for example "XYZ, Inc." In this case, the field should have quotes around the value. This is specified in the Text qualifier box (see Figure 2.11). This second step of the Wizard is handled by these parameters of the `OpenText` method:

```
TextQualifier:=xlDoubleQuote
ConsecutiveDelimiter:=False
Tab:=False
Semicolon:=False
Comma:=True
Space:=False
Other:=False
```

Figure 2.11
Step 2 of the Text Import Wizard is handled by the seven parameters of `OpenText` method.

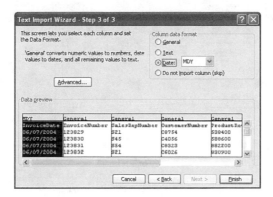

Step 3 of the Wizard is where you actually identify the field types. In our case, we left all fields as General except for the first field, which was marked as a date in MDY (Month, Day, Year) format (see Figure 2.12). This is represented in code by the `FieldInfo` parameter.

Figure 2.12
The third step of the Text Import Wizard is fairly complex. The entire `FieldInfo` parameter of the `OpenText` method duplicates the choices made on this step of the Wizard.

If you would happen to click the Advanced button on Step 3 of the Wizard, you have an opportunity to specify something other than the default Decimal and Thousands separator, plus the setting for Trailing Minus for negative numbers (see Figure 2.13). Note that the macro recorder does not write code for `DecimalSeparator` or `ThousandsSeparator` unless you change these from the defaults. The Macro Recorder does always record the `TrailingMinusNumbers` parameter.

Figure 2.13
The `TrailingMinus Numbers` parameter comes from this Advanced Text Import Settings. If you had changed either of the separator fields, new parameters would have been recorded by the macro recorder.

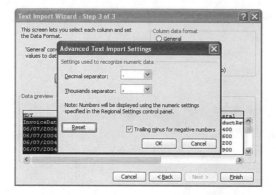

At this point, you can more or less see how just about every option that you do in Excel while the macro recorder is running corresponds to a bit of code in the recorded macro.

Here is another example. The next line of code in the macro is

```
Selection.End(xlDown).Select
```

You can click and get help for three topics in this line of code: `Selection`, `End`, and `Select`. Assuming that `Selection` and `Select` are somewhat self-explanatory, click in the word `End` and press F1 for help. A Context Help dialog box pops up, saying that there are two possible help topics for `End`. There is one in the Excel library and one in the VBA library (see Figure 2.14).

Figure 2.14
Sometimes when you click in a VBA keyword and hit F1, you must guess which help library to use.

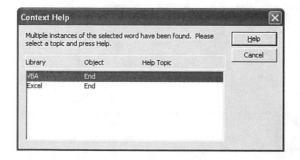

If you are new to VBA, it can be frustrating to know which one to select. Take your best guess and click Help. In this case, the End help topic in the VBA library is talking about the `End` statement (see Figure 2.15), which is not what we have here.

Figure 2.15
If you guess wrong, you are taken to a help topic that is completely off-topic. It is easy enough to try again.

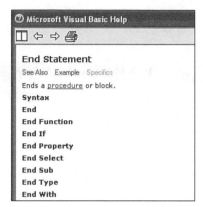

Close Help, press F1 again, and choose the End object in the Excel library. This help topic says that End is a property. It returns a Range object that is equivalent to pressing End+Up or End+Down in the Excel interface. If you click on the blue hyperlink for xlDirection, you will see the valid parameters that can be passed to the End function (see Figure 2.16).

Figure 2.16
The correct help topic for the End property.

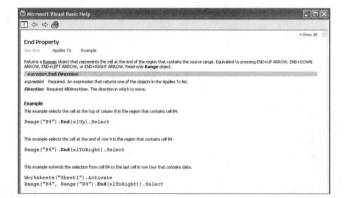

Properties Can Return Objects

In the discussion at the start of this chapter, I said that the basic syntax of VBA is Object.Method. In this particular line of code, the method is .Select. The End keyword is a property, but from the help file, you see that it returns a Range object. Because the .Select method can apply to a Range object, the method is actually appended to a property.

You might then assume that Selection is the object in this line of code. If you click the mouse in the word Selection and press F1, you will see that according to the help topic, Selection is actually a property and not an object. In reality, the proper code would be to say Application.Selection; however, when you are running within Excel, VBA assumes you are referring to the Excel object model, so you can leave off the Application object. If you were to write a program in Word VBA to automate Excel, you would be required to include an object variable before the .Selection property to qualify to which application you are referring.

In this case, the `Application.Selection` can return several different types of objects. If a cell is selected, it returns the `Range` object.

Using Debugging Tools to Figure Out Recorded Code

The Visual Basic Editor features some awesome debugging tools. These are excellent for helping you see what a recorded macro code is doing.

Stepping Through Code

Generally, a macro runs really fast. You start, and less than a second later, it is done. If something goes wrong, you have no opportunity to figure out what it is doing. Using Excel's Step Into feature, it is possible to run one line of code at a time.

Make sure the cursor is in the `ImportInvoice` procedure and from the menu select Debug, Step Into (or press F8) (see Figure 2.17).

Figure 2.17
Stepping into code allows you to run a single line at a time.

Debug	Run	Tools	Add-Ins	Window
Compile VBAProject				
Step Into				F8
Step Over				Shift+F8
Step Out				Ctrl+Shift+F8
Run To Cursor				Ctrl+F8
Add Watch...				
Edit Watch...				Ctrl+W
Quick Watch...				Shift+F9
Toggle Breakpoint				F9
Clear All Breakpoints				Ctrl+Shift+F9
Set Next Statement				Ctrl+F9
Show Next Statement				

The VB Editor is now in step mode. The line about to be executed is highlighted in yellow with a yellow arrow in the margin before the code (see Figure 2.18).

Figure 2.18
The first line of the macro is about to run.

```
Sub ImportInvoice()
'
' ImportInvoice Macro
' Macro recorded 10/23/2003 by Bill Jelen This macro will import invoice.txt and add totals.
'
' Keyboard Shortcut: Ctrl+i
'
    Workbooks.OpenText Filename:= _
        "C:\invoice.txt", Origin _
        :=437, StartRow:=1, DataType:=xlDelimited, TextQualifier:=xlDoubleQuote _
        , ConsecutiveDelimiter:=False, Tab:=True, Semicolon:=False, Comma:=True _
        , Space:=False, Other:=False, FieldInfo:=Array(Array(1, 3), Array(2, 1), _
        Array(3, 1), Array(4, 1), Array(5, 1), Array(6, 1), Array(7, 1)), TrailingMinusNumbers _
        :=True
    Selection.End(xlDown).Select
    Range("A14").Select
    ActiveCell.FormulaR1C1 = "'Total"
    Range("E14").Select
    Selection.FormulaR1C1 = "=SUM(R[-12]C:R[-1]C)"
    Selection.AutoFill Destination:=Range("E14:G14"), Type:=xlFillDefault
    Range("E14:G14").Select
    Rows("1:1").Select
    Selection.Font.Bold = True
    Rows("14:14").Select
    Selection.Font.Bold = True
    Cells.Select
    Selection.Columns.AutoFit
End Sub
```

In this case, the next line to be executed is the `Sub ImportInvoice()` line. This basically says, "We are about to start running this procedure." Press the F8 key to execute the line in yellow and move to the next line of code. The long code for `OpenText` is then highlighted. Press F8 to run this line of code. When you see that `Selection.End(xlDown).Select` is highlighted, you know that Visual Basic has finished running the `OpenText` command. Indeed, you can use Alt+Tab to switch to Excel and see the `Invoice.txt` file has been parsed into Excel. Note that A1 is selected (see Figure 2.19).

Figure 2.19

Switching to Excel shows that the `Invoice.txt` file has indeed been imported.

	A	B	C	D	E	F	G	H
1	InvoiceDat	InvoiceNun	SalesRep	Customer	ProductRe	ServiceRe	ProductCost	
2	6/7/2004	123829	S21	C8754	538400	0	299897	
3	6/7/2004	123830	S45	C4056	588600	0	307563	
4	6/7/2004	123831	S54	C8323	882200	0	521726	
5	6/7/2004	123832	S21	C6026	830900	0	494831	
6	6/7/2004	123833	S45	C3025	673600	0	374953	
7	6/7/2004	123834	S54	C8663	966300	0	528575	
8	6/7/2004	123835	S21	C1508	467100	0	257942	
9	6/7/2004	123836	S45	C7366	658500	10000	308719	
10	6/7/2004	123837	S54	C4533	191700	0	109534	
11								

Switch back to the Visual Basic Editor, using Alt+Tab. The next line about to be executed is `Selection.End(xlDown).Select`. Press F8 to run this code. Switch to Excel to see the results. Now A10 is selected (see Figure 2.20).

Figure 2.20

Verify that the `End(xlDown).Select` command worked as expected. This is equivalent to hitting the End key and then the Down arrow.

	A	B	C	D	E	F	G	H
1	InvoiceDat	InvoiceNun	SalesRep	Customer	ProductRe	ServiceRe	ProductCost	
2	6/7/2004	123829	S21	C8754	538400	0	299897	
3	6/7/2004	123830	S45	C4056	588600	0	307563	
4	6/7/2004	123831	S54	C8323	882200	0	521726	
5	6/7/2004	123832	S21	C6026	830900	0	494831	
6	6/7/2004	123833	S45	C3025	673600	0	374953	
7	6/7/2004	123834	S54	C8663	966300	0	528575	
8	6/7/2004	123835	S21	C1508	467100	0	257942	
9	6/7/2004	123836	S45	C7366	658500	10000	308719	
10	6/7/2004	123837	S54	C4533	191700	0	109534	
11								

Press F8 again to run the `Range("A14").Select` line. If you switch to Excel by using Alt+Tab, you will see that this is where the macro starts to have problems. Instead of moving to the first blank row, the program moved to the wrong row (see Figure 2.21).

Figure 2.21

The recorded macro code blindly moves to Row 14 for the total row.

	A	B	C	D	E	F	G	H
1	InvoiceDat	InvoiceNun	SalesRep	Customer	ProductRe	ServiceRe	ProductCost	
2	6/7/2004	123829	S21	C8754	538400	0	299897	
3	6/7/2004	123830	S45	C4056	588600	0	307563	
4	6/7/2004	123831	S54	C8323	882200	0	521726	
5	6/7/2004	123832	S21	C6026	830900	0	494831	
6	6/7/2004	123833	S45	C3025	673600	0	374953	
7	6/7/2004	123834	S54	C8663	966300	0	528575	
8	6/7/2004	123835	S21	C1508	467100	0	257942	
9	6/7/2004	123836	S45	C7366	658500	10000	308719	
10	6/7/2004	123837	S54	C4533	191700	0	109534	
11								
12								

Now that you have identified the problem area, you can stop the code execution by resetting the program (either by selecting Run, Reset or using the Reset button in the toolbar; see Figure 2.22). After pressing Reset, you should return to Excel and undo anything done by the partially completed macro. In this case, close the `invoice.txt` file without saving.

Figure 2.22

The Reset button in the toolbar stops a macro that is in break mode.

More Debugging Options—Breakpoints

If you have hundreds of lines of code, you may not want to step through each line one by one. You may have a general knowledge that the problem is happening in one particular section of the program. In this case, you can set a breakpoint. You can then have the code start to run, but the macro breaks just before it executes the breakpoint line of code.

To set a breakpoint, click in the grey margin area to the left of the line of code on which you want to break. A large brown dot appears next to this code and the line of code is highlighted in brown (see Figure 2.23).

Figure 2.23

The large brown dot signifies a breakpoint.

```
Sub ImportInvoice()
'
' ImportInvoice Macro
' Macro recorded 10/23/2003 by Bill Jelen This macro will import invoice.txt and add totals.
'
' Keyboard Shortcut: Ctrl+i

    Workbooks.OpenText Filename:= _
        "C:\invoice.txt", Origin _
        :=437, StartRow:=1, DataType:=xlDelimited, TextQualifier:=xlDoubleQuote _
        , ConsecutiveDelimiter:=False, Tab:=True, Semicolon:=False, Comma:=True _
        , Space:=False, Other:=False, FieldInfo:=Array(Array(1, 3), Array(2, 1), _
        Array(3, 1), Array(4, 1), Array(5, 1), Array(6, 1), Array(7, 1)), TrailingMinusNumbers _
        :=True
    Selection.End(xlDown).Select
    Range("A14").Select
    ActiveCell.FormulaR1C1 = "'Total"
    Range("E14").Select
    Selection.FormulaR1C1 = "=SUM(R[-12]C:R[-1]C)"
    Selection.AutoFill Destination:=Range("E14:G14"), Type:=xlFillDefault
    Range("E14:G14").Select
    Rows("1:1").Select
    Selection.Font.Bold = True
    Rows("14:14").Select
    Selection.Font.Bold = True
    Cells.Select
    Selection.Columns.AutoFit
End Sub
```

Now, from the menu select Run, Run Sub or press F5. The program quickly executes but stops just before the breakpoint. The Visual Basic Editor shows the breakpoint line highlighted in yellow. You can now use F8 to begin stepping through the code (see Figure 2.24).

Figure 2.24

The yellow line signifies that the breakpoint line is about to be run next.

```
Sub ImportInvoice()
'
' ImportInvoice Macro
' Macro recorded 10/23/2003 by Bill Jelen This macro will import invoice.txt and add totals.
'
' Keyboard Shortcut: Ctrl+i

    Workbooks.OpenText Filename:= _
        "C:\invoice.txt", Origin _
        :=437, StartRow:=1, DataType:=xlDelimited, TextQualifier:=xlDoubleQuote _
        , ConsecutiveDelimiter:=False, Tab:=True, Semicolon:=False, Comma:=True _
        , Space:=False, Other:=False, FieldInfo:=Array(Array(1, 3), Array(2, 1), _
        Array(3, 1), Array(4, 1), Array(5, 1), Array(6, 1), Array(7, 1)), TrailingMinusNumbers _
        :=True
    Selection.End(xlDown).Select
    Range("A14").Select
    ActiveCell.FormulaR1C1 = "'Total"
    Range("E14").Select
    Selection.FormulaR1C1 = "=SUM(R[-12]C:R[-1]C)"
    Selection.AutoFill Destination:=Range("E14:G14"), Type:=xlFillDefault
    Range("E14:G14").Select
    Rows("1:1").Select
    Selection.Font.Bold = True
    Rows("14:14").Select
    Selection.Font.Bold = True
    Cells.Select
    Selection.Columns.AutoFit
End Sub
```

After you are finished debugging your code, you should remove the breakpoints. You can do this by clicking the dark brown dot in the margin to toggle off the breakpoint. You can also select Debug, Clear All Breakpoints or Ctrl+Shift+F9 to clear all breakpoints that you've set in the project.

Backing Up or Moving Forward in Code

When you are stepping through code, you might want to jump over some lines of code. Or, perhaps you've corrected some lines of code and you want to run them again. In step mode, it is very easy to do this. My favorite method is to use the mouse to grab the yellow arrow. The mouse pointer changes to an icon meaning that you can move the Next line up or down. Drag the yellow line to whichever line you want to execute next (see Figure 2.25). The other option is to click the cursor in the line to which you want to jump and then use Debug, Set Next Statement.

Figure 2.25
The mouse pointer as it appears when dragging the yellow line to a different line of code to be executed next.

```
Range ("E14:G14") .Select
Rows ("1:1") .Select
Selection.Font.Bold = True
```

Not Stepping Through Each Line of Code

When you are stepping through code, you might want to run a section of code without stepping through each line. This is common when you get to a loop. You might want VBA to run through the loop 100 times so you can step through the lines after the loop. It is particularly monotonous to hit the F8 key hundreds of times to step through a loop. Click the cursor on the line you want to step to and hit Ctrl+F8 or select Debug, Run to Cursor.

Querying Anything While Stepping Through Code

We haven't talked about variables yet (the macro recorder never records a variable), but you can query the value of anything while in step mode.

Using the Immediate Window

Press Ctrl+G to display the Immediate window in the VB Editor. While the macro is in break mode, you can ask the VB Editor to tell you the currently selected cell, the name of the active sheet, or the value of any variable. Figure 2.26 shows several examples of queries typed into the Immediate pane.

Figure 2.26
Queries (and their answers), which can be typed into the Immediate window while a macro is in break mode.

When invoked with Ctrl+G, the Immediate window usually appears at the bottom of the code window. You can use the resize handle (above the blue Immediate title bar) to make the Immediate window larger or smaller (see Figure 2.27).

Figure 2.27
Resizing the Immediate window.

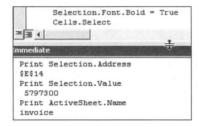

There is a scrollbar on the side of the Immediate window. You can use this to scroll backward or forward through past entries in the Immediate window.

It is not necessary to run queries only at the bottom of the Immediate window. Here is an example. In this case, I've just run one line of code. In the Immediate window, I ask for the Selection.Address to ensure that this line of code worked (see Figure 2.28).

Figure 2.28
The Immediate window shows the results before the current line is executed.

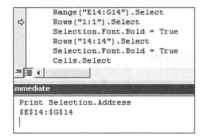

Press the F8 key to run the next line of code. Rather than retyping the same query, I can click in the Immediate window at the end of the line containing the last query (see Figure 2.29).

Figure 2.29
There is no need to type the same commands over in the Immediate window. Place the cursor at the end of the previous command and press Enter.

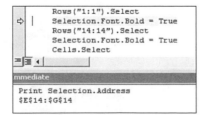

Press Enter, and the Immediate window runs this query again, displaying the results on the next line and pushing the old results farther down the window. In this case, the selected address is $1:$1. The previous answer, $E$14:$G$14, is pushed down the window (see Figure 2.30).

Figure 2.30
The prior answer ($E$14:$G$14) is shifted down and the current answer ($1:$1) appears below the query.

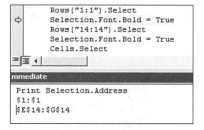

Press F8 four more times to run through the line of code with Cells.Select. Again, position the cursor in the Immediate window just after Print Selection.Address and press Enter. The query is run again, and the most recent address is shown with the prior answers moved down in the Immediate window (see Figure 2.31).

Figure 2.31
After selecting all cells with Cells.Select, place the cursor after the query in the Immediate window and press Enter. The new answer is that the selected range is all rows from 1 to 65536.

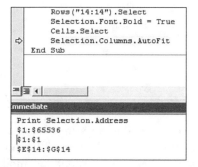

You can also use this method to change the query. Click to the right of the word .Address in the Immediate window. Use the backspace to erase the word Address and instead type **Rows.Count**. Hit Enter and the Immediate window tells you the number of rows in the Selection (see Figure 2.32).

Figure 2.32
Delete part of a query, type something new, and press Enter. The previous answers are pushed down and the current answer is displayed.

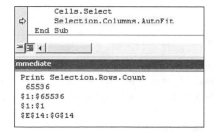

This technique is excellent when you are trying to figure out a sticky bit of code. I may find myself querying the name of the active sheet (`Print Activesheet.Name`), the selection (`Print Selection.Address`), the active cell (`Print ActiveCell.Address`), the formula (`Print ActiveCell.Formula`) in the active cell, the value of the active cell (`Print ActiveCell.Value` or—`Print ActiveCell` because `.Value` is the default property of a cell), and so on.

To dismiss the Immediate window, use the X in the upper-right corner of the Immediate window. (Ctrl+G does not toggle the window on and off.)

Querying by Hovering

In many instances, you can hover your mouse over an expression in the code. Wait a second, and a tooltip pops up showing you the current value of the expression. This is invaluable for you to understand when you get to looping in Chapter 5, "Looping." And it still will come in handy with recorded code. Note that the expression that you hover over does not have to be in the line of code just executed. In Figure 2.33, Visual Basic just selected all cells (making A1 the ActiveCell). If I hover the mouse over `ActiveCell.Formula`, I get a tool tip showing me that the formula in the ActiveCell is the word `InvoiceDate`.

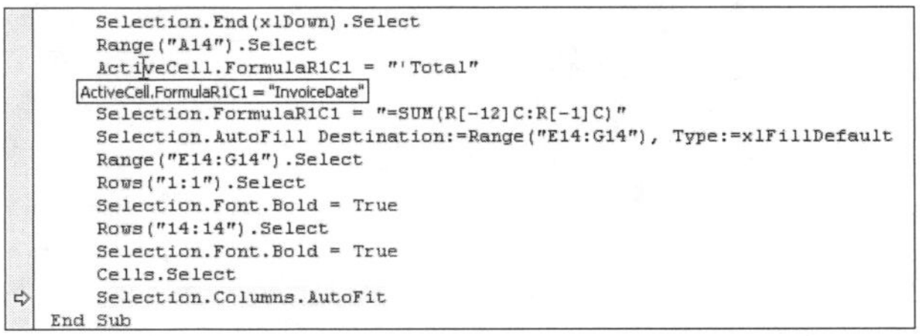

Figure 2.33
Hover the mouse cursor over any expression for a few seconds and a tooltip shows the current value of the expression.

```
        Selection.End(xlDown).Select
        Range("A14").Select
        ActiveCell.FormulaR1C1 = "'Total"
ActiveCell.FormulaR1C1 = "InvoiceDate"
        Selection.FormulaR1C1 = "=SUM(R[-12]C:R[-1]C)"
        Selection.AutoFill Destination:=Range("E14:G14"), Type:=xlFillDefault
        Range("E14:G14").Select
        Rows("1:1").Select
        Selection.Font.Bold = True
        Rows("14:14").Select
        Selection.Font.Bold = True
        Cells.Select
        Selection.Columns.AutoFit
    End Sub
```

Sometimes the VBA window seems to not respond to hovering. Because some expressions are not supposed to show a value, it is difficult to tell whether VBA is not displaying the value on purpose or whether you are in the buggy "not responding" mode. Try hovering over something that you know should respond (such as a variable). If you get no response, then hover, actually click into the variable, and continue to hover. This tends to wake Excel up from the stupor and hovering will work again.

Are you impressed yet? I started the chapter complaining that this didn't seem much like BASIC, but you have to admit that the Visual Basic environment is great to work in. These debugging tools are excellent.

Querying by Using a Watch Window

In Visual Basic, a Watch is not something you wear on your wrist. It allows you to watch the value of any expression while you step through code. Let's say that in the current example, I wanted to watch to see what is selected as the code runs. I would set up a Watch for `Selection.Address`.

From the VBE menu, select Debug, Add Watch.

In the Add Watch dialog, enter `Selection.Address` in the Expression text box and click OK (see Figure 2.34).

Figure 2.34
Setting up a Watch to see the address of the current selection.

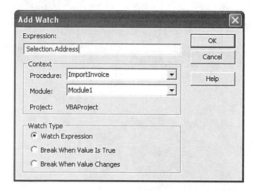

A Watches window is added to the busy Visual Basic window. It is usually added at the bottom of the Code pane. I started running the macro, importing the file and pressing End+Down to move to the last row with data. Right before the `Range("A14").Select` code is executed, the Watches window shows me that `Selection.Address` is $A$10 (see Figure 2.35).

Figure 2.35
Without having to hover or type in the Immediate window, you can always see the value of watched expressions.

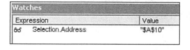

Press the F8 key to run the code `Range("A14").Select`. The Watches window is updated to show the current address of the Selection is now $A$14 (see Figure 2.36).

Figure 2.36
The Watches pane appears at the bottom of the Code pane. Without having to hover or type in the Immediate window, you can always see the value of watched expressions. Here, you see that just before selecting cell A14, the value of `Selection.Addres s` is $A$10.

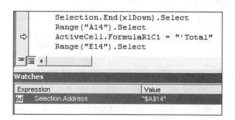

Using a Watch to Set a Breakpoint

Right-click the glasses icon in the Watches window and choose Edit Watch. In the Watch Type section of the Edit Watch dialog, select Break When Value Changes (see Figure 2.37). Click OK.

Figure 2.37
Select Break When Value Changes in the bottom of the Edit Watch dialog.

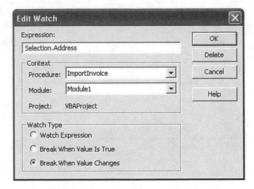

The glasses icon has changed to a hand with triangle icon. You can now press F5 to run the code. The macro starts running lines of code until something new is selected. This is very powerful. Rather than having to step through each line of code, you can now conveniently have the macro stop only when something important has happened. A watch can also be set up to stop when the value of a particular variable changes.

Using a Watch on an Object

In the last example, we watched a specific property—Selection.Address. It is also possible to watch an object, such as Selection. In Figure 2.38, I have set up a Watch on Selection. I get the glasses icon and a + icon.

Figure 2.38
Setting a Watch on an object gives you a + icon next to the glasses.

By clicking on the + icon, I can see all the properties associated with Selection. Look at Figure 2.39! You can now see more than you ever wanted to know about the Selection. There are properties that you probably never realized were available. You can see that the .AddIndent property is set to False and the .AllowEdit property is set to True. There are useful properties in the list—you can see the .Formula of the selection.

In this Watch window, some entries can be expanded. The Borders collection has a plus next to it. Click any + icon to see even more details.

Figure 2.39
Clicking the + icon shows a plethora of properties and their current values.

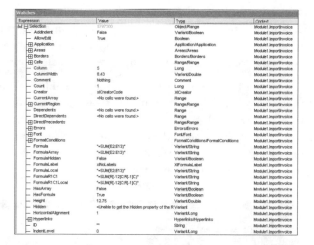

The Ultimate Reference to All Objects, Methods, Properties

In the Visual Basic Editor, press F2 to open the Object Browser (see Figure 2.40). The Object Browser lets you browse and search the entire Excel object library. I own a thick book that is a reprint of this entire object model from the object browser. It took up 409 pages of text. I've never used those 409 pages, because the built-in Object Browser is far more powerful and always available at the touch of F2. I'll take a few pages to teach you how to use the Object Browser.

Figure 2.40
Press F2 to display the Object Browser.

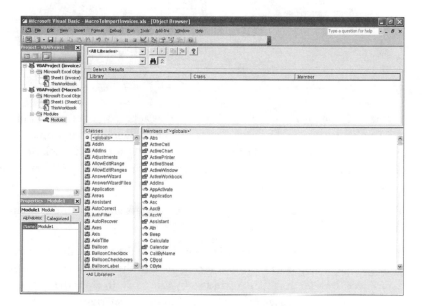

Press F2 and the Object Browser appears where the code window normally appears. The topmost drop-down currently shows <All Libraries>. There is an entry in this dropdown for Excel, Office, VBA, each workbook that you have open, plus additional entries for anything that you check in Tools, References. Go to the drop-down and select only Excel for now.

In the left pane of the Object browser is a list of all classes available for Excel. Click on the `Application` class in the left pane. The right pane adjusts to show all properties and methods that apply to the `Application` object (see Figure 2.41). Click on something in the right pane like `ActiveCell`. The bottom pane of the object browser tells you that `ActiveCell` is a property that returns a Range. It tells you that `ActiveCell` is read only—an alert that you can not assign an address to `ActiveCell` to move the cell pointer.

Figure 2.41

Select a class then a member. The bottom pane tells you the basics about the particular member. Methods appear as green books with speed lines. Properties appear as index cards with a hand pointing to them.

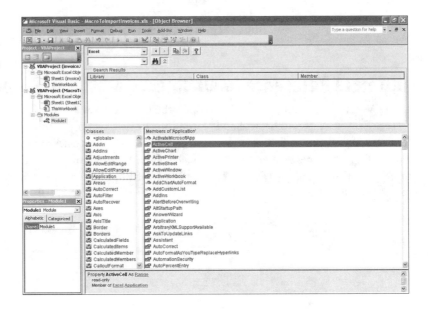

We have learned from the Object Browser that `ActiveCell` returns a range. Click the green hyperlink for `Range` in the bottom pane and you will see all the properties and methods that apply to Range objects and hence to the `ActiveCell` property. Click on any property or method and click the yellow question mark near the top of the Object Browser to go to the help topic for that property or method.

Type any term in the text box next to the binoculars and click the binoculars to find all matching members of the Excel library.

The search capabilities and hyperlinks available in the Object Browser make it far more valuable than an alphabetic printed listing of all of the information. Learn to make use of the Object Browser in the VBA window by using F2. To close the object browser and return to your code window, click on the lower X in the upper-right corner (see Figure 2.42).

Figure 2.42
Close the Object Browser and return to your code window by clicking this X.

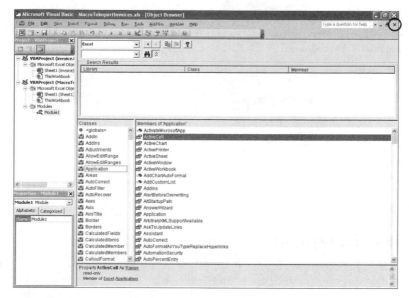

Five Easy Tips for Cleaning Up Recorded Code

I apologize. We are nearly to the end of Chapter 2, and the crazy macro we recorded in Chapter 1 still doesn't work. I am sure you want to get to the heart of the matter and find out how to make the recorded macro work. Here are five easy rules that will quickly have your code running fast and working well.

Tip 1: Don't Select Anything

Nothing screams "recorded code" more than having code that selects things before acting upon them. This makes sense—in the Excel interface, you have to select Row 1 before you can make it bold.

However, in VBA we rarely have to do this. (There are a couple buggy features in charts where you do have to select the chart object in order to make the method work.) It is possible to directly turn on Bold font to Row 1 without selecting it. The following two lines of code turn into one line.

Macro recorder code before being streamlined:

```
Rows("1:1").Select
Selection.Font.Bold = True
```

After streamlining the recorded code:

```
Rows("1:1").Font.Bold = True
```

There are several advantages to this method. First, there will be half as many lines of code in your program. Second, the program will run faster.

After recording code, I literally highlight from before the word `.Select` at the end of one line all the way to the dot after the word `Selection` on the next line and press Delete (see Figures 2.43 and 2.44).

Figure 2.43
Select from here to here...

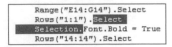

```
Range("E14:G14").Select
Rows("1:1").Select
Selection.Font.Bold = True
Rows("14:14").Select
```

Figure 2.44
...and hit the Delete key. This is basic "101" of cleaning up recorded macros.

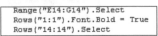

```
Range("E14:G14").Select
Rows("1:1").Font.Bold = True
Rows("14:14").Select
```

Tip 2: Ride the Range from the Bottom to Find Last Row

It is difficult to trust data from anywhere. If you are analyzing data in Excel, remember that the data is often coming from who-knows-what system written who-knows-how-long ago. The universal truth is that sooner or later, some clerk somewhere will find a way to break the source system and will manage to enter a record without an invoice number. Maybe it takes a power failure to do it, but invariably, we cannot count on having every cell filled in.

This is a problem when using End+Down. This key combination does not take you to the last row with data in the worksheet. It takes you to the last row with data in the current range. In Figure 2.45, hitting End+Down would move the cursor to cell A6 instead of cell A10.

Figure 2.45
End+Down fails in the user interface if a record is missing a value. Similarly, End(xlDown) fails in Excel VBA.

	A1	▼	ƒx	InvoiceDate	
	A	B	C	D	
1	InvoiceDat	InvoiceNun	SalesRepN	CustomerN	
2	6/7/2004	123829	S21	C8754	
3	6/7/2004	123830	S45	C4056	
4	6/7/2004	123831	S54	C8323	
5	6/7/2004	123832	S21	C6026	
6	6/7/2004	123833	S45	C3025	
7		123834	S54	C8663	
8	6/7/2004	123835	S21	C1508	
9	6/7/2004	123836	S45	C7366	
10	6/7/2004	123837	S54	C4533	
11					

The better solution is to start at the bottom of the Excel worksheet and press End+Up. Now, this seems silly in the Excel interface because you can easily see whether you are really at the end of the data. But, because it is easy in Excel VBA to start at the last row, get in the habit of using this code to find the true last row.

```
Range("A65536").End(xlUp)
```

> **CAUTION**
>
> Excel has had the same number of rows (65,536) since they increased it from 16,384 in 1995. Although it is very tempting and seemingly safe to hard code 65,536, I firmly believe that we will finally see more rows in Excel 2005. To make your code work with any past or future version of Excel, some advocate using `Rows.Count` as the number of rows in the currently open version of Excel. Using something along the lines of Cells(Row.Count, 1).End(xlUp) ensures your code will work after we have more rows available in Excel. It also ensures your code will be compatible with pre-Excel 97 versions that have fewer than 65,536 rows.

Tip 3: Use Variables to Avoid Hard-coding Rows and Formulas

The macro recorder never records a variable. They are very easy to use. They are discussed in more detail later, but just as in BASIC, a variable can remember a value.

My recommendation is to set the last row with data to a variable. I like to use meaningful variable names, so my favorite for this is `FinalRow`.

```
FinalRow = Range("A65536").End(xlUp).Row
```

Now that you know the row number of the last record, it is easy to put the word Total in Column A of the next row.

```
Range("A" & FinalRow + 1).Value = "Total"
```

→ For simpler methods of referring to this range, **see** "Using the `Offset` Property to Refer to a Range," **p. 65**, in Chapter 3.

You can even use the variable when building the formula. This formula totals everything from E2 to the `FinalRow` of E:

```
Range("E" & FinalRow + 1).Formula = "=SUM(E2:E" & FinalRow & ")"
```

Tip 4: Learn to Copy and Paste in a Single Statement

Recorded code is notorious for copying a range, selecting another range, and then doing an `ActiveSheet.Paste`. The `Copy` method as it applies to a range is actually far more powerful. You can specify what to copy and specify the destination in one statement.

Recorded code:

```
Range("E14").Select
Selection.Copy
Range("F14:G14").Select
ActiveSheet.Paste
```

Better code:

```
Range("E14").Copy Destination:=Range("F14:G14")
```

Tip 5: Use `With...End With` If You Are Performing Multiple Actions to the Same Cell or Range of Cells

If you were going to make the total row bold, double underline, with a larger font and a special color, you might get recorded code like this:

```
Range("A14:G14").Select
Selection.Font.Bold = True
Selection.Font.Size = 12
Selection.Font.ColorIndex = 5
Selection.Font.Underline = xlUnderlineStyleDoubleAccounting
```

For four of those lines of code, VBA must resolve the expression `Selection.Font`. Because you have four lines that all refer to the same object, you can name the object once at the top of a `With` block. Inside the `With...End With` block, everything that starts with a period is assumed to refer to the `With` object:

```
With Range("A14:G14").Font
    .Bold = True
    .Size = 12
    .ColorIndex = 5
    .Underline = xlUnderlineStyleDoubleAccounting
End With
```

Putting It All Together—Fixing the Recorded Code

CASE STUDY

Changing the Recorded Code

Using the five tips given in this chapter, you can convert the recorded code into efficient, professional-looking code. Here is the code as recorded by the macro recorder:

```
' ImportInvoice Macro
' Recorded 10/23/2003 by Bill Jelen This macro will import invoice.txt
' and add totals.
'
' Keyboard Shortcut: Ctrl+i
'

  Workbooks.OpenText Filename:= _
        "C:\invoice.txt", Origin _
        :=437, StartRow:=1, DataType:=xlDelimited, TextQualifier:=xlDoubleQuote _
        , ConsecutiveDelimiter:=False, Tab:=True, Semicolon:=False, Comma:=True _
        , Space:=False, Other:=False, FieldInfo:=Array(Array(1, 3), Array(2, 1), _
        Array(3, 1), Array(4, 1), Array(5, 1), Array(6, 1), Array(7, 1)), _
        TrailingMinusNumbers:=True
    Selection.End(xlDown).Select
    Range("A14").Select
    ActiveCell.FormulaR1C1 = "'Total"
    Range("E14").Select
```

```
        Selection.FormulaR1C1 = "=SUM(R[-12]C:R[-1]C)"
        Selection.AutoFill Destination:=Range("E14:G14"), Type:=xlFillDefault
        Range("E14:G14").Select
        Rows("1:1").Select
        Selection.Font.Bold = True
        Rows("14:14").Select
        Selection.Font.Bold = True
        Cells.Select
        Selection.Columns.AutoFit
End Sub
```

Follow these steps to clean up the macro:

1. The `Workbook.OpenText` lines are fine as recorded.

2. The following lines of code attempt to locate the final row of data so that the program knows where to enter the total row:

   ```
   Selection.End(xlDown).Select
   ```

   You don't need to select anything to find the last row. Also, it helps to assign the row number of the final row and the total row to a variable so that they can be used later. To handle the unexpected case where a single cell in Column A is blank, start at the bottom of the worksheet and go up to find the last used row:

   ```
   ' Find the last row with data. This might change every day
   FinalRow = Range("A65536").End(xlUp).Row
   TotalRow = FinalRow + 1
   ```

3. These lines of code enter the word "Total" in Column A of the total row:

   ```
   Range("A14").Select
   ActiveCell.FormulaR1C1 = "'Total"
   ```

   The better code will use the `TotalRow` variable to locate where to enter the word "Total." Again, there is no need to select the cell before entering the label:

   ```
   ' Build a Total row below this
   Range("A" & TotalRow).Value = "Total"
   ```

4. These lines of code enter the Total formula in Column E and copy it over to the next two columns:

   ```
   Range("E14").Select
   Selection.FormulaR1C1 = "=SUM(R[-12]C:R[-1]C)"
   Selection.AutoFill Destination:=Range("E14:G14"), Type:=xlFillDefault
   Range("E14:G14").Select
   ```

   There is no reason to do all this selecting. The following line enters the formula in three cells. The R1C1 style of formulas is discussed completely in Chapter 6, "R1C1 Style Formulas":

   ```
   Range("E" & TotalRow).Resize(1, 3).FormulaR1C1 = "=SUM(R2C:R[-1]C)"
   ```

5. The macro recorder selects a range and then applies formatting:

   ```
   Rows("1:1").Select
   Selection.Font.Bold = True
   Rows("14:14").Select
   Selection.Font.Bold = True
   ```

There is no reason to select before applying the formatting. These two lines perform the same action and do it much quicker:

```
Rows("1:1").Font.Bold = True
Rows(TotalRow & ":" & TotalRow).Font.Bold = True
```

6. The macro recorder selects all cells before doing the AutoFit command:

```
Cells.Select
Selection.Columns.AutoFit
```

There is no need to select the cells before doing the AutoFit:

```
Cells.Columns.AutoFit
```

7. The macro recorder tags each macro with a line that the macro was recorded on a certain date:

```
' ImportInvoice Macro
' Recorded 10/23/2003 by Bill Jelen This macro will import invoice.txt
'  and add totals.
```

Now that you have changed the recorded macro code into something that will actually work, go ahead and change the "Recorded" to reflect the fact that you've written useful code:

```
' ImportInvoice Macro
' Written 10/23/2003 by Bill Jelen This macro will import invoice.txt
' and add totals.
```

Here is the final macro with the changes:

```
Sub ImportInvoiceFixed()
'
' ImportInvoice Macro
' Written 10/23/2003 by Bill Jelen This macro will import invoice.txt
' and add totals.
'
' Keyboard Shortcut: Ctrl+i
'
    Workbooks.OpenText Filename:= _
        "C:\invoice.txt", Origin _
        :=437, StartRow:=1, DataType:=xlDelimited, TextQualifier:=xlDoubleQuote _
        , ConsecutiveDelimiter:=False, Tab:=True, Semicolon:=False, Comma:=True _
        , Space:=False, Other:=False, FieldInfo:=Array(Array(1, 3), Array(2, 1), _
        Array(3, 1), Array(4, 1), Array(5, 1), Array(6, 1), Array(7, 1)), _
        TrailingMinusNumbers:=True
    ' Find the last row with data. This might change every day
    FinalRow = Range("A65536").End(xlUp).Row
    TotalRow = FinalRow + 1
    ' Build a Total row below this
    Range("A" & TotalRow).Value = "Total"
    Range("E" & TotalRow).Resize(1, 3).FormulaR1C1 = "=SUM(R2C:R[-1]C)"
    Rows("1:1").Font.Bold = True
    Rows(TotalRow & ":" & TotalRow).Font.Bold = True
    Cells.Columns.AutoFit
End Sub
```

Next Steps

Our goal by now is that you know how to record a macro. You can use help and debugging to figure out how the code works. You also have five tools for making the recorded code look like professional code.

The next chapters go into more detail about referring to ranges, looping, and the crazy (but useful) R1C1 style of formulas that the macro recorder loves to use. We'll also introduce you to 30 useful code samples that you can use.

2

Referring to Ranges

A range can be a cell, row, column, or a grouping of any of these. The Range object is probably the most frequently used object in Excel VBA—after all, you're manipulating data on a sheet. But although a range can refer to any grouping of cells on a sheet, it can refer to only one sheet at a time; if you want to refer to ranges on multiple sheets, you have to refer to each sheet separately.

This chapter shows you different ways of referring to ranges, such as specifying a row or column. You'll also learn how to manipulate cells based on the active cell and how to create a new range from overlapping ranges.

The Range **Object**

The following is the Excel object hierarchy:

Application ➜ Workbook ➜ Worksheet ➜ Range

The Range object is a property of the Worksheet object. This means it requires that either a sheet be active or it must reference a worksheet. Both of the following lines mean the same thing *if* Worksheets(1) is the active sheet:

```
Range("A1")
Worksheets(1).Range("A1")
```

There are several ways of referring to a Range object; Range("A1") is the most identifiable because that is how the macro recorder does it. But each of the following is equivalent:

```
Range("D5")
[D5]
Range("B3").Range("C3")
Cells(5,4)
Range("A1").Offset(4,3)
Range("MyRange") 'assuming that D5 has a
Name of MyRange
```

Which format you use depends on your needs. Keep reading—it will all make sense soon!

3

Using the Top-Left and Bottom-Right Corners of a Selection to Specify a Range

There are two acceptable syntaxes for the Range command. To specify a rectangular range in the first syntax, you specify the complete range reference just as you would in a formula in Excel:

```
Range("A1:B5").Select
```

In the alternative syntax, you specify the top-left corner and bottom-right corner of the desired rectangular range. In this syntax, the equivalent statement might be

```
Range("A1", "B5").Select
```

For either corner, you can substitute a named range, the Cells function, or the ActiveCell property. This line of code selects the rectangular range from A1 to the active cell:

```
Range("A1", ActiveCell).Select
```

The following statement would select from the active cell to five rows below the active cell and two columns to the right:

```
Range(ActiveCell, ActiveCell.Offset(5, 2)).Select
```

Shortcut for Referencing Ranges

A shortcut is available when referencing ranges. It uses [square brackets], as shown in Table 3.1:

Table 3.1 Shortcuts for Referring to Ranges	
Standard Method	**Shortcut**
Range("D5")	[D5]
Range("A1:D5")	[A1:D5]
Range ("A1:D5," "G6:I17")	[A1:D5, G6:I17]
Range("MyRange")	[MyRange]

Named Ranges

You've probably already used Named ranges on your sheets and in formulas. You can also use them in VBA.

To refer to the range "MyRange" in Sheet1, do this:

```
Worksheets(1).Range("MyRange")
```

Notice that the Name of the range is in quotes—unlike the use of Named ranges in formulas on the sheet itself. If you forget to put the Name in quotes, Excel thinks you are referring to a variable in the program, unless you are using the shortcut syntax discussed in the previous section, in which case, quotes are not used.

Referencing Ranges in Other Sheets

Switching between sheets by activating the needed sheet can drastically slow down your code. Instead, you can refer to a sheet that is not active by referencing the Worksheet object first:

```
Worksheets("Sheet1").Range("A1")
```

This line of code references Sheet1 of the active workbook even if Sheet2 is the active sheet.

If you need to reference a range in another workbook, then include the Workbook object, the Worksheet object, and then the Range object:

```
Workbooks("InvoiceData.xls").Worksheets("Sheet1").Range("A1")
```

Be careful if you use the Range property as an argument within another Range property. You must identify the range fully each time. Let's say that Sheet1 is your active sheet and you need to total data on Sheet2:

```
WorksheetFunction.Sum(Worksheets("Sheet2").Range(Range("A1"), Range("A7")))
```

This line does not work. Why? Because Range(Range("A1"), Range("A7")) refers to an extra range at the beginning of the code line. Excel does not assume that you want to carry the Worksheet object reference over to the other Range objects. So what do you do? Well, you could write this:

```
WorksheetFunction.Sum(Worksheets("Sheet2").Range(Worksheets("Sheet2"). _
    Range("A1"), Worksheets("Sheet2").Range("A7")))
```

But this is not only a long line of code, it is difficult to read! Thankfully, there is a simpler way, With...End With:

```
With Worksheets("Sheet2")
    WorksheetFunction.Sum(.Range(.Range("A1"), .Range("A7")))
End With
```

Notice now that there is a .Range in your code, but without the preceding object reference. That's because With Worksheets("Sheet2") implies that the object of the Range is the Worksheet.

Referencing a Range Relative to Another Range

Typically, .Range is a property of a worksheet. It is also possible to have .Range be the property of another range. In this case, the .Range property is relative to the original range! This makes for code that it very unintuitive. Consider this example:

```
Range("B5").Range("C3").Select
```

This actually selects cell D7. Think about cell C3. It is located two rows below and two columns to the right of cell A1. The preceding line of code starts at cell B5. If we assumed that B5 were in the A1 position, VBA finds the cell that would be in the C3 position relative to B5. In other words, VBA finds the cell that is two rows below and two columns to the right of B5, and this is D7.

Again, I consider this coding style to be very unintuitive. This line of code mentions two addresses, and the actual cell being selected is neither of these addresses! It seems very misleading when you are trying to read this code.

You might consider using this syntax to refer to a cell relative to the active cell. For example, this line would activate the cell three rows down and four columns to the right of the currently active cell:

```
Selection.Range("E4").Select
```

Although it is a matter of personal preference, I find the Offset property (discussed later in this chapter) to be far more intuitive.

This syntax is mentioned only because the macro recorder uses it. Remember that back in Chapter 1, "Unleash the Power of Excel with VBA!" when we were recording a macro with Relative References on, the following line was recorded:

```
ActiveCell.Offset(0, 4).Range("A2").Select
```

It found the cell four columns to the right of the active cell and from there selected the cell that would correspond to A2. This is not the easiest way to write code, but that's the macro recorder.

Although a worksheet is usually the object of the Range property, on occasion, such as when recording, a Range may be the property of a Range.

Using the Cells Property to Select a Range

The Cells property refers to all the cells of the specified range object, which can be a worksheet or a range of cells. For example, this line selects all the cells of the active sheet:

```
Cells.Select
```

Using the Cells property with the Range object may seem redundant:

```
Range("A1:D5").Cells
```

The line refers to the original Range object. But the Cells property has a property, Item, which makes the Cells property very useful. The Item property enables you to refer to a specific cell relative to the Range object.

The syntax for using the Item property with the Cells object is

```
Cells.Item(Row,Column)
```

You must use a numeric value for Row, but you may use the numeric value or string value for Column. Both the following lines refer to cell C5:

```
Cells.Item(5,"C")
Cells.Item(5,3)
```

Because the Item property is the default property of the Range object, you can shorten these lines to

```
Cells(5,"C")
Cells(5,3)
```

The ability to use numeric values for parameters is especially useful if you need to loop through rows or columns. The macro recorder usually uses something like Range("A1").Select for a single cell and Range("A1:C5").Select for a range of cells. If you are learning to code simply from the recorder, then you might be tempted to write code like

```
FinalRow = Range("A65536").End(xlUp).Row
For i = 1 to FinalRow
    Range("A" & i & ":E" & i).Font.Bold = True
Next i
```

This little piece of code, which loops through rows and bolds the cells in Columns A to E is awkward to read and write. But, how else can you do it?

```
FinalRow = Cells(65536,1).End(xlUp).Row
For i = 1 to FinalRow
    Cells(i,"A").Resize(,5).Font.Bold = True
Next i
```

Instead of trying to type out the range address, the new code uses the Cells and Resize properties to find the required cell based on the active cell.

Using the Cells **Property in the** Range **Property**

You can use Cells properties as parameters in the Range property. The following refers to range A1:E5:

```
Range(Cells(1,1),Cells(5,5))
```

This is especially useful when you need to specify your variables with a parameter, as in the previous looping example.

Using the Offset **Property to Refer to a Range**

You've already seen a reference to Offset; the macro recorder used it when we were recording a relative reference. It enables you to manipulate a cell based off the location of the active cell. In this way, you don't have to know the address of a cell.

The syntax for the Offset property is

```
Range.Offset(RowOffset, ColumnOffset)
```

To affect cell F5 from cell A1, write

```
Range("A1").Offset(RowOffset:=4, ColumnOffset:=5)
```

or, shorter yet:

```
Range("A1").Offset(4,5)
```

The count starts at A1, but does not include A1.

But what if you need to go over only a row or a column, but not both? You don't have to enter both the row and column parameter. If you need to refer to a cell one column over, use one of these:

```
Range("A1").Offset(ColumnOffset:=1)
Range("A1").Offset(,1)
```

Both lines mean the same. The choice is yours. Referring to a cell one row up is similar:

```
Range("B2").Offset(RowOffset:=-1)
Range("B2").Offset(-1)
```

Once again, the choice is yours. It is a matter of readability of the code.

Let's say we had a list of produce with totals next to them. Find any total equal to zero and place **LOW** in the cell next to it. You could do it this way:

```
Set Rng = Range("B1:B16").Find(What:="0", LookAt:=xlWhole, LookIn:=xlValues)
Rng.Offset(, 1).Value = "LOW"
```

The LOW totals are quickly noted by the program, as shown in Figure 3.1.

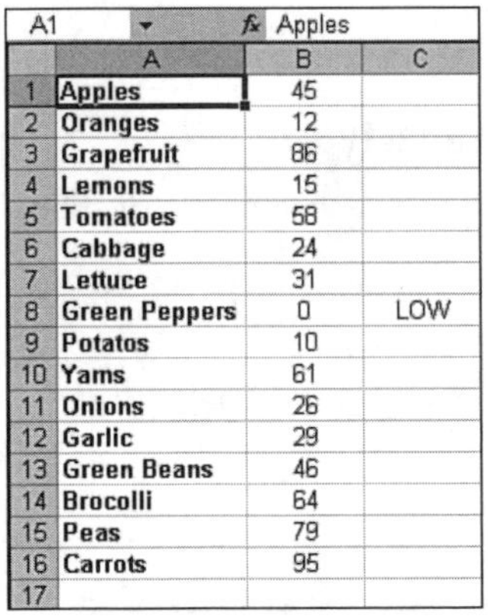

Figure 3.1
Find the produce with the 0 total.

	A	B	C
1	Apples	45	
2	Oranges	12	
3	Grapefruit	86	
4	Lemons	15	
5	Tomatoes	58	
6	Cabbage	24	
7	Lettuce	31	
8	Green Peppers	0	LOW
9	Potatos	10	
10	Yams	61	
11	Onions	26	
12	Garlic	29	
13	Green Beans	46	
14	Brocolli	64	
15	Peas	79	
16	Carrots	95	
17			

Offsetting isn't only for single cells—it can be used with ranges. You can *shift* the focus of a range over in the same way you can shift the active cell. The following line refers to B2:D4 (see Figure 3.2):

```
Range("A1:C3").Offset(1,1)
```

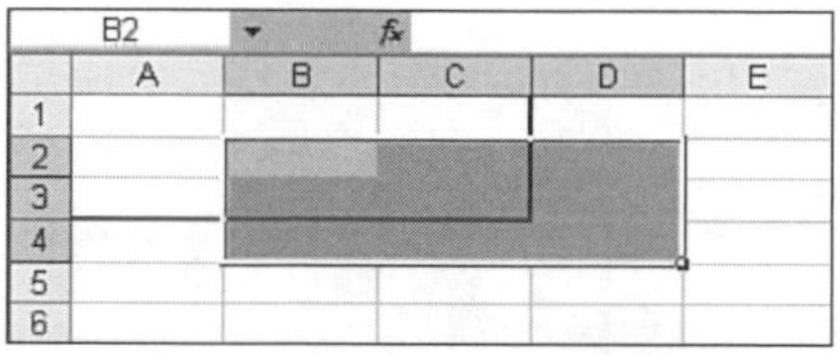

Figure 3.2
Offsetting a range—
`Range("A1:C3").`
`Offset(1,1).`
`Select.`

Using the `Resize` **Property to Change the Size of a Range**

The `Resize` property enables you to change the size of a range based off the location of the active cell. You can create a new range as you need it.

The syntax for the `Resize` property is

```
Range.Resize(RowSize, ColumnSize)
```

To create a range B3:D13, use this:

```
Range("B3").Resize(RowSize:=11, ColumnSize:=3)
```

or, simpler:

```
Range("B3").Resize(11, 3)
```

But what if you need to resize by only a row or a column, not both? You don't have to enter both the row and column parameters. If you need to expand by two columns,

```
Range("B3").Resize(ColumnSize:=2)
Range("B3").ReSize(,2)
```

Both lines mean the same. The choice is yours. Resizing just the rows is similar:

```
Range("B3").Resize(RowSize:=2)
Range("B3").Resize(2)
```

Once again, the choice is yours. It is a matter of readability of the code.

From the list of produce, find the zero total and color the cells of the total and corresponding produce (see Figure 3.3):

```
Set Rng = Range("B1:B16").Find(What:="0", LookAt:=xlWhole, LookIn:=xlValues)
Rng.Offset(, -1).Resize(, 2).Interior.ColorIndex = 15
```

Notice that that the offset property was used first to move the active cell over; when resizing, the top-left corner cell must remain the same.

Resizing isn't only for single cells—it can be used to resize an existing range. For example, if you have a named range but need it and the two columns next to it, use this:

```
Range("Produce").Resize(,2)
```

Remember, the number you resize by is the total number of rows and/or columns you want to include.

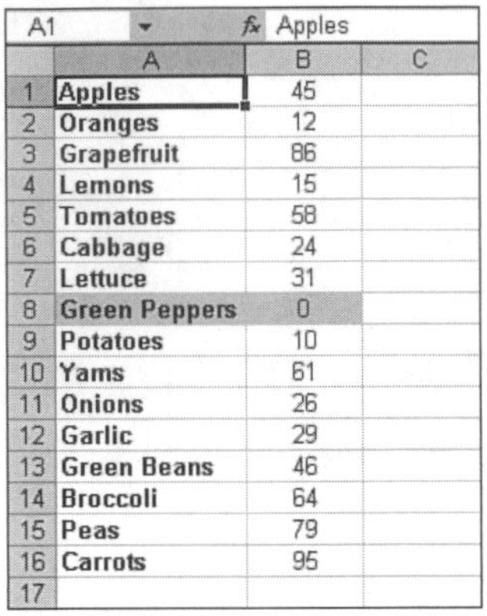

Figure 3.3
Resizing a range to
extend the selection.

	A	B	C
1	Apples	45	
2	Oranges	12	
3	Grapefruit	86	
4	Lemons	15	
5	Tomatoes	58	
6	Cabbage	24	
7	Lettuce	31	
8	Green Peppers	0	
9	Potatoes	10	
10	Yams	61	
11	Onions	26	
12	Garlic	29	
13	Green Beans	46	
14	Broccoli	64	
15	Peas	79	
16	Carrots	95	
17			

Using the `Columns` and `Rows` Properties to Specify a Range

`Columns` and `Rows` refer to the columns and rows of a specified range object, which can be a worksheet or a range of cells. They return a `Range` object referencing the rows or columns of the specified object.

You've seen the following line used, but what is it doing?

```
FinalRow = Range("A65536").End(xlUp).Row
```

This line of code finds the last row in a sheet in which column A has a value and places the row number of that `Range` object into `FinalRow`. This can be very useful when you need to loop through a sheet row by row—you'll know exactly how many rows you need to go through.

CAUTION

Some properties of Columns and Rows require contiguous rows and columns to work properly. For example, if you were to use the following line of code, 9 would be the answer because only the first range would be evaluated:

```
Range("A1:B9, C10:D19").Rows.Count
```

But if the ranges are grouped separately, `Range("A1:B9", "C10:D19").Rows.Count` the answer would be 19.

Using the `Union` Method to Join Multiple Ranges

The `Union` Method enables you to join two or more non-contiguous ranges. It creates a temporary object of the multiple ranges, allowing you to affect them together:

```
Application.Union(argument1, argument2, etc.)
```

The following code joins two named ranges on the sheet, inserts the =RAND() formulas, and bolds them:

```
Set UnionRange = Union(Range("Range1"), Range("Range2"))
With UnionRange
    .Formula = "=RAND()"
    .Font.Bold = True
End With
```

Using the Intersect Method to Create a New Range from Overlapping Ranges

The Intersect method returns the cells that overlap between two or more ranges:

```
Application.Intersect(argument1, argument2, etc.)
```

The following code colors the overlapping cells of the two ranges, as shown in Figure 3.4:

```
Set IntersectRange = Intersect(Range("Range1"), Range("Range2"))
IntersectRange.Interior.ColorIndex = 6
```

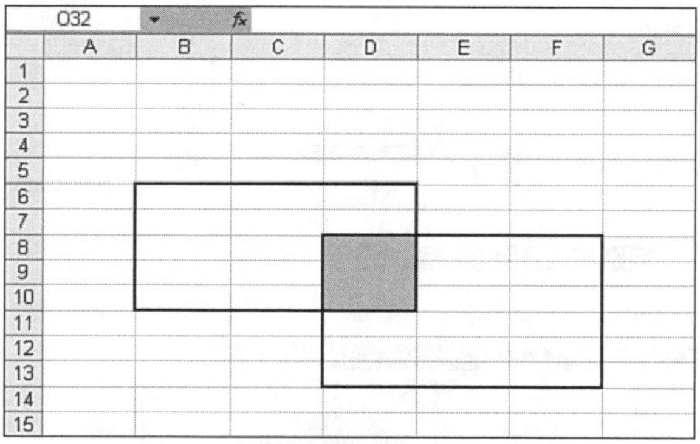

Figure 3.4
The Intersect method returns overlapping cells.

Using the IsEmpty Function to Check Whether a Cell Is Empty

The IsEmpty function returns a Boolean value of whether a single cell is empty or not; True if empty, False if not. The cell must truly be empty. Even if it has a space in it, which you cannot see, Excel does not consider it empty:

```
IsEmpty(Cell)
```

Look at Figure 3.5. You have several groups of data separated by a blank row. You want to make the separations a little more obvious.

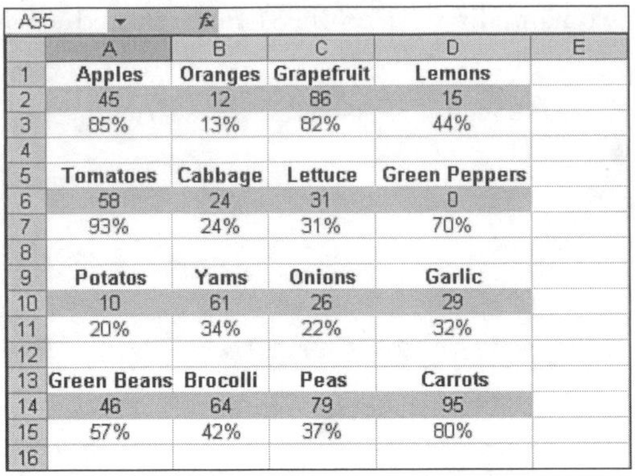

Figure 3.5
Blank empty rows separating data.

The following code goes down the data in Column A and where it finds an empty cell, colors in the first four cells for that row (see Figure 3.6):

```
LastRow = Range("A65536").End(xlUp).Row
For i = 1 To LastRow
    If IsEmpty(Cells(i, 1)) Then
        Cells(i, 1).Resize(1, 4).Interior.ColorIndex = 1
    End If
Next i
```

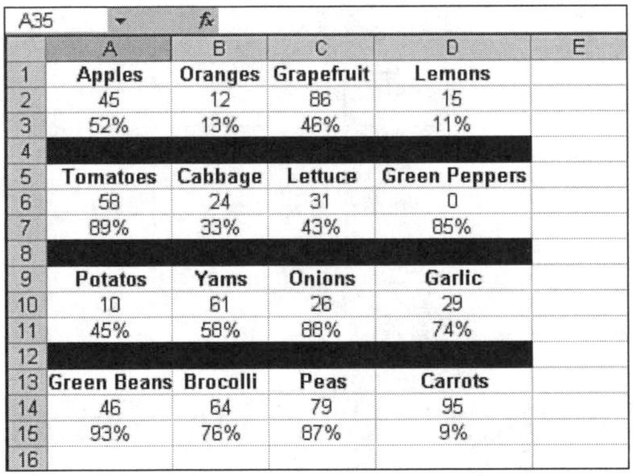

Figure 3.6
Colored rows separating data.

Using the `CurrentRegion` Property to Quickly Select a Data Range

`CurrentRegion` returns a range object representing a set of contiguous data. As long as the data is surrounded by one empty row and one empty column, you can select the table with `CurrentRegion`:

RangeObject.CurrentRegion

Look at Figure 3.7. The following line would select A1:D3, as this is the contiguous range of cells around cell A1:

```
Range("A1").CurrentRegion.Select
```

This is useful if you have a table whose size is in constant flux.

Figure 3.7
Use `CurrentRegion` to quickly select a range of contiguous data around the active cell.

A1	▼	fx	Apples		
	A	B	C	D	E
1	**Apples**	**Oranges**	**Grapefruit**	**Lemons**	
2	45	12	86	15	
3	52%	13%	46%	11%	
4					
5	**Tomatoes**	**Cabbage**	**Lettuce**	**Green Peppers**	
6	58	24	31	0	
7	89%	33%	43%	85%	
8					
9	**Potatos**	**Yams**	**Onions**	**Garlic**	
10	10	61	26	29	
11	45%	58%	88%	74%	
12					
13	**Green Beans**	**Brocolll**	**Peas**	**Carrots**	
14	46	64	79	95	
15	93%	76%	87%	9%	
16					

3

CASE STUDY

Using the `SpecialCells` Method to Select Specific Cells

Even Excel power users may never have encountered the Go To Special dialog box. If you press the F5 key in an Excel worksheet, you get the normal Go To dialog box (see Figure 3.8). In the lower-left corner of this dialog is a button called Special. Click that button to get to the super-powerful Go To Special dialog (see Figure 3.9).

Figure 3.8
While the Go To dialog doesn't seem very useful, press the Special button in the lower-left corner.

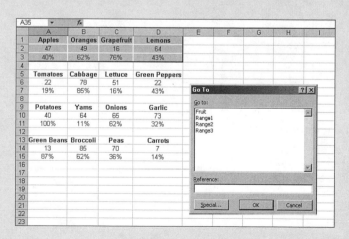

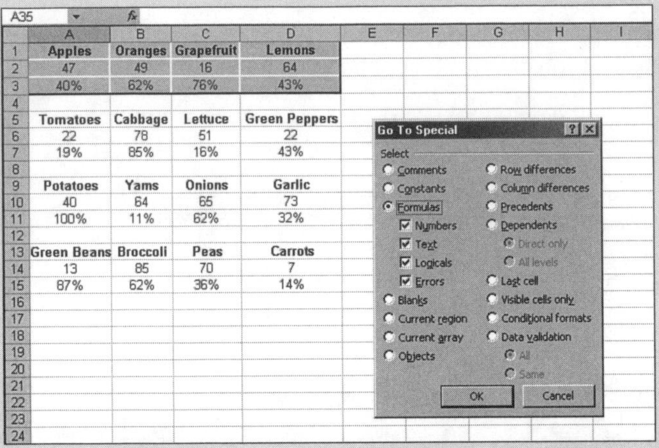

Figure 3.9
The Go To Special dialog has many incredibly useful selection tools.

In the Excel interface, the Go To Special dialog enables you to select only cells with formulas, or only blank cells, or only the visible cells. Selecting visible cells only is excellent for grabbing the visible results of AutoFiltered data.

To simulate the Go To Special dialog in VBA, use the `SpecialCells` method. This enables you to act on cells that meet a certain criteria:

```
RangeObject.SpecialCells(Type, Value)
```

This method has two parameters: `Type` and `Value`. Type is one of the `xlCellType` constants:

```
xlCellTypeAllFormatConditions

xlCellTypeAllValidation

xlCellTypeBlanks

xlCellTypeComments

xlCellTypeConstants

xlCellTypeFormulas

xlCellTypeLastCell

xlCellTypeSameFormatConditions

xlCellTypeSameValidation

xlCellTypeVisible
```

Value is optional and can be one of the following:

```
xlErrors

xlLogical

xlNumbers

xlTextValues.
```

The following returns all the ranges that have conditional formatting set up. It will produce an error if there are no conditional formats. It puts a border around each contiguous section it finds:

```
Set rngCond = ActiveSheet.Cells.SpecialCells(xlCellTypeAllFormatConditions)
If Not rngCond Is Nothing Then
    rngCond.BorderAround xlContinuous
End If
```

Have you ever had someone send you a worksheet without all the labels filled in? Some people consider the data shown in Figure 3.10 to look neat. They enter the Region field only once for each region. This may look aesthetically pleasing, but it is impossible to sort. Even Excel's pivot table routinely returns data in this annoying format.

Figure 3.10

The blank cells in the region column make data tables such as this very difficult to sort.

	A	B	C	D
1	Region	Product	Sales	
2	Central	ABC	766,469	
3		DEF	776,996	
4		XYZ	832,414	
5	East	ABC	703,255	
6		DEF	891,799	
7		XYZ	897,949	
8	West	ABC	631,646	
9		DEF	494,919	
10		XYZ	712,365	
11				
12				

Using the `SpecialCells` property to select all the blanks in this range is one way to quickly fill in all the blank region cells with the region found above them:

```
Sub FillIn()
    Range("A1").CurrentRegion.SpecialCells(xlCellTypeBlanks).FormulaR1C1 _
    = "=R[-1]C"
    Range("A1").CurrentRegion.Value = Range("A1").CurrentRegion.Value
End Sub
```

In this code, `Range("A1").CurrentRegion` refers to the contiguous range of data in the report. The `.SpecialCells` property returns just the blank cells in that range. Although you can read more about R1C1 style formulas in Chapter 6, "R1C1 Style Formulas," this particular formula fills in all the blank cells with a formula that points to the cell above the blank cell. The second line of code is a fast way to simulate doing a Copy and then Paste Special Values. The result is shown in Figure 3.11.

Figure 3.11

After running the macro, the blank cells in the region column have been filled in with data from above.

	A	B	C	D
1	Region	Product	Sales	
2	Central	ABC	766,469	
3	Central	DEF	776,996	
4	Central	XYZ	832,414	
5	East	ABC	703,255	
6	East	DEF	891,799	
7	East	XYZ	897,949	
8	West	ABC	631,646	
9	West	DEF	494,919	
10	West	XYZ	712,365	
11				
12				

Using the Areas Collection to Return a Non-contiguous Range

The Areas Collection is a collection on non-contiguous ranges within a selection. It consists of individual `Range` objects representing contiguous ranges of cells within the selection. If the selection contains only one area, the `Areas` collection contains a single `Range` object corresponding to that selection.

Refer to Figure 3.12. You need to copy only the total numbers (the gray cells) and paste them to a new section. You might be tempted to loop through the sheet, copy a row, and paste it to another section. But there's an easier way (see Figure 3.13):

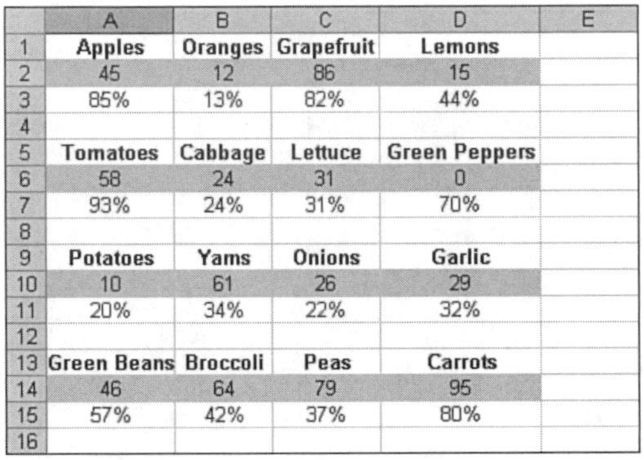

	A	B	C	D	E
1	Apples	Oranges	Grapefruit	Lemons	
2	45	12	86	15	
3	85%	13%	82%	44%	
4					
5	Tomatoes	Cabbage	Lettuce	Green Peppers	
6	58	24	31	0	
7	93%	24%	31%	70%	
8					
9	Potatoes	Yams	Onions	Garlic	
10	10	61	26	29	
11	20%	34%	22%	32%	
12					
13	Green Beans	Broccoli	Peas	Carrots	
14	46	64	79	95	
15	57%	42%	37%	80%	
16					

Figure 3.12
You want to copy the gray cells to another area.

```
Set NewDestination = ActiveSheet.Range("I1")
For Each Rng In Cells.SpecialCells(xlCellTypeConstants, 1).Areas
    Rng.Copy Destination:=NewDestination
    Set NewDestination = NewDestination.Offset(Rng.Rows.Count)
Next Rng
```

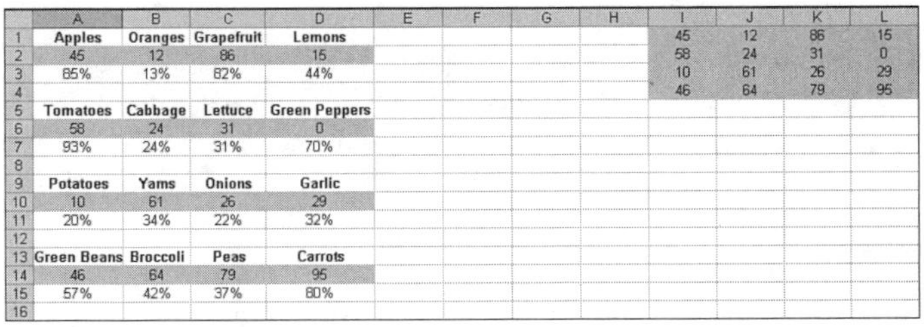

	A	B	C	D	E	F	G	H	I	J	K	L
1	Apples	Oranges	Grapefruit	Lemons					45	12	86	15
2	45	12	86	15					58	24	31	0
3	85%	13%	82%	44%					10	61	26	29
4									46	64	79	95
5	Tomatoes	Cabbage	Lettuce	Green Peppers								
6	58	24	31	0								
7	93%	24%	31%	70%								
8												
9	Potatoes	Yams	Onions	Garlic								
10	10	61	26	29								
11	20%	34%	22%	32%								
12												
13	Green Beans	Broccoli	Peas	Carrots								
14	46	64	79	95								
15	57%	42%	37%	80%								
16												

Figure 3.13
The Areas Collection makes it easy to manipulate non-contiguous ranges.

Next Steps

Now that you're getting an idea of how Excel works, it's time to apply it to useful situations. The next chapter looks at user-defined functions, uses the skills you've learned, and shows you other programming methods that you will learn more about throughout the book.

User-Defined Functions

4

Creating User-Defined Functions

Excel provides many built-in formulas, but there are times when you need a complex custom formula not offered—for example, a formula that sums a range of cells based on their interior color.

So, what do you do? You could go down your list and copy the colored cells to another section. Or, perhaps you have a calculator next to you as you work your way down your list—beware you don't enter the same number twice! Both methods are time consuming and open to accidents. What to do? You could write a procedure—after all, that's what this book is about. But, there is another option: *User-Defined Functions* (UDFs).

You can create functions in VBA that can be used just like Excel's built-in functions, such as SUM. After the custom function is created, a user needs to know only the function name and its arguments.

> **NOTE**
>
> UDFs can be entered only into standard modules. Sheet and ThisWorkbook modules are a special type of module and if you enter the function there, Excel doesn't recognize that you are creating a UDF.

Case Study: Custom Functions—Example and Explanation

Let's build a custom function used to add two values. After we've created it, we'll use it on a worksheet.

Insert a new module in the VBE. Type the following function into the module. It is a function called Add that will total two numbers in different cells. The function has two arguments:

```
Add(Number1,Number2)
```

Number1 is the first number to add; Number2 is the second number to add:

```
Function Add(Number1, Number2) As Integer
Add = Number1 + Number2
End Function
```

Let's break this down:

> Function name—Add.
>
> Arguments are placed in parentheses after the name of the function. This example has two arguments— Number1 and Number2.
>
> As Integer defines the variable type of the result as a whole number.
>
> Add =Number1 + Number2—The result of the function is returned.

Here is how to use the function on a worksheet:

1. Type numbers into cells A1 and A2.
2. Select cell A3.
3. Press Shift+F3 to open the Paste Function dialog box (or choose Insert, Function from the main menu).
4. Select the User Defined category.
5. Select the Add function.
6. In the first argument box, select cell A1.
7. In the second argument box, select cell A2.
8. Click OK.

Congratulations! You have created your first custom function. You can easily share it because the users are not required to know how the function works.

Most of the same functions used on sheets can also be used in VBA and vice-versa. In VBA, though, you would call the user-defined function (Add) from a procedure (Addition):

```
Sub Addition ()
Dim Total as Integer
Total = Add (1,10) 'we use a user-defined function Add
MsgBox "The answer is: " & Total
End Sub
```

Useful Custom Excel Functions

Following is a sampling of functions that can be useful in the everyday Excel world.

Set the Current Workbook's Name in a Cell

The following function is useful to set the name of the active workbook in a cell, as shown in Figure 4.1:

```
MyName()
```

No arguments are used with this function.

```
Function MyName() As String
    MyName = ThisWorkbook.Name
End Function
```

Set the Current Workbook's Name and File Path in a Cell

A variation of the previous function, this one sets the file path and name of the active workbook in a cell, as shown in Figure 4.1:

```
MyFullName()
```

No arguments are used with this function.

```
Function MyFullName() As String
    MyFullName = ThisWorkbook.FullName
End Function
```

Figure 4.1
Use a UDF to show the filename or the filename with directory path.

	A	B	C
1	Chapter 4 samples.xls	=MyName()	
2	C:\Excel VBA 2003 by Jelen & Syrstad\Chapter 4 samples.xls	=MyFullName()	
3			

Check Whether a Workbook Is Open

There may be times you need to check whether a workbook is open. The following function returns `True` if the workbook is open and `False` if it is not:

```
BookOpen(Bk)
```

The argument is

> Bk—The name of the workbook being checked.

```
Function BookOpen(Bk As String) As Boolean
Dim T As Excel.Workbook
Err.Clear 'clears any errors
On Error Resume Next 'if the code runs into an error, it skips it and continues
Set T = Application.Workbooks(Bk)
BookOpen = Not T Is Nothing
'If the workbook is open, then T will hold the workbook object and therefore
'will NOT be Nothing
Err.Clear
On Error GoTo 0
End Function
```

Here is an example of using the function:

```
Sub OpenAWorkbook()
Dim IsOpen As Boolean
Dim BookName As String
BookName = "Chapter 4 samples.xls"
IsOpen = BookOpen(BookName) 'calling our function - don't forget the parameter
If IsOpen Then
    MsgBox BookName & " is already open!"
Else
    Workbooks.Open (BookName)
End If
End Sub
```

Check Whether a Sheet in an Open Workbook Exists

This function requires that the workbook(s) it checks be open. It returns True if the sheet is found and False if it is not:

```
SheetExists(SName, WBName)
```

The arguments are

> SName—The name of the sheet being searched.

> WBName—Optional, the name of the workbook containing the sheet.

```
Function SheetExists(SName As String, Optional WB As Workbook) As Boolean
    Dim WS As Worksheet
    ' Use active workbook by default
    If WB Is Nothing Then
        Set WB = ActiveWorkbook
    End If

    On Error Resume Next
        SheetExists = CBool(Not WB.Sheets(SName) Is Nothing)
    On Error GoTo 0

End Function
```

Here is an example of using this function:

```
Sub CheckForSheet()
Dim ShtExists As Boolean
ShtExists = SheetExists("Sheet9")
'notice that only one parameter was passed; the workbook name is optional
If ShtExists Then
    MsgBox "The worksheet exists!"
Else
    MsgBox "The worksheet does NOT exist!"
End If
End Sub
```

Count the Number of Workbooks in a Directory

This function searches the current directory, and its subfolders if you want, counting all Excel workbook files or just the ones starting with a string of letters.

```
NumFilesInCurDir (LikeText, Subfolders)
```

The arguments are

> LikeText—Optional, a string value to search for, must include "*,"; for example: Mr*.

> Subfolders—Optional; True to search subfolders, False (default) not to.

```
Function NumFilesInCurDir(Optional LikeText As String, _
        Optional Subfolders As Boolean = False)
With Application.FileSearch
    .NewSearch
    If Len(LikeText) > 0 Then
        .Filename = LikeText 'sets a wildcard filename to search for
    End If
    .FileType = msoFileTypeExcelWorkbooks 'specifies to look for workbooks
    .LookIn = CurDir 'specifies to look in the current directory
    .SearchSubFolders = Subfolders 'sets whether subfolders should be searched
    .Execute
    NumFilesInCurDir = .FoundFiles.Count
End With
End Function
```

Here is an example of using this function:

```
Sub CountMyWkbks()
Dim MyFiles As Integer
MyFiles = NumFilesInCurDir("MrE*", True)
MsgBox MyFiles & " file(s) found"
End Sub
```

Retrieve UserID

Ever need to keep a record of who saves changes to a workbook? With this function, you can retrieve the name of the user logged in to a computer. Combine it with *Retrieve*

Permanent Date and Time (following) and you'll have a nice log file. It can also be used to set up user rights to a workbook.

```
WinUserName ()
```

No arguments are used with this function.

> **NOTE**
>
> This function is an advanced function that uses Application Programming Interface (API), which we will review in Chapter 22, "Windows Application Programming Interface (API)."

This first section (`Private` declarations) must be at the *top* of the module.

```
Private Declare Function WNetGetUser Lib "mpr.dll" Alias "WNetGetUserA" _
    (ByVal lpName As String, ByVal lpUserName As String, _
        lpnLength As Long) As Long
Private Const NO_ERROR = 0
Private Const ERROR_NOT_CONNECTED = 2250&
Private Const ERROR_MORE_DATA = 234
Private Const ERROR_NO_NETWORK = 1222&
Private Const ERROR_EXTENDED_ERROR = 1208&
Private Const ERROR_NO_NET_OR_BAD_PATH = 1203&
```

The following section of code can be placed anywhere in the module as long as it is below the previous section.

```
Function WinUsername() As String
    'variables
    Dim strBuf As String, lngUser As Long, strUn As String
    'clear buffer for user name from api func
    strBuf = Space$(255)
    'use api func WNetGetUser to assign user value to lngUser
    'will have lots of blank space
    lngUser = WNetGetUser("", strBuf, 255)
    'if no error from function call
    If lngUser = NO_ERROR Then
        'clear out blank space in strBuf and assign val to function
        strUn = Left(strBuf, InStr(strBuf, vbNullChar) - 1)
        WinUsername = strUn
    Else
    'error, give up
        WinUsername = "Error :" & lngUser
    End If
End Function
```

Function example:

```
Sub CheckUserRights()
Dim UserName As String
UserName = WinUsername
Select Case UserName
    Case "Administrator"
        MsgBox "Full Rights"
    Case "Guest"
        MsgBox "You cannot make changes"
```

```
    Case Else
        MsgBox "Limited Rights"
End Select
End Sub
```

Retrieve Date and Time of Last Save

This function retrieves the saved date and time of any workbook, including the current one, as shown in Figure 4.2.

> **NOTE** The cell must be formatted properly to display the date and/or time.

```
LastSaved(FullPath)
```

The argument is

FullPath—A string showing the full path and filename of the file in question.

```
Function LastSaved(FullPath As String) As Date
LastSaved = FileDateTime(FullPath)
End Function
```

Figure 4.2
Retrieve date and time of last save.

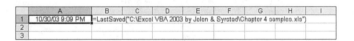

	A	B	C	D	E	F	G	H	I
1	10/30/03 9:09 PM	=LastSaved("C:\Excel VBA 2003 by Jelen & Syrstad\Chapter 4 samples.xls")							
2									
3									

Retrieve Permanent Date and Time

Because of the volatility of Now(), it isn't very useful for stamping a worksheet with the creation or editing date—everytime the workbook is opened, the result of the Now() function gets updated. The following function uses the Now function, but because you need to re-enter the cell to update the function, it is much less volatile, as shown in Figure 4.3.

```
DateTime()
```

No arguments are used with this function.

> **NOTE** The cell must be formatted properly to display the date and/or time.

```
DateTime()
```

Function example:

```
Function DateTime()
    DateTime = Now
End Function
```

Figure 4.3
Retrieve permanent date
and time.

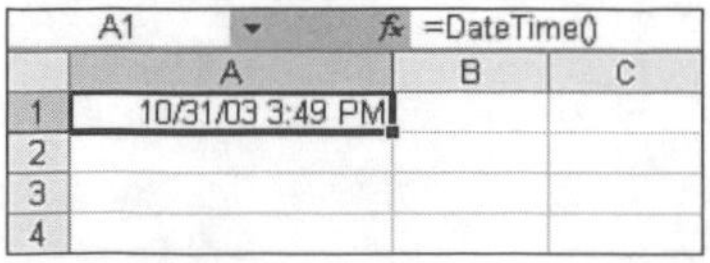

Validate an Email Address

If you manage an email subscription list, you may receive invalid email addresses, such as addresses with a space before the @. The following function can check addresses and confirm that they are proper email addresses (see Figure 4.4).

> **CAUTION**
>
> This function cannot verify that an email address is an existing one. It only checks the syntax to verify that the address may be legitimate.

```
IsEmailValid (StrEmail)
```

The argument is

StrEmail—An email address

```
Function IsEmailValid(strEmail As String) As Boolean
Dim strArray As Variant
Dim strItem As Variant
Dim i As Long
Dim c As String
Dim blnIsItValid As Boolean
blnIsItValid = True
'count the @ in the string
i = Len(strEmail) - Len(Application.Substitute(strEmail, "@", ""))
'if there is more than one @, invalid email
If i <> 1 Then IsEmailValid = False: Exit Function
ReDim strArray(1 To 2)
'the following two lines place the text to the left and right
'of the @ in their own variables
strArray(1) = Left(strEmail, InStr(1, strEmail, "@", 1) - 1)
strArray(2) = Application.Substitute(Right(strEmail, Len(strEmail) - _
    Len(strArray(1))), "@", "")

For Each strItem In strArray
    'verify there is something in the variable.
'If there isn't, then part of the email is missing
    If Len(strItem) <= 0 Then
        blnIsItValid = False
        IsEmailValid = blnIsItValid
        Exit Function
    End If
    'verify only valid characters in the email
    For i = 1 To Len(strItem)
```

```
'lowercases all letters for easier checking
        c = LCase(Mid(strItem, i, 1))
        If InStr("abcdefghijklmnopqrstuvwxyz_-.", c) <= 0 _
        And Not IsNumeric(c) Then
            blnIsItValid = False
            IsEmailValid = blnIsItValid
            Exit Function
        End If
    Next i
'verify that the first character of the left and right aren't periods
    If Left(strItem, 1) = "." Or Right(strItem, 1) = "." Then
        blnIsItValid = False
        IsEmailValid = blnIsItValid
        Exit Function
    End If
Next strItem
'verify there is a period in the right half of the address
If InStr(strArray(2), ".") <= 0 Then
    blnIsItValid = False
    IsEmailValid = blnIsItValid
    Exit Function
End If
i = Len(strArray(2)) - InStrRev(strArray(2), ".") 'locate the period
'verify that the number of letters corresponds to a valid domain extension
If i <> 2 And i <> 3 And i <> 4 Then
    blnIsItValid = False
    IsEmailValid = blnIsItValid
    Exit Function
End If
'verify that there aren't two periods together in the email
If InStr(strEmail, "..") > 0 Then
    blnIsItValid = False
    IsEmailValid = blnIsItValid
    Exit Function
End If
IsEmailValid = blnIsItValid
End Function
```

Figure 4.4
Validating email
addresses.

	A	B	C	D	E
1	Tracy@ MrExcel.com	FALSE	<-a space after the @		
2	Bill@MrExcel.com	TRUE			
3	consult?@MrExcel/com	FALSE	<-invalid characters		
4					
5					

Sum Cells Based on the Interior Color

You have a listing of clients and how much each owes you. You've colored in the amounts of the clients that are 30 days past due and want to sum up just those cells.

> **NOTE**
> Cells colored by conditional formatting will not work; the cells must have an interior color.

```
SumColor(CellColor, SumRange)
```

The arguments are

> CellColor—The address of a cell with the target color.

> SumRange—The range of cells to be searched.

```
Function SumByColor(CellColor As Range, SumRange As Range)
Dim myCell As Range
Dim iCol As Integer
Dim myTotal
iCol = CellColor.Interior.ColorIndex 'get the target color
For Each myCell In SumRange 'look at each cell in the designated range
'if the cell color matches the target color
If myCell.Interior.ColorIndex = iCol Then
'add the value in the cell to the total
myTotal = WorksheetFunction.Sum(myCell) + myTotal
    End If
Next myCell
SumByColor = myTotal
End Function
```

Figure 4.5 shows an example worksheet using the function.

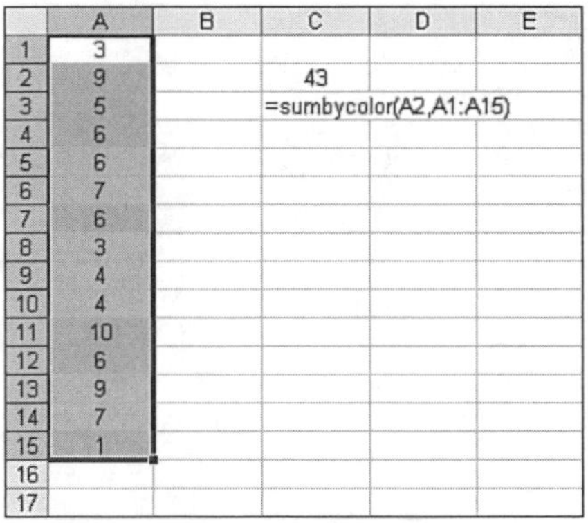

Figure 4.5
Sum cells based on interior color.

Retrieve Interior Cell Color Name or Index

Ever wanted to know the name of a cell color? Or perhaps the index number so you could add interior cell color through code? This function retrieves the cell color and index number for the target cell.

> **NOTE**
> Cells colored by conditional formatting will not work; the cells must have an interior color.

```
CellColor (myCell, ColorIndex)
```

The arguments are

myCell—The target cell.

ColorIndex—Optional; by default, the Color Name is returned, but if this is set to True, the Index number is returned instead.

Function example:

```
Function CellColor(myCell As Range, Optional ColorIndex As Boolean)
Dim myColor As String, IndexNum As Integer

Select Case myCell.Interior.ColorIndex
    Case 1
     myColor = "Black"
     IndexNum = 1
    Case 2
     myColor = "White"
     IndexNum = 2
    Case 3
     myColor = "Red"
     IndexNum = 3
    Case 4
     myColor = "Bright Green"
     IndexNum = 4
    Case 5
     myColor = "Blue"
     IndexNum = 5
    Case 6
     myColor = "Yellow"
     IndexNum = 6
    Case 7
     myColor = "Pink"
     IndexNum = 7
    Case 8
     myColor = "Turquoise"
     IndexNum = 8
    Case 9
     myColor = "Dark Red"
     IndexNum = 9
    Case 10
     myColor = "Green"
     IndexNum = 10
    Case 11
     myColor = "Dark Blue"
     IndexNum = 11
    Case 12
     myColor = "Dark Yellow"
     IndexNum = 12
    Case 13
     myColor = "Violet"
     IndexNum = 13
    Case 14
     myColor = "Teal"
     IndexNum = 14
```

4

```
Case 15
 myColor = "Gray-25%"
 IndexNum = 15
Case 16
 myColor = "Gray-50%"
 IndexNum = 16
Case 33
 myColor = "Sky Blue"
 IndexNum = 33
Case 34
 myColor = "Light Turquoise"
 IndexNum = 34
Case 35
 myColor = "Light Green"
 IndexNum = 35
Case 36
 myColor = "Light Yellow"
 IndexNum = 36
Case 37
 myColor = "Pale Blue"
 IndexNum = 37
Case 38
 myColor = "Rose"
 IndexNum = 38
Case 39
 myColor = "Lavender"
 IndexNum = 39
Case 40
 myColor = "Tan"
 IndexNum = 40
Case 41
 myColor = "Light Blue"
 IndexNum = 41
Case 42
 myColor = "Aqua"
 IndexNum = 42
Case 43
 myColor = "Lime"
 IndexNum = 43
Case 44
 myColor = "Gold"
 IndexNum = 44
Case 45
 myColor = "Light Orange"
 IndexNum = 45
Case 46
 myColor = "Orange"
 IndexNum = 46
Case 47
 myColor = "Blue-Gray"
 IndexNum = 47
Case 48
 myColor = "Gray-40%"
 IndexNum = 48
Case 49
 myColor = "Dark Teal"
 IndexNum = 49
```

```
        Case 50
         myColor = "Sea Green"
         IndexNum = 50
        Case 51
         myColor = "Dark Green"
         IndexNum = 51
        Case 52
         myColor = "Olive Green"
         IndexNum = 52
        Case 53
         myColor = "Brown"
         IndexNum = 53
        Case 54
         myColor = "Plum"
         IndexNum = 54
        Case 55
         myColor = "Indigo"
         IndexNum = 55
        Case 56
         myColor = "Gray-80%"
         IndexNum = 56
        Case Else
         myColor = "Custom color or no fill"
    End Select
    'if the index number is desired or if the cell color was not
    'returned return the index number
    If ColorIndex = True Or _
        myColor = "Custom color or no fill" Then
        CellColor = IndexNum
    Else
        CellColor = myColor
    End If
    End Function
```

Figure 4.6 shows an example worksheet using the function.

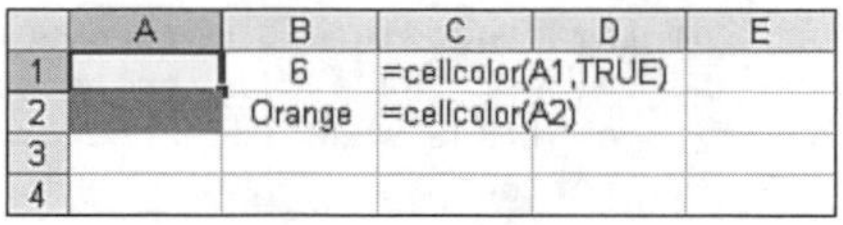

Figure 4.6
Find the cell color or index.

	A	B	C	D	E
1		6	=cellcolor(A1,TRUE)		
2		Orange	=cellcolor(A2)		
3					
4					

Retrieve Text Color Index

You need the color of a cell's text so that you can make some calculations of other similar text-colored cells.

> **NOTE** Text colored by conditional formatting or cell formatting (such as red negative numbers) will not work.

Challenge

Use what you learn in this function to modify the previous function, "Retrieve Interior Cell Color Name or Index," to return the color name.

```
Textcolor(Rng)
```

The argument is

    Rng—The cell to check for text color.

Function example:

```
Function TextColor(Rng As Range) As Long
    TextColor = Rng.Range("A1").Font.ColorIndex
End Function
```

Count Unique Values

How many times have you had a long list of values and needed to know how many were unique values? This function will go through a range and tell you just that, as shown in Figure 4.7.

```
NumUniqueValues(Rng)
```

The argument is

    Rng—The range to search unique values.

Function example:

```
Function NumUniqueValues(Rng As Range) As Long
Dim myCell As Range, UniqueVals As New Collection
Application.Volatile 'forces the function to recalculate when the range changes
On Error Resume Next
'the following places each value from the range into a collection because
'a collection can contain only unique values, there will be no duplicates the
'error statements force the program to continue when the error messages
'appear for duplicate items in the collection
For Each myCell In Rng
    UniqueVals.Add myCell.Value, CStr(myCell.Value)
Next myCell
On Error GoTo 0
'returns the number of items in the collection
NumUniqueValues = UniqueVals.Count
End Function
```

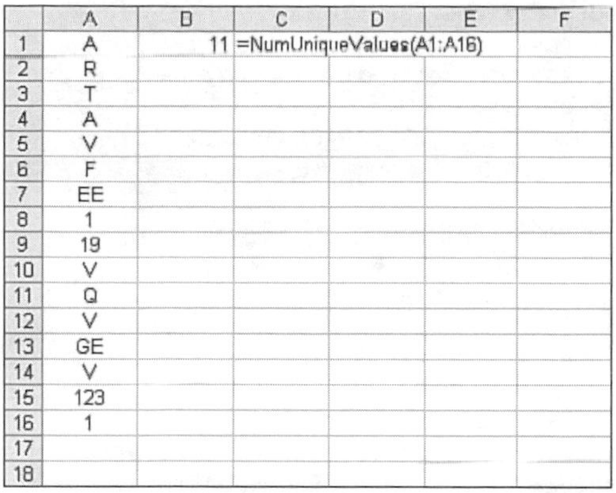

Figure 4.7
Count the number of
unique values in a
range.

	A	B	C	D	E	F
1	A		11	=NumUniqueValues(A1:A16)		
2	R					
3	T					
4	A					
5	V					
6	F					
7	EE					
8	1					
9	19					
10	V					
11	Q					
12	V					
13	GE					
14	V					
15	123					
16	1					
17						
18						

Remove Duplicates from a Range

How often have you had a list of items and needed to list only the unique values? The following function goes through a range and stores only the unique values.

```
UniqueValues (OrigArray)
```

The arguments are

      OrigArray—An array from which to remove duplicates.

This first section (Const declarations) must be at the *top* of the module:

```
Const ERR_BAD_PARAMETER = "Array parameter required"
Const ERR_BAD_TYPE = "Invalid Type"
Const ERR_BP_NUMBER = 20000
Const ERR_BT_NUMBER = 20001
```

The following section of code can be placed anywhere in the module as long as it is below the previous section:

```
Public Function UniqueValues(ByVal OrigArray As Variant) As Variant
    Dim vAns() As Variant
    Dim lStartPoint As Long
    Dim lEndPoint As Long
    Dim lCtr As Long, lCount As Long
    Dim iCtr As Integer
    Dim col As New Collection
    Dim sIndex As String
    Dim vTest As Variant, vItem As Variant
    Dim iBadVarTypes(4) As Integer
    'Function does not work if array element is one of the
    'following types
    iBadVarTypes(0) = vbObject
    iBadVarTypes(1) = vbError
    iBadVarTypes(2) = vbDataObject
```

4

```
            iBadVarTypes(3) = vbUserDefinedType
            iBadVarTypes(4) = vbArray
            'Check to see whether the parameter is an array
            If Not IsArray(OrigArray) Then
                Err.Raise ERR_BP_NUMBER, , ERR_BAD_PARAMETER
                Exit Function
            End If
            lStartPoint = LBound(OrigArray)
            lEndPoint = UBound(OrigArray)
            For lCtr = lStartPoint To lEndPoint
                vItem = OrigArray(lCtr)
                'First check to see whether variable type is acceptable
                For iCtr = 0 To UBound(iBadVarTypes)
                    If VarType(vItem) = iBadVarTypes(iCtr) Or _
                      VarType(vItem) = iBadVarTypes(iCtr) + vbVariant Then
                        Err.Raise ERR_BT_NUMBER, , ERR_BAD_TYPE
                        Exit Function
                    End If
                Next iCtr
                'Add element to a collection, using it as the index
                'if an error occurs, the element already exists
                sIndex = CStr(vItem)
                'first element, add automatically
                If lCtr = lStartPoint Then
                    col.Add vItem, sIndex
                    ReDim vAns(lStartPoint To lStartPoint) As Variant
                    vAns(lStartPoint) = vItem
                Else
                    On Error Resume Next
                    col.Add vItem, sIndex
                    If Err.Number = 0 Then
                        lCount = UBound(vAns) + 1
                        ReDim Preserve vAns(lStartPoint To lCount)
                        vAns(lCount) = vItem
                    End If
                End If
                Err.Clear
            Next lCtr
            UniqueValues = vAns
        End Function
```

Here is an example of using this function. See Figure 4.8 for the result on a worksheet:

```
Function nodupsArray(rng As Range) As Variant
    Dim arr1() As Variant
    If rng.Columns.Count > 1 Then Exit Function
    arr1 = Application.Transpose(rng)
    arr1 = UniqueValues(arr1)
    nodupsArray = Application.Transpose(arr1)
End Function
```

Figure 4.8
List unique values from a range.

C2 ▾ fx {=nodupsArray(A$2:A$1

	A	B	C	D
1	Source		ArrayFunction	
2	A		A	
3	R		R	
4	T		T	
5	A		V	
6	V		F	
7	F		EE	
8	EE		1	
9	1		19	
10	19		Q	
11	V		GE	
12	Q		123	
13	V			
14	GE			
15	V			
16	123			
17	1			
18				

Find the First Non-Zero-Length Cell in a Range

You import a large list of data with a lot of empty cells. Here is a function that evaluates a range of cells and returns the value of the first non-zero-length cell.

```
FirstNonZeroLength(Rng)
```

The argument is

`Rng`—The range to search.

Function example:

```
Function FirstNonZeroLength(Rng As Range)
Dim myCell As Range
FirstNonZeroLength = 0#
For Each myCell In Rng
    If Not IsNull(myCell) And myCell <> "" Then
        FirstNonZeroLength = myCell.Value
        Exit Function
    End If
Next myCell
FirstNonZeroLength = myCell.Value
End Function
```

Figure 4.9 shows the function on an example worksheet.

Figure 4.9
Find the value of the first non-zero-length cell in a range.

	A	B	C	D	E	F
1		2	=FirstNonZeroLength(A1:A7)			
2						
3	2					
4						
5	5					
6	6					
7	7					
8						
9						

Substitute Multiple Characters

Excel has a substitute function, but it is a value-for-value substitution. What if you had several characters you needed to substitute? Figure 4.10 shows several examples of how this function works.

```
MSubstitute(trStr, frStr, toStr)
```

The arguments are

trStr—The string to be search.

frStr—The text being searched for.

toStr—The replacement text.

> **CAUTION**
>
> toStr is assumed to be the same length as frStr. If not, the remaining characters are considered null (""). The function *is* case sensitive. To replace all instances of *a*, use a *and* A. You can't replace one character with two characters. This
> ```
> =MSUBSTITUTE("This is a test","i","$@")
> ```
> results in this:
> ```
> "Th$s $s a test"
> ```

Function example:

```
Function MSUBSTITUTE(ByVal trStr As Variant, frStr As String, _
        toStr As String) As Variant
Dim iRow As Integer
Dim iCol As Integer
Dim j As Integer
Dim Ar As Variant
Dim vfr() As String
Dim vto() As String
ReDim vfr(1 To Len(frStr))
ReDim vto(1 To Len(frStr))
'place the strings into an array
For j = 1 To Len(frStr)
    vfr(j) = Mid(frStr, j, 1)
    If Mid(toStr, j, 1) <> "" Then
        vto(j) = Mid(toStr, j, 1)
    Else
        vto(j) = ""
    End If
Next j
'compare each character and substitute if needed
If IsArray(trStr) Then
    Ar = trStr
    For iRow = LBound(Ar, 1) To UBound(Ar, 1)
        For iCol = LBound(Ar, 2) To UBound(Ar, 2)
            For j = 1 To Len(frStr)
                Ar(iRow, iCol) = Application.Substitute(Ar(iRow, iCol), _
```

```
                vfr(j), vto(j))
            Next j
        Next iCol
    Next iRow
Else
    Ar = trStr
    For j = 1 To Len(frStr)
        Ar = Application.Substitute(Ar, vfr(j), vto(j))
    Next j
End If
MSUBSTITUTE = Ar
End Function
```

Figure 4.10
Multiple substitution.

	A	B	C	D	E	F
1	1 Introduction	Introduction	=msubstitute(A1,"1","")			
2	This wam a test	This was a test	=msubstitute(A2,"wam", "was")			
3	123abc456	abc	=msubstitute(A3,"1234567890","")			
4	Adnothyer Tuiest	Another Test	=msubstitute(A4,"dyui","")			
5						
6						

Retrieve Numbers from Mixed Text

This function extracts and returns numbers from text that is a mix of numbers and letters, as shown in Figure 4.11.

```
RetrieveNumbers (MyString)
```

The argument is

   myString—The text containing the numbers to be extracted.

Function example:

```
Function RetrieveNumbers(myString As String)
Dim i As Integer, j As Integer
Dim OnlyNums As String
'starting at the END of the string and moving backwards (Step -1)
For i = Len(myString) To 1 Step -1
'IsNumeric is a VBA function that returns True if a variable is a number
'When a number is found, it is added to the OnlyNums string
    If IsNumeric(Mid(myString, i, 1)) Then
        j = j + 1
        OnlyNums = Mid(myString, i, 1) & OnlyNums
    End If
    If j = 1 Then OnlyNums = CInt(Mid(OnlyNums, 1, 1))
Next i
RetrieveNumbers = CLng(OnlyNums)
End Function
```

Figure 4.11
Extract numbers from
mixed text.

	B1	▼	ƒx =RetrieveNumbers(A1)		
	A	B	C	D	E
1	123abc456	123456			
2	1b2k3j34ioj	12334			
3	123 abc	123			
4					
5					

4

Convert Week Number into Date

Ever receive a spreadsheet report and all the headers showed the week number? I don't know about you, but I don't know what Week 15 actually is. I'd have to get out my calendar and count the weeks. And what if you need to look at a past year? What we need is a nice little function that will convert Week ## Year into the date of the Monday for that week, as shown in Figure 4.12.

```
Weekday(Str)
```

The argument is

Str—The Week to be converted in "Week ##, YYYY" format.

> **NOTE**
> The result must be formatted as a date.

Function example:

```
Function ConvertWeekDay(Str As String) As Date
Dim Week As Long
Dim FirstMon As Date
Dim TStr As String
FirstMon = DateSerial(Right(Str, 4), 1, 1)
FirstMon = FirstMon - FirstMon Mod 7 + 2
TStr = Right(Str, Len(Str) - 5)
Week = Left(TStr, InStr(1, TStr, " ", 1)) + 0
ConvertWeekDay = FirstMon + (Week - 1) * 7
End Function
```

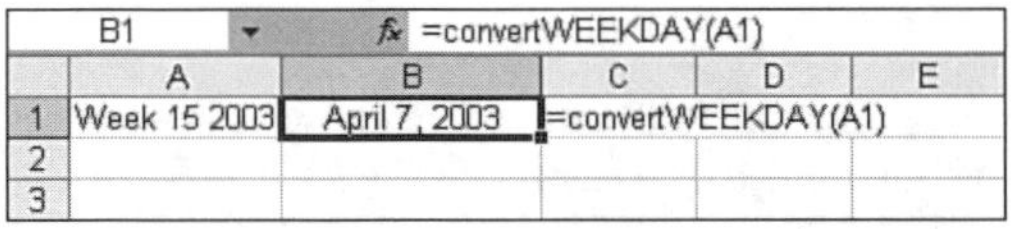

Figure 4.12
Convert a week number into a date more easily referenced.

Separate Delimited String

You need to paste a column of delimited data. You could use Excel's Text to Columns, but you need only an element or two from each cell. Text to Columns parses the entire thing. What you need is a function that lets you specify the number of the element in a string that you need, as shown in Figure 4.13.

```
StringElement(str,chr,ind)
```

The arguments are

str—The string to be parsed.

chr—The delimiter.

ind—The position of the element to be returned.

Function example:

```
Function StringElement(str As String, chr As String, ind As Integer)
Dim arr_str As Variant
arr_str = Split(str, chr) 'Not compatible with XL97
StringElement = arr_str(ind - 1)
End Function
```

Figure 4.13
Extracting a single element from delimited text.

Sort and Concatenate

You need to take a column of data, sort it, and concatenate it, using a "," as the delimiter, as shown in Figure 4.14.

```
SortConcat(Rng)
```

The argument is

Rng—The range of data to be sorted and concatenated.

> **NOTE** SortConcat calls another procedure, BubbleSort, that must be included.

4

Function example:

```
Function SortConcat(Rng As Range) As Variant
Dim MySum As String, arr1() As String
Dim j As Integer, i As Integer
Dim cl As Range
Dim concat As Variant
On Error GoTo FuncFail:
'initialize output
Sortconcat = 0#
'avoid user issues
If Rng.Count = 0 Then Exit Function
'get range into variant variable holding array
ReDim arr1(1 To Rng.Count)
'fill array
i = 1
For Each cl In Rng
    arr1(i) = cl.Value
    i = i + 1
Next
'sort array elements
Call BubbleSort(arr1)
'create string from array elements
```

```
For j = UBound(arr1) To 1 Step -1
    If Not IsEmpty(arr1(j)) Then
        MySum = arr1(j) & ", " & MySum
    End If
Next j
'assign value to function
Sortconcat = Left(MySum, Len(MySum) - 2)
'exit point
concat_exit:
Exit Function
'display error in cell
FuncFail:
Sortconcat = Err.Number & " - " & Err.Description
Resume concat_exit
End Function
```

The following function is the ever-popular `BubbleSort`, a program used by many to do a simple sort of data:

```
Sub BubbleSort(List() As String)
'   Sorts the List array in ascending order
Dim First As Integer, Last As Integer
Dim i As Integer, j As Integer
Dim Temp
First = LBound(List)
Last = UBound(List)
For i = First To Last - 1
    For j = i + 1 To Last
        If UCase(List(i)) > UCase(List(j)) Then
            Temp = List(j)
            List(j) = List(i)
            List(i) = Temp
        End If
    Next j
Next i
End Sub
```

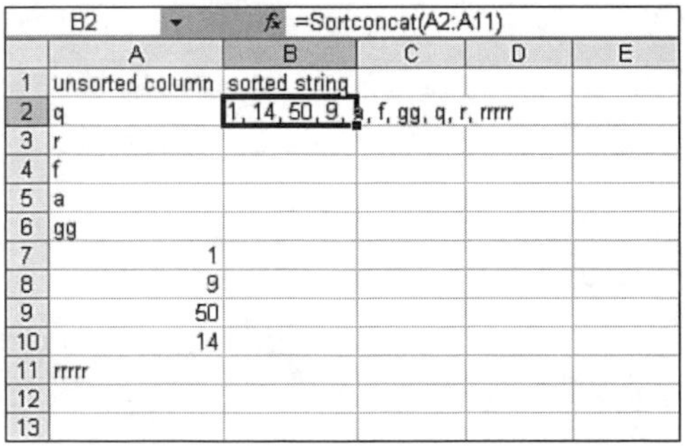

Figure 4.14
Sort and concatenate a range of variables.

	A	B	C	D	E
	unsorted column	sorted string			
1					
2	q	1, 14, 50, 9, , f, gg, q, r, rrrrr			
3	r				
4	f				
5	a				
6	gg				
7		1			
8		9			
9		50			
10		14			
11	rrrrr				
12					
13					

B2   =Sortconcat(A2:A11)

Sort Numeric and Alpha Characters

This function takes a mixed range of numeric and alpha characters and sorts them—numerically first and then alphabetically. The result is placed in an array that can be displayed on a worksheet through the use of an array formula, as shown in Figure 4.15.

```
sorter(Rng)
```

The argument is

> Rng—The range to be sorted.

Function example:

```
Function sorter(Rng As Range) As Variant
'returns an array
Dim arr1() As Variant
If Rng.Columns.Count > 1 Then Exit Function
arr1 = Application.Transpose(Rng)
QuickSort arr1
sorter = Application.Transpose(arr1)
End Function
```

The function uses the following two procedures to sort the data in the range.

```
Public Sub QuickSort(ByRef vntArr As Variant, _
    Optional ByVal lngLeft As Long = -2, _
    Optional ByVal lngRight As Long = -2)
Dim i, j, lngMid As Long
Dim vntTestVal As Variant
If lngLeft = -2 Then lngLeft = LBound(vntArr)
If lngRight = -2 Then lngRight = UBound(vntArr)
If lngLeft < lngRight Then
    lngMid = (lngLeft + lngRight) \ 2
    vntTestVal = vntArr(lngMid)
    i = lngLeft
    j = lngRight
    Do
        Do While vntArr(i) < vntTestVal
            i = i + 1
        Loop
        Do While vntArr(j) > vntTestVal
            j = j - 1
        Loop
        If i <= j Then
            Call SwapElements(vntArr, i, j)
            i = i + 1
            j = j - 1
        End If
    Loop Until i > j
    If j <= lngMid Then
        Call QuickSort(vntArr, lngLeft, j)
        Call QuickSort(vntArr, i, lngRight)
    Else
        Call QuickSort(vntArr, i, lngRight)
        Call QuickSort(vntArr, lngLeft, j)
    End If
End If
End Sub
```

4

```
Private Sub SwapElements(ByRef vntItems As Variant, _
    ByVal lngItem1 As Long, _
    ByVal lngItem2 As Long)
Dim vntTemp As Variant
vntTemp = vntItems(lngItem2)
vntItems(lngItem2) = vntItems(lngItem1)
vntItems(lngItem1) = vntTemp
End Sub
```

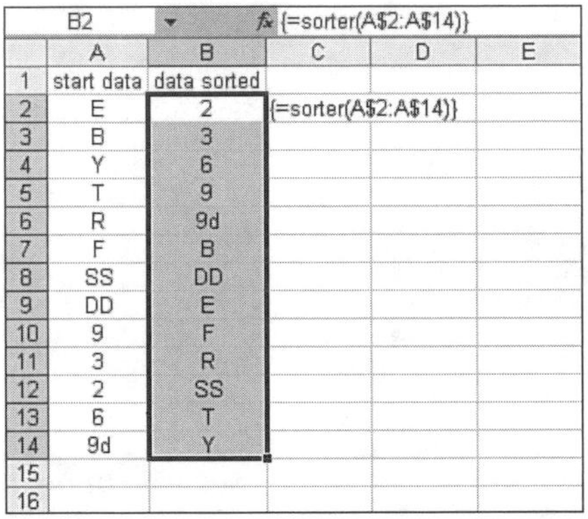

Figure 4.15
Sort a mixed alpha-
numeric list.

Search for a String Within Text

Ever needed to find out which cells contain a specific string of text? This function can search strings in a range, looking for specified text. It returns a result identifying which cells contain the text, as shown in Figure 4.16.

```
ContainsText(Rng,Text)
```

The arguments are

> Rng—The range in which to search.

> Text—The text for which to search.

Function example:

```
Function ContainsText(Rng As Range, Text As String) As String
Dim T As String
Dim myCell As Range
For Each myCell In Rng 'look in each cell
    If InStr(myCell.Text, Text) > 0 Then 'look in the string for the text
        If Len(T) = 0 Then 'if the text is found, add the address to my result
            T = myCell.Address(False, False)
        Else
            T = T & "," & myCell.Address(False, False)
        End If
    End If
Next myCell
ContainsText = T
End Function
```

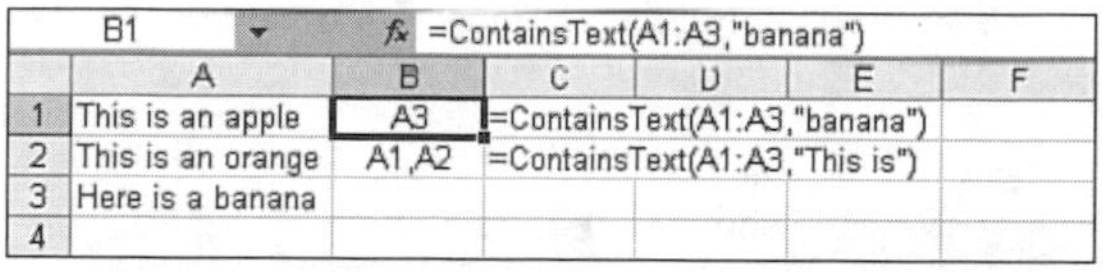

Figure 4.16
Return a result identifying which cell(s) contain(s) a specified string.

	A	B	C	D	E	F
		B1 ▾	fx =ContainsText(A1:A3,"banana")			
1	This is an apple	A3	=ContainsText(A1:A3,"banana")			
2	This is an orange	A1,A2	=ContainsText(A1:A3,"This is")			
3	Here is a banana					
4						

Reverse the Contents of a Cell

This function is mostly fun, but you may find it useful—it reverses the contents of a cell.

```
ReverseContents(myCell, IsText)
```

The arguments are

myCell—The specified cell.

IsText—Optional, should the cell value be treated as Text (Default) or a number.

Function example:

```
Function ReverseContents(myCell As Range, Optional IsText As Boolean = True)
Dim i As Integer
Dim OrigString As String, NewString As String
OrigString = Trim(myCell) 'remove leading and trailing spaces
For i = 1 To Len(OrigString)
'by adding the variable NewString to the character,
'instead of adding the character to NewStringthe string is reversed
    NewString = Mid(OrigString, i, 1) & NewString
Next i
If IsText = False Then
    ReverseContents = CLng(NewString)
Else
    ReverseContents = NewString
End If
End Function
```

Multiple Max

Max finds and returns the maximum value in a range, but it doesn't tell you whether there is more than one maximum value. This function returns the address(es) of the maximum value(s) in a range, as shown in Figure 4.17.

```
ReturnMaxs(Rng)
```

The argument is

Rng—The range to search for the maximum value(s).

Function example:

```
Function ReturnMaxs(Rng As Range) As String
Dim Mx As Double
Dim myCell As Range
'if there is only one cell in the range, then exit
If Rng.Count = 1 Then ReturnMaxs = Rng.Address(False, False): Exit Function
Mx = Application.Max(Rng) 'uses Excel's Max to find the max in the range
'Because you now know what the max value is,
```

4

```
'search the ranging finding matches and return the address
For Each myCell In Rng
    If myCell = Mx Then
        If Len(ReturnMaxs) = 0 Then
            ReturnMaxs = myCell.Address(False, False)
        Else
            ReturnMaxs = ReturnMaxs & ", " & myCell.Address(False, False)
        End If
    End If
Next myCell
End Function
```

Figure 4.17
Return the addresses of all maximum values in a range.

	B1	▼	ƒx	=ReturnMaxs(A1:A15)		
	A	B	C	D	E	F
1	3	A9, A11				
2	9					
3	5					
4	6					
5	6					
6	7					
7	6					
8	3					
9	10					
10	4					
11	10					
12	6					
13	9					
14	7					
15	1					
16						
17						

Return Hyperlink Address

You've received a spreadsheet with a list of hyperlinked information. You would like to see the actual links, not the descriptive text. You could just right-click and Edit Hyperlink, but you want something more permanent. This function extracts the hyperlink address, as shown in Figure 4.18.

```
GetAddress(Hyperlink)
```

The argument is

Hyperlink—The hyperlinked cell from which you want the address extracted.

Function example:

```
Function GetAddress(HyperlinkCell As Range)
    GetAddress = Replace(HyperlinkCell.Hyperlinks(1).Address, "mailto:", "")
End Function
```

Figure 4.18
Extract the hyperlink address from behind a hyperlink.

	B1	▼	ƒx	=GetAddress(A1)		
	A		B		C	D
1	Tracy Syrstad		Tracy@MrExcel.com		=GetAddress(A1)	
2	The Best Site for Your Excel Questions		http://www.mrexcel.com/			
3						
4						

Return the Column Letter of a Cell Address

This function extracts the column letter from a cell address.

```
ColName(Rng)
```

The argument is

Rng—The cell for which you want the column letter.

```
Function ColName(Rng As Range) As String
ColName = Left(Rng.Range("A1").Address(True, False), _
    InStr(1, Rng.Range("A1").Address(True, False), "$", 1) - 1)
End Function
```

Static Random

The function =RAND() can be very useful for creating random numbers, but it constantly recalculates. What if you need random numbers, but don't want them to change constantly? The following function places a random number, but the number changes only if you force the cell to recalculate, as shown in Figure 4.19.

```
StaticRAND ()
```

There are no arguments for this function.

```
Function StaticRAND() As Double
Randomize
STATICRAND = Rnd
End Function
```

Figure 4.19
Produce random numbers not quite so volatile.

	A	B	C	D	E
1	0.866448	=STATICRAND()			
2	0.071667				
3	0.92649				
4	0.706228				
5	0.101437				
6	0.915809				
7	0.738272				
8	0.005305				
9	0.204205				
10	0.873084				
11					
12					

(A1 ▾ fx =STATICRAND())

Using Select Case on a Worksheet

Have you ever nested an If...Then...Else on a worksheet to return a value? The Select...Case statement available in VBA case makes this a lot easier—but you can't use Select Case statements in a worksheet formula. So, create a UDF (see Figure 4.20). The following function shows how you can use `Select` statements to produce the results of a nested `If...Then` statement:

```
Function state_period(mth As Integer, yr As Integer)
Select Case mth
    Case 1
        state_period = "July 1, " & yr - 1 & " through July 31, " & yr - 1
    Case 2
        state_period = "August 1, " & yr - 1 & " through August 31, " & yr - 1
    Case 3
        state_period = "September 1, " & yr - 1 & " _
            through September 30, " & yr - 1
    Case 4
        state_period = "October 1, " & yr - 1 & " through October 31, " & yr - 1
    Case 5
        state_period = "November 1, " & yr - 1 & " _
            through November 30, " & yr - 1
    Case 6
        state_period = "December 1, " & yr - 1 & " _
            through December 31, " & yr - 1
    Case 7
        state_period = "January 1, " & yr & " through January 31, " & yr
    Case 8
        state_period = "February 1, " & yr & " through February 28, " & yr
    Case 9
        state_period = "March 1, " & yr & " through March 31, " & yr
    Case 10
        state_period = "April 1, " & yr & " through April 30, " & yr
    Case 11
        state_period = "May 1, " & yr & " through May 31, " & yr
    Case 12
        state_period = "June 1, " & yr & " through June 30, " & yr
    Case 13
        state_period = "Pre-Final"
    Case 14
        state_period = "Closeout"
End Select
End Function
```

Figure 4.20
An example of using a `Select...Case` structure in a UDF rather than nested `If...Then` statements.

Next Steps

The next chapter describes a fundamental component of any programming language: loops. You will be familiar with basic loop structures if you've taken any programming classes, and VBA supports all the usual loops. You will also learn about a special loop, `For Each...Next`, which is unique to VBA.

Looping and Flow Control

Loops are a fundamental component of any programming language. If you've taken any programming classes, even BASIC, you've likely encountered a For...Next loop. Luckily, VBA supports all the usual loops, plus a special loop that is excellent to use with VBA.

This chapter covers the basic loop constructs:

- For...Next
- Do...While
- Do...Until
- While...Loop
- Until...Loop

We'll also discuss the cool loop construct unique to object oriented languages:

- For Each...Next

For...Next **Loops**

These are common loop constructs. Everything between For and Next is run multiple times. Each time that the code runs, a certain counter variable (specified in the For statement) has a different value.

Consider this code:

```
For I = 1 to 10
    Cells(I, I).value = I
Next I
```

As this program starts to run, we've given the counter variable a name of I. The first time through the code, the variable I is set to 1. The first time that the loop is executed, I is equal to 1 so the cell in Row 1, Column 1 will be set to 1 (see Figure 5.1).

Figure 5.1
After the first iteration through the loop, the cell in Row 1, Column 1 has the value of 1.

A1	▼	fx	1	
	A	B	C	D
1	1			
2				
3				
4				

Let's take a close look at what happens as VBA gets to the line that says Next I. Before running this line, the variable I is equal to 1. During the execution of Next I, VBA must make a decision. VBA adds 1 to the variable I and compares it to the maximum value in the To clause of the For statement. If it is within the limits specified in the To clause, then the loop is not finished. In this case, the value of I will be incremented to 2. Code execution then moves back to the first line of code after the For statement. Figure 5.2 shows the state of the program before running the Next line. Figure 5.3 shows what happens after executing the Next line.

Figure 5.2
Before running the Next I statement, I is equal to 1. VBA can safely add 1 to I and it will be less than the 10 specified in the To clause of the For statement.

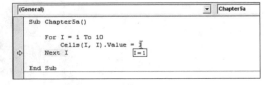

Figure 5.3
After running the Next I statement, I is incremented to 2. Code execution continues with the line of code immediately following the For statement.

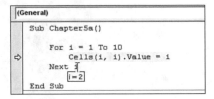

The second time through the loop, the value of I is 2. The cell in Row 2, Column 2 (that is, cell B2) gets a value of 2 (see Figure 5.4).

Figure 5.4
After the second time through the loop, cells A1 and B2 are filled in.

A1	▼	fx	1	
	A	B	C	D
1	1			
2		2		
3				
4				
5				

As the process continues, the Next I statement advances I up to 3, 4, and so on. On the tenth pass through the loop, the cell in Row 10, Column 10 is assigned a value of 10.

It is interesting to watch what happens to the variable I on the last pass through Next I. In Figure 5.5, you can see that before executing Next I the tenth time, the variable I is equal to 10.

Figure 5.5
Before running `Next I` for the tenth time, the variable `I` is equal to 10.

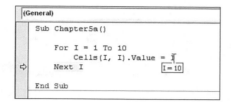

VBA is now at a decision point. It adds 1 to the variable `I`. `I` is now equal to 11, which is greater than the limit in the `For...Next` loop. VBA then moves execution to the next line in the macro after the `Next` statement (see Figure 5.6). In case you are tempted to use the variable `I` later in the macro, it is important to realize that it might be incremented beyond the limit specified in the `To` clause of the `For` statement.

Figure 5.6
After incrementing `I` to 11, code execution moves to the line after the `Next` statement.

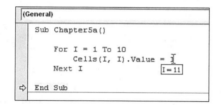

At the end of the loop, you get the result shown in Figure 5.7.

Figure 5.7
After the loop completes all 10 iterations, this is the result.

The common use for such a loop is to walk through all the rows in a dataset and decide to perform some action on the basis of a criteria. For example, if you want to mark all the rows with positive service revenue in Column F, you could use this loop:

```
For I = 2 to 10
    If Cells(I, 6).value > 0 then
        Cells(I, 8).value = "Service Revenue"
        Cells(I, 1).resize(1, 8).Interior.ColorIndex = 4
    End If
Next i
```

This loop checks each item of data from Row 2 through Row 10. If there is a positive number in Column F, then Column H of that row will have a new label and the cells in Columns A:H of the row will be colored green. After running this macro, the results look like Figure 5.8.

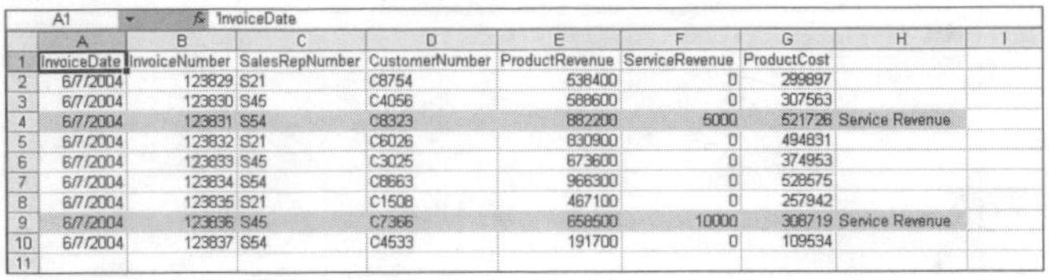

	A	B	C	D	E	F	G	H	I
1	InvoiceDate	InvoiceNumber	SalesRepNumber	CustomerNumber	ProductRevenue	ServiceRevenue	ProductCost		
2	6/7/2004	123829	S21	C8754	538400	0	299897		
3	6/7/2004	123830	S45	C4056	588600	0	307563		
4	6/7/2004	123831	S54	C8323	882200	5000	521726	Service Revenue	
5	6/7/2004	123832	S21	C6026	830900	0	494831		
6	6/7/2004	123833	S45	C3025	673600	0	374953		
7	6/7/2004	123834	S54	C8663	966300	0	528575		
8	6/7/2004	123835	S21	C1508	467100	0	257942		
9	6/7/2004	123836	S45	C7366	658500	10000	308719	Service Revenue	
10	6/7/2004	123837	S54	C4533	191700	0	109534		
11									

Figure 5.8
After the loop completes all 9 iterations, any rows with positive values in Column F are colored green and have the label "Service Revenue" added to Column H.

Using Variables in the `For` Statement

The previous example is not very useful in that it works only when there are exactly 10 rows of data. It is possible to use a variable to specify the upper and/or lower limit of the `For` statement. This code sample identifies the `FinalRow` with data, and then loops from Row 2 to that row:

```
FinalRow = Cells(65536, 1).end(xlup).row
For I = 2 to FinalRow
    If Cells(I, 6).value > 0 then
        Cells(I, 8).value = "Service Revenue"
        Cells(I, 1).resize(1, 8).Interior.ColorIndex = 4
    End If
Next i
```

Be aware when using variables. What if the imported file today is empty and has only a heading row? In this case, the `FinalRow` variable is equal to 1. This makes the first statement of the loop essentially say, "For I = 2 to 1." Because the start number is higher than the end number, the loop does not execute at all. The variable `I` is equal to 2 and code execution jumps to the line after `Next`.

5

Variations on the `For...Next` Loop

In a `For...Next` loop, it is possible to have the loop variable jump up by something other than 1. You might use it to apply greenbar formatting to every other row in a dataset, for example. In this case, you would want to have the counter variable `I` examine every other row in the dataset. Indicate this by adding the `Step` clause to the end of the `For` statement.

```
FinalRow = Cells(65536, 1).end(xlup).row
For I = 2 to FinalRow Step 2
    Cells(I, 1).resize(1, 8).Interior.ColorIndex = 35
Next i
```

While running this code, VBA adds a light green shading to Rows 2, 4, 6, and so on (see Figure 5.9).

The `Step` clause can easily be any number. You might want to check every tenth row of a dataset to extract a random sample. In this case, you would use `Step 10`:

```
FinalRow = Cells(65536, 1).end(xlup).row
NextRow = FinalRow + 5
Cells(NextRow-1, 1).value = "Random Sample of Above Data"
For I = 2 to FinalRow Step 10
    Cells(I, 1).Resize(1, 8).Copy Destination:=Cells(NextRow, 1)
    NextRow = NextRow + 1
Next i
```

	A	B	C	D	E	F	G	H	I
1	InvoiceDate	InvoiceNumber	SalesRepNumber	CustomerNumber	ProductRevenue	ServiceRevenue	ProductCost		
2	6/7/2004	123829	S21	C8754	538400	0	299897		
3	6/7/2004	123830	S45	C4056	588600	0	307563		
4	6/7/2004	123831	S54	C8323	882200	5000	521726		
5	6/7/2004	123832	S21	C6026	830900	0	494831		
6	6/7/2004	123833	S45	C3025	673600	0	374953		
7	6/7/2004	123834	S54	C8663	966300	0	528575		
8	6/7/2004	123835	S21	C1508	467100	0	257942		
9	6/7/2004	123836	S45	C7366	658500	10000	308719		
10	6/7/2004	123837	S54	C4533	191700	0	109534		
11									

Figure 5.9
The `Step` clause in the `For` statement of the loop causes the action to occur on every other row.

You can also have a `For...Next` loop run backward from high to low. This is particularly useful if you are selectively deleting rows. To do this, reverse the order of the `For` statement and have the `Step` clause specify a negative number:

```
' Delete all rows where column C is the Internal rep - S54
FinalRow = Cells(65536, 1).end(xlup).row
For I = FinalRow to 2 Step -1
    If Cells(I, 3).value = "S54" then
        Cells(I, 1).EntireRow.Delete
    End If
Next i
```

Exiting a Loop Early After a Condition Is Met

There are times where you don't need to execute the whole loop. Perhaps you simply need to read through the dataset until you find one record that meets a certain criteria. In this case, you would want to find the first record and then stop the loop. There is a statement called `Exit For` that does this.

The following sample macro looks for a row in the dataset where service revenue in Column F is positive and product revenue in Column E is 0. If such a row is found, you might indicate a message that the file needs manual processing today and move the cell pointer to that row:

```
' Are there any special processing situations in the data?
FinalRow = Cells(65536, 1).end(xlup).row
ProblemFound = False
For I = 2 to FinalRow
    If Cells(I, 6).value > 0 then
        If cells(I, 5).value = 0 then
            Cells(I, 6).Select
            ProblemFound = True
            Exit For
        End if
    End if
Next I
If ProblemFound then
    MsgBox "There is a problem at row " & I
    Exit Sub
End if
```

Nesting One Loop Inside Another Loop

It is okay to run a loop inside another loop. Perhaps the first loop is running through all the rows in your recordset. The second loop then might run through all the columns in your recordset. Consider the dataset in Figure 5.10:

5

Figure 5.10
By nesting one loop inside the other, VBA can loop through each row and then each column.

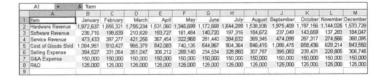

```
' Loop through each row and column
' Add a checkerboard format
FinalRow = Cells(65536, 1).End(xlUp).Row
FinalCol = Cells(1, 255).End(xlToLeft).Column
For I = 2 to FinalRow
    ' For even numbered rows, start in column 1
    ' For odd numbered rows, start in column 2
    if I mod 2 = 1 then
        StartCol = 1
    Else
    StartCol = 2
    End if
    For J = StartCol to FinalCol Step 2
    Cells(I, J).Interior.ColorIndex = 35
    Next J
Next I
```

In this code, the outer loop is using the I counter variable to loop through all the rows in the dataset. The inner loop is using the J counter variable to loop through all the columns in that row. Because Figure 5.10 has 7 data rows, the code runs through the I loop 7 times. Each time through the I loop, the code runs through the J loop 6 or 7 times. This means that the line of code that is inside the J loop ends up being executed several times for each pass through the I loop. The result is shown in Figure 5.11.

Figure 5.11
The result of nesting one loop inside the other; VBA can loop through each row and then each column.

Do **Loops**

There are several variations of the Do loop. The most basic loop is great for doing a bunch of some mundane task. I once had someone send me a list of addresses going down a column, as shown in Figure 5.12.

I needed to rearrange these addresses into a database with name in Column B, street in Column C, city and state in Column D. By setting Relative Recording (see Chapter 1, "Unleash the Power of Excel with VBA!") and using a hot key of Ctrl+A, I recorded this little bit of useful code. The code is designed to copy one single address into database format. It also navigates the cell pointer to the name of the next address in the list. This allowed me to sit at my desk, and each time that I hit Ctrl+A, it would reformat one address for me:

Figure 5.12
Someone sent addresses typed in this format, but it is more useful to have them in a database format so they can later be used in a mail merge.

	A
1	
2	John Smith
3	123 Main Street
4	Akron OH 44308
5	
6	Jane Doe
7	245 State Street
8	Chicago IL 60011
9	
10	Ralph Emerson
11	345 2nd Ave
12	New York NY 10011
13	
14	George Washington
15	456 3rd St
16	Philadelphia PA 12345
17	
18	John Adams
19	543 4th Ave
20	Baltimore MD 12345
21	
22	Thomas Jefferson
23	654 5th Ave
24	Roanoke VA 12345
25	
26	James Madison
27	987 6th St
28	Hollywood CA 12345
29	
30	James Monroe
31	765 7th Ave
32	Houston TX 12345
33	

→ For a discussion of Relative Recording, **see** "A Possible Solution: Using Relative References When Recording," **p. 25**, in Chapter 1.

```
Sub Macro3()
'
' Macro3 Macro
' Macro recorded 10/29/2003 by Bill Jelen
' Move one address into database format.
' Then move the cell pointer to the start of the next address.
'
' Keyboard Shortcut: Ctrl+Shift+A
'
    Selection.Copy
    ActiveCell.Offset(0, 1).Range("A1").Select
    ActiveSheet.Paste
    ActiveCell.Offset(1, -1).Range("A1").Select
    Application.CutCopyMode = False
    Selection.Copy
    ActiveCell.Offset(-1, 2).Range("A1").Select
    ActiveSheet.Paste
    ActiveCell.Offset(2, -2).Range("A1").Select
    Application.CutCopyMode = False
    Selection.Copy
    ActiveCell.Offset(-2, 3).Range("A1").Select
    ActiveSheet.Paste
    ActiveCell.Offset(4, -3).Range("A1").Select
End Sub
```

CAUTION

I am not suggesting that the above code is suitable for a professional application. However, sometimes we are writing macros just to automate a one-time mundane task.

Without a macro, I would have done a lot of copying and pasting manually. Now, with the preceding recorded macro, I could place the cell pointer on a name in Column A and hit Ctrl+Shift+A. That one address would be copied into three columns and the cell pointer would move to the start of the next address (see Figure 5.13).

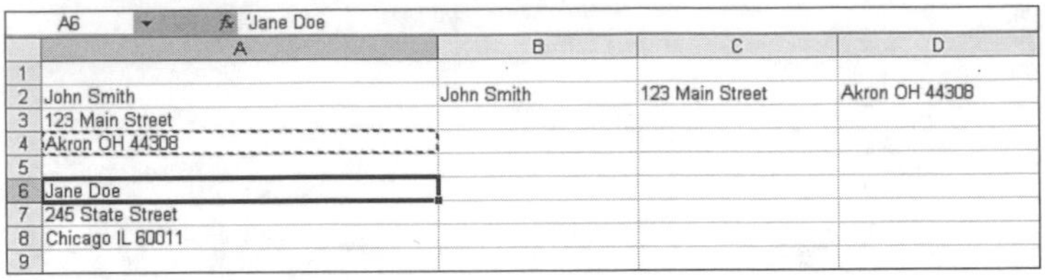

Figure 5.13
After running the macro once, one address is moved into the proper format and the cell pointer is positioned to run the macro again.

I was pretty happy with this macro, as it allowed me to process an address every second using the hot key. I soon realized that I had 5,000 addresses and I didn't want to keep running the same macro over and over.

Using a `Do...Loop`, I could set up the macro to run continuously. If I simply enclosed the recorded code with `Do` at the top and `Loop` at the end, VBA would continuously run my code over and over. This would allow me to sit back and watch the code do the work. This insanely boring task was now done in minutes instead of hours.

Note that this particular `Do...Loop` will run forever. There is no mechanism to stop it. That worked for the task at hand--I could watch the progress on the screen and after the program had advanced past the end of this database, I simply hit Ctrl+Break to stop execution:

```
Sub Macro3()
'
' Macro3 Macro
' Macro recorded 10/29/2003 by Bill Jelen
' Move one address into database format.
' Then move the cell pointer to the start of the next address.
'
' Keyboard Shortcut: Ctrl+Shift+A
'
Do
    Selection.Copy
    ActiveCell.Offset(0, 1).Range("A1").Select
    ActiveSheet.Paste
    ActiveCell.Offset(1, -1).Range("A1").Select
    Application.CutCopyMode = False
    Selection.Copy
    ActiveCell.Offset(-1, 2).Range("A1").Select
    ActiveSheet.Paste
    ActiveCell.Offset(2, -2).Range("A1").Select
    Application.CutCopyMode = False
    Selection.Copy
    ActiveCell.Offset(-2, 3).Range("A1").Select
    ActiveSheet.Paste
    ActiveCell.Offset(4, -3).Range("A1").Select
Loop
End Sub
```

All of these examples are "quick and dirty" loops. They are great where you need to accomplish a task quickly. The Do...Loop provides a number of options to allow you to automatically have the program stop when it accomplishes the end of the task.

The first option is to have a line in the Do...Loop that detects the end of the dataset and exits the loop. In the current example, this could be accomplished by using the Exit Do command in an If statement. If the current cell is on a cell that is empty, you can assume that you've reached the end of the data and stopped processing the loop:

```
Do
    If Not Selection.Value > "" then Exit Do
    Selection.Copy
    ActiveCell.Offset(0, 1).Range("A1").Select
    ActiveSheet.Paste
    ActiveCell.Offset(1, -1).Range("A1").Select
    Application.CutCopyMode = False
    Selection.Copy
    ActiveCell.Offset(-1, 2).Range("A1").Select
    ActiveSheet.Paste
    ActiveCell.Offset(2, -2).Range("A1").Select
    Application.CutCopyMode = False
    Selection.Copy
    ActiveCell.Offset(-2, 3).Range("A1").Select
    ActiveSheet.Paste
    ActiveCell.Offset(4, -3).Range("A1").Select
Loop
End Sub
```

Using the While or Until Clause in Do Loops

There are four variations of using While or Until. These clauses can be added to either the Do statement or the Loop statement. In every case, the While or Until clause includes some test that evaluates to True or False.

With a Do While <test expression>...Loop construct, the loop is never executed if <test expression> is false. If you are reading records from a text file, you can not assume that the file has one or more records, so you need to test to see whether you are already at the end of file with the EOF function before you enter the loop:

```
' Read a text file, skipping the Total lines
    Open "C:\Invoice.txt" For Input As #1
    R = 1
    Do While Not EOF(1)
        Line Input #FileNumber, Data
        If Not Left (Data, 5) = "TOTAL" then
            ' Import this row
            r = r + 1
            Cells(r, 1).Value = Data
        End If
    Loop
    Close #1
```

5

In this example, I used the NOT keyword. EOF(1) evaluates to True after there are no more records to be read from invoice.txt. Some programmers feel it hard to read a program that contains a lot of NOTs. To avoid the use of NOT, use the Do Until <*test expression*>...Loop construct:

```
' Read a text file, skipping the Total lines
    Open "C:\Invoice.txt" For Input As #1
    R = 1
    Do Until EOF(1)
        Line Input #1, Data
        If Not (Data, 5) = "TOTAL" then
            ' Import this row
            r = r + 1
            Cells(r, 1).Value = Data
        End If
    Loop
    Close #1
```

In other examples, you always want the loop to be executed the first time. In these cases, you move the While or Until instruction to the end of the loop. This code sample asks the user to enter sales amounts made that day. It continually asks them for sales amounts until they enter a 0:

```
TotalSales = 0
Do
    x = InputBox(Prompt:="Enter Amount of Next Invoice. Enter 0 when done.")
    TotalSales = TotalSales + x
Loop Until x = 0
MsgBox "The total for today is $" & TotalSales
```

In the following loop, a check amount is entered and then it looks for open invoices to which to apply the check. It is often the case that a single check is received and it covers many invoices. This program sequentially applies the check to the oldest invoices until 100% of the check has been applied.

```
' Ask for the amount of check received
AmtToApply = InputBox("Enter Amount of Check")
' Loop through the list of open invoices.
' Apply the check to the oldest open invoices and Decrement AmtToApply
NextRow = 2
Do While AmtToApply > 0
    OpenAmt = Cells(NextRow, 3)
    If OpenAmt > AmtToApply Then
        ' Apply total check to this invoice
        Cells(NextRow, 4).Value = AmtToApply
        AmtToApply = 0
    Else
        Cells(NextRow, 4).Value = OpenAmt
        AmtToApply = AmtToApply - OpenAmt
    End If
    NextRow = NextRow + 1
Loop
```

Because you can construct the Do...Loop with the While or Until qualifiers at the beginning or end, you have a lot of subtle control over whether the loop is always executed once, even if the condition is True at the beginning.

While...Wend **Loops**

While...Wend loops are included in VBA for backward compatibility. In the VBA help file, Microsoft suggests that Do...Loops are more flexible. However, because you might encounter While...Wend loops in code written by others, here is a quick example. In this loop, the first line is always While *condition*. The last line of the loop is always Wend. Note that there is no Exit While statement. In general, these loops are okay, but the Do...Loop construct is more robust and flexible. Because it offers either the While or Until qualifier, this qualifier can be at the beginning or end of the loop, and there is the possibility to exit a Do loop early:

```
' Read a text file, adding the amounts
    Open "C:\Invoice.txt" For Input As #1
    TotalSales = 0
    While Not EOF(1)
        Line Input #1, Data
        TotalSales = TotalSales + Data
    Wend
    MsgBox "Total Sales=" & TotalSales
    Close #1
```

The VBA Loop: For Each

This is an excellent loop and the macro recorder never records this type of loop. VBA is an object-oriented language. It's common to have a collection of objects in Excel, such as a collection of worksheets in a workbook, cells in a range, PivotTables on a worksheet, or data series on a chart.

This special type of loop is great for looping through all the items in the collection. Before discussing this loop in detail, you need to understand a special kind of variable called *object variables*.

Object Variables

At this point, you've seen a variable that contains a single value. When you have a variable such as TotalSales = 0, then TotalSales is a normal variable and generally contains only a single value. It is also possible to have a more powerful variable called an *object variable*. An object variable holds many values, basically, any property that is associated with the object is associated with the object variable.

I generally do not take the time to declare my variables. Many books implore you to use the DIM statement to identify all your variables at the top of the procedure. This allows you to specify that a certain variable is of a certain type, such as Integer or Double. Although this saves a tiny bit of memory, it requires you to know up front which variables you plan on using. I tend to invent variables as I go, whipping up a new variable on the fly as the need arises. However, there are great benefits to declaring object variables. The VBA autocomplete feature turns on if you declare an object variable at the top of your procedure. The following lines of code declare three object variables, one as a worksheet, one as a range, and one as a PivotTable.

```
Sub Test()
    Dim WSD as Worksheet
    Dim MyCell as Range
    Dim PT as PivotTable
    Set WSD = ThisWorkbook.Worksheets("Data")
    Set MyCell = WSD.Cells(65536, 1).End(xlUp).Offset(1, 0)
    Set PT = WSD.PivotTables(1)
    …
```

In this example, you can see that just an equals statement is not used to assign object variables. You need to use the Set statement to assign a specific object to the object variable.

There are many great reasons for using object variables, not the least of which is the fact that it can be a great shorthand notation. It is a lot easier to have a lot of lines of code referring to WSD instead of ThisWorkbook.Worksheets("Data").

Also, as mentioned earlier, the object variable inherits all the properties of the object to which it refers.

The For Each...Loop employs an object variable rather than a Counter variable. The following code loops through all the cells in Column A. The code uses the .CurrentRegion property to define the current region and then uses the .Resize property to limit the selected range to a single column. The object variable is called Cell. I could have used any name for the object variable, but Cell seems more appropriate than something arbitrary like Fred.

```
For Each cell in Range("A1").CurrentRegion.Resize(, 1)
    If cell.value = "Total" then
        cell.resize(1,8).Font.Bold = True
    End if
Next cell
```

This code sample searches all open workbooks, looking for one with a particular sheet name.

```
For Each wb in Workbooks
    If wb.Worksheets(1).Name = "Menu" then
    WBFound = True
    WBName = wb.Name
    Exit For
End if
Next wb
```

In this code sample, all shapes on the current worksheet are deleted:

```
For Each Sh in ActiveSheet.Shapes
    Sh.Delete
Next Sh
```

This code sample deletes all pivot tables on the current sheet:

```
For Each pt in ActiveSheet.PivotTables
    pt.TableRange2.Clear
Next pt
```

Looping Through All Files in a Directory

Here are some useful procedures that make extensive use of loops. The first procedure uses VBA's FileSearch object to find all JPG picture files in a certain directory. Each file is listed down a column in Excel.

The outer For i loop iterates through each image file found in a particular folder and all its subfolders. Each pass through the outer loop will return a new path and file name in the variable ThisEntry. To separate the path from the file name, the inner For j loop will search the path and file name from the end to the beginning, looking for the final path separator:

```vba
Sub ListJpgFiles()
    ' This macro lists all .jpg files
    ' in a certain directory to a column in Excel

    ' Clear out all cells in the sheet
    Cells.Clear

    ' Add Headings
    Range("A1:D1").Value = Array("FileName", "Path", "FileName", "NewPath")
    NextRow = 2

    ' Use the FileSearch Object
    With Application.FileSearch
        .NewSearch
        .LookIn = "C:\MyPictures\"
        .SearchSubFolders = True
        .Filename = "*.jpg"
        .Execute
        FilesToProcess = .FoundFiles.Count
        ' loop through each workbook in the directory
        For i = 1 To .FoundFiles.Count
            ThisEntry = .FoundFiles(i)
            Cells(NextRow, 1).Value = ThisEntry
            ' Find to path portion. Start looking from the end
            ' of This Entry for a backslash
            For j = Len(ThisEntry) To 1 Step -1
                If Mid(ThisEntry, j, 1) = Application.PathSeparator Then
                    Cells(NextRow, 2) = Left(ThisEntry, j)
                    Cells(NextRow, 3) = Mid(ThisEntry, j + 1)
                    Exit For
                End If
            Next j
            NextRow = NextRow + 1
        Next i

    End With

End Sub
```

My idea in this case is that I want to organize the photos into new folders. In Column D, if I wanted to move a picture to a new folder, I would type the path of that folder. The following For Each loop takes care of copying the pictures. Each time through the loop, the object variable named Cell will contain a reference to a cell in Column A. You can use

Cell.Offset(0, 3) to return the value from the cell three columns to the right of the range represented by the variable Cell:

```
Sub CopyToNewFolder()
    FinalRow = Range("A65536").End(xlUp).Row
    For Each Cell In Range("A2:A" & FinalRow)
        OrigFile = Cell.Value
        NewFile = Cell.Offset(0, 3) & Application.PathSeparator & _
            Cell.Offset(0, 4)
        FileCopy OrigFile, NewFile
    Next Cell
End Sub
```

Flow Control: Using If...Then...Else and Select Case

Another aspect of programming that will never be recorded by the macro recorder is the concept of flow control. Sometimes, you do not want every line of your program to be executed every time you run the macro. VBA offers two excellent choices for flow control: the If...Then...Else construct, and the Select Case construct.

Basic Flow Control: If...Then...Else

The most common device for program flow control is the If statement. Say that you have a list of products as shown in Figure 5.14. You would like to loop through each product in the list and copy it to either a Fruits list or a Vegetables list. As a beginning programmer, I was tempted to loop through the rows twice; I wanted to loop through once looking for fruit, and a second time looking for vegetables. However, there is no need to loop through twice. On a single loop, you can use an If...Then...Else construct to copy each row to the correct place.

Figure 5.14
A single loop can look for fruits or vegetables.

	A	B	C
1	Class	Product	Quantity
2	Fruit	Apples	1
3	Fruit	Apricots	3
4	Vegetable	Apsaragus	62
5	Fruit	Bananas	55
6	Fruit	Blueberry	17
7	Vegetable	Broccoli	56
8	Vegetable	Cabbage	35
9	Fruit	Cherries	59

Conditions

Any If statement needs a condition that is being tested. The condition should always evaluate to TRUE or FALSE. Here are some examples of simple and complex conditions:

- If Range("A1").value = "Title" Then
- If Not Range("A1").Value = "Title" then
- If Range("A1").Value = "Title" And Range("B1").Value = "Fruit"
- If Range("A1").Value = "Title" Or Range("B1").Value = "Fruit"

If...Then...End If

After the If statement, you may include one or more program lines that will be executed only if the condition is met. You should then close the If block with an End If line. Here is a simple example of an If statement.

```
Sub ColorFruitRedBold()
    FinalRow = Cells(65536, 1).End(xlUp).Row

    For i = 2 To FinalRow
        If Cells(i, 1).Value = "Fruit" Then
            Cells(i, 1).Resize(1, 3).Font.Bold = True
            Cells(i, 1).Resize(1, 3).Font.ColorIndex = 3
        End If
    Next i

    MsgBox "Fruit is now bold and red"
End Sub
```

Either/Or Decisions: If...Then...Else...End If

Sometimes you will want to do one set of statements if the condition is true, and another set of statements if the condition is not true. To do this with VBA, the second set of conditions would be coded after the Else statement. There is still only one End If statement associated with this construct. Let's say that you want to color the fruit red and the vegetables green.

```
Sub FruitRedVegGreen()
    FinalRow = Cells(65536, 1).End(xlUp).Row

    For i = 2 To FinalRow
        If Cells(i, 1).Value = "Fruit" Then
            Cells(i, 1).Resize(1, 3).Font.ColorIndex = 3
        Else
            Cells(i, 1).Resize(1, 3).Font.ColorIndex = 50
        End If
    Next i

    MsgBox "Fruit is red / Veggies are green"
End Sub
```

Using If...Else If...End If for Multiple Conditions

You will notice that our product list includes one item that is classified as an herb. We really have three conditions for which to test. It is possible to build an If...End If structure with multiple conditions. First, test to see whether the record is a fruit. Next, use an Else If to test whether the record is a vegetable. Next, test to see whether the record is an herb. Finally, if the record is none of those, highlight the record as an error.

```
Sub MultipleIf()
    FinalRow = Cells(65536, 1).End(xlUp).Row

    For i = 2 To FinalRow
        If Cells(i, 1).Value = "Fruit" Then
            Cells(i, 1).Resize(1, 3).Font.ColorIndex = 3
        ElseIf Cells(i, 1).Value = "Vegetable" Then
            Cells(i, 1).Resize(1, 3).Font.ColorIndex = 50
```

5

```
        ElseIf Cells(i, 1).Value = "Herbs" Then
            Cells(i, 1).Resize(1, 3).Font.ColorIndex = 5
        Else
            ' This must be a record in error
            Cells(i, 1).Resize(1, 3).Interior.ColorIndex = 6
        End If
    Next i

    MsgBox "Fruit is red / Veggies are green / Herbs are blue"
End Sub
```

Using Select Case…End Select for Multiple Conditions

When you have many different conditions, it becomes unwieldy to use many Else If statements. VBA offers another construct known as the Select Case construct. In our running example, we always want to check the value of the Class in column A. This value is called the *test expression*. The basic syntax of this construct starts with the words Select Case followed by the test expression:

```
Select Case Cells(i, 1).Value
```

Thinking about our problem in English, you might say "In cases where the record is fruit, color the record with red." VBA uses a shorthand version of this. You write the word Case followed by the literal "Fruit". Any statements that follow Case "Fruit" will be executed whenever the test expression is a fruit. After these statements, you would have the next Case statement: Case "Vegetables". You would continue in this fashion, writing a Case statement followed by the program lines that will be executed if that case is true.

After you've listed all the possible conditions you can think of, you may optionally include a "Case Else" section at the end. This section will include what the program should do if the test expression matches none of your cases. Finally, close the entire construct with the End Select statement.

The following program does the same operation as the previous macro, but uses a Select Case statement.

```
Sub SelectCase()
    FinalRow = Cells(65536, 1).End(xlUp).Row

    For i = 2 To FinalRow
        Select Case Cells(i, 1).Value
            Case "Fruit"
                Cells(i, 1).Resize(1, 3).Font.ColorIndex = 3
            Case "Vegetable"
                Cells(i, 1).Resize(1, 3).Font.ColorIndex = 50
            Case "Herbs"
                Cells(i, 1).Resize(1, 3).Font.ColorIndex = 5
            Case Else
        End Select
    Next i

    MsgBox "Fruit is red / Veggies are green / Herbs are blue"
End Sub
```

Complex Expressions in Case Statements

It is possible to have fairly complex expressions in case statements. You might want to perform the same actions for all berry records:

```
Case "Strawberry", "Blueberry", "Raspberry"
    AdCode = 1
```

If it makes sense, you might code a range of values in the Case statement:

```
Case 1 to 20
    Discount = 0.05
Case 21 to 100
    Discount = 0.1
```

You can include the keyword Is and a comparison operator, such as > or <:

```
Case Is < 10
    Discount = 0
Case is > 100
    Discount = 0.2
Case Else
    Discount = 0.10
```

Nesting If Statements

It is possible and common to nest an If statement inside another If statement. This is a situation where it is very important to use proper indenting. You will find that you often have several End If lines at the end of the construct. By having proper indenting, it is easier to tell which End If is associated with a particular If.

The final macro has a lot of logic. Our discount rules are as follows:

- For Fruit, quantities under 5 cases get no discount
- Quantities from 5 to 20 cases get a 10% discount
- Quantities above 20 cases get a 15% discount
- For Herbs, quantities under 10 cases get no discount
- Quantities from 10 cases to 15 cases get a 3% discount
- Quantities above 15 cases get a 6% discount
- For Vegetables except Asparagus, 5 cases and above earn a 12% discount
- Asparagus requires 20 cases for a discount of 12%
- None of the discounts apply if the product is on sale this week. The sale price is 25% off the normal price. This week's sale items are Strawberry, Lettuce, and Tomatoes.

The code to execute this logic follows:

```
Sub ComplexIf()
    FinalRow = Cells(65536, 1).End(xlUp).Row
```

5

```vba
For i = 2 To FinalRow
    ThisClass = Cells(i, 1).Value
    ThisProduct = Cells(i, 2).Value
    ThisQty = Cells(i, 3).Value

    ' First, figure out if the item is on sale
    Select Case ThisProduct
        Case "Strawberry", "Lettuce", "Tomatoes"
            Sale = True
        Case Else
            Sale = False
    End Select

    ' Figure out the discount
    If Sale Then
        Discount = 0.25
    Else
        If ThisClass = "Fruit" Then
            Select Case ThisQty
                Case Is < 5
                    Discount = 0
                Case 5 To 20
                    Discount = 0.1
                Case Is > 20
                    Discount = 0.15
            End Select
        ElseIf ThisClass = "Herbs" Then
            Select Case ThisQty
                Case Is < 10
                    Discount = 0
                Case 10 To 15
                    Discount = 0.03
                Case Is > 15
                    Discount = 0.05
            End Select
        ElseIf ThisClass = "Vegetables" Then
            ' There is a special condition for asparagus
            If ThisProduct = "Asparagus" Then
                If ThisQty < 20 Then
                    Discount = 0
                Else
                    Discount = 0.12
                End If
            Else
                If ThisQty < 5 Then
                    Discount = 0
                Else
                    Discount = 0.12
                End If
            End If ' Is the product asparagus or not?
        End If ' Is the product a vegetable?
    End If ' Is the product on sale?

    Cells(i, 4).Value = Discount

    If Sale Then
        Cells(i, 4).Font.Bold = True
    End If
```

```
    Next i

    Range("D1").Value = "Discount"

    MsgBox "Discounts have been applied"
End Sub
```

Next Steps

Loops add a tremendous amount of power to your recorded macros. Any time that you need to repeat a process over all worksheets or all rows in a worksheet, a loop is the way to go. Excel VBA supports the traditional programming loops of For...Next and Do...Loop, as well as the object-oriented loop of For Each...Next. Next, Chapter 6, "R1C1 Style Formulas," discusses the seemingly arcane R1C1 style of formulas and shows you why it is important in Excel VBA.

5

R1C1 Style Formulas

6

Referring to Cells: A1 Versus R1C1 References

We can trace the "A1" style of referencing back to VisiCalc. Dan Bricklin and Bob Frankston used A1 to refer to the cell in the upper-left corner of the spreadsheet. Mitch Kapor used this same addressing scheme in Lotus 1-2-3. Upstart Multiplan from Microsoft attempted to buck the trend and used something called R1C1-style addressing. In R1C1 addressing, the cell known as A1 is referred to as "R1C1" because it is in Row 1, Column 1.

With the dominance of Lotus 1-2-3 in the 1980s and early 1990s, the A1 style became the standard. Microsoft realized they were fighting a losing battle and eventually offered either R1C1-style addressing or A1-style addressing in Excel. When you open Excel today, the A1 style is used by default. Officially, however, Microsoft supports both styles of addressing.

Why Care About R1C1 Style?

You would think that this chapter would be a non-issue. Anyone who uses the Excel interface would agree that the R1C1 style is dead. However, we have what on the face of it would seem to be an annoying problem: The macro recorder records formulas in the R1C1 style. So you might be thinking that you just need to learn R1C1 addressing so that you can read the recorded code and switch it back to the familiar A1 style.

Not Just an Annoyance

I have to give Microsoft credit. After you understand R1C1-style formulas, they are actually more efficient, especially when you are dealing with writing formulas in VBA. Using R1C1-style addressing allows you to write more efficient code. Plus, there are some features, such as setting up array formulas or conditional formatting with the Formula Is option, where you are required to enter the formula in R1C1 style.

I can hear the collective groan from Excel users everywhere. I would be all for skipping 14 pages of this old-fashioned addressing style if it were only an annoyance or an efficiency issue. However, because it is necessary to understand R1C1 addressing to effectively use important features such as array formulas or conditional formatting, we'll have to dive in and learn this style.

Switching Excel to Display R1C1 Style References

To switch to R1C1-style addressing, select Tools, Options from the main menu. On the General tab, check the box for R1C1 reference style (see Figure 6.1).

Figure 6.1
Checking R1C1 reference style on the General tab of the Options box causes Excel to revert to R1C1 style in the Excel user interface.

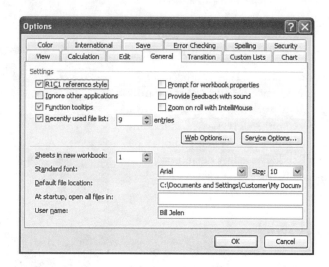

After you switch to R1C1 style, the column letters A, B, C across the top of the worksheet are replaced by numbers 1, 2, 3 (see Figure 6.2).

Figure 6.2
In R1C1 style, the column letters are replaced by numbers.

In this format, the cell that you know as B5 is called R5C2 because it is in Row 5, Column 2.

Every couple of weeks, someone manages to accidentally turn this option on, and we get an urgent support request at MrExcel; the style is very foreign to 99% of spreadsheet users.

The Miracle of Excel Formulas

Automatically recalculating thousands of cells is the main benefit of electronic spreadsheets over the green ledger paper used up until 1979. However, I would say a close second prize award would be that you can enter one formula and copy that formula to thousands of cells.

Enter a Formula Once and Copy 1,000 Times

Consider this simple worksheet in Figure 6.3. Enter a simple formula like `=C4*B4` in Cell D4, double-click the AutoFill handle, and the formula intelligently changes as at is copied down the range.

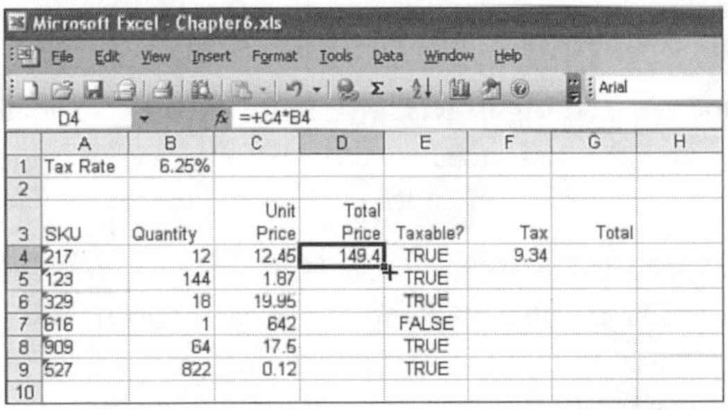

	A	B	C	D	E	F	G	H
1	Tax Rate	6.25%						
2								
3	SKU	Quantity	Unit Price	Total Price	Taxable?	Tax	Total	
4	217	12	12.45	149.4	TRUE	9.34		
5	123	144	1.87		TRUE			
6	329	18	19.95		TRUE			
7	616	1	642		FALSE			
8	909	64	17.5		TRUE			
9	527	822	0.12		TRUE			
10								

Figure 6.3
Double-click the AutoFill handle and Excel intelligently copies this relative-reference formula down the column.

The formula in F4 includes both relative and absolute formulas: `=IF(E4,ROUND(D4*$B$1,2),0)`. Thanks to the dollar signs inserted in B1, you can copy this formula down and it always multiplies the Total Price in this row by the tax rate in Cell B1.

The numerical results in Figure 6.4 are achieved by the formulas shown in Figure 6.5. (Ctrl+~ in Excel switches between normal view and formula view.) Considering that I had to enter formulas only in Rows 4 and 10, I think it is amazing that Excel was able to intelligently copy the formulas down the column.

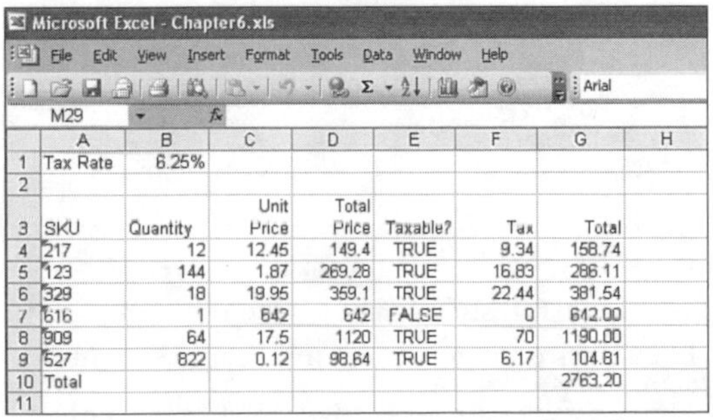

	A	B	C	D	E	F	G	H
1	Tax Rate	6.25%						
2								
3	SKU	Quantity	Unit Price	Total Price	Taxable?	Tax	Total	
4	217	12	12.45	149.4	TRUE	9.34	158.74	
5	123	144	1.87	269.28	TRUE	16.83	286.11	
6	329	18	19.95	359.1	TRUE	22.44	381.54	
7	616	1	642	642	FALSE	0	642.00	
8	909	64	17.5	1120	TRUE	70	1190.00	
9	527	822	0.12	98.64	TRUE	6.17	104.81	
10	Total						2763.20	
11								

Figure 6.4
These results in Columns D, F, and G are achieved by the formulas shown in Figure 6.5.

6

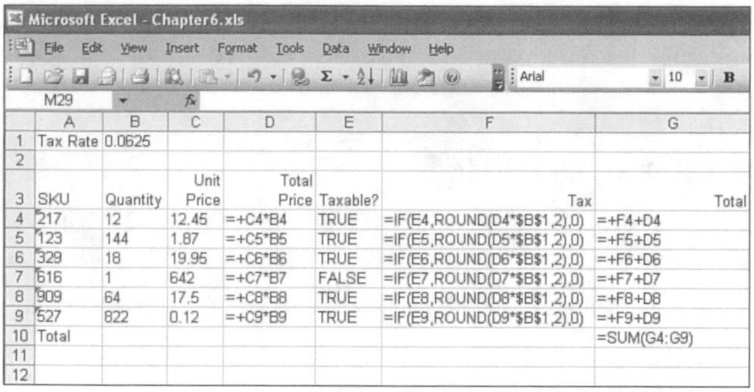

Microsoft Excel - Chapter6.xls

M29

	A	B	C	D	E	F	G
1	Tax Rate	0.0625					
2							
3	SKU	Quantity	Unit Price	Total Price	Taxable?	Tax	Total
4	217	12	12.45	=+C4*B4	TRUE	=IF(E4,ROUND(D4*$B$1,2),0)	=+F4+D4
5	123	144	1.87	=+C5*B5	TRUE	=IF(E5,ROUND(D5*$B$1,2),0)	=+F5+D5
6	329	18	19.95	=+C6*B6	TRUE	=IF(E6,ROUND(D6*$B$1,2),0)	=+F6+D6
7	616	1	642	=+C7*B7	FALSE	=IF(E7,ROUND(D7*$B$1,2),0)	=+F7+D7
8	909	64	17.5	=+C8*B8	TRUE	=IF(E8,ROUND(D8*$B$1,2),0)	=+F8+D8
9	527	822	0.12	=+C9*B9	TRUE	=IF(E9,ROUND(D9*$B$1,2),0)	=+F9+D9
10	Total						=SUM(G4:G9)
11							
12							

Figure 6.5
Hit Ctrl+~ to switch to showing formulas rather than their results. It is amazing that Excel adjusts the cell references in each formula as you copy down the column.

As Excel users, we take this behavior for granted, but people in my beginning Excel class are fairly amazed that the formula `=F4+D4` in Cell G4 automatically changed to `=F5+D5` when it was copied to Cell G5.

The Secret—It Is Not That Amazing

Remember that Excel does everything in R1C1-style formulas. Excel shows addresses and formulas in A1 style merely because it needs to adhere to the standard made popular by VisiCalc and Lotus.

If you switch the worksheet in Figure 6.5 to use R1C1 notation, you will notice that the "different" formulas in D4:D9 are all actually identical formulas in R1C1 notation. The same is true of F4:F9 and G4:G9. Use the Options dialog to change the sample worksheet to R1C1-style addresses. If you examine the formulas in Figure 6.6, you will see that in R1C1 language, every formula in Column D is exactly identical. Given that Excel is storing the formulas in R1C1 style, copying them, and then merely translating to A1 style for us to understand, it is no longer that amazing that Excel can easily manipulate A1-style formulas as it does.

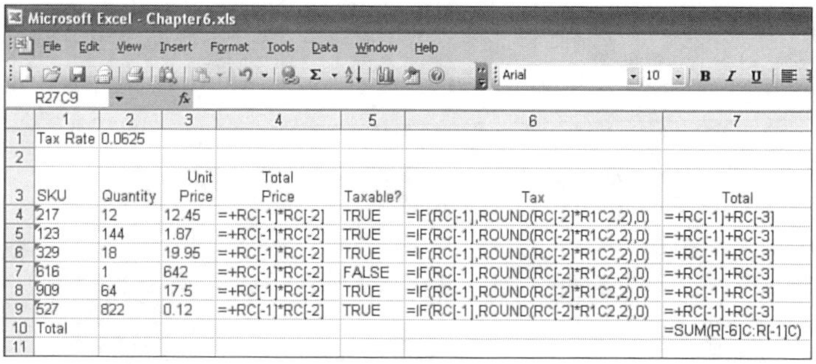

Microsoft Excel - Chapter6.xls

R27C9

	1	2	3	4	5	6	7
1	Tax Rate	0.0625					
2							
3	SKU	Quantity	Unit Price	Total Price	Taxable?	Tax	Total
4	217	12	12.45	=+RC[-1]*RC[-2]	TRUE	=IF(RC[-1],ROUND(RC[-2]*R1C2,2),0)	=+RC[-1]+RC[-3]
5	123	144	1.87	=+RC[-1]*RC[-2]	TRUE	=IF(RC[-1],ROUND(RC[-2]*R1C2,2),0)	=+RC[-1]+RC[-3]
6	329	18	19.95	=+RC[-1]*RC[-2]	TRUE	=IF(RC[-1],ROUND(RC[-2]*R1C2,2),0)	=+RC[-1]+RC[-3]
7	616	1	642	=+RC[-1]*RC[-2]	FALSE	=IF(RC[-1],ROUND(RC[-2]*R1C2,2),0)	=+RC[-1]+RC[-3]
8	909	64	17.5	=+RC[-1]*RC[-2]	TRUE	=IF(RC[-1],ROUND(RC[-2]*R1C2,2),0)	=+RC[-1]+RC[-3]
9	527	822	0.12	=+RC[-1]*RC[-2]	TRUE	=IF(RC[-1],ROUND(RC[-2]*R1C2,2),0)	=+RC[-1]+RC[-3]
10	Total						=SUM(R[-6]C:R[-1]C)
11							

Figure 6.6
The same formulas in R1C1 style. Note that every formula in Column 4 or Column 6 is the same as all other formulas in that column.

This is one of the reasons that R1C1-style formulas are more efficient in VBA. You can enter the same formula in an entire range of data in a single statement.

CASE STUDY

Entering A1 Versus R1C1 in VBA

Think about how you would set this spreadsheet up in the Excel interface. First, you would enter a formula in Cells D4, F4, G4. Next, you would copy these cells, then paste them the rest of the way down the column. The code might look something like this:

```
Sub A1Style()
    ' Locate the FinalRow
    FinalRow = Range("B65536").End(xlUp).Row
    ' Enter the first formula
    Range("D4").Formula = "=B4*C4"
    Range("F4").Formula = "=IF(E4,ROUND(D4*$B$1,2),0)"
    Range("G4").Formula = "=F4+D4"
    ' Copy the formulas from Row 4 down to the other cells
    Range("D4").Copy Destination:=Range("D5:D" & FinalRow)
    Range("F4:G4").Copy Destination:=Range("F5:G" & FinalRow)
    ' Enter the Total Row
    Cells(FinalRow + 1, 1).Value = "Total"
    Cells(FinalRow + 1, 6).Formula = "=SUM(G4:G" & FinalRow & ")"
End Sub
```

In this code, it takes three lines to enter the formulas at the top of the row, then another two lines to copy the formulas down the column.

The equivalent code in R1C1 style allows the formulas to be entered for the entire column in a single statement. Remember, the advantage of R1C1 style formulas is that all the formulas in Columns D, F, and most of G are identical:

```
Sub R1C1Style()
    ' Locate the FinalRow
    FinalRow = Range("B65536").End(xlUp).Row
    ' Enter the first formula
    Range("D4:D" & FinalRow).FormulaR1C1 = "=RC[-1]*RC[-2]"
    Range("F4:F" & FinalRow).FormulaR1C1 = "=IF(RC[-1],ROUND(RC[-2]*R1C2,2),0)"
    Range("G4:G" & FinalRow).FormulaR1C1 = "=+RC[-1]+RC[-3]"
    ' Enter the Total Row
    Cells(FinalRow + 1, 1).Value = "Total"
    Cells(FinalRow + 1, 6).Formula = "=SUM(G4:G" & FinalRow & ")"
End Sub
```

6

Explanation of R1C1 Reference Style

A R1C1-style reference includes the letter *R* to refer to Row and the letter *C* to refer to Column. Because the most common reference in a formula is a relative reference, let's look at relative references in R1C1 style first.

Using R1C1 with Relative References

Imagine you are entering a formula in a cell. To point to a cell in a formula, you use the letters *R* and *C*. After each letter, enter the number of rows or columns in square brackets.

For columns, a positive number means to move to the right a certain number of columns, and a negative number means to move to the left a certain number of columns. From cell E5, use RC[1] to refer to F5 and RC[-1] to refer to D5.

For rows, a positive number means to move down the spreadsheet a certain number of rows. A negative number means to move toward the top of the spreadsheet a certain number of rows. From cell E5, use R[1]C to refer to E6 and use cell R[-1]C to refer to E4.

If you leave off the square brackets for either the *R* or the *C*, it means that you are pointing to a cell in the same row or column as the cell with the formula.

If you enter =R[-1]C[-1] in cell E5, you are referring to a cell one row up and one column to the left. This would be cell D4.

If you enter =RC[-1] in cell E5, you are referring to a cell in the same row, but one column to the left. This would be cell D5.

If you enter =RC[1] in cell E5, you are referring to a cell in the same row, but one column to the right. This would be cell F5.

If you enter =RC in cell E5, you are referring to a cell in the same row and column, which is cell E5 itself. You would generally never do this because it would create a circular reference.

Figure 6.7 shows how you would enter a reference in cell E5 to point to various cells around E5.

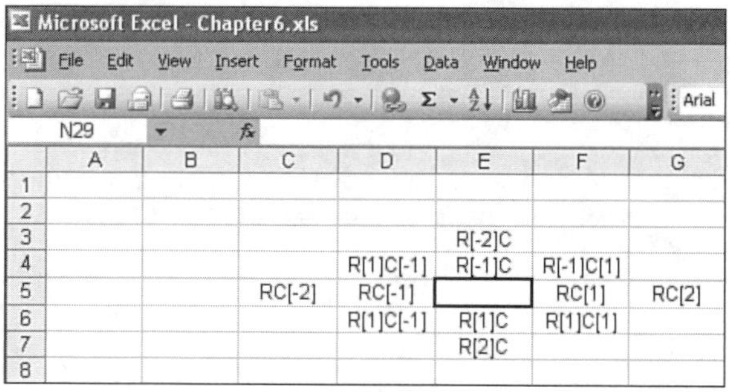

Figure 6.7
Here are various relative references. These would be entered in cell E5 to describe each cell around E5.

You can use R1C1 style to refer to a range of cells. If you wanted to add up the 12 cells to the left of the current cell, the formula would be

=SUM(RC[-12]:RC[-1])

Using R1C1 with Absolute References

An *absolute reference* is one where the row and column remain fixed when the formula is copied to a new location. In A1-style notation, Excel uses a $ before the row number or column letter to keep that row or column absolute as the formula is copied.

To always refer to an absolute row or column number, simply leave off the square brackets. This reference refers to cell $B$2 no matter where it is entered:

```
=R2C2
```

Using R1C1 with Mixed References

A *mixed reference* is one where the row is fixed and the column is allowed to be relative, or where the column is fixed and the row is allowed to be relative. There are many situations where this will be useful.

Imagine you've written a macro to import Invoice.txt into Excel. Using .End(xlUp), you find where the total row should go. As you are entering totals, you know that you want to sum from the row above the formula up to Row 2. The following code would handle that:

```
Sub MixedReference()
    TotalRow = Cells(65536, 1).End(xlUp).Row + 1
    Cells(TotalRow, 1).Value = "Total"
    Cells(TotalRow, 5).Resize(1, 3).FormulaR1C1 = "=SUM(R2C:R[-1]C)"
End Sub
```

In this code, the reference R2C:R[1]C indicates that the formula should add from Row 2 in the same column to the row just above the formula in the current column. Do you see the advantage to R1C1 formulas in this case? A single R1C1 formula with a mixed reference can be used to easily enter a formula to handle an indeterminate number of rows of data (see Figure 6.8).

Figure 6.8
After running the macro, the formulas in Columns E:G of the total row will have a reference to a range that is locked to Row 2, but all other aspects are relative.

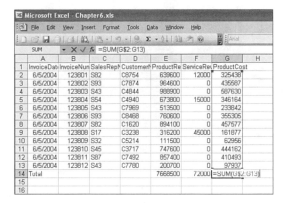

Referring to Entire Columns or Rows with R1C1 Style

You will occasionally write a formula that refers to an entire column. For example, you may want to know the maximum value in Column G. If you don't know how many rows you will have in G, you can write =MAX($G:$G) in A1 style or =MAX(C7) in R1C1 style. To find the minimum value in Row 1, use =MIN($1:$1) in A1 style or =MIN(R1) in R1C1 style. You can use relative reference for either rows or columns. To find the average of the row above the current cell, use =AVERAGE(R[-1]).

Replacing Many A1 Formulas with a Single R1C1 Formula

After you get used to R1C1-style formulas, they actually seem a lot more intuitive to build. One classic example to illustrate R1C1-style formulas is building a multiplication table. It is easy to build a multiplication table in Excel using a single mixed reference formula.

Building the Table

Enter the numbers 1 through 12 going across B1:M1. Copy and transpose these so the same numbers are going down A2:A13. Now the challenge is to build a single formula that will work in all cells of B2:M13 and that will show the multiplication of the number in Row 1 times the number in Column 1. Using A1-style formulas, you must press the F4 key five times to get the dollar signs in the proper locations. The following is a far simpler formula in R1C1 style:

```
Sub MultiplicationTable()
    ' Build a multiplication table using a single formula
    Range("B1:M1").Value = Array(1, 2, 3, 4, 5, 6, 7, 8, 9, 10, 11, 12)
    Range("B1:M1").Font.Bold = True
    Range("B1:M1").Copy
    Range("A2:A13").PasteSpecial Transpose:=True
    Range("B2:M13").FormulaR1C1 = "=RC1*R1C"
    Cells.EntireColumn.AutoFit
End Sub
```

The R1C1-style reference `=RC1*R1C` couldn't be simpler. In English, it is saying, "Take this row's Column 1 and multiply it by Row 1 of this column." It works perfectly to build the multiplication table shown in Figure 6.9.

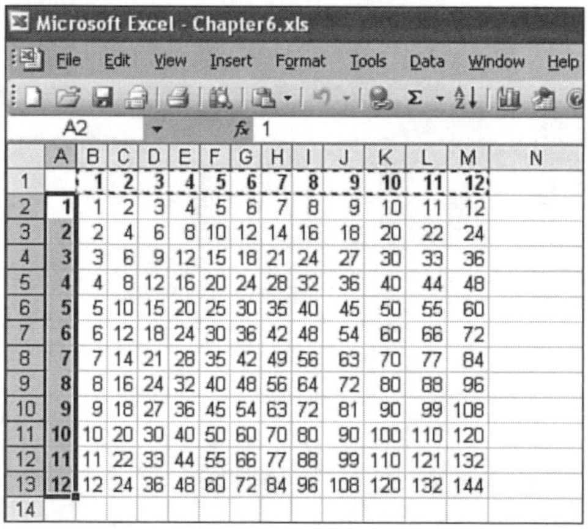

	A	B	C	D	E	F	G	H	I	J	K	L	M	N
1		1	2	3	4	5	6	7	8	9	10	11	12	
2	1	1	2	3	4	5	6	7	8	9	10	11	12	
3	2	2	4	6	8	10	12	14	16	18	20	22	24	
4	3	3	6	9	12	15	18	21	24	27	30	33	36	
5	4	4	8	12	16	20	24	28	32	36	40	44	48	
6	5	5	10	15	20	25	30	35	40	45	50	55	60	
7	6	6	12	18	24	30	36	42	48	54	60	66	72	
8	7	7	14	21	28	35	42	49	56	63	70	77	84	
9	8	8	16	24	32	40	48	56	64	72	80	88	96	
10	9	9	18	27	36	45	54	63	72	81	90	99	108	
11	10	10	20	30	40	50	60	70	80	90	100	110	120	
12	11	11	22	33	44	55	66	77	88	99	110	121	132	
13	12	12	24	36	48	60	72	84	96	108	120	132	144	
14														

Figure 6.9
The macro creates a multiplication table. The formula in B2 uses two mixed references: `=$A2*B$1`.

6

> **CAUTION**
>
> After running the macro and producing the multiplication table in Figure 6.9, note that Excel still has the copied range from line 2 of the macro as the active clipboard item. If the user of this macro would select a cell and press Enter, the contents of those cells would copy to the new location. This is generally not desirable. To get Excel out of Cut/Copy mode, add this line of code before your programs ends:
>
> ```
> Application.CutCopyMode = False
> ```

An Interesting Twist

Try this experiment. Move the cell pointer to F6. Turn on macro recording using Tools, Macros, Record New Macro. Click the Relative Recording button on the Record Macro toolbar. Enter the formula =A1 and press Ctrl+Enter to stay in F6. Click the Stop Recording button on the floating toolbar.

You get this single line macro, which enters a formula that points to a cell five rows up and five columns to the left:

```
Sub Macro1()
    ActiveCell.FormulaR1C1 = "=R[-5]C[-5]"
End Sub
```

Now, move the cell pointer to cell A1 and run the macro that you just recorded. You might think that pointing to a cell five rows above A1 would lead to the ubiquitous Run Time Error 1004. But it doesn't! When you run the macro, the formula in Cell A1 is pointing to =IR65532, meaning that R1C1 style formulas actually wrap from the left side of the workbook to the right side. I cannot think of any instance where this would be actually useful, but for those of you who rely on Excel to error out when you ask for something that doesn't make sense, be aware that your macro will happily provide a result, and probably not the one that you expected!

Remembering Column Numbers Associated with Column Letters

I like these formulas enough to use them regularly in VBA. I don't like them enough to change my Excel interface over to R1C1 style numbers. So I routinely have to know that the cell known as U21 is really R21C21.

Knowing that U is the 21st letter of the alphabet is not something that comes naturally. We have 26 letters, so A is 1 and Z is 26. M is the halfway point of the alphabet and is Column 13. The rest of the letters are pretty non-intuitive. I found that by playing this little game for a few minutes each day, I soon had memorized the column numbers:

```
Sub QuizColumnNumbers()
    Do
        i = Int(Rnd() * 26) + 1
        Ans = InputBox("What column number is the letter " & Chr(64 + i) & "?")
        If Ans = "" Then Exit Do
```

```
        If Not (Ans + 0) = i Then
            MsgBox "Letter " & Chr(64 + i) & " is column # " & i
        End If
    Loop
End Sub
```

If you don't think that memorizing column numbers sounds like fun, or even if you have to figure out the column number of Column DG someday, there is a fairly easy way that uses the Excel interface. Move the cell pointer to Cell A1. Hold down the Shift key and start pressing the right arrow key. For the first screen of columns, the column number appears in the name box to the left of the formula bar (see Figure 6.10).

Figure 6.10
While you select cells with the keyboard, the Name box displays how many columns are selected for the first screen full of columns.

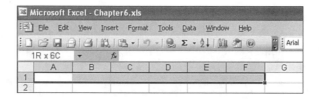

As you keep pressing the right arrow key beyond the first screen, a tool tip box to the right of the current cell tells you how many columns are selected. When you get to Column DG, it informs you that you are at Column 111 (see Figure 6.11).

Figure 6.11
After the first screen of columns, a tool tip bar keeps track of the column number.

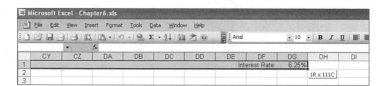

Conditional Formatting—R1C1 Required

When you set up conditional formatting, it is important to use R1C1-style formulas. This is not documented. The problem is very intermittent, but I find that one out of every fifty cells set up with conditional formatting will exhibit strange behavior if you use A1-style formulas.

Setting Up Conditional Formatting in the User Interface

There are two basic kinds of conditional formatting. If you select Conditional Formatting from the Format menu, the Conditional Formatting dialog defaults to the syntax, where you specify that the Cell Value Is. For example, you might set up a conditional format where the Cell Value is less than 0. The other syntax is far more powerful. The Formula Is syntax allows you to build any formula or function that evaluates to True or False. This formula may point to cells other than the current cell, or it may combine multiple conditions with the OR or AND function. You can combine up to three different conditions for each cell.

Here is a fairly advanced example. We want to hide any error cells and then color negative numbers in red. The basic idea is to set up a conditional format that checks to see whether the cell contains an error or NA. If either is true, then we set the font color up to match the background. This first condition relies on the Formula Is syntax. The second condition is straightforward and relies on the Cell Value Is syntax. Figure 6.12 shows how this would be set up in the Excel user interface.

Figure 6.12
This cell contains a pair of conditional formats. The first is designed to hide any error value and uses the powerful Formula Is syntax. The second condition uses the more common Cell Value Is syntax.

Setting Up Conditional Formats in VBA

In the previous example, you saw that the workbook made very liberal use of cell interior colors. We needed a way to turn the font to light blue when an error occurred in a light blue cell, and to turn the font to light yellow when an error occurred in a yellow cell. A quick macro in VBA was the perfect way to do this.

The FormatConditions object is used to set up conditional formats. Because each cell can have three FormatConditions, the following code first deletes all the existing conditional ~~format~~ on the sheet. The code then loops through all non-blank cells in the worksheet and ~~adds~~ conditional formats. In the first conditional format, the type is xlExpression, ~~a~~s we are using the Formula Is syntax. Note that the formula specified for ~~this~~ in R1C1-style notation. The second conditional format uses the xlCellValue ~~which~~ requires both specifying an operator and a value. After we've added the condi-~~tions, se~~t the ColorIndex for the font for conditions 1 and 2:

```
Sub SpecialFormattingAll()
For Each ws In ThisWorkbook.Worksheets
    ws.UsedRange.FormatConditions.Delete
    For Each cell In ws.UsedRange.Cells
        If Not IsEmpty(cell) Then
            cell.FormatConditions.Add Type:=xlExpression, _
                Formula1:="=or(ISERR(RC),isna(RC))"
            cell.FormatConditions(1).Font.Color = cell.Interior.Color
            cell.FormatConditions.Add Type:=xlCellValue, Operator:=xlLess, _
                Formula1:="0"
            cell.FormatConditions(2).Font.ColorIndex = 3
        End If
    Next cell
Next ws
End Sub
```

6

CAUTION

Do not use A1-style formulas for Formula1 in conditional formats. The code appears to work on one cell or a few cells. However, if you apply this to 50 or more cells, you will find some cells where the Formula starts pointing to a totally different cell. If you use R1C1-style formulas for Formula1, you do not have this problem. See the following case study for more specifics.

CASE STUDY

Identifying Row with Largest Value in G

One of the classic examples to illustrate conditional formatting is this example to highlight the row with the minimum and maximum value. Figure 6.13 shows how to set this up in the Excel interface.

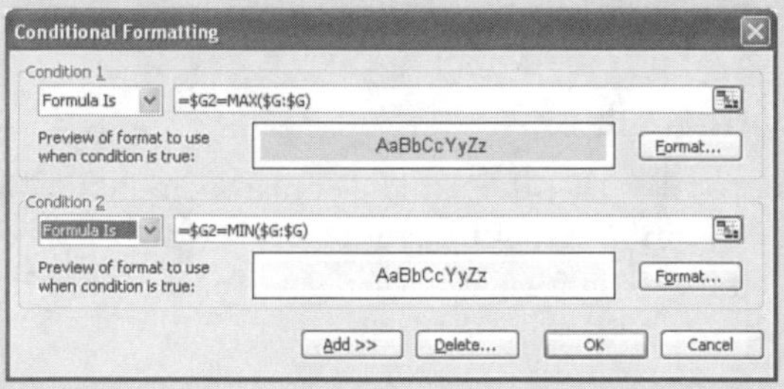

Figure 6.13
This classic conditional formatting example points out an interesting problem in VBA code.

Look at the code to create this conditional format. The formula to find the highest value in Column G, expressed in R1C1-style, is MAX(C7). This can be resolved two ways: either as an A1-style formula or as an R1C1-style formula. Remember—Microsoft started with the R1C1 style and offered the A1 style only to be compatible with Lotus 1-2-3. This is undocumented, but clearly Excel first tries to resolve the formula using R1C1-style formatting and the following code works perfectly.

```
Sub FindMinMax()
    ' Highlight row with highest revenue in Green
    ' Highlight row with lowest revenue in Yellow
    FinalRow = Cells(Application.Rows.Count, 1).End(xlUp).Row
    With Range("A2:I" & FinalRow)
        .FormatConditions.Delete
        .FormatConditions.Add Type:=xlExpression, Formula1:="=RC7=MAX(C7)"
        .FormatConditions(1).Interior.ColorIndex = 4
        .FormatConditions.Add Type:=xlExpression, Formula1:="=RC7=MIN(C7)"
        .FormatConditions(2).Interior.ColorIndex = 6
    End With
End Sub
```

Now, imagine what happens if you try to set up a conditional format pointing to cell C7 or R22. Any of these formats is likely to fail because Excel will interpret the C7 as a reference to Column 7.

With conditional formatting, Excel tries to accommodate either A1 or R1C1 formulas, but there are clearly situations where the formula can be interpreted as either style formula. In this case, Excel always assumes it is R1C1 style, so I recommend using R1C1 style for every conditional format that you set up.

Array Formulas Require Conditional Formatting

Array formulas are powerful "super-formulas." At MrExcel.com, I call these CSE formulas, because you have to use Ctrl+Shift+Enter to enter them. If you are not familiar with array formulas, they look like they would not work.

The array formula in E20 in Figure 6.14 shows a formula that does 18 multiplications and then sums the result. It looks like this would be an illegal formula, and if you happen to enter it without using Ctrl+Shift+Enter, you get the expected `#VALUE!` error. However, if you enter it with Ctrl+Shift+Enter, the formula miraculously multiplies row by row and then sums the result. (You do not type the curly braces when entering the formula.)

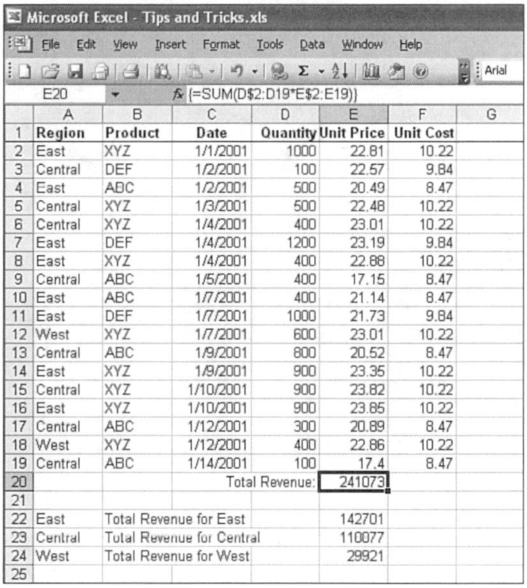

	A	B	C	D	E	F	G
1	Region	Product	Date	Quantity	Unit Price	Unit Cost	
2	East	XYZ	1/1/2001	1000	22.81	10.22	
3	Central	DEF	1/2/2001	100	22.57	9.84	
4	East	ABC	1/2/2001	500	20.49	8.47	
5	Central	XYZ	1/3/2001	500	22.48	10.22	
6	Central	XYZ	1/4/2001	400	23.01	10.22	
7	East	DEF	1/4/2001	1200	23.19	9.84	
8	East	XYZ	1/4/2001	400	22.88	10.22	
9	Central	ABC	1/5/2001	400	17.15	8.47	
10	East	ABC	1/7/2001	400	21.14	8.47	
11	East	DEF	1/7/2001	1000	21.73	9.84	
12	West	XYZ	1/7/2001	600	23.01	10.22	
13	Central	ABC	1/9/2001	800	20.52	8.47	
14	East	XYZ	1/9/2001	900	23.35	10.22	
15	Central	XYZ	1/10/2001	900	23.82	10.22	
16	East	XYZ	1/10/2001	900	23.85	10.22	
17	Central	ABC	1/12/2001	300	20.89	8.47	
18	West	XYZ	1/12/2001	400	22.86	10.22	
19	Central	ABC	1/14/2001	100	17.4	8.47	
20				Total Revenue:	241073		
21							
22	East	Total Revenue for East			142701		
23	Central	Total Revenue for Central			110077		
24	West	Total Revenue for West			29921		
25							

Figure 6.14
The array formula in E20 does 18 multiplications and then sums them. You must use Ctrl+Shift+Enter to enter this formula.

The array formulas in E22:E24 are also powerful array formulas. The formula for E22 is

```
=SUM(IF(A$2:A$19=$A22,D$2:D$19*E$2:E$19,0))
```

The code to enter these formulas follows. Although the formulas appear in the user interface in A1-style notation, you must use R1C1-style notation for entering array formulas:

```
Sub EnterArrayFormulas()
    ' Add a formula to multiply unit price x quantity
    FinalRow = Cells(65536, 1).End(xlUp).Row
    Cells(FinalRow + 1, 5).FormulaArray = "=SUM(R2C[-1]:R[-1]C[-1]*R2C:R[-1]C)"
End Sub
```

Next Steps

Now that you've seen how using R1C1-style formulas can save you lots of time and effort, you're ready to move on to Chapter 7, "Names," which discusses using named ranges to simplify your coding.

6

Names

You've named ranges in a worksheet by highlighting a range and typing a name in the Name box to the left of the formula field. Perhaps you've also created more complicated names containing formulas—such as for a dynamic table. The ability to set a name to a range makes it much easier to write formulas and set tables.

The ability to create and manipulate names is also available in VBA and provides the same benefits as Naming ranges in a worksheet: You can store, for example, a new range in a name.

This chapter explains different types of names and the various ways they can be used.

Global Versus Local Names

Names can be *global*—that is, available anywhere in the workbook—or *local*—available only on a specific worksheet. With local names, you can have multiple references in the workbook with the same name. Global names must be unique to the workbook. You can tell the difference between a local name and a global name because, in the reference, the name of the sheet is in front of the name, as in Sheet1!Fruits, whereas for a global name, you would reference only the name, Fruits.

When looking at the Define Name dialog box, you may see the mixture of global and local listings, as shown in Figure 7.1.

The sheet names of the local names are listed to the right of the names.

If the same name is assigned to both a local reference and a global reference, only the local name appears on the list when you activate the sheet (see Figure 7.2). When the focus is on another worksheet, you see only the global name (see Figure 7.3).

7

Figure 7.1
Identifying local and global names.

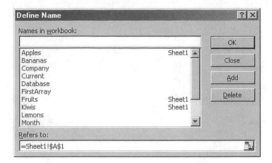

Figure 7.2
When a name is shared by a local and a global reference, the local reference's sheet displays only the local name.

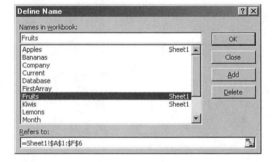

Figure 7.3
When a name is shared by a local reference and a global reference, the other sheets display only the global name.

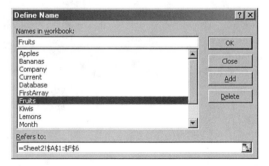

Adding Names

If you record the creation of a named range and then view the code, you see something similar to

```
ActiveWorkbook.Names.Add Name:="Fruits", RefersToR1C1:="=Sheet2!R1C1:R6C6"
```

This creates a global name "Fruits", which includes the range A1:F6 (R1C1:R6C6). The formula is enclosed in quotes and the equal sign in the formula must be included. Also, the range reference must be absolute (include the $ sign) or in R1C1 notation. If the sheet on which the name is created is the active sheet, the sheet reference does not have to be included; however, it can make the code easier to understand.

To create a local name, include the sheet name:

```
ActiveWorkbook.Names.Add Name:="Sheet2!Fruits", _
    RefersToR1C1:="=Sheet2!R1C1:R6C6"
```

Or specify that the `Names` collection belongs to a worksheet:

```
Worksheets("Sheet1").Names.Add Name:="Fruits", _
    RefersToR1C1:="=Sheet1!R1C1:R6C6"
```

The preceding example is what you would learn from the macro recorder. There is a simpler way:

```
Range("A1:F6").Name = "Fruits"
```

Or, for a local variable only:

```
Range("A1:F6").Name = "Sheet1!Fruits"
```

Although this is much easier and quicker than what the macro recorder creates, it is limited in that it works *only for ranges*. Formulas, strings, numbers, and arrays require the use of the `Add` method.

The `Name` Property of the `Name ObjectName` is an object but still has a `Name` property. The following line renames an existing name:

```
Names("Fruits").Name = "Produce"
```

"Fruits" no longer exists; "Produce" is now the name of the range.

When renaming names in which a local and global reference both carry the same name, the previous line renames the local reference first.

If `Range("A1:F6").Name = "Fruits"` exists early in the code and then `Range ("A1:F6").Name = "Produce"` is added later on, `"Produce"` overwrites `"Fruits"`, as shown in Figure 7.4. An attempt to access the local name `"Fruits"` later in the program creates an error because it no longer exists.

Figure 7.4
It's easy to overwrite an existing name if you aren't careful. The local name Fruits has been overwritten by the local name Produce. The name Fruits you see is the global variable, not the local one.

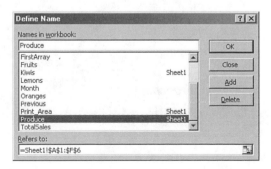

Deleting Names

Use the `Delete` method to delete a name:

```
Names("ProduceNum").Delete
```

An error occurs if you attempt to delete a name that doesn't exist.

CAUTION

If both local and global references with the same name exist, be more specific as to which name is being deleted.

Types of Names

The most common use of names is for storing ranges. But names can store more than that; after all, that's what they're for: Names store *information*. They make it simple to remember and use potentially complex or large amounts of information. And, unlike variables, Names remember what they store beyond the life of the program.

We've already covered creating range names, but we can also assign names to name formulas, strings, numbers, and arrays.

Formulas

The syntax for storing a formula in a name is the same as for a range because the range is, in essence, a formula:

```
Names.Add Name:="ProductList", _
    RefersTo:="=OFFSET(Sheet2!A2,0,0,COUNTA(Sheet2!$A:$A))"
```

The preceding line of code allows for a dynamic named column, which is very useful in creating dynamic tables or referencing any dynamic listing on which calculations may be performed, as shown in Figure 7.5.

Figure 7.5
Dynamic formulas can be assigned to names.

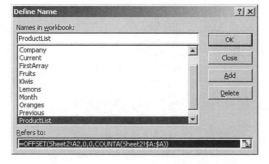

Strings

When using names to hold strings, such as the name of the current fruit producer, enclose the string value in quotes. Because there is no formula involved, an equal sign is not needed:

```
Names.Add Name: = "Company", RefersTo:="CompanyA"
```

Figure 7.6 shows how the coded name would appear in the Define Name window.

Figure 7.6
A string value can be assigned to a name.

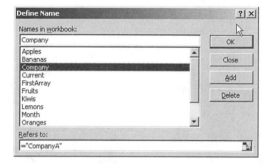

> **TIP**
> Because names do not lose their references between sessions, this is a great way of storing values as opposed to storing values in cells from which the information would have to be retrieved. For example, to track the leading producer between seasons, create a name "Leader." If the new season's leading producer matches the name reference, a special report comparing the seasons could be created. The other option is to create a special sheet to track the values between sessions and then retrieve the values when needed. With names, the values are readily available.

The following procedure shows how cells in a Variable sheet are used to retain information between sessions.

```
Sub NoNames(ByRef CurrentTop As String)
TopSeller = Worksheets("Variables").Range("A1").Value
If CurrentTop = TopSeller Then
    MsgBox ("Top Producer is " & TopSeller & " again.")
Else
    MsgBox ("New Top Producer is " & CurrentTop)
End If
End Sub
```

The following procedure shows how names are used to store information between sessions:

```
Sub WithNames()
If Evaluate("Current") = Evaluate("Previous") Then
    MsgBox ("Top Producer is " & Evaluate("Previous") & " again.")
Else
    MsgBox ("New Top Producer is " & Evaluate("Current"))
End If
End Sub
```

7

If "Current" and "Previous" are previously declared names, you access them directly rather than create variables to pass them in. Note the use of the `Evaluate` method to extract the values in `Names`.

> **CAUTION**
>
> The string being stored cannot have more than 255 characters.

Numbers

Names can also be used to store numbers between sessions. Use

```
NumofSales = 5123
Names.Add Name:="TotalSales", RefersTo:=NumofSales
```

Or

```
Names.Add Name:="TotalSales", RefersTo:=5123
```

Notice the lack of quotes or an equal sign. Using quotes changes the number to a string; and with the addition of an equal sign, the number changes to a formula.

To retrieve the value in the name, there are two options:

```
NumofSales = Names("TotalSales").Value
```

Or the shorter version:

```
NumofSales = [TotalSales]
```

Keep in mind that someone reading your code may not be familiar with the use of the `Evaluate` method (square brackets). If you know that someone else will be reading your code, avoid the use of the `Evaluate` method or add a comment explaining it.

Using Arrays in Names

A name can also store the data stored in an array. The array size is limited to 256 columns and 5,461 total elements. See Chapter 16, "Automating Word," for more information on arrays.

An array reference is stored in a name the same way as a numeric reference.

```
Sub NamedArray()
Dim myArray(10, 5)
Dim i As Integer, j As Integer
'The following For loops fill the array myArray
For i = 1 To 10
    For j = 1 To 5
        myArray(i, j) = i + j
    Next j
Next i
'The following line takes our array and gives it a name
Names.Add Name:="FirstArray", RefersTo:=myArray
End Sub
```

Because the name is referencing a variable, no quotes or equal signs are required.

Reserved Names

Excel uses local names of its own to keep track of information. These local names are considered reserved and, if you use them for your own references, may cause problems.

Highlight an area on a sheet and select, from the Excel menu, File, Print Area, Set Print Area.

As shown in Figure 7.7, a `Print_Area` listing is in the range name field. Deselect the area and look again in the range name field. The name is still there; select it and the print area previously set is now highlighted. If you save, close, and re-open the workbook, `Print_Area` is still set to the same range. `Print_Area` is a name reserved by Excel for its own use.

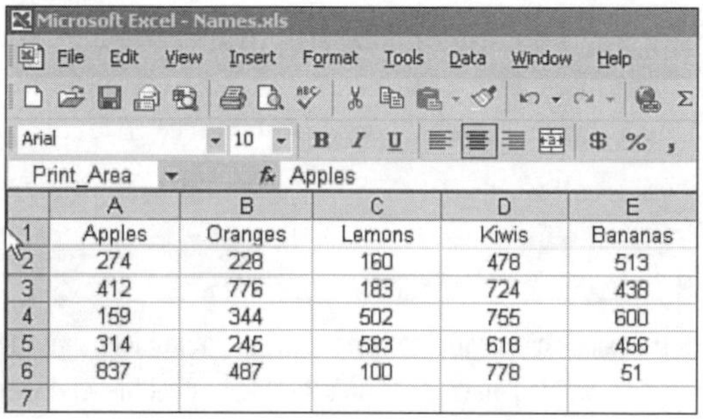

Figure 7.7
Excel creates its own names.

> **CAUTION**
>
> Each sheet has its own print area. Also, setting a new print area on a sheet with an existing print area overwrites the original print area name.

Luckily, Excel does not have a large list of reserved names:

- `Criteria`
- `Database`
- `Extract`
- `Print_Area`
- `Print_Titles`

`Criteria` and `Extract` are used when the Advanced Filter (Data, Filter, Advanced Filter) is configured to extract the results of the filter to a new location.

`Database` is no longer required in Excel, but there are some features, such as Data, Form, that do recognize it. Older versions of Excel used it to identify the data you wanted to manipulate in certain functions.

7

Print_Area is used when a print area is set (File, Print Area, Set Print Area) or when Page Setup options that designate the print area (File, Page Setup, Scaling) are changed.

Print_Titles is used when print titles are set (File, Page Setup, Sheet, Print Titles).

These names should be avoided and variations used with caution. For example, if you create a name "PrintTitles," you may accidentally code

```
Worksheets("Sheet4").Names("Print_Titles").Delete
```

You've deleted the Excel name instead of your custom name.

Hiding Names

Names are incredibly useful, but you don't necessarily want to see all the names created. Like many other objects, Names has a Visible property. To hide a name, set the Visible property to False; to unhide a name, set the Visible property to True:

```
Names.Add Name:="ProduceNum", RefersTo:="=$A$1", Visible:=False
```

> **CAUTION**
>
> If a user creates a Name object with the same name as your hidden one, the hidden name is overwritten without any warning message. To prevent this, protect the worksheet.

Checking for the Existence of a Name

The following function can be used to check for the existence of a user-defined name, even a hidden one, but does not return the existence of Excel's reserved names. It's a handy addition to your arsenal of "programmer's useful code":

```
Function NameExists(FindName As String) As Boolean
Dim Rng As Range
Dim myName As String
On Error Resume Next
myName = ActiveWorkbook.Names(FindName).Name
If Err.Number = 0 Then NameExists = True
End Function
```

The preceding code is also an example of how to use errors to your advantage. If the name for which you are searching doesn't exist, an error message is generated. By adding the On Error Resume Next line at the beginning, you force the code to continue. Then you use the Err.Number to tell you whether you ran into an error. If you didn't, then Err.Number is zero, which means the name exists; else, you had an error and the name does not exist.

Using Named Ranges for VLookups

Every day, you import a file of sales data from a chain of retail stores. The file includes store number but not the store name. You obviously don't want to have to type store names every day, but you would like to have store names appear on all the reports that you run.

Normally, you enter a table of store numbers and names in an out-of-the-way spot on a back worksheet. You can use VBA to help maintain the list of stores each day and then use the VLOOKUP function to get store names from the list into our dataset.

The basic steps are as follows:

1. Import the data file.
2. Find all the unique store numbers in today's file.
3. See whether any of these store numbers are not in your current table of store names.
4. For any stores that are new, add them to the table and ask the user for a store name.
5. The Store Names table is now larger, so re-assign the named range used to describe the store table.
6. Use a VLOOKUP in the original dataset to add a store name to all records. This VLOOKUP references the named range of the newly expanded Store Names table.

The following code handles these six steps:

```
Sub ImportData()
    ' This routine imports sales.csv to the data sheet
    ' Check to see whether any stores in column A are new
    ' If any are new, then add them to the StoreList table
    Dim WSD As Worksheet
    Dim WSM As Worksheet
    Dim WB As Workbook
    Set WB = ThisWorkbook
    ' Data is stored on the Data worksheet
    Set WSD = ThisWorkbook.Worksheets("Data")
    ' StoreList is stored on a menu worksheet
    Set WSM = ThisWorkbook.Worksheets("Menu")

    ' Open the file. This makes the csv file active
    Workbooks.Open Filename:="C:\Sales.csv"

    ' Copy the data to WSD and close
    Range("A1").CurrentRegion.Copy Destination:=WSD.Range("A1")
    ActiveWorkbook.Close SaveChanges:=False

    ' Activate the data sheet. Find a list of unique stores from column A
    WSD.Activate
    FinalRow = Cells(65536, 1).End(xlUp).Row
    Range("A1").Resize(FinalRow, 1).AdvancedFilter Action:=xlFilterCopy, _
    CopyToRange:=Range("Z1"), Unique:=True
```

7

```
    ' For all the unique stores, see whether they are in the
    ' current store list.
    FinalStore = Range("Z65536").End(xlUp).Row
    Range("AA1").Value = "There?"
    Range("AA2:AA" & FinalStore).FormulaR1C1 = _
    "=ISNA(VLOOKUP(RC[-1],StoreList,1,False))"

    ' Find the next row for a new store. Because StoreList starts in A1
    ' of the Menu sheet, find the next available row
    NextRow = WSM.Range("A65536").End(xlUp).Row + 1

    ' Loop through the list of today's stores. If they are shown
    ' as missing, then add them at the bottom of the StoreList
    For i = 2 To FinalStore
        If Cells(i, 27).Value = True Then
            ThisStore = Cells(i, 26).Value
            WSM.Cells(NextRow, 1).Value = ThisStore
            WSM.Cells(NextRow, 2).Value = _
            InputBox(Prompt:="What is.name of store " _
            & ThisStore, Title:="New Store Found")
            NextRow = NextRow + 1
        End If
    Next i

    ' Delete the temporary list of stores in Z & AA
    Range("Z1:AA" & FinalStore).Clear

    ' In case any stores were added, re-define StoreList name
    FinalStore = WSM.Range("A65536").End(xlUp).Row
    WSM.Range("A1:B" & FinalStore).Name = "StoreList"

    ' Use VLOOKUP to add StoreName to column B of the dataset
    WSD.Range("B1").EntireColumn.Insert
    Range("B1").Value = "StoreName"
    Range("B2:B" & FinalRow).FormulaR1C1 = "=VLOOKUP(RC1,StoreList,2,False)"
    ' Change Formulas to Values
    Range("B2:B" & FinalRow).Value = Range("B2:B" & FinalRow).Value

End Sub
```

Next Steps

In the next chapter, we'll learn how code can be written to run automatically based on users' actions, such as activating a sheet or selecting a cell. This is done with *events*, which are actions in Excel that can be captured and used to our advantage.

Event Programming

Levels of Events

Earlier in the book you saw mention of workbook events and have seen examples of worksheet events. Events are Excel's way of letting you execute code based on certain actions that take place in a workbook.

These events can be found at the following levels:

- Application level—Control based on application actions, such as `Application_NewWorkbook`
- Workbook level—Control based on workbook actions, such as `Workbook_Open`
- Worksheet level—Control based on worksheet actions, such as `Worksheet_SelectionChange`
- Chart sheet level—Control based on chart actions, such as `Chart_Activate`

Workbook events go into the `ThisWorkbook` module; worksheet events go into the module of the sheet they affect (such as Sheet1); chart sheet events go into the module of the chart sheet they affect (such as Chart1); embedded charts and application events go into class modules. The events can still make procedure or function calls outside their own modules. So if you want the same action to take place for two different sheets, you don't have to copy the code twice—instead, place the code in a module and have each sheet event call the procedure.

In this chapter, you'll learn about the different levels of events, where to find them, and how to use them.

Using Events

Each level consists of several types of events, and memorizing the syntax of them all would be a feat. Excel makes it easy to view and insert the available events in their proper modules right from the VBE.

When a `ThisWorkbook`, `Sheet`, `Chart Sheet`, or `Class` module is active, the corresponding events are available through the Object and Procedure drop-downs, as shown in Figure 8.1.

Figure 8.1
The different events are easy to access from the VBE Object and Procedure drop-downs.

After the object is selected, the Procedure drop-down updates to list the events available for that object. Selecting a procedure automatically places the procedure header (Private Sub) and footer (End Sub) in the editor, as shown in Figure 8.2.

Figure 8.2
The procedure header and footer are automatically placed.

Event Parameters

Some events have parameters, such as `Target` or `Cancel`. These parameters allow values to be passed into the procedure. For example, some procedures are triggered before the actual event—such as `BeforeRightClick`. Assigning `True` to the `Cancel` parameter prevents the default action from taking place; in this case, the shortcut menu is prevented from appearing:

```
Private Sub Worksheet_BeforeRightClick(ByVal Target As Range, Cancel As Boolean)
Cancel = True
End Sub
```

Enabling Events

Some events can trigger other events, including themselves. For example, the `Worksheet_Change` event is triggered by a change in a cell. If the event is triggered and the procedure itself changes a cell, then the event gets triggered again, which changes a cell, triggering the event, and so on. The procedure gets stuck in an endless loop.

To prevent this, disable the events and then re-enable them at the end of the procedure:

```
Private Sub Worksheet_Change(ByVal Target As Range)
Application.EnableEvents = False
Range("A1").Value = Target.Value
Application.EnableEvents = True
End Sub
```

NOTE To interrupt a macro, press Esc or Ctrl+Break.

Workbook Events

The following event procedures are available at the workbook level:

- Activate
- Deactivate
- Open
- BeforeSave
- BeforePrint
- BeforeClose
- NewSheet
- SheetActivate
- SheetDeactivate
- SheetCalculate

- SheetBeforeDoubleClick
- SheetSelectionChange
- SheetBeforeRightClick
- SheetChange
- WindowResize
- WindowActivate
- WindowDeactivate
- AddInInstall
- AddInUninstall

Workbook_Activate()

Workbook_Activate occurs when the workbook containing this event becomes the active workbook.

Workbook_Deactivate()

Workbook_Deactivate occurs when the active workbook is switched from the workbook containing the event to another workbook.

Workbook_Open()

Workbook_Open is the default workbook event. This procedure is activated when a workbook is opened—no user interface is required. It has a variety of uses, such as checking the username and then customizing the user's privileges in the workbook.

The following code checks the UserName and if it is not Admin, protects each sheet from user changes (UserInterfaceOnly allows macros to make changes, but not the user):

```
Private Sub Workbook_Open()
Dim sht As Worksheet
If Application.UserName <> "Admin" Then
    For Each sht In Worksheets
        sht.Protect UserInterfaceOnly:=True
    Next sht
End If
End Sub
```

Workbook_Open can also be used to create custom menus or toolbars. The following code adds the menu MrExcel Programs with two options underneath it (see Figure 8.3).

➔ For more information on custom menus, **see** "Creating a Custom Menu," **p. 487**, in Chapter 24.

```
Sub Workbook_Open()
Dim cbWSMenuBar As CommandBar
Dim Ctrl As CommandBarControl, muCustom As CommandBarControl
Dim iHelpIndex As Integer
Set cbWSMenuBar = Application.CommandBars("Worksheet menu bar")
iHelpIndex = cbWSMenuBar.Controls("Help").Index
Set muCustom = cbWSMenuBar.Controls.Add(Type:=msoControlPopup, _
    Before:=iHelpIndex, Temporary:=True)
For Each Ctrl In cbWSMenuBar.Controls
    If Ctrl.Caption = "&MrExcel Programs" Then
        cbWSMenuBar.Controls("MrExcel Programs").Delete
    End If
Next Ctrl
With muCustom
    .Caption = "&MrExcel Programs"
    With .Controls.Add(Type:=msoControlButton)
        .Caption = "&Import and Format"
        .OnAction = "ImportFormat"
    End With
    With .Controls.Add(Type:=msoControlButton)
        .Caption = "&Calculate Year End"
        .OnAction = "CalcYearEnd"
    End With
End With
End Sub
```

Figure 8.3
The Open event can be used to create custom menus.

Workbook_BeforeSave(ByVal SaveAsUI As Boolean, Cancel As Boolean)

Workbook_BeforeSave occurs when the workbook is saved. SaveAsUI is set to True if the Save As dialog box is to be displayed; Cancel set to True prevents the workbook from being saved.

Workbook_BeforePrint(Cancel As Boolean)

Workbook_BeforePrint occurs when any print command is used—menu, toolbar, keyboard, or macro. Cancel set to True prevents the workbook from being printed.

The following code tracks each time a sheet is printed. It logs the date, time, username, and the sheet printed in a hidden print log (see Figure 8.4):

```
Private Sub Workbook_BeforePrint(Cancel As Boolean)
Dim LastRow As Long
Dim PrintLog As Worksheet
Set PrintLog = Worksheets("PrintLog")
LastRow = PrintLog.Range("A65536").End(xlUp).Row + 1
```

```
With PrintLog
    .Cells(LastRow, 1).Value = Now()
    .Cells(LastRow, 2).Value = Application.UserName
    .Cells(LastRow, 3).Value = ActiveSheet.Name
End With
End Sub
```

Figure 8.4
The BeforePrint event can be used to keep a hidden print log in a workbook.

	A	B	C	D
1	Date and Time	UserName	Sheet Name	
2	11/25/2003 19:37	Tracy	Sheet1	
3	11/29/2003 19:40	Bill	Sheet2	
4				

The BeforePrint event can also be used to add information to a header or footer before the sheet is printed. Though you can now enter the file path into a header or footer through the Page Setup, before XP, the only way to add the file path was with code. This piece of code was commonly used:

```
Private Sub Workbook_BeforePrint(Cancel As Boolean)
    ActiveSheet.PageSetup.RightFooter = ActiveWorkbook.FullName
End Sub
```

Workbook_BeforeClose(Cancel As Boolean)

Workbook_BeforeClose occurs when a workbook is closed. Cancel set to True prevents the workbook from closing.

If the Open event is used to create a custom menu, then the BeforeClose event is used to delete it:

```
Private Sub Workbook_BeforeClose(Cancel As Boolean)
Dim cbWSMenuBar As CommandBar
On Error Resume Next
Set cbWSMenuBar = Application.CommandBars("Worksheet menu bar")
cbWSMenuBar.Controls("MrExcel Programs").Delete
End Sub
```

This is a nice little procedure, but there is one problem: If changes are made to the workbook and it isn't saved, Excel pops up the Do You Want to Save? dialog box. This dialog box pops up *after* the BeforeClose event has run. So, if the user decides to Cancel, the menu is now gone.

The solution is to create your own Save dialog in the event:

```
Private Sub Workbook_BeforeClose(Cancel As Boolean)
Dim Msg As String
Dim Response
Dim cbWSMenuBar As CommandBar
If Not ThisWorkbook.Saved Then
    Msg = "Do you want to save the changes you made to " & Me.Name & "?"
    Response = MsgBox(Msg, vbQuestion + vbYesNoCancel)
    Select Case Response
        Case vbYes
            ThisWorkbook.Save
```

```
              Case vbNo
                  ThisWorkbook.Saved = True
              Case vbCancel
                  Cancel = True
                  Exit Sub
          End Select
      End If
      On Error Resume Next
      Set cbWSMenuBar = Application.CommandBars("Worksheet menu bar")
      cbWSMenuBar.Controls("MrExcel Programs").Delete
      End Sub
```

Workbook_NewSheet(ByVal Sh As Object)

Workbook_NewSheet occurs when a new sheet is added to the active workbook. Sh is the new worksheet or chart sheet object.

Workbook_WindowResize(ByVal Wn As Window)

Workbook_WindowResize occurs when the active workbook is resized. Wn is the window.

> **NOTE**
> Only resizing the active workbook window starts this event. Resizing the application window is an application-level event and is not affected by the workbook-level event.

This code disables the resizing of the active workbook:

```
Private Sub Workbook_WindowResize(ByVal Wn As Window)
Wn.EnableResize = False
End Sub
```

> **CAUTION**
> If you disable the capability to resize, the minimize and maximize buttons are removed and the workbook cannot be resized. To undo this, type **ActiveWindow.EnableResize = True** in the Immediate window.

Workbook_WindowActivate(ByVal Wn As Window)

Workbook_WindowActivate occurs when *any* workbook window is activated. Wn is the window.

> **NOTE**
> Only activating the workbook window starts this event.

Workbook_WindowDeactivate(ByVal Wn As Window)

Workbook_WindowDeactivate occurs when *any* workbook window is deactivated. Wn is the window.

> **NOTE** Only deactivating the workbook window starts this event.

Workbook_AddInInstall()

`Workbook_AddInInstall` occurs when the workbook is installed as an add-in (by selecting Tools, Add-Ins). Double-clicking on an `.xla` file (an add-in) to open it does not activate the event.

Workbook_AddInUninstall

`Workbook_AddInUninstall` occurs when the workbook (add-in) is uninstalled. The add-in is not automatically closed.

Workbook_SheetActivate(ByVal Sh As Object)

`Workbook_SheetActivate` occurs when any chart sheet or worksheet in the workbook is activated. `Sh` is the active sheet.

To affect a specific worksheet, refer to `Worksheet_Activate`; for chart sheets, refer to `Chart_Activate`.

Workbook_SheetBeforeDoubleClick (ByVal Sh As Object, ByVal Target As Range, Cancel As Boolean)

`Workbook_SheetBeforeDoubleClick` occurs when the user double-clicks on any chart sheet or worksheet in the active workbook. `Sh` is the active sheet; `Target` is the object double-clicked; `Cancel` set to `True` prevents the default action from taking place.

To affect a specific worksheet, refer to `Worksheet_BeforeDoubleClick`; for chart sheets, refer to `Chart_BeforeDoubleClick`.

Workbook_SheetBeforeRightClick(ByVal Sh As Object, ByVal Target As Range, Cancel As Boolean)

`Workbook_SheetBeforeRightClick` occurs when the user right-clicks on any worksheet in the active workbook. `Sh` is the active worksheet; `Target` is the object right-clicked on; `Cancel` set to `True` prevents the default action from taking place.

To affect a specific worksheet, refer to `Worksheet_BeforeRightClick`; for chart sheets, refer to `Chart_BeforeRightClick`.

Workbook_SheetCalculate (ByVal Sh As Object)

`Workbook_SheetCalculate` occurs when any worksheet is recalculated or any updated data is plotted on a chart. `Sh` is the active sheet.

To affect a specific worksheet, refer to `Worksheet_Calculate`; for chart sheets, refer to `Chart_Calculate`.

Workbook_SheetChange (ByVal Sh As Object, ByVal Target As Range)

`Workbook_SheetChange` occurs when any range in a worksheet is changed. `Sh` is the worksheet; `Target` is the changed range.

To affect a specific worksheet, refer to `Worksheet_Change`.

Workbook_SheetDeactivate (ByVal Sh As Object)

`Workbook_SheetDeactivate` occurs when any chart sheet or worksheet in the workbook is deactivated. `Sh` is the sheet being switched from.

To affect a specific worksheet, refer to `Worksheet_Deactivate`; for chart sheets, refer to `Chart_Deactivate`.

Workbook_SheetFollowHyperlink (ByVal Sh As Object, ByVal Target As Hyperlink)

`Workbook_SheetFollowHyperlink` occurs when any hyperlink is clicked in Excel. `Sh` is the active worksheet; `Target` is the hyperlink.

To affect a specific worksheet, refer to `Worksheet_FollowHyperlink`.

Workbook_SheetSelectionChange (ByVal Sh As Object, ByVal Target As Range)

`Workbook_SheetSelectionChange` occurs when a new range is selected on any sheet. `Sh` is the active sheet; `Target` is the affected range.

To affect a specific worksheet, refer to `Worksheet_SelectionChange`.

Worksheet Events

The following event procedures are available at the worksheet level:

- `Activate`
- `BeforeDoubleClick`
- `BeforeRightClick`
- `Calculate`
- `Change`
- `Deactivate`
- `FollowHyperlink`
- `SelectionChange`

Worksheet_Activate()

Worksheet_Activate occurs when the sheet on which the event is becomes the active sheet. A good use for activate and deactivate events is a custom floating toolbar on a sheet:

```
Private Sub Worksheet_Activate()
    Application.CommandBars("TYS Editing Tools").Visible = True
End Sub
```

Worksheet_Deactivate()

Worksheet_Deactivate occurs when another sheet becomes the active sheet:

```
Private Sub Worksheet_Deactivate()
On Error Resume Next
    Application.CommandBars("TYS Editing Tools").Visible = False
End Sub
```

> **NOTE** If a Deactivate event is on the active sheet and you switch to a sheet with an Activate event, the Deactivate event runs first, followed by the Activate event.

Worksheet_BeforeDoubleClick(ByVal Target As Range, Cancel As Boolean)

Worksheet_BeforeDoubleClick allows control over what happens when the user double-clicks on the sheet. Target is the selected range on the sheet; Cancel is set to False by default, but if set to True, it prevents the default action (such as entering a cell) from happening.

The following code prevents the user from entering a cell with a double-click. And if the formula field is also hidden, the user cannot enter information in the traditional way:

```
Private Sub Worksheet_BeforeDoubleClick(ByVal Target As Range, _
    Cancel As Boolean)
Cancel = True
End Sub
```

> **NOTE** The previous code does not prevent the user from sizing a row or column with a double-click.

Preventing the double-click from entering a cell allows it to be used for something else, such as highlighting a cell. The following code changes a cell's interior color to red when it is double-clicked:

```
Private Sub Worksheet_BeforeDoubleClick(ByVal Target As Range, _
    Cancel As Boolean)
Dim myColor As Integer
Target.Interior.ColorIndex = 3
End Sub
```

Worksheet_BeforeRightClick(ByVal Target As Range, Cancel As Boolean)

Worksheet_BeforeRightClick is triggered when the user right-clicks on a range. Target is the object right-clicked on; Cancel set to True prevents the default action from taking place.

Worksheet_Calculate()

Worksheet_Calculate occurs after a sheet is recalculated.

The following sample compares a month's profits between the previous and the current year. If profit has fallen, a red down arrow appears below the month; if profit has risen, a green up arrow appears (see Figure 8.5):

```
Private Sub Worksheet_Calculate()
Select Case Range("C3").Value
    Case Is > Range("C4").Value
        SetArrow 10, msoShapeDownArrow
    Case Is < Range("C4").Value
        SetArrow 3, msoShapeUpArrow
End Select
End Sub

Private Sub SetArrow(ByVal ArrowColor As Integer, ByVal ArrowDegree)
ActiveSheet.Shapes.AddShape(ArrowDegree, 17.25, 43.5, 5, 10).Select
With Selection.ShapeRange
    With .Fill
    .Visible = msoTrue
    .Solid
    .ForeColor.SchemeColor = ArrowColor
    .Transparency = 0#
    End With
    With .Line
    .Weight = 0.75
    .DashStyle = msoLineSolid
    .Style = msoLineSingle
    .Transparency = 0#
    .Visible = msoTrue
    .ForeColor.SchemeColor = 64
    .BackColor.RGB = RGB(255, 255, 255)
    End With
End With
End Sub
```

Worksheet_Change(ByVal Target As Range)

Worksheet_Change is triggered by a change to a cell's value, such as when text is entered, edited, or deleted. Target is the cell that has been changed.

> NOTE
> The event can also be triggered by pasting values. Recalculation does not trigger the event; use the Calculation event instead.

Figure 8.5
Use the `Calculate` event to add graphics emphasizing the change in profits.

8

	A	B	C	D
1	2002 vs 2003 Profit			
2				
3	October	Current	5308	
4	↓	Previous	2090	
5				
6				
7		2002	2003	
8	January	3018	7258	
9	February	9704	3459	
10	March	3950	3874	
11	April	7518	3907	
12	May	4542	9774	
13	June	1383	3307	
14	July	2888	4741	
15	August	8493	8232	
16	September	642	9775	
17	October	5308	2090	
18	November	6040	7490	
19	December	6845	6845	
20				

CASE STUDY

You're entering arrival and departure times and want the times to be formatted with a 24-hour clock (Military Time). You've tried formatting the cell, but no matter how you enter the times, they are displayed in the 0:00 hours and minutes format.

The only way to get the time to appear correctly, such as with 23:45, is to have it entered in the cell as such. But typing the colon is time-consuming—it would be much more efficient to simply enter the numbers and let Excel format it for you.

The solution? Use a `Change` event to take what is in the cell and insert the colon for you:

```
Private Sub Worksheet_Change(ByVal Target As Range)
Dim ThisColumn As Integer
Dim UserInput As String, NewInput As String
ThisColumn = Target.Column
If ThisColumn < 3 Then
    UserInput = Target.Value
    If UserInput > 1 Then
        NewInput = Left(UserInput, Len(UserInput) - 2) & ":" & _
        Right(UserInput, 2)
        Application.EnableEvents = False
        Target = NewInput
        Application.EnableEvents = True
    End If
End If
End Sub
```

An entry of 2345 will display as 23:45. Note that the format change is limited to Columns A and B (`If ThisColumn < 3`)—without this, entering numbers anywhere on a sheet, such as in a totals column, would force it to be reformatted.

CAUTION

Use `Application.EnableEvents = False` to prevent the procedure from calling itself when the value in the target is updated.

Worksheet_SelectionChange(ByVal Target As Range)

`Worksheet_SelectionChange` occurs when a new range is selected. Target is the newly selected range.

The following example helps identify the selected cell by highlighting the row and column:

> ___ CAUTION _____
>
> This example makes use of conditional formatting and overwrites any existing conditional format-
> ting on the sheet. Also the code may clear the clipboard, making it difficult to copy and paste on the
> sheet.

```
Private Sub Worksheet_SelectionChange(ByVal Target As Range)
Dim iColor As Integer
On Error Resume Next
iColor = Target.Interior.ColorIndex
If iColor < 0 Then
    iColor = 36
Else
    iColor = iColor + 1
End If
If iColor = Target.Font.ColorIndex Then iColor = iColor + 1
Cells.FormatConditions.Delete
With Range("A" & Target.Row, Target.Address)
    .FormatConditions.Add Type:=2, Formula1:="TRUE"
    .FormatConditions(1).Interior.ColorIndex = iColor
End With
With Range(Target.Offset(1 - Target.Row, 0).Address & ":" & _
    Target.Offset(-1, 0).Address)
    .FormatConditions.Add Type:=2, Formula1:="TRUE"
    .FormatConditions(1).Interior.ColorIndex = iColor
End With
End Sub
```

Worksheet_FollowHyperlink(ByVal Target As Hyperlink)

`Worksheet_FollowHyperlink` occurs when a hyperlink is clicked on. `Target` is the hyperlink.

Chart Sheet Events

Chart events occur when a chart is changed or activated. Embedded charts require the use of class modules to access the events.

→ For more information on class modules, **see** "Creating Classes, Records and Collections," **p. 421**.

- Activate
- BeforeDoubleClick
- BeforeRightClick
- Calculate
- Deactivate
- DragOver
- DragPlot

- MouseDown
- MouseMove
- MouseUp
- Resize
- Select
- SeriesChange

Embedded Charts

Because embedded charts do not create chart sheets, the chart events are not as readily available. You can make them available by adding a class module.

1. Insert a class module.

2. Rename the module to cl_ChartEvents.

3. Enter the following line of code in the class module:

```
Public WithEvents myChartClass As Chart
```

The chart events are now available to the chart, as shown in Figure 8.6. They are accessed in the class module rather than on a chart sheet.

4. Insert a standard module.

5. Enter the following lines of code in a standard module:

```
Dim myClassModule As New cl_ChartEvents
Sub InitializeChart()
    Set myClassModule.myChartClass = _
        Worksheets(1).ChartObjects(1).Chart
End Sub
```

These lines initialize the embedded chart to be recognized as a chart object. The procedure must be run once per session (use Workbook_Open to automate this).

Figure 8.6
Embedded chart events are now available in the class module.

Chart_Activate()

Chart_Activate occurs when a chart sheet is activated or changed.

Chart_BeforeDoubleClick(ByVal ElementID As Long, ByVal Arg1 As Long, ByVal Arg2 As Long, Cancel As Boolean)

`Chart_BeforeDoubleClick` occurs when any part of a chart is double-clicked. `ElementID` is the part of the chart that is double-clicked, such as the Legend; `Arg1` and `Arg2` are dependent upon the `ElementID`; `Cancel` set to `True` prevents the default double-click action from occurring.

The following sample hides the legend when it is double-clicked; double-clicking on the chart area brings back the legend:

```
Private Sub MyChartClass_BeforeDoubleClick(ByVal ElementID As Long, _
    ByVal Arg1 As Long, ByVal Arg2 As Long, Cancel As Boolean)
Select Case ElementID
    Case xlLegend
        Me.HasLegend = False
        Cancel = True
    Case xlChartArea
        Me.HasLegend = True
        Cancel = True
End Select
End Sub
```

Chart_BeforeRightClick(Cancel As Boolean)

`Chart_BeforeRightClick` occurs when a chart is right-clicked. `Cancel` set to `True` prevents the default right-click action from occurring.

Chart_Calculate()

`Chart_Calculate` occurs when a chart's data is changed.

Chart_Deactivate()

`Chart_Deactivate` occurs when another sheet becomes the active sheet.

Chart_DragOver()

`Chart_DragOver` occurs when a range is dragged over to a chart.

Chart_DragPlot()

`Chart_DragPlot` occurs when a range is dragged and dropped on a chart.

Chart_MouseDown(ByVal Button As Long, ByVal Shift As Long, ByVal x As Long, ByVal y As Long)

`Chart_MouseDown` occurs when the cursor is over the chart and any mouse button is pressed. `Button` is the mouse button that was clicked; `Shift` is whether a Shift, Ctrl, or Alt key was pressed; `x` is the X coordinate of the cursor when the button is pressed; `y` is the Y coordinate of the cursor when the button is pressed.

The following code zooms in on a left mouse click and zoom out on a right mouse click. Use the `Cancel` argument in the `BeforeRightClick` event to handle the menus that appear when right-clicking on a chart:

```
Private Sub MyChartClass_MouseDown(ByVal Button As Long, ByVal Shift _
    As Long, ByVal x As Long, ByVal y As Long)
If Button = 1 Then
    ActiveChart.Axes(xlValue).MaximumScale = _
    ActiveChart.Axes(xlValue).MaximumScale - 50
End If
If Button = 2 Then
    ActiveChart.Axes(xlValue).MaximumScale = _
    ActiveChart.Axes(xlValue).MaximumScale + 50
End If
End Sub
```

Chart_MouseMove(ByVal Button As Long, ByVal Shift As Long, ByVal x As Long, ByVal y As Long)

`Chart_MouseMove` occurs as the cursor is moved over a chart. `Button` is the mouse button being held down, if any; `Shift` is whether a Shift, Ctrl, or Alt key was pressed; `x` is the X coordinate of the cursor on the chart; `Y` is the Y coordinate of the cursor on the chart.

Chart_MouseUp(ByVal Button As Long, ByVal Shift As Long, ByVal x As Long, ByVal y As Long)

`Chart_MouseUp` occurs when any mouse button is released while the cursor is on the chart. `Button` is the mouse button that was clicked; `Shift` is whether a Shift, Ctrl, or Alt key was pressed; `x` is the X coordinate of the cursor when the button is released; `Y` is the Y coordinate of the cursor when the button is released.

Chart_Resize()

`Chart_Resize` occurs when a chart is resized. If the chart is on a chart sheet, this event can be triggered when the Sized with Window option under the View menu is enabled.

Chart_Select(ByVal ElementID As Long, ByVal Arg1 As Long, ByVal Arg2 As Long)

`Chart_Select` occurs when a chart element is selected. `ElementID` is the part of the chart selected, such as the Legend; `Arg1` and `Arg2` are dependent upon the `ElementID`.

The following program highlights the data set when a point on the chart is selected:

```
Private Sub MyChartClass_Select(ByVal ElementID As Long, ByVal Arg1 _
    As Long, ByVal Arg2 As Long)
If Arg1 = 0 Then Exit Sub
Sheets("sheet1").Cells.Interior.ColorIndex = xlNone
```

```
        If ElementID = 3 Then
          If Arg2 = -1 Then
              ' Selected the entire series in Arg1
              Sheets("Sheet1").Range("A2:A22").Offset(0, Arg1).Interior.ColorIndex = 19
          Else
              ' Selected a single point in range Arg1, Point Arg2
              Sheets("Sheet1").Range("A1").Offset(Arg2, Arg1).Interior.ColorIndex = 19
          End If
       End If
    End Sub
```

Chart_SeriesChange(ByVal SeriesIndex As Long, ByVal PointIndex As Long)

Chart_SeriesChange occurs when a chart data point is updated. SeriesIndex is the offset in the Series collection of updated series; PointIndex is the offset in the Point collection of updated point.

Application-Level Events

Application-level events affect all open workbooks in an Excel session. They require a class module to access them (similar to the class module used to access events for embedded chart events). Follow these steps to create the class module:

1. Insert a class module.

2. Rename the module to cl_AppEvents.

3. Enter the following line of code in the class module:

   ```
   Public WithEvents AppEvent As Application
   ```

   The application events are now available to the workbook, as shown in Figure 8.7. They are accessed in the class module rather than in a standard module.

4. Insert a standard module.

5. Enter the following lines of code in the standard module:

   ```
   Dim myAppEvent As New cl_AppEvents
   Sub InitializeAppEvent()
       Set myAppEvent.AppEvent = Application
   End Sub
   ```

   These lines initialize the application to recognize application events. The procedure must be run once per session (use Workbook_Open to automate this).

Figure 8.7
Application events are
now available through
the class module.

The following application-level events are now available for applying code to all open workbooks.

- NewWorkbook
- SheetActivate
- SheetBeforeDoubleClick
- SheetBeforeRightClick
- SheetCalculate
- SheetChange
- SheetDeactivate
- SheetFollowHyperlink
- SheetSelectionChange
- WindowActivate
- WindowDeactivate

- WindowResize
- WorkbookActivate
- WorkbookAddinInstall
- WorkbookAddinUninstall
- WorkbookBeforeClose
- WorkbookBeforePrint
- WorkbookBeforeSave
- WorkbookDeactivate
- WorkbookNewSheet
- WorkbookOpen

CAUTION

The object in front of the event, such as AppEvent, is dependent on the name given in the class module.

AppEvent_NewWorkbook(ByVal Wb As Workbook)

AppEvent_NewWorkbook occurs when a new workbook is created. Wb is the new workbook. The following sample arranges the open workbooks in a tiled configuration:

```
Private Sub AppEvent_NewWorkbook(ByVal Wb As Workbook)
    Application.Windows.Arrange xlArrangeStyleTiled
End Sub
```

AppEvent_SheetActivate(ByVal Sh As Object)

AppEvent_SheetActivate occurs when a sheet is activated. Sh is the sheet (worksheet or chart sheet).

8

AppEvent_SheetBeforeDoubleClick(ByVal Sh As Object, ByVal Target As Range, Cancel As Boolean)

`AppEvent_SheetBeforeDoubleClick` occurs when the user double-clicks on a worksheet. `Target` is the selected range on the sheet; `Cancel` is set to `False` by default, but if set to `True`, it prevents the default action (such as entering a cell) from happening.

AppEvent_SheetBeforeRightClick(ByVal Sh As Object, ByVal Target As Range, Cancel As Boolean)

`AppEvent_SheetBeforeRightClick` occurs when the user right-clicks on any worksheet. `Sh` is the active worksheet; `Target` is the object right-clicked on; `Cancel` set to `True` prevents the default action from taking place.

AppEvent_SheetCalculate(ByVal Sh As Object)

`AppEvent_SheetCalculate` occurs when any worksheet is recalculated or any updated data is plotted on a chart. `Sh` is the active sheet.

AppEvent_SheetChange(ByVal Sh As Object, ByVal Target As Range)

`AppEvent_SheetChange` occurs when the value of any cell is changed. `Sh` is the worksheet; `Target` is the changed range.

AppEvent_SheetDeactivate(ByVal Sh As Object)

`AppEvent_SheetDeactivate` occurs when any chart sheet or worksheet in a workbook is deactivated. `Sh` is the sheet being deactivated.

AppEvent_SheetFollowHyperlink(ByVal Sh As Object, ByVal Target As Hyperlink)

`AppEvent_SheetFollowHyperlink` occurs when any hyperlink is clicked in Excel. `Sh` is the active worksheet; `Target` is the hyperlink.

AppEvent_SheetSelectionChange(ByVal Sh As Object, ByVal Target As Range)

`AppEvent_SheetSelectionChange` occurs when a new range is selected on any sheet. `Sh` is the active sheet; `Target` is the selected range.

AppEvent_WindowActivate(ByVal Wb As Workbook, ByVal Wn As Window)

`AppEvent_WindowActivate` occurs when *any* workbook window is activated. `Wb` is the workbook being deactivated; `Wn` is the window.

AppEvent_WindowDeactivate(ByVal Wb As Workbook, ByVal Wn As Window)

AppEvent_WindowDeactivate occurs when *any* workbook window is deactivated. Wb is the active workbook; Wn is the window.

AppEvent_WindowResize(ByVal Wb As Workbook, ByVal Wn As Window)

AppEvent_WindowResize occurs when the active workbook is resized. Wb is the active workbook; Wn is the window.

> **CAUTION**
>
> If you disable the capability to resize (EnableResize = False), the minimize and maximize buttons are removed and the workbook cannot be resized. To undo this, type **ActiveWindow. EnableResize = True** in the Immediate window.

AppEvent_WorkbookActivate(ByVal Wb As Workbook)

AppEvent_WorkbookActivate occurs when *any* workbook is activated. Wn is the window. The following sample maximizes any workbook when it is activated:

```
Private Sub AppEvent_WorkbookActivate(ByVal Wb as Workbook)
    Wb.WindowState = xlMaximized
End Sub
```

AppEvent_WorkbookAddinInstall(ByVal Wb As Workbook)

AppEvent_WorkbookAddinInstall occurs when a workbook is installed as an add-in (Tools, Add-Ins). Double-clicking on an .xla file to open it does not activate the event. Wb is the workbook being installed.

AppEvent_WorkbookAddinUninstall(ByVal Wb As Workbook)

AppEvent_WorkbookAddinUninstall occurs when a workbook (add-in) is uninstalled. The add-in is not automatically closed. Wb is the workbook being uninstalled.

AppEvent_WorkbookBeforeClose(ByVal Wb As Workbook, Cancel As Boolean)

AppEvent_WorkbookBeforeClose occurs when a workbook closes. Wb is the workbook; Cancel set to True prevents the workbook from closing.

AppEvent_WorkbookBeforePrint(ByVal Wb As Workbook, Cancel As Boolean)

`AppEvent_WorkbookBeforePrint` occurs when any print command is used—menu, toolbar, keyboard, or macro. `Wb` is the workbook; `Cancel` set to `True` prevents the workbook from being printed.

The following sample places the username in the footer of each sheet printed:

```
Private Sub AppEvent_WorkbookBeforePrint(ByVal Wb As Workbook, _
    Cancel As Boolean)
Wb.ActiveSheet.PageSetup.LeftFooter = Application.UserName
End Sub
```

AppEvent_WorkbookBeforeSave(ByVal Wb As Workbook, ByVal SaveAsUI As Boolean, Cancel As Boolean)

`AppEvent_Workbook_BeforeSave` occurs when the workbook is saved. `Wb` is the workbook; `SaveAsUI` is set to `True` if the Save As dialog box is to be displayed; `Cancel` set to `True` prevents the workbook from being saved.

AppEvent_WorkbookNewSheet(ByVal Wb As Workbook, ByVal Sh As Object)

`AppEvent_WorkbookNewSheet` occurs when a new sheet is added to the active workbook. `Wb` is the workbook; `Sh` is the new worksheet or chart sheet object.

AppEvent_WorkbookOpen(ByVal Wb As Workbook)

`AppEvent_WorkbookOpen` occurs when a workbook is opened. `Wb` is the workbook that was just opened.

Next Steps

In this chapter, you learned more about interfacing with Excel. The next chapter introduces you to tools you can use to interact with the users, prompting them for information to use in your code, warning them of illegal actions, or just providing them with an interface to work with other than the spreadsheet.

UserForms—An Introduction

User Interaction Methods

User forms allow you to display information and allow the user to input information. InputBox and MsgBox are simple ways of doing this; the UserForm controls in the VBE can be used to create more complex forms.

This chapter covers simple user interface using InputBoxes and Messageboxes and the basics of creating UserForms in the VBE; for more advanced programming, see Chapter 21, "Advanced UserForm Techniques."

InputBox

The InputBox function is a basic interface requesting input from the user before the program can continue. You can configure the prompt, the title for the window, a default value, the window position, and user help files. Only two buttons are provided: OK and Cancel. The returned value is a string. The following code asks the user for the number of months to be averaged. The resulting InputBox is shown in Figure 9.1.

```
AveMos = InputBox(Prompt:="Enter the number " & _
" of months to average", Title:="Enter Months", _
Default:="3")
```

MsgBox

The MsgBox function displays information and waits for the user to press a button before continuing. Whereas InputBox only has OK and Cancel buttons, MsgBox allows you to choose from several configurations of buttons, including Yes, No, OK, and Cancel. You can also configure the prompt, title, and help files. The following code is a simple prompt to find out whether the user wishes to continue. A Select Case statement is then used to continue the program with the appropriate action. Figure 9.2 shows the resulting customized message box.

Figure 9.1
A simple, but effective,
`InputBox`.

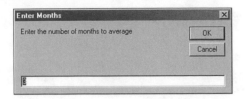

```
MyMsg = "Do you want to Continue?"
Response = MsgBox(myMsg, vbExclamation + vbYesNoCancel, myTitle)
Select Case Response
    Case Is = vbYes
        ActiveWorkbook.Close SaveChanges:=False
    Case Is = vbNo
        ActiveWorkbook.Close SaveChanges:=True
    Case Is = vbCancel
        Exit Sub
End Select
```

Figure 9.2
A `MsgBox` can be used
to display information
and obtain a basic
response from the user.

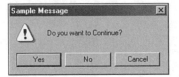

Creating a Userform

UserForms combine the capabilities of `InputBox` and `MsgBox` to create a more efficient way of interacting with the user. For example, rather than have the user fill out personal information on a sheet, you can create a UserForm that prompts for the required data (see Figure 9.3).

Figure 9.3
You can create a custom
userform to get more
information from the
user.

Insert a UserForm in the VBE by choosing Insert, UserForm from the main menu. A UserForm module is added to the Project Explorer, a blank form appears in the window where your code usually is, and the Controls Toolbox appears (see Figure 9.4).

Figure 9.4
Preliminary userform
and toolbox.

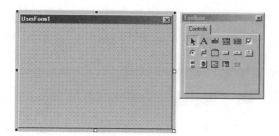

You can resize the form by grabbing and dragging the handles on the right side, bottom edge, or lower right corner of the UserForm. To add controls to the form, click on the desired control in the toolbox and draw it on the form. Controls can be moved and resized at any time.

 NOTE The toolbox, by default, displays the most common controls. To access more controls, right-click on the toolbox and select Additional Controls.

After a control is added to a form, its properties can be changed from the properties window. These properties can be set now, manually, or later programmatically.

TIP It's a good idea to give the userform and its controls descriptive names. For example, the default name for a userform is UserForm1. But, if you have multiple userforms, it can get difficult to tell the difference. Instead, rename the form in a way that will make sense to you later, for example, frm_AddEmp.

Calling and Hiding a Userform

A userform can be called from any module. `FormName.Show` pops up a form for the user:

```
frm_AddEmp.Show
```

The `Load` method can also be used to call a userform. This allows a form to be loaded, but remain hidden.

To hide a userform, use the `Hide` method. The form is still active but is now hidden from the user. The controls on the form can still be accessed programmatically.

The `Unload` method unloads the form from memory and removes it from the user's view. The form can no longer be accessed by the user or programmatically:

```
Unload Me
```

Programming the UserForm

The code for a control goes in the forms module. Unlike the other modules, double-clicking the forms module opens up the form in design view. To view the code, right-click on the module or the UserForm in design mode and select View Code.

To program a control, highlight it and select View, Code. The footer, header, and default action for the control is automatically entered in the programming field. To see what other actions are available for a control, select the control from the Object drop-down and view the actions in the Properties drop-down, as shown in Figure 9.5.

Figure 9.5
Various actions for a control can be selected from the VBE drop-downs.

The controls are objects, like `ActiveWorkbook`. They have properties and methods, dependent on the type of control. Most of the programming for the controls is done behind the form, but if another module needs to refer to a control, the parent, which is the form, needs to be included with the object.

```
Private Sub btn_EmpCancel_Click()
Unload Me
End Sub
```

The previous code can be broken down into three sections:

- `btn_EmpCancel`—Name given to the control
- `Click`—Action of the control
- `Unload Me`—The code behind the control, in this case, unloading the form

CASE STUDY

Case Study: Bug—Adding Controls to an Existing Form

If you have a userform that you've been using for some time and later try to add a new control, you might find that Excel seems to get confused about the control. You will see that the control is added to the form, but when you right-click the control and choose View Code, the code module does not seem to acknowledge that the control exists. The control name will not be available in the left drop-down at the top of the code module.

To work around this situation, follow these steps:

1. Add all the controls you need to add to the existing form.

2. In the project explorer, right-click the userform and choose Export File. Choose Save to save the file in the default location.

> 3. In the project explorer, right-click the userform and choose Remove. Because you just exported, you can click No to the question about exporting.
>
> 4. Right-click anywhere in the project explorer and choose Import File. Select the filename that you saved in step 2.
>
> The new controls will now be available in the code pane of the userform.

Using Basic Form Controls

Our basic form, as shown in Figure 9.6, consists of labels, text boxes, and command buttons. It is a simple yet effective method of requesting information from the user. After the text boxes have been filled in, the user clicks OK and the information is added to a sheet (see Figure 9.7):

Figure 9.6
A simple form to collect information from the user.

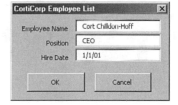

```
Private Sub btn_EmpOK_Click()
Dim LastRow As Long
LastRow = Worksheets("Sheet2").Range("A65536").End(xlUp).Row + 1
Cells(LastRow, 1).Value = tb_EmpName.Value
Cells(LastRow, 2).Value = tb_EmpPosition.Value
Cells(LastRow, 3).Value = tb_EmpHireDate.Value
End Sub
```

Figure 9.7
The information gets added to the sheet.

	A	B	C	D
1	Add	View		
2	**Name**	**Position**	**Hire Date**	
3	Tracy Syrstad	Project Consultant	7/20/2003	
4	Cort Chilldon-Hoff	CEO	1/1/2003	
5				

With a change in code as shown in the following sample, the same form design can be used to retrieve information. The following sample retrieves the position and hire date after the employee name has been entered:

```
Private Sub btn_EmpOK_Click()
Dim EmpFound As Range
With Range("EmpList")
    Set EmpFound = .Find(tb_EmpName.Value)
    If EmpFound Is Nothing Then
        MsgBox ("Employee not found!")
        tb_EmpName.Value = ""
        Exit Sub
```

```
    Else
        With Range(EmpFound.Address)
            tb_EmpPosition = .Offset(0, 1)
            tb_HireDate = .Offset(0, 2)
        End With
    End If
End With
End Sub
```

Deciding Whether to Use ListBoxes or ComboBoxes in Your Forms

You can let users type in an employee name to search for, but what if they misspell the name? You need a way of making sure that the name is entered correctly. Which do you use: a ListBox or a ComboBox?

 ■ A ListBox displays a list of values from which the user can choose.

■ A ComboBox displays a list of values from which the user can choose and allows the user to enter a new value.

In this case, where we want to limit users' options, we use a ListBox to list the employee names, as shown in Figure 9.8.

Figure 9.8
Use a ListBox to control user input.

In the RowSource property of the ListBox, enter the range from which the control should draw its data. Use a dynamic named range to keep the list updated if employees are added:

```
Private Sub btn_EmpOK_Click()
Dim EmpFound As Range
With Range("EmpList")
    Set EmpFound = .Find(lb_EmpName.Value)
    If EmpFound Is Nothing Then
        MsgBox ("Employee not found!")
        lb_EmpName.Value = ""
        Exit Sub
    Else
        With Range(EmpFound.Address)
            tb_EmpPosition = .Offset(0, 1)
            tb_HireDate = .Offset(0, 2)
        End With
    End If
End With
End Sub
```

Using the Multi-Select Property of a ListBox

ListBoxes have a multi-select property, which allows the user to select multiple items from the choices in the ListBox, as shown in Figure 9.9:

- `fmMultiSelectSingle` — The default setting allows only a single item selection at a time.

- `fmMultiSelectMulti` — Allows an item to be deselected by clicking on it again; multiple items can also be selected.

- `fmMultiSelectExtended` — Allows the Ctrl and Shift keys to be used to select multiple items.

Figure 9.9
Multiselect can allow the user to select multiple items from a ListBox.

If multiple items are selected, the Value property cannot be used to retrieve the items. Instead, check whether the item is selected, then manipulate it as needed:

```
Private Sub btn_EmpOK_Click()
Dim LastRow As Long, i As Integer
LastRow = Worksheets("Sheet2").Range("A65536").End(xlUp).Row + 1
Cells(LastRow, 1).Value = tb_EmpName.Value
'check the selection status of the items in the ListBox
For i = 0 To lb_EmpPosition.ListCount - 1
'if the item is selected, add it to the sheet
    If lb_EmpPosition.Selected(i) = True Then
        Cells(LastRow, 2).Value = Cells(LastRow, 2).Value & _
        lb_EmpPosition.List(i) & ","
    End If
Next i
Cells(LastRow, 3).Value = tb_HireDate.Value
End Sub
```

The items in a ListBox start counting at 0, so if you use the ListCount property, you must subtract 1 from the result:

```
For i = 0 To lb_EmpPosition.ListCount - 1
```

Adding Option Buttons to a UserForm

Using the Frame tool, draw a frame to separate the next set of controls from the other controls on the userform. The frame is used to group option buttons together, as shown in Figure 9.10.

Figure 9.10
Use a frame to group option buttons together.

Option buttons have a Group property. If you assign the same group name, Buildings, to a set of option buttons, you force them to act collectively as a toggle, so that only one button in the set can be selected:

> **TIP**
>
> For users who prefer to select the option button's label instead of the button itself, such as in Figure 9.11, add code to the label to trigger the option button.
>
> ```
> Private Sub Lbl_Bldg1_Click()
> Obtn_Bldg1.Value = True
> End Sub
> ```

Figure 9.11
Add code to the label to allow the user to select the option button.

Adding Graphics to a UserForm

 A listing on a form can be even more helpful if a corresponding graphic is added to the form, as shown in Figure 9.12.

The following code displays the photograph corresponding to the selected employee from the ListBox:

```
Private Sub lb_EmpName_Change()
Dim EmpFound As Range
With Range("EmpList")
    Set EmpFound = .Find(lb_EmpName.Value)
    If EmpFound Is Nothing Then
        MsgBox ("Employee not found!")
        lb_EmpName.Value = ""
```

```
            Exit Sub
        Else
            With Range(EmpFound.Address)
                tb_EmpPosition = .Offset(0, 1)
                tb_HireDate = .Offset(0, 2)
                On Error Resume Next
                Img_Employee.Picture = LoadPicture _
            ("C:\Excel VBA 2003 by Jelen & Syrstad\" & EmpFound & ".bmp")
                On Error GoTo 0
            End With
        End If
    End With
End With
```

Figure 9.12
Use a graphic to
enhance identification.

Using Spinbutton on a Userform

As it is, the Hire Date field allows the user to enter the date in any format: 1/1/1 or January 1, 2001. This possible inconsistency can create problems later on if you need to use or search for dates. The solution? Force users to enter dates in a unified manner.

Spinbuttons allow the user to increment/decrement through a series of numbers. In this way, the user is forced to enter numbers rather than text.

Draw a spinbutton for a Month entry on the form. In the properties, set the Min to 1 (for January) and the Max to 12 (for December). In the Value property, enter 1, the first month. Next, draw a text box next to the spinbutton. This is the text box that will reflect the value of the spinbutton (labels can also be used).

```
Private Sub SpBtn_Month_Change()
tb_Month.Value = SpBtn_Month.Value
End Sub
```

Finish building the form as shown in Figure 9.13. Use a Min of 1 and Max of 31 for days; Min of 1900 and a Max of 2100 for Year.

```
Private Sub btn_EmpOK_Click()
Dim LastRow As Long, i As Integer
LastRow = Worksheets("Sheet2").Range("A65536").End(xlUp).Row + 1
Cells(LastRow, 1).Value = tb_EmpName.Value
For i = 0 To lb_EmpPosition.ListCount - 1
    If lb_EmpPosition.Selected(i) = True Then
        Cells(LastRow, 2).Value = Cells(LastRow, 2).Value & _
        lb_EmpPosition.List(i) & ","
    End If
```

```
Next i
'Concatenate the values from the textboxes to create the date
Cells(LastRow, 3).Value = tb_Month.Value & "/" & tb_Day.Value & __
    "/" & tb_Year.Value
End Sub
```

Figure 9.13
Use spinbuttons to control the date entry.

Using the Multipage Control to Combine Forms

 The Multipage control provides a neat way of organizing multiple forms. Instead of having a form for personal employee information and one for on-the-job information, combine the information into one multipage form, as shown in Figure 9.14.

> **TIP**
> Multipage forms should be planned from the beginning—adding them after the rest of the form is created is not an easy task. If you decide at a later point you need a multipage form, insert a new form, draw the multipage, and copy/paste the controls from the other forms to the new form.

Figure 9.14
Use the Multipage control to combine multiple forms.

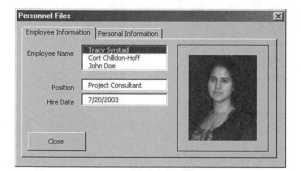

Verifying Field Entry

Even if users are told to fill in all the fields, there is no way of forcing them to do so—except with an electronic form. As a programmer, you can ensure that all required fields are filled in by not allowing the user to continue until all requirements are met:

```
If tb_EmpName.Value = "" Then
    frm_AddEmp.Hide
    MsgBox ("Please enter an Employee Name")
    frm_AddEmp.Show
    Exit Sub
End If
```

Illegal Window Closing

The userforms created in the VBE are not that different than normal windows: They also include the X close button in the upper right-hand corner. Though using the button is not wrong, it can cause problems, depending on the objective of the userform. In cases like this, you may want to control what happens if the user presses the button. Use the `QueryClose` event of the userform to find out what method is used to close the form and code an appropriate action:

```
Private Sub UserForm_QueryClose(Cancel As Integer, CloseMode As Integer)
If CloseMode = vbFormControlMenu Then
    MsgBox "Please use the OK or Cancel buttons to close the form", vbCritical
    Cancel = True
End If
End Sub
```

After you know the method the user used to try and close the form, you can create a `MsgBox` similar to Figure 9.15, to warn the user that the method was illegal.

Figure 9.15
Control what happens when the user clicks the X button.

The `QueryClose` event can be triggered in three other ways:

- `vbFormCode` — The `Unload` statement was used.
- `vbAppWindows` — Windows shuts down.
- `vbAppTaskManager` — The application was shut down by the Task Manager.

Next Steps

Now that you've seen how to work with UserForms, the next chapter examines charts. You'll learn how spreadsheet charting has become a highly customizable resource capable of handling large amounts of data.

Automating Excel Power in VBA

IN THIS PART

Charts

My guess is that you are probably a numbers person. Excel power users tend to be analytical types. We can look at a table of data and spot the spikes and trends. Unfortunately, our managers need some help. They say a picture is worth a thousand words. And for a picture of numbers, nothing works better than a well-conceived chart that draws data from an Excel table. Charts linked with tables of spreadsheet data have been in use from the early spreadsheet days and, over this period, spreadsheet charting has evolved tremendously. It has metamorphosed from a rudimentary graphical spreadsheet tool to a highly customizable resource capable of handling large amounts of data.

Overview

You probably know how to do all the following tasks in the Excel user interface, but this chapter covers the VBA needed to perform them:

- Creating charts on a chart sheet or as an embedded chart on a worksheet.
- Selecting from among the chart types available in Excel.
- Changing the type of an existing chart.
- Formatting, moving, and deleting a chart and chart elements.
- Customizing a chart through the user interface.

As with earlier chapters, you might find that recording a bit of code reveals the methods and properties that are relevant. One of the most frustrating aspects of charts is that two different object models are used, depending on the chart's location.

10

Embedded Charts Versus ChartSheets

If you go back far enough, you find that all charts used to be created as their own ChartSheets. Then, in the mid-1990s, Excel added the amazing capability to embed a chart right onto an existing worksheet. This allowed a report to be created with tables of numbers and charts all on the same page, something we all take for granted today.

This separate evolution of charts has made it necessary for us to deal with two separate object models for charts. When a chart is on its own stand-alone ChartSheet, then we are dealing with a Chart object. When a chart is embedded in a worksheet, then we have to deal with a ChartObject object.

Embedded Charts in a ChartObject Container

The ChartObject object represents the "container" for an embedded chart. The purpose of having this container is to enable you to specify its size (height, width) and location (top, left) on the worksheet. These properties apply to all objects (such as pictures or autoshapes) that can be embedded on a chart.

To illustrate, go to any worksheet with an embedded chart. With the Ctrl or Shift key depressed, click the chart. The eight resize handles appear white as shown in Figure 10.1. You have now selected the chart object. The Name box to the left of the formula bar shows Chart 1 (or whatever the name of the chart is). You can rename the embedded chart object by entering another name, say MyChart, in the Name box. Subsequently, you can use this name in your VBA code to refer to the embedded chart object. For example:

```
ActiveSheet.ChartObjects("Chart 1").Select
```

Figure 10.1
By holding down the Ctrl key or the Shift key before clicking the chart, you get the white resize handles indicating that the ChartObject container has been selected. This is the easiest way to learn that this ChartObject is named "Chart 1" (see Name box).

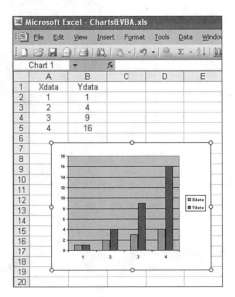

While the `ChartObject` is selected, you can go to the Immediate pane in the Visual Basic Editor and query the location with `Print Selection.Top` to learn that this `ChartObject` container is 75 points from the top of the spreadsheet.

Deselect the chart and reselect it by clicking between the chart boundary and the plot area. Now, the sizing handles appear black, indicating that you have selected the chart area inside the `ChartObject`. Note in Figure 10.2 that the Name box now includes the generic `Chart Area` name. The VBA code corresponding to this action would be

```
ActiveSheet.ChartObjects("Chart 1").Activate
ActiveChart.ChartArea.Select
```

Figure 10.2
By simply clicking the chart, you get the black resize handles indicating that the `Chart Area` within the `ChartObject` container is selected. The Name box would show that all charts have the same `Chart Area` name.

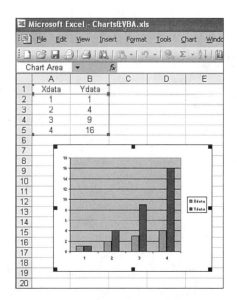

While the `Chart Area` inside the container is selected, go to the Immediate pane in the Visual Basic Editor, and query the location with `Print Selection.Top`. This time, the Immediate pane returns an answer of 4 points. It is obvious that the chart is more than 4 points from the top of the worksheet. In fact, you are learning that the `Chart Area` is located 4 points from the top of the `ChartObject` container. This is a confusing distinction. To find the location of the `Chart` container on the worksheet, remember to hold down the Ctrl key or the Shift key to select the `Chart` object to correctly find the position of the container object on the worksheet.

In VBA, to change the color of the `ChartArea` in a chart embedded on a worksheet, you have to reference the `Chart` object inside the `ChartObjects` object inside the worksheet:

```
Worksheets("Sheet3").ChartObjects("Chart 2").Chart.ChartArea. _
    Interior.ColorIndex = 2
```

Charts on a Chart Sheet Have No Container

When the same chart is moved to its own chart sheet, the object model changes. We no longer refer to a `Chart` object inside a `ChartObject` container. In this model, the `Chart` object belongs to the `Sheet`. To change the color of the `ChartArea`, the reference is much simpler:

```
Sheets("Chart2").ChartArea.Interior.ColorIndex = 2
```

Creating a Chart with VBA

The fastest way to create a chart in the Excel user interface is to select some chartable data and press the F11 key. Let's look at the macro code recorded during this operation. I set up a simple table, shown in Figure 10.3.

Figure 10.3
Highlight some chartable data and press the F11 key to create a chart quickly in the user interface.

After pressing F11, you get the default chart type, located on a new sheet, as shown in Figure 10.4.

Figure 10.4
After you press F11, Excel provides the default chart on a new sheet.

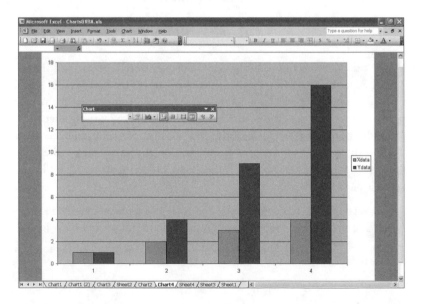

The following code is produced by using the macro recorder while hitting F11.

```
Charts.Add
ActiveChart.SetSourceData Source:=Sheets("Sheet4").Range("A1:B5")
ActiveChart.Location Where:=xlLocationAsNewSheet
```

Let's examine that code line by line:

```
Charts.Add
```

You are already familiar with the concept of collections. The Charts collection is the collection of all chart sheets in a workbook. Every collection has an Add method, which adds a new member to the collection. This line does just that—adds a new chart sheet (Chart4) to the workbook. At this point, the newly added chart is a blank chart sheet because the data source specs for the chart are yet to come.

After the new (as yet blank) chart sheet is added, Excel automatically makes it active—just as any object last accessed/modified in the user interface is active when you have finished with it. VBA has an ActiveChart object that refers to the currently active chart (if one is really active).

10

> ___ CAUTION ___
>
> Use of the ActiveChart object in code when something other than a chart is active (selected) results in an error.

Of course, the chart can also be referred to as Charts("Chart4") just as effectively.

```
ActiveChart.SetSourceData Source:=Sheets("Sheet4").Range("A1:B5")
```

This line specifies the data source (the range that contains the source data for the chart) for the new chart, using the SetSourceData method. It is interesting to note that VBA has a corresponding method for all that you do through the user interface. In the current instance, if you right-click the chart, and select Source Data from the shortcut menu, the Source Data dialog box appears (see Figure 10.5). The Data Range tab of this dialog takes two inputs: the data range and whether the data series is in rows or columns.

The SetSourceData method is the VBA equivalent of doing just this. The complete syntax of this method is

```
SetSourceData(Source, PlotBy)
```

Where Source is a range reference and PlotBy is an Excel constant that can have one of two values: xlColumns or xlRows.

Thus, the explicitly complete line of code for specifying the data source for the sample chart would be

```
ActiveChart.SetSourceData Source:=Sheets("Sheet4").Range("A1:B5"),_
PlotBy:=xlColumns
```

Figure 10.5
The Source Data dialog is emulated by the `SetSourceData` method in VBA code.

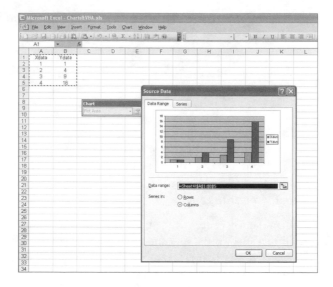

Note that the recorded code does not contain the `PlotBy` argument. This is probably because the data structure (field names in A1 and B1) itself suggests that the data is in columns and therefore the macro recorder perceives this argument as being redundant and omits to record it. However, the macro recorder is not consistently as efficient. More often than not, it spews out large quantities of redundant code that you will find yourself deleting in the end.

```
ActiveChart.Location Where:=xlLocationAsNewSheet
```

This line corresponds to the last step, when you use the Chart Wizard (see Figure 10.6) to create a chart. In this step you specify where the newly created chart should be located: either as a new chart sheet or as an embedded object on a specific worksheet.

Figure 10.6
The `Location` method in VBA answers the final question in the Chart Wizard.

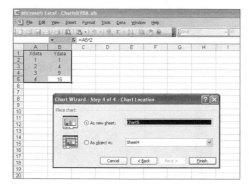

The complete syntax is

```
Cht.Location(Where, Name)
```

The possible values of the `Where` argument are `xlLocationAsNewSheet` and `xlLocationAsObject`, or `xlLocationAutomatic`.

`Name` is a string which specifies

- The name of the chart sheet to convert the embedded chart to when `Where` is `xlLocationAsNewSheet`
- The name of the sheet that will hold the embedded chart sheet when `Where` is `xlLocationAsObject`

The macro recorder often records unnecessary code. This is one such example. Notice that when we used the line `Charts.Add`, we already specified that the chart would be on a new chart sheet. So when a chart is created on a new sheet, the code works even if this line is deleted.

Moving from Embedded to Chart Sheet and Vice-Versa

The `Location` method is the equivalent of right-clicking a chart (embedded or in its own sheet) and selecting Location from the shortcut menu. The method is put to use when you want to change an embedded chart to a chart sheet or vice versa.

Consider the code:

```
Worksheets("Sheet1").ChartObjects("Chart 1").Activate
ActiveChart.Location Where:=xlLocationAsNewSheet, Name:= "MyChart"
```

When this code is run, it changes the embedded chart, Chart 1 on Sheet1, to a chart sheet named MyChart.

The Default Chart Type

You will notice that code does not specify the chart type being created, yet a column chart was produced. On my machine, the default chart type for Excel is a column chart. This is an important feature of Excel VBA. Defaults that are saved as Excel settings need not be explicitly specified in VBA code.

This can work for you or against you. On the positive side, if you need to create many charts of one particular type, you can change the default chart type on your machine and produce code to create that default chart. However, be aware that this also can work against you. Probably 98% of people don't know how to change their default chart type and so `Charts.Add` works as you expect in many cases. However, as you distribute your code to all the department managers, you will undoubtedly find the regional manager in Sioux City read a book and changed his default chart type to a pie chart. He will end up with dramatically different charts if you rely on `Charts.Add` without explicitly coding which type of chart you want.

10

When you want to override any default chart parameter, you need to add several lines of code. For example, the plot area of the default chart is an ugly gray. If you want to replace this with white, you need to add the following line of code:

```
ActiveChart.PlotArea.Interior.ColorIndex = xlNone
```

> **TIP**
>
> To change your default chart type, right-click any chart and choose Chart Type from the popup menu. Select a chart type, and click Set As Default Chart in the lower-left corner of the dialog.

Using Object Variables to Streamline Code

Object variables make for much simpler and more efficient code. With an object variable, you can refer to a chart without actually activating the chart. In the confusing world of Charts and ChartObjects and ChartSheets, it is easier to define an object variable as a Chart object and then refer to that variable instead of ActiveChart or Worksheets("Sheet1").ChartObject("Chart 2").Chart. To define an object variable as a Chart, use this line of code:

```
Dim Cht as Chart
Set Cht = Charts.Add
Cht.SourceData = Source:=Sheets("Sheet4").Range("A1:B5")
```

As you go through the following section to learn how to customize various chart options, we'll use object variables extensively.

Another advantage of declaring object variables is that the Visual Basic Editor (VBE) can help you write code. In the VBE, go to Tools, Options and select the Editor tab. Make sure that "Auto List Members" is checked (see Figure 10.7).

Figure 10.7
Use Auto List Members to allow the VBE to show you a list of possible property settings.

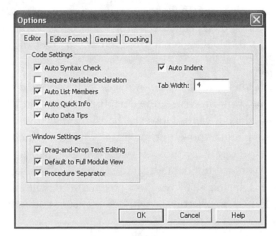

With this setting enabled, the VBE automatically displays a list that contains information that would logically complete the statement at the current insertion point. This happens as you are typing. All you need to do is select an item from the list and it is put in place in the code. In Figure 10.8, I typed `Cht.ChartType =`. Excel pops up a window with the possible constants. It is far easier to select `xlLineMarkers` from the list, as shown in Figure 10.8, than to try to remember the proper name for a particular type of chart.

Figure 10.8
If your object variables are properly declared, the VBE pops up a list of valid values as you type.

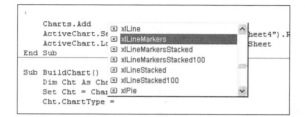

CAUTION

If the Auto List Members ever suddenly stops working, you may have inadvertently introduced a compile error into your code. From the VBE menu, select Debug, Compile VBA Project to identify the problem. After you solve the compile error, the Auto List Members begins working again.

The Anatomy of a Chart

Now that you have made VBA plot a chart for you, we can look at the ways in which you can use code to manipulate the chart. The first step in the process is to get familiar with the VBA equivalents of the various elements of a chart. Then you will learn to apply the available methods to and modify the properties of these elements to achieve your objectives.

Some elements (for example, chart area, plot area, chart title, legend) are common to all chart types, whereas others (such as the start angle of a pie chart or the perspective settings of a 3D chart) apply to specific types only. Line, scatter, and area charts have two axes, a radar chart has one axis for each category, and pie and doughnut charts have none.

As you progress, you will find that the VBA names of all objects, properties, and methods are logically devised and very similar to the terms you normally use to refer to them. For example, the VBA name for `Chart Area` is `ChartArea` and the `Plot Area` is referred to as `PlotArea`. Notice that the only difference is that there are no spaces in each name. This is a basic feature of VBA—no VBA entity name can contain a space.

The Chart Area—VBA Name: ChartArea

`ChartArea` is the container for all the other elements of a chart, including the plot area, axes, legend, series, data labels, and so on. The most common action performed with the chart area is modifying its format (border, fill color, and pattern) and the font settings for the entire chart, including chart and axis titles, legend, and data labels.

Take any existing chart that is loaded on a chart sheet. Turn on the macro recorder and use the Excel user interface to format the chart by right-clicking the chart area and selecting Format Chart Area. In the Patterns tab, borders section, select red color and the third of the four line weights. Click the Shadow check box so it is checked (has a tick mark). In the Area section, select a color (say, Light Turquoise). In the Font tab, select font size 14 and uncheck the Autoscale Font check box. The recorded code will look like this:

```
Sub Macro2()
    ActiveChart.ChartArea.Select
    With Selection.Border
        .ColorIndex = 3
        .Weight = xlMedium
        .LineStyle = xlContinuous
    End With
    Selection.Shadow = True
    With Selection.Interior
        .ColorIndex = 34
        .PatternColorIndex = 1
        .Pattern = xlSolid
    End With
    Selection.AutoScaleFont = False
    With Selection.Font
        .Name = "Arial"
        .FontStyle = "Regular"
        .Size = 14
        .Strikethrough = False
        .Superscript = False
        .Subscript = False
        .OutlineFont = False
        .Shadow = False
        .Underline = xlUnderlineStyleNone
        .ColorIndex = xlAutomatic
        .Background = xlAutomatic
    End With
End Sub
```

Note that the recorder has recorded all you did with the chart area (including many things you didn't even touch). The next step is to clean the code to limit its contents to your actions. I've reproduced the macro with redundant lines in bold and comments added at the appropriate places:

```
Sub Macro2()
    ActiveChart.ChartArea.Select
    With Selection.Border
        .ColorIndex = 3 'Red border
        .Weight = xlMedium '3rd of the four line weights available
        '.LineStyle = xlContinuous (default)
    End With
    Selection.Shadow = True
    With Selection.Interior
        .ColorIndex = 34   'Light turquoise fill
        '.PatternColorIndex = 1 (default)
        '.Pattern = xlSolid (default)
    End With
    Selection.AutoScaleFont = False
```

```
    With Selection.Font
        .Name = "Arial" (unchanged)
        .FontStyle = "Regular" (unchanged)
        .Size = 14
        '.Strikethrough = False (unchanged)
        '.Superscript = False (unchanged)
        '.Subscript = False (unchanged)
        '.OutlineFont = False (unchanged)
        '.Shadow = False (unchanged)
        '.Underline = xlUnderlineStyleNone (unchanged)
        '.ColorIndex = xlAutomatic (unchanged)
        '.Background = xlAutomatic (unchanged)
    End With
End Sub
```

Here is the macro with all the unneeded lines removed:

```
Sub Macro2()
    ActiveChart.ChartArea.Select
    With Selection.Border
        .ColorIndex = 3
        .Weight = xlMedium
    End With
    Selection.Shadow = True
    With Selection.Interior
        .ColorIndex = 34
    End With
    Selection.AutoScaleFont = False
    With Selection.Font
        .Size = 14
    End With
End Sub
```

You can see that when we limit the code to only those items we are changing, it is much more compact. You can make the code even slicker.

Because this section of the code is meant for the chart area only, declare an object variable to stand for the chart area. Use this variable for all the remaining code. Notice that with VBA, you need not actually select the chart area to format it. The following code works even if a sheet other than the chart sheet is active at the time the macro is run:

```
Sub ChartArDemo()
    Dim ChtArea As ChartArea
    Set ChtArea = Charts("Chart1").ChartArea
    With ChtArea
        .Shadow = True
        With .Border
            .ColorIndex = 3
            .Weight = xlMedium
        End With
        .Interior.ColorIndex = 34
        .AutoScaleFont = False
        .Font.Size = 14
    End With
End Sub
```

A Word About Using Colors

When you use the line, fill, or font color from the Formatting toolbar or Format dialog box, Excel displays a palette of 56 colors to choose from. Excel comes with its own default color palette, which you can modify. You can define your own color palette on the Color tab in Tools, Options by selecting the color you want to change and clicking the Modify button. Your modified palette is saved with the workbook. The palette colors can be set or accessed from the workbook's Colors property.

Thus, instead of

```
.Border.ColorIndex = 3
```

you can write

```
.Border.Color = ThisWorkbook.Colors(3)
```

You will notice that the order of the colors as they appear in the palette is not the same as the ColorIndex value. For example, in the default color palette, red (row 3, column 1) has a ColorIndex value of 3, whereas turquoise (row 4, column 5) has a ColorIndex value of 8. This can be confusing. The easiest way out is to record a macro for setting a particular color and use the ColorIndex value from the recorded code into your own code.

All colors can be derived from the three monitor colors: red, green, and blue. VBA has a RGB function to enable full control over the colors you use by specifying different intensities for each of these three components. The syntax is RGB (red, green, blue); each of the arguments can have a value from 0 to 255. For pure red, the RGB equivalent would be RGB(255,0,0). Thus, instead of

```
.Border.ColorIndex = 3
```

you can write (in RGB terms)

```
.Border.Color = RGB(255,0,0)
```

The Plot Area—VBA Name: PlotArea

This is the area where the data series are plotted. The plot area also contains the axes and axis labels. The plot area can be formatted just like the chart area. In addition, you can also resize and reposition the plot area within the chart. To do this, specify the Top, Left, Height, and Width properties of the plot area.

Sizing and Positioning an Object

Every drawing or chart object has a container. For example, the container for an autoshape (say, rectangle) is the worksheet on which it is drawn. Similarly, the container for a plot area is the chart itself. Each such object has a *bounding rectangle*. You can visualize the bounding rectangle as the smallest rectangle that can fully enclose the object.

In Excel VBA, distances and size are measured in points, one point being equal to 1/72 of an inch.

The position of the object is specified as the horizontal and vertical distance of the top-left corner of the object from the top-left corner of its container. The vertical distance corresponds to the Top property of the object, and the horizontal distance to its Left property. The height and width of such an object are defined as the height and width of the bounding rectangle for the object (see Figure 10.9).

Figure 10.9
Every object has a width and height, and is also located a certain number of points from the top and left of its container.

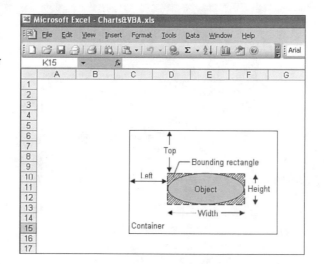

These properties are read-write in nature. This means that you can either query these properties to determine them or use their current values:

```
ObjHt = obj.Height
```

or set their values to reposition or resize the object:

```
obj.Top = 75
obj.Left = 80
```

Consider the code:

```
Sub PlotArDemo()
    Dim PltArea As PlotArea
    Set PltArea = Charts("Chart1").PlotArea
    With PltArea
        .Top = 100
        .Left = 100
        .Height = 300
        .Width = 400
    End With
End Sub
```

Running this procedure in the sample workbook resizes and relocates the plot area to look like Figure 10.10.

Figure 10.10
Adjusting the Top, Left, Height, and Width properties of an object in VBA provides very precise control of the size and location of an object. Although the chart on a chart sheet typically is full size, you can control it with this code.

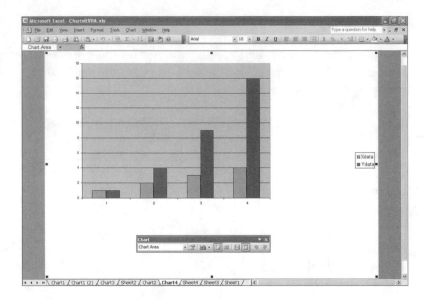

The ability to set the Top, Left, Width and Height properties of an object is very important when you need to customize it at runtime. A major advantage is that you can perform this with the highest precision possible in Excel, which is something one can never hope to achieve manually. Care needs to be taken so that invalid values are not used. For example, the sum of an object's Left and Width properties cannot exceed the Width of its container.

The Data Series—VBA Name: Series

Each series in a chart is a member of the SeriesCollection collection. The sample chart has two data series (Xdata and Ydata). The VBA syntax for specifying a given series is

```
Cht.SeriesCollection(Index)
```

Index can be a number ranging from 1 to the number of series in the chart or the name of the series. When you click any data point (column) belonging to Xdata on the chart, you see the following formula in the formula bar:

```
=SERIES(Sheet1!$A$1,,Sheet1!$A$2:$A$5,1)
```

Sheet1!$A$1 represents the name of the data series (Xdata).

By default, the second argument is null because the x-axis of a column chart is ordinal in nature: It ranges from 1 to the number of data points. However, this argument can contain a range reference if you intend to show custom x-axis labels.

Sheet1!$A$2:$A$5 is the data range for the series.

Lastly, the 1 represents the index number of the series. In the user interface, you can change the index number of the series with Format Data Series, Series Order.

To specify series Xdata you can use either

```
Charts("Chart1").SeriesCollection("Xdata")
```

or

```
Charts("Chart1").SeriesCollection(1)
```

Here is a macro to create a combination chart with series Xdata as a line series. The code needs to change the Xdata series to Line type, set the line weight to the heaviest value, and place black circular markers of size 10 points.

```
Sub SeriesDemo()
    Dim Ser As Series
    Set Ser = Charts("Chart1").SeriesCollection("XData")
    With Ser
        .ChartType = xlLine
        .Border.Weight = xlThick
        .MarkerStyle = xlMarkerStyleCircle
        .MarkerBackgroundColorIndex = xlAutomatic
        .MarkerForegroundColorIndex = xlAutomatic
        .MarkerSize = 10
    End With
End Sub
```

Running this macro modifies the chart as shown in Figure 10.11.

Figure 10.11
Setting a different ChartType for a single series allows you to make interesting combination charts.

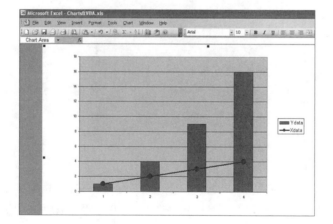

The Chart Axes—VBA Name: Axis

Each axis in a chart is a member of the Axes collection. The sample chart has two axes (X and Y), known respectively as the category axis and the value axis. The simplest VBA syntax for specifying a given axis is

```
Cht.Axes(Type)
```

where Type is an Excel VBA constant specifying the axis. For our chart, the value of Type can be xlCategory (for the X axis) or xlValue (for the Y axis).

Using `Cht.Axes` without the `Type` argument returns the entire `Axes` collection for the chart.

The following code demonstrates how you can use VBA to add axis titles to the chart and set the number format of the Y axis (value axis) to 2 decimals:

```
Sub AxisDemo()
    Dim Axs As Axis
    Set Axs = Charts("Chart1").Axes(xlValue)
    With Axs
        .HasTitle = True
        .AxisTitle.Caption = "Performance index"
        .TickLabels.NumberFormat = "0.00"
    End With
    Set Axs = Charts("Chart1").Axes(xlCategory)
    With Axs
        .HasTitle = True
        .AxisTitle.Caption = "Year of production"
    End With
End Sub
```

The resulting chart is shown in Figure 10.12.

Figure 10.12
The number format for the Y axis has been changed and axis titles have been added.

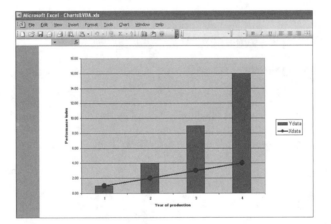

Note that the plot area is automatically resized to accommodate the axis titles. You cannot set the axis caption unless the `HasTitle` property for the axis is set to `True`.

Secondary Axes

If the data series have very different scales, you need to use a secondary axis. This can be done for either or both of the horizontal and vertical axes. In this context, the VBA syntax for specifying a given axis is

```
Cht.Axes(Type, AxisGroup)
```

The following macro specifies a secondary value (Y) axis for the chart and plots the Xdata series on the secondary Y axis. It results in the chart shown in Figure 10.13:

```
Sub SecondaryAxisDemo()
    Dim Cht As Chart
    Set Cht = Charts("Chart1")
    Cht.SeriesCollection("Xdata").AxisGroup = 2
End Sub
```

Figure 10.13
When one series has numbers of a vastly different scale, add a secondary axis to the chart.

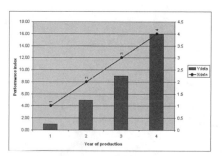

Grid Lines—VBA Name: `HasMajorGridlines` and `HasMinorGridlines`

Gridlines are extensions of the axis tick marks. Just as there are major and minor tick marks on the axes, there are also major and minor gridlines. Gridlines help you to estimate the ordinates of a data point lying at some distance from the axis. Depending upon your requirement and taste, you can choose to either display or do away with either or both of the major and minor gridlines. If the gridlines are displayed, you can set the patterns (color, line weight, line style, and so on) of the lines.

The following code removes all gridlines from the chart:

```
Sub GridlineDemo()
    Dim Cht As Chart
    Set Cht = Charts("Chart1")
    With Cht
        With .Axes(xlValue)
            .HasMajorGridlines = False
            .HasMinorGridlines = False
        End With
        With Cht.Axes(xlValue)
            .HasMajorGridlines = False
            .HasMinorGridlines = False
        End With
    End With
End Sub
```

Data Labels—VBA Name: `DataLabels` and `DataLabel`

A series comprises data points. Some or all of the data points in a series may have data labels. The data labels may show the X (category) value, Y (value) value, or some custom value that you specify. A custom value can be literal or a cell reference. You can use VBA to

- Specify that all points of all series in a chart show data labels of a particular kind (either value or category) or show no data labels:

```
ActiveChart.ApplyDataLabels Type:=xlDataLabelsShowNone
```

- Specify that a particular series show the values (Y) as data labels:

```
With ActiveChart.SeriesCollection("Xdata")
    .HasDataLabels=True
    .ApplyDataLabels Type:= xlDataLabelsShowValue
End With
```

- Specify that a particular point on a series show a literal in its data label

```
With ActiveChart.SeriesCollection("Xdata").Points(1)
    .HasDataLabel=True
    .DataLabel.Text="MyLabel"
End With
```

- Put a formula (single cell reference) in the data label for a particular point on a series (note that you need to use the RC style in the formula):

```
With ActiveChart.SeriesCollection("Xdata").Points(1)
    .HasDataLabel=True
    .DataLabel.Text="=Sheet1!R1C1"
End With
```

You can also use code to specify the location and orientation of data labels with respect to the data points, similar to how you do it in the user interface.

Try the following macro to set the data labels for series Xdata:

```
Sub DataLabelDemo()
    With Charts("Chart1").SeriesCollection("Xdata")
        .HasDataLabels = True
        .ApplyDataLabels Type:=xlDataLabelsShowValue
        With .DataLabels
            .HorizontalAlignment = xlCenter
            .VerticalAlignment = xlCenter
            .Position = xlLabelPositionAbove
            .Orientation = xlUpward
        End With
    End With
End Sub
```

Notice that the properties and methods have names appropriate to their functions.

Chart Title, Legend, and Data Table—VBA Name: `ChartTitle`, `HasLegend`, and `HasDataTable`

You can specify the location, text, and text format of the chart title and legend with VBA. You can also specify whether the chart has a data table containing the source data. The following code adds a chart title to the chart, sets the font size to 16, and places the title at the top-left corner of the chart. The legend is moved to the bottom. It also adds the data table to the chart.

Notice that it is necessary to set the HasProperty value to True before working with any of these elements:

```
Sub DemoMisc()
    With Charts("Chart1")
        .HasTitle = True
        With .ChartTitle
            .Text = "Company Performance"
            .Font.Size = 16
            .Top = 0
            .Left = 0
        End With
        .HasLegend = True
        .Legend.Position = xlBottom
        .HasDataTable = True
    End With
End Sub
```

Trendlines and Error Bars—VBA Name: `Trendlines` and `ErrorBar`

If you have observed values, you might want to chart both the values and then add a trend line to help illustrate the trend. Excel offers several types of trend lines: linear, logarithmic, polynomial, power, exponential, and moving average. After you've added the trend line, you might want to add error bars to show how the actual values differ from the trend.

Figure 10.14 shows an XY chart plotting sales by year for a product line.

Figure 10.14
Historical sales figures in an XY chart. If you right-click the series and select Trend Line, Excel can add one of six different trend lines and forecast *n* years into the future.

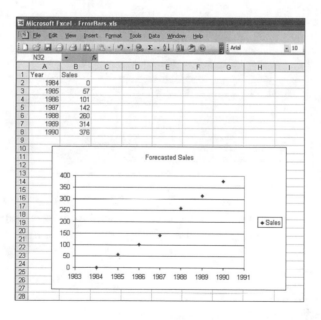

The following code adds a trend line to the chart based on a straight-line trend. It tells Excel to forecast forward 5 years and to display the series equation plus the R-squared value on the chart:

```
Sub AddTrendLine()
    Dim Ser As Series
    Dim Trnd As Trendline
    Dim Cht As Chart

    Set Cht = Worksheets("Sheet1").ChartObjects("Chart 2").Chart
    Set Ser = Cht.SeriesCollection(1)
    Set Trnd = Ser.Trendlines.Add(Type:=xlLinear, Forward:=5, _
        Backward:=0, DisplayEquation:=True, DisplayRSquared:=True)
    Trnd.Border.LineStyle = xlDot
    With Cht
        .HasTitle = True.ChartTitle.Characters.Text = "Forecasted Sales"
    End With
End Sub
```

After the trend line is added, you can see projected sales for the next 5 years. An R-Squared value near 1 means that the observed data fits fairly closely to the trend line (see Figure 10.15).

Figure 10.15
Use Excel's curve-fitting power to find a trend line for the existing points and then forecast 5 years into the future.

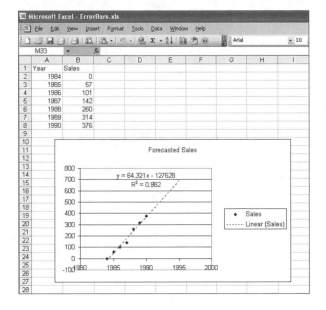

Whenever you have actual and forecasted data, it is useful to show error bars above and below the series. The following code adds error bars that extend a fixed 25 units above and below the sales data series:

```
Sub AddErrorBars()
    Dim Ser As Series
    Dim Trnd As Trendline
    Dim Cht As Chart

    Set Cht = Worksheets("Sheet1").ChartObjects("Chart 2").Chart
    Set Ser = Cht.SeriesCollection(1)
    Ser.ErrorBar Direction:=xlY, Include:=xlBoth, Type:=xlFixedValue, Amount:=25
End Sub
```

Error bars can be set to be above and/or below the bar and can be a fixed width, a percentage of the data point, a certain number of standard deviations, or a custom formula. In Figure 10.16, the fixed-width error bars show that each year's forecasted sales were within an acceptable error range except for 1987.

Figure 10.16
A myriad of error bar options is available.

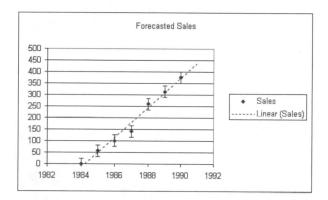

Table of Chart Types

Excel includes many built-in chart types. Now that you've learned to manipulate the elements of a chart, Table 10.1 presents you with the complete list of standard chart types and sub-types.

Table 10.1	**Excel's Standard Chart Types**	
Chart Type	**Description**	**Excel VBA Constant Identifier**
Column	Clustered Column	xlColumnClustered
	3D Clustered Column	xl3DColumnClustered
	Stacked Column	xlColumnStacked
	3D Stacked Column	xl3DColumnStacked
	100% Stacked Column	xlColumnStacked100
	3D 100% Stacked Column	xl3DColumnStacked100
	3D Column	xl3DColumn
Bar	Clustered Bar	xlBarClustered
	3D Clustered Bar	xl3DBarClustered
	Stacked Bar	xlBarStacked
	3D Stacked Bar	xl3DBarStacked
	100% Stacked Bar	xlBarStacked100
	3D 100% Stacked Bar	xl3DBarStacked100

continued

10

Table 10.1 Continued

Chart Type	Description	Excel VBA Constant Identifier
Line	Line	xlLine
	Line with Markers	xlLineMarkers
	Stacked Line	xlLineStacked
	Stacked Line with Markers	xlLineMarkersStacked
	100% Stacked Line	xlLineStacked100
	100% Stacked Line with Markers	xlLineMarkersStacked100
	3D Line	xl3DLine
Pie	Pie	xlPie
	Exploded Pie	xlPieExploded
	3D Pie	xl3DPie
	Exploded 3D Pie	xl3DPieExploded
	Pie of Pie	xlPieOfPie
	Bar of Pie	xlBarOfPie
XY (Scatter)	Scatter	xlXYScatter
	Scatter with Smoothed Lines	xlXYScatterSmooth
	Scatter with Smoothed Lines and No Data Markers	xlXYScatterSmoothNoMarkers
	Scatter with Lines	xlXYScatterLines
	Scatter with Lines and No Data Markers	xlXYScatterLinesNoMarkers
Bubble	Bubble	xlBubble
	Bubble with 3D effects	xlBubble3DEffect
Area	Area	xlArea
	3D Area	xl3DArea
	Stacked Area	xlAreaStacked
	3D Stacked Area	xl3DAreaStacked
	100% Stacked Area	xlAreaStacked100
	3D 100% Stacked Area	xl3DAreaStacked100
Doughnut	Doughnut	xlDoughnut
	Exploded Doughnut	xlDoughnutExploded
Radar	Radar	xlRadar
	Radar with Data Markers	xlRadarMarkers
	Filled Radar	xlRadarFilled

Table 10.1	Continued	
Chart Type	**Description**	**Excel VBA Constant Identifier**
Surface	3D Surface	`xlSurface`
	Surface (Top View)	`xlSurfaceTopView`
	3D Surface (wireframe)	`xlSurfaceWireframe`
	Surface (Top View wireframe)	`lSurfaceTopViewWireframe`
Stock Quotes	High-Low-Close	`xlStockHLC`
	Volume-High-Low-Close	`xlStockVHLC`
	Open-High-Low-Close	`xlStockOHLC`
	Volume-Open-High-Low-Close	`xlStockVOHLC`
Cylinder	Clustered Cylinder Column	`xlCylinderColClustered`
	Clustered Cylinder Bar	`xlCylinderBarClustered`
	Stacked Cylinder Column	`xlCylinderColStacked`
	Stacked Cylinder Bar	`xlCylinderBarStacked`
	100% Stacked Cylinder Column	`xlCylinderColStacked100`
	100% Stacked Cylinder Bar	`xlCylinderBarStacked100`
	3D Cylinder Column	`xlCylinderCol`
Cone	Clustered Cone Column	`xlConeColClustered`
	Clustered Cone Bar	`xlConeBarClustered`
	Stacked Cone Column	`xlConeColStacked`
	Stacked Cone Bar	`xlConeBarStacked`
	100% Stacked Cone Column	`xlConeColStacked100`
	100% Stacked Cone Bar	`xlConeBarStacked100`
	3D Cone Column	`xlConeCol`
Pyramid	Clustered Pyramid Column	`xlPyramidColClustered`
	Clustered Pyramid Bar	`xlPyramidBarClustered`
	Stacked Pyramid Column	`xlPyramidColStacked`
	Stacked Pyramid Bar	`xlPyramidBarStacked`
	100% Stacked Pyramid Column	`xlPyramidColStacked100`
	100% Stacked Pyramid Bar	`xlPyramidBarStacked100`
	3D Pyramid Column	`xlPyramidCol`

10

Do not be daunted by the size of this table. For all practical purposes, Cluster, Cone, Cylinder, and Pyramid types (and sub-types) are the same as the Column type except for appearance. You can look upon the Bar chart type as the Column chart type rotated 90°. In most cases, you can arrive at all sub-types of a given chart type by changing very few features of the basic sub-type.

For example, the only difference between an xlXYScatter chart and an xlXYScatterLines chart is that the SeriesCollection(1).Border.LineStyle is set to xlAutomatic for the xlXYScatterLines chart.

Details of Various Chart Types

Certain settings apply uniquely to various chart types. Although we've covered most of the conceivable options for bar and column charts, you should know the possibilities when working with other types of charts.

Settings for 3D Charts

All 3D charts have settings that apply to the appearance of the 3D effect. All these properties apply to the Chart object:

- Elevation—This controls the height from which the viewer sees the chart. With an elevation of 0, the top plane of each column is not visible to the viewer. With an elevation of 90, the viewer looks straight down upon the top of the chart.

- Rotation—This is a value from 0 to 359. With a small rotation number, you appear to be standing off to the right of the chart. With a number around 330 to 350, you appear to be standing a little to the left of the chart. Numbers in the 150-210 range are useful for turning the chart around and viewing it from the back.

- Perspective—Valid values are 0 to 100. With a high perspective value, the floor of the chart becomes distorted.

- BaseSize—The HeightPercent option controls how narrow or wide the base of the markers is. To have normal-size columns, set the height to 100% of the base. To make the columns skinnier, use a higher value, such as 150%.

- RightAngleAxes—This value must be set to False if you want to control perspective. Note that bar charts always have this value set to True, so perspective cannot be adjusted on a bar chart.

There are objects that apply only to 3D charts. You can now adjust the fill color of Walls and a Floor.

In addition, each series in the 3D chart includes a few properties. These control how closely each column is drawn to the next column:

- GapWidth—If this value is set to zero, then the individual columns in a series touch each other, making them appear as a series of stair steps. With a higher value, the gap between each column in a series grows, making the width of each column narrower. GapWidth must be applied to a new object called a ChartGroup. A single ChartGroup includes all series of the same chart type. Thus, if you had 2 series identified as 3DColumns and 1 series as Lines, the `Column3DGroup` object would control the `GapWidth` for all series formatted as 3DColumns.

- GapDepth—Again, if this value is zero, the columns in one series touch the columns in the next series. With a higher value, the depth of each column lessens. Interestingly, although this is set in the `Format` Series dialog box, the `GapDepth` must be the same for all series, so this property applies to the `Chart` object.

- ChartDepth—This controls how deep the floor of the chart appears to be. With a low `ChartDepth` of 20, the entire chart appears very flat, sort of like it was created by the people who used to make the Gumby and Pokey characters. With a large chart depth, you can see some floor between the two series. The `DepthPercent` property must be the same for all series, so it applies to the `Chart` object.

The following macro code adjusts all these values. The resulting chart is shown in Figure 10.17:

```
Sub Format3D()
    Dim Cht As Chart
    Set Cht = Worksheets("3d").ChartObjects(1).Chart
    With Cht
        .Elevation = 30
        .Perspective = 25
        .Rotation = 30
        .RightAngleAxes = False
        .HeightPercent = 150
        .AutoScaling = True
        .DepthPercent = 280
        .GapDepth = 160
    End With
    Cht.Column3DGroup.GapWidth = 0
    With Cht.Walls.Fill
        .TwoColorGradient Style:=msoGradientHorizontal, Variant:=1
        .Visible = True
        .ForeColor.SchemeColor = 2
        .BackColor.SchemeColor = 1
    End With
    With Cht.Floor.Fill
        .PresetGradient Style:=msoGradientHorizontal, Variant:=1, _
            PresetGradientType:=msoGradientCalmWater
        .Visible = True
    End With
End Sub
```

Settings for Pie Charts

Pie charts can be problematic, especially when a whole bunch of small categories are grouped together. The pie labels tend to overwrite each other, as in Figure 10.18. A couple of properties unique to pie charts can help with this.

Figure 10.17
You have exacting control over elevation, perspective, and rotation in 3D charts.

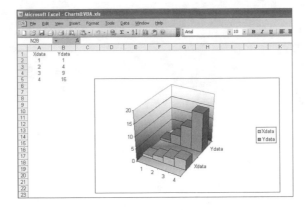

Figure 10.18
Data labels for the small pie slices tend to overwrite each other, leading to an unreadable chart.

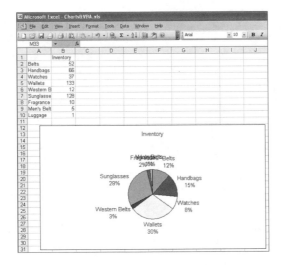

If only two data labels overwrite each other, rotating the angle of the first pie slice may solve the problem. Use the `FirstSliceAngle` property to rotate the pie. However, this exposes one of the most frustrating aspects of creating charts with VBA. If you are creating a chart in the user interface, you can tell whether labels are overlapping each other and know to adjust the `FirstAngleSlice`. There is no method or property in VBA that alerts you that your chart looks bad because of overlapping labels. I've found that using a `FirstSliceAngle` to rotate the chart 80–100° often gives the most room for the smaller pie slices:

```
Sub RotateFirstSlice()
    Dim Cht As Chart
    Set Cht = Worksheets("Pie").ChartObjects(1).Chart
    Cht.PieGroups(1).FirstSliceAngle = 100
End Sub
```

If many slices overwrite each other, then the solution might lie in taking all the slices under 5% of the total, grouping them into a single slice, and showing the detail from this slice in a bar chart. This can all be accomplished with VBA code:

```
Sub CreateBarOfPie()
    Dim Cht As Chart
    Dim CG As ChartGroup
    Set Cht = Worksheets("Pie").ChartObjects(1).Chart
    Cht.ChartType = xlBarOfPie
    Set CG = Cht.PieGroups(1)
    With CG
        .SplitType = xlSplitByPercentValue
        .SplitValue = 5 ' smaller than 5% combined
        .GapWidth = 200 ' gap between pie and bars
        .SecondPlotSize = 55 ' % relative to pie size
    End With
End Sub
```

The resulting chart is shown in Figure 10.19.

Figure 10.19
Using the
`xlBarOfPie` chart
type allows the smaller
categories to be com-
bined and exploded into
a separate bar. This usu-
ally alleviates the prob-
lems with overlapping
labels.

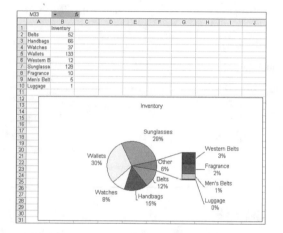

> **TIP**
>
> The leader lines shown in Figure 10.19 are automatically added by Excel whenever the data label is
> located more than a few points away from the corresponding data slice. To turn off these lines, set
> the chart's `HasLeaderLines` property to False.

Interactive Charts

Charts provide many opportunities to create interactivity. Even without using VBA, there are clever tricks you can use on a worksheet to show different charts as the user selects a value from a dropdown on a worksheet. Here, though, let's address the things that you can do with VBA.

Using Events with Charts

One frustration of working with charts is that as the shape of the data changes, Excel often changes aspects of the chart to fit the data. This can cause perfect formatting to go astray.

Luckily, some events associated with charts can be trapped. (To learn more about event programming, read Chapter 8, "Event Programming.") Code for ChartSheet events should be placed on the worksheet module for the sheet that contains the chart. If you need to do event-based programming for embedded charts, you need to write a class module to work when one of the chart events is triggered. Some very useful events for charts include the following:

- SeriesChange—Detects whenever a change is made to a series

- Calculate—Detects whenever the values in a chart change

- Activate—Detects that the chart has been activated

- Deactivate—Detects that the chart has been deactivated

The following macro runs whenever the chart is recalculated (for example, when you change the data series). It makes the series line on the sample XY chart red if the number of data points is greater than 5 and blue if less than or equal to 5:

```
Private Sub Chart_Calculate()
    Dim Ser As Series
    Set Ser = Me.SeriesCollection(1)
    If Ser.Points.Count > 5 Then
        Ser.Border.ColorIndex = 3
    Else
        Ser.Border.ColorIndex = 5
    End If
End Sub
```

Exporting Charts as Images

It is very easy to export a chart as a GIF image file. The following code saves a picture of a chart to your hard drive as a GIF file:

```
Sub SaveChart()
    Dim Cht as Chart
    Set Cht = Worksheets("Pie").ChartObjects(1).Chart
    Cht.Export FileName:="C:\MyChart.gif", FilterName:="GIF"
End Sub
```

This can come in useful in three possible scenarios:

- Displaying Charts in a Web Page—You might have a Web page that displays charts. It is easy to set up the Web page to always display <Img src="MyChart.gif">. You can use Excel to import data, produce the chart, and save it as MyChart.gif.

- Saving Resources—Charts are very memory intensive. I have seen client projects that can handle 40MB of numerical data with ease. I have also seen small 2MB files run out of memory when they have 128 charts in a workbook. If you need to display a hundred or more charts in a workbook, it might make sense to use VBA to individually create each chart, save it as a GIF file, and then load the GIF files into the workbook. The saved GIF files are not "live," but you can fit more images into the workbook than live charts without running into memory problems. To load a picture onto a worksheet, use this code:

```
ActiveSheet.Pictures.Insert("C:\MyChart.gif")
```

■ Displaying a Chart on a Userform—The only way to display a chart on a userform is to save the chart as a GIF file and then load the chart into an image on the userform. To load a chart into an `Image` control on a userform, use this code:

```
Me.Image1.Picture = LoadPicture("C:\MyChart.gif")
```

Drawing with X-Y Charts

I realize this is Excel and not Auto-CAD, but you can draw some pretty amazing shapes if you use Scatter charts. Figure 10.20 shows a really simple example: 15 points are plotted to draw a logo in the chart.

Figure 10.20
XY points were plotted in a scatter chart to draw this shape.

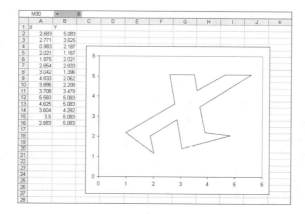

The concept of using XY charts for drawing has been perfected by Mala Singh of XLSoft Consulting in India. Mala has been able to use XY charts to draw just about anything. This blueprint is actually an XY chart in Excel (see Figure 10.21).

Figure 10.21
This blueprint is actually an XY Chart in Excel. It takes about 25 seconds to draw the chart.

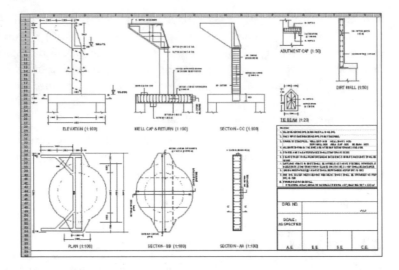

Custom Charts with VBA

It is beyond the scope of this book, but you can use VBA to draw some incredible charts that are not in the standard Excel toolkit. All the charts in this section were created with VBA and are courtesy of XLSoft Consulting.

Pie Bubble Chart

Figure 10.22 shows a pie bubble chart. A bubble chart is like a scatter (XY) chart with a third data series that is represented by the size of the bubble. The chart you see here is an extension of the bubble chart concept where a fourth parameter (the breakup of each bubble) is shown with the bubble depicted as a pie chart. This is done by having VBA loop through the number of points in the data series, and for each point, update a (hidden) pie chart with the corresponding value and paste a picture of the pie chart in place of the bubble for the point.data series.

Speedometer Chart

Figure 10.23 shows data plotted on a speedometer chart. It is perfect for dashboard reports for your boss. This is a customized XY chart with two autoshapes (circles to represent the outer periphery and dial hub). The circles are sized and placed each time the chart is updated. The rest of the chart is made up of several series and data labels that derive data from the spreadsheet. The actual dial reading, as well as the range of each color zone, is completely customizable. Several dials can be generated for different parameters to make an attractive dashboard. The various dials on the dashboard are pictures of individual speedometer charts: The dials are generated when you click a button that runs a macro to read data for the various parameters from an Excel table (one row of data for each dial), update the XY chart in the background, and paste a (static) picture of this in a selected worksheet. The code arranges the pictures in a grid to give you the dashboard.

Figure 10.22
Each bubble Is replaced with a picture of a pie chart.

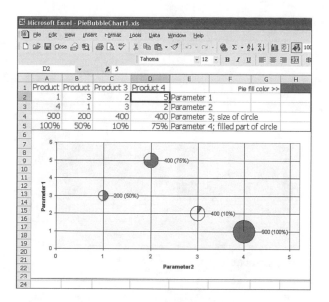

Figure 10.23
These custom speedometer charts are perfect for the management dashboard report.

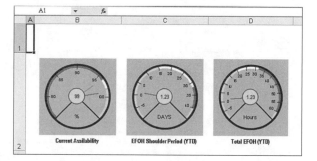

Supply Curve Chart

Figure 10.24 shows a macro-economic supply curve chart. Excel does not allow you to create a column chart with different widths for different columns. In a typical supply curve chart, the height of the bar indicates supplier cost, and the width of the bar indicates units supplied. This chart is created as an XY chart; colored rectangles are placed onto the plot area to simulate data columns. These rectangles are sized and placed according to the plot area scale so that they correctly represent the data.

Hierarchical Donut Chart

Conceptually, a hierarchical donut chart is like a pie chart with each slice exploded twice. The unique thing is that each layer holds the proportion of the one inside. Each data label optionally shows the data value, as well as what percent it is of the preceding layer(s) it encloses (see Figure 10.25).

10

Figure 10.24
In a macro-economic supply curve chart, both the height and width of the bars represent data.

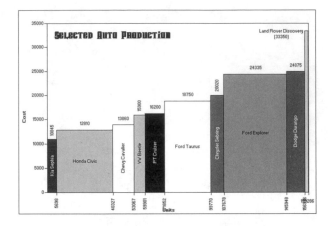

Figure 10.25
This is like a pie chart that has been exploded two times.

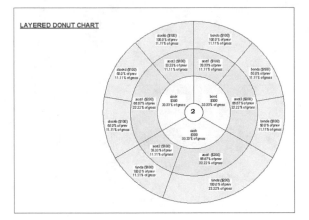

Next Steps

Charts provide a visual picture that can help to summarize data for a manager. In Chapter 11, "Data Mining with Advanced Filter," you will learn about using the Advanced Filter tools to quickly produce reports.

Data Mining with Advanced Filter

11

Advanced Filter Is Easier in VBA Than in Excel

The arcane Advanced Filter command is so hard in the Excel user interface that it is pretty rare to find someone who enjoys using it regularly. I predict that Microsoft will totally rework this command for Excel 2005 to make it easier to use.

However, in VBA, advanced filters are a joy to use. With a single line of code, you can rapidly extract a subset of records from a database or quickly get a unique list of values in any column. This is critical when you want to run reports for a specific region or customer.

Because not many people use the Advanced Filter feature, I will walk you through examples, using the user interface to build an advanced filter, and then show you the analogous code. You will be amazed at how complex the user interface seems and yet how easy it is to program a powerful advanced filter to extract records.

One reason why Advanced Filter is hard to use is that there are several different ways to use the filter. You must make three basic choices in the Advanced Filter dialog box. As each choice has two options, there are eight (2×2×2) possible combinations of these choices. The three choices are shown in Figure 11.1 and described here:

- **Action:** You can choose to Filter The List, In-Place or Copy To Another Location. Choosing to filter the records in place will hide rows. Choosing to copy to a new location will copy the records that match the filter to a new range.

- **Criteria:** You can filter with or without criteria. Filtering with criteria is appropriate for getting a subset of rows. Filtering without criteria is still useful when you want a subset of columns or when you are using the Unique Records Only option.

- **Unique:** You can choose to request Unique Records Only or all matching records. The Unique option makes the Advanced Filter command one of the fastest ways to find a unique list of values in one field.

Figure 11.1
The Advanced Filter dialog is complicated to use in the Excel user interface. Luckily, it is far easier in VBA.

Using Advanced Filter to Extract a Unique List of Values

One of the simplest uses of Advanced Filter is to extract a unique list of one field from a dataset. In this example, we want to get a unique list of customers from a sales report. We know that customer is in Column D of the dataset. We have an unknown number of records starting in cell A2 (Row 1 is the header row). There is nothing located to the right of the dataset.

Extracting a Unique List of Values with the User Interface

With the cell pointer anywhere in the data range, select Data, Filter, Advanced Filter from the menu. The first time that you use the Advanced Filter command on a worksheet, Excel automatically populates the List Range text box with the entire range of your dataset. On subsequent uses of the Advanced Filter command, this dialog box remembers the settings from the prior Advanced Filter.

Choose the Unique Records Only check box at the bottom of the dialog.

In the Action section, choose Copy To Another Location. Type **J1** in the Copy To text box. When you exit that field, Excel changes your entry to $J$1.

By default, Excel would copy all of the columns in the dataset. You can filter just the Customer column by either limiting the List Range to include only Column D, or by specifying one or more headings in the Copy To range. Either method has its own drawbacks.

Change the List Range to a Single Column

Edit the List range to point to the Customer column. In this case it means changing the default $A$1:$H$1127 to $D$1:$D$1127. The Advanced Filter dialog should appear, as shown in Figure 11.2.

Figure 11.2
These settings copy a unique list of customers from Column D to Column J.

The drawback of this method is that Excel remembers the list range on subsequent uses of the Advanced Filter command. If you later want to get a unique list of regions, you will be constantly respecifying the list range.

Change the List Range to a Single Column

With a little forethought before invoking the Advanced Filter command, you can allow Excel to keep the default list range of $A$1:$H$1127. In cell J1, type the Customer heading. In Figure 11.3, you leave the List Range field pointing to Columns A through H. Because the Copy To range of J1 already contains a valid heading from the list range, Excel copies data only from the Customer column. I prefer this method, particularly if you will be doing multiple advanced filters. Because Excel remembers the prior settings from the last Advanced Filter, it is more convenient to always filter the entire columns of the list range and limit the columns by setting up headings in the Copy To range.

Figure 11.3
By setting up a heading in the Copy To range of J1, you can avoid having to re-specify the list range for each Advanced Filter.

After using either of these methods to perform the Advanced Filter, a concise list of the unique customers appears in Column J (see Figure 11.4).

Extracting a Unique List of Values with VBA Code

In VBA, you use the .AdvancedFilter method to carry out the Advanced Filter command. Again, there are three choices to make.

- **Action:** Choose to either filter in place with the parameter Action:=xlFilterInPlace or to copy with Action:=xlFilterCopy. If you want to copy, you also have to specify the parameter CopyToRange:=Range("J1").

Figure 11.4

The Advanced Filter extracted a unique list of customers from the dataset and copied it to Column J. Extracting a unique list of values from a dataset has many uses. For example, you may now offer to produce a report for any or all of those customers.

	A	B	C	D	E	F	G	H	I	J	K
1	Region	Product	Date	Customer	Quantity	Revenue	COGS	Profit		Customer	
2	East	XYZ	7/24/04	QRS INC.	1000	22810	10220	12590		QRS INC.	
3	Central	DEF	7/25/04	JKL, CO	100	2257	984	1273		JKL, CO	
4	East	ABC	7/25/04	JKL, CO	500	10245	4235	6010		WXY, CO	
5	Central	XYZ	7/26/04	WXY, CO	500	11240	5110	6130		RST INC.	
6	Central	XYZ	7/27/04	WXY, CO	400	9204	4088	5116		FGH, CO	
7	East	DEF	7/27/04	RST INC.	800	18552	7872	10680		EFG S.A.	
8	East	XYZ	7/27/04	FGH, CO	400	9152	4088	5064		FGH LTD.	
9	Central	ABC	7/28/04	EFG S.A.	400	6860	3388	3472		UVW, INC.	
10	East	ABC	7/30/04	FGH LTD.	400	8456	3388	5068		MNO S.A.	
11	East	DEF	7/30/04	UVW, INC.	1000	21730	9840	11890		OPQ, INC.	
12	West	XYZ	7/30/04	FGH, CO	600	13806	6132	7674		TUV GMBH	
13	Central	ABC	8/1/04	FGH LTD.	800	16416	6776	9640		LMN PTY LTD	
14	East	XYZ	8/1/04	MNO S.A.	900	21015	9198	11817		DEF, LLC	
15	Central	XYZ	8/2/04	OPQ, INC.	900	21438	9198	12240		LMN LTD.	
16	East	XYZ	8/2/04	WXY, CO	900	21465	9198	12267		GHI, CO	
17	Central	ABC	8/4/04	EFG S.A.	300	6267	2541	3726		HIJ GMBH	
18	West	XYZ	8/4/04	WXY, CO	400	9144	4088	5056		MNO CORP	
19	Central	ABC	8/6/04	TUV GMBH	100	1740	847	893		LMN INC.	
20	East	XYZ	8/6/04	TUV GMBH	100	2401	1022	1379		VWX GMBH	
21	West	ABC	8/6/04	OPQ, INC.	1000	19110	8470	10640		RST PTY LTD	
22	East	ABC	8/7/04	JKL, CO	500	9345	4235	5110		BCD LTD.	
23	Central	XYZ	8/8/04	OPQ, INC.	900	21888	9198	12690		XYZ S.A.	
24	Central	ABC	8/8/04	LMN PTY LTD	600	11628	5082	6546		CDE INC.	
25	East	DEF	8/9/04	DEF, LLC	300	5961	2952	3009		XYZ GMBH	
26	West	DEF	8/11/04	JKL, CO	100	2042	984	1058		VWX PTY LTD	
27	Central	ABC	8/12/04	LMN PTY LTD	900	17505	7623	9882		RST S.A.	
28	East	ABC	8/13/04	LMN LTD.	800	14440	6776	7664		UVW INC.	
29	West	ABC	8/13/04	RST INC.	200	3552	1694	1858			

■ **Criteria:** To filter with criteria, include the parameter `CriteriaRange:=Range("L1:L2")`. To filter without criteria, omit this optional parameter.

■ **Unique:** To return only unique records, specify the parameter `Unique:=True`.

This code sets up a single column output range two columns to the right of the last used column in the data range.

By default, an advanced filter copies all columns. If you just want one particular column, use that column heading as the heading in the output range.

The first bit of code finds the final row and column in the dataset. Although it is not necessary to do so, I will define an object variable for the output range (`ORange`) and for the input range (`IRange`):

```
Sub GetUniqueCustomers()
    Dim IRange As Range
    Dim ORange As Range

    ' Find the size of today's dataset
    FinalRow = Cells(65536, 1).End(xlUp).Row
    NextCol = Cells(1, 255).End(xlToLeft).Column + 2

    ' Set up output range. Copy heading from D1 there
    Range("D1").Copy Destination:=Cells(1, NextCol)
    Set ORange = Cells(1, NextCol)

    ' Define the Input Range
    Set IRange = Range("A1").Resize(FinalRow, NextCol - 2)

    ' Do the Advanced Filter to get unique list of customers
    IRange.AdvancedFilter Action:=xlFilterCopy, CopyToRange:=ORange, Unique:=True

End Sub
```

This code is generic enough that it will not have to be rewritten if new columns are added to the dataset at a later time. Setting up the object variables for the input and output range is done for readability instead of out of necessity. The previous code could be written just as easily like this shortened version:

```
Sub UniqueCustomerRedux()
    ' Copy a heading to create an output range
    Range("J1").Value = Range("D1").Value
    ' Do the Advanced Filter
    Range("A1").CurrentRegion.AdvancedFilter xlFilterCopy, _
        CopyToRange:=Range("J1"), Unique:=True
End Sub
```

If you run either code on the sample dataset, you will get a unique list of customers off to the right of the data. In Figure 11.4, you will see the original dataset in Columns A:H and the unique customers in Column J. The key to getting a unique list of customers is copying the header from the Customer field to a blank cell and specifying this cell as the output range.

After you have the unique list of customers, you could easily sort the list and add an array formula to get total revenue by customer. The following code gets the unique list of customers, sorts it, and then builds an array formula to total revenue by customer. The results are shown in Figure 11.5.

```
Sub RevenueByCustomers()
    Dim IRange As Range
    Dim ORange As Range

    ' Find the size of today's dataset
    FinalRow = Cells(65536, 1).End(xlUp).Row
    NextCol = Cells(1, 255).End(xlToLeft).Column + 2

    ' Set up output range. Copy heading from D1 there
    Range("D1").Copy Destination:=Cells(1, NextCol)
    Set ORange = Cells(1, NextCol)

    ' Define the Input Range
    Set IRange = Range("A1").Resize(FinalRow, NextCol - 2)

    ' Do the Advanced Filter to get unique list of customers
    IRange.AdvancedFilter Action:=xlFilterCopy, _
        CopyToRange:=ORange, Unique:=True

    ' Determine how many unique customers we have
    LastRow = Cells(65536, NextCol).End(xlUp).Row

    ' Sort the data
    Cells(1, NextCol).Resize(LastRow, 1).Sort Key1:=Cells(1, NextCol), _
        Order1:=xlAscending, Header:=xlYes

    ' Add an array formula to get totals
    Cells(1, NextCol + 1).Value = "Revenue"
    Cells(2, NextCol + 1).FormulaArray = _
        "=SUM((R2C4:R" & FinalRow & "C4=RC[-1])*R2C6:R" & FinalRow & "C6)"
    If LastRow > 2 Then
        Cells(2, NextCol + 1).Copy Cells(3, NextCol + 1).Resize(LastRow - 2, 1)
    End If

End Sub
```

Figure 11.5

This simple macro produced a summary report by customer from a lengthy dataset. Using `AdvancedFilter` is the key to powerful macros such as these.

J	K
Customer	Revenue
BCD LTD.	101016
CDE INC.	105650
DEF, LLC	1543677
EFG S.A.	947025
FGH LTD.	1448081
FGH, CO	53170
GHI, CO	104205
HIJ GMBH	768598
JKL, CO	820384
LMN INC.	113114
LMN LTD.	130220
LMN PTY LTD	1277848
MNO CORP	92544
MNO S.A.	97107
OPQ, INC.	1529209
QRS INC.	1274519
RST INC.	60109
RST PTY LTD	77518
RST S.A.	115202
TUV GMBH	977561
UVW INC.	92789
UVW, INC.	104323
VWX GMBH	105937
VWX PTY LTD	97545
WXY, CO	1154712
XYZ GMBH	106442
XYZ S.A.	117119

Another use of a unique list of values is to quickly populate a list box or a combo box on a userform. Say that you have a macro that can run a report for any one specific customer. To allow your clients to choose which customers to report, create a simple userform. Add a list box to the userform and set the list box's `MultiSelect` property to `1-fmMultiSelectMulti`. I named my form frmReport. In addition to the list box, I have four command buttons: OK, Cancel, Mark All, Clear All. The code to run the form follows. Note the `Userform_Initialize` procedure includes an Advanced Filter to get the unique list of customers from the dataset:

```
Private Sub CancelButton_Click()
    Unload Me
End Sub

Private Sub cbSubAll_Click()
    For i = 0 To lbCust.ListCount - 1
        Me.lbCust.Selected(i) = True
    Next i
End Sub

Private Sub cbSubClear_Click()
    For i = 0 To lbCust.ListCount - 1
        Me.lbCust.Selected(i) = False
    Next i
End Sub

Private Sub OKButton_Click()
    For i = 0 To lbCust.ListCount - 1
        If Me.lbCust.Selected(i) = True Then
            ' Call a routine to produce this report
            RunCustReport WhichCust:=Me.lbCust.List(i)
```

```
        End If
    Next i
    Unload Me
End Sub

Private Sub UserForm_Initialize()
    Dim IRange As Range
    Dim ORange As Range

    ' Find the size of today's dataset
    FinalRow = Cells(65536, 1).End(xlUp).Row
    NextCol = Cells(1, 255).End(xlToLeft).Column + 2

    ' Set up output range. Copy heading from D1 there
    Range("D1").Copy Destination:=Cells(1, NextCol)
    Set ORange = Cells(1, NextCol)

    ' Define the Input Range
    Set IRange = Range("A1").Resize(FinalRow, NextCol - 2)

    ' Do the Advanced Filter to get unique list of customers
    IRange.AdvancedFilter Action:=xlFilterCopy, _
        CopyToRange:=ORange, Unique:=True

    ' Determine how many unique customers we have
    LastRow = Cells(65536, NextCol).End(xlUp).Row

    ' Sort the data
    Cells(1, NextCol).Resize(LastRow, 1).Sort Key1:=Cells(1, NextCol), _
        Order1:=xlAscending, Header:=xlYes

With Me.lbCust
    .RowSource = ""
    .List = Cells(2, NextCol).Resize(LastRow - 1, 1).Value
End With

    ' Erase the temporary list of customers
    Cells(1, NextCol).Resize(LastRow, 1).Clear
End Sub
```

Launch this form with a simple module such as this:

```
Sub ShowCustForm()
    frmReport.Show
End Sub
```

Your clients are presented with a list of all valid customers from the dataset. Because the list box's MultiSelect property is set to allow it, they can select any number of customers, as shown in Figure 11.6.

Figure 11.6

Your clients will have a list of customers from which to select quickly. Using an advanced filter on even a 60,000-row dataset is far faster than setting up a class to populate the list box.

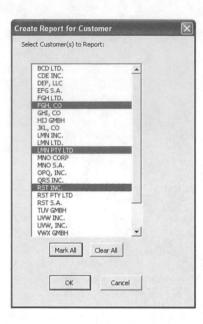

Getting Unique Combinations of Two or More Fields

To get all unique combinations of two (or more) fields, build the output range to include the additional fields. This code sample builds a list of unique combinations of two fields; Customer and Product:

```
Sub UniqueCustomerProduct()
    Dim IRange As Range
    Dim ORange As Range

    ' Find the size of today's dataset
    FinalRow = Cells(65536, 1).End(xlUp).Row
    NextCol = Cells(1, 255).End(xlToLeft).Column + 2

    ' Set up output range. Copy headings from D1 & B1
    Range("D1").Copy Destination:=Cells(1, NextCol)
    Range("B1").Copy Destination:=Cells(1, NextCol + 1)
    Set ORange = Cells(1, NextCol).Resize(1, 2)

    ' Define the Input Range
    Set IRange = Range("A1").Resize(FinalRow, NextCol - 2)

    ' Do the Advanced Filter to get unique list of customers & product
    IRange.AdvancedFilter Action:=xlFilterCopy, _
        CopyToRange:=ORange, Unique:=True

    ' Determine how many unique rows we have
    LastRow = Cells(65536, NextCol).End(xlUp).Row

    ' Sort the data
```

```
Cells(1, NextCol).Resize(LastRow, 2).Sort Key1:=Cells(1, NextCol), _
    Order1:=xlAscending, Key2:=Cells(1, NextCol + 1), _
    Order2:=xlAscending, Header:=xlYes

End Sub
```

In the result shown in Figure 11.7, you can see that customer BCD buys only one product, and customer CDE buys three products. This might be useful to use as a guide in running reports on either customer by product or product by customer.

Figure 11.7

By including two columns in the Output range on a Unique Values query, we get every combination of Customer and Product.

J	K
Customer	Product
BCD LTD.	ABC
CDE INC.	ABC
CDE INC.	DEF
CDE INC.	XYZ
DEF, LLC	XYZ
EFG S.A.	ABC
EFG S.A.	DEF
EFG S.A.	XYZ
FGH LTD.	ABC
FGH LTD.	DEF
FGH LTD.	XYZ
FGH, CO	ABC
FGH, CO	DEF
FGH, CO	XYZ
GHI, CO	ABC
GHI, CO	DEF
GHI, CO	XYZ
HIJ GMBH	ABC
HIJ GMBH	DEF
HIJ GMBH	XYZ
JKL, CO	ABC
JKL, CO	DEF
JKL, CO	XYZ
LMN INC.	ABC
LMN INC.	DEF
LMN INC.	XYZ
LMN LTD.	ABC
LMN LTD.	DEF
LMN LTD.	XYZ

NOTE Using advanced filters to get a unique set of values is usually the only case where you will perform an advanced filter without using criteria cells.

Using Advanced Filter with Criteria Ranges

As the name implies, Advanced Filter is usually used to filter records—in other words, to get a subset of data. You specify the subset by setting up a criteria range. Even if you are familiar with criteria, be sure to check out using the powerful Boolean formula in criteria ranges later in this chapter, in the section "The Most Complex Criteria—Replacing the List of Values with a Condition Created as the Result of a Formula."

Set up a criteria range in a blank area of the worksheet. A criteria range always includes two or more rows. The first row of the criteria range contains one or more field header values to match the one(s) in the data range you want to filter. The second row contains a value showing what records to extract. In Figure 11.8, range J1:J2 is the criteria range and range L1 is the output range.

Figure 11.8

This is about the simplest criteria there is; to learn a unique list of products purchased by customer CDE, set up the criteria range shown in J1:J2.

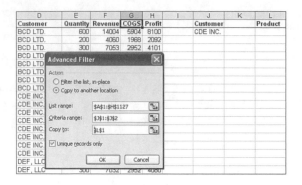

In the Excel user interface, to extract a unique list of products that were purchased by customer ABC, select Advanced Filter and set up the Advanced Filter dialog as shown earlier in Figure 11.8. The results are shown in Figure 11.9.

In VBA, you would use the following code to perform an equivalent advanced filter.

```
Sub UniqueProductsOneCustomer()
    Dim IRange As Range
    Dim ORange As Range
    Dim CRange As Range

    ' Find the size of today's dataset
    FinalRow = Cells(65536, 1).End(xlUp).Row
    NextCol = Cells(1, 255).End(xlToLeft).Column + 2

    ' Set up the Output Range with one customer
    Cells(1, NextCol).Value = Range("D1").Value
    ' In reality, this value should be passed from the userform
    Cells(2, NextCol).Value = "CDE INC."
    Set CRange = Cells(1, NextCol).Resize(2, 1)

    ' Set up output range. Copy heading from B1 there
    Range("B1").Copy Destination:=Cells(1, NextCol + 2)
    Set ORange = Cells(1, NextCol + 2)

    ' Define the Input Range
    Set IRange = Range("A1").Resize(FinalRow, NextCol - 2)

    ' Do the Advanced Filter to get unique list of customers & product
    IRange.AdvancedFilter Action:=xlFilterCopy, _
        CriteriaRange:=CRange, CopyToRange:=ORange, Unique:=True
    ' The above could also be written as:
    'IRange.AdvancedFilter xlFilterCopy, CRange, ORange, True

    ' Determine how many unique rows we have
    LastRow = Cells(65536, NextCol + 2).End(xlUp).Row

    ' Sort the data
    Cells(1, NextCol + 2).Resize(LastRow, 1).Sort Key1:=Cells(1, NextCol + 2), _
        Order1:=xlAscending, Header:=xlYes

End Sub
```

Figure 11.9
The results of the advanced filter that uses a criteria range and asks for a unique list of products. Of course, more complex and interesting criteria can be built.

	B	C	D	E	F	G	H	I	J	K	L	M
1	Product	Date	Customer	Quantity	Revenue	COGS	Profit		Customer		Product	
2	ABC	11/4/04	BCD LTD.	800	14004	5904	8100		CDE INC.		ABC	
3	ABC	1/15/05	BCD LTD.	200	4060	1968	2092				DEF	
4	ABC	1/19/05	BCD LTD.	300	7053	2952	4101				XYZ	
5	ABC	3/15/05	BCD LTD.	500	11530	4920	6610					
6	ABC	3/24/05	BCD LTD.	800	18072	8176	9896					
7	ABC	5/28/05	BCD LTD.	800	15104	6776	8328					
8	ABC	8/21/05	BCD LTD.	700	12131	5929	6202					
9	ABC	11/29/05	BCD LTD.	900	19062	9198	9864					
10	DEF	11/21/04	CDE INC.	800	19520	7872	11648					
11	XYZ	2/9/05	CDE INC.	400	9240	4088	5152					
12	XYZ	2/10/05	CDE INC.	1000	22840	10220	12620					
13	DEF	3/10/05	CDE INC.	600	14634	6132	8502					
14	ABC	3/19/05	CDE INC.	100	1819	847	972					
15	XYZ	6/17/05	CDE INC.	100	2538	1022	1516					
16	ABC	7/19/05	CDE INC.	900	18756	9198	9558					
17	ABC	9/6/05	CDE INC.	700	16303	6888	9415					

Joining Multiple Criteria with a Logical OR

You may wish to filter records that match one criteria or another. For example, extract customers who purchased either product ABC or product XYZ. This is called a *logical OR* criteria.

When your criteria should be joined by a logical OR, place the criteria on subsequent rows of the criteria range. For example, the criteria range shown in J1:J3 of Figure 11.10 tells you which customers order product ABC or product XYZ.

Figure 11.10
Place criteria on successive rows to join them with an OR. This criteria range gets customers who ordered either product ABC or XYZ.

I	J	K	L	M
	Product		Customer	
	ABC			
	XYZ			

Joining Two Criteria with a Logical AND

Other times, you will want to filter records that match one criteria *and* another criteria. For example, you may want to extract records where the product sold was XYZ and the region was the West region. This is called a *logical AND*.

To join two criteria by AND, put both criteria on the same row of the criteria range. For example, the criteria range shown in J1:K2 of Figure 11.11 gets the customers who ordered product XYZ in the West region.

Figure 11.11
Place criteria on the same row to join them with an AND. The criteria range in J1:K2 gets customers from the West region who ordered product XYZ.

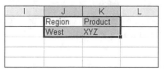

I	J	K	L
	Region	Product	
	West	XYZ	

Other Slightly Complex Criteria Ranges

The criteria range shown in Figure 11.12 is based on two different fields. They are joined with an OR. The query finds all records from either the West region or records where the product is XYZ.

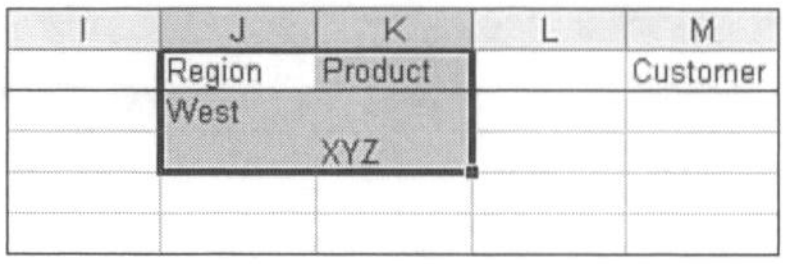

Figure 11.12
The criteria range in J1:K3 returns records where either the Region is West or the Product is XYZ.

> **TIP**
> Joining two criteria with OR might be useful where new California legislation will impact shipments made to California or products sourced at the California XYZ plant.

The Most Complex Criteria—Replacing the List of Values with a Condition Created as the Result of a Formula

It is possible to have a criteria range with multiple logical AND and logical OR criteria joined together. Although this may work in some situations, there are others where it quickly gets out of hand. Luckily, Excel allows for criteria where the records are selected as the result of a formula to handle this situation.

CASE STUDY

Case Study—Working with Very Complex Criteria

Your clients so loved the "Create a Customer" report, they hired you to write a new report. In this case, they could select any customer, any product, any region, or any combination of them. You can quickly adapt the frmReport userform to show three list boxes, as shown in Figure 11.13.

In your first test, imagine that you select two customers and two products. In this case, your program has to build a 5-row criteria range, as shown in Figure 11.14. This isn't too bad.

This gets crazy if someone selects 10 products, all regions but the house region, and all customers except the internal customer. Your criteria range would need unique combinations of the selected fields. This could easily be 10 products times 9 regions times 499 customers, or more than 44,000 rows of criteria range. You can quickly end up with a criteria range that spans thousands of rows and three columns. I was once foolish enough to actually try running an Advanced Filter with such a criteria range. It would still be trying to compute if I hadn't rebooted the computer.

The solution for this report is to replace the lists of values with a formula-based condition.

Figure 11.13
This super-flexible form lets clients run any types of reports that they can imagine. It creates some nightmarish criteria ranges, unless you know the way out.

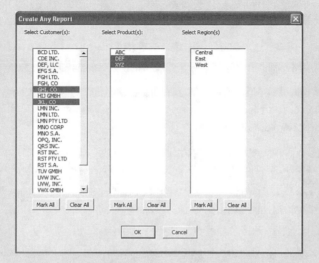

Figure 11.14
This criteria range returns any records where the two selected customers ordered any of the two selected products.

I	J	K	L
	Customer	Product	
	GHI, CO	DEF	
	GHI, CO	XYZ	
	JKL, CO	DEF	
	JKL, CO	XYZ	

11

Setting Up a Condition as the Result of a Formula

Amazingly, there is an incredibly obscure version of Advanced Filter criteria that can replace the 44,000-row criteria range in the case study. In the alternate form of criteria range, the top row is left blank. There is no heading above the criteria. The criteria set up in Row 2 are a formula that results in True or False. If the formula contains any relative references to Row 2 of the input range, then Excel compares that formula to every row of the input range, one by one.

For example, if we wanted all records where the Gross Profit Percentage was below 53%, the formula built in J2 would reference the Profit in H2 and the Revenue in F2. We would leave J1 blank to tell Excel that we are using a formula-based criterion. Cell J2 would contain the formula =(H2/F2)<0.53. The criteria range for the advanced filter would be specified as J1:J2.

As Excel performs the Advanced Filter, it logically copies the formula and applies it to all rows in the database. Anywhere that the formula evaluates to True, the record is included in the output range.

This is incredibly powerful and it runs remarkably quickly. You can combine multiple formulas in adjacent columns or rows to join the formula criteria with AND or OR, just as you do with regular criteria.

Case Study—Using Formula Based Conditions in the Excel User Interface

You can use formula-based conditions to easily solve the report introduced in the prior case study.

To illustrate, off to the right of the criteria range, set up a column of cells with the list of selected customers. Assign a name to the range such as `MyCust`. In cell J2 of the criteria range enter a formula such as

`=Not(ISNA(Match(D2,MyCust,False)))`.

To the right of the `MyCust` range, set up a range with a list of selected products. Assign this range the name of `MyProd`. In the K2 of the criteria range, add a formula to check products, `=NOT(ISNA(Match(B2,MyProd,False)))`.

To the right of the `MyProd` range, set up a range with a list of selected regions. Assign this range the name of `MyRegion`. In L2 of the criteria range, add a formula to check for selected Regions, `=NOT(ISNA(Match(A2,MyRegion,False)))`.

Now, with a criteria range of J1:L2, you can effectively retrieve the records matching any combination of selections from the user form.

Using Formula Based Conditions with VBA

The following is the code for this new userform. Note the logic in OKButton_Click that builds the formula. Figure 11.15 shows the Excel sheet just before the Advanced Filter is run.

```
Private Sub CancelButton_Click()
    Unload Me
End Sub

Private Sub cbSubAll_Click()
    For i = 0 To lbCust.ListCount - 1
        Me.lbCust.Selected(i) = True
    Next i
End Sub

Private Sub cbSubClear_Click()
    For i = 0 To lbCust.ListCount - 1
        Me.lbCust.Selected(i) = False
    Next i
End Sub

Private Sub CommandButton1_Click()
    ' Clear all products
    For i = 0 To lbProduct.ListCount - 1
        Me.lbProduct.Selected(i) = False
    Next i
End Sub

Private Sub CommandButton2_Click()
    ' Mark all products
    For i = 0 To lbProduct.ListCount - 1
        Me.lbProduct.Selected(i) = True
```

```vba
        Next i
    End Sub

    Private Sub CommandButton3_Click()
        ' Clear all regions
        For i = 0 To lbRegion.ListCount - 1
            Me.lbRegion.Selected(i) = False
        Next i
    End Sub

    Private Sub CommandButton4_Click()
        ' Mark all regions
        For i = 0 To lbRegion.ListCount - 1
            Me.lbRegion.Selected(i) = True
        Next i
    End Sub

    Private Sub OKButton_Click()
        Dim CRange As Range, IRange As Range, ORange As Range
        ' Build a complex criteria that ANDS all choices together
        NextCCol = 10
        NextTCol = 15

        For j = 1 To 3
            Select Case j
                Case 1
                    MyControl = "lbCust"
                    MyColumn = 4
                Case 2
                    MyControl = "lbProduct"
                    MyColumn = 2
                Case 3
                    MyControl = "lbRegion"
                    MyColumn = 1
            End Select
            NextRow = 2
            ' Check to see what was selected.
            For i = 0 To Me.Controls(MyControl).ListCount - 1
                If Me.Controls(MyControl).Selected(i) = True Then
                    Cells(NextRow, NextTCol).Value = _
                        Me.Controls(MyControl).List(i)
                    NextRow = NextRow + 1
                End If
            Next i
            ' If anything was selected, build a new criteria formula
            If NextRow > 2 Then
                ' the reference to Row 2 must be relative in order to work
                MyFormula = "=NOT(ISNA(MATCH(RC" & MyColumn & ",R2C" & NextTCol & _
                    ":R" & NextRow - 1 & "C" & NextTCol & ",False)))"
                Cells(2, NextCCol).FormulaR1C1 = MyFormula
                NextTCol = NextTCol + 1
                NextCCol = NextCCol + 1
            End If
        Next j
        Unload Me
```

11

```
        ' Figure 11.14 shows the worksheet at this point
        ' if we built any criteria, define the criteria range
        If NextCCol > 10 Then
            Set CRange = Range(Cells(1, 10), Cells(2, NextCCol - 1))
            Set IRange = Range("A1").CurrentRegion
            Set ORange = Cells(1, 20)
            IRange.AdvancedFilter xlFilterCopy, CRange, ORange

            ' Clear out the criteria
            Cells(1, 10).Resize(1, 10).EntireColumn.Clear
        End If

        ' At this point, the matching records are in T1

End Sub

Private Sub UserForm_Initialize()
    Dim IRange As Range
    Dim ORange As Range

    ' Find the size of today's dataset
    FinalRow = Cells(65536, 1).End(xlUp).Row
    NextCol = Cells(1, 255).End(xlToLeft).Column + 2

    ' Define the input range
    Set IRange = Range("A1").Resize(FinalRow, NextCol - 2)

    ' Set up output range for Customer. Copy heading from D1 there
    Range("D1").Copy Destination:=Cells(1, NextCol)
    Set ORange = Cells(1, NextCol)

    ' Do the Advanced Filter to get unique list of customers
    IRange.AdvancedFilter Action:=xlFilterCopy, CriteriaRange:="", _
        CopyToRange:=ORange, Unique:=True

    ' Determine how many unique customers we have
    LastRow = Cells(65536, NextCol).End(xlUp).Row

    ' Sort the data
    Cells(1, NextCol).Resize(LastRow, 1).Sort Key1:=Cells(1, NextCol), _
        Order1:=xlAscending, Header:=xlYes

    With Me.lbCust
        .RowSource = ""
        FinalRow = Range("J65536").End(xlUp).Row
        For Each cell In Cells(2, NextCol).Resize(LastRow - 1, 1)
            .AddItem cell.Value
        Next cell
    End With

    ' Erase the temporary list of customers
    Cells(1, NextCol).Resize(LastRow, 1).Clear
```

```vba
    ' Set up output range for product. Copy heading from D1 there
    Range("B1").Copy Destination:=Cells(1, NextCol)
    Set ORange = Cells(1, NextCol)

    ' Do the Advanced Filter to get unique list of customers
    IRange.AdvancedFilter Action:=xlFilterCopy, _
        CopyToRange:=ORange, Unique:=True

    ' Determine how many unique customers we have
    LastRow = Cells(65536, NextCol).End(xlUp).Row

    ' Sort the data
    Cells(1, NextCol).Resize(LastRow, 1).Sort Key1:=Cells(1, NextCol), _
        Order1:=xlAscending, Header:=xlYes

    With Me.lbProduct
        .RowSource = ""
        FinalRow = Range("J65536").End(xlUp).Row
        For Each cell In Cells(2, NextCol).Resize(LastRow - 1, 1)
            .AddItem cell.Value
        Next cell
    End With

    ' Erase the temporary list of customers
    Cells(1, NextCol).Resize(LastRow, 1).Clear

    ' Set up output range for Region. Copy heading from A1 there
    Range("A1").Copy Destination:=Cells(1, NextCol)
    Set ORange = Cells(1, NextCol)

    ' Do the Advanced Filter to get unique list of customers
    ' Figure 11.15 shows the worksheet state just before this line
    IRange.AdvancedFilter Action:=xlFilterCopy, CopyToRange:=ORange, _
        Unique:=True

    ' Determine how many unique customers we have
    LastRow = Cells(65536, NextCol).End(xlUp).Row

    ' Sort the data
    Cells(1, NextCol).Resize(LastRow, 1).Sort Key1:=Cells(1, NextCol), _
        Order1:=xlAscending, Header:=xlYes

    With Me.lbRegion
        .RowSource = ""
        FinalRow = Range("J65536").End(xlUp).Row
        For Each cell In Cells(2, NextCol).Resize(LastRow - 1, 1)
            .AddItem cell.Value
        Next cell
    End With

    ' Erase the temporary list of customers
    Cells(1, NextCol).Resize(LastRow, 1).Clear

End Sub
```

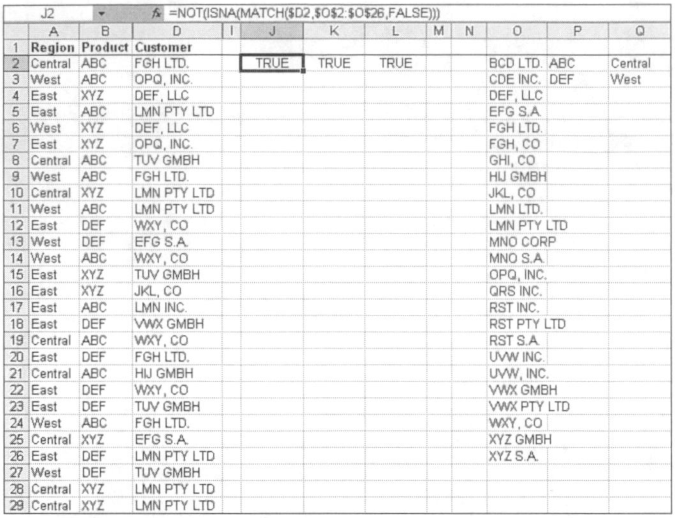

Figure 11.15
The worksheet just
before the macro runs
the advanced filter.

	J2	▼	fx	=NOT(ISNA(MATCH($D2,$O$2:$O$26,FALSE)))								

	A	B	D	I	J	K	L	M	N	O	P	Q
1	Region	Product	Customer									
2	Central	ABC	FGH LTD.		TRUE	TRUE	TRUE			BCD LTD.	ABC	Central
3	West	ABC	OPQ, INC.							CDE INC.	DEF	West
4	East	XYZ	DEF, LLC							DEF, LLC		
5	East	ABC	LMN PTY LTD							EFG S.A.		
6	West	XYZ	DEF, LLC							FGH LTD.		
7	East	XYZ	OPQ, INC.							FGH, CO		
8	Central	ABC	TUV GMBH							GHI, CO		
9	West	ABC	FGH LTD.							HIJ GMBH		
10	Central	XYZ	LMN PTY LTD							JKL, CO		
11	West	ABC	LMN PTY LTD							LMN LTD.		
12	East	DEF	WXY, CO							LMN PTY LTD		
13	West	DEF	EFG S.A.							MNO CORP		
14	West	ABC	WXY, CO							MNO S.A.		
15	East	XYZ	TUV GMBH							OPQ, INC.		
16	East	XYZ	JKL, CO							QRS INC.		
17	East	ABC	LMN INC.							RST INC.		
18	East	DEF	VWX GMBH							RST PTY LTD		
19	Central	ABC	WXY, CO							RST S.A.		
20	East	DEF	FGH LTD.							UVW INC.		
21	Central	ABC	HIJ GMBH							UVW, INC.		
22	East	DEF	WXY, CO							VWX GMBH		
23	East	DEF	TUV GMBH							VWX PTY LTD		
24	West	ABC	FGH LTD.							WXY, CO		
25	Central	XYZ	EFG S.A.							XYZ GMBH		
26	East	DEF	LMN PTY LTD							XYZ S.A.		
27	West	DEF	TUV GMBH									
28	Central	XYZ	LMN PTY LTD									
29	Central	XYZ	LMN PTY LTD									

11

Figure 11.15 shows the worksheet just before the AdvancedFilter method is called. The user has selected customers, products, and regions. The macro has built temporary tables in Columns O, P, Q to show which values the user selected. The criteria range is J1:L2. That criteria formula in J2 looks to see whether the value in $D2 is in the list of selected customers in O. The formulae in K2 and L2 compare $B2 to Column P and $A2 to Column Q.

CAUTION

Excel VBA help says that if you do not specify a criteria range, then no criteria is used. This is not true in Excel 2003—if no criteria range is specified, the AdvancedFilter inherits the CriteriaRange from the prior AdvancedFilter. You should include CriteriaRange:="" to clear the prior value.

Using Formula-Based Conditions to Return Above-Average Records

The formula-based conditions formula criteria are cool, but are a rarely used feature in a rarely used function. There are some interesting business applications that use this technique. For example, this criteria formula would find all the above-average rows in the dataset:

```
=$A2>Average($A$2:$A$60000)
```

Being Prepared for No Records After the Filter

If you are doing a filter, you might encounter a day when no records match the criteria. This is easy to detect: The output range will have nothing below the heading in Row 1. I usually add code to find the last row in the output range after performing the Advanced Filter. If the final row is 1, I notify the user that the report is not going to be meaningful and exit out of the procedure.

Using "Filter in Place" in Advanced Filter

It is possible to filter a large dataset in place. In this case, you do not need an output range. You would normally specify criteria range—otherwise you return 100% of the records and there is no need to do the AutoFilter!

In the user interface of Excel, doing a Filter In Place makes sense: You can easily peruse the filtered list looking for something in particular.

Doing a Filter In Place in VBA is a little less convenient. The only good way to programmatically peruse through the filtered records is to use the xlCellTypeVisible option of the SpecialCells method. In the Excel user interface, the equivalent action is to select Edit, Go To from the menu. On the Go To dialog, choose the Special button. In the Go To Special dialog, select Visible Cells Only, as shown in Figure 11.16.

Figure 11.16
The Filter In Place option hides rows that do not match the selected criteria, but the only way to programmatically see the matching records is to do the equivalent of selecting Visible Cells Only from the Go To Special dialog box.

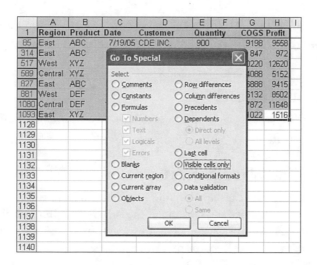

To do a Filter In Place, use the constant XLFilterInPlace as the Action parameter in the AdvancedFilter command and remove the CopyToRange from the command:

```
lRange.AdvancedFilter Action:=xlFilterInPlace, CriteriaRange:=CRange,
➥Unique:=False
```

Then the programmatic equivalent to loop through Visible Cells Only is this code:

```
For Each cell In Range("A2:A" & FinalRow).SpecialCells(xlCellTypeVisible)
    Ctr = Ctr + 1
Next cell
MsgBox Ctr & " cells match the criteria"
```

Catching No Records When Using Filter In Place

Just as when using Copy, you have to watch out for the possibility of having no records match the criteria. In this case, however, it is more difficult to realize that nothing is returned. You generally find out when the `SpecialCells` method returns a Run-time error 1004—no cells were found.

To catch this condition, you have to set up an error trap to anticipate the 1004 error with the `.SpecialCells` method. (See Chapter 23, "Handling Errors," for more information on catching errors.)

```
    On Error GoTo NoRecs
    For Each cell In Range("A2:A" & FinalRow).SpecialCells(xlCellTypeVisible)
        Ctr = Ctr + 1
    Next cell
    On Error GoTo 0
    MsgBox Ctr & " cells match the criteria"
    Exit Sub
NoRecs:
    MsgBox "No records match the criteria"
End Sub
```

This error trap works because I specifically exclude the header row from the SpecialCells range. The header row is always visible after an advanced filter. Including it in the range and would prevent the 1004 error from being raised.

Showing All Records After Filter In Place

After doing a Filter In Place, you can get all records to show again by using `.ShowAllData`:

`ActiveSheet.ShowAllData`

Using Filter In Place with Unique Records Only

It is possible to use `FilterInPlace` and Unique Records Only. However, when you specified an output range of only Product and Customer, the Advanced Filter was able to give you only the unique combinations of Customer and Product. If you ask for unique records from a dataset with 10 fields, the only records that will not be shown are those records where all 10 fields are exact duplicates.

The Real Workhorse: `xlFilterCopy` with All Records Instead of Unique Records Only

The examples at the beginning of this chapter talked about using `xlFilterCopy` to get a unique list of values in a field. We used unique lists of customer, region, and product to populate the list boxes in our report specification userforms.

A more common scenario, though, is to use an advanced filter to return all records that match the criteria. After the client selects which customer to report, an advanced filter can extract all records for that customer.

In all these examples, you want to leave the Unique Records Only check box unselected. You do this in VBA by specifying `Unique:=False` as a parameter to the `AdvancedFilter` method.

This is easy to do and there are some powerful options. If you need only a subset of fields for a report, then copy only those field headings to the output range. If you want to resequence the fields to appear exactly as you need them in the report, you can do this by changing the sequence of the headings in the output range.

I will walk you through three quick examples to show the options available.

Copying All Columns

To copy all columns, specify a single blank cell as the output range. You will get all columns for those records that match the criteria as shown in Figure 11.17.

```
Sub AllColumnsOneCustomer()
    Dim IRange As Range
    Dim ORange As Range
    Dim CRange As Range

    ' Find the size of today's dataset
    FinalRow = Cells(65536, 1).End(xlUp).Row
    NextCol = Cells(1, 255).End(xlToLeft).Column + 2

    ' Set up the criteria range with one customer
    Cells(1, NextCol).Value = Range("D1").Value
    ' In reality, this value should be passed from the userform
    Cells(2, NextCol).Value = "CDE INC."
    Set CRange = Cells(1, NextCol).Resize(2, 1)

    ' Set up output range. It is a single blank cell
    Set ORange = Cells(1, NextCol + 2)

    ' Define the Input Range
    Set IRange = Range("A1").Resize(FinalRow, NextCol - 2)

    ' Do the Advanced Filter to get unique list of customers & product
    IRange.AdvancedFilter Action:=xlFilterCopy, CriteriaRange:=CRange,
➡CopyToRange:=ORange


End Sub
```

Figure 11.17
When using
xlFilterCopy with
a blank output range,
you get all columns in
the same order as they
appear in the original list
range. If you are taking
the data to another
report, you may want
only a subset of these
columns and in a differ-
ent order.

	L	M	N	O	P	Q	R	S	T
	Region	Product	Date	Customer	Quantity	Revenue	COGS	Profit	
	East	ABC	7/19/05	CDE INC.	900	18756	9198	9558	
	East	ABC	3/19/05	CDE INC.	100	1819	847	972	
	West	XYZ	2/10/05	CDE INC.	1000	22840	10220	12620	
	Central	XYZ	2/9/05	CDE INC.	400	9240	4088	5152	
	East	ABC	9/6/05	CDE INC.	700	16303	6888	9415	
	West	DEF	3/10/05	CDE INC.	600	14634	6132	8502	
	Central	DEF	11/21/04	CDE INC.	800	19520	7872	11648	
	East	XYZ	6/17/05	CDE INC.	100	2538	1022	1516	

Copying a Subset of Columns and Reordering

If you are doing the AdvancedFilter to send records to a report, it is likely that you may only need a subset of columns and you might need them in a different sequence.

Here is an example that will finish off the frmReport example from earlier in the chapter. As you remember, frmReport would allow the client to select a customer. The OK button would then call the RunCustReport routine, passing a parameter to identify for which customer to prepare a report.

Imagine this is a report being sent to the customer. The customer really doesn't care about the surrounding region, and we definitely do not want to reveal our cost of goods sold or profit. Assuming that we will put the customer in the title of the report, the fields that we really need to produce the report are Date, Quantity, Product, Revenue.

The following code copies those headings to the Output range. The AdvancedFilter produces data, as shown in Figure 11.18. The program then goes on to copy the matching records to a new workbook. A title and total row is added and the report is saved with the customer's name. The final report is shown in Figure 11.19.

```
Sub RunCustReport(WhichCust As Variant)
    Dim IRange As Range
    Dim ORange As Range
    Dim CRange As Range
    Dim WBN As Workbook
    Dim WSN As Worksheet
    Dim WSO As Worksheet

    Set WSO = ActiveSheet
    ' Find the size of today's dataset
    FinalRow = Cells(65536, 1).End(xlUp).Row
    NextCol = Cells(1, 255).End(xlToLeft).Column + 2

    ' Set up the criteria range with one customer
    Cells(1, NextCol).Value = Range("D1").Value
    Cells(2, NextCol).Value = WhichCust
    Set CRange = Cells(1, NextCol).Resize(2, 1)

    ' Set up output range. We want Date, Quantity, Product, Revenue
    ' These columns are in C, E, B, and F
    Cells(1, NextCol + 2).Resize(1, 4).Value = _
        Array(Cells(1, 3), Cells(1, 5), Cells(1, 2), Cells(1, 6))
    Set ORange = Cells(1, NextCol + 2).Resize(1, 4)

    ' Define the Input Range
    Set IRange = Range("A1").Resize(FinalRow, NextCol - 2)

    ' Do the Advanced Filter to get unique list of customers & products
    IRange.AdvancedFilter Action:=xlFilterCopy, _
        CriteriaRange:=CRange, CopyToRange:=ORange

    ' At this point, the data looks like Figure 11.18

    ' Create a new workbook with one blank sheet to hold the output
    Set WBN = Workbooks.Add(xlWBATWorksheet)
```

```
        Set WSN = WBN.Worksheets(1)

        ' Set up a title on WSN
        WSN.Cells(1, 1).Value = "Report of Sales to " & WhichCust

        ' Copy data from WSO to WSN
        WSO.Cells(1, NextCol + 2).CurrentRegion.Copy Destination:=WSN.Cells(3, 1)
        TotalRow = WSN.Cells(65536, 1).End(xlUp).Row + 1
        WSN.Cells(TotalRow, 1).Value = "Total"
        WSN.Cells(TotalRow, 2).FormulaR1C1 = "=SUM(R2C:R[-1]C)"
        WSN.Cells(TotalRow, 4).FormulaR1C1 = "=SUM(R2C:R[-1]C)"

        ' Format the new report with bold
        WSN.Cells(3, 1).Resize(1, 4).Font.Bold = True
        WSN.Cells(TotalRow, 1).Resize(1, 4).Font.Bold = True
        WSN.Cells(1, 1).Font.Size = 18

        WBN.SaveAs "C:\" & WhichCust & ".xls"
        WBN.Close SaveChanges:=False

        WSO.Select

        ' clear the output range, etc.
        Range("J1:Z1").EntireColumn.Clear

End Sub
```

	A	B	C	D	E	F	G	H	I	J	K	L	M	N	O	P
1	Region	Product	Date	Customer	Qua	Revenı	COGS	Profit		Customer		Date	Quantity	Product	Revenue	
2	Central	ABC	10/16/04	FGH LTD.	700	11858	5929	5929		CDE INC.		7/19/05	900	ABC	18756	
3	West	ABC	4/20/05	OPQ, INC.	800	13552	6776	6776				3/19/05	100	ABC	1819	
4	East	XYZ	6/14/05	DEF, LLC	700	11858	5929	5929				2/10/05	1000	XYZ	22040	
5	East	ABC	11/3/05	LMN PTY LTD	800	13552	6776	6776				2/9/05	400	XYZ	9240	
6	West	XYZ	2/11/05	DEF, LLC	200	3390	1694	1696				9/6/05	700	ABC	16303	
7	East	XYZ	3/16/05	OPQ, INC.	200	3390	1694	1696				3/10/05	600	DEF	14634	
8	Central	ABC	6/7/05	TUV GMBH	900	15255	7623	7632				#######	800	DEF	19520	
9	West	ABC	10/3/05	FGH LTD.	900	15255	7623	7632				6/17/05	100	XYZ	2538	
10	Central	XYZ	11/22/04	LMN PTY LTD	200	3942	1968	1974								

Figure 11.18
Immediately after the Advanced Filter, we have just the columns and records needed for the report.

Microsoft Excel - CDE INC..xls

	A	B	C	D	E
1	Report of Sales to CDE INC.				
2					
3	Date	Quantity	Product	Revenue	
4	7/19/05	900	ABC	18756	
5	3/19/05	100	ABC	1819	
6	2/10/05	1000	XYZ	22840	
7	2/9/05	400	XYZ	9240	
8	9/6/05	700	ABC	16303	
9	3/10/05	600	DEF	14634	
10	11/21/04	800	DEF	19520	
11	6/17/05	100	XYZ	2538	
12	Total	4600		105650	
13					
14					

Figure 11.19
After copying the filtered data to a new sheet and applying some formatting, we have a good-looking report to send to each customer.

This report macro is simple but powerful. There are 200 million people using Excel in a work environment. Just about every one of them could use a simple reporting tool like the one shown here.

CASE STUDY

Case Study: Utilizing Two Kinds of Advanced Filters to Create a Report for Each Customer

The final `AdvancedFilter` example for this chapter uses several advanced filter techniques. Let's say that after importing invoice records, you want to send a purchase summary to each customer. The process would be as follows:

1. Do an advanced filter requesting unique values to get a list of customers in J. This `.AdvancedFilter` would specify the `Unique:=True` parameter and use a `CopyToRange` that includes a single heading for Customer:

```
' Set up output range. Copy heading from D1 there
Range("D1").Copy Destination:=Cells(1, NextCol)
Set ORange = Cells(1, NextCol)

' Define the Input Range
Set IRange = Range("A1").Resize(FinalRow, NextCol - 2)

' Do the Advanced Filter to get unique list of customers
IRange.AdvancedFilter Action:=xlFilterCopy, CriteriaRange:="", _
    CopyToRange:=ORange, Unique:=True
```

2. For each customer in the list of unique customers in Column J, perform steps 3 through 7. Find the number of customers in the output range from step 1. Then, use a For Each Cell loop to loop through the customers.

```
' Loop through each customer
FinalCust = Cells(65536, NextCol).End(xlUp).Row
For Each cell In Cells(2, NextCol).Resize(FinalCust - 1, 1)
    ThisCust = cell.Value
    ' … Steps 3 through 7 here
Next Cell
```

3. Build a criteria range in L1:L2 to be used in a new advanced filter. The criteria range would include a heading of "Customer" in L1 and the customer name from this iteration of the loop in cell L2.

```
' Set up the Criteria Range with one customer
Cells(1, NextCol + 2).Value = Range("D1").Value
Cells(2, NextCol + 2).Value = ThisCust
Set CRange = Cells(1, NextCol + 2).Resize(2, 1)
```

4. Do an advanced filter to copy matching records for this customer to Column N. This `AdvancedFilter` statement would specify the `Unique:=False` parameter. Because we want only the columns for Date, Quantity, Product, and Revenue, the `CopyToRange` specifies a four-column range with those headings copied in the proper order.

```
' Set up output range. We want Date, Quantity, Product, Revenue
' These columns are in C, E, B, and F
Cells(1, NextCol + 4).Resize(1, 4).Value = _
    Array(Cells(1, 3), Cells(1, 5), Cells(1, 2), Cells(1, 6))
Set ORange = Cells(1, NextCol + 4).Resize(1, 4)

' Do the Advanced Filter to get unique list of customers & product
IRange.AdvancedFilter Action:=xlFilterCopy, CriteriaRange:=CRange, _
    CopyToRange:=ORange
```

5. Copy the customer records to a report sheet in a new workbook. The VBA code uses the Workbooks.Add method to create a new blank workbook. The extracted records from step 4 are copied to cell A3 of the new workbook.

```
' Create a new workbook with one blank sheet to hold the output
Set WBN = Workbooks.Add(xlWBATWorksheet)
Set WSN = WBN.Worksheets(1)

' Copy data from WSO to WSN
WSO.Cells(1, NextCol + 4).CurrentRegion.Copy _
    Destination:=WSN.Cells(3, 1)
```

6. Format the report with a title and totals. In VBA, add a title that reflects the customer's name in cell A1. Make the headings bold and add a total below the final row.

```
' Set up a title on WSN
WSN.Cells(1, 1).Value = "Report of Sales to " & ThisCust

TotalRow = WSN.Cells(65536, 1).End(xlUp).Row + 1
WSN.Cells(TotalRow, 1).Value = "Total"
WSN.Cells(TotalRow, 2).FormulaR1C1 = "=SUM(R2C:R[-1]C)"
WSN.Cells(TotalRow, 4).FormulaR1C1 = "=SUM(R2C:R[-1]C)"

' Format the new report with bold
WSN.Cells(3, 1).Resize(1, 4).Font.Bold = True
WSN.Cells(TotalRow, 1).Resize(1, 4).Font.Bold = True
WSN.Cells(1, 1).Font.Size = 18
```

7. Use SaveAs to save the workbook based on customer name. After the workbook is saved, close the new workbook. Return to the original workbook and clear the output range to prepare for the next pass through the loop.

```
WBN.SaveAs "C:\Reports\" & ThisCust & ".xls"
WBN.Close SaveChanges:=False

WSO.Select
Set WSN = Nothing
Set WBN = Nothing

' clear the output range, etc.
Cells(1, NextCol + 2).Resize(1, 10).EntireColumn.Clear
```

The complete code is as follows:

```
Sub RunReportForEachCustomer()
    Dim IRange As Range
    Dim ORange As Range
    Dim CRange As Range
    Dim WBN As Workbook
    Dim WSN As Worksheet
    Dim WSO As Worksheet

    Set WSO = ActiveSheet
    ' Find the size of today's dataset
    FinalRow = Cells(65536, 1).End(xlUp).Row
    NextCol = Cells(1, 255).End(xlToLeft).Column + 2
```

11

```
' First - get a unique list of customers in J
' Set up output range. Copy heading from D1 there
Range("D1").Copy Destination:=Cells(1, NextCol)
Set ORange = Cells(1, NextCol)

' Define the Input Range
Set IRange = Range("A1").Resize(FinalRow, NextCol - 2)

' Do the Advanced Filter to get unique list of customers
IRange.AdvancedFilter Action:=xlFilterCopy, CriteriaRange:="", _
    CopyToRange:=ORange, Unique:=True

' Loop through each customer
FinalCust = Cells(65536, NextCol).End(xlUp).Row
For Each cell In Cells(2, NextCol).Resize(FinalCust - 1, 1)
    ThisCust = cell.Value

    ' Set up the Criteria Range with one customer
    Cells(1, NextCol + 2).Value = Range("D1").Value
    Cells(2, NextCol + 2).Value = ThisCust
    Set CRange = Cells(1, NextCol + 2).Resize(2, 1)

    ' Set up output range. We want Date, Quantity, Product, Revenue
    ' These columns are in C, E, B, and F
    Cells(1, NextCol + 4).Resize(1, 4).Value = _
        Array(Cells(1, 3), Cells(1, 5), Cells(1, 2), Cells(1, 6))
    Set ORange = Cells(1, NextCol + 4).Resize(1, 4)

    ' Do the Advanced Filter to get unique list of customers & product
    IRange.AdvancedFilter Action:=xlFilterCopy, CriteriaRange:=CRange, _
        CopyToRange:=ORange

    ' Create a new workbook with one blank sheet to hold the output
    Set WBN = Workbooks.Add(xlWBATWorksheet)
    Set WSN = WBN.Worksheets(1)

    ' Copy data from WSO to WSN
    WSO.Cells(1, NextCol + 4).CurrentRegion.Copy _
        Destination:=WSN.Cells(3, 1)

    ' Set up a title on WSN
    WSN.Cells(1, 1).Value = "Report of Sales to " & ThisCust

    TotalRow = WSN.Cells(65536, 1).End(xlUp).Row + 1
    WSN.Cells(TotalRow, 1).Value = "Total"
    WSN.Cells(TotalRow, 2).FormulaR1C1 = "=SUM(R2C:R[-1]C)"
    WSN.Cells(TotalRow, 4).FormulaR1C1 = "=SUM(R2C:R[-1]C)"

    ' Format the new report with bold
    WSN.Cells(3, 1).Resize(1, 4).Font.Bold = True
    WSN.Cells(TotalRow, 1).Resize(1, 4).Font.Bold = True
    WSN.Cells(1, 1).Font.Size = 18

    WBN.SaveAs "C:\Reports\" & ThisCust & ".xls"
    WBN.Close SaveChanges:=False
```

```
            WSO.Select
            Set WSN = Nothing
            Set WBN = Nothing

            ' clear the output range, etc.
            Cells(1, NextCol + 2).Resize(1, 10).EntireColumn.Clear
     Next cell

        Cells(1, NextCol).EntireColumn.Clear
        MsgBox FinalCust - 1 & " Reports have been created!"
End Sub
```

This is a remarkable 75 lines of code. Incorporating a couple of Advanced Filters and not much else, we've managed to produce a tool that created 27 reports in less than 1 minute (see Figure 11.20). Even an Excel power user would normally take 2–3 minutes per report to create these manually. In less than 60 seconds, this code easily will save someone a few hours every time these reports need to be created. Imagine the real scenario where there are hundreds of customers. I guarantee that there are people in every city who are manually creating these reports in Excel because they simply don't realize the power of Excel VBA.

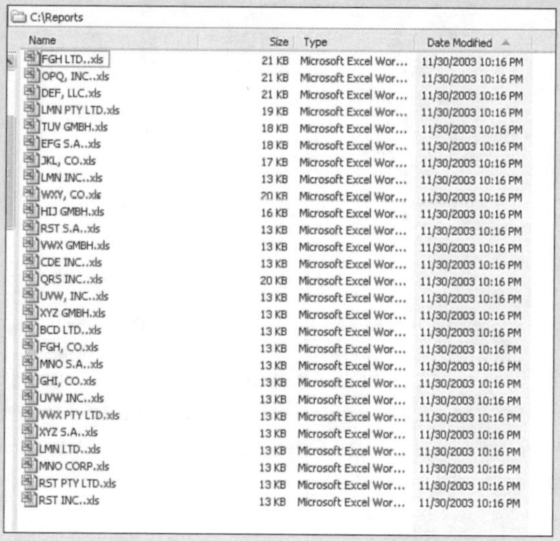

Figure 11.20
White collar productivity would skyrocket if everyone knew how to create 27 reports in less than a minute.

AutoFilters

The AutoFilter feature was added to Excel because people found Advanced Filters too hard. They are cool when used in the Excel user interface. I rarely have an occasion to use them in Excel VBA.

However, one cool feature is available only in Excel VBA. When you AutoFilter a list in the Excel user interface, every column in the dataset gets a field drop-down in the heading row. Sometimes, you have a field that doesn't make a lot of sense to AutoFilter. For example, in our current dataset, you might want to provide AutoFilter drop-downs for Region, Product,

Customer, but not the numeric or date fields. After setting up the AutoFilter, you need one line of code to turn off each drop-down that you do not want to appear. The following code turns off the drop-downs for Columns C, E, F, G, H:

```
Sub AutoFilterCustom()
    Range("A1").AutoFilter Field:=3, VisibleDropDown:=False
    Range("A1").AutoFilter Field:=5, VisibleDropDown:=False
    Range("A1").AutoFilter Field:=6, VisibleDropDown:=False
    Range("A1").AutoFilter Field:=7, VisibleDropDown:=False
    Range("A1").AutoFilter Field:=8, VisibleDropDown:=False
End Sub
```

I think using this tool is a fairly rare treat. Most of the time, Excel VBA lets us do things that are possible in the user interface (although it lets us do them very rapidly). This VisibleDropDown parameter actually allows us to do something in VBA that is generally not available in the Excel user interface. Your knowledgeable clients will be scratching their heads trying to figure out how you set up the cool AutoFilter with only a few filterable columns (see Figure 11.21).

Figure 11.21
Using VBA, you can set up an AutoFilter where only certain columns have the AutoFilter drop-down. There is no way to selectively hide the AutoFilter drop-down by column in the Excel user interface.

	A	B	C	D	E	F	G	H	I
1	Region	Product	Date	Customer	Quantity	Revenue	COGS	Profit	
112	East	DEF	3/31/05	MNO S.A.	600	12570	6132	6438	
194	West	DEF	1/24/05	MNO S.A.	400	8556	4088	4468	
224	East	ABC	2/18/05	MNO S.A.	1000	17840	8470	9370	
278	East	XYZ	10/2/04	MNO S.A.	100	2178	1022	1156	
640	East	XYZ	8/1/04	MNO S.A.	900	21015	9198	11817	
783	Central	DEF	4/2/05	MNO S.A.	500	11550	4920	6630	
809	Central	ABC	8/19/05	MNO S.A.	800	18552	7872	10680	
838	West	XYZ	12/10/04	MNO S.A.	200	4846	2044	2802	
1128									

Next Steps

Using techniques from Chapter 11, you have many reporting techniques available to you by using the arcane Advanced Filter tool. Chapter 12, "Pivot Tables," introduces the most powerful feature in Excel: the Pivot Table. The combination of Advanced Filter and Pivot Tables creates reporting tools that enable amazing applications.

Pivot Tables

Pivot tables are the most powerful tools that Excel has to offer. The concept was first put into practice by Lotus with their Improv product.

I love pivot tables because they are a really fast way to summarize massive amounts of data. The basic vanilla pivot table can be used to produce a concise summary in seconds. However, pivot tables come in so many flavors that they can be the tools of choice for many different uses. You can build pivot tables to act as the calculation engine to produce reports by store, by style, or to quickly find the top 5 or bottom 10 of anything.

I am not suggesting you use VBA to build pivot tables to give to your user! I am suggesting you use pivot tables as a means to an end—use a pivot table to extract a summary of data, and then take this summary on to better uses.

Versions

Pivot tables have been evolving. They were introduced in Excel 95 and perfected in Excel 97. In Excel 2000, pivot table creation in VBA was dramatically altered. Some new parameters were added in Excel 2002. Thus, you need to be extremely careful when writing code in Excel 2003 that might be run in Excel 2000 or Excel 97.

Just a few simple tweaks make 2003 code run in 2000, but a major overhaul is required to make 2003 code run in Excel 97. Given that we are 6 years out from Excel 97 and given that Microsoft has not supported the product for 2+ years, I will write most of the chapter using only the pivot cache method introduced in Excel 2000. At the end of the chapter, I'll briefly cover the Pivot Table Wizard method, which is your only option if you need code to run in Excel 97.

12

Creating a Vanilla Pivot Table in Excel Interface

Although they are the most powerful feature in Excel, Microsoft estimates that pivot tables are used by only 7% of Excel users overall. Based on surveys at MrExcel.com, about 42% of advanced Excel users have used pivot tables. Because a significant portion of you have never used pivot tables, I will walk through the steps of building a pivot table in the user interface. If you are already a pivot table pro, jump ahead to the next section.

Let's say you have 50,000 rows of data, as shown in Figure 12.1. You want a summary of revenue by region and product. Regions should go down the side, products across the top. To build the pivot table to the right of the data, follow these steps:

Figure 12.1

If you need to quickly summarize 50,000 rows of transactional data, a pivot table can do so in seconds. Your goal is to produce a summary of revenue by region and product.

	A	B	C	D	E	F	G	H
1	Region	Product	Date	Customer	Quantity	Revenue	COGS	Profit
2	East	XYZ	1/1/2004	VWX GMBH	1000	22810	10220	12590
3	Central	DEF	1/2/2004	MNO CORP	100	2257	984	1273
4	East	ABC	1/2/2004	MNO CORP	500	10245	4235	6010
5	Central	XYZ	1/3/2004	HIJ GMBH	500	11240	5110	6130
6	Central	XYZ	1/4/2004	HIJ GMBH	400	9204	4088	5116
7	East	DEF	1/4/2004	FGH, CO	800	18552	7872	10680
8	East	XYZ	1/4/2004	RST PTY LTD	400	9152	4088	5064
9	Central	ABC	1/5/2004	CDE INC.	400	6860	3388	3472
10	East	ABC	1/7/2004	RST S.A.	400	8456	3388	5068
11	East	DEF	1/7/2004	LMN LTD.	1000	21730	9840	11890
12	West	XYZ	1/7/2004	RST PTY LTD	600	13806	6132	7674
13	Central	ABC	1/9/2004	RST S.A.	800	16416	6776	9640
14	East	XYZ	1/9/2004	XYZ GMBH	900	21015	9198	11817
15	East	XYZ	1/10/2004	HIJ GMBH	900	21465	9198	12267
16	Central	XYZ	1/10/2004	RST INC.	900	21438	9198	12240
17	West	XYZ	1/12/2004	HIJ GMBH	400	9144	4088	5056
18	Central	ABC	1/12/2004	CDE INC.	300	6267	2541	3726
19	Central	ABC	1/14/2004	OPQ, INC.	100	1740	847	893
20	East	XYZ	1/14/2004	OPQ, INC.	100	2401	1022	1379
21	West	ABC	1/14/2004	RST INC.	1000	19110	8470	10640
22	East	ABC	1/15/2004	MNO CORP	500	9345	4235	5110
23	East	ABC	1/16/2004	WXY, CO	600	11628	5082	6546
24	Central	XYZ	1/16/2004	RST INC.	900	21888	9198	12690
25	East	DEF	1/17/2004	LMN INC.	300	5961	2952	3009
26	West	DEF	1/19/2004	MNO CORP	100	2042	984	1058
27	Central	ABC	1/20/2004	WXY, CO	900	17505	7623	9882
28	West	DEF	1/21/2004	LMN INC.	300	7032	2952	4080
29	West	ABC	1/21/2004	FGH, CO	200	3552	1694	1858
30	East	ABC	1/21/2004	GHI, CO	800	14440	6776	7664
31	West	DEF	1/22/2004	LMN INC.	300	6735	2952	3783
32	East	ABC	1/23/2004	LMN INC.	400	8164	3388	4776
33	West	ABC	1/23/2004	RST S.A.	800	14592	6776	7816

1. Select a singe cell in the transaction data. Click the Data menu item, and from the drop-down select PivotTable and PivotChart Report.

2. In the Pivot Table and PivotChart Wizard Step 1 of 3, confirm that you are creating a pivot table from an Excel list by selecting the option button next to Microsoft Excel List or Database.

3. In Step 2 of the Wizard, confirm that Excel selected the correct range for your data.

4. In Step 3 of the Wizard, specify a location for the pivot table results. Click the Layout button, shown in Figure 12.2.

5. In the Layout dialog, drag the Region button and drop it in the Row area. Drag Product and drop it in the Column area. Leave the Page area blank for now. Drag the Revenue button and drop it in the Data area. If your Revenue column contains 100% numeric data with no blank cells, the Revenue button changes to say Sum of Revenue when it is dropped in the Data area, as shown in Figure 12.3. Click OK to return to the Pivot Table Wizard.

Figure 12.2
Click on the Layout button in Step 3 to draw the initial state of the pivot table summary report.

Figure 12.3
To use a pivot table to build a summary report, drag field names from the right and drop them in the Row, Column, and Data areas of the Pivot Table Layout dialog.

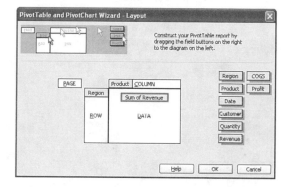

6. In Step 3 of the Wizard, click Finish. Almost instantly, Excel produces a summary of the transactional data, and you have a summary report, as shown in Figure 12.4.

Figure 12.4
The pivot table results are a concise summary of the transactional data.

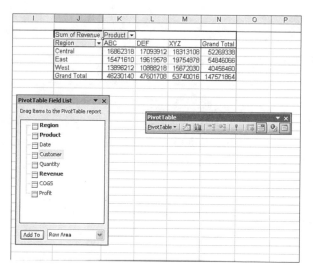

12

CAUTION

In Excel 97, the Pivot Table Wizard involved four steps instead of three. The former third step—dragging fields onto the Layout dialog—was moved to the Layout button in the final step of the Pivot Table Wizard.

After a Pivot Table has been created on your worksheet, you may easily change the data summarized in the report by dragging fields from the Pivot Table Field list and dropping them on the appropriate section of the pivot table. In Figure 12.5, Customer was added to the Row area of the existing pivot table.

Figure 12.5
The name "pivot table" comes from the ability you have to drag or drop new fields on the table and have them recalculate. In a couple of clicks, you can move Region across the top, move Product down the side, and add a summary by Customer.

J	K	L	M	N	O	P
Sum of Revenue		Region				
Product	Customer	Central	East	West	Grand Total	
ABC	BCD LTD.			378180	378180	
	CDE INC.	652168	864006	673794	2189968	
	DEF, LLC	528066	1979120		2507186	
	EFG S.A.			379500	379500	
	FGH LTD.			332288	332288	
	FGH, CO			78144	78144	
	GHI, CO		317680		317680	
	HIJ GMBH	1709026	1356520	836858	3902404	
	JKL, CO		121704		121704	
	LMN INC.	3009028	1332232	2129776	6471036	
	LMN LTD.			304766	304766	
	LMN PTY LTD		211970		211970	
	MNO CORP	901098	1419594	417582	2738274	
	MNO S.A.			128898	128898	
	OPQ, INC.	827200	1670064	635800	3133064	
	QRS INC.			91476	91476	
	RST INC.	2384690	1765896	1940048	6090634	
	RST PTY LTD		156992		156992	
	RST S.A.	2744236	1518880	1918158	6181274	
	TUV GMBH		178552	402380	580932	
	UVW INC.	336864			336864	
	UVW, INC.		40018		40018	
	VWX GMBH	2001890	606100	1607826	4215816	
	VWX PTY LTD			274428	274428	
	WXY, CO	1768052	1539802	1169630	4477484	
	XYZ GMBH		392480		392480	
	XYZ S.A.			196680	196680	
ABC Total		16862318	15471610	13896212	46230140	
DEF	BCD LTD.		318934		318934	
	CDE INC.	1447270	1334014	1140304	3921588	

Building a Pivot Table in Excel VBA

In Excel 2000 and newer, you first build a pivot cache object to describe the input area of the data:

```
Dim WSD As Worksheet
Dim PTCache As PivotCache
Dim PT As PivotTable
Dim PRange As Range
Dim FinalRow as Long
Set WSD = Worksheets("Pivot Table")

' Delete any prior pivot tables
For Each PT In WSD.PivotTables
    PT.TableRange2.Clear
Next PT
```

```
' Define input area and set up a Pivot Cache
FinalRow = WSD.Cells(65536, 1).End(xlUp).Row
Set PRange = WSD.Cells(1, 1).Resize(FinalRow, 8)
Set PTCache = ActiveWorkbook.PivotCaches.Add(SourceType:=xlDatabase, _
SourceData:=PRange.Address)
```

After the pivot cache is defined, use the CreatePivotTable method to create a blank pivot table based on the defined PivotCache:

```
Set PT = PTCache.CreatePivotTable(TableDestination:=WSD.Range("J2"), _
    TableName:="PivotTable1")
```

In the CreatePivotTable method, you specify the output location and give the table a name. After running this line of code, you have a strange-looking blank pivot table that looks like Figure 12.6.

Figure 12.6

Immediately after using the CreatePivotTable method, Excel gives you a 4-cell blank pivot table that is not very useful. You now have to use code to drop fields on to the table.

If you are using the Layout dialog in the user interface to build the pivot table, Excel does not recalculate the pivot table after you drop each field on to the table. By default in VBA, Excel calculates the pivot table as you execute each step of building the table. This could require the pivot table to be executed a half-dozen times before you get to the final result. To speed up your code execution, you can temporarily turn off calculation of the pivot table by using the ManualUpdate property:

```
PT.ManualUpdate = True
```

You can now run through the steps needed to lay out the pivot table. In the .AddFields method, you can specify one or more fields that should be in the Row, Column, or Page area of the pivot table:

```
' Set up the row & column fields
PT.AddFields RowFields:=Array("Product", "Customer"), ColumnFields:="Region"
```

To add a field such as Revenue to the Data area of the table, you change the `Orientation` property of the field to be `xlDataField`.

Getting a Sum Instead of Count

Excel is smart. When you build a report with revenue, it assumes you want to sum the revenue. But, there is a problem. Say that one of the revenue cells is accidentally blank. When you build the pivot table, even though 99.9% of fields are numeric, Excel assumes you have alphanumeric data and offers to count this field. This is annoying. It seems to me to be an anomaly that on one hand, you are expected to make sure that 100% of your cells have numeric data, but the results of the pivot table are often filled with non-numeric blank cells.

When you build the pivot table in the Excel interface, you should take care in the Layout dialog to notice that the field says Count of Revenue instead of Sum of Revenue. At that point, the right thing is to go back and fix the data, but what people usually do is double-click the Count of Revenue button and change it to Sum of Revenue.

In VBA, you should always explicitly define that you are creating a sum of revenue by explicitly setting the `Function` property to `xlSum`:

```
' Set up the data fields
With PT.PivotFields("Revenue")
    .Orientation = xlDataField
    .Function = xlSum
    .Position = 1
End With
```

At this point, we've given VBA all the settings required to correctly generate the pivot table. If you set the `ManualUpdate` to False, Excel calculates and draws the pivot table. You can immediately thereafter set this setting back to `True`:

```
' Calc the pivot table
PT.ManualUpdate = False
PT.ManualUpdate = True
```

At this point, you will have a complete pivot table like the one shown in Figure 12.5. Here is the complete code used to generate the pivot table:

```
Sub CreatePivot()
    Dim WSD As Worksheet
    Dim PTCache As PivotCache
    Dim PT As PivotTable
    Dim PRange As Range
    Dim FinalRow as Long
    Set WSD = Worksheets("Pivot Table")

    ' Delete any prior pivot tables
    For Each PT In WSD.PivotTables
        PT.TableRange2.Clear
    Next PT
```

```
' Define input area and set up a Pivot Cache
FinalRow = WSD.Cells(65536, 1).End(xlUp).Row
Set PRange = WSD.Cells(1, 1).Resize(FinalRow, 8)
Set PTCache = ActiveWorkbook.PivotCaches.Add(SourceType:=xlDatabase, _
    SourceData:=PRange.Address)
Set PT = PTCache.CreatePivotTable(TableDestination:=WSD.Range("J2"), _
    TableName:="PivotTable1")
PT.ManualUpdate = True
' Set up the row & column fields
PT.AddFields RowFields:=Array("Product", "Customer"), ColumnFields:="Region"
' Set up the data fields
With PT.PivotFields("Revenue")
    .Orientation = xlDataField
    .Function = xlSum
    .Position = 1
End With

' Calc the pivot table
PT.ManualUpdate = False
PT.ManualUpdate = True
End Sub
```

Cannot Move or Change Part of a Pivot Report

Although pivot tables are incredible, they have annoying limitations. You cannot move or change just a part of the pivot table. For example, try to run a macro that would delete Column O. This column contains the Grand Total column of the pivot table. The macro comes to a screeching halt with an error 1004, as shown in Figure 12.7.

Figure 12.7
You can not delete just a part of a pivot table. To get around this limita-tion, you can change the summary from a pivot table to just values.

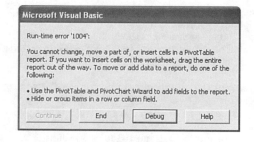

Figuring the Size of a Finished Pivot Table

It is difficult to know the size of a pivot table in advance. If you run a report of transactional data on one day, you may or may not have sales from the West region. This could cause your table to either be 5 or 6 columns wide. Use the special property `TableRange2` to refer to the entire resultant pivot table.

Because of the limitation of a pivot table, I generally copy the results of a pivot table to a new location on the worksheet and then delete the original pivot table. The code shown in `CreateSummaryReportUsingPivot()` creates a small pivot table. Note that you can set the `ColumnGrand` and `RowGrand` properties of the table to `False` to prevent the totals from being added to the table.

`PT.TableRange2` includes the entire pivot table. In this case, this includes the extra row at the top with the button Sum of Revenue. To eliminate that row, the code copies `PT.TableRange2`, but offsets this selection by one row by using `.Offset(1, 0)`. Depending on the nature of your pivot table, you might need to use an offset of 2 or more rows to get rid of extraneous information at the top of the pivot table.

The code copies `PT.TableRange2` and does a `PasteSpecial` to cell J10. At that point in the code, your worksheet appears like Figure 12.8. The table in J2 is a live pivot table and the table in J10 is just the copied results.

You can then totally eliminate the pivot table by applying the `Clear` method to the entire table. If your code is then going on to do additional formatting, you should remove the `PivotCache` from memory by setting `PTCache` equal to `Nothing`:

```
Sub CreateSummaryReportUsingPivot()
    ' Use a Pivot Table to create a static summary report
    ' with Region going down the rows and products across

    Dim WSD As Worksheet
    Dim PTCache As PivotCache
    Dim PT As PivotTable
    Dim PRange As Range
    Set WSD = Worksheets("Pivot Table")

    ' Delete any prior pivot tables
    For Each PT In WSD.PivotTables
        PT.TableRange2.Clear
    Next PT

    ' Define input area and set up a Pivot Cache
    FinalRow = WSD.Cells(65536, 1).End(xlUp).Row
    Set PRange = WSD.Cells(1, 1).Resize(FinalRow, 8)
    Set PTCache = ActiveWorkbook.PivotCaches.Add(SourceType:=xlDatabase, _
        SourceData:=PRange.Address)

    Set PT = PTCache.CreatePivotTable(TableDestination:=WSD.Range("J2"), _
        TableName:="PivotTable1")
    PT.ManualUpdate = True
    ' Set up the row fields
    PT.AddFields RowFields:="Region", ColumnFields:="Product"

    ' Set up the data fields
    With PT.PivotFields("Revenue")
        .Orientation = xlDataField
        .Function = xlSum
        .Position = 1
    End With

    With PT
        .ColumnGrand = False
        .RowGrand = False
        .NullString = "0"
    End With
```

```
' Calc the pivot table
PT.ManualUpdate = False
PT.ManualUpdate = True

' PT.TableRange2 contains the results. Move these to J10
' as just values and not a real pivot table.
PT.TableRange2.Offset(1, 0).Copy
WSD.Range("J10").PasteSpecial xlPasteValues

' At this point, the worksheet looks like Figure 12.8

' Delete the original Pivot Table & the Pivot Cache
PT.TableRange2.Clear
Set PTCache = Nothing
End Sub
```

Figure 12.8

Create the pivot table, copy the results, and paste them as values to a new area of the worksheet. This is the worksheet just before the macro uses the `PT.TableRange2.Clear` command to erase the original pivot table. You'll then be left with a summary in J10:M13.

So far, we've walked through building the simplest of pivot table reports. Pivot tables offer far more flexibility. Read on for more complex reporting examples.

Revenue by Customer for a Product Line Manager

A typical report might provide a list of customers who purchased each product. This report could be given to product line managers to show them which customers are buying their products. In this example, you want to show the customers in descending order by revenue with regions going across the columns. A sample report is shown in Figure 12.9.

The key to producing this data quickly is to use a pivot table. Although pivot tables are an incredible tool for summarizing data, they are quirky and their presentation is downright ugly. The final result is rarely formatted in a manner that is acceptable to line managers. There is not a good way to insert page breaks between each product in the pivot table.

To create this report, start with a pivot table that has product and customer as row fields, region as a column field, and revenue as the data field. Figure 12.10 shows the default pivot table created with these settings.

Figure 12.9

A typical request is to take transactional data and produce a summary by customer for each product line manager. You can use a pivot table to get 90% of this report, and then a little formatting to finish it.

Revenue by Product & Customer

	Product	Customer	Central	East	West	Total
4	ABC	LMN INC.	3,009K	1,332K	2,130K	6,471K
5	ABC	RST S.A.	2,744K	1,519K	1,918K	6,181K
6	ABC	RST INC.	2,385K	1,766K	1,940K	6,091K
7	ABC	WXY, CO	1,768K	1,540K	1,170K	4,477K
8	ABC	VWX GMBH	2,002K	606K	1,608K	4,216K
9	ABC	HIJ GMBH	1,709K	1,357K	837K	3,902K
10	ABC	OPQ, INC.	827K	1,670K	636K	3,133K
11	ABC	MNO CORP	901K	1,420K	418K	2,738K
12	ABC	DEF, LLC	528K	1,979K	0K	2,507K
13	ABC	CDE INC.	652K	864K	674K	2,190K
14	ABC	TUV GMBH	0K	179K	402K	581K
15	ABC	LMN LTD.	0K	0K	305K	305K
16	ABC	VWX PTY LTD	0K	0K	274K	274K
17	ABC	LMN PTY LTD	0K	212K	0K	212K
18	ABC	XYZ S.A.	0K	0K	197K	197K
19	ABC	RST PTY LTD	0K	157K	0K	157K
20	ABC	MNO S.A.	0K	0K	129K	129K
21	ABC	JKL, CO	0K	122K	0K	122K
22	ABC	QRS INC.	0K	0K	91K	91K
23	ABC	FGH, CO	0K	0K	78K	78K
24	ABC	UVW, INC.	0K	40K	0K	40K
25	ABC Total		16,525K	14,761K	12,806K	44,093K
26	DEF	RST INC.	1,630K	3,434K	1,629K	6,692K
27	DEF	RST S.A.	1,042K	2,923K	1,171K	5,136K
28	DEF	WXY, CO	1,412K	1,805K	1,276K	4,493K

Figure 12.10

Use the power of the pivot table feature to get the summarized data, but then use your own common sense in formatting the report.

Sum of Revenue		Region			
Product	Customer	Central	East	West	Grand Total
ABC	BCD LTD.			378180	378180
	CDE INC.	652168	864006	673794	2189968
	DEF, LLC	528066	1979120		2507186
	EFG S.A.			379500	379500
	FGH LTD.			332288	332288
	FGH, CO			78144	78144
	GHI, CO		317680		317680
	HIJ GMBH	1709026	1356520	836858	3902404
	JKL, CO		121704		121704
	LMN INC.	3009028	1332232	2129776	6471036
	LMN LTD.			304766	304766
	LMN PTY LTD		211970		211970
	MNO CORP	901098	1419594	417582	2738274
	MNO S.A.			128898	128898
	OPQ, INC.	827200	1670064	635800	3133064
	QRS INC.			91476	91476
	RST INC.	2384690	1765896	1940048	6090634
	RST PTY LTD		156992		156992
	RST S.A.	2744236	1518880	1918158	6181274
	TUV GMBH		178552	402380	580932
	UVW INC.	336864			336864
	UVW, INC.		40018		40018
	VWX GMBH	2001890	606100	1607826	4215816
	VWX PTY LTD			274428	274428
	WXY, CO	1768052	1539802	1169630	4477484
	XYZ GMBH		392480		392480
	XYZ S.A.			196680	196680
ABC Total		16862318	15471610	13896212	46230140
DEF	BCD LTD.		318934		318934

Here is what I hate about the default pivot table with two column fields:

- The outline view is horrible. In Figure 12.10, the value "ABC" appears in the product column only once and is followed by 26 blank cells. This is the worst feature of pivot tables and there is absolutely no way to correct it. Although humans can understand that this entire section is for product ABC, it is radically confusing if your ABC section spills to a second or third page. Page 2 starts without any indication that these customers purchased product ABC. If you intend to repurpose the data, you need the ABC value to be on every row.

- The report contains blank cells instead of zeroes. In Figure 12.10, customer BCD Ltd bought only from the Western region. Excel produces a pivot table where the sales values for Central and East are blank instead of zero. This is simply bad form. Excel experts rely on being able to "ride the range," using the End and arrow keys. Blank cells ruin this ability.

- The title is boring. I've never tried to pass a report off to a manager with the title of "Sum of Revenue." It is an annoying title.

- Some captions are extraneous. The word "Region" floating in cell L2 of Figure 12.10 really does not belong in a report.

- The default alphabetical sort order is rarely useful. Product line managers are going to want the top customers at the top of the list. It would be helpful to have the report sorted in descending order by revenue. The default region sequence of Central, East, West does not correspond to how those regions actually appear on a map. It would be helpful to re-sequence them as West, Central, East.

- The borders are ugly. Excel draws in a myriad of borders that really make the report look awful.

- The default number format is General. It would be better to set this up as data with commas to serve as thousands separators or perhaps even data in thousands or millions.

- Pivot tables offer no intelligent page break logic. If you want to be able to produce one report for each product manager, there is no fast method for indicating that each product should be on a new page.

- Because of the page break problem, you may find it is easier to do away with the pivot table's subtotal rows and have the Subtotal method add subtotal rows with page breaks. You need a way to turn off the pivot table subtotal rows offered for Product in Figure 12.10. These show up automatically whenever you have two or more row fields. If you would happen to have four row fields, you would want to turn off the automatic subtotals for the three outermost row fields.

Even with all these problems in default pivot tables, they are still the way to go. Each complaint can be overcome, either by using special settings within the pivot table, or by entering a few lines of code after the pivot table is created and then copied to a regular dataset.

Eliminating Blank Cells in the Data Area

People started complaining about the blank cells immediately when pivot tables were introduced in Excel 95. Anyone using Excel 97 or later can replace the blank cells with zeroes. In the user interface, the setting can be found in the PivotTable Options dialog. This dialog can be accessed in Pivot Table Wizard Step 3, or from the Table Options choice in the Pivot Table drop-down on the left side of the Pivot Table toolbar. Choose the For Empty Cells, Show option and type **0** in the box, as shown in Figure 12.11.

Figure 12.11
Fill the empty cells in the data area of a pivot table with the For Empty Cells, Show setting in the PivotTable dialog.

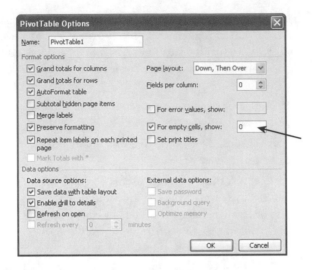

The equivalent operation in VBA is to set the `NullString` property for the pivot table to `"0"`.

> **NOTE** It always alarms me that the proper code is to set this value to a text zero. Luckily, Excel actually puts a real zero in the empty cells.

Using AutoSort to Control the Sort Order

The Excel user interface offers an AutoSort option that enables you to show customers in descending order based on revenue. It is possible to create pivot tables for years without ever finding this setting. In the Excel user interface, double-click the Customer button in the pivot report. This brings up the PivotTable Field dialog, as shown in Figure 12.12.

Figure 12.12
This dialog is the gateway to the AutoSort feature.

From the PivotTable Field dialog, click the Advanced button. Clicking this button opens the PivotTable Field Advanced Options dialog. Change the AutoSort option from Manual to Descending. When you select the Descending option, the drop-down for Using Field: appears. Change that drop-down to be Sum of Revenue. The dialog then looks like Figure 12.13.

Figure 12.13
After clicking Advanced, you get to the powerful PivotTable Field Advanced Options dialog. Here, you can specify that customers should be sorted based on Descending revenue.

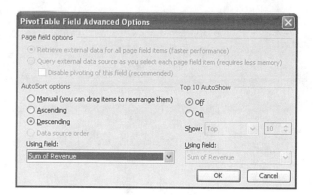

The equivalent code in VBA to sort the customer field by descending revenue uses the AutoSort method:

```
PT.PivotFields("Customer").AutoSort Order:=xlDescending, Field:="Sum of Revenue"
```

Controlling the Sort Order Manually

If your company has been reporting regions in the sequence of West, Central, East forever, it is an uphill battle getting managers to accept seeing the report ordered Central, East, West just because this is the default alphabetical order offered by Pivot Tables.

Strangely enough, Microsoft offers a bizarre method for handling a custom sort order in a pivot table. They call this a manual sort order. In Figure 12.10, the regions start in an alphabetic sort order of Central, East, West. These headings are in cells L3:N3. To change the sort order in the user interface, you simply go to cell L3—the cell with the word "Central." In that cell, type **West** and press Enter. As if by magic, Central and East move over and West is now the first column. Of course, all the numbers for West move from column N to Column L. This is not intuitive. See the results in Figure 12.14.

The VBA code to do a manual sort involves setting the Position property for a specific PivotItem. This is somewhat dangerous because you don't know whether the underlying data will have data for "West" on any given day. Be sure to set Error Checking to resume in case West doesn't exist today (see Chapter 23, "Handling Errors," for more information on error handling):

```
On Error Resume Next
PT.PivotFields("Region").PivotItems("West").Position = 1
On Error GoTo 0
```

Changing the Default Number Format

To change the number format in the user interface, double-click the Sum of Revenue title, click the Number button, and set an appropriate number format.

12

Figure 12.14

The default sequence for Region was Central, East, West. To manually resequence, simply click into cell L3 and type the word **West**. The pivot table resequences as if by magic.

		Region			
Sum of Revenue					
Product	Customer	West	Central	East	Grand Total
ABC	LMN INC.	2129776	3009028	1332232	6471036
	RST S.A.	1918158	2744236	1518880	6181274
	RST INC.	1940048	2384690	1765896	6090634
	WXY, CO	1169630	1768052	1539802	4477484
	VWX GMBH	1607826	2001890	606100	4215816
	HIJ GMBH	836858	1709026	1356520	3902404
	OPQ, INC.	635800	827200	1670064	3133064
	MNO CORP	417582	901098	1419594	2738274
	DEF, LLC	0	528066	1979120	2507186
	CDE INC.	673794	652168	864006	2189968
	TUV GMBH	402380	0	178552	580932
	XYZ GMBH	0	0	392480	392480
	EFG S.A.	379500	0	0	379500
	BCD LTD.	378180	0	0	378180
	UVW INC.	0	336864	0	336864
	FGH LTD.	332288	0	0	332288
	GHI, CO	0	0	317680	317680
	LMN LTD.	304766	0	0	304766
	VWX PTY LTD	274428	0	0	274428
	LMN PTY LTD	0	0	211970	211970
	XYZ S.A.	196680	0	0	196680
	RST PTY LTD	0	0	156992	156992
	MNO S.A.	128898	0	0	128898
	JKL, CO	0	0	121704	121704
	QRS INC.	91476	0	0	91476
	FGH, CO	78144	0	0	78144
	UVW, INC.	0	0	40018	40018
ABC Total		13896212	16862318	15471610	46230140
DEF	RST INC.	1628506	1629914	3433936	6692356
	RST S.A.	1170796	1042206	2922568	5135570

When you have large numbers, it helps to have the thousands separator displayed. To set this up in VBA code, use

```
PT.PivotFields("Sum of Revenue").NumberFormat = "#,##0"
```

Some companies often have customers who typically buy thousands or millions of dollars of goods. You can display numbers in thousands by using a single comma after the number format. Of course, you will want to include a "K" abbreviation to indicate that the numbers are in thousands:

```
PT.PivotFields("Sum of Revenue").NumberFormat = "#,##0,K"
```

Of course, local custom dictates the thousands abbreviation. I grew up in a young computer company where everyone was computer literate and we used "K" for the thousands separator. My fellow accountants at the 100+ year old soap company down the street always needed to use "M" for thousands and "MM" for millions. Microsoft is clearly a young computer company and makes it easy to use the K abbreviation, but hard to use the M abbreviation. You are required to prefix the M character with a backslash to have it work:

```
PT.PivotFields("Sum of Revenue").NumberFormat = "#,##0,\M"
```

Alternatively, you can surround the M character with a double quote. To put a double quote inside a quoted string in VBA, you must put two sequential quotes. To set up a format in tenths of millions that uses the #,##0.0,,"MM" format, you would use this line of code:

```
PT.PivotFields("Sum of Revenue").NumberFormat = "#,##0.0,,""MM"""
```

In case it is hard to read, the format is Quote, Pound, Comma, Pound, Pound, Zero, Period, Zero, Comma, Comma, Quote, Quote, M, M, Quote, Quote, Quote. The three quotes at the end are correct. Use two quotes to simulate typing one quote in the custom number format box and a final quote to close the string in VBA.

Suppressing Subtotals for Multiple Row Fields

As soon as you have more than one row field, Excel automatically adds subtotals for all but the innermost row field. Because I am unhappy with the pivot table's lack of capability to add a page break at each change in the product field, I have resigned myself that the subtotals are better added if I use the Subtotals method after converting the pivot table to a table.

Thus, while creating the pivot table in code, you will want to turn off the subtotal rows for the product field. To do this in the Excel user interface, double-click the Product button, and change the Subtotals option to None, as shown in Figure 12.15.

Figure 12.15
When you have more than one row field, eliminate the product subtotals. Double-click the Product button, and choose the None option under Subtotals.

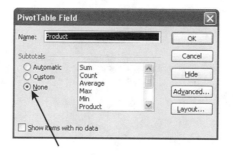

The VBA code to suppress subtotals is incredibly complex. You must set the Subtotals property equal to an array of 12 False values. Read the VBA help for all the gory details, but it goes something like this: The first False turns off automatic subtotals, the second False turns off the Sum subtotal, the third False turns off the Count subtotal, and so on. It is interesting that you have to turn off all 12 possible subtotals even though Excel displays only one subtotal. This line of code suppresses the Product subtotal:

```
PT.PivotFields("Product").Subtotals = Array(False, False, False, False, _
    False, False, False, False, False, False, False, False)
```

Keep in mind there is absolutely no readability here. You cannot name the individual members of the array, so no other coder will be able to know that you are turning on the Count subtotal instead of the Min subtotal. If you have a report with three row fields, you might find it easier to define an array of 12 Falses once and assign this array to both row fields:

```
NoSubtotalArray = Array(False, False, False, False, False, False, False, False, _
    False, False, False, False)
PT.PivotFields("Product").Subtotals = NoSubtotalArray
PT.PivotFields("Date").Subtotals = NoSubtotalArray
```

12

Suppressing Grand Total for Rows

Because you are going to be using VBA code to add automatic subtotals, you can get rid of the Grand Total row. Two settings in the PivotTable Options dialog (back in Figure 12.11) control Grand Totals. It is not entirely intuitive. If you uncheck Grand Total for Rows, you delete the column called Grand Total. Thus, to get rid of the Grand Total row, you must uncheck Grand Total for Columns. This is handled in the code with this line:

```
PT.ColumnGrand = False
```

Handling Additional Annoyances

You've reached the end of the adjustments that you can make to the pivot table. To achieve the final report, you have to make the remaining adjustments after converting the pivot table from a pivot table to regular data.

Figure 12.16 shows the pivot table with all of the adjustments described in the previous sections made and with `PT.TableRange2` selected.

Figure 12.16

It took less than 1 second and 30 lines of code to get 90% of the way to the final report. To solve the last five annoying problems, you have to change this data from a pivot table to regular data.

Sum of Revenue		Region ▾			
Product ▾	Customer ▾	West	Central	East	Grand Total
ABC	LMN INC.	2,130K	3,009K	1,332K	6,471K
	RST S.A.	1,918K	2,744K	1,519K	6,181K
	RST INC.	1,940K	2,385K	1,766K	6,091K
	WXY, CO	1,170K	1,768K	1,540K	4,477K
	VWX GMBH	1,608K	2,002K	606K	4,216K
	HIJ GMBH	837K	1,709K	1,357K	3,902K
	OPQ, INC.	636K	827K	1,670K	3,133K
	MNO CORP	418K	901K	1,420K	2,738K
	DEF, LLC	0K	528K	1,979K	2,507K
	CDE INC.	674K	652K	864K	2,190K
	TUV GMBH	402K	0K	179K	581K
	XYZ GMBH	0K	0K	392K	392K
	EFG S.A.	380K	0K	0K	380K
	BCD LTD.	378K	0K	0K	378K
	UVW INC.	0K	337K	0K	337K
	FGH LTD.	332K	0K	0K	332K
	GHI, CO	0K	0K	318K	318K
	LMN LTD.	305K	0K	0K	305K
	VWX PTY LTD	274K	0K	0K	274K
	LMN PTY LTD	0K	0K	212K	212K
	XYZ S.A.	197K	0K	0K	197K
	RST PTY LTD	0K	0K	157K	157K
	MNO S.A.	129K	0K	0K	129K
	JKL, CO	0K	0K	122K	122K
	QRS INC.	91K	0K	0K	91K
	FGH, CO	78K	0K	0K	78K
	UVW, INC.	0K	0K	40K	40K
DEF	RST INC.	1,629K	1,630K	3,434K	6,692K
	RST S.A.	1,171K	1,042K	2,923K	5,136K
	WXY, CO	1,276K	1,412K	1,805K	4,493K

Creating a New Workbook to Hold the Report

Let's say that you want to build the report in a new workbook so that it can be easily mailed to the product managers. This is fairly easy to do. To make the code more portable, assign object variables to the original workbook, the new workbook, and the first worksheet in the new workbook. This code is similar to the code used in the Chapter 11 case study. At the top of the procedure, add these statements:

```
Dim WSD As Worksheet
Dim WSR As Worksheet
Dim WBO As Workbook
Dim WBN As Workbook
Dim PTCache As PivotCache
Dim PT As PivotTable
Dim PRange As Range
Set WBO = ActiveWorkbook
Set WSD = Worksheets("Pivot Table")
```

After the pivot table has been successfully created, build a blank Report workbook with this code:

```
' Create a New Blank Workbook with one Worksheet
Set WBN = Workbooks.Add(xlWBATWorksheet)
Set WSR = WBN.Worksheets(1)
WSR.Name = "Report"
' Set up Title for Report
With WSR.[A1]
    .Value = "Revenue by Product and Customer"
    .Font.Size = 14
End With
```

Moving the Summary to a Blank Report Worksheet

In Figure 12.16, I hate the borders. I hate the title. I hate the word "Region" in cell L2. You can solve all three of these problems by excluding the first row(s) of PT.TableRange2 from the .Copy and then using PasteSpecial(xlPasteValuesAndNumberFormats) to copy the data to the report sheet.

In the current example, the .TableRange2 property includes only one row to eliminate: Row 2 as shown in Figure 12.16. If you had a more complex pivot table with several column fields and/or one or more page fields, you would have to eliminate more than just the first row of the report. It helps to run your macro to this point, look at the result, and figure out how many rows you need to delete. You can effectively not copy these rows to the report by using the Offset property. Copy the TableRange2 property, offset by 1 row. Purists will note that this code does copy one extra blank row from below the pivot table, but this really does not matter, because the row is blank. After doing the copy, you can erase the original pivot table and destroy the PivotCache:

```
' Copy the Pivot Table data to row 3 of the Report sheet
' Use Offset to eliminate the title row of the pivot table
PT.TableRange2.Offset(1, 0).Copy
WSR.[A3].PasteSpecial Paste:=xlPasteValuesAndNumberFormats
PT.TableRange2.Clear
Set PTCache = Nothing
```

Note that we used the Paste Special option to paste just values and number formats. This gets rid of both borders and the pivot nature of the table. You might be tempted to use the All Except Borders option under Paste, but this keeps the data in a pivot table, and you won't be able to insert new rows in the middle of the data.

12

Filling in the Outline View

The report is almost complete. We are nearly a Data-Subtotals command away from having everything we need. However, there is this useless Outline view where most of the product values in Column A are blank, as shown in Figure 12.17.

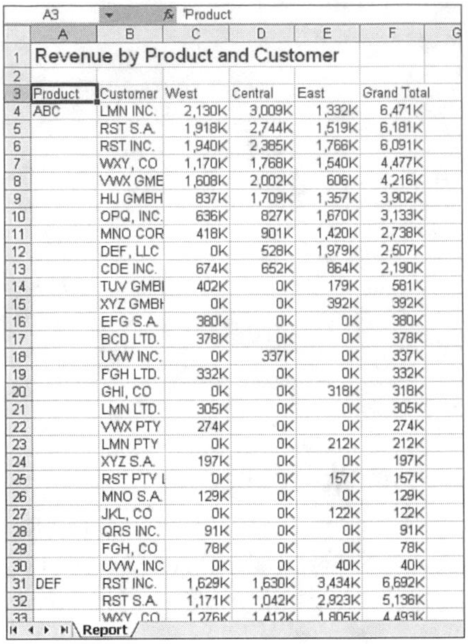

	A	B	C	D	E	F
1	Revenue by Product and Customer					
2						
3	Product	Customer	West	Central	East	Grand Total
4	ABC	LMN INC.	2,130K	3,009K	1,332K	6,471K
5		RST S.A.	1,918K	2,744K	1,519K	6,181K
6		RST INC.	1,940K	2,385K	1,766K	6,091K
7		WXY, CO	1,170K	1,768K	1,540K	4,477K
8		VWX GME	1,608K	2,002K	606K	4,216K
9		HIJ GMBH	837K	1,709K	1,357K	3,902K
10		OPQ, INC.	636K	827K	1,670K	3,133K
11		MNO COR	418K	901K	1,420K	2,738K
12		DEF, LLC	0K	528K	1,979K	2,507K
13		CDE INC.	674K	652K	864K	2,190K
14		TUV GMBI	402K	0K	179K	581K
15		XYZ GMBH	0K	0K	392K	392K
16		EFG S.A.	380K	0K	0K	380K
17		BCD LTD.	378K	0K	0K	378K
18		UVW INC.	0K	337K	0K	337K
19		FGH LTD.	332K	0K	0K	332K
20		GHI, CO	0K	0K	318K	318K
21		LMN LTD.	305K	0K	0K	305K
22		VWX PTY	274K	0K	0K	274K
23		LMN PTY	0K	0K	212K	212K
24		XYZ S.A.	197K	0K	0K	197K
25		RST PTY L	0K	0K	157K	157K
26		MNO S.A.	129K	0K	0K	129K
27		JKL, CO	0K	0K	122K	122K
28		QRS INC.	91K	0K	0K	91K
29		FGH, CO	78K	0K	0K	78K
30		UVW, INC	0K	0K	40K	40K
31	DEF	RST INC.	1,629K	1,630K	3,434K	6,692K
32		RST S.A.	1,171K	1,042K	2,923K	5,136K
33		WXY, CO	1,276K	1,412K	1,805K	4,493K

Figure 12.17
The final major hurdle is filling in the outline view of this report. Luckily, this requires only four non-intuitive, obscure commands that you've likely never used before.

Fixing the outline view requires just a few obscure steps. Here are the steps in the user interface:

1. Select all the cells in Column A that make up the report.
2. Select Edit, GoTo to bring up the GoTo dialog. Select the Special button to bring up the GoTo Special dialog. Select Blanks to select only the blank cells. See Figure 12.18 for this obscure dialog box that is accessed from the Edit, GoTo dialog.
3. Enter an R1C1 style formula to fill the blank with the cell above it. This formula is `=R[-1]C`. In the user interface you would type the equals sign, the up arrow, and then press Ctrl+Enter.
4. Re-select all the cells in Column A that make up the report. This is necessary because the PasteSpecial step cannot work with non-contiguous selections.
5. Copy the formulas in Column A and convert to values by using the Values option in the PasteSpecial dialog.

Figure 12.18
The Go To Special dialog holds the key to selecting only the Blank cells in Column A. After selecting the blanks, fill in the missing cells using a formula that points to the cell above it.

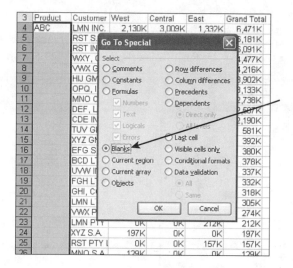

The equivalent VBA code is a bit easier:

1. Find the last row of the report.

2. Enter the formula `=R[-1]C` in the blank cells in A.

3. Change those formulas to values.

The code to do this follows:

```
' Fill in the Outline view in column A
' Look for last row in column B since many rows
' in column A are blank
FinalReportRow = WSR.Range("B65536").End(xlUp).Row
With WSR.Range("A3").Resize(FinalReportRow - 2, 1)
    With .SpecialCells(xlCellTypeBlanks)
        .FormulaR1C1 = "=R[-1]C"
    End With
    .Value = .Value
End With
```

Final Formatting

The last steps for the report involve some basic formatting tasks and then adding the subtotals. You can bold and right-justify the headings in Row 3. Set Rows 1–3 up so that the top three rows print on each page:

```
' Do some basic formatting
' Autofit columns, bold the headings, right-align
Selection.Columns.AutoFit
Range("A3").EntireRow.Font.Bold = True
Range("A3").EntireRow.HorizontalAlignment = xlRight
Range("A3:B3").HorizontalAlignment = xlLeft

' Repeat rows 1-3 at the top of each page
WSR.PageSetup.PrintTitleRows = "$1:$3"
```

Adding Subtotals

Automatic subtotals were discussed in Chapter 11, "Data Mining with Advanced Filter." You want to make sure that you select the Page Break Between Groups option, as shown in Figure 12.19.

Figure 12.19
Use automatic subtotals because doing so enables you to add a page break after each product. This ensures that each product manager has a clean report with only his or her product on it.

If you were sure that you would always have three regions and a total, the code to add subtotals for each product group would be

```
' Add Subtotals by Product.
' Be sure to add a page break at each change in product
Selection.Subtotal GroupBy:=1, Function:=xlSum, TotalList:=Array(3, 4, 5, 6), _
    PageBreaks:=True
```

However, this code fails if you ever have a day where one region has no sales and is not included in the report, or if a new region is added to the company. The solution is to use this convoluted code to dynamically build a list of the columns to total, based on the number of columns in the report:

```
Dim TotColumns()
FinalCol = Cells(3, 255).End(xlToLeft).Column
ReDim Preserve TotColumns(1 To FinalCol - 2)
For i = 3 To FinalCol
    TotColumns(i - 2) = i
Next i
Selection.Subtotal GroupBy:=1, Function:=xlSum, TotalList:=TotColumns _
    , Replace:=True, PageBreaks:=True, SummaryBelowData:=True
```

Finally, with the new totals added to the report, you need to AutoFit the numeric columns again with this code:

```
' Make sure the columns are wide enough for totals
GrandRow = Range("A65536").End(xlUp).Row
Cells(GrandRow, 3).Resize(1, 4).Columns.AutoFit
Cells(GrandRow, 3).Resize(1, 4).NumberFormat = "#,##0,K"
' Add a page break before the Grand Total row, otherwise
' the product manager for XYZ will have two totals
WSR.HPageBreaks.Add Before:=Cells(GrandRow, 1)
```

Putting It All Together

The following code listing produces the product line manager reports in a few seconds:

```
Sub ProductLineManagerReport()
    Dim WSD As Worksheet
    Dim WSR As Worksheet
    Dim WBO As Workbook
    Dim WBN As Workbook
    Dim PTCache As PivotCache
    Dim PT As PivotTable
    Dim PRange As Range
    Dim TotColumns()
    Dim FinalRow As Long
    Dim FinalReportRow As Long
    Dim FinalCol As Integer
    Dim i As Integer
    Dim GrandRow As Long
    Dim NoSubtotalArray As Variant

    Set WBO = ActiveWorkbook
    Set WSD = Worksheets("Pivot Table")

    ' Delete any prior pivot tables
    For Each PT In WSD.PivotTables
        PT.TableRange2.Clear
    Next PT

    ' Define input area and set up a Pivot Cache
    FinalRow = WSD.Cells(65536, 1).End(xlUp).Row
    Set PRange = WSD.Cells(1, 1).Resize(FinalRow, 8)
    Set PTCache = ActiveWorkbook.PivotCaches.Add(SourceType:=xlDatabase, _
        SourceData:=PRange.Address)

    Set PT = PTCache.CreatePivotTable(TableDestination:=WSD.Range("J2"), _
        TableName:="PivotTable1")
    PT.ManualUpdate = True
    ' Set up the row fields
    PT.AddFields RowFields:=Array("Product", "Customer"), ColumnFields:="Region"

    ' Set up the data fields
    With PT.PivotFields("Revenue")
        .Orientation = xlDataField
        .Function = xlSum
        .Position = 1
        .NumberFormat = "#,##0,K"
    End With

    ' Ensure that we get zeroes instead of blanks in the data area
    PT.NullString = "0"

    ' Eliminate the Grand Total Row
    PT.ColumnGrand = False

    ' Suppress the subtotals for the outer row field
    NoSubtotalArray = Array(False, False, False, False, False, False, _
    False, False, False, False, False, False)
```

12

```
PT.PivotFields("Product").Subtotals = NoSubtotalArray

' Sort customers descending by sum of revenue
PT.PivotFields("Customer").AutoSort Order:=xlDescending, _
Field:="Sum of Revenue"

' Manually re-sort the Regions to put West first
' In case West does not exist, eliminate the error message
On Error Resume Next
PT.PivotFields("Region").PivotItems("West").Position = 1
On Error GoTo 0

' Calc the pivot table
PT.ManualUpdate = False
PT.ManualUpdate = True

' Create a New Blank Workbook with one Worksheet
Set WBN = Workbooks.Add(xlWBATWorksheet)
Set WSR = WBN.Worksheets(1)
WSR.Name = "Report"
' Set up Title for Report
With WSR.[A1]
    .Value = "Revenue by Product and Customer"
    .Font.Size = 14
End With

' Copy the pivot table data to row 3 of the Report sheet
' Use Offset to eliminate the title row of the pivot table
PT.TableRange2.Offset(1, 0).Copy
WSR.[A3].PasteSpecial Paste:=xlPasteValuesAndNumberFormats
PT.TableRange2.Clear
Set PTCache = Nothing

' Fill in the Outline view in column A
' Look for last row in column B because many rows
' in column A are blank
FinalReportRow = WSR.Range("B65536").End(xlUp).Row
With Range("A3").Resize(FinalReportRow - 2, 1)
    With .SpecialCells(xlCellTypeBlanks)
        .FormulaR1C1 = "=R[-1]C"
    End With
    .Value = .Value
End With

' Do some basic formatting
' Autofit columns, bold the headings, right-align
Selection.Columns.AutoFit
Range("A3").EntireRow.Font.Bold = True
Range("A3").EntireRow.HorizontalAlignment = xlRight
Range("A3:B3").HorizontalAlignment = xlLeft

' Repeat rows 1-3 at the top of each page
WSR.PageSetup.PrintTitleRows = "$1:$3"

' Add Subtotals by Product.
' Be sure to add a page break at each change in product
```

```
'Selection.Subtotal GroupBy:=1, Function:=xlSum, TotalList:=_
'   Array(3, 4, 5, 6), Replace:=True, PageBreaks:=True, _
'   SummaryBelowData:=True

' The above code would fail if there were no sales
' for the West region on any given day. Build a dynamic
' list of which columns to total.
FinalCol = Cells(3, 255).End(xlToLeft).Column
ReDim Preserve TotColumns(1 To FinalCol - 2)
For i = 3 To FinalCol
    TotColumns(i - 2) = i
Next i
Selection.Subtotal GroupBy:=1, Function:=xlSum, TotalList:=TotColumns _
    , Replace:=True, PageBreaks:=True, SummaryBelowData:=True

' Make sure the columns are wide enough for totals
GrandRow = Range("A65536").End(xlUp).Row
Cells(GrandRow, 3).Resize(1, 4).Columns.AutoFit
Cells(GrandRow, 3).Resize(1, 4).NumberFormat = "#,##0,K"
' Add a page break before the Grand Total row; otherwise
' the product manager for XYZ will have two totals
WSR.HPageBreaks.Add Before:=Cells(GrandRow, 1)
' Change the heading in the final column to Total instead of Grand Total
Cells(3, FinalCol).Value = "Total"

MsgBox "Product Report has been Created"
End Sub
```

Figure 12.20 shows the report produced by this code.

Figure 12.20
It takes less than two seconds to convert 10,000 rows of transactional data to this useful report if you use the code that produced this example. Without pivot tables, the code would be far more complex.

Revenue by Product and Customer

Product	Customer	West	Central	East	Total
ABC	LMN INC.	2,130K	3,009K	1,332K	6,471K
ABC	RST S.A.	1,918K	2,744K	1,519K	6,181K
ABC	RST INC.	1,940K	2,385K	1,766K	6,091K
ABC	WXY, CO	1,170K	1,768K	1,540K	4,477K
ABC	VWX GMBH	1,608K	2,002K	606K	4,216K
ABC	HIJ GMBH	837K	1,709K	1,357K	3,902K
ABC	OPQ, INC.	636K	827K	1,670K	3,133K
ABC	MNO CORP	418K	901K	1,420K	2,738K
ABC	DEF, LLC	0K	528K	1,979K	2,507K
ABC	CDE INC.	674K	652K	864K	2,190K
ABC	TUV GMBH	402K	0K	179K	581K
ABC	XYZ GMBH	0K	0K	392K	392K
ABC	EFG S.A.	380K	0K	0K	380K
ABC	BCD LTD.	378K	0K	0K	378K
ABC	UVW INC.	0K	337K	0K	337K
ABC	FGH LTD.	332K	0K	0K	332K
ABC	GHI, CO	0K	0K	318K	318K
ABC	LMN LTD.	305K	0K	0K	305K
ABC	VWX PTY LTD	274K	0K	0K	274K
ABC	LMN PTY LTD	0K	0K	212K	212K
ABC	XYZ S.A.	197K	0K	0K	197K
ABC	RST PTY LTD	0K	0K	157K	157K
ABC	MNO S.A.	129K	0K	0K	129K
ABC	JKL, CO	0K	0K	122K	122K
ABC	QRS INC.	91K	0K	0K	91K
ABC	FGH, CO	78K	0K	0K	78K
ABC	UVW, INC.	0K	0K	40K	40K
ABC Total		13,896K	16,862K	15,472K	46,230K

12

Product Profitability—Issues with Two or More Data Fields

So far, we've built some powerful summary reports. We've touched only a portion of the powerful features available in pivot tables. The prior example produced a report but had only one data field—revenue.

It is possible to have multiple fields in a pivot report. Microsoft also teases us, pretending to offer calculated fields and calculated items in pivot tables, but these rarely produce the intended calculation and should be avoided.

The data in this example includes not just revenue, but quantity, cost of goods sold (COGS), and profit. The CFO will probably appreciate a report by product that shows quantity sold, revenue, average price, cost of goods sold, average cost, gross profit, and gross profit percent.

If you started to build this report through the user interface, you might end up with a Layout dialog that looks like Figure 12.21.

Figure 12.21
Pivot tables can have many data fields.

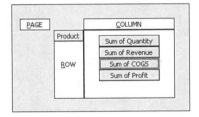

By default, the user interface stacks the data fields on top of each other, as shown in Figure 12.22.

Figure 12.22
The default view of a pivot table with multiple data fields is to have the data fields appear in subsequent rows. This is not a standard method of presenting data.

Product	Data	Total
ABC	Sum of Quantity	2420000
	Sum of Revenue	46230140
	Sum of COGS	20497400
	Sum of Profit	25732740
DEF	Sum of Quantity	2151600
	Sum of Revenue	47601708
	Sum of COGS	21171744
	Sum of Profit	26429964
XYZ	Sum of Quantity	2334200
	Sum of Revenue	53740016
	Sum of COGS	23855524
	Sum of Profit	29884492
Total Sum of Quantity		6905800
Total Sum of Revenue		147571864
Total Sum of COGS		65524668
Total Sum of Profit		82047196

In the Excel user interface, you can drag the Data button and drop it to the left of the Product field to produce a report, as shown in Figure 12.23.

Figure 12.23
Move the Data button to the left of the Product field and you have this also bizarre view of the data. I really hate that the line with Total Sum of Quantity is located so far away from the individual Quantity subtotals.

Data ▾	Product ▾	Total
Sum of Quantity	ABC	2420000
	DEF	2151600
	XYZ	2334200
Sum of Revenue	ABC	46230140
	DEF	47601708
	XYZ	53740016
Sum of COGS	ABC	20497400
	DEF	21171744
	XYZ	23855524
Sum of Profit	ABC	25732740
	DEF	26429964
	XYZ	29884492
Total Sum of Quantity		6905800
Total Sum of Revenue		147571864
Total Sum of COGS		65524668
Total Sum of Profit		82047196

The solution in the current case is to grab the data field and drag it over to become a column field. Keep a close eye on the mouse cursor as you drag. The blue shaded area indicates whether you are about to drop in the column field or row field area. Figure 12.24 shows the various mouse cursors when pivot table fields are being dragged.

Figure 12.24
As you drag a pivot field in the user interface, the blue portion of the mouse cursor indicates where you are dropping the field.

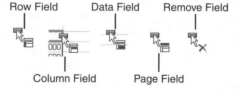

Row Field   Data Field   Remove Field

Column Field   Page Field

With the data fields set up as a column field in the pivot table, the various data fields run from left to right, as shown in Figure 12.25.

12

Figure 12.25
With the data fields set up as a column field, you get a typical accounting-type report.

	Data ▾			
Product ▾	Sum of Quantity	Sum of Revenue	Sum of COGS	Sum of Profit
ABC	2420000	46230140	20497400	25732740
DEF	2151600	47601708	21171744	26429964
XYZ	2334200	53740016	23855524	29884492
Grand Total	6905800	147571864	65524668	82047196

When a pivot table is going to have more that one data field, you have a virtual field name called Data. Where you place the data field in the `.AddFields` method determines which view of the data you get.

The default setup, as shown in Figure 12.22, would have this `AddFields` line:

```
PT.AddFields RowFields:=Array("Product", "Data")
```

The view shown in Figure 12.23 would use this code:

```
PT.AddFields RowFields:=Array("Data", "Product")
```

The view that you need for this report would have Data as a column field:

```
PT.AddFields RowFields:="Product", ColumnFields:="Data"
```

After adding a column field called Data, you would then go on to define four data fields:

```
' Set up the data fields
With PT.PivotFields("Quantity")
    .Orientation = xlDataField
    .Function = xlSum
    .Position = 1
    .NumberFormat = "#,##0"
End With

With PT.PivotFields("Revenue")
    .Orientation = xlDataField
    .Function = xlSum
    .Position = 2
    .NumberFormat = "#,##0"
End With

With PT.PivotFields("COGS")
    .Orientation = xlDataField
    .Function = xlSum
    .Position = 3
    .NumberFormat = "#,##0"
End With

With PT.PivotFields("Profit")
    .Orientation = xlDataField
    .Function = xlSum
    .Position = 4
    .NumberFormat = "#,##0"
End With
```

Defining Calculated Data Fields

Pivot tables offer two types of formulas. The most useful type defines a formula for a calculated field. This adds a new field to the pivot table. Calculations for calculated fields are always done at the summary level. If you define a calculated field for average price as Revenue divided by Quantity, Excel first adds up the total revenue and the total quantity, and then does the division of these totals to get the result. In many cases, this is exactly what you need. If your calculation does not follow the associative law of mathematics, it may not work as you expect.

To set up a calculated field, use the Add method with the CalculatedFields object. You have to specify a field name and a formula. Note that if you create a field called Average Price, the default pivot table produces a field called Sum of Average Price. This is misleading and downright silly. What you have is actually the average of the sums of prices. The solution is to use the Name property when defining the data field to replace Sum of Average Price with something like Avg Price. Note that this name must be different than the name for the calculated field.

The following code produces the report shown in Figure 12.26:

```
Sub AccountingReport()
    Dim WSD As Worksheet
    Dim PTCache As PivotCache
    Dim PT As PivotTable
    Dim PRange As Range
    Dim FinalRow As Long

    Set WSD = Worksheets("Pivot Table")

    ' Delete any prior pivot tables
    For Each PT In WSD.PivotTables
        PT.TableRange2.Clear
    Next PT

    ' Define input area and set up a pivot cache
    FinalRow = WSD.Cells(65536, 1).End(xlUp).Row
    Set PRange = WSD.Cells(1, 1).Resize(FinalRow, 8)
    Set PTCache = ActiveWorkbook.PivotCaches.Add(SourceType:=xlDatabase, _
        SourceData:=PRange.Address)

    Set PT = PTCache.CreatePivotTable(TableDestination:=WSD.Range("J2"), _
        TableName:="PivotTable1")
    PT.ManualUpdate = True
    ' Set up the row fields
    PT.AddFields RowFields:="Product", ColumnFields:="Data"

    ' Define Calculated Fields
    PT.CalculatedFields.Add Name:="AveragePrice", Formula:="=Revenue/Quantity"
    PT.CalculatedFields.Add Name:="AverageCost", Formula:="=COGS/Quantity"
    PT.CalculatedFields.Add Name:="GP_Pct", Formula:="=Profit/Revenue"

    ' Set up the data fields
    With PT.PivotFields("Quantity")
        .Orientation = xlDataField
        .Function = xlSum
        .Position = 1
        .NumberFormat = "#,##0"
        .Name = "Total Qty"
    End With

    With PT.PivotFields("Revenue")
        .Orientation = xlDataField
        .Function = xlSum
        .Position = 2
        .NumberFormat = "#,##0"
        .Name = "Total Revenue"
    End With

    With PT.PivotFields("AveragePrice")
        .Orientation = xlDataField
        .Function = xlSum
        .Position = 3
```

12

```vba
        .NumberFormat = "#,##0.00"
        .Name = "Avg Price"
    End With

    With PT.PivotFields("COGS")
        .Orientation = xlDataField
        .Function = xlSum
        .Position = 4
        .NumberFormat = "#,##0"
        .Name = "Total COGS"
    End With

    With PT.PivotFields("AverageCost")
        .Orientation = xlDataField
        .Function = xlSum
        .Position = 5
        .NumberFormat = "#,##0.00"
        .Name = "Avg Cost"
    End With

    With PT.PivotFields("Profit")
        .Orientation = xlDataField
        .Function = xlSum
        .Position = 6
        .NumberFormat = "#,##0"
        .Name = "Gross Profit"
    End With

    With PT.PivotFields("GP_Pct")
        .Orientation = xlDataField
        .Function = xlSum
        .Position = 7
        .NumberFormat = "#0.0%"
        .Name = "GP%"
    End With

    ' Ensure that we get zeroes instead of blanks in the data area
    PT.NullString = "0"

    ' Calc the pivot table
    PT.ManualUpdate = False
    PT.ManualUpdate = True

End Sub
```

Figure 12.26
All these calculations are straightforward and produce a useful report that enables the CFO to measure product line profitability.

	J	K	L	M	N	O	P	Q
		Data ▼						
	Product ▼	Total Qty	Total Revenue	Avg Price	Total COGS	Avg Cost	Gross Profit	GP%
	ABC	2,420,000	46,230,140	19.10	20,497,400	8.47	25,732,740	55.7%
	DEF	2,151,600	47,601,708	22.12	21,171,744	9.84	26,429,964	55.5%
	XYZ	2,334,200	53,740,016	23.02	23,855,524	10.22	29,884,492	55.6%
	Grand Total	6,905,800	147,571,864	21.37	65,524,668	9.49	82,047,196	55.6%

Avoid Calculated Items

I have never found a situation where the calculated item is useful. The concept of a calculated item is that you can add a new item to an existing field.

Let's say that your company makes three product lines. One division of the company is responsible for product lines ABC and DEF. Another division handles product line XYZ. The theory is that you can add a calculated item to total ABC and DEF. The following code produces the report shown in Figure 12.27:

```
Sub CalculatedItemsAreEvil()
    Dim WSD As Worksheet
    Dim PTCache As PivotCache
    Dim PT As PivotTable
    Dim PRange As Range
    Dim FinalRow As Long

    Set WSD = Worksheets("Pivot Table")

    ' Delete any prior pivot tables
    For Each PT In WSD.PivotTables
        PT.TableRange2.Clear
    Next PT

    ' Define input area and set up a Pivot Cache
    FinalRow = WSD.Cells(65536, 1).End(xlUp).Row
    Set PRange = WSD.Cells(1, 1).Resize(FinalRow, 8)
    Set PTCache = ActiveWorkbook.PivotCaches.Add(SourceType:=xlDatabase, _
        SourceData:=PRange.Address)

    Set PT = PTCache.CreatePivotTable(TableDestination:=WSD.Range("J2"), _
        TableName:="PivotTable1")
    PT.ManualUpdate = True
    ' Set up the row fields
    PT.AddFields RowFields:="Product", ColumnFields:="Data"

    ' Define calculated item along the product dimension
    PT.PivotFields("Product").CalculatedItems.Add "DIVISION1", "=ABC+DEF"
    ' Resequence so that it appears as the 3rd product
    PT.PivotFields("Product").PivotItems("DIVISION1").Position = 3

    With PT.PivotFields("Revenue")
        .Orientation = xlDataField
        .Function = xlSum
        .Position = 1
        .NumberFormat = "#,##0"
        .Name = "Total Revenue"
    End With

    With PT.PivotFields("Profit")
        .Orientation = xlDataField
        .Function = xlSum
        .Position = 2
        .NumberFormat = "#,##0"
        .Name = "Gross Profit"
    End With
```

12

```
' Ensure that we get zeroes instead of blanks in the data area
PT.NullString = "0"

' Calc the pivot table
PT.ManualUpdate = False
PT.ManualUpdate = True

End Sub
```

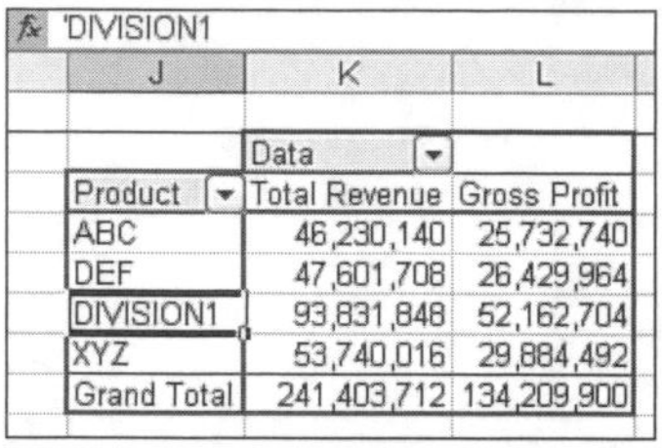

Figure 12.27
Unless you love restating numbers to the SEC, avoid using calculated items.

Product	Total Revenue	Gross Profit
	Data	
ABC	46,230,140	25,732,740
DEF	47,601,708	26,429,964
DIVISION1	93,831,848	52,162,704
XYZ	53,740,016	29,884,492
Grand Total	241,403,712	134,209,900

Look closely at the results shown in Figure 12.27. The calculation for DIVISION1 is correct. Division1 is a total of ABC + DEF. Some quick math confirms that 46 million + 47 million is about 93 million. However, the Grand Total should be 93 million + 53 million, or about 146 million. Instead, Excel gives you a grand total of $241 million. The total revenue for the company just increased by almost $100 million. Excel clearly whacks out and doesn't know how to deal with calculated items added to a field. The only plausible method for dealing with this is to attempt to hide the products that make up Division1. The results are shown in Figure 12.28:

```
With PT.PivotFields("Product")
    .PivotItems("ABC").Visible = False
    .PivotItems("DEF").Visible = False
End With
```

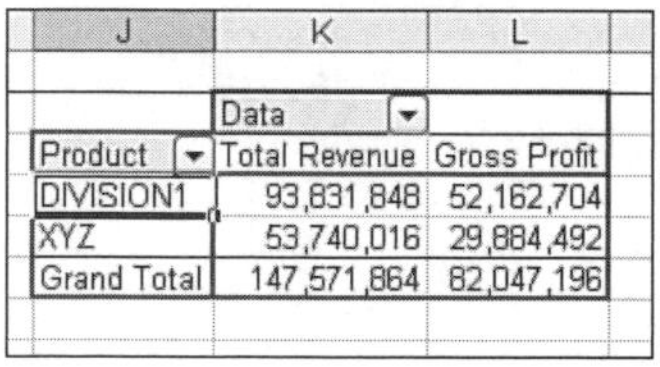

Figure 12.28
After the components that make up the calculated Division1 item are hidden, the total revenue for the company is again correct. However, it would be easier to add a new field to the original data with a Division field.

Product	Total Revenue	Gross Profit
	Data	
DIVISION1	93,831,848	52,162,704
XYZ	53,740,016	29,884,492
Grand Total	147,571,864	82,047,196

Summarizing Date Fields with Grouping

With transactional data, you will often find your date-based summaries having one row per day. Figure 12.29 shows a revenue summary by region and date. There are hundreds of rows in the summary because products were shipped every day. Although daily data might be useful to a plant manager, most people in the company want to see totals by month or quarter and year.

The great news is that Excel handles the summarization of dates in a pivot table with ease. For anyone who has ever had to use the arcane formula =A2+1-Day(A2) to change daily dates into monthly dates, you will appreciate the ease with which you can group transactional data into months or quarters.

Figure 12.29

Before grouping, the summary of this transactional data has hundreds of rows—one row for every ship date in the dataset. The pivot table grouping feature enables you to easily roll this up to month or quarter.

Sum of Revenue	Region			
ShipDate	Central	East	West	Grand Total
1/1/2004		501820		501820
1/2/2004	49654	225390		275044
1/3/2004	247280			247280
1/4/2004	202488	609488		811976
1/5/2004	150920			150920
1/7/2004		664092	303732	967824
1/9/2004	361152	462330		823482
1/10/2004	471636	472230		943866
1/12/2004	137874		201168	339042
1/14/2004	38280	52822	420420	511522
1/15/2004		205590		205590
1/16/2004	481536	255816		737352
1/17/2004		131142		131142
1/19/2004			44924	44924
1/20/2004	385110			385110
1/21/2004		317680	232848	550528
1/22/2004			148170	148170
1/23/2004		179608	321024	500632

To group in the Excel user interface, select a cell in the ShipDate column of the pivot table. From the PivotTable drop-down in the PivotTable toolbar, select Group and Show Detail and then Group. In the Grouping dialog box shown in Figure 12.30, select Months, Quarters, and Years, and then click OK.

Figure 12.30

The Group dialog offers many standard groupings, such as Month, Quarter, and Year.

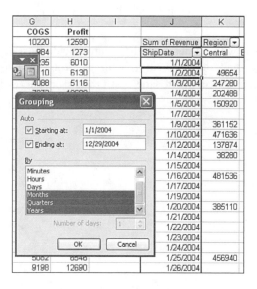

After you select to roll the dates up to Month, Quarter, and Year, an interesting thing happens. Before the operation, you had a PivotField named ShipDate that was grouped by day. We still have a PivotField named ShipDate, but this field is now grouped by month. Two new fields are available in the PivotTable Field list: Years and Quarters. When you group dates, the least aggregated field always takes on the name of the underlying field. Any additional groupings are added as new fields to the Field list.

The new summary and the new field names are shown in Figure 12.31.

Figure 12.31
The Pivot Table quickly summarized the daily information by month, quarter, and year.

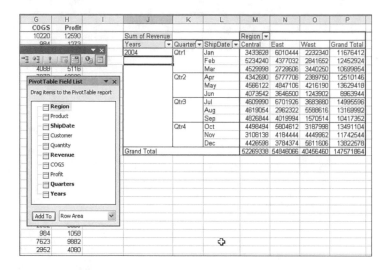

Creating a group with VBA is a bit quirky. The .Group method can be applied to only a single cell in the pivot table and that cell must contain a date or the ShipDate label. This is the first example in this chapter where you must allow Excel to calculate an intermediate pivot table result.

You must define a pivot table with ShipDate in the column field. Turn off ManualCalculation to allow the ShipDate field to be drawn. You can then use the LabelRange property to locate the ShipDate label and group from there. The code to produce Figure 12.31 follows:

```
Sub ReportByMonth()
    Dim WSD As Worksheet
    Dim PTCache As PivotCache
    Dim PT As PivotTable
    Dim PRange As Range
    Dim FinalRow As Long

    Set WSD = Worksheets("Pivot Table")

    ' Delete any prior pivot tables
    For Each PT In WSD.PivotTables
        PT.TableRange2.Clear
    Next PT

    ' Define input area and set up a Pivot Cache
    FinalRow = WSD.Cells(65536, 1).End(xlUp).Row
    Set PRange = WSD.Cells(1, 1).Resize(FinalRow, 8)
```

```
      Set PTCache = ActiveWorkbook.PivotCaches.Add(SourceType:=xlDatabase, _
          SourceData:=PRange.Address)

      Set PT = PTCache.CreatePivotTable(TableDestination:=WSD.Range("J2"), _
          TableName:="PivotTable1")
      PT.ManualUpdate = True
      ' Set up the row fields
      PT.AddFields RowFields:="ShipDate", ColumnFields:="Region"

      With PT.PivotFields("Revenue")
          .Orientation = xlDataField
          .Function = xlSum
          .Position = 1
          .NumberFormat = "#,##0"
          .Name = "Total Revenue"
      End With

      ' Ensure that we get zeroes instead of blanks in the data area
      PT.NullString = "0"

      ' Calc the pivot table to allow the ShipDate label to be drawn
      PT.ManualUpdate = False
      PT.ManualUpdate = True

      ' Group ShipDate by Month, Quarter, Year
      PT.PivotFields("ShipDate").LabelRange.Group Start:=True, _
          End:=True, Periods:= _
          Array(False, False, False, False, True, True, True)

      ' Calc the pivot table
      PT.ManualUpdate = False
      PT.ManualUpdate = True

  End Sub
```

Grouping by Week

You probably noticed that Excel allows you to group by day, month, quarter, year. There is no standard grouping for week. You can define a group that bunches up groups of 7 days.

By default Excel starts the week based on the first date found in the data. This means that the default week would run from Thursday January 1, 2004 through Wednesday January 7, 2004. You can override this by changing the Start parameter from True to an actual date. Use the WeekDay function to determine how many days to adjust the start date.

There is one limitation to grouping by week. When you group by week, you cannot also group by any other measure. It is not valid to group by week and quarter.

The following code creates the report shown in Figure 12.32:

```
Sub ReportByWeek()
    Dim WSD As Worksheet
    Dim PTCache As PivotCache
```

```
Dim PT As PivotTable
Dim PRange As Range
Dim FinalRow As Long

Set WSD = Worksheets("Pivot Table")

' Delete any prior pivot tables
For Each PT In WSD.PivotTables
    PT.TableRange2.Clear
Next PT

' Define input area and set up a Pivot Cache
FinalRow = WSD.Cells(65536, 1).End(xlUp).Row
Set PRange = WSD.Cells(1, 1).Resize(FinalRow, 8)
Set PTCache = ActiveWorkbook.PivotCaches.Add(SourceType:=xlDatabase, _
    SourceData:=PRange.Address)

Set PT = PTCache.CreatePivotTable(TableDestination:=WSD.Range("J2"), _
    TableName:="PivotTable1")
PT.ManualUpdate = True
' Set up the row fields
PT.AddFields RowFields:="ShipDate", ColumnFields:="Region"

With PT.PivotFields("Revenue")
    .Orientation = xlDataField
    .Function = xlSum
    .Position = 1
    .NumberFormat = "#,##0"
    .Name = "Total Revenue"
End With

' Ensure that we get zeroes instead of blanks in the data area
PT.NullString = "0"

' Calc the pivot table to allow the ShipDate label to be drawn
PT.ManualUpdate = False
PT.ManualUpdate = True

' Group ShipDate by Week.
'Figure out the first Monday before the minimum date
FirstDate = PT.PivotFields("ShipDate").LabelRange.Offset(1, 0).Value
WhichDay = Application.WorksheetFunction.Weekday(FirstDate, 3)
StartDate = FirstDate - WhichDay
PT.PivotFields("ShipDate").LabelRange.Group _
    Start:=StartDate, End:=True, By:=7, _
    Periods:=Array(False, False, False, True, False, False, False)

' Re-calc the pivot table with the grouped dates
PT.ManualUpdate = False
PT.ManualUpdate = True

End Sub
```

Figure 12.32
Use the Number of Days setting to group by week.

Total Revenue	Region ⏷			
ShipDate ⏷	Central	East	West	Grand Total
12/29/2003 - 1/4/2004	499,422	1,336,698	0	1,836,120
1/5/2004 - 1/11/2004	983,708	1,598,652	303,732	2,886,092
1/12/2004 - 1/18/2004	657,690	645,370	621,588	1,924,648
1/19/2004 - 1/25/2004	842,050	911,900	883,520	2,637,470
1/26/2004 - 2/1/2004	450,758	1,900,888	545,204	2,896,850
2/2/2004 - 2/8/2004	427,042	610,566	815,100	1,852,708
2/9/2004 - 2/15/2004	271,414	632,082	0	903,496
2/16/2004 - 2/22/2004	1,674,310	885,720	1,407,868	3,967,898
2/23/2004 - 2/29/2004	2,861,474	1,865,600	496,980	5,224,054
3/1/2004 - 3/7/2004	181,984	780,208	816,222	1,778,414
3/8/2004 - 3/14/2004	1,241,636	280,588	461,428	1,983,652
3/15/2004 - 3/21/2004	780,538	847,550	591,668	2,219,756
3/22/2004 - 3/28/2004	1,710,060	441,980	1,089,682	3,241,722

Measuring Order Lead Time by Grouping Two Date Fields

Recall in the last section how Excel adds field names when you group by month and year. The less-aggregated measure (month) inherits the name of the original field. Any more-aggregated measures receive the name of the grouping—for example, "Years."

Your manufacturing plant may be concerned with a measure of how far in advance the orders are received. If the plant has a 12-week lead time to procure components, they would love to have all orders placed 13 weeks in advance. When this doesn't happen, it is critical that you have an excellent forecasting system in place to accurately predict orders.

If you can add an OrderDate field to your transactional data, you could build a table to show how much revenue is received x months in advance of the ship date.

Follow these steps to set up an interesting potential anomaly:

1. Build a pivot table with ShipDate down the side. Group ShipDate by month and year. This creates fields called ShipDate and Year.
2. Move these fields to the column field section of the pivot table.
3. Add OrdDate to the row field of the pivot table.
4. Group OrdDate by month and year. This creates a field called OrdDate with data by month. The grouping of OrdDate by year would tend to also be called "Years," but Excel instead calls it "Year2."

Newer versions of Excel correctly deal with the second set of grouped date fields by changing the field name to Year2 instead of having a second Year.

The following code produces the report shown in Figure 12.33:

```
Sub MeasureLeadtime()
    Dim WSD As Worksheet
    Dim PTCache As PivotCache
    Dim PT As PivotTable
    Dim PRange As Range

    Set WSD = Worksheets("OrderDate")
```

12

```vba
' Delete any prior pivot tables
For Each PT In WSD.PivotTables
    PT.TableRange2.Clear
Next PT

' Define input area and set up a pivot cache
FinalRow = WSD.Cells(65536, 1).End(xlUp).Row
Set PRange = WSD.Cells(1, 1).Resize(FinalRow, 8)
Set PTCache = ActiveWorkbook.PivotCaches.Add(SourceType:=xlDatabase, _
    SourceData:=PRange.Address)

Set PT = PTCache.CreatePivotTable(TableDestination:=WSD.Range("K2"), _
    TableName:="PivotTable1")
PT.ManualUpdate = True
' Set up the row fields
PT.AddFields RowFields:="ShipDate"

With PT.PivotFields("Revenue")
    .Orientation = xlDataField
    .Function = xlSum
    .Position = 1
    .NumberFormat = "#,##0"
    .Name = "Total Revenue"
End With

' Ensure that we get zeroes instead of blanks in the data area
PT.NullString = "0"

' Calc the pivot table to allow the ShipDate label to be drawn
PT.ManualUpdate = False
PT.ManualUpdate = True

' Group ShipDate by month and year
PT.PivotFields("ShipDate").LabelRange.Group Start:=True, End:=True, _
    Periods:=Array(False, False, False, False, True, False, True)

' Now that we have less than 365 data points, move to column field
With PT.PivotFields("Years")
    .Orientation = xlColumnField
    .Position = 1
End With
With PT.PivotFields("ShipDate")
    .Orientation = xlColumnField
    .Position = 2
End With

' Add Order Date as a row field
With PT.PivotFields("OrdDate")
    .Orientation = xlRowField
    .Position = 1
End With

' Calc the pivot table to allow the OrdDate label to be drawn
PT.ManualUpdate = False
PT.ManualUpdate = True

PT.PivotFields("OrdDate").LabelRange.Group Start:=True, End:=True, _
    Periods:=Array(False, False, False, False, True, False, True)
```

12

```
' Re-Calc the pivot table with the grouped dates
PT.ManualUpdate = False
PT.ManualUpdate = True

End Sub
```

Figure 12.33
This order lead time report shows if this manufacturing plant has a 90-day cumulative lead time on components, they'd better have an excellent sales and operations planning system in place.

Total Revenue		Years	▼	ShipDate ▼						
		2004								
Years2 ▼	OrdDate ▼	Jan	Feb	Mar	Apr	May	Jun	Ju
2003	Sep	88,292	0	0	0	0	0	
	Oct	528,323	124,828	0	0	0	0	
	Nov	1,342,765	282,646	138,156	0	0	0	
	Dec	6,868,972	1,319,178	351,004	86,406	0	0	
2004	Jan	2,848,060	6,797,362	1,374,454	556,340	144,329	0	
	Feb	0	3,928,910	5,543,141	1,305,274	512,516	37,790	
	Mar	0	0	3,293,099	7,364,615	1,894,690	359,977	
	Apr	0	0	0	3,197,511	7,554,206	1,187,010	
	May	0	0	0	0	3,523,677	5,782,648	
	Jun	0	0	0	0	0	1,596,519	
	Jul	0	0	0	0	0	0	
	Aug	0	0	0	0	0	0	
	Sep	0	0	0	0	0	0	
	Oct	0	0	0	0	0	0	
	Nov	0	0	0	0	0	0	
	Dec	0	0	0	0	0	0	
Grand Total		11,676,412	12,452,924	10,699,854	12,510,146	13,629,418	8,963,944	

Advanced Pivot Table Techniques

You may be a pivot table pro and never have run into some of the really advanced techniques available with pivot tables. The next four sections discuss such techniques.

Using the Top 10 AutoShow Feature to Produce Executive Overviews

Suppose that 80% of your revenue comes from 20% of your customers. In a real dataset, there would be some large customers at the top of the report, a page of medium-size customers, and then pages of tiny customers who bought just a few hundred dollars of product.

If you are designing an executive dashboard utility, you probably want to provide a snapshot of just the top 5 or top 10 customers. This gives your CEO an idea of who matters most.

As with the AutoSort option, you could be a pivot table pro and never have stumbled across the AutoShow feature in Excel. Accessed from the Advanced button on each Pivot Field dialog, this setting lets you select either the top or bottom *n* records based on any data field in the report. Figure 12.34 shows the settings in the Excel user interface to produce the top 6 customers based on revenue.

Figure 12.34
The Top 10 AutoShow feature lets you spotlight the top or bottom performing customers in a dataset.

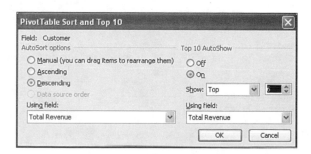

12

> **NOTE** Despite the name of this feature being Top 10 Autoshow, you can actually highlight the bottom 5 or the top 6 or any conceivable combination of top or bottom values.

The code to use Top 10 Autoshow in VBA uses the `.AutoShow` method.

```
' Show only the top 6 customers
PT.PivotFields("Customer").AutoShow Top:=xlAutomatic, Range:=xlTop, _
Count:=6, Field:="Total Revenue"
```

When you create a report using the `AutoShow` method, it is often helpful to copy the data and then go back to the original pivot report to get the totals for all customers. In the following code, this is achieved by removing the customer from the pivot table and copying the grand total to the report. The following code below produces the report shown in Figure 12.35:

```
Sub Top6CEOReport()
    ' Produce a report of top 6 customers with
    ' Revenue, GP, and GP%
    Dim WSD As Worksheet
    Dim WSR As Worksheet
    Dim WBN As Workbook
    Dim PTCache As PivotCache
    Dim PT As PivotTable
    Dim PRange As Range
    Dim FinalRow As Long

    Set WSD = Worksheets("Pivot Table")

    ' Delete any prior pivot tables
    For Each PT In WSD.PivotTables
        PT.TableRange2.Clear
    Next PT

    ' Define input area and set up a pivot cache
    FinalRow = WSD.Cells(65536, 1).End(xlUp).Row
    Set PRange = WSD.Cells(1, 1).Resize(FinalRow, 8)
    Set PTCache = ActiveWorkbook.PivotCaches.Add(SourceType:=xlDatabase, _
        SourceData:=PRange.Address)

    Set PT = PTCache.CreatePivotTable(TableDestination:=WSD.Range("J2"), _
        TableName:="PivotTable1")
    PT.ManualUpdate = True
    ' Set up the row fields
    PT.AddFields RowFields:="Customer", ColumnFields:="Data"

    ' Define Calculated Fields
    PT.CalculatedFields.Add Name:="GP_Pct", Formula:="=Profit/Revenue"

    ' Set up the data fields
    With PT.PivotFields("Revenue")
        .Orientation = xlDataField
        .Function = xlSum
        .Position = 1
```

```
        .NumberFormat = "#,##0,K"
        .Name = "Total Revenue"
End With

With PT.PivotFields("Profit")
    .Orientation = xlDataField
    .Function = xlSum
    .Position = 2
    .NumberFormat = "#,##0,K"
    .Name = "Gross Profit"
End With

With PT.PivotFields("GP_Pct")
    .Orientation = xlDataField
    .Function = xlSum
    .Position = 3
    .NumberFormat = "#0.0%"
    .Name = "GP%"
End With

' Sort customers descending by sum of revenue
PT.PivotFields("Customer").AutoSort Order:=xlDescending, _
    Field:="Total Revenue"

' Show only the top 6 customers
PT.PivotFields("Customer").AutoShow Type:=xlAutomatic, Range:=xlTop, _
    Count:=6, Field:="Total Revenue"

' Ensure that we get zeroes instead of blanks in the data area
PT.NullString = "0"

' Calc the pivot table
PT.ManualUpdate = False
PT.ManualUpdate = True

' Create a new blank workbook with one worksheet
Set WBN = Workbooks.Add(xlWBATWorksheet)
Set WSR = WBN.Worksheets(1)
WSR.Name = "Report"
' Set up ritle for report
With WSR.[A1]
    .Value = "Top 6 Customers"
    .Font.Size = 14
End With

' Copy the pivot table data to row 3 of the report sheet
' Use offset to eliminate the title row of the pivot table
PT.TableRange2.Offset(1, 0).Copy
WSR.[A3].PasteSpecial Paste:=xlPasteValuesAndNumberFormats
LastRow = WSR.Cells(65536, 1).End(xlUp).Row
WSR.Cells(LastRow, 1).Value = "Top 6 Total"

' Go back to the pivot table to get totals without the AutoShow
PT.PivotFields("Customer").Orientation = xlHidden
PT.ManualUpdate = False
PT.ManualUpdate = True
PT.TableRange2.Offset(2, 0).Copy
```

```
WSR.Cells(LastRow + 2, 1).PasteSpecial Paste:=xlPasteValuesAndNumberFormats
WSR.Cells(LastRow + 2, 1).Value = "Total Company"

' Clear the pivot table
PT.TableRange2.Clear
Set PTCache = Nothing

' Do some basic formatting
' Autofit columns, bold the headings, right-align
WSR.Range(WSR.Range("A2"), WSR.Cells(LastRow + 2, 4)).Columns.AutoFit
Range("A3").EntireRow.Font.Bold = True
Range("A3").EntireRow.HorizontalAlignment = xlRight
Range("A3").HorizontalAlignment = xlLeft
Range("B3").Value = "Revenue"

Range("A2").Select
MsgBox "CEO Report has been Created"

End Sub
```

Figure 12.35
The Top 6 Customers report contains two pivot tables.

Top 6 Customers

Customer	Revenue	Gross Profit	GP%
RST INC.	19,128K	10,720K	56.0%
RST S.A.	16,504K	9,142K	55.4%
LMN INC.	15,496K	8,646K	55.8%
VWX GMBH	13,701K	7,652K	55.8%
WXY, CO	13,497K	7,445K	55.2%
HIJ GMBH	12,515K	6,959K	55.6%
Top 6 Total	90,841K	50,564K	55.7%
Total Company	147,572K	82,047K	55.6%

The Top 6 Customers report actually contains two snapshots of a pivot table. After using the AutoShow feature to grab the top 6 customers with their totals, the macro went back to the pivot table, removed the AutoShow option, and grabbed the total of all customers to produce the Total Company row.

Using Pivot Table ShowDetail to Filter a Recordset

Take any pivot table in the Excel user interface. Double-click any number in the table. Excel inserts a new sheet in the workbook and copies all the source records that represent that number. In the Excel user interface, this is a great way to ad-hoc query a data set.

The equivalent VBA property is called ShowDetail. By setting this property to True for any cell in the pivot table, you will generate a new worksheet with all the records that make up that cell:

```
PT.TableRange2.Offset(2, 1).Resize(1, 1).ShowDetail = True
```

The following code produces a pivot table with the total revenue for the top 3 customers and then ShowDetail for each of those customers. This is an alternative method to using the

Advanced Filter report in the case study at the end of Chapter 11. The results of this macro are three new sheets. Figure 12.36 shows the first sheet created:

```
Sub RetrieveTop3CustomerDetail()
    Dim WSD As Worksheet
    Dim PTCache As PivotCache
    Dim PT As PivotTable
    Dim PRange As Range
    Dim FinalRow As Long

    Set WSD = Worksheets("Pivot Table")

    ' Delete any prior pivot tables
    For Each PT In WSD.PivotTables
        PT.TableRange2.Clear
    Next PT

    ' Define input area and set up a pivot cache
    FinalRow = WSD.Cells(65536, 1).End(xlUp).Row
    Set PRange = WSD.Cells(1, 1).Resize(FinalRow, 8)
    Set PTCache = ActiveWorkbook.PivotCaches.Add(SourceType:=xlDatabase, _
        SourceData:=PRange.Address)

    Set PT = PTCache.CreatePivotTable(TableDestination:=WSD.Range("J2"), _
        TableName:="PivotTable1")
    PT.ManualUpdate = True
    ' Set up the row fields
    PT.AddFields RowFields:="Customer", ColumnFields:="Data"

    ' Set up the data fields
    With PT.PivotFields("Revenue")
        .Orientation = xlDataField
        .Function = xlSum
        .Position = 1
        .NumberFormat = "#,##0,K"
        .Name = "Total Revenue"
    End With

    ' Sort customers descending by sum of revenue
    PT.PivotFields("Customer").AutoSort Order:=xlDescending, _
    Field:="Total Revenue"

    ' Show only the top 3 customers
    PT.PivotFields("Customer").AutoShow Type:=xlAutomatic, _
    Range:=xlTop, Count:=3, Field:="Total Revenue"

    ' Ensure that we get zeroes instead of blanks in the data area
    PT.NullString = "0"

    ' Calc the pivot table
    PT.ManualUpdate = False
    PT.ManualUpdate = True

    ' Produce summary reports for each customer
    For i = 1 To 3
        PT.TableRange2.Offset(i + 1, 1).Resize(1, 1).ShowDetail = True
        ' The active sheet has changed to the new detail report
```

12

```
' Add a title
Range("A1:A2").EntireRow.Insert
Range("A1").Value = "Detail for " & _
    PT.TableRange2.Offset(i + 1, 0).Resize(1, 1).Value & _
    " (Customer Rank: " & i & ")"

    Next i

    MsgBox "Detail for Top 3 customers has been created"

End Sub
```

Figure 12.36
Pivot table applications are incredibly diverse. This macro created a pivot table of the top three customers, then used the `ShowDetail` property to retrieve the records for each of those customers.

	A	B	C	D	E	F	G	H
1	Detail for RST INC. (Customer Rank: 1)							
2								
3	Region	Product	ShipDate	Customer	Quantity	Revenue	COGS	Profit
4	West	DEF	12/26/2004	RST INC.	700	14560	6888	7672
5	Central	XYZ	12/24/2004	RST INC.	200	4690	2044	2646
6	West	XYZ	12/19/2004	RST INC.	800	18560	8176	10384
7	East	ABC	12/4/2004	RST INC.	900	18243	7623	10620
8	East	DEF	11/29/2004	RST INC.	800	19280	7872	11408
9	West	ABC	11/19/2004	RST INC.	400	6880	3388	3492
10	Central	ABC	11/14/2004	RST INC.	500	8970	4235	4735
11	East	DEF	11/12/2004	RST INC.	700	14784	6888	7896
12	East	DEF	10/22/2004	RST INC.	1000	23040	9840	13200
13	East	XYZ	10/6/2004	RST INC.	700	15715	7154	8561
14	West	XYZ	10/4/2004	RST INC.	1000	24070	10220	13850
15	West	XYZ	10/2/2004	RST INC.	500	12760	5110	7650
16	West	ABC	9/27/2004	RST INC.	800	13552	6776	6776
17	East	ABC	9/27/2004	RST INC.	700	13139	5929	7210
18	Central	XYZ	1/10/2004	RST INC.	900	21438	9198	12240

Using a Page Field to Create Reports for Each Region or Product

In addition to row fields, column fields, and data fields, a pivot table can have one or more page fields. A page field goes in a separate set of rows above the pivot report. It can serve to filter the report to a certain region, or a certain customer, or a certain combination of region and customers. Figure 12.37 shows a pivot report showing the top 10 customers for product ABC in the West region.

Figure 12.37
This report has two page fields—Region and Product. The page field serves to filter the pivot table results to one particular region or customer. In this case, the report shows the top 10 customers for product ABC in the West region.

	J	K	L	M
	Region	West ▾		
	Product	ABC ▾		
		Data ▾		
	Customer ▾	Total Revenue	Gross Profit	GP%
	LMN INC.	2,130K	1,179K	55.4%
	RST INC.	1,940K	1,064K	54.9%
	RST S.A.	1,918K	1,061K	55.3%
	VWX GMBH	1,608K	900K	56.0%
	WXY, CO	1,170K	667K	57.0%
	HIJ GMBH	837K	464K	55.5%
	CDE INC.	674K	376K	55.8%
	OPQ, INC.	636K	356K	56.0%
	MNO CORP	418K	250K	59.8%
	TUV GMBH	402K	216K	53.7%
	Grand Total	11,732K	6,533K	55.7%

To set up a page field in VBA, add the `PageFields` parameter to the `AddFields` method. The following line of code creates a pivot table with Region in the page field:

```
PT.AddFields RowFields:="Customer", ColumnFields:="Data", PageFields:="Region"
```

The preceding line of code sets up the Region page field set to the value of (All), which returns all regions. To limit the report to just the East region, use the `CurrentPage` property:

```
PT.PivotFields("Region").CurrentPage = "East"
```

One use of a page field is to build a userform where someone can select a particular region or a particular product. You then use this information to set the `CurrentPage` property and display the results of the userform.

Another interesting use is to loop through all `PivotItems` and display them one at a time in the page field. You can quickly produce top 10 reports for each region using this method.

To determine how many regions are available in the data, use `PT.PivotFields("Region").PivotItems.Count`. Either of these loops would work:

```
For i = 1 To PT.PivotFields("Region").PivotItems.Count
    PT.PivotFields("Region").CurrentPage = _
            PT.PivotFields("Region").PivotItems(i).Name
    PT.ManualUpdate = False
    PT.ManualUpdate = True
Next i

For Each PivItem In PT.PivotFields("Region").PivotItems
    PT.PivotFields("Region").CurrentPage = PivItem.Name
    PT.ManualUpdate = False
    PT.ManualUpdate = True
Next PivItem
```

Of course, in both of these loops, the three region reports fly by too quickly to see. In practice, you would want to save each report while it is displayed.

So far in this chapter, we have been using `PT.TableRange2` when copying the data from the pivot table. The `TableRange2` property includes all rows of the pivot table, including the page fields. There is also a `.TableRange1` property, which excludes the page fields. In Figure 12.37, you can use either statement to get the rows starting with Customer:

```
PT.TableRange2.Offset(3, 0)
PT.TableRange1.Offset(1, 0)
```

Which you use is your preference. I prefer to always use `TableRange2`, so that way when I try to delete the pivot table with `PT.TableRange2.Clear`, I never have any problems. If you were to accidentally attempt to clear `TableRange1` when there are page fields, you would end up with the dreaded `Cannot move or change part of a pivot table` error.

The code that follows produces a new workbook for each region, as shown in Figure 12.38:

```
Sub Top10ByRegionReport()
    ' Produce a report of top 10 customers for each region
    Dim WSD As Worksheet
    Dim WSR As Worksheet
```

12

```
Dim WBN As Workbook
Dim PTCache As PivotCache
Dim PT As PivotTable
Dim PRange As Range
Dim FinalRow As Long

Set WSD = Worksheets("Pivot Table")

' Delete any prior pivot tables
For Each PT In WSD.PivotTables
    PT.TableRange2.Clear
Next PT

' Define input area and set up a pivot cache
FinalRow = WSD.Cells(65536, 1).End(xlUp).Row
Set PRange = WSD.Cells(1, 1).Resize(FinalRow, 8)
Set PTCache = ActiveWorkbook.PivotCaches.Add(SourceType:=xlDatabase, _
    SourceData:=PRange.Address)

Set PT = PTCache.CreatePivotTable(TableDestination:=WSD.Range("J2"), _
    TableName:="PivotTable1")
PT.ManualUpdate = True
' Set up the row fields
PT.AddFields RowFields:="Customer", ColumnFields:="Data", _
    PageFields:="Region"

' Define Calculated Fields
PT.CalculatedFields.Add Name:="GP_Pct", Formula:="=Profit/Revenue"

' Set up the data fields
With PT.PivotFields("Revenue")
    .Orientation = xlDataField
    .Function = xlSum
    .Position = 1
    .NumberFormat = "#,##0,K"
    .Name = "Total Revenue"
End With

With PT.PivotFields("Profit")
    .Orientation = xlDataField
    .Function = xlSum
    .Position = 2
    .NumberFormat = "#,##0,K"
    .Name = "Gross Profit"
End With

With PT.PivotFields("GP_Pct")
    .Orientation = xlDataField
    .Function = xlSum
    .Position = 3
    .NumberFormat = "#0.0%"
    .Name = "GP%"
End With

' Sort customers descending by sum of revenue
PT.PivotFields("Customer").AutoSort Order:=xlDescending, _
    Field:="Total Revenue"
```

```vba
' Show only the top 10 customers
PT.PivotFields("Customer").AutoShow Type:=xlAutomatic, Range:=xlTop, _
    Count:=10, Field:="Total Revenue"

' Ensure that we get zeroes instead of blanks in the data area
PT.NullString = "0"

' Calc the pivot table
PT.ManualUpdate = False
PT.ManualUpdate = True
Ctr = 0


' Loop through each region
For Each PivItem In PT.PivotFields("Region").PivotItems
    Ctr = Ctr + 1
    PT.PivotFields("Region").CurrentPage = PivItem.Name
    PT.ManualUpdate = False
    PT.ManualUpdate = True

    ' Create a new blank workbook with one worksheet
    Set WBN = Workbooks.Add(xlWBATWorksheet)
    Set WSR = WBN.Worksheets(1)
    WSR.Name = PivItem.Name
    ' Set up Title for Report
    With WSR.[A1]
        .Value = "Top 10 Customers in the " & PivItem.Name & " Region"
        .Font.Size = 14
    End With

    ' Copy the pivot table data to row 3 of the report sheet
    ' Use offset to eliminate the page & title rows of the pivot table
    PT.TableRange2.Offset(3, 0).Copy
    WSR.[A3].PasteSpecial Paste:=xlPasteValuesAndNumberFormats
    LastRow = WSR.Cells(65536, 1).End(xlUp).Row
    WSR.Cells(LastRow, 1).Value = "Top 10 Total"

    ' Do some basic formatting
    ' Autofit columns, bold the headings, right-align
    WSR.Range(WSR.Range("A3"), WSR.Cells(LastRow, 4)).Columns.AutoFit
    Range("A3").EntireRow.Font.Bold = True
    Range("A3").EntireRow.HorizontalAlignment = xlRight
    Range("A3").HorizontalAlignment = xlLeft
    Range("B3").Value = "Revenue"

    Range("A2").Select

Next PivItem

' Clear the pivot table
PT.TableRange2.Clear
Set PTCache = Nothing

MsgBox Ctr & " Region reports have been created"

End Sub
```

12

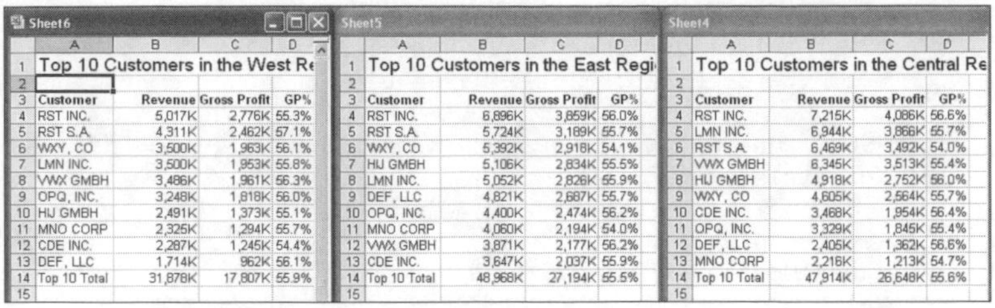

Sheet6

	A	B	C	D
1	Top 10 Customers in the West Re			
2				
3	Customer	Revenue	Gross Profit	GP%
4	RST INC.	5,017K	2,776K	55.3%
5	RST S.A.	4,311K	2,462K	57.1%
6	WXY, CO	3,500K	1,963K	56.1%
7	LMN INC.	3,500K	1,953K	55.8%
8	VWX GMBH	3,486K	1,961K	56.3%
9	OPQ, INC.	3,248K	1,818K	56.0%
10	HIJ GMBH	2,491K	1,373K	55.1%
11	MNO CORP	2,325K	1,294K	55.7%
12	CDE INC.	2,287K	1,245K	54.4%
13	DEF, LLC	1,714K	962K	56.1%
14	Top 10 Total	31,878K	17,807K	55.9%
15				

Sheet5

	A	B	C	D
1	Top 10 Customers in the East Regi			
2				
3	Customer	Revenue	Gross Profit	GP%
4	RST INC.	6,896K	3,859K	56.0%
5	RST S.A.	5,724K	3,189K	55.7%
6	WXY, CO	5,392K	2,918K	54.1%
7	HIJ GMBH	5,106K	2,834K	55.5%
8	LMN INC.	5,052K	2,826K	55.9%
9	DEF, LLC	4,821K	2,687K	55.7%
10	OPQ, INC.	4,400K	2,474K	56.2%
11	MNO CORP	4,060K	2,194K	54.0%
12	VWX GMBH	3,871K	2,177K	56.2%
13	CDE INC.	3,647K	2,037K	55.9%
14	Top 10 Total	48,968K	27,194K	55.5%
15				

Sheet4

	A	B	C	D
1	Top 10 Customers in the Central Re			
2				
3	Customer	Revenue	Gross Profit	GP%
4	RST INC.	7,215K	4,086K	56.6%
5	LMN INC.	6,944K	3,866K	55.7%
6	RST S.A.	6,469K	3,492K	54.0%
7	VWX GMBH	6,345K	3,513K	55.4%
8	HIJ GMBH	4,918K	2,752K	56.0%
9	WXY, CO	4,605K	2,564K	55.7%
10	CDE INC.	3,468K	1,954K	56.4%
11	OPQ, INC.	3,329K	1,845K	55.4%
12	DEF, LLC	2,405K	1,362K	56.6%
13	MNO CORP	2,216K	1,213K	54.7%
14	Top 10 Total	47,914K	26,648K	55.6%
15				

Figure 12.38
By looping through all items found in the Region page field, the macro produced one workbook for each regional manager.

Manually Filtering to Two or More Items in a `PivotField`

In addition to setting up a calculated pivot item to display the total of a couple of products that make up a dimension, it is possible to manually filter a particular `PivotField`.

For example, I have one client who sells shoes. In the report showing sales of sandals, he wants to see just the stores that are in warm weather states. The code to hide a particular store is

```
PT.PivotFields("Store").PivotItems("Minneapolis").Visible = False
```

You need to be very careful to never set all items to `False` or the macro will end with an error. This tends to happen more than you would expect. An application may first show products A and B, then on the next loop show products C and D. If you attempt to make A and B not visible before making C and D visible, you will be in the situation of having no products visible along the PivotField, which causes an error. To correct this, always loop through all PivotItems, making sure to turn them back to Visible before the second pass through the loop.

The process of manually filtering records seems to offer a way to filter a particular `PageField` to two items. Let's say that you want to produce a pivot report showing Revenue, Profit, and GP% by Region for the sum of product lines ABC and DEF.

Conceptually, you would follow these steps in the user interface:

1. Produce a pivot table with Region down the side, Products across the top, and Revenue in the data field.
2. Manually filter the Product PivotField to include only products ABC and DEF.
3. Move the Product page field to the page area.
4. Add Profit and GP% to the column field area.

This seems pretty dangerous to do in the user interface because you have absolutely no indication that the Product dimension in the page field is limited by any criteria. Figure 12.39 shows the resulting pivot table. There is no indication that the numbers exclude XYZ until you happen to touch the Product drop-down, as shown in Figure 12.40.

Figure 12.39
The Product page field excludes XYZ, but there is no visible indication of this.

J	K	L	M
Product	(All) ▾		
	Data ▾		
Region ▾	Total Revenue	Gross Profit	GP%
Central	33,956K	18,910K	55.7%
East	35,091K	19,566K	55.8%
West	24,784K	13,687K	55.2%
Grand Total	93,832K	52,163K	55.6%

Figure 12.40
As soon as someone touches the Product drop-down, he may realize that the report has been filtered to include only two products.

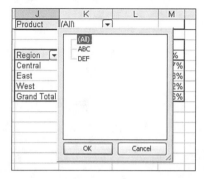

This seems to be a pretty misleading state in which to leave your pivot table. However, if you are in control with VBA and add a proper title to the copied report, this seems to be a fine way to produce reports for a certain division.

This process is even easier in VBA. You can immediately build the table with Product in the page field and then loop through to change the `Visible` property to show only the total of the products in a certain division. The following code produces the report shown in Figure 12.41:

```
Sub ProduceReportOfTwoProducts()
    ' Exploit an apparent anomaly to put
    ' two products in a single page field to
    ' produce a summary report of just products ABC and DEF

    Dim WSD As Worksheet
    Dim WSR As Worksheet
    Dim WBN As Workbook
    Dim PTCache As PivotCache
    Dim PT As PivotTable
    Dim PRange As Range
    Dim FinalRow As Long

    Set WSD = Worksheets("Pivot Table")

    ' Delete any prior pivot tables
    For Each PT In WSD.PivotTables
        PT.TableRange2.Clear
    Next PT

    ' Define input area and set up a pivot cache
    FinalRow = WSD.Cells(65536, 1).End(xlUp).Row
    Set PRange = WSD.Cells(1, 1).Resize(FinalRow, 8)
```

```
Set PTCache = ActiveWorkbook.PivotCaches.Add(SourceType:=xlDatabase, _
    SourceData:=PRange.Address)

Set PT = PTCache.CreatePivotTable(TableDestination:=WSD.Range("J2"), _
    TableName:="PivotTable1")
PT.ManualUpdate = True
' Set up the row fields
PT.AddFields RowFields:="Region", ColumnFields:="Data", _
    PageFields:="Product"

' Define calculated fields
PT.CalculatedFields.Add Name:="GP_Pct", Formula:="=Profit/Revenue"

' Set up the data fields
With PT.PivotFields("Revenue")
    .Orientation = xlDataField
    .Function = xlSum
    .Position = 1
    .NumberFormat = "#,##0,K"
    .Name = "Total Revenue"
End With

' Calc the pivot table
PT.ManualUpdate = False
PT.ManualUpdate = True

' Make sure all PivotItems along product are visible
For Each PivItem In PT.PivotFields("Product").PivotItems
    PivItem.Visible = True
Next PivItem

' Now - loop through and keep only certain items visible
For Each PivItem In PT.PivotFields("Product").PivotItems
    Select Case PivItem.Name
        Case "ABC", "DEF"
            PivItem.Visible = True
        Case Else
            PivItem.Visible = False
    End Select
Next PivItem

' Add the remaining data fields
With PT.PivotFields("Profit")
    .Orientation = xlDataField
    .Function = xlSum
    .Position = 2
    .NumberFormat = "#,##0,K"
    .Name = "Gross Profit"
End With

With PT.PivotFields("GP_Pct")
    .Orientation = xlDataField
    .Function = xlSum
    .Position = 3
    .NumberFormat = "#0.0%"
    .Name = "GP%"
End With
```

```
' Ensure that we get zeroes instead of blanks in the data area
PT.NullString = "0"

' Calc the pivot table
PT.ManualUpdate = False
PT.ManualUpdate = True
Ctr = 0

' Create a new blank workbook with one worksheet
Set WBN = Workbooks.Add(xlWBATWorksheet)
Set WSR = WBN.Worksheets(1)
WSR.Name = "Report"
' Set up Title for Report
With WSR.[A1]
    .Value = "Sales by Region - Products ABC & DEF Only"
    .Font.Size = 14
End With

' Copy the pivot table data to row 3 of the report sheet
' Use offset to eliminate the page & title rows of the pivot table
PT.TableRange2.Offset(3, 0).Copy
WSR.[A3].PasteSpecial Paste:=xlPasteValuesAndNumberFormats
LastRow = WSR.Cells(65536, 1).End(xlUp).Row
WSR.Cells(LastRow, 1).Value = "Division Total"

' Do some basic formatting
' Autofit columns, bold the headings, right-align
WSR.Range(WSR.Range("A3"), WSR.Cells(LastRow, 4)).Columns.AutoFit
Range("A3").EntireRow.Font.Bold = True
Range("A3").EntireRow.HorizontalAlignment = xlRight
Range("A3").HorizontalAlignment = xlLeft
Range("B3").Value = "Revenue"

Range("A2").Select

' Clear the Pivot Table
PT.TableRange2.Clear
Set PTCache = Nothing


MsgBox "ABC/DEF Division report has been created"

End Sub
```

Figure 12.41
VBA makes it fairly easy to exploit the filtered page field anomaly and build a pivot report for two products at one tIme.

Sales by Region - Products ABC & DEF Only			
Region	**Revenue**	**Gross Profit**	**GP%**
Central	33,956K	18,910K	55.7%
East	35,091K	19,566K	55.8%
West	24,784K	13,687K	55.2%
Division Total	93,832K	52,163K	55.6%

Sum, Average, Count, Min, Max, and More

So far, every example in this chapter has involved summing data. It is also possible to get an average, minimum, or maximum of data. In VBA, change the xlFunction property of the data field and give the data field a unique name. For example, the following code fragment produces five different summaries of the quantity field, each with a unique name:

```
Sub ReportManyDetailsByCustomer()
    ' Show Sum, Count, Average, Min, Max Revenue by Customer

    Dim WSD As Worksheet
    Dim PTCache As PivotCache
    Dim PT As PivotTable
    Dim PRange As Range
    Dim FinalRow As Long

    Set WSD = Worksheets("Pivot Table")

    ' Delete any prior pivot tables
    For Each PT In WSD.PivotTables
        PT.TableRange2.Clear
    Next PT

    ' Define input area and set up a pivot cache
    FinalRow = WSD.Cells(65536, 1).End(xlUp).Row
    Set PRange = WSD.Cells(1, 1).Resize(FinalRow, 8)
    Set PTCache = ActiveWorkbook.PivotCaches.Add(SourceType:=xlDatabase, _
        SourceData:=PRange.Address)

    Set PT = PTCache.CreatePivotTable(TableDestination:=WSD.Range("J2"), _
        TableName:="PivotTable1")
    PT.ManualUpdate = True
    ' Set up the row fields
    PT.AddFields RowFields:="Customer", ColumnFields:="Data"

    ' Set up the data fields
    With PT.PivotFields("Revenue")
        .Orientation = xlDataField
        .Function = xlSum
        .Position = 1
        .NumberFormat = "#,##0,K"
        .Name = "Total Revenue"
    End With

    With PT.PivotFields("Revenue")
        .Orientation = xlDataField
        .Function = xlCount
        .Position = 2
        .NumberFormat = "#,##0"
        .Name = "Number Orders"
    End With

    With PT.PivotFields("Revenue")
        .Orientation = xlDataField
        .Function = xlAverage
        .Position = 3
```

```
          .NumberFormat = "#,##0"
          .Name = "Average Revenue"
    End With

    With PT.PivotFields("Revenue")
          .Orientation = xlDataField
          .Function = xlMin
          .Position = 4
          .NumberFormat = "#,##0"
          .Name = "Smallest Order"
    End With

    With PT.PivotFields("Revenue")
          .Orientation = xlDataField
          .Function = xlMax
          .Position = 5
          .NumberFormat = "#,##0"
          .Name = "Largest Order"
    End With

    ' Ensure that we get zeroes instead of blanks in the data area
    PT.NullString = "0"

    ' Calc the pivot table
    PT.ManualUpdate = False
    PT.ManualUpdate = True
    Ctr = 0

End Sub
```

The resulting pivot table provides a number of statistics about the average revenue, largest order, smallest order, and so on. The results are shown in Figure 12.42.

Figure 12.42
All five data columns here are various statistics about revenue. From left to right, there is total, count, average, min, and max.

Customer	Total Revenue	Number Orders	Average Revenue	Smallest Order	Largest Order
BCD LTD.	1,380K	88	15,686	7,167	23,890
CDE INC.	9,402K	968	9,712	1,819	21,366
DEF, LLC	8,939K	616	14,512	6,156	25,350
EFG S.A.	864K	88	9,813	4,380	17,250
FGH LTD.	1,127K	88	12,810	4,060	18,072
FGH, CO	931K	88	10,579	2,484	18,552
GHI, CO	1,599K	88	18,170	11,680	24,420
HIJ GMBH	12,515K	1,144	10,939	1,741	22,014
JKL, CO	1,265K	88	14,379	5,532	18,264
LMN INC.	15,496K	1,452	10,672	1,878	21,762
LMN LTD.	1,317K	88	14,970	4,754	21,730
LMN PTY LTD	1,576K	88	17,913	9,635	24,130
MNO CORP	8,602K	792	10,861	2,042	21,880
MNO S.A.	682K	88	7,755	2,358	17,856
OPQ, INC.	10,977K	880	12,473	1,740	25,310
QRS INC.	690K	88	7,842	2,029	13,962
RST INC.	19,128K	1,430	13,376	2,012	25,140
RST PTY LTD	756K	88	8,591	4,270	13,806
RST S.A.	16,504K	1,320	12,503	1,704	25,080
TUV GMBH	1,189K	88	13,512	7,032	20,610
UVW INC.	1,101K	88	12,508	4,614	19,344
UVW, INC.	1,028K	88	11,679	1,819	22,840
VWX GMBH	13,701K	1,232	11,121	1,836	25,060
VWX PTY LTD	1,327K	88	15,075	9,660	20,408
WXY, CO	13,497K	1,056	12,782	1,817	26,010
XYZ GMBH	1,216K	88	13,813	4,846	21,015
XYZ S.A.	764K	88	8,678	4,282	12,612
Grand Total	147,572K	12,386	11,914	1,704	25,350

12

Reporting Percentages

In addition to the available choices such as Sum, Min, Max, and Average, there is another set of pivot table options called the calculation options. As shown in Figure 12.43, these allow you to show a particular field as a Percentage of the Total, Percentage of the Row, Percentage of the Column, and Percent Difference from the previous or next item. All these settings are controlled through the `.Calculation` property of the page field.

Figure 12.43
There are a myriad of possibilities for the `Calculation` property of a data field.

The valid properties for `.Calculation` are `xlPercentOf`, `xlPercentOfColumn`, `xlPercentOfRow`, `xlPercentOfTotal`, `xlRunningTotal`, `xlPercentDifferenceFrom`, `xlDifferenceFrom`, `xlIndex`, and `xlNoAdditionalCalculation`. Each has its own unique set of rules. Some require that you specify a `BaseField` and others require that you specify both a `BaseField` and a `BaseItem`. The following sections have some specific examples.

Percentage of Total

To get the percentage of the total, specify `xlPercentOfTotal` as the `Calculation` property for the page field:

```
' Set up a percentage of total
With PT.PivotFields("Revenue")
    .Orientation = xlDataField
    .Caption = "PctOfTotal"
    .Function = xlSum
    .Position = 2
    .NumberFormat = "#0.0%"
    .Calculation = xlPercentOfTotal
End With
```

Percentage Growth from Previous Month

With ship months going down the columns, you might want to see the percentage of revenue growth from month to month. You can set this up with the `xlPercentDifferenceFrom` setting. In this case, you must specify that the `BaseField` is `ShipDate` and that the `BaseItem` is something called (`previous`):

```
' Set up % change from prior month
With PT.PivotFields("Revenue")
    .Orientation = xlDataField
    .Function = xlSum
    .Caption = "%Change"
    .Calculation = xlPercentDifferenceFrom
    .BaseField = "ShipDate"
    .BaseItem = "(previous)"
    .Position = 3
    .NumberFormat = "#0.0%"
End With
```

Note that with positional calculations, you cannot use the `AutoShow` or `AutoSort` methods. This is too bad; it would be interesting to sort the customers high to low and to see their sizes in relation to each other.

Percentage of a Specific Item

Another client sells computer hardware and then software and service plans. The sales reps have a goal to have software and service both exceed 10% of the hardware revenue. You can use the `xlPercentDifferenceFrom` setting to express revenues as a percentage of the Hardware product line:

```
' Show revenue as a percentage of hardware
With PT.PivotFields("Revenue")
    .Orientation = xlDataField
    .Function = xlSum
    .Caption = "% of HW"
    .Calculation = xlPercentDifferenceFrom
    .BaseField = "ProductLine"
    .BaseItem = "Hardware"
    .Position = 3
    .NumberFormat = "#0.0%"
End With
```

Running Total

It is not intuitive, but to set up a running total, you must define a `BaseField`. In this example, you have `ShipDate` running down the column. To define a running total column for revenue, you must specify that the `BaseField` is `ShipDate`:

```
' Set up Running Total
With PT.PivotFields("Revenue")
    .Orientation = xlDataField
    .Function = xlSum
    .Caption = "YTD Total"
    .Calculation = xlRunningTotal
    .Position = 4
    .NumberFormat = "#,##0,K"
    .BaseField = "ShipDate"
End With
```

12

Figure 12.44 shows the results of a pivot table with three custom calculation settings, as discussed earlier.

Figure 12.44
This pivot table presents four views of Sum of Revenue. Column K is the normal calculation. Column L is % of Total. Column M is % change from previous month. Column N is the running total.

	Data			
ShipDate	Total Revenue	PctOfTotal	%Change	YTD Total
Jan	11,676K	7.9%		11,676K
Feb	12,453K	8.4%	6.7%	24,129K
Mar	10,700K	7.3%	-14.1%	34,829K
Apr	12,510K	8.5%	16.9%	47,339K
May	13,629K	9.2%	8.9%	60,969K
Jun	8,964K	6.1%	-34.2%	69,933K
Jul	14,996K	10.2%	67.3%	84,928K
Aug	13,170K	8.9%	-12.2%	98,098K
Sep	10,417K	7.1%	-20.9%	108,516K
Oct	13,491K	9.1%	29.5%	122,007K
Nov	11,743K	8.0%	-13.0%	133,749K
Dec	13,823K	9.4%	17.7%	147,572K
Grand Total	147,572K	100.0%		

CASE STUDY

Case Study—Excel 97

Pivot tables and VBA took a radical turn in Excel 2000. In Excel 2000, Microsoft introduced the `PivotCache` object. This object allows you to define one `PivotCache` and then build many pivot reports from the `PivotCache`.

Officially, Microsoft quit supporting Excel 97 a few years ago. But, in practical terms, there are still many companies using Excel 97. If you need your code to work on a legacy platform, then you should be aware of how pivot tables were created in Excel 97.

In Excel 97, you would use the PivotTableWizard method. By way of illustration, I will show the code for building a simple pivot table showing Revenue by Region and Product. Where current code uses two steps—add a PivotCache, and then use CreatePivotTable—Excel 97 would use just one step, using the PivotTableWizard method to create the table:

```
Sub PivotExcel97Compatible()
    ' Pivot Table Code for Excel 97 Users

    Dim WSD As Worksheet
    Dim PT As PivotTable
    Dim PRange As Range
    Dim FinalRow As Long

    Set WSD = Worksheets("Pivot Table")

    ' Delete any prior pivot tables
    For Each PT In WSD.PivotTables
        PT.TableRange2.Clear
    Next PT

    ' Define input area and set up a pivot cache
    FinalRow = WSD.Cells(65536, 1).End(xlUp).Row
    Set PRange = WSD.Cells(1, 1).Resize(FinalRow, 8)

    ' Create pivot table using PivotTableWizard
```

12

```vba
    Set PT = WSD.PivotTableWizard(SourceType:=xlDatabase, _
        SourceData:=PRange.Address, _
        TableDestination:="R2C10", TableName:="PivotTable1")

    PT.ManualUpdate = True
    ' Set up the row fields
    PT.AddFields RowFields:="Region", ColumnFields:="Product"

    ' Set up the data fields
    With PT.PivotFields("Revenue")
        .Orientation = xlDataField
        .Function = xlSum
        .Position = 1
        .NumberFormat = "#,##0,K"
        .Name = "Total Revenue"
    End With

    PT.ManualUpdate = False
    PT.ManualUpdate = True

End Sub
```

Next Steps

If you couldn't already tell, pivot tables are my favorite feature in Excel. They are incredibly powerful and flexible. Combined with VBA, they provide an excellent calculation engine and power many of the reports that I build for clients. In Chapter 13, "Excel Power," you will learn a myriad of techniques for handling various tasks in VBA.

12

Excel Power

A major secret of successful programmers is to never waste time writing the same code twice. They all have little bits—or even big bits—of code that are used over and over again. Another big secret is to never take 8 hours doing something that can be done in 10 minutes—which is what this book is about!

This chapter contains programs donated by several Excel power programmers. These are programs that they have found useful and they hope will be of help to you, too. Not only can they save you time, but they may teach you new ways of solving common problems.

Different programmers have different programming styles and we did not rewrite the submissions. As you review the lines of code, you will notice different ways of doing the same task, such as referring to ranges.

Using VBA to Extend Excel

Excel VBA can be used to make Excel appear to do things that are not possible in the Excel user interface. To start off, a couple of our experts will demonstrate how to use VBA to extend the Conditional Formatting and Advanced Filter commands.

Conditional Formatting with More Than Three Conditions

Submitted by Russell Hauf of Beaverton, OR.

The title of this example is deceptive—this isn't a true conditional format. By using a control sheet, you duplicate the functionality of the conditional format command. This new command allows more than the usual three conditions in a conditional format.

The control sheet consists of two columns: Column A holds the variables being watched, and Column B holds the number conforming to the desired color. After the control sheet is configured, the variables can be entered on the main sheet and colored accordingly:

```
Private Sub Worksheet_Change(ByVal Target As Range)
' Conditional Formatting for more than 3 conditions

    Dim rng As Range

    ' Target is a range: therefore, it can be more than one cell
    ' For example, someone could delete the contents of a range,
    ' or someone could enter an array.
    Set rng = Intersect(Target, Range("D:D"))
    If rng Is Nothing Then
        Exit Sub
    Else
        Dim cl As Range

        For Each cl In rng
            On Error Resume Next
            ' — The preceding line doesn't change the cell's background
            ' — color if the cell's value is not found in the range
            ' — that we specified (rngcolors).
            cl.Interior.ColorIndex = _
                Application.WorksheetFunction.VLookup(cl.Value, _
                ThisWorkbook.Sheets("Sheet3").Range("rngColors"), _
                2, False)
            If Err.Number <> 0 Then
                cl.Interior.ColorIndex = xlNone
            End If
        Next cl
    End If

End Sub
```

AutoFilter with More Than Two Conditions

Submitted by Richie Sills of Worcester, England. Richie is a tax manager at a firm of chartered accountants.

The autofilter in Excel VBA allows only two criteria. The following code shows how three or more criteria can be used with the autofilter:

```
Sub MultiFilter()

    Dim rngTarget As Range, rng1 As Range, rng2 As Range, rngMyRange As Range

    Const Crit1 As String = "Crit1"
    Const Crit2 As String = "Crit2"
    Const Crit3 As String = "Crit3"
    'the AutoFilter criteria to use

    Application.ScreenUpdating = False
    With Worksheets("Sheet1")
        .Rows(1).Insert
        .Range("A1").Value = "dummy"
```

```
                'set up dummy header
                Set rngTarget = .Range("A1:A" & .Cells(Rows.Count, 1).End(xlUp).Row)
                'set the range to work with
                rngTarget.AutoFilter Field:=1, Criteria1:=Crit1, _
                    Operator:=xlOr, Criteria2:=Crit2
                'get first two criteria
                Set rng1 = .AutoFilter.Range.Offset(1, 0) _
                    .Resize(.AutoFilter.Range.Rows.Count - 1). _
                        SpecialCells(xlCellTypeVisible)
                'range with first 2 (use offset and resize to exclude header)
                rngTarget.AutoFilter
                'reset autofilter
                rngTarget.AutoFilter Field:=1, Criteria1:=Crit3
                'get third criteria
                Set rng2 = .AutoFilter.Range.Offset(1, 0) _
                    .Resize(.AutoFilter.Range.Rows.Count - 1). _
                        SpecialCells(xlCellTypeVisible)
                'range with 3rd
                rngTarget.AutoFilter
                .Rows(1).Delete
                'remove dummy header
                Set rngMyRange = Union(rng1, rng2)
                'combine the range
                rngMyRange.EntireRow.Copy Destination:=Worksheets("Sheet2").Range("A1")
                'or whatever you want to do ...
            End With
            Application.ScreenUpdating = True

        End Sub
```

File Operations

The next group of utilities deal with handling files in folders. Being able to loop through a list of files in a folder is a useful task.

List Files in a Directory

Submitted by Nathan P. Oliver of Minneapolis, MN. Nathan is a financial consultant and application developer.

This program returns the filename, size, and date modified of all files in the selected directory and its subfolders:

```
Private Sub Srch()
Dim i As Long, z As Long, ws As Worksheet, y As Variant
Dim fLdr As String
y = Application.InputBox("Please Enter File Extension", "Info Request")
If y = False And Not TypeName(y) = "String" Then Exit Sub
Application.ScreenUpdating = False
fLdr = BrowseForFolderShell
With Application.FileSearch
    .NewSearch
    .LookIn = fLdr
    .SearchSubFolders = True
    .Filename = y
```

```
        Set ws = ThisWorkbook.Worksheets.Add(Sheets(1))
        On Error GoTo 1
2:      ws.Name = "FileSearch Results"
        On Error GoTo 0
        If .Execute() > 0 Then
            For i = 1 To .FoundFiles.Count
                If Left$(.FoundFiles(i), 1) = Left$(fLdr, 1) Then
                    If CBool(Len(Dir(.FoundFiles(i)))) Then
                        z = z + 1
                        ws.Cells(z + 1, 1).Resize(, 3) = _
                            Array(Dir(.FoundFiles(i)), _
                                FileLen(.FoundFiles(i)) \ 1000, _
                                FileDateTime(.FoundFiles(i)))
                        ws.Hyperlinks.Add Anchor:=Cells(z + 1, 1), _
                            Address:=.FoundFiles(i)
                    End If
                End If
            Next i
        End If
    End With
    ActiveWindow.DisplayHeadings = False
    With ws
        With .[a1:c1]
            .Value = [{"Full Name","Kilobytes","Last Modified"}]
            .Font.Underline = xlUnderlineStyleSingle
            .EntireColumn.AutoFit
            .HorizontalAlignment = xlCenter
        End With
        .[d1:iv1].EntireColumn.Hidden = True
        Range(.[a65536].End(3)(2), _
            .[a65536]).EntireRow.Hidden = True
        Range(.[a2], .[c65536]).Sort [a2], xlAscending, header:=xlNo
    End With
    Application.ScreenUpdating = True
    Exit Sub

1:  Application.DisplayAlerts = False
    Worksheets("FileSearch Results").Delete
    Application.DisplayAlerts = True
    GoTo 2


End Sub

Function BrowseForFolderShell() As String
Dim objShell As Object, objFolder As Object

Set objShell = CreateObject("Shell.Application")
' Uncomment next line to start at desktop
'Set objFolder = objShell.BrowseForFolder(0, "Please select a folder", 0, 0)
'*** Specify Starting Browse Location
Set objFolder = objShell.BrowseForFolder(0, _
    "Please select a folder", 0, "c:\")
If (Not objFolder Is Nothing) Then
    On Error Resume Next
    If IsError(objFolder.Items.Item.Path) Then BrowseForFolderShell = _
        CStr(objFolder): GoTo Here
    On Error GoTo 0
```

```
    If Len(objFolder.Items.Item.Path) > 3 Then
        BrowseForFolderShell = objFolder.Items.Item.Path & _
            Application.PathSeparator
    Else
        BrowseForFolderShell = objFolder.Items.Item.Path
    End If
Else: Application.ScreenUpdating = True: End
End If

Here:
    Set objFolder = Nothing:     Set objShell = Nothing

End Function
```

Delete a Workbook After a Specific Date

Submitted by Tom Urtis of San Francisco, CA. Tom is the principal of Atlas Programming Management, an Excel consulting firm in the Bay Area.

This program deletes the active workbook if the system date is after the one specified in the Workbook Open procedure:

> **CAUTION**
>
> The file does *not* go into the Recycle Bin. It is permanently deleted.

```
Sub Workbook_Open()
If Date <= #12/31/2004# Then Exit Sub
    MsgBox "Good-bye cruel world !!"
With ThisWorkbook
    .Saved = True
    .ChangeFileAccess xlReadOnly
    Kill .FullName
    .Close False
End With
End Sub
```

Close and Delete

Submitted by Tommy Miles of Houston, TX.

A common task in Excel is to open data files, grab some information, and then close the data file, never to open it again. Over time, these temporary files build up, unless they are meticulously deleted.

This sample adds a new option to the File menu—Close & Delete (see Figure 13.1). This allows the active workbook to be closed and deleted. It also removes the filename from the list of recently opened files. Good-bye temporary files!

13

Figure 13.1
Close and delete temporary files.

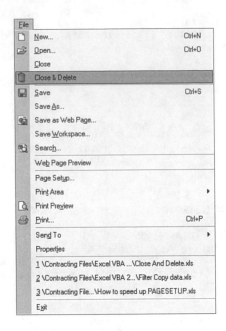

```
Private Sub Workbook_AddinInstall()
    Dim cmdControl As CommandBarButton

    On Error Resume Next
    Set cmdControl = Application.CommandBars(1).Controls("File"). _
        Controls(CONTROLNAME)
    If cmdControl Is Nothing Then
        Set cmdControl = Application.CommandBars(1).Controls("File")._
            Controls.Add(Type:=msoControlButton, _
            Before:=Application.CommandBars(1).Controls("File"). _
            Controls("Save").Index)

        With cmdControl
            .Caption = CONTROLNAME
            .FaceId = 67
            .Style = msoButtonIconAndCaption
            .DescriptionText = "Close and delete the current workbook"
            .OnAction = "CloseAndKill"
        End With

        Set cmdControl = Nothing
    End If
    On Error GoTo 0
End Sub

Private Sub Workbook_AddinUninstall()
    On Error Resume Next
    Application.CommandBars(1).Controls("File").Controls(CONTROLNAME).Delete
End Sub

Public Const CONTROLNAME As String = "Close && De&lete"
```

```
Private Sub CloseAndKill()
    Dim tmpAnswer As Variant

    If ActiveWorkbook Is Nothing Then Exit Sub

    tmpAnswer = MsgBox("Are you sure you want to delete """ & _
        ActiveWorkbook.FullName & """?", _
        vbYesNoCancel + vbInformation)

    If tmpAnswer = vbYes Then
        Dim tmpFileName As String
        Dim RecentFle As RecentFile


        tmpFileName = ActiveWorkbook.FullName

        'this removes the file from the recent used list so
        'that you don't accidentally try to open it again
        For Each RecentFle In Application.RecentFiles
            If RecentFle.Path = tmpFileName Then RecentFle.Delete
        Next

        ActiveWorkbook.Close SaveChanges:=False

        On Error Resume Next
        Kill tmpFileName 'deletes the file
        If Err.Number <> 0 Then
            MsgBox "Unable to delete """ & tmpFileName & """."
        End If
    End If
End Sub
```

Import CSV

Submitted by Masaru Kaji of Kobe-City, Japan. Masaru provides Excel Consultation through Colo's Junkroom (www.interq.or.jp/sun/puremis/colo/).

If you find yourself importing a lot of CSV files and then having to go back and delete them, this program is for you. It quickly opens up a CSV in Excel and deletes the original file:

```
Option Base 1

Sub OpenLargeCSVFast()
    Dim buf(1 To 256) As Variant
    Dim i As Long
    Const strFilePath As String = "C:\temp\Test.CSV" 'Change here

    Dim strRenamedPath As String
    strRenamedPath = Split(strFilePath, ".")(0) & "txt"

    With Application
        .ScreenUpdating = False
        .DisplayAlerts = False
    End With
    'Setting an array for FieldInfo to open CSV
    For i = 1 To 256
        buf(i) = Array(i, 2)
```

13

```
            Next
            Name strFilePath As strRenamedPath
            Workbooks.OpenText Filename:=strRenamedPath, DataType:=xlDelimited, _
                            Comma:=True, FieldInfo:=buf
            Erase buf
            ActiveSheet.UsedRange.Copy ThisWorkbook.Sheets(1).Range("A1")
            ActiveWorkbook.Close False
            Kill strRenamedPath
            With Application
                .ScreenUpdating = True
                .DisplayAlerts = True
            End With
    End Sub
```

Read Entire CSV to Memory and Parse

Submitted by Suat Mehmet Ozgur of Istanbul, Turkey. Suat develops applications in Excel, Access, and Visual Basic for MrExcel.com and TheOfficeExperts.com.

This sample takes a different approach to reading a text file. Rather than read one record at a time, the macro loads the entire text file into memory in a single string variable. The macro then parses the string into individual records. The advantage of this method is that you access the file on disk only once. All subsequent processing occurs in memory and is very fast.

```
Sub ReadTxtLines()
'No need to install Scripting Runtime library since we used late binding
Dim sht As Worksheet
Dim fso As Object
Dim fil As Object
Dim txt As Object
Dim strtxt As String
Dim tmpLoc As Long

    'Working on active sheet
    Set sht = ActiveSheet
    'Clear data in the sheet
    sht.UsedRange.ClearContents

    'File system object that we need to manage files
    Set fso = CreateObject("Scripting.FileSystemObject")
    'File that we like to open and read
    Set fil = fso.GetFile("c:\test.txt")
    'Opening file as a TextStream
    Set txt = fil.OpenAsTextStream(1)
    'Reading file include into a string variable at once
    strtxt = txt.ReadAll
    'Close textstream and free the file. We don't need it anymore.
    txt.Close
    'Find the first placement of new line char
    tmpLoc = InStr(1, strtxt, vbCrLf)
    'Loop until no more new line
    Do Until tmpLoc = 0
        'Use A column and next empty cell to write the text file line
        sht.Cells(65536, 1).End(xlUp).Offset(1).Value = _
            Left(strtxt, tmpLoc - 1)
```

```
            'Remove the parsed line from the variable
            ' that we stored file include
            strtxt = Right(strtxt, Len(strtxt) - tmpLoc - 1)
            'Find the next placement of new line char
            tmpLoc = InStr(1, strtxt, vbCrLf)
        Loop
        'Last line that has data but no new line char
        sht.Cells(65536, 1).End(xlUp).Offset(1).Value = strtxt

        'It will be already released by the ending of this procedure but
        ' as a good habit, set the object as nothing.
        Set fso = Nothing
    End Sub
```

Combining and Separating Workbooks

The next four utilities demonstrate how to combine worksheets into single workbooks or separate a single workbook into individual worksheets or Word documents.

Separate Worksheets into Workbooks

Submitted by Tommy Miles.

This sample goes through the active workbook and saves each sheet as its own workbook in the same path as the original workbook. It names the new workbooks based upon the sheet name. It does not overwrite files without prompting:

```
Sub SplitWorkbook()
    Dim ws As Worksheet
    Dim DisplayStatusBar As Boolean

    DisplayStatusBar = Application.DisplayStatusBar

    Application.DisplayStatusBar = True
    Application.ScreenUpdating = False

    For Each ws In ThisWorkbook.Sheets
        Dim NewFileName As String

        Application.StatusBar = ThisWorkbook.Sheets.Count & " Remaining Sheets"

        If ThisWorkbook.Sheets.Count <> 1 Then
            NewFileName = ThisWorkbook.Path & "\" & ws.Name & ".xls"

            ws.Copy

            ActiveWorkbook.Sheets(1).Name = "Sheet1"

            ActiveWorkbook.SaveAs Filename:=NewFileName

            ActiveWorkbook.Close SaveChanges:=False
        Else
            NewFileName = ThisWorkbook.Path & "\" & ws.Name & ".xls"
```

13

```
                ws.Name = "Sheet1"

                ThisWorkbook.SaveAs Filename:=NewFileName
            End If
        Next

        Application.StatusBar = False
        Application.DisplayStatusBar = DisplayStatusBar
        Application.ScreenUpdating = True
    End Sub
```

Combine Workbooks

Submitted by Tommy Miles.

This sample goes through all the Excel files in a specified directory and combines them into a single workbook. It renames the sheets based on the name of the original workbook:

```
Sub CombineWorkbooks()
    Dim CurFile As String

    Dim DestWB As Workbook
    Dim ws As Object 'allows for different sheet types

    Const DirLoc As String = "C:\Data\" 'location of files

    Application.ScreenUpdating = False

    Set DestWB = Workbooks.Add(xlWorksheet)

    CurFile = Dir(DirLoc & "*.xls")

    Do While CurFile <> vbNullString
        Dim OrigWB As Workbook

        Set OrigWB = Workbooks.Open(Filename:=DirLoc & CurFile, ReadOnly:=True)

        ' Limit to valid sheet names and remove .xls
        CurFile = Left(Left(CurFile, Len(CurFile) - 4), 29)

        For Each ws In OrigWB.Sheets
            ws.Copy After:=DestWB.Sheets(DestWB.Sheets.Count)

            If OrigWB.Sheets.Count > 1 Then
                DestWB.Sheets(DestWB.Sheets.Count).Name = CurFile & ws.Index
            Else
                DestWB.Sheets(DestWB.Sheets.Count).Name = CurFile
            End If
        Next

        OrigWB.Close SaveChanges:=False

        CurFile = Dir
    Loop

    Application.DisplayAlerts = False
        DestWB.Sheets(1).Delete
```

```
        Application.DisplayAlerts = True

        Application.ScreenUpdating = True

    Set DestWB = Nothing
End Sub
```

Filter and Copy Data to Separate Worksheets

Submitted by Dennis Wallentin of Ostersund, Sweden. Dennis provides Excel Tips and Tricks at www.xldennis.com.

This sample uses a specified column as shown in Figure 13.2 to filter data and copies the results to new worksheets in the active workbook as shown in Figure 13.3.

Figure 13.2
Data to be filtered and copied to new sheets.

	A	B	C
1	Article	Catego	Number
2	AA1	A	76
3	AA1	B	23
4	AA1	C	80
5	AA2	A	25
6	AA2	B	43
7	AA2	C	54
8	AA3	A	40
9	AA3	B	54
10	AA3	C	21
11	AA4	A	10
12	AA4	B	90
13	AA4	C	20
14	AA5	A	25
15	AA5	B	30
16	AA5	C	40
17			

Figure 13.3
Filtered data on its own sheet.

	A	B	C
1			
2	AA5	A	25
3	AA5	B	30
4	AA5	C	40
5			

```
Sub Filter_NewSheet()
Dim wbBook As Workbook
Dim wsSheet As Worksheet
Dim rnStart As Range, rnData As Range
Dim i As Long

Set wbBook = ThisWorkbook
Set wsSheet = wbBook.Worksheets("Sheet1")

With wsSheet
    'Make sure that the first row contains headings.
    Set rnStart = .Range("A2")
    Set rnData = .Range(.Range("A2"), .Range("C65536").End(xlUp))
End With

Application.ScreenUpdating = True
```

13

```
For i = 1 To 5
    'Here we filter the data with the first criterion.
    rnStart.AutoFilter Field:=1, Criteria1:="AA" & i
    'Copy the filtered list
    rnData.SpecialCells(xlCellTypeVisible).Copy
    'Add a new worksheet to the active workbook.
    Worksheets.Add Before:=wsSheet
    'Name the added new worksheets.
    ActiveSheet.Name = "AA" & i
    'Paste the filtered list.
    Range("A2").PasteSpecial xlPasteValues
Next i

'Reset the list to its original status.
rnStart.AutoFilter Field:=1

With Application
    'Reset the clipboard.
    .CutCopyMode = False
    .ScreenUpdating = False
End With

End Sub
```

Export Data to Word

Submitted by Dennis Wallentin.

This program transfers data from Excel to a Word document. It uses early binding, so a reference must be established in the VBE (Tools, References) to the Microsoft Word Object Library.

```
Sub Export_Data_Word_Table()
Dim wdApp As Word.Application
Dim wdDoc As Word.Document
Dim wdCell As Word.Cell
Dim i As Long
Dim wbBook As Workbook
Dim wsSheet As Worksheet
Dim rnData As Range
Dim vaData As Variant

Set wbBook = ThisWorkbook
Set wsSheet = wbBook.Worksheets("Sheet1")

With wsSheet
    Set rnData = .Range("A1:A10")
End With

'Add the values in the range to a one-dimensional variant-array.
vaData = rnData.Value

'Here we instantiate the new object.
Set wdApp = New Word.Application
'Here the target document resides in the same folder as the workbook.
Set wdDoc = wdApp.Documents.Open(ThisWorkbook.Path & "\Test.doc")
```

```
'Import data to the first table and in the first column of a ten-row table.
For Each wdCell In wdDoc.Tables(1).Columns(1).Cells
    i = i + 1
    wdCell.Range.Text = vaData(i, 1)
Next wdCell

'Save and close the document.
With wdDoc
    .Save
    .Close
End With

'Close the hidden instance of Microsoft Word.
wdApp.Quit
'Release the external variables from the memory
Set wdDoc = Nothing
Set wdApp = Nothing

MsgBox "The data has been transfered to Test.doc.", vbInformation

End Sub
```

Working with Cell Comments

Cell comments are often underused features of Excel. The following four utilities help you to get the most out of cell comments.

List Comments

Submitted by Tommy Miles.

Excel allows the user to print the comments in a workbook, but it doesn't specify the workbook or worksheet on which the comments appear. The following sample places comments, author, and location of each comment on a new sheet for easy viewing, saving, or printing. Sample results are shown in Figure 13.4.

Figure 13.4
Easily list all the information pertaining to comments.

	A	B	C	D	E	F	G	H
1	Author	Book	Sheet	Range	Comment			
2	Tracy	Chapter 13 - Contributors.xls	Sheet1	$B$2	modify to handle "cancel" of input box			
3	Tracy	Chapter 13 - Contributors.xls	Sheet1	$B$8	Only works with keyboard			
4	Tracy	Chapter 13 - Contributors.xls	Sheet1	$B$19	fix error msgs			
5								
6								

```
Sub ListComments()
    Dim wb As Workbook
    Dim ws As Worksheet

    Dim cmt As Comment

    Dim cmtCount As Long

    cmtCount = 2
```

```
    On Error Resume Next
        Set ws = ActiveSheet
            If ws Is Nothing Then Exit Sub
    On Error GoTo 0

    Application.ScreenUpdating = False

    Set wb = Workbooks.Add(xlWorksheet)

    With wb.Sheets(1)
        .Range("$A$1") = "Author"
        .Range("$B$1") = "Book"
        .Range("$C$1") = "Sheet"
        .Range("$D$1") = "Range"
        .Range("$E$1") = "Comment"
    End With

    For Each cmt In ws.Comments
        With wb.Sheets(1)
            .Cells(cmtCount, 1) = cmt.author
            .Cells(cmtCount, 2) = cmt.Parent.Parent.Parent.Name
            .Cells(cmtCount, 3) = cmt.Parent.Parent.Name
            .Cells(cmtCount, 4) = cmt.Parent.Address
            .Cells(cmtCount, 5) = CleanComment(cmt.author, cmt.Text)
        End With

        cmtCount = cmtCount + 1
    Next

    wb.Sheets(1).UsedRange.WrapText = False

    Application.ScreenUpdating = True

    Set ws = Nothing
    Set wb = Nothing
End Sub

Private Function CleanComment(author As String, cmt As String) As String
    Dim tmp As String

    tmp = Application.WorksheetFunction.Substitute(cmt, author & ":", "")
    tmp = Application.WorksheetFunction.Substitute(tmp, Chr(10), "")

    CleanComment = tmp
End Function
```

Resize Comments

Submitted by Tom Urtis.

This sample resizes all the comment boxes on a sheet so that, when selected, the entire comment is easily viewable (see Figure 13.5):

Figure 13.5
Resize comments.

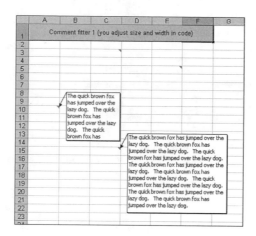

```
Sub CommentFitter1()
Application.ScreenUpdating = False
Dim x As Range, y As Long

For Each x In Cells.SpecialCells(xlCellTypeComments)
    Select Case True
        Case Len(x.NoteText) <> 0
            With x.Comment
                .Shape.TextFrame.AutoSize = True
                If .Shape.Width > 250 Then
                    y = .Shape.Width * .Shape.Height
                    .Shape.Width = 150
                    .Shape.Height = (y / 200) * 1.2
                End If
            End With
    End Select
Next x
Application.ScreenUpdating = True
End Sub
```

Resize Comments with Centering

Submitted by Tom Urtis.

This sample resizes all the comment boxes on a sheet by centering the comments (see Figure 13.6):

Figure 13.6
Center comments.

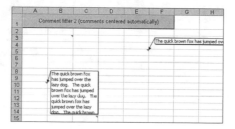

```
Sub CommentFitter2()
Application.ScreenUpdating = False
Dim x As Range, y As Long

For Each x In Cells.SpecialCells(xlCellTypeComments)
    Select Case True
        Case Len(x.NoteText) <> 0
            With x.Comment
                .Shape.TextFrame.AutoSize = True
                If .Shape.Width > 250 Then
                    y = .Shape.Width * .Shape.Height
                    .Shape.ScaleHeight 0.9, msoFalse, msoScaleFromTopLeft
                    .Shape.ScaleWidth 1#, msoFalse, msoScaleFromTopLeft
                End If
            End With
    End Select
Next x
Application.ScreenUpdating = True
End Sub
```

Place a Chart in a Comment

Submitted by Tom Urtis.

A live chart cannot exist in a shape, but you can take a picture of the chart and load it into the comment shape as shown in Figure 13.7.

Figure 13.7
Place a chart in a cell comment.

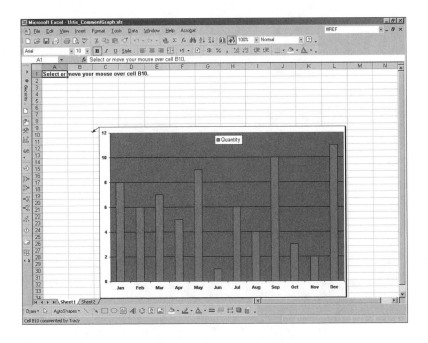

The steps to do this manually follow:

1. Create and/or save the picture image you want the comment to display.

2. Create the comment, if you have not already done so, and select the cell in which the comment is.

3. From the menu bar, click Insert, Edit Comment, or right-click the cell and select Edit Comment.

4. Right-click on the comment border and select Format Comment.

5. Select the Colors and Lines tab, and click the down arrow belonging to the Color field of the Fill section.

6. Select Fill Effects, then select the Picture tab and click the Select Picture button.

7. Navigate to your desired image, select it, and click OK twice.

The effect of having a "live chart" in a comment can be achieved if, for example, the code is part of a SheetChange event when the chart's source data is being changed. Also, business charts are updated often so you might want a macro to keep the comment updated and to avoid repeating the same steps. The following macro does just that: modifies the macro for file path name, chart name, destination sheet, and cell, and size of comment shape, depending on the size of the chart:

```
Sub PlaceGraph()
Dim x As String, z As Range

Application.ScreenUpdating = False
x = "C:\Excel VBA 2003 by Jelen & Syrstad\Graph.gif"

Set z = Worksheets("Sheet1").Range("B10")

On Error Resume Next
z.Comment.Delete
On Error GoTo 0

ActiveSheet.ChartObjects("Chart 1").Activate
ActiveChart.Export x

With z.AddComment
    With .Shape
        .Height = 322
        .Width = 465
        .Fill.UserPicture x
    End With
End With

Range("A1").Activate
Application.ScreenUpdating = True

Set z = Nothing
End Sub
```

13

Utilities to Wow Your Clients

The next four utilities will amaze and impress your clients.

Using Conditional Formatting to Highlight Selected Cell

Submitted by Ivan F. Moala of Auckland, New Zealand. Ivan is the site author of "The XcelFiles" (www.xcelfiles.com), where you will find out things you thought you couldn't do in Excel.

Conditional formatting is used to highlight the row and column of the active cell to help you visually locate it. Important: Do not use this method if you already have conditional formats on the worksheet. Any existing conditional formats will be overwritten. Also, this program clears the clipboard, so it is not possible to use while doing copy, cut, or paste:

```
Const iInternational As Integer = Not (0)

Private Sub Worksheet_SelectionChange(ByVal Target As Range)
Dim iColor As Integer
'// On error resume in case
'// user selects a range of cells
On Error Resume Next
iColor = Target.Interior.ColorIndex
'// Leave On Error ON for Row offset errors

If iColor < 0 Then
    iColor = 36
Else
    iColor = iColor + 1
End If

'// Need this test in case font color is the same
If iColor = Target.Font.ColorIndex Then iColor = iColor + 1

Cells.FormatConditions.Delete

'// Horizontal color banding
With Range("A" & Target.Row, Target.Address) 'Rows(Target.Row)
    .FormatConditions.Add Type:=2, Formula1:=iInternational 'Or just 1 '"TRUE"
    .FormatConditions(1).Interior.ColorIndex = iColor
End With

'// Vertical color banding
With Range(Target.Offset(1 - Target.Row, 0).Address & ":" & _
    Target.Offset(-1, 0).Address)
    .FormatConditions.Add Type:=2, Formula1:=iInternational 'Or just 1 '"TRUE"
    .FormatConditions(1).Interior.ColorIndex = iColor
End With

End Sub
```

13

Highlight Selected Cell Without Using Conditional Formatting

Submitted by Ivan F. Moala.

This example visually highlights the active cell without using conditional formatting when the keyboard arrow keys are used to move around the sheet:

```
Dim strCol As String
Dim iCol As Integer
Dim dblRow As Double

Sub HighlightRight()
    HighLight 0, 1
End Sub

Sub HighlightLeft()
    HighLight 0, -1
End  Sub

Sub HighlightUp()
    HighLight -1, 0, -1
End Sub

Sub HighlightDown()
    HighLight 1, 0, 1
End Sub

Sub HighLight(dblxRow As Double, iyCol As Integer, Optional dblZ As Double = 0)

On Error GoTo NoGo
strCol = Mid(ActiveCell.Offset(dblxRow, iyCol).Address, _
        InStr(ActiveCell.Offset(dblxRow, iyCol).Address, "$") + 1, _
        InStr(2, ActiveCell.Offset(dblxRow, iyCol).Address, "$") - 2)
iCol = ActiveCell.Column
dblRow = ActiveCell.Row

Application.ScreenUpdating = False

With Range(strCol & ":" & strCol & "," & dblRow + dblZ & ":" & dblRow + dblZ)
    .Select
    Application.ScreenUpdating = True
    .Item(dblRow + dblxRow).Activate
End With

NoGo:
End Sub

Sub DisableDelete()
    Cells(ActiveCell.Row, ActiveCell.Column).Select
    Application.OnKey "{DEL}"
End Sub

Sub ReSet()
    Application.OnKey "{RIGHT}"
    Application.OnKey "{LEFT}"
    Application.OnKey "{UP}"
    Application.OnKey "{DOWN}"
End Sub
```

13

Custom Transpose Data

Submitted by Masaru Kaji.

This program does a customized data transposition based on the specified column:

```
Sub TransposeData()
    Dim shOrg As Worksheet, shRes As Worksheet
    Dim rngStart As Range, rngPaste As Range
    Dim lngData As Long

    Application.ScreenUpdating = False
    On Error Resume Next
    Application.DisplayAlerts = False
    Sheets("Result").Delete
    Application.DisplayAlerts = True
    On Error GoTo 0

    On Error GoTo terminate

    Set shOrg = Sheets(1)
    Set shRes = Sheets.Add(After:=shOrg)
    shRes.Name = "Result"
    With shOrg
        '--Sort
        .Cells.CurrentRegion.Sort Key1:=.[B2], Order1:=1, _
            Key2:=.[C2], Order2:=1, Key3:=.[E2], Order3:=1, Header:=xlYes
        '--Copy title
        .Rows(1).Copy shRes.Rows(1)
        '--Set start range
        Set rngStart = .[C2]
        Do Until IsEmpty(rngStart)
            Set rngPaste = shRes.[A65536].End(xlUp).Offset(1)
            lngData = GetNextRange(rngStart)
            rngStart.Offset(, -2).Resize(, 5).Copy rngPaste

            'Copy to V1 toV14
            rngStart.Offset(, 2).Resize(lngData).Copy
            rngPaste.Offset(, 5).PasteSpecial Paste:=xlAll, _
                Operation:=xlNone, SkipBlanks:=False, Transpose:=True
            'Copy to V1FP to V14FP
            rngStart.Offset(, 1).Resize(lngData).Copy
            rngPaste.Offset(, 19).PasteSpecial Paste:=xlAll, Operation:=xlNone, _
                SkipBlanks:=False, Transpose:=True
            Set rngStart = rngStart.Offset(lngData)
        Loop
    End With
    Application.GoTo shRes.[A1]
    shRes.Cells.Columns.AutoFit
    Application.ScreenUpdating = True
    Application.CutCopyMode = False
    If MsgBox("Do you want to delete an original worksheet?", 36) = 6 Then
        Application.DisplayAlerts = False
        Sheets(1).Delete
        Application.DisplayAlerts = True
    End If
    Set rngPaste = Nothing
    Set rngStart = Nothing
```

13

```
        Set shRes = Nothing
        Exit Sub
terminate:

End Sub

Function GetNextRange(ByVal rngSt As Range) As Long
        Dim i As Long
        i = 0
        Do Until rngSt.Value <> rngSt.Offset(i).Value
            i = i + 1
        Loop
        GetNextRange = i
End Function
```

Select/Deselect Non-contiguous Cells

Submitted by Tom Urtis.

Ordinarily, to deselect a single cell or range on a sheet, you must click on an unselected cell to deselect all cells and then start over by reselecting all the correct cells. This is inconvenient if you need to reselect a lot of non-contiguous cells.

This sample adds two new options to the right-click menu of a selection: Deselect ActiveCell and Deselect ActiveArea. With the non-contiguous cells selected, right-click (to make active) the cell you want to deselect. The right-click menu shown in Figure 13.8 appears. Left-click the menu item that deselects either that one active cell or the contiguously selected area of which it is a part of.

Figure 13.8
The `ModifyRightClick` procedure provides a custom right-click menu for deselecting non-contiguous cells.

Enter the following procedures in a standard module:

```
Sub ModifyRightClick()
Dim O1 As Object, O2 As Object
On Error Resume Next
With CommandBars("Cell")
.Controls("Deselect ActiveCell").Delete
```

```
.Controls("Deselect ActiveArea").Delete
End With
On Error GoTo 0
Set O1 = CommandBars("Cell").Controls.Add
With O1
.Caption = "Deselect ActiveCell"
.OnAction = "DeselectActiveCell"
End With
Set O2 = CommandBars("Cell").Controls.Add
With O2
.Caption = "Deselect ActiveArea"
.OnAction = "DeselectActiveArea"
End With
End Sub

Sub DeselectActiveCell()
Dim x As Range, y As Range
If Selection.Cells.Count > 1 Then
For Each y In Selection.Cells
If y.Address <> ActiveCell.Address Then
If x Is Nothing Then
Set x = y
Else
Set x = Application.Union(x, y)
End If
End If
Next y
If x.Cells.Count > 0 Then
x.Select
End If
End If
End Sub
Sub DeselectActiveArea()
Dim x As Range, y As Range
If Selection.Areas.Count > 1 Then
For Each y In Selection.Areas
If Application.Intersect(ActiveCell, y) Is Nothing Then
If x Is Nothing Then
Set x = y
Else
Set x = Application.Union(x, y)
End If
End If
Next y
x.Select
End If
End Sub
Dim x As Range, y As Range
```

Add the following procedures to the ThisWorkbook module:

```
Private Sub Workbook_Activate()
Dim x As Range, y As Range
```

```
ModifyRightClick
End Sub

Private Sub Workbook_Deactivate()
Application.CommandBars("Cell").Reset
End Sub
```

Techniques for VBA Pros

The next 11 utilities amaze me. In the various message board communities on the Internet, VBA programmers are constantly coming up with new ways to do something faster or better. When someone posts some new code which obviously runs circles around the prior generally accepted best code, everyone benefits.

Speedy Page Setup

Submitted by Juan Pablo González of Bogotá, Colombia. Juan Pablo is the developer of the F&I Menu Wizard and handles all Spanish programming requests at MrExcel.com.

The following examples compare the runtimes of variations on changing the margins from the defaults to 1.5" and the footer/header to 1" in the Page Setup. The macro recorder was used to create Macro1. Macros 2, 3, and 4 show how the recorded code's runtime can be decreased. Figure 13.9 shows the results of the speed test running each variation:

Figure 13.9

Page setup speed tests.

	A	B	C	D
1	**Macro1**	**Macro2**	**Macro3**	**Macro4**
2	0.4467	0.1206	0.1147	0.0193
3	0.4776	0.115	0.1156	0.0194
4	0.4467	0.117	0.1178	0.0194
5	0.4362	0.1145	0.1151	0.026
6	0.4485	0.1149	0.122	0.0189
7	0.4473	0.1153	0.1143	0.0196
8	0.4458	0.1145	0.116	0.0192
9	0.4396	0.1141	0.1141	0.0186
10	0.4451	0.121	0.1229	0.0187
11	0.4369	0.1152	0.1144	0.0192
12	0.4388	0.1145	0.1174	0.0187
13	0.4454	0.114	0.1137	0.0201
14	0.4421	0.1212	0.1217	0.0188
15	0.4508	0.1157	0.1147	0.0192
16	0.4471	0.1169	0.1174	0.0188
17	0.4403	0.1381	0.1176	0.0201
18	0.4399	0.1305	0.1157	0.0188
19	0.4436	0.1152	0.1145	0.0195
20	0.4446	0.1129	0.1136	0.0197
21	0.4429	0.1146	0.1161	0.0202
22	**45%**	**12%**	**12%**	**2%**
23	**4**	**3**	**2**	**1**

```
Sub Macro1()
'
' Macro1 Macro
' Macro recorded 12/2/2003 by Juan Pablo Gonzalez
'
    With ActiveSheet.PageSetup
        .PrintTitleRows = ""
        .PrintTitleColumns = ""
```

```
        End With
        ActiveSheet.PageSetup.PrintArea = ""
        With ActiveSheet.PageSetup
            .LeftHeader = ""
            .CenterHeader = ""
            .RightHeader = ""
            .LeftFooter = ""
            .CenterFooter = ""
            .RightFooter = ""
            .LeftMargin = Application.InchesToPoints(1.5)
            .RightMargin = Application.InchesToPoints(1.5)
            .TopMargin = Application.InchesToPoints(1.5)
            .BottomMargin = Application.InchesToPoints(1.5)
            .HeaderMargin = Application.InchesToPoints(1)
            .FooterMargin = Application.InchesToPoints(1)
            .PrintHeadings = False
            .PrintGridlines = False
            .PrintComments = xlPrintNoComments
            .CenterHorizontally = False
            .CenterVertically = False
            .Orientation = xlPortrait
            .Draft = False
            .PaperSize = xlPaperLetter
            .FirstPageNumber = xlAutomatic
            .Order = xlDownThenOver
            .BlackAndWhite = False
            .Zoom = 100
        End With
End Sub
```

The macro recorder is doing a *lot* of extra work, which requires extra processing time. Considering that, plus the fact that the PageSetup object is one of the slowest objects to update, and you can have quite a mess…so, a cleaner version (that uses just the delete key!) follows:

```
Sub Macro1_Version2()
    With ActiveSheet.PageSetup
        .LeftMargin = Application.InchesToPoints(1.5)
        .RightMargin = Application.InchesToPoints(1.5)
        .TopMargin = Application.InchesToPoints(1.5)
        .BottomMargin = Application.InchesToPoints(1.5)
        .HeaderMargin = Application.InchesToPoints(1)
        .FooterMargin = Application.InchesToPoints(1)
    End With
End Sub
```

Okay, this runs faster than Macro1 (the average reduction is around 70% on some simple tests!), but it can be improved even further. As noted earlier, the PageSetup object takes a long time to process, so if you reduce the number of operations that VBA has to make *and* include some IF functions to update only the properties which require changing, you can get much better results.

In the following case, the `Application.InchesToPoints` function was hardcoded to the inches value. The third version of Macro1 looks like this:

```
Sub Macro1_Version3()
    With ActiveSheet.PageSetup
        If .LeftMargin <> 108 Then .LeftMargin = 108
        If .RightMargin <> 108 Then .RightMargin = 108
        If .TopMargin <> 108 Then .TopMargin = 108
        If .BottomMargin <> 108 Then .BottomMargin = 108
        If .HeaderMargin <> 72 Then .HeaderMargin = 72
        If .FooterMargin <> 72 Then .FooterMargin = 72
    End With
End Sub
```

You should see the difference on this one when you're not changing all the default margins.

Another option can reduce the runtime by over 95%! It uses the `PAGE.SETUP` XLM method. The necessary parameters are `left`, `right`, `top`, `bot`, `head_margin`, and `foot_margin`. They are measured in inches, not points. So, using the same margins that we have been changing already, a fourth version of Macro1 looks like this:

```
Sub Macro1_Version4()
    Dim St As String
    St = "PAGE.SETUP(, , " & _
                     "1.5, 1.5, 1.5, 1.5" & _
                     ", 0, False, False, False, 1, 1, True, 1, 1,False, , " & _
                     "1, 1" & _
                     ", False)"
    Application.ExecuteExcel4Macro St
End Sub
```

The second and fourth lines of `St` correspond to these parameters. But there are some simple precautions to follow. First, this macro relies on XLM language, which is still included in Excel for backward compatibility, but we don't know when Microsoft will drop it. Second, be careful when setting the parameters of `PAGE.SETUP` because if one of them is wrong, the `PAGE.SETUP` is not executed and doesn't generate an error, which can possibly leave you with the wrong page setup.

Calculating Time to Execute Code

You may wonder how to calculate elapsed time down to the thousandth of a second as shown in Figure 13.9.

This is the code used to generate the time results for the macros in this section:

```
Public Declare Function QueryPerformanceFrequency _
    Lib "kernel32" (lpFrequency As Currency) As Long
Public Declare Function QueryPerformanceCounter _
    Lib "kernel32.dll" (lpPerformanceCount As Currency) As Long

Sub Test()
    Dim Ar(1 To 20, 1 To 4) As Currency, WS As Worksheet
    Dim n As Currency, str As Currency, fin As Currency
    Dim y As Currency
```

13

```
        Dim i As Long, j As Long

        Application.ScreenUpdating = False
        For i = 1 To 4
            For j = 1 To 20
                Set WS = ThisWorkbook.Sheets.Add
                WS.Range("A1").Value = 1
                QueryPerformanceFrequency y
                QueryPerformanceCounter str
                Select Case i
                Case 1: Macro1
                Case 2: Macro1_Version2
                Case 3: Macro1_Version3
                Case 4: Macro1_Version4
                End Select
                QueryPerformanceCounter fin
                Application.DisplayAlerts = False
                WS.Delete
                Application.DisplayAlerts = True
                n = (fin - str)
                Ar(j, i) = CCur(Format(n, "##########.############") / y)
            Next j
        Next i
        With Range("A1").Resize(1, 4)
            .Value = Array("Macro1", "Macro1_Version2", "Macro1_Version3", _
            "Macro1_Version4")
            .Font.Bold = True
        End With
        Range("A2").Resize(20, 4).Value = Ar

        With Range("A22").Resize(1, 4)
            .FormulaR1C1 = "=AVERAGE(R2C:R21C)"
            .Offset(1).FormulaR1C1 = "=RANK(R22C,R22C1:R22C4,1)"
            .Resize(2).Font.Bold = True
        End With
        Application.ScreenUpdating = True
    End Sub
```

Disable Cut, Copy, and Paste

Submitted by Ivan F. Moala.

There are times when you do not want your clients to interfere with the structure of a worksheet. This program disables/enables all methods of cutting, copying, and pasting data in Excel:

```
Option Private Module

Dim ComBar As CommandBar
Dim ComBarCtrl As CommandBarControl

Sub EnableAllClear()
    '// Insert
    EnableControl 295, True  '// ..cells
    EnableControl 296, True  '// ..Rows
    EnableControl 297, True  '// ..Cols
    '// &Delete...
```

```vba
        EnableControl 478, True   '// &Delete...
        EnableControl 292, True   '// &Delete...
        EnableControl 293, True   '// ...Row
        EnableControl 294, True   '// ...Column
        EnableControl 847, True   '// RightClick Tab..
        '// Clear
        EnableControl 3125, True  '// Clear Contents
        EnableControl 1964, True  '// All
        EnableControl 872, True   '// Formats
        EnableControl 873, True   '// Contents
        EnableControl 874, True   '// Comments
        '// CutCopyPaste
        EnableControl 21, True    '// cut
        EnableControl 19, True    '// copy
        EnableControl 22, True    '// paste
        EnableControl 755, True   '// pastespecial
        '// ShortCut Keys
        With Application
            .OnKey "^c" ', ""
            .OnKey "^v" ', ""
            .OnKey "+{DEL}" ', ""
            .OnKey "+{INSERT}" ', ""
            .CellDragAndDrop = True
            .OnDoubleClick = ""
        End With
        '// ToolBar Change
        CommandBars("ToolBar List").Enabled = True

End Sub

Sub DisAbleAllCLear()
        '// Insert
        EnableControl 295, False  '// ..cells
        EnableControl 296, False  '// ..Rows
        EnableControl 297, False  '// ..Cols
        '// &Delete...
        EnableControl 478, False  '// Edit > Delete...
        EnableControl 292, False  '// &Delete...
        EnableControl 293, False  '// Row
        EnableControl 294, False  '// Column
        EnableControl 847, False  '// RightClick Tab
        '// Clear
        EnableControl 21, False   '// cut
        EnableControl 19, False   '// copy
        EnableControl 22, False   '// paste
        EnableControl 755, False  '// pastespecial
        '// CutCopyPaste
        EnableControl 3125, False '// Clear Contents
        EnableControl 1964, False '// All
        EnableControl 872, False  '// Formats
        EnableControl 873, False  '// Contents
        EnableControl 874, False  '// Comments
        '// Short cut keys
        With Application
            .OnKey "^c", "Dummy"
            .OnKey "^v", "Dummy"
            .OnKey "+{DEL}", "Dummy"
```

13

```
        .OnKey "+{INSERT}", "Dummy"
        .CellDragAndDrop = False
        .OnDoubleClick = "Dummy"
    End With
    '// Toolbar change
    CommandBars("ToolBar List").Enabled = False

End Sub

Sub EnableControl(iId As Integer, blnState As Boolean)
Dim ComBar As CommandBar
Dim ComBarCtrl As CommandBarControl

On Error Resume Next
For Each ComBar In Application.CommandBars
    Set ComBarCtrl = ComBar.FindControl(Id:=iId, recursive:=True)
    If Not ComBarCtrl Is Nothing Then ComBarCtrl.Enabled = blnState
Next

End Sub

Sub Dummy()
    '// NoGo
    MsgBox "Sorry command not Available!"
End Sub
```

Custom Sort Order

Submitted by Wei Jiang of Shiyan City, China. Jiang is a consultant for MrExcel.com.

By default, Excel enables you to sort lists numerically or alphabetically, but sometimes that is not what is needed. In Figure 13.10, the client needs each day's sales data sorted by the default division order of belts, handbags, watches, wallets, and everything else. This sample uses a custom sort order list to sort a range of data into default division order. The results are shown in Figure 13.11:

Figure 13.10
Unsorted list in Columns A:C and the custom sort list in Column I.

	A	B	C	D	E	F	G	H	I	J
1	Date	Category	# sold						Belts	
2	1/1/2004	Belts	15						Handbags	
3	1/1/2004	Wallets	17						Watches	
4	1/2/2004	Belts	17						Wallets	
5	1/2/2004	Wallets	18						Everything Else	
6	1/3/2004	Wallets	19							
7	1/3/2004	Handbags	20							
8	1/2/2004	Handbags	21							
9	1/3/2004	Belts	21							
10	1/1/2004	Handbags	23							
11	1/3/2004	Watches	35							
12	1/1/2004	Everything Else	36							
13	1/1/2004	Watches	42							
14	1/2/2004	Everything Else	42							
15	1/2/2004	Watches	43							
16	1/3/2004	Everything Else	45							
17										

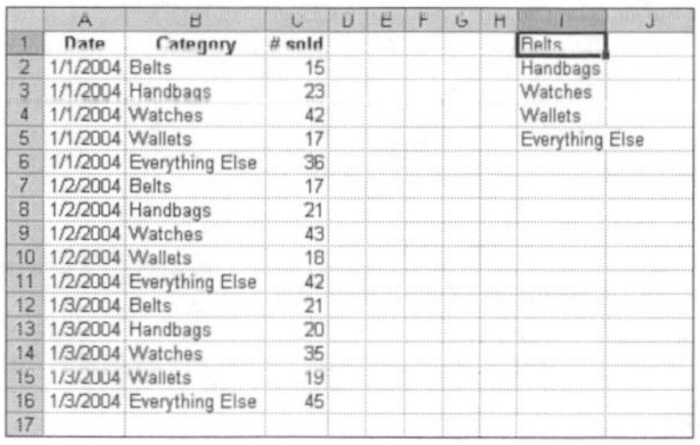

	A	B	C	D	E	F	G	H	I	J
1	Date	Category	# sold						Belts	
2	1/1/2004	Belts	15						Handbags	
3	1/1/2004	Handbags	23						Watches	
4	1/1/2004	Watches	42						Wallets	
5	1/1/2004	Wallets	17						Everything Else	
6	1/1/2004	Everything Else	36							
7	1/2/2004	Belts	17							
8	1/2/2004	Handbags	21							
9	1/2/2004	Watches	43							
10	1/2/2004	Wallets	18							
11	1/2/2004	Everything Else	42							
12	1/3/2004	Belts	21							
13	1/3/2004	Handbags	20							
14	1/3/2004	Watches	35							
15	1/3/2004	Wallets	19							
16	1/3/2004	Everything Else	45							
17										

Figure 13.11
After using the macro, the list in A:C is sorted first by date, then by the custom sort list in Column I.

```
Sub CustomSort()

    ' add the custom list to Custom Lists
    Application.AddCustomList ListArray:=Range("I1:I5")

    ' get the list number
    nIndex = Application.GetCustomListNum(Range("I1:I5").Value)

    ' Now, we could sort a range with the custom list.
    ' Note, we should use nIndex + 1 as the custom list number here,
    ' for the first one is Normal order
    Range("A2:C16").Sort Key1:=Range("B2"), Order1:=xlAscending, _
                         Header:=xlNo, Orientation:=xlSortColumns, _
                         OrderCustom:=nIndex + 1
    Range("A2:C16").Sort Key1:=Range("A2"), Order1:=xlAscending, _
                         Header:=xlNo, Orientation:=xlSortColumns

    ' At the end, we should remove this custom list...
    Application.DeleteCustomList nIndex
End Sub
```

Cell Progress Indicator

Submitted by Tom Urtis.

This example builds a progress indicator in Column C based on entries in Columns A and B (see Figure 13.12):

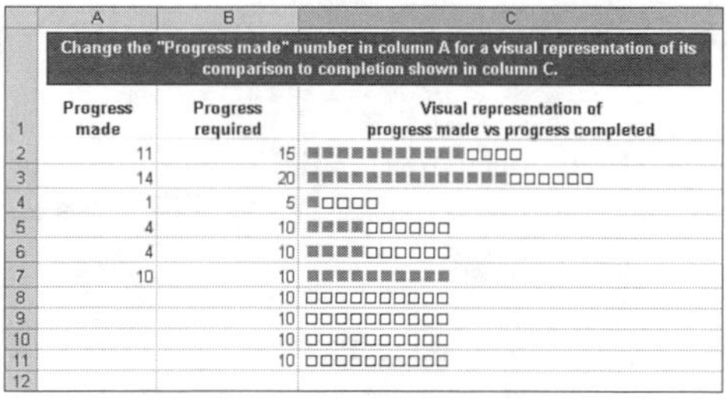

Change the "Progress made" number in column A for a visual representation of its comparison to completion shown in column C.

	A	B	C
1	Progress made	Progress required	Visual representation of progress made vs progress completed
2	11	15	■■■■■■■■■■■□□□□
3	14	20	■■■■■■■■■■■■■■□□□□□□
4	1	5	■□□□□
5	4	10	■■■■□□□□□□
6	4	10	■■■■□□□□□□
7	10	10	■■■■■■■■■■
8		10	□□□□□□□□□□
9		10	□□□□□□□□□□
10		10	□□□□□□□□□□
11		10	□□□□□□□□□□
12			

Figure 13.12
Cell progress indicator.

```
Private Sub Worksheet_Change(ByVal Target As Range)
If Target.Column > 2 Or Target.Cells.Count > 1 Then Exit Sub
If Application.IsNumber(Target.Value) = False Then
    Application.EnableEvents = False
    Application.Undo
```

```
        Application.EnableEvents = True
        MsgBox "Numbers only please."
        Exit Sub
    End If
    Select Case Target.Column
        Case 1
            If Target.Value > Target.Offset(0, 1).Value Then
                Application.EnableEvents = False
                Application.Undo
                Application.EnableEvents = True
                MsgBox "Value in column A may not be larger than value in column B."
                Exit Sub
            End If
        Case 2
            If Target.Value < Target.Offset(0, -1).Value Then
                Application.EnableEvents = False
                Application.Undo
                Application.EnableEvents = True
                MsgBox "Value in column B may not be smaller " & _
                    "than value in column A."
                Exit Sub
            End If
    End Select
    Dim x As Long
    x = Target.Row
    Dim z As String
    z = Range("B" & x).Value - Range("A" & x).Value
    With Range("C" & x)
        .Formula = "=IF(RC[-1]<=RC[-2],REPT(""n"",RC[-1]) _
            &REPT(""n"",RC[-2]-RC[-1]),REPT(""n"",RC[-2]) _
            &REPT(""o"",RC[-1]-RC[-2]))"
        .Value = .Value
        .Font.Name = "Wingdings"
        .Font.ColorIndex = 1
        .Font.Size = 10
        If Len(Range("A" & x)) <> 0 Then
            .Characters(1, (.Characters.Count - z)).Font.ColorIndex = 3
            .Characters(1, (.Characters.Count - z)).Font.Size = 12
        End If
    End With
End Sub
```

Protected Password Box

Submitted by Daniel Klann of Sydney, Australia. Daniel works mainly with VBA in Excel and Access but dabbles in all sorts of languages. He maintains a Web site at www.danielklann.com.

Using an input box for password protection has a major security flaw: The characters being entered are easily viewable. This program changes the characters to asterisks as they are entered—just like a real password field (see Figure 13.13):

Figure 13.13
Use an input box as a
secure password field.

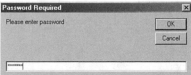

```
Private Declare Function CallNextHookEx Lib "user32" (ByVal hHook As Long, _
ByVal ncode As Long, ByVal wParam As Long, lParam As Any) As Long

Private Declare Function GetModuleHandle Lib "kernel32" _
    Alias "GetModuleHandleA" (ByVal lpModuleName As String) As Long

Private Declare Function SetWindowsHookEx Lib "user32" _
    Alias "SetWindowsHookExA" _
    (ByVal idHook As Long, ByVal lpfn As Long, _
    ByVal hmod As Long,ByVal dwThreadId As Long) As Long

Private Declare Function UnhookWindowsHookEx Lib "user32" _
    (ByVal hHook As Long) As Long

Private Declare Function SendDlgItemMessage Lib "user32" _
    Alias "SendDlgItemMessageA" _
    (ByVal hDlg As Long, _
    ByVal nIDDlgItem As Long, ByVal wMsg As Long, _
    ByVal wParam As Long, ByVal lParam As Long) As Long

Private Declare Function GetClassName Lib "user32" _
    Alias "GetClassNameA" (ByVal hwnd As Long, _
    ByVal lpClassName As String, _
    ByVal nMaxCount As Long) As Long

Private Declare Function GetCurrentThreadId _
    Lib "kernel32" () As Long

'Constants to be used in our API functions
Private Const EM_SETPASSWORDCHAR = &HCC
Private Const WH_CBT = 5
Private Const HCBT_ACTIVATE = 5
Private Const HC_ACTION = 0

Private hHook As Long

Public Function NewProc(ByVal lngCode As Long, _
    ByVal wParam As Long, ByVal lParam As Long) As Long
    Dim RetVal
    Dim strClassName As String, lngBuffer As Long

    If lngCode < HC_ACTION Then
        NewProc = CallNextHookEx(hHook, lngCode, wParam, lParam)
        Exit Function
    End If

    strClassName = String$(256, " ")
    lngBuffer = 255
```

13

```
        If lngCode = HCBT_ACTIVATE Then      'A window has been activated

            RetVal = GetClassName(wParam, strClassName, lngBuffer)

            'Check for class name of the Inputbox
            If Left$(strClassName, RetVal) = "#32770" Then
                'Change the edit control to display the password character *.
                'You can change the Asc("*") as you please.
                SendDlgItemMessage wParam, &H1324, EM_SETPASSWORDCHAR, Asc("*"), &H0
            End If

        End If

        'This line will ensure that any other hooks that may be in place are
        'called correctly.
        CallNextHookEx hHook, lngCode, wParam, lParam

End Function

Public Function InputBoxDK(Prompt, Optional Title, _
    Optional Default, Optional XPos, _
Optional YPos, Optional HelpFile, Optional Context) As String
    Dim lngModHwnd As Long, lngThreadID As Long

    lngThreadID = GetCurrentThreadId
    lngModHwnd = GetModuleHandle(vbNullString)

    hHook = SetWindowsHookEx(WH_CBT, AddressOf NewProc, lngModHwnd, lngThreadID)
    On Error Resume Next
    InputBoxDK = InputBox(Prompt, Title, Default, XPos, YPos, HelpFile, Context)
    UnhookWindowsHookEx hHook

End Function
Sub PasswordBox()
If InputBoxDK("Please enter password", "Password Required") <> "password" Then
        MsgBox "Sorry, that was not a correct password."
    Else
        MsgBox "Correct Password!  Come on in."
    End If
End Sub
```

Change Case

Submitted by Ivan F. Moala.

Word can change the case of selected text, but that capability is notably lacking in Excel.
This program enables the Excel user to change the case of text in any selected range:

```
Sub TextCaseChange()
Dim RgText As Range
Dim oCell As Range
Dim Ans As String
Dim strTest As String
Dim sCap As Integer, _
    lCap As Integer, _
    i As Integer
```

```vba
'// You need to select a range to alter first!

Again:
Ans = Application.InputBox("[L]owercase" & vbCr & "[U]ppercase" & vbCr & _
        "[S]entence" & vbCr & "[T]itles" & vbCr & "[C]apsSmall", _
        "Type in a Letter", Type:=2)

If Ans = "False" Then Exit Sub
If InStr(1, "LUSTC", UCase(Ans), vbTextCompare) = 0 _
    Or Len(Ans) > 1 Then GoTo Again

On Error GoTo NoText
If Selection.Count = 1 Then
    Set RgText = Selection
Else
    Set RgText = Selection.SpecialCells(xlCellTypeConstants, 2)
End If
On Error GoTo 0

For Each oCell In RgText
    Select Case UCase(Ans)
        Case "L": oCell = LCase(oCell.Text)
        Case "U": oCell = UCase(oCell.Text)
        Case "S": oCell = UCase(Left(oCell.Text, 1)) & _
            LCase(Right(oCell.Text, Len(oCell.Text) - 1))
        Case "T": oCell = Application.WorksheetFunction.Proper(oCell.Text)
        Case "C"
                lCap = oCell.Characters(1, 1).Font.Size
                sCap = Int(lCap * 0.85)
                'Small caps for everything.
                oCell.Font.Size = sCap
                oCell.Value = UCase(oCell.Text)
                strTest = oCell.Value
                'Large caps for 1st letter of words.
                strTest = Application.Proper(strTest)
                For i = 1 To Len(strTest)
                    If Mid(strTest, i, 1) = UCase(Mid(strTest, i, 1)) Then
                        oCell.Characters(i, 1).Font.Size = lCap
                    End If
                Next i
    End Select
Next

Exit Sub
NoText:
MsgBox "No text in your selection @ " & Selection.Address

End Sub
```

Custom Delete Event

Submitted by Masaru Kaji. Excel doesn't provide an event for capturing the deletion of a row or column. The following code is an "Event Hack": By replacing the built-in deletion choices, it provides the programmer control over what the user can delete. In the sample provided, a message box appears, informing the user of what has been deleted:

```
Sub EventHack()
    AssignMacro "JudgeRng"
End Sub

Sub EventReset()
    AssignMacro ""
End Sub

Private Sub AssignMacro(ByVal strProc As String)
    Dim lngId As Long
    Dim CtrlCbc As CommandBarControl
    Dim CtrlCbcRet As CommandBarControls
    Dim arrIdNum As Variant

    '// 293=Delete menu of the right click on row
    '// 294=Delete menu of the right click on column
    '// 293=Delete menu of the Edit of main menu
    arrIdNum = Array(293, 294, 478)

    For lngId = LBound(arrIdNum) To UBound(arrIdNum)
        Set CtrlCbcRet = CommandBars.FindControls(ID:=arrIdNum(lngId))
        For Each CtrlCbc In CtrlCbcRet
            CtrlCbc.OnAction = strProc
        Next
        Set CtrlCbcRet = Nothing
    Next
End Sub

Private Sub JudgeRng()
    If Not TypeOf Selection Is Range Then Exit Sub
    With Selection
        If .Address = .EntireRow.Address Then
            Call DelExecute("Row:" & .Row, xlUp)
        ElseIf .Address = .EntireColumn.Address Then
            Call DelExecute("Column:" & .Column, xlToLeft)
        Else
            Application.Dialogs(xlDialogEditDelete).Show
        End If
    End With
End Sub

Private Sub DelExecute(ByVal str, ByVal lngDerec As Long)
    MsgBox "deleted:" & str
    Selection.Delete lngDerec
End Sub
```

Selecting with `SpecialCells`

Submitted by Ivan F. Moala.

Typically, when you want to find certain values, text, or formulas in a range, the range is selected and each cell is tested. The following example shows how `SpecialCells` can be used to select only the desired cells. Having fewer cells to check will speed up your code:

```
Sub SpecialRange()
Dim TheRange As Range
Dim oCell As Range

    Set TheRange = Range("A1:Z200").SpecialCells(_
    xlCellTypeConstants, xlTextValues)

    For Each oCell In TheRange
        If oCell.Text = "Your Text" Then
            MsgBox oCell.Address
            MsgBox TheRange.Cells.Count
        End If
    Next oCell

End Sub
```

Delete Rows with Conditions

Submitted by Dennis Wallentin.

The following macro deletes a specified number of rows after a certain condition (the cell in Column A is empty) is met:

```
Sub Delete_rows_with_conditions()
Dim wbBook As Workbook
Dim wsSheet As Worksheet
Dim rnArea As Range
Dim lnLastRow As Long, lnMoreRows As Long
Dim i As Long, j As Long, k As Long

Set wbBook = ThisWorkbook
Set wsSheet = wbBook.Worksheets("Sheet1")

Application.ScreenUpdating = False

'Here we set the number of rows to be deleted.
j = 5

With wsSheet
'Here we identify the number of filled rows in column A, which will
'be compared with the last row of the other columns in the next step.

    lnLastRow = .Cells(Rows.Count, 1).End(xlUp).Row + 1

    'Here we loop through columns B and C, and if one column contains
    'more filled cells than column A or the previously checked column,
    'the variable lnMoreRows will be updated accordingly.
    For k = 2 To 3
        lnMoreRows = .Cells(Rows.Count, k).End(xlUp).Row + 1
        If lnLastRow < lnMoreRows Then
            lnLastRow = lnMoreRows
        End If
    Next k

    'Here we delete the rows where the cell in the Column A is empty
    'by stepping backward in the For-loop.
```

13

```
        For i = lnLastRow To 1 Step -1
            If IsEmpty(.Cells(i, 1)) Then
                .Cells(i, 1).Resize(j, 1).EntireRow.Delete
            End If
        Next i
    End With

    Application.ScreenUpdating = True

End Sub
```

Hide the Formula Bar

Submitted by Tom Urtis.

The Excel formula bar drops down and covers cells when a cell containing more than 50 characters is selected. The following sample prevents this from happening by hiding the formula bar. In Figure 13.14, the formula bar would normally obscure most of this worksheet. Thanks to the following macro, the formula bar is hidden:

Figure 13.14
Normally, the formula bar would obscure most of this worksheet. The macro causes the formula bar to be selectively hidden whenever the cell contains more than 50 characters.

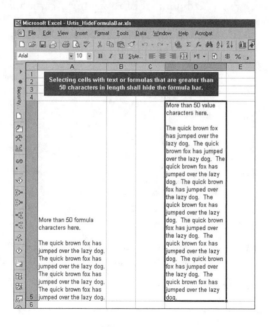

```
Private Sub Worksheet_SelectionChange(ByVal Target As Range)
If Target.Cells.Count > 1 Then Exit Sub
On Error Resume Next
If Len(Target.Text) > 50 Or Len(Target.Formula) > 50 Then
    Application.DisplayFormulaBar = False
Else
    Application.DisplayFormulaBar = True
End If
End Sub
```

Cool Applications

These last samples are interesting applications that you might be able to incorporate into your own projects.

Historical Stock/Fund Quotes

Submitted by Nathan P. Oliver.

The following retrieves the average of a valid ticker or the close of a fund for the specified date (see Figure 13.15):

Figure 13.15
Retrieve stock information.

	A	B	C
1	Symbol	Date	Average/Close
2	Dell	1/12/1994	25.3125
3	MSFT	1/30/2003	49.18
4	VFINX	1/20/2000	133.21
5	INNDX	1/6/2003	20.02
6	INSTX	1/6/2003	15.35
7			

```
Private Sub GetQuote()
Dim ie As Object, lCharPos As Long, sHTML As String
Dim HistDate As Date, HighVal As String, LowVal As String
Dim cl As Range

Set cl = ActiveCell
HistDate = cl(, 0)

If Intersect(cl, [c2:c65366]) Is Nothing Then
    MsgBox "You must select a cell in column C."
    Exit Sub
End If

If Not CBool(Len(cl(, -1))) Or Not CBool(Len(cl(, 0))) Then
    MsgBox "You must enter a symbol and date."
    Exit Sub
End If

Set ie = CreateObject("InternetExplorer.Application")

With ie
    .Navigate _
        http://bigcharts.marketwatch.com/historical & _
        "/default.asp?detect=1&symbol=" _
        & cl(, -1) & "&close_date=" & Month(HistDate) & "%2F" & _
        Day(HistDate) & "%2F" & Year(HistDate) & "&x=31&y=26"
    Do While .Busy And .ReadyState <> 4
        DoEvents
    Loop
    sHTML = .Document.body.innertext
    .Quit
End With

Set ie = Nothing
```

13

```
lCharPos = InStr(1, sHTML, "High:", vbTextCompare)
If lCharPos Then HighVal = Mid$(sHTML, lCharPos + 5, 15)

If Not Left$(HighVal, 3) = "n/a" Then
    lCharPos = InStr(1, sHTML, "Low:", vbTextCompare)
    If lCharPos Then LowVal = Mid$(sHTML, lCharPos + 4, 15)
    cl.Value = (Val(LowVal) + Val(HighVal)) / 2
Else: lCharPos = InStr(1, sHTML, "Closing Price:", vbTextCompare)
    cl.Value = Val(Mid$(sHTML, lCharPos + 14, 15))
End If

Set cl = Nothing
End Sub
```

Using VBA Extensibility to Add Code to New Workbooks

You have a macro which moves data to a new workbook for the regional managers. What if you need to also copy macros to the new workbook? You can use Visual Basic for Application Extensibility to import modules to a workbook or to actually write lines of code to the workbook.

In order to use any of these examples, you must first open the VB editor, choose References from the Tools menu, and select the reference for Microsoft Visual Basic for Applications Extensibility 5.3.

The easiest way to use VBA Extensibility is to export a complete module or userform from the current project and import it to the new workbook. Perhaps you have an application with thousands of lines of code. You want to create a new workbook with data for the regional manager and give her three macros to enable custom formatting and printing. Place all of these macros in a module called modToRegion. Macros in this module also call the frmRegion userform. The following code will transfer this code from the current workbook to the new workbook.

```
Sub MoveDataAndMacro()
    Dim WSD as worksheet
    Set WSD = Worksheets("Report")
    ' Copy Report to a new workbook
    WSD.Copy
    ' The active workbook is now the new workbook
    ' Delete any old copy of the module from C
    On Error Resume Next
    ' Delete any stray copies from hard drive
    Kill ("C:\ModToRegion.bas")
    Kill ("C:\frmRegion.frm")
    On Error GoTo 0
    ' Export module & form from this workbook
    ThisWorkbook.VBProject.VBComponents("ModPics").Export ("C:\ModToRegion.bas")
    ThisWorkbook.VBProject.VBComponents("frmModPics").Export ("C:\frmRegion.frm")
```

```
      ' Import to new workbook
      ActiveWorkbook.VBProject.VBComponents.Import ("C:\ModToRegion.bas")
      ActiveWorkbook.VBProject.VBComponents.Import ("C:\frmRegion.frm")
      On Error Resume Next
      Kill ("C:\ModToRegion.bas")
      Kill ("C:\frmRegion.bas")
      On Error GoTo 0
End Sub
```

The above method will work if you need to move modules or userforms to a new workbook. However, what if you need to write some code to the Workbook_Open macro in the ThisWorkbook module? There are two tools to use. The Lines method will allow you to return a particular set of code lines from a given module. The .InsertLines method will allow you to insert code lines to a new module.

> **CAUTION**
>
> With each call to InsertLines, you must insert a complete macro. Excel will attempt to compile the code after each call to InsertLines. If you insert lines which do not completely compile, Excel may crash with a GPF.

```
Sub MoveDataAndMacro()
    Dim WSD as worksheet
    Dim WBN as Workbook
    Set WSD = Worksheets("Report")
    ' Copy Report to a new workbook
    WSD.Copy
    ' The active workbook is now the new workbook
    Set WBN = ActiveWorkbook
    ' Copy the Workbook level Event handlers
    Set WBCodeMod1 =
ThisWorkbook.VBProject.VBComponents("ThisWorkbook").CodeModule
    Set WBCodeMod2 = WBN.VBProject.VBComponents("ThisWorkbook").CodeModule
    WBCodeMod2.insertlines 1, WBCodeMod1.Lines(1, WBCodeMod1.countoflines)
End Sub
```

Next Steps

In Chapter 14, "Reading from and Writing to the Web," you will learn how to use Web queries to automatically import data from the Internet to your Excel applications.

Reading from and Writing to the Web

14

The Internet has become pervasive and has really changed our lives. From your desktop, there are millions of answers available at your fingertips. Alternatively, publishing a report on the Web allows millions of others to instantly access your information.

This chapter discusses automated ways to pull data from the Web into spreadsheets, using Web queries. It also shows how to save data from your spreadsheet directly to the Web.

Getting Data from the Web

Someone at a desk anywhere can get up-to-the-minute stock prices for a portfolio. Figure 14.1 shows a Web page from Finance.Yahoo.com, which shows current stock quotes for a theoretical portfolio. Clearly, the people at Yahoo understand how important spreadsheets are, because they offer a link to download the data to a spreadsheet.

Figure 14.1
A wealth of nearly-realtime data is available for free on Web sites everywhere. Finance. Yahoo.com even offers a link to download the portfolio to a spreadsheet. Web queries offer something so much more amazing than manually downloading the file each day.

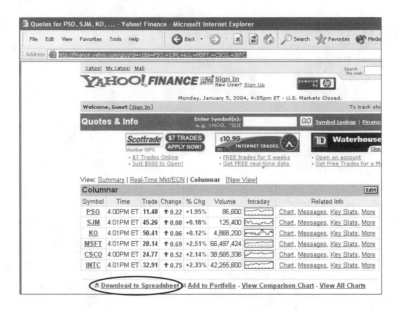

Manually Creating a Web Query and Refreshing with VBA

The easiest way to get started with Web queries is to create your first one manually. Using any Web browser, navigate to a Web site and enter the settings needed to display the information of interest to you. In the case of Figure 14.1, the URL to display that portfolio is

`http://finance.yahoo.com/q/cq?d=v1&s=PSO,+SJM,+KO,+MSFT,+CSCO,+INTC`

Open Excel. Find a blank area of the worksheet. From the Excel menu, choose Data, Import External Data, New Web Query. Excel shows the New Web Query dialog with your Internet Explorer home page displayed. Copy the preceding URL to the Address text box and click Go. In a moment, the desired Web page will be displayed in the dialog box. Note that in addition to the Web page, there are a number of yellow squares with a black arrow. These squares are in the upper-left corner of various tables on the Web page. Click the square that contains the data that you want to import to Excel. In this case, we want the portfolio information, so in Figure 14.2, I have clicked the square by the table of quotes. While clicking, a blue border confirms the table that will be imported. After clicking, the yellow arrow changes to a green check mark.

Click the Import button on the New Web Query dialog. Click OK on the Import Data dialog. In a few seconds, you will see the live data imported into a range on your spreadsheet, as shown in Figure 14.3.

Figure 14.2
Use the New Web Query dialog to browse to a Web page. Highlight the table that you want to import to Excel by clicking on a yellow arrow adjacent to the table.

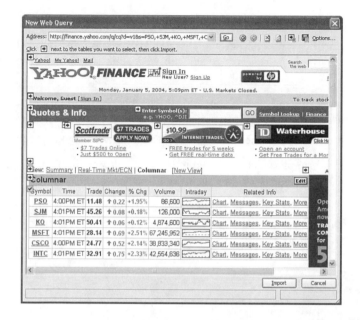

Figure 14.3
Data from the Web page is automatically copied to your worksheet. You can now use VBA to automatically refresh this data at your command or periodically.

Using VBA to Update an Existing Web Query

To update all Web queries on the current sheet, use this code:

```
Sub RefreshAllWebQueries()
    Dim QT As QueryTable
    For Each QT In ActiveSheet.QueryTables
        Application.StatusBar = "Refreshing " & QT.Connection
        QT.Refresh
    Next QT
    Application.StatusBar = False
End Sub
```

You could assign this macro to a hot key or to a macro button and refresh all queries on demand.

14

Building a New Web Query with VBA

The problem with the previous examples is that the Web query URL is hardcoded into the VBA. Someone would be required to edit the VBA code every time that the portfolio changed.

It is fairly simple to build a Web query on the fly. The key is to build a connect string. The connect string for the Yahoo Finance stock quote is

```
URL;http://finance.yahoo.com/q/cq?d=v1&s=PSO,+SJM,+KO,+MSFT,+CSCO,+INTC
```

To build a flexible application, you need to use the concatenation character to join the first part of the connect string with the various stock symbols.

Figure 14.4 shows a simple front end for a Web query engine. Anyone can enter stock symbols of interest in the shaded area of Column A. The Get Quotes button is set up to call the CreateNewQuery macro.

Figure 14.4

This worksheet serves as a front end to allow different stock symbols to be entered in Column A. Click the Get Quotes button to run a macro that builds a Web query on the fly on a second worksheet and then copies the data to this sheet.

When the button is clicked, the macro builds a connect string by concatenating the first part of the URL with the first stock symbol from cell A2:

```
ConnectString = "URL;http://finance.Yahoo.com/q/cq?d=v1&s=" & _
    WSD.Cells(i, 1).Value
```

As the program loops through additional stock symbols, it takes the existing connect string and adds a comma and a plus sign, and then the next stock symbol:

```
ConnectString = ConnectString & ",+" & WSD.Cells(i, 1).Value
```

After the connect string has been built, then the macro uses a worksheet called "Workspace" to build the Web query. This hides the unformatted Web query results from view. Because it is possible that the list of stock symbols has changed since the last Web query, the program deletes any old query and then builds the new query.

It is important to set the query up with BackgroundRefresh set to False. This ensures that the macro pauses to give the query time to refresh before continuing.

After the results have been received, the program assigns a range name to the results and uses VLOOKUP formulas to retrieve the desired columns from the Web query:

```vba
Sub CreateNewQuery()
    Dim WSD As Worksheet
    Dim WSW As Worksheet
    Dim QT As QueryTable
    Dim FinalRow As Long
    Dim i As Integer
    Dim ConnectString As String
    Dim FinalResultRow As Long
    Dim RowCount As Long

    Set WSD = Worksheets("Portfolio")
    Set WSW = Worksheets("Workspace")

    ' Read column A of Portfolio to find all stock symbols
    FinalRow = WSD.Cells(65536, 1).End(xlUp).Row
    For i = 2 To FinalRow
        Select Case i
            Case 2
                ConnectString = "URL;http://finance.Yahoo.com/q/cq?d=v1&s=" & _
                    WSD.Cells(i, 1).Value
            Case Else
                ConnectString = ConnectString & ",+" & WSD.Cells(i, 1).Value
        End Select
    Next i

    ' On the Workspace worksheet, clear all existing query tables
    For Each QT In WSW.QueryTables
        QT.Delete
    Next QT

    ' Define a new Web Query
    Set QT = WSW.QueryTables.Add(Connection:=ConnectString, _
        Destination:=WSW.Range("A1"))
    With QT
        .Name = "portfolio"
        .FieldNames = True
        .RowNumbers = False
        .FillAdjacentFormulas = False
        .PreserveFormatting = True
        .RefreshOnFileOpen = False
        .BackgroundQuery = False
        .RefreshStyle = xlInsertDeleteCells
        .SavePassword = False
        .SaveData = True
        .AdjustColumnWidth = True
        .RefreshPeriod = 0
        .WebSelectionType = xlSpecifiedTables
        .WebFormatting = xlWebFormattingNone
        .WebTables = "20"
        .WebPreFormattedTextToColumns = True
        .WebConsecutiveDelimitersAsOne = True
        .WebSingleBlockTextImport = False
        .WebDisableDateRecognition = False
        .WebDisableRedirections = False
    End With

    ' Refresh the query
    QT.Refresh BackgroundQuery:=False
```

14

```
    ' Define a named range for the results
    FinalResultRow = WSW.Cells(65536, 1).End(xlUp).Row
    WSW.Cells(1, 1).Resize(FinalResultRow, 7).Name = "WebInfo"

    ' Build a VLOOKUP to get quotes from WSW to WSD
    RowCount = FinalRow - 1
    WSD.Cells(2, 2).Resize(RowCount, 1).FormulaR1C1 = _
        "=VLOOKUP(RC1,WebInfo,3,False)"
    WSD.Cells(2, 3).Resize(RowCount, 1).FormulaR1C1 = _
        "=VLOOKUP(RC1,WebInfo,4,False)"
    WSD.Cells(2, 4).Resize(RowCount, 1).FormulaR1C1 = _
        "=VLOOKUP(RC1,WebInfo,5,False)"
    WSD.Cells(2, 5).Resize(RowCount, 1).FormulaR1C1 = _
        "=VLOOKUP(RC1,WebInfo,6,False)"
    WSD.Cells(2, 6).Resize(RowCount, 1).FormulaR1C1 = _
        "=VLOOKUP(RC1,WebInfo,2,False)"

    MsgBox "Data Updated"
End Sub
```

When the program runs, you will get nicely formatted results, as shown in Figure 14.5.

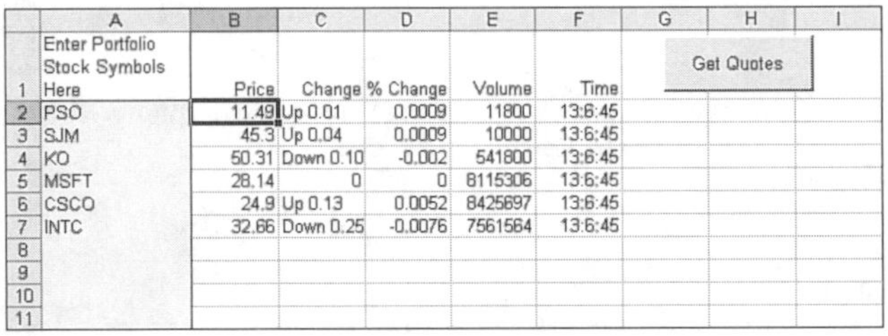

	A	B	C	D	E	F	G	H	I
1	Enter Portfolio Stock Symbols Here	Price	Change	% Change	Volume	Time	Get Quotes		
2	PSO	11.49	Up 0.01	0.0009	11800	13:6:45			
3	SJM	45.3	Up 0.04	0.0009	10000	13:6:45			
4	KO	50.31	Down 0.10	-0.002	541800	13:6:45			
5	MSFT	28.14	0	0	8115306	13:6:45			
6	CSCO	24.9	Up 0.13	0.0052	8425697	13:6:45			
7	INTC	32.66	Down 0.25	-0.0076	7561564	13:6:45			
8									
9									
10									
11									

Figure 14.5
After running the macro, only the relevant columns are shown on the report. The back worksheet contains the unformatted Web query from the Web site.

Using Streaming Data

A number of services offer live streaming data into your spreadsheet. These services use a technology such as DDE to automatically pipe information directly into cells in your worksheet. Although these services require a monthly subscription, it is pretty amazing to watch your spreadsheet automatically change every second with real-time stock prices.

These real-time DDE services typically use a formula that identifies the external `.exe` program, then a pipe character (|), and data for the external program to use.

In Figure 14.6, the formula in cell A2 is calling the `MktLink.exe` program to return price data for stock symbol AA.

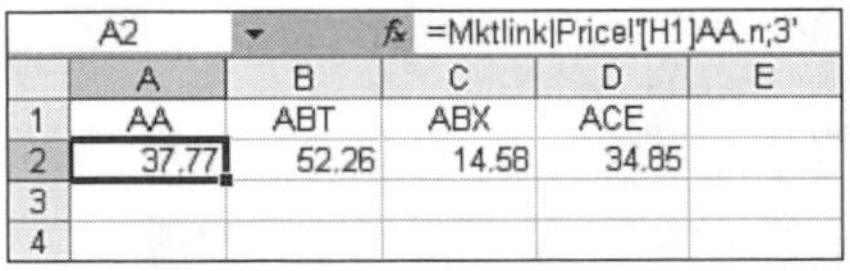

A2 =Mktlink|Price!'[H1]AA.n;3'

	A	B	C	D	E
1	AA	ABT	ABX	ACE	
2	37.77	52.26	14.58	34.85	
3					
4					

Figure 14.6
The `MktLink.exe` service allows live streaming data to be piped into cells on the spreadsheet.

Although these services are amazing to watch, the data is fleeting. What do you do with information that flies by, updating every few seconds? The real power is using Excel to capture and save the data every so often to look for trends.

Using Application.OnTime to Periodically Analyze Data

VBA offers the .OnTime method for running any VBA procedure at a specific time of day or after a specific amount of time has passed.

You could write a macro that would capture data every hour throughout the day. This macro would have times hard-coded. The following code will theoretically capture data from a Web site every hour throughout the day:

```
Sub ScheduleTheDay()
    Application.OnTime EarliestTime:=TimeValue("8:00 AM"), _
        Procedure:=CaptureData
    Application.OnTime EarliestTime:=TimeValue("9:00 AM"), _
        Procedure:=CaptureData
    Application.OnTime EarliestTime:=TimeValue("10:00 AM"), _
        Procedure:=CaptureData
    Application.OnTime EarliestTime:=TimeValue("11:00 AM"), _
        Procedure:=CaptureData
    Application.OnTime EarliestTime:=TimeValue("12:00 AM"), _
        Procedure:=CaptureData
    Application.OnTime EarliestTime:=TimeValue("1:00 PM"), _
        Procedure:=CaptureData
    Application.OnTime EarliestTime:=TimeValue("2:00 PM"), _
        Procedure:=CaptureData
    Application.OnTime EarliestTime:=TimeValue("3:00 PM"), _
        Procedure:=CaptureData
    Application.OnTime EarliestTime:=TimeValue("4:00 PM"), _
        Procedure:=CaptureData
    Application.OnTime EarliestTime:=TimeValue("5:00 PM"), _
        Procedure:=CaptureData
End Sub

Sub CaptureData()
    Dim WSQ As Worksheet
    Dim NextRow As Long
    Set WSQ = Worksheets("MyQuery")
    ' Refresh the Web query
    WSQ.Range("A2").QueryTable.Refresh BackgroundQuery:=False
    ' Make sure the data is updated
    Application.Wait (Now + TimeValue("0:00:10"))
    ' Copy the Web query results to a new row
    NextRow = WSQ.Range("A65536").End(xlUp).Row + 1
    WSQ.Range("A2:B2").Copy WSQ.Cells(NextRow, 1)
End Sub
```

Scheduled Procedures Require Ready Mode

The .OnTime method will run provided only that Excel is in Ready, Copy, Cut, or Find mode at the prescribed time. If you start to edit a cell at 7:59:55 a.m. and keep that cell in Edit mode, Excel cannot run the CaptureData macro at 8:00 a.m. as directed.

14

In the previous code example, I've specified only the start time for the procedure to run. Excel waits anxiously until the spreadsheet is returned to Ready mode and then runs the scheduled program as soon as it can.

The classic example is that you start to edit a cell at 7:59 a.m. and then your manager walks in and asks you to attend a surprise staff meeting down the hall. If you leave your spreadsheet in Edit mode and attend the staff meeting until 10:30 a.m., the program cannot run the first three scheduled hours of updates. As soon as you return to your desk and hit Enter to exit Edit mode, the program runs all previously scheduled tasks. In the previous code, you will find that the first three scheduled updates of the program all happen between 10:30 and 10:31 a.m.

Specifying a Window of Time for an Update

One alternative is to provide Excel with a window of time within which to make the update. The following code tells Excel to run the update at anytime between 8:00 a.m. and 8:05 a.m. If the Excel session remains in Edit mode for the entire five minutes, then the scheduled task is skipped:

```
Application.OnTime EarliestTime:=TimeValue("8:00 AM"), Procedure:=CaptureData,
LatestTime:=TimeValue("8:05 AM")
```

Cancelling a Previously Scheduled Macro

It is fairly difficult to cancel a previously scheduled macro. You must know the exact time that the macro is scheduled to run. To cancel a pending operation, call the `OnTime` method again, using the `Schedule:=False` parameter to unschedule the event. The following code cancels the 11:00 a.m. run of `CaptureData`:

```
Sub CancelEleven()
Application.OnTime EarliestTime:=TimeValue("11:00 AM"), _
    Procedure:=CaptureData, Schedule:=False
End Sub
```

It is interesting to note that the `.OnTime` schedules are remembered by a running instance of Excel. If you keep Excel open but close the workbook with the scheduled procedure, it still runs. Consider this hypothetical series of events:

1. Open Excel at 7:30 a.m.
2. Open `Schedule.XLS` and run a macro to schedule a procedure at 8:00 a.m.
3. Close `Schedule.xls` but keep Excel open.
4. Open a new workbook and begin entering data.

At 8:00 a.m., Excel re-opens `Schedule.xls` and runs the scheduled macro. Excel doesn't close `Schedule.xls`. As you can imagine, this is fairly annoying and alarming if you are not expecting it. If you are going to make extensive use of `Application.Ontime`, you might want to have it running in one instance of Excel while you work in a second instance of Excel.

Closing Excel Cancels All Pending Scheduled Macros

If you close Excel with File, Exit, then all future scheduled macros are automatically cancelled. When you have a macro that has scheduled a bunch of macros at indeterminate times, closing Excel is the only way to prevent the macros from running.

Scheduling a Macro to Run x Minutes in the Future

You can schedule a macro to run at a time at a certain point in the future. The following macro runs something 2 minutes and 30 seconds from now:

```
Sub ScheduleAnything()
    ' This macro can be used to schedule anything
    WaitHours = 0
    WaitMin = 2
    WaitSec = 30
    NameOfScheduledProc = "CaptureData"
    ' --- End of Input Section -------

    ' Determine the next time this should run
    NextTime = Time + TimeSerial(WaitHours, WaitMin, WaitSec)

    ' Schedule ThisProcedure to run then
    Application.OnTime EarliestTime:=NextTime, Procedure:=NameOfScheduledProc

End Sub
```

Scheduling a Macro to Run Every Two Minutes

My favorite method is to ask Excel to run a certain macro every two minutes. However, I realize that if a macro gets delayed because I accidently left the workbook in Edit mode while going to the staff meeting, then I don't want dozens of updates to happen in a matter of seconds.

The easy solution is to have the `ScheduleAnything` procedure recursively schedule itself to run again in two minutes. The following code schedules a run in two minutes and then performs Capture Data:

```
Sub ScheduleAnything()
    ' This macro can be used to schedule anything
    ' Enter how often you want to run the macro in hours and minutes
    WaitHours = 0
    WaitMin = 2
    WaitSec = 0
    NameOfThisProcedure = "ScheduleAnything"
    NameOfScheduledProc = "CaptureData"
    ' --- End of Input Section -------

    ' Determine the next time this should run
    NextTime = Time + TimeSerial(WaitHours, WaitMin, WaitSec)

    ' Schedule ThisProcedure to run then
    Application.OnTime EarliestTime:=NextTime, Procedure:=NameOfThisProcedure
```

14

```
' Get the Data
Application.Run NameOfScheduledProc

End Sub
```

There are some advantages of this method. I have not scheduled a million updates in the future. I have only one future update scheduled at any given time. Thus, if I decide that I am tired of seeing the national debt every 15 seconds, I only need to comment out the `Application.OnTime` line of code and wait 15 seconds for the last update to happen.

CASE STUDY

Case Study: Tracking the National Debt

Figure 14.7 shows a worksheet. Cell A2 contains a Web query to return the national debt from `http://brillig.com/debt_clock/`. Cell B2 contains the function =NOW().

I thought it would be interesting to demonstrate to my Junior Achievement students how the national debt changes over time. Starting in Row 5, I added headings for my desired table.

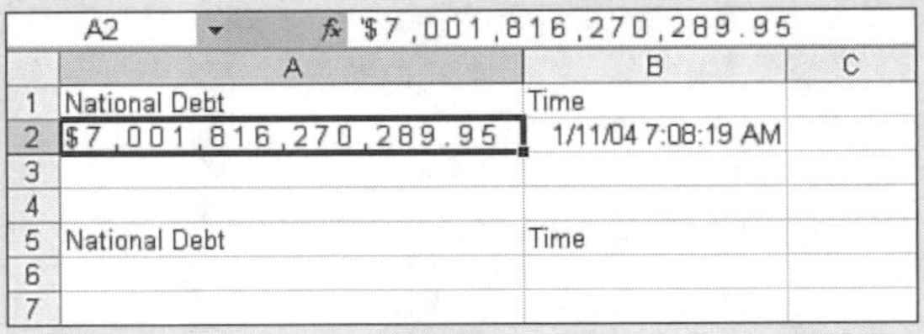

Figure 14.7
Cell A2 contains a Web query and B2 contains current date and time. The goal is to periodically capture the results in the table starting in Row 5 every 15 seconds.

	A	B	C
	A2 ▼ fx $7,001,816,270,289.95		
1	National Debt	Time	
2	$7,001,816,270,289.95	1/11/04 7:08:19 AM	
3			
4			
5	National Debt	Time	
6			
7			

The macro below updates the Web query, copies the data to a new row, and schedules an update for 15 seconds later:

```
Sub DebtClock()
    Dim WSQ As Worksheet
    Set WSQ = Worksheets("MyQuery")

    ' Cell A2 of MyQuery contains a  Web query to
    ' http://brillig.com/debt_clock
    WaitSec = 15
    NameOfThisProcedure = "DebtClock"
    ' --- End of Input Section -------

    ' Determine the next time this should run
    NextTime = Time + TimeSerial(0, 0, WaitSec)

    ' Schedule ThisProcedure to run then
    Application.OnTime EarliestTime:=NextTime, Procedure:=NameOfThisProcedure

    ' Update Web query, capture data
    ' Refresh the Web query
    WSQ.Range("A2").QueryTable.Refresh BackgroundQuery:=False
    ' Make sure the data is updated
    Application.Wait (Now + TimeValue("0:00:05"))
```

```
' Copy the Web query results to a new row
NextRow = WSQ.Range("A65536").End(xlUp).Row + 1
WSQ.Range("A2:B2").Copy WSQ.Cells(NextRow, 1)
'Freeze date & time
WSQ.Cells(NextRow, 2).Value = WSQ.Cells(NextRow, 2).Value

End Sub
```

At the beginning of the period, I ran the macro and turned the class's attention to something else. After 30 minutes, I had an impressive table showing in real time how the national debt was climbing by a little over $1 million every minute (see Figure 14.8).

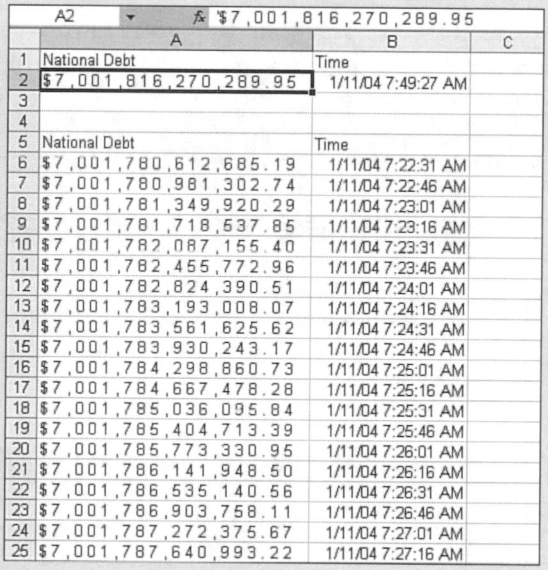

Figure 14.8
After several minutes, you have an impressive trend of real-time data.

	A2	▼	fx	$7,001,816,270,289.95	
	A		B		C
1	National Debt		Time		
2	$7,001,816,270,289.95		1/11/04 7:49:27 AM		
3					
4					
5	National Debt		Time		
6	$7,001,780,612,685.19		1/11/04 7:22:31 AM		
7	$7,001,780,981,302.74		1/11/04 7:22:46 AM		
8	$7,001,781,349,920.29		1/11/04 7:23:01 AM		
9	$7,001,781,718,537.85		1/11/04 7:23:16 AM		
10	$7,001,782,087,155.40		1/11/04 7:23:31 AM		
11	$7,001,782,455,772.96		1/11/04 7:23:46 AM		
12	$7,001,782,824,390.51		1/11/04 7:24:01 AM		
13	$7,001,783,193,008.07		1/11/04 7:24:16 AM		
14	$7,001,783,561,625.62		1/11/04 7:24:31 AM		
15	$7,001,783,930,243.17		1/11/04 7:24:46 AM		
16	$7,001,784,298,860.73		1/11/04 7:25:01 AM		
17	$7,001,784,667,478.28		1/11/04 7:25:16 AM		
18	$7,001,785,036,095.84		1/11/04 7:25:31 AM		
19	$7,001,785,404,713.39		1/11/04 7:25:46 AM		
20	$7,001,785,773,330.95		1/11/04 7:26:01 AM		
21	$7,001,786,141,948.50		1/11/04 7:26:16 AM		
22	$7,001,786,535,140.56		1/11/04 7:26:31 AM		
23	$7,001,786,903,758.11		1/11/04 7:26:46 AM		
24	$7,001,787,272,375.67		1/11/04 7:27:01 AM		
25	$7,001,787,640,993.22		1/11/04 7:27:16 AM		

Publishing Data to a Web Page

This chapter has highlighted many ways to capture data from the Web. It is also very useful for publishing Excel data back to the Web.

In Chapter 13, "Excel Power," a macro was able to produce reports for each region in a company. Rather than printing and faxing the report, it would be cool to save the Excel file as HTML and post the results on a company intranet so that the regional manager could instantly access the latest version of the report.

Consider a report like the one shown in Figure 14.9. Using the Excel user interface, it is easy to use File, Save as Web Page to create an HTML view of the data.

14

Figure 14.9

A macro from Chapter 13 was used to automatically generate this Excel workbook. Rather than email the report, we could save it as a Web page and post it on the company intranet.

	A	B	C	D	E
1	Top 10 Customers in the West Region				
2					
3	Customer	Revenue	Gross Profit	GP%	
4	RST INC.	5,017K	2,776K	55.3%	
5	RST S.A.	4,311K	2,462K	57.1%	
6	WXY, CO	3,500K	1,963K	56.1%	
7	LMN INC.	3,500K	1,953K	55.8%	
8	VWX GMBH	3,486K	1,961K	56.3%	
9	OPQ, INC.	3,248K	1,818K	56.0%	
10	HIJ GMBH	2,491K	1,373K	55.1%	
11	MNO CORP	2,325K	1,294K	55.7%	
12	CDE INC.	2,287K	1,245K	54.4%	
13	DEF, LLC	1,714K	962K	56.1%	
14	Top 10 Total	31,878K	17,807K	55.9%	
15					

When saving the Web page in the Excel user interface, be sure to leave Add Interactivity unchecked. This ensures that the Web page's viewers do not have to have Excel available to view it (see Figure 14.10).

Figure 14.10

When saving a worksheet to a static HTML page, be sure to leave Add Interactivity unchecked. This allows the greatest number of people to view the Web page.

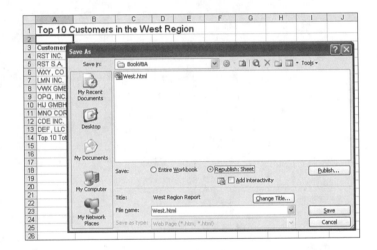

The result is a file which can be viewed in any Web browser. The Web page accurately shows our number formats and font sizes (see Figure 14.11).

Several versions ago, Microsoft became enamored of saving a worksheet as HTML, then later opening the HTML file in Excel and having the original formulas intact. They called this feature "round tripping." This feature causes Excel to write out incredibly bloated HTML files. The data presented in Figure 14.11 is about 457 bytes of data, yet Excel requires 9,105 bytes of data to store both the data for presentation and the data needed to load the file back into Excel.

Although the data is accurately presented in Figure 14.11, it is not extremely fancy. We don't have a company logo or navigation bar to examine other reports.

14

Figure 14.11
Excel does a nice job of rendering the worksheet as HTML.

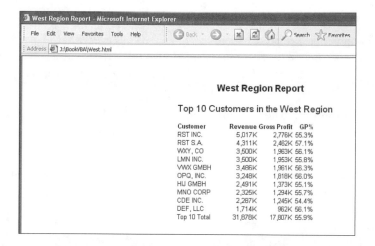

Using VBA to Create Custom Web Pages

Long before Microsoft introduced the Save as Web Page functionality, people had been using VBA to take Excel data and publish it as HTML. The advantage of this method is that you can write out specific HTML statements to display company logos and navigation bars.

Consider a typical Web page template. There is code to display a logo and navigation bar at the top and/or side. There is data specific to the page, and then there is data to close the HTML file. Build an HTML template with the words "PUT DATA HERE" and examine the resulting HTML in Notepad, as shown in Figure 14.12.

Figure 14.12
Examining the `sample.html` file in notepad and locating the words "PUT DATA HERE" allows you to separate the HTML file into three pieces: the top portion of the code used to write the navigation bar, the data, and the bottom portion used to close the HTML page.

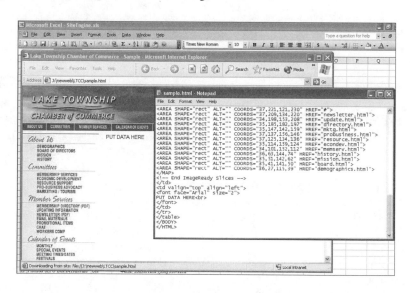

After you examine the code in Notepad, the task of creating a custom Web page is fairly simple. First, write out the HTML needed to draw the navigation bars. Then write the data from Excel. Then write the few lines of HTML to close the table and finish the Web page.

Using Excel as a Content Management System

200 million people are proficient in Excel. Companies everywhere have data in Excel and many staffers who are comfortable in maintaining that data. Rather than force these people to learn how to create HTML pages, why not build a content management system to take their Excel data and write out custom Web pages?

Figure 14.13 shows a typical membership database. We had a Web designer offer to build an expensive php database on the Web to display the membership directory and allow maintenance of members.

The organization is already maintaining this data in Excel. Using the code from Figure 14.12, you pretty much know the top and bottom portions of the HTML needed to render the Web page.

Figure 14.13
Companies everywhere are maintaining all sorts of data in Excel and are comfortable updating the data in Excel. Why not marry Excel with a simple bit of VBA so that custom HTML can be produced from Excel?

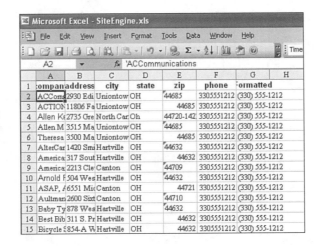

Building a content management system with these tools is simple. To the membership directory Excel file, I added two worksheets. In the worksheet called "Top," I copied the HTML needed to generate the navigation bar of the Web site. To the worksheet called "Bottom," I copied the HTML needed to generate the end of the HTML page. The simple Bottom worksheet is shown in Figure 14.14.

Figure 14.14
Two worksheets are added to the membership directory workbook. One lists the HTML code necessary to draw the navigation bar. The second lists the HTML code necessary to finish the Web page after displaying the data.

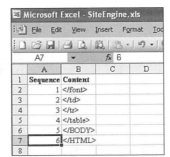

The macro code opens a text file called `directory.html` for output. First, all the HTML code from the Top worksheet is written to the file.

Then the macro loops through each row in the membership directory, writing data to the file.

After completing this loop, the macro writes out the HTML code from the Bottom worksheet to finish the file:

```
Sub WriteMembershipHTML()
    ' Write Web Pages
    Dim WST As Worksheet
    Dim WSB As Worksheet
    Dim WSM As Worksheet
    Set WSB = Worksheets("Bottom")
    Set WST = Worksheets("Top")
    Set WSM = Worksheets("Membership")

    ' Figure out the path
    MyPath = ThisWorkbook.Path

    LineCtr = 0

    FinalT = WST.Cells(65536, 1).End(xlUp).Row
    FinalB = WSB.Cells(65536, 1).End(xlUp).Row
    FinalM = WSM.Cells(65536, 1).End(xlUp).Row

    MyFile = "sampledirectory.html"

    ThisFile = MyPath & Application.PathSeparator & MyFile
    ThisHostFile = MyFile

    ' Delete the old HTML page
    On Error Resume Next
    Kill (ThisFile)
    On Error GoTo 0

    ' Build the title
    ThisTitle = "<Title>LTCC Membership Directory</Title>"
    WST.Cells(3, 2).Value = ThisTitle

    ' Open the file for output
    Open ThisFile For Output As #1

    ' Write out the top part of the HTML
    For j = 2 To FinalT
        Print #1, WST.Cells(j, 2).Value
    Next j

    ' For each row in Membership, write out lines of data to HTML file
    For j = 2 To FinalM
        ' Surround Member name with bold tags
        Print #1, "<b>" & WSM.Cells(j, 1).Value & "</b><br>"
        ' Member Address
        Print #1, WSM.Cells(j, 2).Value & "<br>"
        ' City, State, Zip code
        Addr = WSM.Cells(j, 3) & " " & WSM.Cells(j, 4) & " " & WSM.Cells(j, 5)
```

```
        Print #1, Addr & "<br>"
        ' Telephone number with 2 line breaks after it
        Print #1, WSM.Cells(j, 6).Value & "<br><br>"
    Next j

    ' Close old file
    ' Write date updated, but make sure there are 20 rows first
    Print #1, "<br>"
    Print #1, "This page current as of " & Format(Date, "mmmm dd, yyyy") & _
        " " & Format(Time, "h:mm AM/PM")

    ' Write out HTML code from Bottom worksheet
    For j = 2 To FinalB
        Print #1, WSB.Cells(j, 2).Value
    Next j
    Close #1

    Application.StatusBar = False
    Application.CutCopyMode = False
    MsgBox "Web pages updated"

End Sub
```

The finished Web page is shown in Figure 14.15. This Web page looks a lot better than the generic page created by Excel's Save As Web Page option. It can maintain the look and feel of the rest of the site.

Figure 14.15
A simple content management system in Excel was used to generate this Web page. The look and feel matches the rest of the Web site. Excel achieved it without any expensive Web database coding.

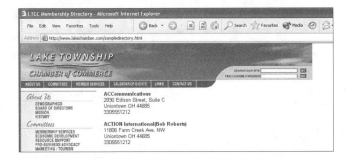

There are many advantages to this system. The person who maintains the membership directory is comfortable working in Excel. She has already been maintaining the data in Excel on a regular basis. Now, after updating some records, she presses a button to produce a new version of the Web page.

Of course, the Web designer is clueless about Excel. However, if he ever wants to change the Web design, it is a simple matter to open his new sample.html file in Notepad and copy the new code to the Top and Bottom worksheet.

The resulting Web page has a small file size—about one-sixth the size of the equivalent page created by Excel's Save As Web Page.

14

In real life, the content management system in this example was extended to allow easy maintenance of the organization's calendar, board members, and so on. The resulting workbook made it possible to maintain 41 Web pages at the click of a button.

Bonus—FTP from Excel

After you are able to update Web pages from Excel, you still have the hassle of using an FTP program to upload the pages from your hard drive to the Internet. Again, we have lots of people proficient in Excel, but not so many comfortable with using an FTP client.

Ken Anderson has written a cool command-line FTP freeware utility. Download WCL_FTP from `http://www.pacific.net/~ken/software/`. Save `WCL_FTP.exe` to the root directory of your hard drive, and then use this code to automatically upload your recently created HTML files to your Web server:

```
Sub DoFTP(fname, pathfname)
' To have this work, copy wcl_ftp.exe to the C:\ root directory
' Download from http://www.pacific.net/~ken/software/

' Build a string to FTP. The syntax is
' WCL_FTP.exe "Caption" hostname username password host-directory _
' host-filename local-filename get-or-put 0Ascii1Binanry 0NoLog _
' 0Background 1CloseWhenDone 1PassiveMode  1ErrorsText

If Not Worksheets("Menu").Range("I1").Value = True Then Exit Sub

s = """c:\wcl_ftp.exe "" " _
    & """Upload File to Web site"" " _
    & "ftp.MySite.com FTPUser FTPPassword www " _
    & fname & " " _
    & """" & pathfname & """ " _
    & "put " _
    & "0 0 0 1 1 1"

Shell s, vbMinimizedNoFocus
End Sub
```

Next Steps

Chapter 15, "XML in Excel 2003 Professional," examines passing data between applications with XML. Some Web sites, such as Amazon, are offering data in XML today, which makes for a tool more powerful than Web queries.

14

XML in Excel 2003 Professional

15

One of the most exciting new features in Office 2003 is the capability to better handle XML data. If you are working with a company that offers XML data and schemas, then the opportunities are endless. Even if your company does not offer XML data, you can still test out these features using publicly available XML data. Later in this chapter, we will look at using XML to retrieve data from Amazon.com.

What Is XML?

If you have ever looked at the source code for a Web page, you are familiar with HTML tags. Near the top of a Web page's HTML source, you will see a tag that defines the Web page title to appear in the blue bar at the top of the browser window. The tag might look something like this:

```
<TITLE>Ask Mr. Excel - Tips and Solutions for
➥Excel</TITLE>
```

A Web page can contain tags to identify titles, paragraphs, tables, rows within tables, and so on. This is the language of HTML.

XML is like HTML on steroids. With XML, you can define absolutely any fields in XML. The following XML file contains information about today's orders received. There is no magic in creating an XML file; I actually typed this into Notepad:

```
<TodaysOrders>
    <SalesOrder>
        <Customer>BCA Co</Customer>
        <Address>123 North</Address>
        <City>Stow</City>
        <State>OH</State>
        <Zip>44224</Zip>
        <ItemSKU>23456</ItemSKU>
```

```
        <Quantity>500</Quantity>
        <UnitPrice>21.75</UnitPrice>
    </SalesOrder>
    <SalesOrder>
        <Customer>DEF Co</Customer>
        <Address>234 Carapace Lane</Address>
        <City>South Bend</City>
        <State>IN</State>
        <Zip>44685</Zip>
        <ItemSKU>34567</ItemSKU>
        <Quantity>20</Quantity>
        <UnitPrice>50.00</UnitPrice>
    </SalesOrder>
</TodaysOrders>
```

Simple XML Rules

If you are familiar with HTML, then there are a few simple rules that differentiate XML from HTML:

- Every data element has to begin and end with an identical tag. Tag names are case sensitive. `<TagName>Data</Tagname>` is not valid. `<TagName>Data</TagName>` is valid.

- The XML file must begin and end with a root tag. There can be only one root tag in the file. In the example earlier, the root tag is `<TodaysOrders>`.

- It is valid to have an empty tag. Put a slash at the end of the tag. If there is no zip code for an international order, for example, use `<Zip/>` to indicate that there is no data for this field for this record.

- If you nest tags, the inner tag must be closed before you close the outer tag. This is different from HTML. In HTML it is valid to code `<b>XML is very <i>cool</b></i>`. This is not valid in XML. `<Item><a>data</a></Item>` will work, but `<Item><a>data</Item></a>` will not.

For a more thorough discussion of XML, see Benoit Marchal's *XML by Example* (0-7897-2504-5).

Universal File Format

For many years, CSV was considered the universal file format. Just about any application could produce data in comma-separated values and just about any spreadsheet could read in CSV data. XML promises to become the universal file format of the future and it is far more powerful.

You may deal with CSV data every day. As developers, we need to talk to the other developer who is generating the CSV data, and we have to understand that the fifth column contains a zip code and the sixth column contains a product SKU. If the source system ever leaves out a field, we are likely to end up with wrong results. Open a CSV file and you may have this confusing view of the data (see Figure 15.1).

Figure 15.1

For years, CSV has been the universal format to get data from another system into a spreadsheet. With CSV, both developers must understand that the fifth column contains a zip code and the sixth column contains a product SKU.

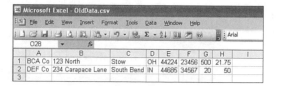

XML as the New Universal File Format

XML is far more powerful. If you use Excel to open the simple XML file shown in Figure 15.1, Excel can offer headings and can even infer something called the *schema* of the data. A schema is a separate file that describes the columns and relationships inherent in the data. If the source system would happen to be missing a zip code for a record, we do not have to worry about the SKU moving over from Column F. Compare Figure 15.2 with the CSV example shown in Figure 15.1. Excel can present a much more meaningful view of the data.

Figure 15.2

Data can be written in XML format by any system and intelligently read in to Excel. Unlike CSV data, the format of XML data is something Excel can understand.

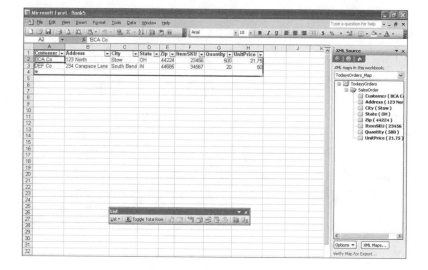

If you insert new records into the XML list in Excel, you can save the file back out as just the XML data. Use File, Save As and select XML Data for Save As Type, as shown in Figure 15.3. Excel can natively read from and write to XML files, allowing you to share data between applications.

15

Figure 15.3
Excel offers two choices for saving XML. You can save the file as an ExcelML spreadsheet file, or choose to save the data only in an XML data file.

The Alphabet Soup of XML

Note that in the previous example, we had only an XML file and Excel was able to accurately read the data, allow editing, and write the data back out for use by another application.

Two additional file types—schemas and transforms—enhance XML files.

Although the XML file contains the data and field names, an XML Schema file defines data relationships and data validation requirements. For example, a zip code field could require five numeric digits. XML Schemas are typically stored in XSD files.

XSL files are called Transforms or Solutions. A Transform describes how the fields in the XML file should be mapped to your document. If your data contains 20 elements, you can define in the transform file that you want to see only particular elements in this spreadsheet. You can have many XSL files for a particular schema to enable many views of the same data.

If you are reading someone else's XML data, XSD and XSL files have probably been provided for you. If you are reading your own XML data, Excel actually infers a data schema for you. After opening the XML file with TodaysOrders introduced at the start of this chapter, you can go to the immediate pane of the Visual Basic Editor (VBE) and retrieve the XSD file. Type

```
Print ActiveWorkbook.XmlMaps(1).Schemas(1).xml
```

Copy the result to a Notepad window and save as TodaysOrders.xsd. Figure 15.4 shows the inferred XSD file, although I have added line breaks and spacing to improve the readability.

The final step to fully use XML in Office 2003 is to create XSL transform files. There is no easy way to create this with the tools in Excel. For a discussion of the rather awkward process of manually creating an XSL file, see http://www.mrexcel.com/tip064.shtml.

Figure 15.4
Excel is able to infer a default schema for any XML file that it encounters. Having an .XSD schema file is a requirement to use any higher level XML features such as repurposing data.

```
NewOrders.xsd - Notepad
File  Edit  Format  View  Help
<xsd:schema xmlns:xsd="http://www.w3.org/2001/XMLSchema">
  <xsd:element nillable="true" name="iudaysorders">
  <xsd:complexType>
  <xsd:sequence minOccurs="0">
  <xsd:element minOccurs="0" maxOccurs="unbounded" nillable="true" name="salesorder" form="unqualified">
    <xsd:complexType>
    <xsd:sequence minOccurs="0">
      <xsd:element minOccurs="0" nillable="true" type="xsd:string" name="Customer" form="unqualified">
      </xsd:element>
      <xsd:element minOccurs="0" nillable="true" type="xsd:string" name="Address" form="unqualified">
      </xsd:element>
      <xsd:element minOccurs="0" nillable="true" type="xsd:string" name="City" form="unqualified">
      </xsd:element>
      <xsd:element minOccurs="0" nillable="true" type="xsd:string" name="State" form="unqualified">
      </xsd:element>
      <xsd:element minOccurs="0" nillable="true" type="xsd:integer" name="Zip" form="unqualified">
      </xsd:element>
      <xsd:element minOccurs="0" nillable="true" type="xsd:integer" name="ItemSKU" form="unqualified">
      </xsd:element>
      <xsd:element minOccurs="0" nillable="true" type="xsd:integer" name="Quantity" form="unqualified">
      </xsd:element>
      <xsd:element minOccurs="0" nillable="true" type="xsd:double" name="UnitPrice" form="unqualified">
      </xsd:element>
    </xsd:sequence>
    </xsd:complexType>
  </xsd:element>
  </xsd:sequence>
  </xsd:complexType>
  </xsd:element>
</xsd:schema>
```

Using XML to Round-Trip a Workbook from Excel to HTML and Back

Microsoft is thrilled that you can now save Excel 2003 and Word 2003 documents as XML files. They consider XML files to be native Office documents now. This is cool, because it means that any program that can write XML can, in theory, produce an Excel file on the fly.

Round-tripping is the process of saving an Excel file as XML, and then opening the XML file back into Excel. Figure 15.5 shows the results of round-tripping an Excel file. The file on the left contains greenbar formatting, strange fonts, and a chart. The formatted spreadsheet on the left was saved as an XML Spreadsheet file, closed, and re-opened as the file on the right. Excel did warn that the chart and any VBA code would be lost. Other than the chart, all other formatting was preserved perfectly on the round-trip to XML and back.

Figure 15.5
Excel 2003 now supports XML as a native file format.

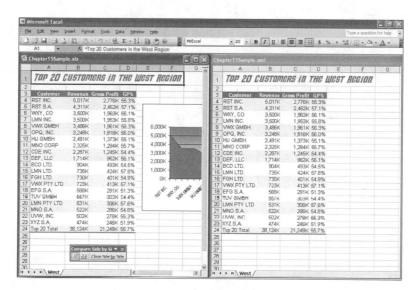

Figure 15.6 shows a subset of the XML code created when an Excel file is saved as an XML spreadsheet file.

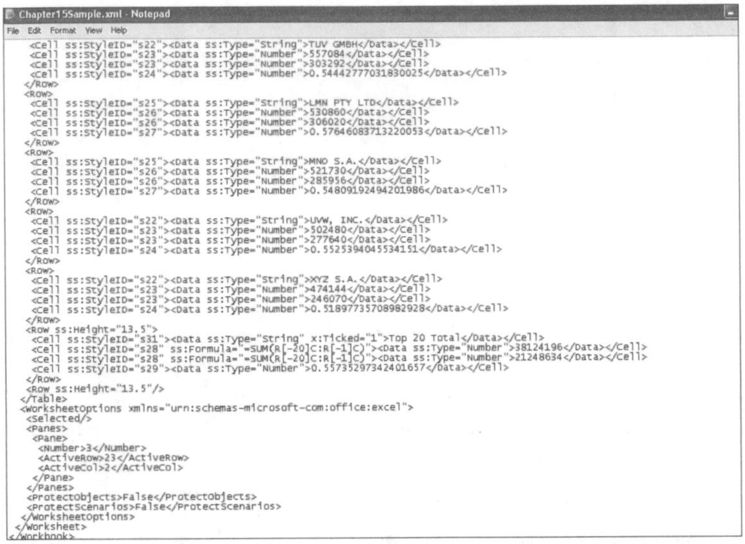

Chapter15Sample.xml - Notepad

File Edit Format View Help

```
    <Cell ss:StyleID="s22"><Data ss:Type="String">TUV GMBH</Data></Cell>
    <Cell ss:StyleID="s23"><Data ss:Type="Number">557084</Data></Cell>
    <Cell ss:StyleID="s23"><Data ss:Type="Number">303292</Data></Cell>
    <Cell ss:StyleID="s24"><Data ss:Type="Number">0.5444277031830025</Data></Cell>
   </Row>
   <Row>
    <Cell ss:StyleID="s25"><Data ss:Type="String">LMN PTY LTD</Data></Cell>
    <Cell ss:StyleID="s26"><Data ss:Type="Number">530860</Data></Cell>
    <Cell ss:StyleID="s26"><Data ss:Type="Number">306020</Data></Cell>
    <Cell ss:StyleID="s27"><Data ss:Type="Number">0.5764608371322053</Data></Cell>
   </Row>
   <Row>
    <Cell ss:StyleID="s25"><Data ss:Type="String">MNO S.A.</Data></Cell>
    <Cell ss:StyleID="s26"><Data ss:Type="Number">521730</Data></Cell>
    <Cell ss:StyleID="s26"><Data ss:Type="Number">285956</Data></Cell>
    <Cell ss:StyleID="s27"><Data ss:Type="Number">0.5480919249420198</Data></Cell>
   </Row>
   <Row>
    <Cell ss:StyleID="s22"><Data ss:Type="String">UVW, INC.</Data></Cell>
    <Cell ss:StyleID="s23"><Data ss:Type="Number">502480</Data></Cell>
    <Cell ss:StyleID="s23"><Data ss:Type="Number">277640</Data></Cell>
    <Cell ss:StyleID="s24"><Data ss:Type="Number">0.552539404553415l</Data></Cell>
   </Row>
   <Row>
    <Cell ss:StyleID="s22"><Data ss:Type="String">XYZ S.A.</Data></Cell>
    <Cell ss:StyleID="s23"><Data ss:Type="Number">474144</Data></Cell>
    <Cell ss:StyleID="s23"><Data ss:Type="Number">246070</Data></Cell>
    <Cell ss:StyleID="s24"><Data ss:Type="Number">0.5189773570898292</Data></Cell>
   </Row>
   <Row ss:Height="13.5">
    <Cell ss:StyleID="s31"><Data ss:Type="String" x:Ticked="1">Top 20 Total</Data></Cell>
    <Cell ss:StyleID="s28" ss:Formula="=SUM(R[-20]C:R[-1]C)"><Data ss:Type="Number">38124196</Data></Cell>
    <Cell ss:StyleID="s28" ss:Formula="=SUM(R[-20]C:R[-1]C)"><Data ss:Type="Number">21248634</Data></Cell>
    <Cell ss:StyleID="s29"><Data ss:Type="Number">0.5573529734240165</Data></Cell>
   </Row>
   <Row ss:Height="13.5"/>
  </Table>
  <WorksheetOptions xmlns="urn:schemas-microsoft-com:office:excel">
   <Selected/>
   <Panes>
    <Pane>
     <Number>3</Number>
     <ActiveRow>23</ActiveRow>
     <ActiveCol>2</ActiveCol>
    </Pane>
   </Panes>
   <ProtectObjects>False</ProtectObjects>
   <ProtectScenarios>False</ProtectScenarios>
  </WorksheetOptions>
 </Worksheet>
</Workbook>
```

Figure 15.6
This simple text file is now considered a valid native Excel 2003 file format. Using the specification from Microsoft, any program can now create native Excel files on the fly.

CASE STUDY

Case Study: Using XML Data from Amazon.com

The promise is that all sorts of XML data will soon be available. One high-profile example available now is Amazon.com. They now offer a wide variety of queryable data that is returned in XML format.

It is possible to use VBA to query data from Amazon and have the results returned to Excel.

Amazon.com offers a software development kit for download from `http://amazon.com/webservices`. To get the kit, follow these steps.

1. Follow the link to download the free developer's kit.
2. Click the Download Now button.
3. Unzip the kit.zip file to your hard drive.
4. The development kit describes two schemas: a lite schema and a heavy schema. In `ReadMeFirst.txt`, there will be a link to the heavy XSD. At press time, this link was located at `http://xml.amazon.com/schemas3/dev-heavy.xsd`.
5. Open that file in a browser and save it to your hard drive.

Starting with a blank Excel workbook, I first attach the schema to the workbook:

1. From the menu, select Data, XML, XML Source.
2. In the XML Source pane, click the XML Maps button.

3. In the XML Maps Dialog, click the Add button.

4. In the File Name box, type the URL for the Amazon heavy XSD file: `http://xml.amazon.com/schemas3/dev-heavy.xsd`. Select Open.

5. In the Multiple Roots dialog, select the ProductInfo as the root note of interest.

6. Click OK to close the XML Maps dialog.

All the fields available in the Amazon.com ProductInfo schema now appear in the XML Source pane. Drag any fields of interest to your spreadsheet, as shown in Figure 15.7.

Figure 15.7
After the XSD Schema is attached to the workbook, you can drag fields of interest from the XML Source pane to the spreadsheet.

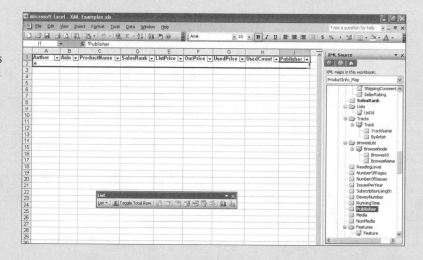

Now that the workbook is set up, you can switch to VBA to enter the code needed to retrieve data from Amazon.com.

The first step is to go to Tools, References and add a reference to Microsoft WinHTTP Services.

The Amazon Development Kit provides many sample URL strings to return various searches by author, publisher, ISBN, and so on.

After defining the proper URL string, the string is sent as a WinHttpRequest. The results are then mapped to the worksheet through the use of the `.ImportXML` method.

This sample code queries Amazon for all books written by Bill Jelen and published in 2002:

```
Sub QuerybyAuthor()
    ' Query all Bill Jelen books published in 2002
    Dim ws As Worksheet
    Dim whr As New WinHttpRequest
    Dim lobj As ListObject
    Dim nCount As Integer
    Dim objSelected As Object

    Dim sURI As String
```

```
        Set objSelected = Selection
        Set ws = Worksheets("Sheet1")
        Set lobj = ws.ListObjects(1)

        Application.Cursor = xlWait

        sURI = "http://xml.amazon.com/onca/xml2?t=webservices-20" _
            & "&dev-t=D3VCCO47XZEQFA" _
            & "&PowerSearch=author:Bill Jelen and pubdate:2002" _
            & "&mode=books&type=heavy&page=1&f=xml"

        whr.Open "GET", sURI
        whr.Send

        ActiveWorkbook.XmlMaps(1).ImportXml whr.ResponseText

        Application.Cursor = xlDefault

    End Sub
```

After the query has run, the results are written to the List object on sheet1. Note that because I asked for an Author field and Author is a repeating element along the ProductInfo node, any titles with two authors appear twice: one with each author. This query is useful for tracking sales rank and knowing the current used price for various titles (see Figure 15.8).

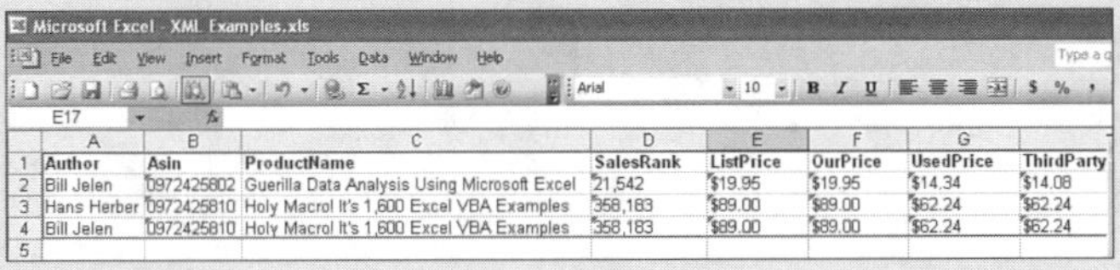

Figure 15.8
The .ImportXML method returns the search results to the worksheet. Only the mapped fields that were dragged from the XML Source pane are displayed.

Returning More Than One Page of Results

If you expect that a query will return more than one page of results, you can call the ImportXML query once for Page=1 and again for Page=2. Note that on the second call, the OverWrite parameter for the ImportXML is set to False to add the results to the current list object. This code returns two pages of results for books published by Que in 2003:

```
Sub QuerybyPublisher()
    Dim ws As Worksheet
    Dim whr As New WinHttpRequest
    Dim lobj As ListObject
    Dim nCount As Integer
    Dim objSelected As Object

    Dim sURI As String

    Set objSelected = Selection
    Set ws = Worksheets("Sheet1")
    Set lobj = ws.ListObjects(1)
```

```
Application.Cursor = xlWait

sURI = "http://xml.amazon.com/onca/xml2?t=webservices-20" _
    & "&dev-t=D3VCCO47XZEQFA" _
    & "&PowerSearch=publisher:Que and pubdate:2003" _
    & "&mode=books&type=heavy&page=1&f=xml"

' Get first 20 results
whr.Open "GET", sURI
whr.Send
ActiveWorkbook.XmlMaps(1).ImportXml whr.ResponseText, Overwrite:=True

' Get next 20 results
sURI = "http://xml.amazon.com/onca/xml2?t=webservices-20" _
    & "&dev-t=D3VCCO47XZEQFA" _
    & "&PowerSearch=publisher:Que and pubdate:2003" _
    & "&mode=books&type=heavy&page=2&f=xml"

whr.Open "GET", sURI
whr.Send
ActiveWorkbook.XmlMaps(1).ImportXml whr.ResponseText, Overwrite:=False

Application.Cursor = xlDefault

End Sub
```

The results are shown in Figure 15.9.

Figure 15.9
Because the results exceeded one page of data as returned by Amazon, this query made two calls to return XML and made sure that the Overwrite option was false for the second call.

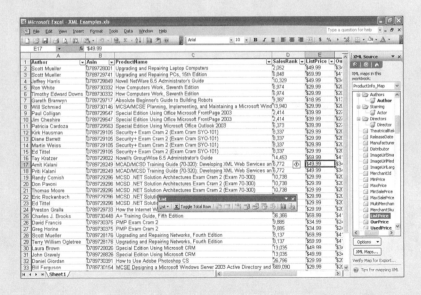

It is interesting to note that the `ProductInfo_Map` offers six dozen fields and the results of the query are very easily changed by dragging and dropping new data from the XML Source pane to the workbook. Without changing one line of VBA code, the query can easily focus on SalesRank or Lists or the number of Marketplace vendors offering the book for sale.

15

Next Steps

Although XML enables you to transfer data between unrelated applications, you already can transfer data programmatically between applications in the Microsoft Office suite. Chapter 16, "Automating Word," looks at using Excel VBA to automate and control Microsoft Word.

Automating Word

Word, Excel, PowerPoint, Outlook, and Access all use the same VBA language; the only difference between them is their object models (for example, Excel has a `Workbooks` object, Word has `Documents`). Any one of these applications can access another application's object model as long as the second application is installed.

To access Word's object library, Excel must establish a link to it. There are two ways of doing this: *early binding* or *late binding*. With early binding, the reference to the application object is created when the program is compiled; with late binding, it is created when the program is run.

This chapter is an introduction to accessing Word from Excel; we will not be reviewing Word's entire object model or the object models of other applications. Refer to the VBA Object Browser in the appropriate application to learn about other object models.

Early Binding

Code written with early binding executes faster than code with late binding. A reference is made to Word's object library before the code is written so that Word's objects, properties, and methods are available in the Object Browser. Tips also appear as shown in Figure 16.1, such as a list of members of an object.

The disadvantage of early binding is that the referenced object library must exist on the system. For example, if you write a macro referencing Word 2003's object library and someone with Word 2002 attempts to run the code, the program fails because the program cannot find the 2003 object library.

Figure 16.1
Early binding allows
easy access to the Word
object's syntax.

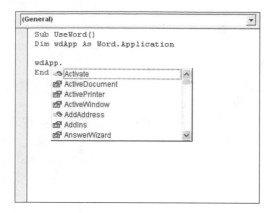

The object library is added through the VBE:

1. Select Tools, References.

2. Check Microsoft Word 11.0 Object Library in the Available References list (see Figure 16.2).

3. Click OK.

> **NOTE**
> If the object library is not found, then Word is not installed. If another version is found in the list (such as 10.0), then another version of Word is installed.

Figure 16.2
Select the object library
from the References list.

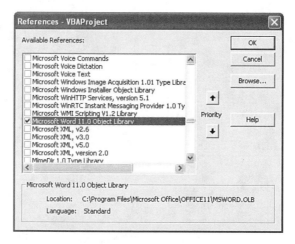

After the reference is set, Word variables can be declared with the correct (Word) variable type. However, if the object variable is declared As Object, this will force the program to use late binding:

Excel searches through the selected libraries to find the reference for the object type. If the type is found in more than one library, the first reference is selected. You can influence which library is chosen by changing the priority of the reference in the listing.

16

```
Sub WordEarlyBinding()
Dim wdApp As Word.Application
Dim wdDoc As Document
Set wdApp = New Word.Application
Set wdDoc = wdApp.Documents.Open(ThisWorkbook.Path & _
    "\Chapter 16 - Automating Word.doc")
wdApp.Visible = True
Set wdApp = Nothing
Set wdDoc = Nothing
End Sub
```

This example opens an existing Word document from Excel. The declared variables, wdApp and wdDoc, are of Word object types. wdApp is used to create a reference to the Word Application in the same way the Application object is used in Excel. New Word.Application is used to create a new instance of Word.

TIP If no other session of Word is active when it is opened in the macro, Word is not visible. If the application needs to be shown, it must be unhidden (wdApp.Visible = True).

When finished, it's a good idea to set the object variables to Nothing and release the memory being used by the application.

Compile Error: Can't Find Object or Library

If the referenced version of Word does not exist on the system, then an error message appears. View the Reference List and the missing object is highlighted with the words "MISSING" (see Figure 16.3).

If a previous version of Word is available, you can try running the program with that version referenced. Many objects are the same between versions.

Figure 16.3
Excel cannot compile if
references are missing.

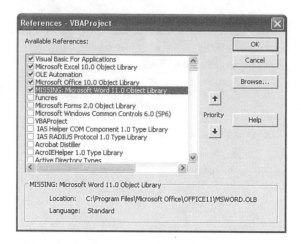

Late Binding

With late binding, you create an object that refers to the Word application before linking to
the Word library. Because you do not set up a reference beforehand, the only constraint on
the Word version is that the objects, properties, and methods must exist. In the case where
there are differences, the version can be verified and the correct object used accordingly.

The disadvantage of late binding is that Excel doesn't know what is going on—it doesn't
understand that you are referring to Word. This prevents the tips from appearing when referencing Word objects. Also, built-in constants are not available and, when compiling, Excel
cannot verify that the references to Word are correct. After the program is executed, the
links to Word begin to build, and any coding errors are detected at that point.

The following example opens and makes visible an existing Word document:

```
Sub WordLateBinding()
Dim wdApp As Object, wdDoc As Object
Set wdApp = CreateObject("Word.Application")
Set wdDoc = wdApp.Documents.Open(ThisWorkbook.Path & _
"\Chapter 16 - Automating Word.doc")
wdApp.Visible = True
Set wdApp = Nothing
Set wdDoc = Nothing
End Sub
```

An object variable (wdApp) is declared and set to reference the application
(CreateObject("Word.Application")). Other required variables are then declared (wdDoc)
and the application object is used to refer these variables to Word's object model.

> **NOTE**
> Declaring wdApp and wdDoc as objects forces the use of late binding. The program cannot create
> the required links to the Word object model until it executes the CreateObject function.

Creating and Referencing Objects

The following sections describe how to create new objects as well as reference currently open objects.

Keyword New

In the early binding example, the keyword New was used to reference the Word application. The New keyword can be used only with early binding; it does not work with late binding. CreateObject or GetObject would also work, but New was best for the example. If an instance of the application is running and you want to use it, use the GetObject function instead.

16

> **CAUTION**
>
> If your code to open Word runs smoothly but you don't see an instance of Word (and should), open your Task Manager and look for the process WinWord.exe. If it exists, from the Immediate Window in Excel's VBE, type the following (early binding):
>
> ```
> Word.Application.Visible = True
> ```
>
> If multiple instances of WinWord.exe are found, you must make each visible and close the extra instance(s) of WinWord.exe.

CreateObject **Function**

The CreateObject function was used in the late binding example, but can also be used in early binding. CreateObject has a *class* parameter consisting of the name and type of the object to be created (Name.Type).

It creates a new instance of the object; in this case, the Word application is created.

GetObject **Function**

The GetObject function can be used to reference an instance of Word that is already running. It creates an error if no instance can be found.

GetObject's two parameters are optional. The first parameter specifies the full path and filename to open and the second the application program:

```
Sub UseGetObject()
Dim wdDoc As Object
Set wdDoc = GetObject(ThisWorkbook.Path & "\Chapter 16 - Automating Word.doc")
wdDoc.Application.Visible = True
Set wdDoc = Nothing
End Sub
```

This example opens a document in an existing instance of Word and ensures the Word application's Visible property is true. Note that to make the document visible, you have to refer to the application object (wdDoc.Application.Visible) because wdDoc is referencing a document rather than the application.

> **NOTE**
> Although the Word application's `Visible` property is set to `True`, this code does not make the Word application the active application. In most cases, the Word application icon stays in the taskbar and Excel remains the active application on the user's screen.

The following example uses errors to learn whether Word is already open before pasting a chart at the end of a document. If not, it opens Word and creates a new document:

```
Sub IsWordOpen()
    Dim wdApp As Object
    ActiveChart.ChartArea.Copy
    On Error Resume Next
    Set wdApp = GetObject(, "Word.Application")
    If wdApp Is Nothing Then
        Set wdApp = GetObject("", "Word.Application")
    End If
    If wdApp.ActiveDocument Is Nothing Then
        With wdApp
            .Documents.Add
            .Visible = True
        End With
    End If
    On Error GoTo 0
    With wdApp.Selection
        .EndKey Unit:=6 ' wdStory=6
        .TypeParagraph
        ' wdPasteOLEObject=0, wdInLine=0 so this works
        .PasteSpecial link:=False, DataType:=wdPasteOLEObject, _
            Placement:=wdInLine, DisplayAsIcon:=False
    End With
    Set wdApp = Nothing
End Sub
```

Using `On Error Resume Next` forces the program to continue even if it runs into an error. In this case, an error occurs when we attempt to link wdApp to an object that does not exist. wdApp will have no value. The next line, `If wdApp Is Nothing then`, takes advantage of this and opens an instance of Word, adding an empty document and making the application visible. Note the use of empty quotes for the first parameter in `GetObject("", "Word.Application")`—this is how to use the `GetObject` function to open a new instance of Word. Use `On Error Goto 0` to return to normal VBA handling behavior.

Word's Objects

Word's macro recorder can be used to get a preliminary understanding of the Word object model. However, much like Excel's macro recorder, the results will be long winded. Keep this in mind and use the recorder to lead you toward the objects, properties, and methods in Word.

> **CAUTION**
> The macro recorder is limited in what it will allow you to record. The mouse cannot be used to move the cursor or select objects, but there are no limits on doing so with the keyboard.

The following example is what the Word macro recorder produces when adding a new, blank document.

```
Documents.Add Template:="Normal", NewTemplate:=False, DocumentType:=0
```

Making this more efficient (still in Word) produces this:

```
Documents.Add
```

`Template`, `NewTemplate`, and `DocumentType` are all optional properties that the recorder includes but are not required unless you need to change a default property or ensure that a property is as you require.

To use the same line of code in Excel, a link to the Word object library is required, as we learned earlier. After that link is established, an understanding of Word's objects is all you need. Following is a review of *some* of Word's objects—enough to get you off the ground. For a more detailed listing, refer to the object model in Word's VBE.

Document **Object**

Word's `Document` object is equivalent to Excel's `Workbook` object. It consists of characters, words, sentences, paragraphs, sections, and headers/footers. It is through the `Document` object that methods and properties affecting the entire document, such as printing, closing, searching, and reviewing, are accomplished.

Create

To create a blank document in an existing instance of Word, use the `Add` method (we already learned how to create a new document when Word is closed—refer to `GetObject` and `CreateObject`):

```
Sub NewDocument()
Dim wdApp As Word.Application

Set wdApp = GetObject(, "Word.Application")

wdApp.Documents.Add

Set wdApp = Nothing
End Sub
```

This example opens a new, blank document that uses the default template. To create a new document that uses a specific template:

```
wdApp.Documents.Add Template:="Contemporary Memo.dot"
```

This creates a new document that uses the Contemporary Memo template. `Template` can be either just the name of a template from the default template location or the file path and name.

Open

To open an existing document, use the `Open` method. Several parameters are available, including `Read Only` and `AddtoRecentFiles`. The following example opens an existing document as `Read Only`, but prevents the file from being added to the Recent File List under the File menu:

```
wdApp.Documents.Open _
    Filename:="C:\Excel VBA 2003 by Jelen & Syrstad\Chapter 17 - Arrays.Doc", _
    ReadOnly:=True, AddtoRecentFiles:=False
```

After changes have been made to a document, you most likely will want to save it. To save a document with its existing name:

```
wdApp.Documents.Save
```

If the `Save` command is used with a new document without a name, the Save As dialog box appears. To save a document with a new name, you can use the `SaveAs` method instead.

```
wdApp.ActiveDocument.SaveAs "C:\Excel VBA 2003 by Jelen & Syrstad\MemoTest.doc"
```

> **NOTE** SaveAs requires the use of members of the `Document` object, such as `ActiveDocument`.

Close

Use the `Close` method to close a specified document or all open documents. By default, a Save dialog appears for any documents with unsaved changes. The `SaveChanges` argument can be used to change this. To close all open documents without saving changes, use this code:

```
wdApp.Documents.Close SaveChanges:=wdDoNotSaveChanges
```

To close a specific document, you can close the active document or you can specify a document name:

```
wdApp.ActiveDocument.Close
```

or

```
wdApp.Documents("Chapter 17 - Arrays.Doc").Close
```

Print

Use the `PrintOut` method to print part or all of a document. To print a document with all the default print settings:

```
wdApp.ActiveDocument.PrintOut
```

By default, the print range is the entire document, but this can be changed by setting the `Range` and `Pages` arguments of the `PrintOut` method:

```
wdApp.ActiveDocument.PrintOut Range:=wdPrintRangeOfPages, Pages:="2"
```

Selection **Object**

The Selection object represents what is selected in the document—that is, a word, sentence, or the insertion point. It has a Type property that returns the type of what is selected (wdSelectionIP, wdSelectionColumn, wdSelectionShape, and so on).

HomeKey/EndKey

The HomeKey and EndKey methods are used to change the selection; they correspond to using the Home and End keys, respectively, on the keyboard. They have two parameters: Unit and Extend. Unit is the range of movement to make, either to the beginning (Home) or end (End) of a line (wdLine), document (wdStory), column (wdColumn), or row (wdRow). Extend is the type of movement: wdMove moves the selection, wdExtend extends the selection from the original insertion point to the new insertion point.

To move the cursor to the beginning of the document, use this code:

```
wdApp.Selection.HomeKey Unit:=wdStory, Extend:=wdMove
```

To select the document from the insertion point to the end of the document, use this code:

```
.wdApp.Selection.EndKey Unit:=wdStory, Extend:=wdExtend
```

TypeText

The TypeText method is used to insert text into a Word document. User settings, such as the Overtype setting, can affect what will happen when text is inserted into the document:

```
Sub InsertText()
Dim wdApp As Word.Application
Dim wdDoc As Document
Dim wdSln As Selection

Set wdApp = GetObject(, "Word.Application")
Set wdDoc = wdApp.ActiveDocument
Set wdSln = wdApp.Selection

wdDoc.Application.Options.Overtype = False
With wdSln
    If .Type = wdSelectionIP Then
        .TypeText ("Inserting at insertion point. ")
    ElseIf .Type = wdSelectionNormal Then
            If wdApp.Options.ReplaceSelection Then
                .Collapse Direction:=wdCollapseStart
            End If
            .TypeText ("Inserting before a text block. ")
    End If
End With
Set wdApp = Nothing
Set wdDoc = Nothing
End Sub
```

16

Range **Object**

The Range object represents a contiguous area, or areas, in the document. It has a starting character position and an ending character position. The object can be the insertion point, a range of text, or the entire document, including non-printing characters (such as spaces or paragraph marks).

The Range object is similar to the Selection object but, in some ways, is better: It requires less code to accomplish the same tasks; it has more capabilities; and it saves time and memory because the Range object doesn't require Word to move the cursor or highlight objects in the document to manipulate them.

Define a Range

To define a range, enter a starting and ending position, as shown in this code segment:

```
Range(StartPosition, EndPosition)
Sub RangeText()
Dim wdApp As Word.Application
Dim wdDoc As Document
Dim wdRng As Word.Range

Set wdApp = GetObject(, "Word.Application")
Set wdDoc = wdApp.ActiveDocument

Set wdRng = wdDoc.Range(0, 22)
wdRng.Select

Set wdApp = Nothing
Set wdDoc = Nothing
Set wdRng = Nothing
End Sub
```

Figure 16.4 shows the results of running this code. The first 22 characters, including non-printing characters such as paragraph returns, are selected.

> **NOTE**
> The range was selected for easier viewing. It is not required that the range be selected to be manipulated.

Figure 16.4
The Range object selects everything in its path.

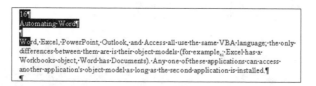

The first character position in a document is always zero and the last is equivalent to the number of characters in the document.

The Range object also selects paragraphs. The following example selects the third paragraph in the active document and pastes it in Excel. Depending on how the paste is done, the text can be pasted into a text box (see Figure 16.5) or into a cell (see Figure 16.6):

```
Sub SelectSentence()
Dim wdApp As Word.Application
Dim wdRng As Word.Range

Set wdApp = GetObject(, "Word.Application")

With wdApp.ActiveDocument
    If .Paragraphs.Count >= 3 Then
        Set wdRng = .Paragraphs(3).Range
        wdRng.Copy
    End If
End With

'This line pastes the copied text into a text box
Worksheets("Sheet2").PasteSpecial

'These two lines paste the copied text in cell A1
'Note that the range must be selected and then we can paste the text
Worksheets("Sheet2").Range("A1").Activate
ActiveSheet.Paste

Set wdApp = Nothing
Set wdRng = Nothing
End Sub
```

Figure 16.5
Paste Word text into an Excel text box.

Figure 16.6
Paste Word text into an Excel cell.

Format a Range

After a range is selected, formatting can be applied to it (see Figure 16.7). The following program loops through all the paragraphs of the active document and bolds the first word of each paragraph:

```
Sub ChangeFormat()
Dim wdApp As Word.Application
Dim wdRng As Word.Range
Dim count As Integer

Set wdApp = GetObject(, "Word.Application")

With wdApp.ActiveDocument
    For count = 1 To .Paragraphs.count
        Set wdRng = .Paragraphs(count).Range
```

```
            With wdRng
                .Words(1).Font.Bold = True
                .Collapse
            End With
        Next count
    End With

    Set wdApp = Nothing
    Set wdRng = Nothing
    End Sub
```

Figure 16.7
Format the first word of each paragraph in a document.

Word, Excel, PowerPoint, Outlook, and Access all use the same VBA language; the only differences between them are their object models (for example,: Excel has a Workbooks object, Word has Documents). Any one of these applications can access another application's object model as long as the second application is installed.

To access Word's object library, Excel must establish a link to it. There are two ways of doing this: early binding or late binding. With early binding, the reference to the application object is created when the program is compiled; with late binding, it is created when the program is run.

Note: This chapter is an introduction to accessing Word from Excel; we will not be reviewing Word's entire object model or the object models of other applications. Refer to the VBA Object Browser in the appropriate application to learn about other object models.
—

A quick way of changing the formatting of entire paragraphs is to change the style (see Figure 16.8). The program below finds the paragraph with the "NO" style and changes it to "HA":

```
Sub ChangeStyle()
Dim wdApp As Word.Application
Dim wdRng As Word.Range
Dim count As Integer

Set wdApp = GetObject(, "Word.Application")

With wdApp.ActiveDocument
    For count = 1 To .Paragraphs.count
        Set wdRng = .Paragraphs(count).Range
        With wdRng
            If .Style = "NO" Then
                .Style = "HA"
                .Collapse
            End If
        End With
    Next count
End With

Set wdApp = Nothing
Set wdRng = Nothing
End Sub
```

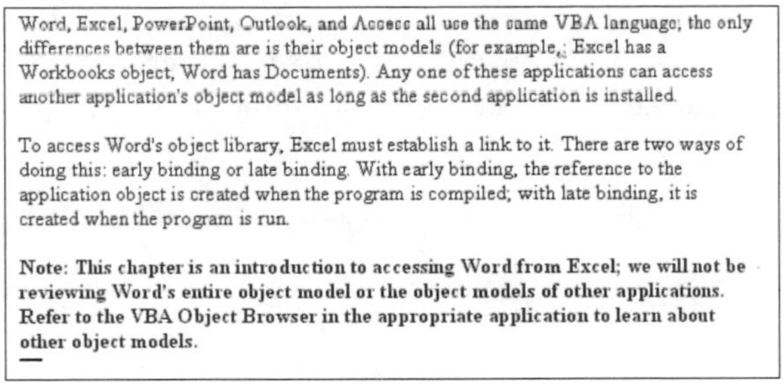

Figure 16.8
Use styles to quickly
change paragraph for-
matting.

> Word, Excel, PowerPoint, Outlook, and Access all use the same VBA language; the only
> differences between them are is their object models (for example, Excel has a
> Workbooks object; Word has Documents). Any one of these applications can access
> another application's object model as long as the second application is installed.
>
> To access Word's object library, Excel must establish a link to it. There are two ways of
> doing this: early binding or late binding. With early binding, the reference to the
> application object is created when the program is compiled; with late binding, it is
> created when the program is run.
>
> Note: This chapter is an introduction to accessing Word from Excel; we will not be
> reviewing Word's entire object model or the object models of other applications.
> Refer to the VBA Object Browser in the appropriate application to learn about
> other object models.

Bookmarks

Bookmarks are members of the Document, Selection, and Range objects. They can help make
it easier to navigate around Word. Instead of having to choose words, sentences, or paragraphs, use bookmarks to swiftly manipulate sections of a document.

> **NOTE**
> Bookmarks do not have to be existing; they can be created via code.

Bookmarks appear as grey I-bars in Word documents. Go to Tools, Options, View to turn
on bookmarks (see Figure 16.9).

Figure 16.9
Turn on bookmarks to
find them in a docu-
ment.

After you've set up bookmarks in a document, you can use the bookmarks to quickly move to a range. The following code automatically inserts text after four bookmarks that were previously set up in the document. The results are shown in Figure 16.10.

```
Sub UseBookmarks()
Dim myArray()
Dim wdBkmk As String

Dim wdApp As Word.Application
Dim wdRng As Word.Range

myArray = Array("To", "CC", "From", "Subject")
Set wdApp = GetObject(, "Word.Application")

Set wdRng = wdApp.ActiveDocument.Bookmarks(myArray(0)).Range
wdRng.InsertBefore ("Bill Jelen")
Set wdRng = wdApp.ActiveDocument.Bookmarks(myArray(1)).Range
wdRng.InsertBefore ("Tracy Syrstad")
Set wdRng = wdApp.ActiveDocument.Bookmarks(myArray(2)).Range
wdRng.InsertBefore ("MrExcel")
Set wdRng = wdApp.ActiveDocument.Bookmarks(myArray(3)).Range
wdRng.InsertBefore ("Fruit Sales")

Set wdApp = Nothing
Set wdRng = Nothing
End Sub
```

Figure 16.10
Use bookmarks to quickly enter text into a Word document.

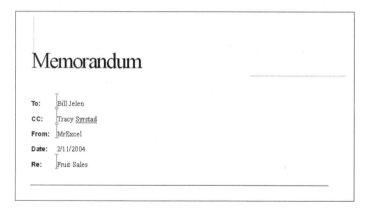

Bookmarks can also be used as markers for bringing in Charts created in Excel (see Figure 16.11). The following links an Excel chart to the memo:

```
Sub CreateMemo()
Dim myArray()
Dim wdBkmk As String

Dim wdApp As Word.Application
Dim wdRng As Word.Range

myArray = Array("To", "CC", "From", "Subject", "Chart")
Set wdApp = GetObject(, "Word.Application")
```

```
Set wdRng = wdApp.ActiveDocument.Bookmarks(myArray(0)).Range
wdRng.InsertBefore ("Bill Jelen")
Set wdRng = wdApp.ActiveDocument.Bookmarks(myArray(1)).Range
wdRng.InsertBefore ("Tracy Syrstad")
Set wdRng = wdApp.ActiveDocument.Bookmarks(myArray(2)).Range
wdRng.InsertBefore ("MrExcel")
Set wdRng = wdApp.ActiveDocument.Bookmarks(myArray(3)).Range
wdRng.InsertBefore ("Fruit & Vegetable Sales")

Set wdRng = wdApp.ActiveDocument.Bookmarks(myArray(4)).Range
ActiveSheet.ChartObjects("Chart 1").Copy
wdRng.Select
wdRng.Application.Selection.PasteAndFormat Type:=2

wdApp.Activate

Set wdApp = Nothing
Set wdRng = Nothing
End Sub
```

16

Figure 16.11
Use bookmarks to bring charts into Word documents.

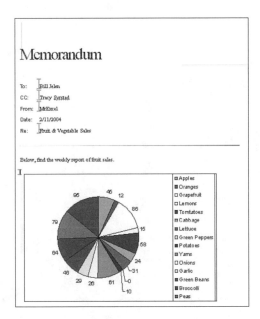

Case Study: Creating a Filtered Report in Word

In Chapter 11,"Data Mining with Advanced Filter," we showed you how to use filtering to create custom reports for multiple clients. The results were saved on individual sheets in new workbooks. This time, you need to include the results in a document report that will be sent to each customer:

1. Create a new document in Word. In this document, add bookmarks called Client and Table. Add styles to place the title in a large font. Save the document as a template called SalesReport.dot.

2. Modify the Filter program from Chapter 11. After creating the report in Excel, use `Documents.Add` to add a new Word document based on the `SalesReport.dot` template.
3. Use the `InsertBefore` method to write the customer name at the Client bookmark in the new Word document.
4. Copy the report table to the Word document after the Table bookmark. After pasting, use `Selection.Rows(1)` to add a heading style to the first row of the table.

The final result is shown in Figure 16.12.

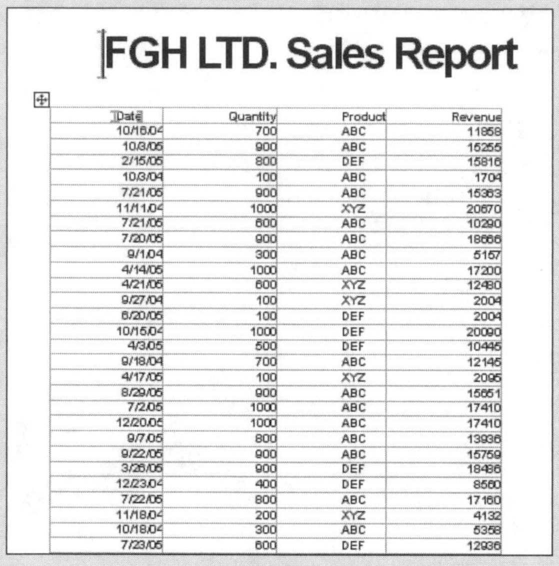
FGH LTD. Sales Report

Date	Quantity	Product	Revenue
10/16/04	700	ABC	11858
10/3/05	900	ABC	15255
2/15/05	800	DEF	15816
10/3/04	100	ABC	1704
7/21/05	900	ABC	15363
11/11/04	1000	XYZ	20670
7/21/05	600	ABC	10290
7/20/05	900	ABC	18666
9/1/04	300	ABC	5157
4/14/05	1000	ABC	17200
4/21/05	600	XYZ	12480
9/27/04	100	XYZ	2004
6/20/05	100	DEF	2004
10/15/04	1000	DEF	20090
4/3/05	500	DEF	10445
9/18/04	700	ABC	12145
4/17/05	100	XYZ	2095
8/29/05	900	ABC	15651
7/2/05	1000	ABC	17410
12/20/05	1000	ABC	17410
9/7/05	800	ABC	13936
9/22/05	900	ABC	15759
3/26/05	900	DEF	18486
12/23/04	400	DEF	8560
7/22/05	800	ABC	17160
11/18/04	200	XYZ	4132
10/18/04	300	ABC	5358
7/23/05	600	DEF	12936

Figure 16.12
Send filtered reports to Word for distribution.

The complete code follows:

```
Sub RunReportForEachCustomer()
    Dim IRange As Range
    Dim ORange As Range
    Dim CRange As Range
    Dim WBN As Workbook
    Dim WSN As Worksheet
    Dim WSO As Worksheet

    Dim wdApp As Word.Application
    Dim wdDoc As Word.Document
    Dim wdRng As Word.Range

    Application.ScreenUpdating = False

    Set WSO = ActiveSheet
    ' Find the size of today's dataset
    FinalRow = Cells(65536, 1).End(xlUp).Row
    NextCol = Cells(1, 255).End(xlToLeft).Column + 2
```

```vba
    ' First - get a unique list of customers in J
    ' Set up output range. Copy heading from D1 there
    Range("D1").Copy Destination:=Cells(1, NextCol)
    Set ORange = Cells(1, NextCol)

    ' Define the Input Range
    Set IRange = Range("A1").Resize(FinalRow, NextCol - 2)

    ' Do the Advanced Filter to get unique list of customers
    IRange.AdvancedFilter Action:=xlFilterCopy, CriteriaRange:="", _
        CopyToRange:=ORange, Unique:=True

    FinalCust = Cells(65536, NextCol).End(xlUp).Row

    ' Loop through each customer
    For Each cell In Cells(2, NextCol).Resize(FinalCust - 1, 1)
        ThisCust = cell.Value

        ' Set up the Criteria Range with one customer
        Cells(1, NextCol + 2).Value = Range("D1").Value
        Cells(2, NextCol + 2).Value = ThisCust
        Set CRange = Cells(1, NextCol + 2).Resize(2, 1)

        ' Set up output range. We want Date, Quantity, Product, Revenue
        ' These columns are in C, E, B, and F
        Cells(1, NextCol + 4).Resize(1, 4).Value = _
            Array(Cells(1, 3), Cells(1, 5), _
            Cells(1, 2), Cells(1, 6))
        Set ORange = Cells(1, NextCol + 4).Resize(1, 4)

' Do the Advanced Filter to get unique list of customers & product
IRange.AdvancedFilter Action:=xlFilterCopy, CriteriaRange:=CRange, _
    CopyToRange:=ORange
' Add Total information
totalrow = WSO.Cells(65536, ORange.Columns(1).Column).End(xlUp).Row + 1
WSO.Cells(totalrow, ORange.Columns(1).Column).Value = "Total"
WSO.Cells(totalrow, ORange.Columns(2).Column).FormulaR1C1 = _
    "=SUM(R2C:R[-1]C)"
WSO.Cells(totalrow, ORange.Columns(4).Column).FormulaR1C1 = _
     "=SUM(R2C:R[-1]C)"
' Create a new document to hold the output
On Error Resume Next
'Set wdDoc = New Word.Document
Set wdApp = GetObject(, "Word.Application")
If wdApp Is Nothing Then Set wdApp = GetObject("", "Word.Application")
Set wdDoc = wdApp.Documents.Add(Template:= _
    "C:\Reports\MrExcel SalesTemplate.dot")
        wdDoc.Activate

        ' Set up a title on the document
        wdDoc.Bookmarks("Client").Range.InsertBefore (ThisCust)

        ' Copy data from WSO to wdDoc
        WSO.Cells(1, NextCol + 4).CurrentRegion.Copy
        Set wdRng = wdApp.ActiveDocument.Bookmarks("Table").Range
        wdRng.Select
```

```vba
            ' Format the table
            With wdDoc.Application.Selection
                .Paste
                With wdDoc.Application.ActiveDocument.Tables(1)
                    .Rows.Alignment = wdAlignRowCenter
                    With .Rows(1)
                        .HeadingFormat = True
                        .Select
                        wdApp.Selection.Font.Bold = True
                    End With
                End With
                .HomeKey Unit:=wdStory, Extend:=Move
            End With

            ' Save the document with a unique title and then close it
            wdDoc.SaveAs "C:\Reports\" & ThisCust & ".doc"
            wdDoc.Close savechanges:=False

            WSO.Select

            Set wdApp = Nothing
            Set wdDoc = Nothing
            Set wdRng = Nothing

            ' clear the output range, etc.
            Cells(1, NextCol + 2).Resize(1, 10).EntireColumn.Clear
        Next cell
        Application.ScreenUpdating = True
        Cells(1, NextCol).EntireColumn.Clear
        MsgBox FinalCust - 1 & " Reports have been created!"
    End Sub
```

Next Steps

In Chapter 17, "Arrays," you will learn how to use multi-dimensional arrays. Reading data into a multi-dimensional array, performing calculations on the array, and then writing the array back to a range can dramatically speed up your macros.

Techie Stuff You Will Need to Produce Applications for the Administrator to Run

IN THIS PART

III

Arrays

An *array* is a type of variable that can be used to hold more than one piece of data. For example, if you had to work with the name and address of a client, your first thought might be to assign one variable for the name and another for the address of the client. Instead, consider using an array, which can hold both pieces of information—and not for just one client, but for hundreds.

Declare an Array

Declare an array by adding parentheses after the array name. The parentheses contain the number of elements in the array:

```
Dim myArray (2)
```

This creates an array, myArray, that contains three elements. Why three? Because, by default, the index count starts at zero:

```
myArray(0) = 10
myArray(1) = 20
myArray(2) = 30
```

If the index count needs to start on one, then use Option Base 1. This forces the count to start at one. The option base statement is placed in the declarations section of the module:

```
Option Base 1

Dim myArray(2)
```

This now forces the array to have only two elements.

You can also create an array independent of the Option Base statement by declaring its lower bound:

```
Dim myArray (1 to 10)
```

```
Dim BigArray (100 to 200)
```

17

Every array has a lower bound (Lbound) and an upper bound (Ubound). When you declare `Dim myArray (2)`, you are declaring the upper bound and allowing the option base to declare the lower bound. By declaring `Dim myArray (1 to 10)`, you declare the lower bound, 1, and the upper bound, 10.

Multidimensional Arrays

The arrays just discussed are considered *one-dimensional arrays*—only one number designates the location of an element of the array. The array is like a single row of data, but because there can be only one row, you don't have to worry about the row number—only the column number. For example, to retrieve the second element (`Option Base 0`) use `myArray (1)`.

In some cases, a single dimension isn't enough. This is where multidimensional arrays come in. Where a one-dimensional array is a single row of data, a multidimensional array contains rows *and* columns.

> **NOTE**
>
> Another word for array is *matrix*, which is what a spreadsheet is. The `Cells` object refers to *elements* of a spreadsheet—and a Cell consists of a row and a column. You've been using arrays all along!

To declare another dimension to an array, add another argument. The following creates an array of 10 rows and 20 columns:

```
Dim myArray (1 to 10, 1 to 20)
```

This fills the first row:

```
myArray (1,1) = 10, myArray (1,2) = 20
```

This fills the second row:

```
myArray (2,1) = 20, myArray (2,2) = 40
```

and so on. Of course, this is very time consuming and could take a lot of lines of code. There are other ways to fill an array, which are discussed in the next section.

Fill an Array

Now that you can declare an array, you need to fill it. One method was shown earlier—individually entering a value for each element of the array. There's a quicker way, as shown in the following sample code and Figure 17.1:

```
Option Base 1

Sub ColumnHeaders()
Dim myArray As Variant
Dim myCount As Integer
```

```
' Fill the array
myArray = Array("Name", "Address", "Phone", "Email")

' Empty the array
With Worksheets("Sheet2")
    For myCount = 1 To UBound(myArray)
        .Cells(1, myCount).Value = myArray(myCount)
    Next myCount
End With
End Sub
```

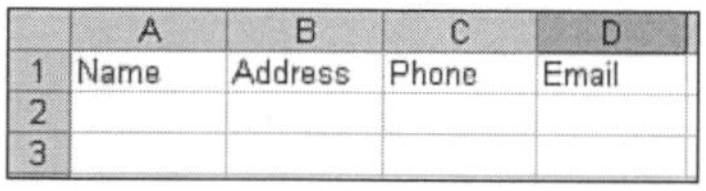

Figure 17.1

Use an array to quickly create column headers.

	A	B	C	D
1	Name	Address	Phone	Email
2				
3				

Remember that Variant variables can hold any type of information. To quickstack the array, create a variant-type variable that can be treated like an array. When the data is shoved into the variant, it is forced to take on the properties of an array.

But what if the information needed in the array is on the sheet already? Use the following to quickly fill an array (see Figure 17.2):

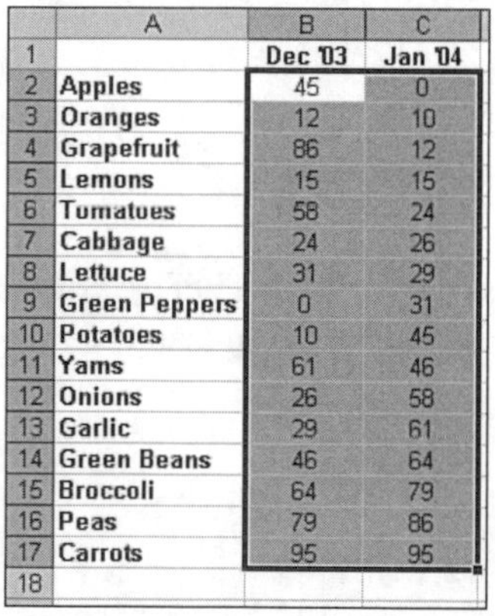

Figure 17.2

Quickly fill an array from a sheet.

	A	B	C
1		Dec '03	Jan '04
2	Apples	45	0
3	Oranges	12	10
4	Grapefruit	86	12
5	Lemons	15	15
6	Tomatoes	58	24
7	Cabbage	24	26
8	Lettuce	31	29
9	Green Peppers	0	31
10	Potatoes	10	45
11	Yams	61	46
12	Onions	26	58
13	Garlic	29	61
14	Green Beans	46	64
15	Broccoli	64	79
16	Peas	79	86
17	Carrots	95	95
18			

```
Dim myArray As Variant

myArray = Worksheets("Sheet1").Range("B2:C17")
```

Although these two methods are quick and easy, they may not always suit the situation. What if you needed every other row in the array? The code to do this follows (see Figure 17.3):

```
Sub EveryOtherRow()
Dim myArray(1 To 8, 1 To 2)
Dim i As Integer, j As Integer, myCount As Integer
```

```
'Fill the array with every other row
For i = 1 To 8
    For j = 1 To 2
        myArray(i, j) = Worksheets("Sheet1").Cells(i * 2, j + 1).Value
    Next j
Next i

'Empty the array
For myCount = LBound(myArray) To UBound(myArray)
    Worksheets("Sheet1").Cells(myCount * 2, 4) = _
    WorksheetFunction.Sum(myArray(myCount, 1), myArray(myCount, 2))
Next myCount
End Sub
```

Figure 17.3

Fill the array with only the data needed.

	A	B	C	D
1		Dec '03	Jan '04	Sum
2	Apples	45	0	45
3	Oranges	12	10	
4	Grapefruit	86	12	98
5	Lemons	15	15	
6	Tomatoes	58	24	82
7	Cabbage	24	26	
8	Lettuce	31	29	60
9	Green Peppers	0	31	
10	Potatoes	10	45	55
11	Yams	61	46	
12	Onions	26	58	84
13	Garlic	29	61	
14	Green Beans	46	64	110
15	Broccoli	64	79	
16	Peas	79	86	165
17	Carrots	95	95	
18				

Empty an Array

After an array is filled, the data needs to be retrieved. But before you do that, you can manipulate it or return information about it, such as the maximum integer, as shown in the following code (see Figure 17.4):

```
Sub QuickFillMax()
Dim myArray As Variant

myArray = Worksheets("Sheet1").Range("B2:C17")
MsgBox "Maximum Integer is: " & WorksheetFunction.Max(myArray)

End Sub
```

Figure 17.4

Return the Max variable in an array.

	A	B	C	D	E	F
1		Dec '03	Jan '04			
2	Apples	45	0			
3	Oranges	12	10			
4	Grapefruit	86	12			
5	Lemons	15	15			
6	Tomatoes	58	24	Microsoft Excel		
7	Cabbage	24	26	Maximum Integer is: 95		
8	Lettuce	31	29			
9	Green Peppers	0	31	OK		
10	Potatoes	10	45			
11	Yams	61	46			
12	Onions	26	58			
13	Garlic	29	61			
14	Green Beans	46	64			
15	Broccoli	64	79			
16	Peas	79	86			
17	Carrots	95	95			
18						

Data can also be manipulated as it is returned to the sheet. In the following example, we use Lbound and Ubound with a For loop to loop through the elements of the array and average each set. The result is then placed on the sheet in a new column (see Figure 17.5):

MyCount + 1 is used to place the results back on the sheet because the Lbound is 1 and the data starts in row 2.

```
Sub QuickFillAverage()
Dim myArray As Variant
Dim myCount As Integer

myArray = Worksheets("Sheet1").Range("B2:C17")

For myCount = LBound(myArray) To UBound(myArray)
    Worksheets("Sheet1").Cells(myCount + 1, 5).Value = _
    WorksheetFunction.Average(myArray(myCount, 1), myArray(myCount, 2))
Next myCount

End Sub
```

Figure 17.5
Calculations can be done on the data as it is returned to the sheet.

	A	B	C	D	E
1		Dec '03	Jan '04	Sum	Average
2	Apples	45	0	45	22.5
3	Oranges	12	10		11
4	Grapefruit	86	12	98	49
5	Lemons	15	15		15
6	Tomatoes	58	24	82	41
7	Cabbage	24	26		25
8	Lettuce	31	29	60	30
9	Green Peppers	0	31		15.5
10	Potatoes	10	45	55	27.5
11	Yams	61	46		53.5
12	Onions	26	58	84	42
13	Garlic	29	61		45
14	Green Beans	46	64	110	55
15	Broccoli	64	79		71.5
16	Peas	79	86	165	82.5
17	Carrots	95	95		95
18					

Arrays Can Make It Easier to Manipulate Data, But Is That All?

Okay, so arrays can make it easier to manipulate data and get information from it—but is that all they're good for? NO! Arrays are so powerful because they can actually make the code run *faster*!

Typically, if there are columns of data to average, as in the previous example, your first thought might be for the following:

```
Sub SlowAverage()
Dim myCount As Integer, LastRow As Integer

LastRow = Worksheets("Sheet1").Range("A65536").End(xlUp).Row

For myCount = 2 To LastRow
    With Worksheets("Sheet1")
        .Cells(myCount, 6).Value = _
        WorksheetFunction.Average(Cells(myCount, 2), Cells(myCount, 3))
```

```
      End With
Next myCount

End Sub
```

Although this works fine, the program is having to look at each row of the sheet individually, get the data, do the calculation, and place it in the correct column. Wouldn't it be easier to grab all the data at one time, then do the calculations and place it back on the sheet? Also, with the slower code, you need to know which columns on the sheet to manipulate (Columns 2 and 3 in our example). With an array, you need to know only what element of the array.

To make this even more useful, rather than use an address range to fill the array, you could use a named range. With a named range in an array, it really doesn't matter where on the sheet the range is.

Instead of:

```
myArray = Range("B2:C17")
```

use:

```
myArray = Range("myData")
```

Whereas with the slow method you need to know where `myData` is so you can return the correct columns, with an array all you need to know is that you want the first and second columns.

TIP

Make your array even faster! Technically, if you place a column of data into an array, it is a two-dimensional array. If you want to process it, you must process the row and column.

You can process the column more easily if it is just a single row. Use the `Transpose` function to turn the one column into one row (see Figure 17.6):

```
Sub TransposeArray()
Dim myArray As Variant

myArray = WorksheetFunction.Transpose(Range("myTran"))

'return the 5th element of the array
MsgBox "The 5th element of the Array is: " & myArray(5)
End Sub
```

Figure 17.6
Use the `Transpose` function to turn a two-dimensional array into a one-dimensional array.

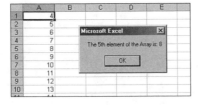

Dynamic Arrays

You can't always know how big of an array you will need. You could create an array based on how big it could ever need to be, but that's not only a waste of memory. What if it turns out it needs to be bigger? In this case, you can use a *dynamic array*.

A dynamic array is an array that does not have a set size. Declare the array, but leave the parentheses empty:

```
Dim myArray ()
```

Later, as the program needs to use the array, use Redim to set the size of the array:

```
Sub MySheets()
Dim myArray() As String
Dim myCount As Integer, NumShts As Integer

NumShts = ActiveWorkbook.Worksheets.Count

' Size the array
ReDim myArray(1 To NumShts)

For myCount = 1 To NumShts
    myArray(myCount) = ActiveWorkbook.Sheets(myCount).Name
Next myCount

End Sub
```

Using Redim re-initializes the array, so if you were to use it many times, such as in a loop, you would lose all the data it holds. Use Preserve to prevent that from happening. The following example looks for all the Excel files in a directory and puts the results in an array. Because we don't know how many files there will be until we look at them, we can't size the array before the program is run:

```
Sub XLFiles()
Dim FName As String
Dim arNames() As String
Dim myCount As Integer

FName = Dir("C:\Contracting Files\Excel VBA 2003 by Jelen & Syrstad\*.xls")
Do Until FName = ""
    myCount = myCount + 1
    ReDim Preserve arNames(1 To myCount)
    arNames(myCount) = FName
    FName = Dir
Loop

End Sub
```

> **CAUTION**
>
> Using Preserve with large amounts of data in a loop can slow down the program. If possible, use code to figure out the Max size of the array.

Passing an Array

Just like strings, integers, and other variables, arrays can be passed into other procedures. This makes for more efficient and easier-to-read code. The following sub, `PassAnArray`, passes the array, `myArray`, into the function `RegionSales`. The data in the array is summed for the specified region and the result returned to the sub (see Figure 17.7).

```
Sub PassAnArray()
Dim myArray() As Variant
Dim myRegion As String

myArray = Range("mySalesData")
myRegion = InputBox("Enter Region - Central, East, West")
MsgBox myRegion & " Sales are: " & Format(RegionSales(myArray, _
    myRegion), "$#,#00.00")

End Sub

Function RegionSales(ByRef BigArray As Variant, sRegion As String) As Long
Dim myCount As Integer

RegionSales = 0
For myCount = LBound(BigArray) To UBound(BigArray)
    If BigArray(myCount, 1) = sRegion Then
        RegionSales = BigArray(myCount, 6) + RegionSales
    End If
Next myCount

End Function
```

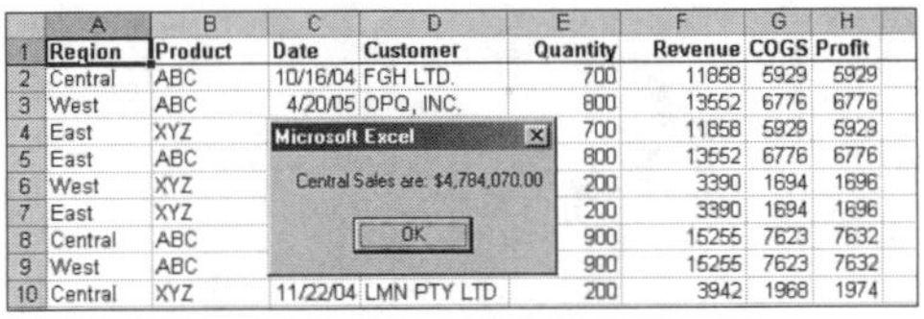

	A	B	C	D	E	F	G	H
1	Region	Product	Date	Customer	Quantity	Revenue	COGS	Profit
2	Central	ABC	10/16/04	FGH LTD.	700	11858	5929	5929
3	West	ABC	4/20/05	OPQ, INC.	800	13552	6776	6776
4	East	XYZ			700	11858	5929	5929
5	East	ABC			800	13552	6776	6776
6	West	XYZ			200	3390	1694	1696
7	East	XYZ			200	3390	1694	1696
8	Central	ABC			900	15255	7623	7632
9	West	ABC			900	15255	7623	7632
10	Central	XYZ	11/22/04	LMN PTY LTD	200	3942	1968	1974

Figure 17.7
Arrays can be passed into other functions or procedures for data extraction.

Next Steps

Arrays are a type of variable used for holding more than one piece of data. Chapter 18, "Text File Processing," covers importing from a text file and writing to a text file. Being able to write to a text file is useful when you need to write out data for another system to read, or even when you need to produce HTML files.

Text File Processing

Despite the promise in Chapter 15, "XML in Excel 2003 Professional," that XML will be the next great file format of the future, we still have a lot of files in CSV or TXT file format today.

VBA makes it easy to both read and write from text files. This chapter covers importing from a text file and writing to a text file. Being able to write to a text file is useful when you need to write out data for another system to read, or even when you need to produce HTML files.

Importing from Text Files

There are three basic scenarios when reading from text files. If the file contains less than 65,536 records, it is easy to import the file using the `Workbooks.OpenText` method. If the file contains more than 65,536 records and less than 98,304 records, then it is possible to open the text file using two calls to `Workbooks.OpenText`. If the file contains more than 98,304, then you have to read the file one record at a time.

Importing Text Files with Less Than 65,536 Rows

Text files typically come in one of two formats. In one format, the fields in each record are separated by some delimiter, such as a comma, pipe, or tab. In the second format, each field takes a particular number of character positions. This is called a fixed-width file and was very popular in the days of COBOL.

Excel can import either type of file easily. You can open both types using the `OpenText` method. In both cases, it is best to record the process of opening the file and use the recorded snippet of code.

Opening a Fixed-Width File

Figure 18.1 shows a text file where each field takes up a certain amount of space in the record. Writing the code to open this type of file is slightly arduous, because you need to specify the length of each field. In my antique drawer, I still have the metal ruler used by COBOL programmers to measure the number of characters in a field printed on a greenbar printer. You could, in theory, change the font of your file to a monospace font and use this same method. However, using the macro recorder is a slightly more up-to-date method.

Figure 18.1
This file is space-delimited or fixed width. Opening this file is fairly involved, as you need to specify the exact length of each field in the file.

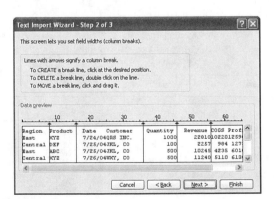

Turn on the macro recorder by selecting Tools, Macros, Record New Macro from the main menu. From the File menu, select Open. Change the Files of Type to All Files and find your text file.

In the Text Import Wizard's Step 1, specify that the data is Fixed Width and click Next.

Excel then looks at your data and attempts to figure out where each field begins and ends. Figure 18.2 shows Excel's guess on this particular file. Because the Date field is too close to the Customer field, Excel missed drawing that line.

Figure 18.2
Excel guesses at where each field starts. In this case, it missed two fields and probably did not leave enough room for a longer product name.

To add a new field indicator in Step 2 of the Wizard, simply click in the appropriate place in the Data Preview window. If you click in the wrong column, click on the line and drag it to the right place. If Excel inadvertently put in an extra field line, double-click the line to remove it. Figure 18.3 shows the data preview after the appropriate changes have been made. Note the little ruler above the data. When you click to add a field marker, Excel is actually handling the tedious work of figuring out that the Customer field starts in position 25 for a length of 11.

Figure 18.3

After adding two new field markers and moving the marker between Product and Date to the right place, Excel can build the code that gives us an idea of start position and length of each field.

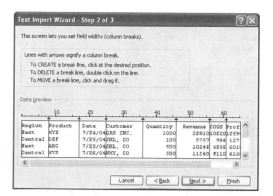

In Step 3 of the Wizard, Excel always assumes that every field is in General format.

Change the format of any fields that require special handling. Click the column and choose the appropriate format from the Column data format section of the dialog box. Figure 18.4 shows the selections for this file.

Figure 18.4

Here, I've indicated that the third column is a date and that I do not want to import the Cost and Profit columns. If you ever receive files from say, Italy, where they use periods as a thousands separator, you will need to choose the Advanced button to handle this.

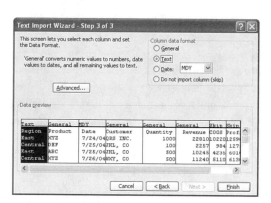

If you have date fields, click the heading above that column, and change the column data format choice to a date. If you have a file with dates in year month-day format or day-month-year format, select the drop-down next to date and choose the appropriate date sequence.

18

If you would prefer to skip some fields, click that column and select Do Not Import Column (Skip) from the Column Data Format selection. There are a couple of times where this is useful. If the file includes sensitive data that you would not want to show to the client, you can leave it out of the import. For example, perhaps this report is for a customer and I don't want to show our cost of goods sold or profit. I can choose to skip these fields in the import. Also, you will occasionally run into a text file that is both fixed width and delimited by a character such as the pipe character. Setting the 1-wide pipe columns as "do not import" is a great way to get rid of the pipe characters, as shown in Figure 18.5.

Figure 18.5
This file is both fixed width and pipe delimited. Liberal use of the Do Not Import setting for each pipe column eliminates the pipe characters from the file.

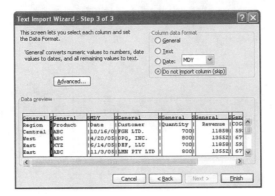

If you have text fields that contain alphabetic characters, you can use the General format. The only time you should use the Text format is if you have a numeric field that you explicitly need imported as text. One example of this would be an account number with leading zeroes or a column of zip codes. To ensure that zip code 01234 does not lose the leading zero, change the field to text.

CAUTION

After you import a text file and specify that one field is text, then that field will exhibit seemingly bizarre behavior. Try inserting a new row and entering a formula in the middle of a column imported as text. Instead of getting the results of the formula, Excel enters the formula as text. The solution is to delete the formula, format the entire column as general, then enter the formula again.

After opening the file, turn off the macro recorder and examine the recorded code:

```
Workbooks.OpenText Filename:="C:\sales.prn", Origin:=437, StartRow:=1, _
DataType:=xlFixedWidth, FieldInfo:=Array(Array(0, 1), Array(8, 1), _
Array(17, 3), Array(25, 1), Array(36, 1), Array(46, 1), Array(56, 9), _
Array(61, 9)), TrailingMinusNumbers:=True
```

The most confusing part of this code is the FieldInfo parameter. You are supposed to code an array of two-element arrays. Each field in the file gets a two-element array to identify where the field starts and the field type.

The field start position is zero-based; because the Region field is in the first character position, its start position is listed as 0.

The field type is a numeric code. If you were coding this by hand, you would use the xlColumnDataType constant names, but for some reason, the macro recorder uses the harder to understand numeric equivalents.

With Table 18.1, you can decode the meaning of the individual arrays in the FieldInfo array. Array(0, 1) means that this field starts 0 characters from the left edge of the file and is a general format. Array(8, 1) indicates that the next field starts 8 characters from the left edge of the file and is also general format. Array(17, 3) indicates that the next field starts 17 characters from the left edge of the file and is a date format in month-day-year sequence.

Table 18.1 *xlColumnDataType* **Values**

Value	Constant	Used For
1	xlGeneralFormat	General
2	xlTextFormat	Text
3	xlMDYFormat	MDY date
4	xlDMYFormat	DMY date
5	xlYMDFormat	YMD date
6	xlMYDFormat	MYD date
7	xlDYMFormat	DYM date
8	xlYDMFormat	YDM date
9	xlSkipColumn	Skip Column
10	xlEMDFormat	EMD date

As you can see, the FieldInfo parameter for fixed-width files is arduous to code and confusing to look at. It is really one situation where it is easier to record the macro and copy the code snippet.

> **CAUTION**
>
> The xlTrailingMinusNumbers parameter is new in Excel 2002. If you have any clients who might be using Excel 97 or Excel 2000, take the recorded parameter out. The code runs fine without the parameter in newer versions, but if left in, it leads to a compile error on older versions.

Opening a Delimited File

Figure 18.6 shows a text file where each field is comma-separated. The main task in opening such a file is to tell Excel that the delimiter in the file is a comma and then identify any special processing for each field. In this case, we definitely want to identify the third column as being a date in mm/dd/yyyy format.

CAUTION

If you try to record the process of opening a comma-delimited file where the filename ends in .csv, Excel records the `Workbooks.Open` method rather than `Workbooks.OpenText`. If you need to control the formatting of certain columns, rename the file to have a .txt extension before recording the macro.

Figure 18.6
This file is comma delimited. Opening this file involves telling Excel to look for a comma as the delimiter and then identifying any special handling, such as treating the third column as a date. This is far easier than handling fixed-width files.

Turn on the macro recorder and record the process of opening the text file. In Step 1 of the wizard, specify that the file is Delimited.

In the Text Import Wizard—Step 2 of 3, the data preview may initially look horrible. This is because Excel defaults to assuming that each field is separated by a tab character (see Figure 18.7).

Figure 18.7
While you import a delimited text file, the initial data preview looks like a confusing mess of data because Excel is looking for tab characters between each field.

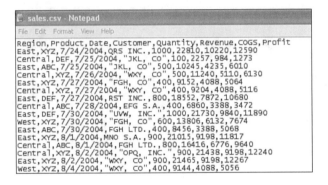

After unchecking the Tab box and checking the proper delimiter choice (in this case, a comma), the data preview in step 2 looks perfect, as shown in Figure 18.8.

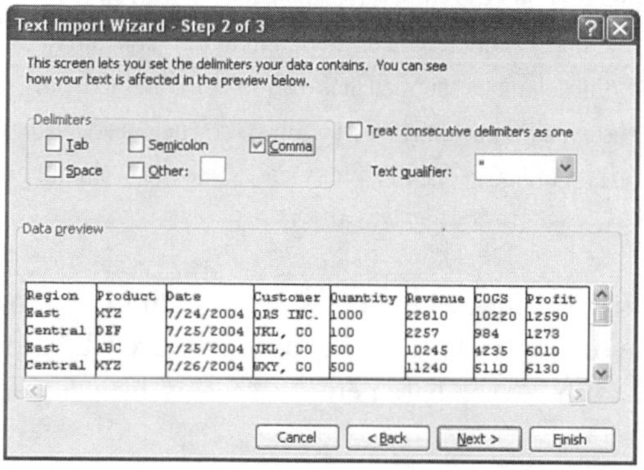

Figure 18.8
After changing the delimiter field from a tab to a comma, the Data Preview looks perfect. This is certainly easier than the cumbersome process in Step 2 for a fixed-width file.

Step 3 of the wizard is identical to step 3 for a fixed-width file. In this case, specify that the third column has a date format. Click Finish, and you will have this code:

```
Workbooks.OpenText Filename:="C:\sales.txt", Origin:=437, _
    StartRow:=1, DataType:=xlDelimited, TextQualifier:=xlDoubleQuote, _
    ConsecutiveDelimiter:=False, Tab:=False, Semicolon:=False, Comma:=True _
    , Space:=False, Other:=False, FieldInfo:=Array(Array(1, 1), Array(2, 1), _
    Array(3, 3), Array(4, 1), Array(5, 1), Array(6, 1), Array(7, 1), _
    Array(8, 1)), TrailingMinusNumbers:=True
```

Although this code appears longer, it is actually far simpler. In the `FieldInfo` parameter, the two element arrays consist of a sequence number (starting at 1 for the first field) and then an `xlColumnDataType` from Table 18.1. In this example, `Array(2, 1)` is simply saying "the second field is of general type." `Array(3, 3)` is saying, "the third field is a date in M-D-Y format." The code is longer because they explicitly specify each possible delimiter is set to `False`. Because `False` is the default for all delimiters, you really need only the one that you will use. The following code is equivalent:

```
Workbooks.OpenText Filename:="C:\sales.txt", DataType:=xlDelimited, Comma:=True, _
    FieldInfo:=Array(Array(1, 1), Array(2, 1), Array(3, 3), Array(4, 1), _
    Array(5, 1), Array(6, 1), Array(7, 1), Array(8, 1))
```

Finally, to make the code more readable, you can use the constant names instead of the code numbers.

```
Workbooks.OpenText Filename:="C:\sales.txt", DataType:=xlDelimited, Comma:=True, _
    FieldInfo:=Array(Array(1, xlGeneralFormat), Array(2, xlGeneralFormat), _
    Array(3, xlMDYFormat), Array(4, xlGeneralFormat), Array(5, xlGeneralFormat), _
    Array(6, xlGeneralFormat), Array(7, xlGeneralFormat), Array(8, xlGeneralFormat))
```

> **CAUTION**
>
> For the remainder of your Excel session, Excel will remember the delimiter settings. There is an annoying bug (feature?) in Excel. After Excel remembers that you are using a comma or a tab as a delimiter, any time that you attempt to paste data from the clipboard to Excel, the data is parsed automatically by the delimiters specified in the `OpenText` method. Thus, if you attempted to paste some text that included the customer ABC, Inc., the text would be parsed automatically into two columns, with text up to ABC in one column and Inc. in the next column.

Excel has built-in options to read files where fields are delimited by tabs, semicolons, commas, or spaces. Excel can actually handle anything as a delimiter. If someone sends pipe-delimited text, you would set the `Other` parameter to `True` and specify an `OtherChar` parameter:

```
Workbooks.OpenText Filename:="C:\sales.txt", Origin:=437, _
    DataType:=xlDelimited, Other:=True, OtherChar:="¦", FieldInfo:=...
```

Reading Text Files with More Than 65,536 Rows

If you use the Text Import wizard to read a file with more than 65,536 rows of data, you will get an error saying `File not loaded completely`. The first 65,536 rows of the file will load correctly.

If you use `Workbooks.OpenText` to open a file with more than 65,536 rows of data, you are given no indication that the file did not load completely. Excel 2003 loads the first 65,536 rows and allows macro execution to continue. Your only real indication that there is a problem is if someone notices that the reports aren't reporting all the sales. If you think that your files will ever get this large, it would be good to check whether cell A65536 is non-blank after an import. If it is, the odds are that the entire file was not loaded.

Reading Text Files with Less Than 98,304 Rows

There is an easy built-in workaround. On the Text Import Wizard, there is a field where you can specify Start Import At Row. This is equivalent to using the `StartRow` parameter in the `OpenText` method. This would be a perfect solution. In theory, you could specify a `StartRow` of 65537 and continue reading the file. However, if you attempt to specify a `StartRow` higher than 32767, you get runtime error 1004. Microsoft wrote this import code back in the days when there were only 16,000+ rows in a worksheet. This field is assigned an integer datatype, which limits it to values between 1 and 32767. One would think that in the five versions released since they bumped up to 65,536 rows, someone would have remembered to change the datatype on this variable, but it hasn't happened.

I can think of some examples where you specifically know that you will have less than 98,304 rows. Imagine you are importing inventory records for a chain of retail stores. You know each store has roughly 2,000 rows and your company just opened stores 31 through 35. All of a sudden, the text file goes from 60,000 to 70,000. When that happens, you could code something like the following to completely load the file:

```
Sub ImportFile()
    Dim WBO As Workbook
    Dim WBC As Workbook

    Set WBO = ActiveWorkbook
    ThisFile = "C:\inventory.csv"
    Workbooks.OpenText Filename:=ThisFile
    Cells.Copy WBO.Worksheets("Data").Range("A1")

    If Cells(65536, 1).Value > "" Then
        ' The file was too large. Import again, starting at row 32767
        Workbooks.OpenText Filename:=ThisFile, StartRow:=32767
        ' There are some rows that have already been copied
        ' Everything from 32767 to 65,536 is already on the data sheet.
        ' Delete the first 32,770 rows from this second pass of the file
        RowsToSkip = Application.Rows + 1 - 32767
        Cells(1, 1).Resize(RowsToSkip, 1).EntireRow.Delete
        Cells.Copy WBO.Worksheets("Data").Range("AA1")
    End If
End Sub
```

Reading Text Files One Row at a Time

Continuing the example, as the retail chain keeps opening more stores, they will eventually get to store 50. Fifty stores times 2,000 SKUs means a file with 100,000 rows. After this happens, the alternative is to read the text file one row at a time. The code for doing this is the same code you might remember in your first high school BASIC class.

You need to open the file for INPUT as #1. You can then use the Line Input #1 statement to read a line of the file into a variable. The following code opens sales.txt, reads 10 lines of the file into the first 10 cells of the worksheet, and closes the file.

```
Sub Import10()
    ThisFile = "C\sales.txt"
    Open ThisFile For Input As #1
    For i = 1 To 10
        Line Input #1, Data
        Cells(i, 1).Value = Data
    Next i
    Close #1
End Sub
```

Rather than read only 10 records, you will want to read until you get to the end of the file. A variable called EOF is automatically updated by Excel. If you open a file for input as #1, then checking EOF(1) will tell you whether you've read the last record or not.

Use a Do...While Loop to keep reading records until you've reached the end of the file.

```
Sub ImportAll()
    ThisFile = "C:\sales.txt"
    Open ThisFile For Input As #1
    Ctr = 0
    Do
        Line Input #1, Data
        Ctr = Ctr + 1
```

18

```
        Cells(Ctr, 1).Value = Data
    Loop While EOF(1) = False
    Close #1
End Sub
```

After reading records with code such as this, you will note in Figure 18.9 that the data is not parsed into columns. All the fields are in Column A of the file.

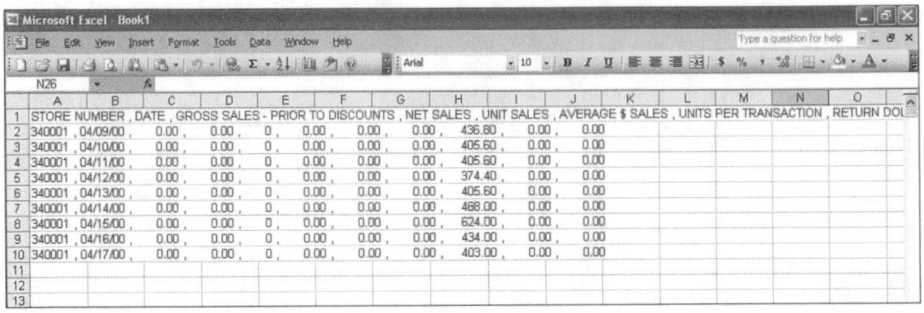

Figure 18.9
When reading a text file one row at a time, all the data fields end up in one long entry in Column A.

Use the `TextToColumns` method to parse the records into columns. The parameters for `TextToColumns` are nearly identical to the `OpenText` method.

```
Cells(1, 1).Resize(Ctr, 1).TextToColumns Destination:=Range("A1"), _
DataType:=xlDelimited, Comma:=True, FieldInfo:=Array(Array(1, _
xlGeneralFormat), Array(2, xlMDYFormat), Array(3, xlGeneralFormat), _
Array(4, xlGeneralFormat), Array(5, xlGeneralFormat), Array(6, _
xlGeneralFormat), Array(7,xlGeneralFormat), Array(8, xlGeneralFormat), _
Array(9, xlGeneralFormat), Array(10,xlGeneralFormat), Array(11, _
xlGeneralFormat))
```

Rather than hard-code that you are using the #1 designator to open the text file, it is safer to use the `FreeFile` function. This returns an integer representing the next file number available for use by the `Open` statement. The complete code to read a text file smaller than 65,536 rows would be

```
Sub ImportAll()
    ThisFile = "C:\sales.txt"
    FileNumber = FreeFile
    Open ThisFile For Input As #FileNumber
    Ctr = 0
    Do
        Line Input #FileNumber, Data
        Ctr = Ctr + 1
        Cells(Ctr, 1).Value = Data
    Loop While EOF(FileNumber) = False
    Close #FileNumer
    Cells(1, 1).Resize(Ctr, 1).TextToColumns Destination:=Range("A1"), _
        DataType:=xlDelimited, Comma:=True, _
        FieldInfo:=Array(Array(1, xlGeneralFormat), _
        Array(2, xlMDYFormat), Array(3, xlGeneralFormat), _
        Array(4, xlGeneralFormat), Array(5, xlGeneralFormat), _
        Array(5, xlGeneralFormat), Array(6, xlGeneralFormat), _
        Array(7, xlGeneralFormat), Array(8, xlGeneralFormat), _
```

```
            Array(9, xlGeneralFormat), Array(10, xlGeneralFormat), _
            Array(10, xlGeneralFormat), Array(11, xlGeneralFormat))
End Sub
```

Reading Text Files with More Than 98,304 Rows

You can use the Line Input method for reading a large text file. My strategy is to read rows into cells A1:A65534, then begin reading additional rows into cell AA2. I start in Row 2 on the second set so that the headings can be copied from Row 1 of the first dataset. If the file is large enough that it fills up Column AA, then move to BA2, CA2, and so on. Also, I stop writing columns when I get to Row 65,534, leaving 2 blank rows at the bottom. This ensures that the code Range("A65536").End(xlup).Row finds the final row. The following code reads a large text file into several sets of columns:

```
Sub ReadLargeFile()
    ThisFile = "C:\sales.txt"
    FileNumber = FreeFile
    Open ThisFile For Input As #FileNumber

    NextRow = 1
    NextCol = 1
    Do While Not EOF(1)
        Line Input #FileNumber, Data
        Cells(NextRow, NextCol).Value = Data
        NextRow = NextRow + 1
        If NextRow = 65534 Then
            ' Parse these records
            Range(Cells(1, NextCol), Cells(65536, NextCol)).TextToColumns _
                Destination:=Cells(1, NextCol), DataType:=xlDelimited, _
                Comma:=True, FieldInfo:=Array(Array(1, xlGeneralFormat), _
                Array(2, xlMDYFormat), Array(3, xlGeneralFormat), _
                Array(4, xlGeneralFormat), Array(5, xlGeneralFormat), _
                Array(6, xlGeneralFormat), Array(7, xlGeneralFormat), _
                Array(8, xlGeneralFormat), Array(9, xlGeneralFormat), _
                Array(10, xlGeneralFormat), Array(11, xlGeneralFormat))
            ' Copy the headings from section 1
            If NextCol > 1 Then
                Range("A1:K1").Copy Destination:=Cells(1, NextCol)
            End If
            ' Set up the next section
            NextCol = NextCol + 26
            NextRow = 2
        End If
    Loop
    Close #FileNumber
    ' Parse the final Section of records
    FinalRow = NextRow - 1
    If FinalRow = 1 Then
        ' Handle if the file coincidentally had 65536 rows exactly
        NextCol = NextCol - 26
    Else
        Range(Cells(2, NextCol), Cells(FinalRow, NextCol)).TextToColumns _
                Destination:=Cells(1, NextCol), DataType:=xlDelimited, _
                Comma:=True, FieldInfo:=Array(Array(1, xlGeneralFormat), _
                Array(2, xlMDYFormat), Array(3, xlGeneralFormat), _
                Array(4, xlGeneralFormat), Array(5, xlGeneralFormat), _
```

18

```
                    Array(6, xlGeneralFormat), Array(7, xlGeneralFormat), _
                    Array(8, xlGeneralFormat), Array(9, xlGeneralFormat), _
                    Array(10, xlGeneralFormat), Array(11, xlGeneralFormat))
        If NextCol > 1 Then
            Range("A1:K1").Copy Destination:=Cells(1, NextCol)
        End If
    End If

    DataSets = (NextCol - 1) / 26 + 1

End Sub
```

I usually write the `DataSets` variable to a named cell somewhere in the workbook so I know how many datasets I have in the worksheet later.

As you can imagine, it is possible, using this method, to read 655,000 rows of data into a single worksheet. The code that you formerly used to filter and report the data now becomes more complex. You might find yourself creating pivot tables from each set of columns to create a dataset summary, and then finally summarizing all the summary tables with a final pivot table. At some point, you need to consider that the application really belongs in Access, or the data should be stored in Access with an Excel front end, as discussed in Chapter 19, "Using Access as a Back End to Enhance Multi-User Access to Data."

Writing Text Files

The code for writing text files is similar to reading text files. You need to open a specific file for output as #1. Then, as you loop through various records, you write them to the file using the `Print #1` statement.

Before you open a file for output, you should make sure that any prior examples of the file have been deleted. You can use the `Kill` statement to delete a file. `Kill` returns an error if the file wasn't there in the first place, so you will want to use `On Error Resume Next` to prevent an error.

The following code writes out a text file for use by another application.

```
Sub WriteFile()
    ThisFile = "C:\Results.txt"

    ' Delete yesterday's copy of the file
    On Error Resume Next
    Kill (ThisFile)
    On Error GoTo 0

    ' Open the file
    Open ThisFile For Output As #1
    FinalRow = Range("A65536").End(xlUp).Row
    ' Write out the file
    For j = 1 To FinalRow
        Print #1, Cells(j, 1).Value
    Next j
End Sub
```

This is a fairly trivial example. You can use this method to write out any type of text-based file. The code at the end of Chapter 14, "Reading from and Writing to the Web," uses the same concept to write out HTML files.

Next Steps

You will sometimes find yourself writing to text files out of necessity—either to import data from another system or to produce data compatible with another system. Using text files is a slow method for reading and writing data. In Chapter 19 you will learn about writing to MDB files. These files are faster, indexable, and allow multi-user access to data.

18

Using Access as a Back End to Enhance Multi-User Access to Data

19

The example near the end of Chapter 18, "Text File Processing," proposed a method for storing 650,000 records in an Excel worksheet. At some point, you need to admit that even though Excel is the greatest product in the world, there is a time to move to Access and take advantage of the Access Multidimensional Database (MDB) files.

Even before you have more than 65,000 rows, another compelling reason to use MDB data files is to allow multi-user access to data without the headaches associated with shared workbooks.

Microsoft Excel offers an option to share a workbook, but you automatically lose a number of important Excel features when you share a workbook. After you share a workbook, you cannot use automatic subtotals, pivot tables, group and outline mode, scenarios, protection, Autoformat, Styles, Pictures, Add Charts, or Insert worksheets.

By using an Excel VBA front end and storing data in an MDB database, you have the best of both worlds. You have the power and flexibility of Excel, and the multi-user access capability available in Access.

> **NOTE**
> MDB is the official file format of both Microsoft Access and Microsoft Visual Basic. This means that you can deploy an Excel solution that reads and writes from an MDB to customers who do not have Microsoft Access. Of course, it helps if you as the developer have a copy of Access because you can use the Access front end to set up tables and queries.

ADO Versus DAO

For several years, Microsoft recommended DAO (Data Access Objects) for accessing data in external database. With Excel 2000 and VB6, Microsoft still supports DAO, but recommends ADO (ActiveX Data Objects). The concepts are similar and the syntax is only slightly different. I am going to use the newer ADO in this chapter. Realize that if you start going through code written a while ago, you might run into DAO code. Other than a few syntax changes, the code for both ADO and DAO looks similar. The Microsoft Knowledge Base articles you can find at the following address discuss the differences:

`http://support.microsoft.com/default.aspx?scid=KB;EN-US;q225048&`

The following two articles provide the Rosetta Stone between DAO and ADO. The ADO code is shown at

`http://support.microsoft.com/default.aspx?scid=KB;EN-US;q146607&`

and the equivalent DAO code is shown at

`http://support.microsoft.com/default.aspx?scid=KB;EN-US;q142938&`

To use any code in this chapter, open the Visual Basic Editor. Select Tools, References from the main menu, and then select Microsoft ActiveX Data Objects 2.1 Library (or higher) from the available references list, as shown in Figure 19.1.

Figure 19.1
To read or write from an Access MDB file, add the reference for Microsoft ActiveX Data Objects 2.1 or higher.

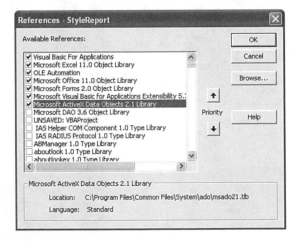

Linda and Virginia are two buyers for a retail chain of stores. Each morning, they import data from the cash registers to get current information on sales and inventory for 2,000 styles. Throughout the day, either buyer may enter transfers of inventory from one store to another. It would be ideal if Linda could see the pending transfers entered by Virginia and vice-versa.

Each buyer has an Excel application with VBA running on her desktop. They each import the cash register data and have VBA routines that facilitate the creation of pivot table reports to help them make buying decisions.

Attempting to store the transfer data in a common Excel file causes problems. When either buyer attempts to write to the Excel file, the entire file becomes read-only for the other buyer. With a shared workbook, Excel turns off the capability to create Pivot Tables, and this is required in our application.

Neither Linda nor Virginia have the professional version of Office, so they do not have Access running on their desktop PCs.

The solution is to produce an Access database on a network drive that both Linda and Virginia can see:

1. Using Access on another PC, produce a new database called `transfers.mdb` and add a table called tblTransfer, as shown in Figure 19.2.

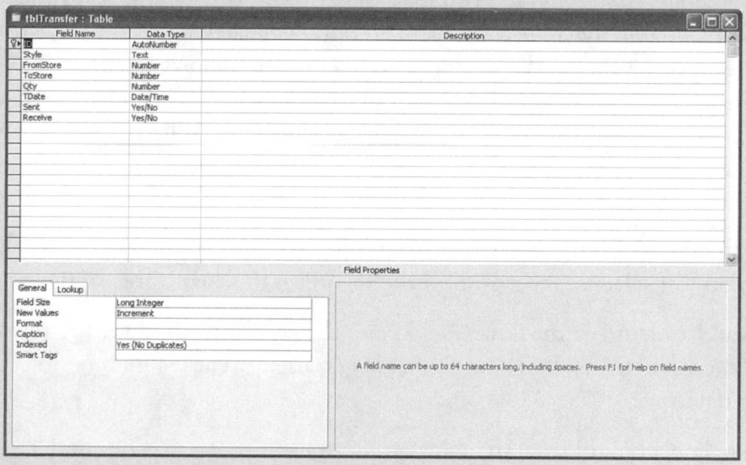

Figure 19.2
Multiple people using their own Excel workbooks will read and write to this table inside an MDB file on a network drive.

2. Move the `Transfers.mdb` file to a network drive. You might find that this common folder uses different drive letter mappings on each machine. It might be `H:\Common\` on Linda's machine and `I:\Common\` on Virginia's machine.

3. On both machines, go to the VB Editor and under Tools, References, add a reference to ActiveX Data Objects 2.1 Library (or higher).

4. In both their applications, find an out-of-the-way cell to store the path to `transfers.mdb`. Name this cell TPath.

5. Whenever the application needs to read or write data from the tblTransfer table, use the code shown in the rest of this chapter.

19

The application provides nearly seamless multi-user access to both buyers. Both Linda and Virginia can read or write to the table at the same time. The only time a conflict would occur is if they both happened to try to update the same record at the same time.

Other than the out-of-the-way cell reference to the path to `transfers.mdb`, neither buyer is aware that her data is being stored in a shared Access table and neither computer needs to have Access installed.

The Tools of ADO

The primary objects needed to access data in an MDB file are an ADO Connection and an ADO Recordset.

The ADO Connection defines the path to the database and specifies that the connection is based on the Microsoft Jet Engine.

After you have established the connection to the database, then you usually will use that connection to define a recordset. A recordset can be a table or a subset of records in the table or a pre-defined query in the Access database. To open a recordset, you have to specify the connection and the values for the `CursorType`, `CursorLocation`, `LockType`, and `Options` parameters. Assuming that you have only two users trying to access the table at a time, I generally use a dynamic cursor and an optimistic lock type. For large datasets, the `adUseServer` value of the `CursorLocation` property allows the database server to process records without using up RAM on the client machine. If you have a small dataset, it might be faster to use `adUseClient` for the `CursorLocation`. When the recordset is opened, all of the records are transferred to memory of the client machine. This allows faster navigation from record to record.

Reading data from the Access database is easy. You can use the `CopyFromRecordset` method to copy all selected records from the recordset to a blank area of the worksheet.

To add a record to the Access table, use the `AddNew` method for the recordset. You then specify the value for each field in the table and use the `Update` method to commit the changes to the database.

To delete a record from the table, you can use a pass-through query to delete records that match a certain criteria.

Other tools are available that let you make sure a table exists or that a particular field exists in a table. You can also use VBA to add new fields to a table definition on the fly.

Adding a Record to the Database

The application has a userform where buyers can enter transfers. To make the calls to the Access database as simple as possible, a series of utility modules handle the ADO connection to the database. This way, the userform code can simply call `AddTransfer(Style, FromStore, ToStore, Qty)`.

The technique for adding records, after the connection is defined, is as follows:

1. Open a recordset that points to the table.
2. Use `AddNew` to add a new record.
3. Update each field in the new record.
4. Use `Update` to update the recordset.
5. Close the recordset and the connection.

The following code adds a new record to the tblTransfer table.

```
Sub AddTransfer(Style As Variant, FromStore As Variant, _
    ToStore As Variant, Qty As Integer)
    Dim cnn As ADODB.Connection
    Dim rst As ADODB.Recordset

    MyConn = "J:\transfers.mdb"

    ' open the connection
    Set cnn = New ADODB.Connection
    With cnn
        .Provider = "Microsoft.Jet.OLEDB.4.0"
        .Open MyConn
    End With

    ' Define the Recordset
    Set rst = New ADODB.Recordset
    rst.CursorLocation = adUseServer

    ' open the table
    rst.Open Source:="tblTransfer", _
        ActiveConnection:=cnn, _
        CursorType:=adOpenDynamic, _
        LockType:=adLockOptimistic, _
        Options:=adCmdTable

    ' Add a record
    rst.AddNew

    ' Set up the values for the fields. The first four fields
    ' are passed from the calling userform. The date field
    ' is filled with the current date.
    rst("Style") = Style
    rst("FromStore") = FromStore
    rst("ToStore") = ToStore
    rst("Qty") = Qty
    rst("tDate") = Date
    rst("Sent") = False
    rst("Receive") = False

    ' Write the values to this record
    rst.Update
```

19

```
                ' Close
                rst.Close
                cnn.Close

        End Sub
```

Retrieving Records from the Database

Reading records from the Access database is very easy. As you define the recordset, you pass a SQL string to return the records in which you are interested.

After the recordset is defined, use the `CopyFromRecordSet` to copy all the matching records from Access to a specific area of the worksheet.

The following routine queries the Transfer table to find all records where the Sent flag is not yet set to True. The results are placed on a blank worksheet. The final few lines display the results in a userform to illustrate how to update a record in the next section:

```
Sub GetUnsentTransfers()
    Dim cnn As ADODB.Connection
    Dim rst As ADODB.Recordset
    Dim WSOrig As Worksheet
    Dim WSTemp As Worksheet
    Dim sSQL as String
    Dim FinalRow as Long

    Set WSOrig = ActiveSheet

    'Build a SQL String to get all fields for unsent transfers
    sSQL = "SELECT ID, Style, FromStore, ToStore, Qty, tDate FROM tblTransfer"
    sSQL = sSQL & " WHERE Sent=FALSE"

    ' Path to Transfers.mdb
    MyConn = "J:\transfers.mdb"

    Set cnn = New ADODB.Connection
    With cnn
        .Provider = "Microsoft.Jet.OLEDB.4.0"
        .Open MyConn
    End With

    Set rst = New ADODB.Recordset
    rst.CursorLocation = adUseServer
    rst.Open Source:=sSQL, ActiveConnection:=cnn, _
        CursorType:=AdForwardOnly, LockType:=adLockOptimistic, _
            Options:=adCmdText

    ' Create the report in a new worksheet
    Set WSTemp = Worksheets.Add

    ' Add Headings
    Range("A1:F1").Value = Array("ID", "Style", "From", "To", "Qty", "Date")

    ' Copy from the recordset to row 2
    Range("A2").CopyFromRecordset rst
```

```
    ' Close the connection
    rst.Close
    cnn.Close

    ' Format the report
    FinalRow = Range("A65536").End(xlUp).Row

    ' If there were no records, then stop
    If FinalRow = 1 Then
        Application.DisplayAlerts = False
        WSTemp.Delete
        Application.DisplayAlerts = True
        WSOrig.Activate
        MsgBox "There are no transfers to confirm"
        Exit Sub
    End If

    ' Format column F as a date
    Range("F2:F" & FinalRow).NumberFormat = "m/d/y"

    ' Show the userform - used in next section
    frmTransConf.Show

    ' Delete the temporary sheet
    Application.DisplayAlerts = False
    WSTemp.Delete
    Application.DisplayAlerts = True

End Sub
```

The `CopyFromRecordSet` method copies records that match the SQL query to a range on the worksheet. Note that you receive only the data rows. The headings do not come along automatically. You must use code to write the headings to Row 1. The results are shown in Figure 19.3.

Figure 19.3
`Range("A2").CopyFromRecordSet` brought matching records from the Access database to the worksheet.

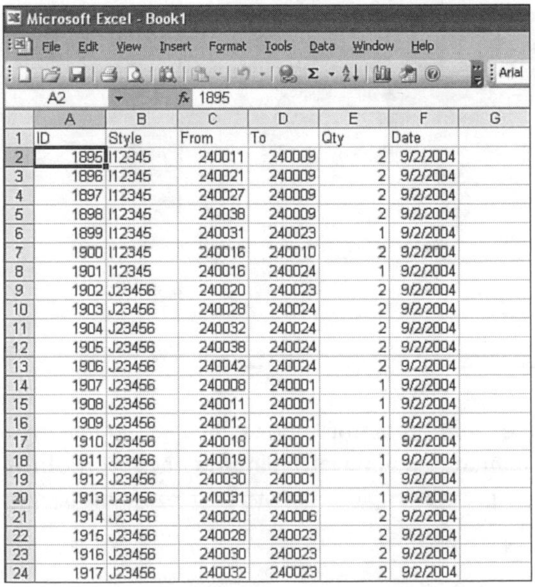

	A	B	C	D	E	F	G
1	ID	Style	From	To	Qty	Date	
2	1895	I12345	240011	240009	2	9/2/2004	
3	1896	I12345	240021	240009	2	9/2/2004	
4	1897	I12345	240027	240009	2	9/2/2004	
5	1898	I12345	240038	240009	2	9/2/2004	
6	1899	I12345	240031	240023	1	9/2/2004	
7	1900	I12345	240016	240010	2	9/2/2004	
8	1901	I12345	240016	240024	1	9/2/2004	
9	1902	J23456	240020	240023	2	9/2/2004	
10	1903	J23456	240028	240024	2	9/2/2004	
11	1904	J23456	240032	240024	2	9/2/2004	
12	1905	J23456	240038	240024	2	9/2/2004	
13	1906	J23456	240042	240024	2	9/2/2004	
14	1907	J23456	240008	240001	1	9/2/2004	
15	1908	J23456	240011	240001	1	9/2/2004	
16	1909	J23456	240012	240001	1	9/2/2004	
17	1910	J23456	240018	240001	1	9/2/2004	
18	1911	J23456	240019	240001	1	9/2/2004	
19	1912	J23456	240030	240001	1	9/2/2004	
20	1913	J23456	240031	240001	1	9/2/2004	
21	1914	J23456	240020	240006	2	9/2/2004	
22	1915	J23456	240028	240023	2	9/2/2004	
23	1916	J23456	240030	240023	2	9/2/2004	
24	1917	J23456	240032	240023	2	9/2/2004	

Updating an Existing Record

To update an existing record, you need to build a recordset with exactly one record. This requires that the user select some sort of unique key when identifying the records. After you have opened the recordset, use the `.Fields` property to change the field in question and then the `.Update` method to commit the changes to the database.

The earlier example returned a recordset to a blank worksheet and then called a userform frmTransConf. This form uses a simple `Userform_Initialize` to display the range in a large list box. The list box's properties have the `MultiSelect` property set to True:

```
Private Sub UserForm_Initialize()

    ' Determine how Records we have
    FinalRow = Cells(65536, 1).End(xlUp).Row
    If FinalRow > 1 Then
        Me.lbXlt.RowSource = "A2:F" & FinalRow
    End If

End Sub
```

After the initialize procedure is run, the unconfirmed records are displayed in a list box. The logistics planner can mark all the records that have been actually sent, as shown in Figure 19.4.

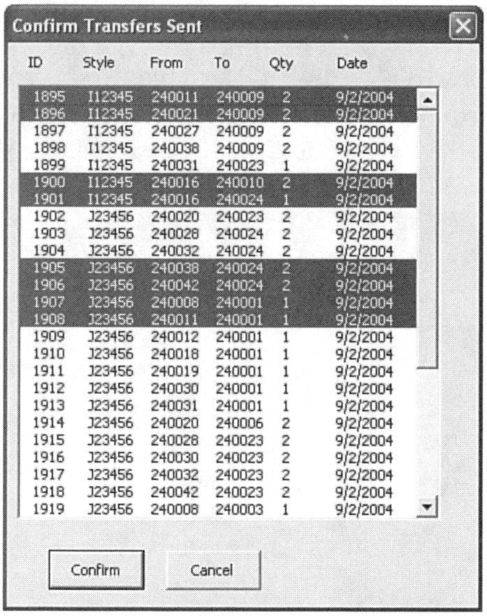

Figure 19.4
This userform displays particular records from the Access recordset. When the buyer selects certain records and then chooses the Confirm button, you'll have to use ADO's `Update` method to update the Sent field on the selected records.

The code attached to the Confirm button follows. The key to making this work is being able to build a SQL statement that uniquely identifies one record. Including the ID field in the fields returned in the prior example is important if you want to narrow the information down to a single record:

```vb
Private Sub cbConfirm_Click()
    Dim cnn As ADODB.Connection
    Dim rst As ADODB.Recordset

    ' If nothing is selected, warn them
    CountSelect = 0
    For x = 0 To Me.lbXlt.ListCount - 1
        If Me.lbXlt.Selected(x) Then
            CountSelect = CountSelect + 1
        End If
    Next x

    If CountSelect = 0 Then
        MsgBox "There were no transfers selected. " & _
            "To exit without confirming any tranfers, use Cancel."
        Exit Sub
    End If

    ' Establish a connection transfers.mdb
    ' Path to Transfers.mdb is on Menu
    MyConn = "J:\transfers.mdb"

    Set cnn = New ADODB.Connection

    With cnn
        .Provider = "Microsoft.Jet.OLEDB.4.0"
        .Open MyConn
    End With

    ' Mark as complete
    For x = 0 To Me.lbXlt.ListCount - 1
        If Me.lbXlt.Selected(x) Then
            ThisID = Cells(2 + x, 1).Value
            ' Mark ThisID as complete
            'Build SQL String
            sSQL = "SELECT * FROM tblTransfer Where ID=" & ThisID
            Set rst = New ADODB.Recordset
            With rst
                .Open Source:=sSQL, ActiveConnection:=cnn, _
                    CursorType:=adOpenKeyset, LockType:=adLockOptimistic
                ' Update the field
                .Fields("Sent").Value = True
                .Update
                .Close
            End With
        End If
    Next x

    ' Close the connection
    cnn.Close
    Set rst = Nothing
    Set cnn = Nothing

    ' Close the userform
    Unload Me

End Sub
```

19

Deleting Records via ADO

Like updating a record, the key is being able to write a bit of SQL to uniquely identify the record(s) to be deleted. The following code uses the Execute method to pass the Delete command through to Access:

```
Public Sub ADOWipeOutAttribute(RecID)
    ' Establish a connection transfers.mdb
    MyConn = "J:\transfers.mdb"

    With New ADODB.Connection
        .Provider = "Microsoft.Jet.OLEDB.4.0"
        .Open MyConn
        .Execute "Delete From tblTransfer Where ID = " & RecID
        .Close
    End With
End Sub
```

Summarizing Records via ADO

One of Access's strengths is running summary queries that group by a particular field. If you build a summary query in Access and examine the SQL view, you will see that complex queries can be written. Similar SQL can be built in Excel VBA and passed to Access via ADO.

The following code uses a fairly complex query to get a net total by store:

```
Sub NetTransfers(Style As Variant)
    ' This builds a table of net open transfers
    ' on Styles AI1
    Dim cnn As ADODB.Connection
    Dim rst As ADODB.Recordset

    ' Build the large SQL query
    ' Basic Logic:  Get all open Incoming Transfers by store,
    ' union with -1* outgoing transfers by store
    ' Sum that union by store, and give us min date as well
    ' A single call to this macro will replace 60 _
    ' calls to GetTransferIn, GetTransferOut, TransferAge
    sSQL = "Select Store, Sum(Quantity), Min(mDate) From _
        (SELECT ToStore AS Store, Sum(Qty) AS Quantity, _
        Min(TDate) AS mDate FROM tblTransfer where Style='" & Style _
        & "' AND Receive=FALSE GROUP BY ToStore "
    sSQL = sSQL & " Union All SELECT FromStore AS Store, _
        Sum(-1*Qty) AS Quantity, Min(TDate) AS mDate _
        FROM tblTransfer where Style='" & Style & "' AND _
        Sent=FALSE GROUP BY FromStore)"
    sSQL = sSQL & " Group by Store"

    MyConn = "J:\transfers.mdb"

    ' open the connection.
    Set cnn = New ADODB.Connection
```

```
    With cnn
        .Provider = "Microsoft.Jet.OLEDB.4.0"
        .Open MyConn
    End With

    Set rst = New ADODB.Recordset

    rst.CursorLocation = adUseServer

    ' open the first query
    rst.Open Source:=sSQL, _
        ActiveConnection:=cnn, _
        CursorType:=AdForwardOnly, _
        LockType:=adLockOptimistic, _
        Options:=adCmdText

    Range("A1:C1").Value = Array("Store", "Qty", "Date")
    ' Return Query Results
    Range("A2").CopyFromRecordset rst
    rst.Close
    cnn.Close

End Sub
```

Other Utilities via ADO

The rest of the chapter provides some useful utilities. Thinking about the application you provided for your clients, they now have an Access database located on their network, but possibly no copy of Access. It would be ideal if you could deliver changes to the Access database on the fly as their application opens up. In the case study in Chapter 25, "Add-Ins," I discuss burying an Update macro that gets called with Workbook_Open. The update macro might be responsible for making database enhancements.

Checking for Existence of Tables

If the application needs a new table in the database, you can use the code in the next section. However, because we have a multi-user application, only the first person who opens the application has to add the table on the fly. When the next buyer shows up, the table may have already been added by the first buyer's application.

This code uses the OpenSchema method to actually query the database schema:

```
Function TableExists(WhichTable)
    Dim cnn As ADODB.Connection
    Dim rst As ADODB.Recordset
    Dim fld As ADODB.Field
    TableExists = False


    ' Path to Transfers.mdb is on Menu
    MyConn = "J:\transfers.mdb"

    Set cnn = New ADODB.Connection
```

19

```
    With cnn
        .Provider = "Microsoft.Jet.OLEDB.4.0"
        .Open MyConn
    End With

    Set rst = cnn.OpenSchema(adSchemaTables)

    Do Until rst.EOF
        If LCase(rst!Table_Name) = LCase(WhichTable) Then
            TableExists = True
            GoTo ExitMe
        End If
        rst.MoveNext
    Loop

ExitMe:
    rst.Close
    Set rst = Nothing
    ' Close the connection
    cnn.Close

End Function
```

Checking for Existence of a Field

Sometimes, you will want to add a new field to an existing table. Again, this code uses the OpenSchema method, but this time looks at the columns in the tables:

```
Function ColumnExists(WhichColumn, WhichTable)
    Dim cnn As ADODB.Connection
    Dim rst As ADODB.Recordset
    Dim WSOrig As Worksheet
    Dim WSTemp As Worksheet
    Dim fld As ADODB.Field
    ColumnExists = False

    ' Path to Transfers.mdb is on menu
    MyConn = ActiveWorkbook.Worksheets("Menu").Range("TPath").Value
    If Right(MyConn, 1) = "\" Then
        MyConn = MyConn & "transfers.mdb"
    Else
        MyConn = MyConn & "\transfers.mdb"
    End If

    Set cnn = New ADODB.Connection

    With cnn
        .Provider = "Microsoft.Jet.OLEDB.4.0"
        .Open MyConn
    End With

    Set rst = cnn.OpenSchema(adSchemaColumns)

    Do Until rst.EOF
        If LCase(rst!Column_Name) = LCase(WhichColumn) And _
            LCase(rst!Table_Name) = LCase(WhichTable) Then
            ColumnExists = True
```

```
                GoTo ExitMe
            End If
            rst.MoveNext
        Loop

ExitMe:
        rst.Close
        Set rst = Nothing
        ' Close the connection
        cnn.Close

End Function
```

Adding a Table on the Fly

This code uses a pass-through query to tell Access to run a `Create Table` command:

```
Sub ADOCreateReplenish()
    ' This creates tblReplenish
    ' There are five fields:
    ' Style
    ' A = Auto replenishment for A
    ' B = Auto replenishment level for B stores
    ' C = Auto replenishment level for C stores
    ' RecActive = Yes/No field
    Dim cnn As ADODB.Connection
    Dim cmd As ADODB.Command

    ' Define the connection
    MyConn = "J:\transfers.mdb"

    ' open the connection
    Set cnn = New ADODB.Connection
    With cnn
        .Provider = "Microsoft.Jet.OLEDB.4.0"
        .Open MyConn
    End With

    Set cmd = New ADODB.Command
    Set cmd.ActiveConnection = cnn
    'create table
    cmd.CommandText = "CREATE TABLE tblReplenish (Style Char(10) Primary Key, _
        A int, B  int, C Int, RecActive YesNo)"
    cmd.Execute , , adCmdText
    Set cmd = Nothing
    Set cnn = Nothing
    Exit Sub
End Sub
```

Adding a Field on the Fly

If you determine that a field does not exist, you can use a pass-through query to add a field to the table:

```
Sub ADOAddField()
    ' This adds a grp field to tblReplenish
    Dim cnn As ADODB.Connection
```

```
        Dim cmd As ADODB.Command

        ' Define the connection
        MyConn = "J:\transfers.mdb"
        End If

        ' open the connection
        Set cnn = New ADODB.Connection
        With cnn
            .Provider = "Microsoft.Jet.OLEDB.4.0"
            .Open MyConn
        End With


        Set cmd = New ADODB.Command
        Set cmd.ActiveConnection = cnn
        'create table
        cmd.CommandText = "ALTER TABLE tblReplenish Add Column Grp Char(25)"
        cmd.Execute , , adCmdText
        Set cmd = Nothing
        Set cnn = Nothing

    End Sub
```

Next Steps

In Chapter 20, "Creating Classes, Records, and Collections," you will learn about the powerful technique of setting up your own `Class` module. With this technique, you can set up your own object with its own methods and properties.

Creating Classes, Records, and Collections

20

Excel already has many objects available, but there are times when a custom object would be better suited for the job at hand. You can create custom objects that you use in the same way as Excel's built-in objects. These special objects are created in *class modules*.

You've already had some experience with class modules. In the VBE, the workbook, worksheet, chart, and userform modules are all types of enhanced class modules. They are specific to the object with which they are associated and contain events.

Class modules are used to create custom objects with custom properties and methods. They can trap application events, embedded chart events, ActiveX control events, and more.

Inserting a Class Module

From the VBE, select Insert, Class Module. A new module, Class1, is added to the VBAProject Workbook and can be seen in the Project Explorer window (see Figure 20.1). Two things to keep in mind concerning class modules:

- Each custom object must have its own module. (Event trapping can share a module.)
- The class module should be renamed to reflect the custom object.

Figure 20.1
Custom objects are created in class modules.

Trapping Application and Embedded Chart Events

Chapter 8, "Event Programming," showed you how certain actions in workbooks, worksheets, and non-embedded charts could be trapped and used to activate code. Briefly, it reviewed how to set up a class module to trap application and chart events. The following goes into more detail on what was shown in that chapter.

Application Events

The Workbook_BeforePrint event is triggered when the workbook in which it resides is printed. If you wanted to run the same code in every workbook available, you would have to copy the code to each workbook. Or, you could use an application event, Workbook_BeforePrint, which is triggered when any workbook is printed.

The application events already exist, but a class module must be set up first so that they can be seen. To create a class module, follow these steps:

1. Insert a class module into the project. Rename it to something that will make sense to you, such as clsAppEvents.

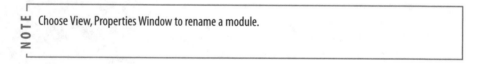

    NOTE   Choose View, Properties Window to rename a module.

2. Enter the following into the class module:
    `Public WithEvents xlApp As Application`

    The name of the variable, xlApp, can be any variable name. The WithEvents keyword exposes the events associated with the Application object.

3. xlApp is now available from that class module's Object drop-down list. Select it from the drop-down, and then click on the Procedure drop-down menu to the right of it to view the list of events that is available for the xlApps object type (Application), as shown in Figure 20.2.

→ For a review of the various Application Events, **see** "Application-Level Events," **p. 162**, in Chapter 8.

Figure 20.2
Events are made available after the object is created.

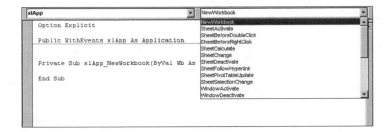

Any of the events listed can by captured, just as workbook and worksheet events were captured in an earlier chapter. The following example uses the NewWorkbook event to automatically set up footer information. This code is placed in the class module, below the xlApp declaration line you just added:

```
Private Sub xlApp_NewWorkbook(ByVal Wb As Workbook)
Dim wks As Worksheet

With Wb
    For Each wks In .Worksheets
        wks.PageSetup.LeftFooter = "Created by: " & .Application.UserName
        wks.PageSetup.RightFooter = Now
    Next wks
End With

End Sub
```

The procedure placed in a class module does not run automatically as events in workbook or worksheet modules would. An instance of the class module must be created and the Application object assigned to the xlApp property. After that is complete, the TrapAppEvent procedure needs to run. As long as the procedure is running, the footer will be created on each sheet every time a new workbook is added (see Figure 20.3):

```
Public myAppEvent As New clsAppEvents

Sub TrapAppEvent()

Set myAppEvent.xlApp = Application

End Sub
```

Figure 20.3
Use an application event to automate the creation of a footer in each new workbook.

Created by: Tracy   1/17/2004 8:32:39 PM

20

In this example, the public `myAppEvent` declaration was placed in a standard module with the
`TrapAppEvent` procedure. To automate the running of the entire event trapping, all the modules could be transferred to the `Personal.xls` and the procedure transferred to a
`Workbook_Open` event. In any case, the `Public` declaration of `myAppEvent` *must* remain in a
standard module so that it can be shared between modules.

Embedded Chart Events

Preparation to trap embedded chart events is the same as the preparation for trapping application events. Create a class module, insert the public declaration for a chart type, create a
procedure for the desired event, and then add a standard module procedure to initiate the
trapping.

> **NOTE**
> The same class module used for the application event can be used for the embedded chart event.

Place the following line in the declaration section of the class module. The available chart
events are now viewable (see Figure 20.4):

```
Public WithEvents xlChart As Chart
```

→ For a review of the various charts events, see "Chart Sheet Events," **p. 158**, in Chapter 8.

Figure 20.4
The chart events are
available after the chart
type variable has been
declared.

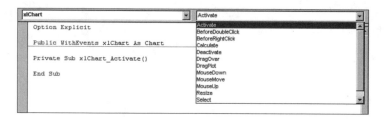

Three events are set up. The primary event, `MouseDown`, changes the chart scale with a
right-click or double-click. Because these actions also have actions associated with them,
you need two more events, `BeforeRightClick` and `BeforeDoubleClick`, to prevent the usual
action from taking place:

This BeforeDoubleClick event prevents the normal result of a double-click from taking place:

```
Private Sub xlChart_BeforeDoubleClick(ByVal ElementID As Long, _
    ByVal Arg1 As Long, ByVal Arg2 As Long, Cancel As Boolean)
Cancel = True
End Sub
```

This BeforeRightClick event prevents the normal result of a right-click from taking place:

```
Private Sub xlChart_BeforeRightClick(Cancel As Boolean)
Cancel = True
End Sub
```

Now that the normal actions of the double-click and right-click have been controlled, ChartMouseDown rewrites what actions are initiated by a right-click and double-click of the mouse.

```
Private Sub xlChart_MouseDown(ByVal Button As Long, ByVal Shift As Long, _
    ByVal x As Long, ByVal y As Long)
    If Button = 1 Then
       XLChart.Axes(xlValue).MaximumScale = _
    XLChart.Axes(xlValue).MaximumScale - 50
    End If

    If Button = 2 Then
       XLChart.Axes(xlValue).MaximumScale = _
    XLChart.Axes(xlValue).MaximumScale + 50
    End If

End Sub
```

After the events are set in the class module, all that's left to do is declare the variable in a standard module, as follows:

```
Public myChartEvent As New clsEvents
```

Then create a procedure that will capture the events on the embedded chart (see Figure 20.5):

```
Sub TrapChartEvent()

Set myChartEvent.xlChart = Worksheets("EmbedChart"). _
    ChartObjects("Chart Area").Chart

End Sub
```

20

Figure 20.5
Use a class module to capture embedded chart events.

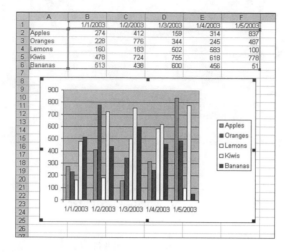

Creating a Custom Object

Class modules are useful for trapping events, but they are also valuable because they can be used to create custom objects. When you are creating a custom object, the class module becomes a template of the object's properties and methods. To better understand this, we are going to create an employee object to track employee name, ID, hourly wage rate, and hours worked.

Insert a class module and rename it to `clsEmployee`. The `clsEmployee` object has four properties:

- `EmpName`—Employee name
- `EmpID`—Employee ID
- `EmpRate`—Hourly wage rate
- `EmpWeeklyHrs`—Hours worked

Properties are variables that can be declared `Private` or `Public`. These properties need to be accessible to the standard module so they will be declared `Public`. Place the following lines at the top of the class module:

```
Public EmpName As String
Public EmpID As String
Public EmpRate As Double
Public EmpWeeklyHrs As Double
```

Methods are actions that the object can take. In the class module, these actions take shape as procedures and functions. The following code creates a method, `EmpWeeklyPay()`, for the object that calculates weekly pay:

```
Public Function EmpWeeklyPay() As Double
EmpWeeklyPay = EmpRate * EmpWeeklyHrs
End Function
```

The object is now complete. It has four properties and one method. The next step is using the object in an actual program.

Using a Custom Object

After a custom object is properly configured in a class module, it can be referenced from another module. Declare a variable as the custom object type in the declarations section:

```
Dim Employee As clsEmployee
```

In the procedure, Set the variable to be a New object:

```
Set Employee = New clsEmployee
```

Continue entering the rest of the procedure. As you refer to the properties and method of the custom object, a tip screen appears, just as with Excel's standard objects (see Figure 20.6).

Figure 20.6
The properties and method of the custom object are just as easily accessible as they are for standard objects.

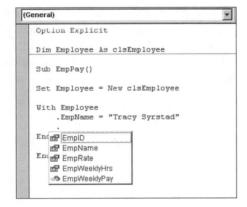

```
Option Explicit

Dim Employee As clsEmployee

Sub EmpPay()

Set Employee = New clsEmployee

With Employee
    .EmpName = "Tracy Syrstad"
    .EmpID = "1651"
    .EmpRate = 25
    .EmpWeeklyHrs = 40
    MsgBox .EmpName & " earns $" & .EmpWeeklyPay & " per week."
End With

End Sub
```

The sub procedure declares an object Employee as a new instance of clsEmployee. It then assigns values to the four properties of the object and generates a message box displaying the employee name and weekly pay (see Figure 20.7). The object's method, `EmpWeeklyPay`, is used to generate the displayed pay.

Figure 20.7
Create custom objects to make code more efficient.

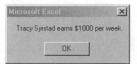

Using `Property Let` and `Property Get` to Control How Users Utilize Custom Objects

Public variables, as declared in the earlier example, have read/write properties. When they are used in a program, the values of the variables can be retrieved or changed. To assign read/write limitations, use `Property Let` and `Property Get` procedures.

`Property Let` procedures give you control of how properties can be assigned values. `Property Get` procedures give you control of how the properties are accessed. In the custom object example, there is a public variable for weekly hours. This variable is used in a method for calculating pay for the week, but doesn't take overtime pay into consideration. Variables for normal hours and overtime hours are needed, but the variables must be read only.

To accomplish this, the class module must be reconstructed. It needs two new properties, `EmpNormalHrs` and `EmpOverTimeHrs`. But because these two properties are to be confined to read-only, they are not declared as variables. `Property Get` procedures are used to create them.

If `EmpNormalHrs` and `EmpOverTimeHrs` are going to be read-only, they must have values assigned somehow. Their values are a calculation of the `EmpWeeklyHrs`. Because `EmpWeeklyHrs` is going to be used to set the property values of these two object properties, it can no longer be a public variable. There are two `Private` variables. These private variables, `NormalHrs` and `OverHrs`, are used within the confines of the class module:

```
Public EmpName As String
Public EmpID As String
Public EmpRate As Double

Private NormalHrs As Double
Private OverHrs As Double
```

A `Property Let` procedure is created for `EmpWeeklyHrs` to break the hours down into normal and overtime hours:

```
Property Let EmpWeeklyHrs(Hrs As Double)

NormalHrs = WorksheetFunction.Min(40, Hrs)
OverHrs = WorksheetFunction.Max(0, Hrs - 40)

End Property
```

The Property Get EmpWeeklyHrs totals these hours and returns a value to this property. Without it, a value cannot be retrieved from EmpWeeklyHrs:

```
Property Get EmpWeeklyHrs() As Double

EmpWeeklyHrs = NormalHrs + OverHrs

End Property
```

Property Get procedures are created for EmpNormalHrs and EmpOverTimeHrs to set their values. If you use Property Get procedures only, the values of these two properties are read-only. They can be assigned values only through the EmpWeeklyHrs property:

```
Property Get EmpNormalHrs() As Double

EmpNormalHrs = NormalHrs

End Property
Property Get EmpOverTimeHrs() As Double

EmpOverTimeHrs = OverHrs

End Property
```

Finally, the method EmpWeeklyPay is updated to reflect the changes in the properties and goal:

```
Public Function EmpWeeklyPay() As Double

EmpWeeklyPay = (EmpNormalHrs * EmpRate) + (EmpOverTimeHrs * EmpRate * 1.5)

End Function
```

Update the procedure in the standard module to take advantage of the changes in the class module. The new message box resulting from this updated procedure is shown in Figure 20.8:

```
Sub EmpPayOverTime()
Dim Employee As New clsEmployee

With Employee
    .EmpName = "Tracy Syrstad"
    .EmpID = "1651"
    .EmpRate = 25
    .EmpWeeklyHrs = 45
    MsgBox .EmpName & Chr(10) & Chr(9) & _
    "Normal Hours: " & .EmpNormalHrs & Chr(10) & Chr(9) & _
    "OverTime Hours: " & .EmpOverTimeHrs & Chr(10) & Chr(9) & _
    "Weekly Pay : $" & .EmpWeeklyPay
End With

End Sub
```

20

Figure 20.8
Use `Property Let`
and `Property Get`
procedures for more
control over custom
object properties.

Collections

Up to now, you've been able to have only one record at a time of the custom object. To create more, a *collection* is needed. A collection allows more than a single record to exist at a time. For example, `Worksheet` is a member of the `Worksheets` collection. You can add, remove, count, and refer to each worksheet in a workbook by item. This functionality is also available to your custom object.

There are two ways of creating a collection: in the standard module or in a class module. Which you choose depends on your needs.

Creating a Collection in a Standard Module

The quickest way to create a collection is to use the built-in `Collection` method. By setting up a collection in a standard module, you can access the four default collection methods: `Add`, `Remove`, `Count`, and `Item`.

The following example reads a list of employees off a sheet and into an array. It then processes the array, supplying each property of the object with a value, and places each record in the collection:

```
Sub EmpPayCollection()
Dim colEmployees As New Collection
Dim recEmployee As New clsEmployee
Dim LastRow As Integer, myCount As Integer
Dim EmpArray As Variant

LastRow = ActiveSheet.Range("A65536").End(xlUp).Row
EmpArray = ActiveSheet.Range(Cells(1, 1), Cells(LastRow, 4))

For myCount = 1 To UBound(EmpArray)
    With recEmployee
        .EmpName = EmpArray(myCount, 1)
        .EmpID = EmpArray(myCount, 2)
        .EmpRate = EmpArray(myCount, 3)
        .EmpWeeklyHrs = EmpArray(myCount, 4)
        colEmployees.Add recEmployee, .EmpID
    End With
Next myCount

MsgBox "Number of Employees: " & colEmployees.Count & Chr(10) & _
    "Employee(2) Name: " & colEmployees(2).EmpName
MsgBox "Tracy's Weekly Pay: $" & colEmployees("1651").EmpWeeklyPay

Set recEmployee = Nothing

End Sub
```

The collection, `colEmployees`, is declared as a new collection and the record, `recEmployee`, as a new variable of the custom object type.

After the object's properties are given values, the record, `recEmployee`, is added to the collection. The second parameter of the `Add` method applies a unique key to the record—in this case, the employee ID number. This allows a specific record to be quickly accessed, as in the second message box (`colEmployees("1651").EmpWeeklyPay`) (see Figure 20.9).

> **NOTE** The unique key is an optional parameter. An error message appears if a duplicate key is entered.

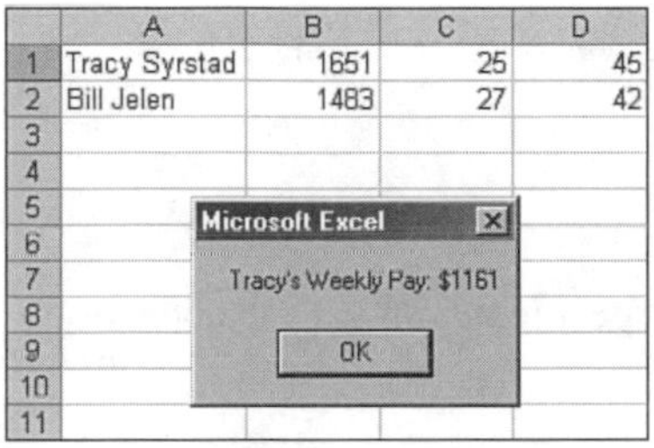

Figure 20.9
Individual records in a collection can be easily accessed.

Creating a Collection in a Class Module

Collections can be created in a class module but, in this case, the innate methods of the collection (`Add`, `Remove`, `Count`, `Item`) are not available; they have to be created in the class module. The advantages of creating a collection in a class module are that the entire code is in one module, you have more control over what is done with the collection, and you can prevent access to the collection.

Insert a new class module for the collection and rename it `clsEmployees`. Declare a private collection to be used within the class module:

```
Option Explicit
Private AllEmployees As New Collection
```

Add the new properties and methods required to make the collection work. The innate methods of collection are available within the class module and can be used to create the custom methods and properties:

Insert an `Add` method for adding new items to the collection:

```
Public Sub Add(recEmployee As clsEmployee)

AllEmployees.Add recEmployee, recEmployee.EmpID

End Sub
```

20

Insert a `Count` property to return the number of items in the collection:

```
Public Property Get Count() As Long

Count = AllEmployees.Count

End Property
```

Insert an `Items` property to return the entire collection:

```
Public Property Get Items() As Collection

Set Items = AllEmployees

End Property
```

Insert an `Item` property to return a specific item from the collection:

```
Public Property Get Item(myItem As Variant) As clsEmployee

Set Item = AllEmployees(myItem)

End Property
```

Insert a `Remove` property to remove a specific item from the collection:

```
Public Sub Remove(myItem As Variant)

AllEmployees.Remove (myItem)

End Sub
```

Because you have to create your own methods, you can improve on their functionality. For example, in the `Add` procedure, you can have it create the unique key automatically.

`Property Get` is used with `Count`, `Item`, and `Items` because these are read-only properties. `Item` returns a reference to a single member of the collection, whereas `Items` returns the entire collection (so that it can be used in `For Each Next` loops).

After the collection is configured in the class module, a procedure can be written in a standard module to use it:

```
Sub EmpAddCollection()
Dim colEmployees As New clsEmployees
Dim recEmployee As New clsEmployee
Dim LastRow As Integer, myCount As Integer
Dim EmpArray As Variant

LastRow = ActiveSheet.Range("A65536").End(xlUp).Row
EmpArray = ActiveSheet.Range(Cells(1, 1), Cells(LastRow, 4))

For myCount = 1 To UBound(EmpArray)
    With recEmployee
        .EmpName = EmpArray(myCount, 1)
        .EmpID = EmpArray(myCount, 2)
        .EmpRate = EmpArray(myCount, 3)
```

```
            .EmpWeeklyHrs = EmpArray(myCount, 4)
            colEmployees.Add recEmployee
        End With
    Next myCount

    MsgBox "Number of Employees: " & colEmployees.Count & Chr(10) & _
        "Employee(2) Name: " & colEmployees.Item(2).EmpName
    MsgBox "Tracy's Weekly Pay: $" & colEmployees.Item("1651").EmpWeeklyPay

    For Each recEmployee In colEmployees.Items
        recEmployee.EmpRate = recEmployee.EmpRate * 1.5
    Next recEmployee

    MsgBox "Tracy's Weekly Pay (after Bonus): $" & colEmployees.Item("1651"). _
        EmpWeeklyPay

End Sub
```

This program isn't that different from the one used with the standard collection, but there are a few key differences. colEmployees is declared as type clsEmployees, the new class module collection, instead of as Collection. The array and collection are filled the same way, but the way the records in the collection are referenced has changed. When referencing a member of the collection, such as employee record 2, the Item property must be used. Compare the syntax of the message boxes in this program to the previous program.

The For Each Next loop goes through each record in the collection and multiplies the EmpRate by 1.5, changing its value. The result of this "Bonus" is shown in a message box (see Figure 20.10).

Figure 20.10
Create custom procedures and methods in a class module collection.

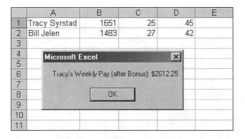

CASE STUDY

Help Buttons

You have a complex sheet that requires a way for the user to get help. You could place the information in comment boxes, but they aren't very obvious, especially to the novice Excel user. Another option is to create help buttons. The user could click on a button and a help form would appear.

On the worksheet, create small labels with a question mark in each one. To get the button-like appearance shown in Figure 20.11, set the SpecialEffect property of the labels to Raised and darken the BackColor. Place one label per row. Two columns over from the button, enter the help text you want to appear when the label is clicked. Hide this help text column.

Figure 20.11
Attach help buttons to
the sheet and enter help
text.

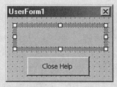

	1	2	3	4	5	6	7	8	9
1									
2		?		You can create a collection of custom help buttons.					
3									
4		?		It makes it much easier for someone to update the help text.					
5									
6		?		And the buttons are easy to see.					
7									

Create a simple userform with a label and a Close button, as shown in Figure 20.12. Rename the form to HelpForm, the button to CloseHelp, and the label to HelpText. Size the label large enough to hold the help text. Add a macro behind the form to hide the form when the button is clicked:

```
Private Sub CloseHelp_Click()
Unload Me
End Sub
```

Figure 20.12
Create a userform with a
label and button.

Insert a class module named clsLabel. You'll need a variable, Lbl, to capture the control events and a variable, ws, to capture on what worksheet the event occurs:

```
Public WithEvents Lbl As MSForms.Label
```

Also, you need a method of finding and displaying the corresponding help text:

```
Private Sub Lbl_Click()
Dim Rng As Range

Set Rng = Lbl.TopLeftCell

If Lbl.Caption = "?" Then
    HelpForm.Caption = "Label in cell " & Rng.Address(0, 0)
    HelpForm.HelpText.Caption = Rng.Offset(, 2).Value
    HelpForm.Show
End If

End Sub
```

In the ThisWorkbook module, create a Workbook_Open procedure to create a collection of the labels in the workbook:

```
Option Explicit
Option Base 1
Dim col As Collection

Sub Workbook_Open()
Dim WS As Worksheet
Dim cLbl As clsLabel
Dim OleObj As OLEObject
```

```
    Set col = New Collection

    For Each WS In ThisWorkbook.Worksheets
        For Each OleObj In WS.OLEObjects
            If OleObj.OLEType = xlOLEControl Then
                If TypeName(OleObj.Object) = "Label" Then
                    Set cLbl = New clsLabel
                    Set cLbl.Lbl = OleObj.Object
                    col.Add cLbl
                End If
            End If
        Next OleObj
    Next WS

    End Sub
```

Run `Workbook_Open` to create the collection. Click a label on the worksheet. The corresponding help text appears in the help form, as shown in Figure 20.13.

Figure 20.13
Help text is only a click away.

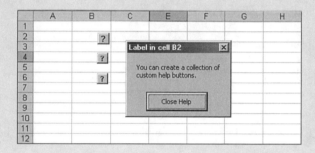

User-Defined Types (UDTs)

User-Defined Types provide some of the power of a custom object but without the need of a class module. A class module allows the creation of custom properties and methods, whereas a UDT allows only custom properties. But sometimes, that's all you need.

A UDT is declared with a `Type..End Type` statement. It can be `Public` or `Private`. A name that is treated like an object is given to the UDT. Within the `Type`, individual variables are declared that become the properties of the UDT.

Within an actual procedure, a variable is defined of the custom type. When that variable is used, the properties are available, just as they are in a custom object (see Figure 20.14).

The following example uses two UDTs to summarize a report of product styles in various stores.

20

Figure 20.14
The properties of a UDT are available as they are in a custom object.

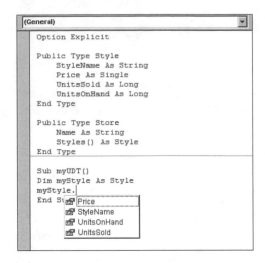

The first UDT consists of properties for each product style.

```
Option Explicit
Public Type Style
    StyleName As String
    Price As Single
    UnitsSold As Long
    UnitsOnHand As Long
End Type
```

The second UDT consists of the store name and an array whose type is the first UDT.

```
Public Type Store
    Name As String
    Styles() As Style
End Type
```

After the UDTs are established, the main program is written. Only a variable of the second UDT type, Store, is needed because that type contains the first type, Style (see Figure 20.15). But all the properties of the UDTs are easily available. And with the use of the UDT, the various variables are easy to remember—they're only a "." away:

```
Sub Main()
Dim FinalRow As Integer, ThisRow As Integer, ThisStore As Integer
Dim CurrRow As Integer, TotalDollarsSold As Integer, TotalUnitsSold As Integer
Dim TotalDollarsOnHand As Integer, TotalUnitsOnHand As Integer
Dim ThisStyle As Integer
Dim StoreName As String

ReDim Stores(0 To 0) As Store ' The UDT is declared

FinalRow = Range("A65536").End(xlUp).Row

' The following For loop fills both arrays. The outer array is filled with the
' store name and an array consisting of product details.
' To accomplish this, the store name is tracked and when it changes,
'the outer array is expanded.
```

```
'The inner array for each outer array expands with each new product
For ThisRow = 2 To FinalRow
    StoreName = Range("A" & ThisRow).Value
' Checks whether this is the first entry in the outer array
    If LBound(Stores) = 0 Then
        ThisStore = 1
        ReDim Stores(1 To 1) As Store
        Stores(1).Name = StoreName
        ReDim Stores(1).Styles(0 To 0) As Style
    Else
        For ThisStore = LBound(Stores) To UBound(Stores)
            If Stores(ThisStore).Name = StoreName Then Exit For
        Next ThisStore
        If ThisStore > UBound(Stores) Then
            ReDim Preserve Stores(LBound(Stores) To UBound(Stores) + 1) As Store
            Stores(ThisStore).Name = StoreName
            ReDim Stores(ThisStore).Styles(0 To 0) As Style
        End If
    End If
    With Stores(ThisStore)
        If LBound(.Styles) = 0 Then
            ReDim .Styles(1 To 1) As Style
        Else
            ReDim Preserve .Styles(LBound(.Styles) To _
        UBound(.Styles) + 1) As Style
        End If
        With .Styles(UBound(.Styles))
            .StyleName = Range("B" & ThisRow).Value
            .Price = Range("C" & ThisRow).Value
            .UnitsSold = Range("D" & ThisRow).Value
            .UnitsOnHand = Range("E" & ThisRow).Value
        End With
    End With
Next ThisRow

' Create a report on a new sheet
Sheets.Add
Range("A1:E1").Value = Array("Store Name", "Units Sold", _
    "Dollars Sold", "Units On Hand", "Dollars On Hand")
CurrRow = 2

For ThisStore = LBound(Stores) To UBound(Stores)
    With Stores(ThisStore)
        TotalDollarsSold = 0
        TotalUnitsSold = 0
        TotalDollarsOnHand = 0
        TotalUnitsOnHand = 0
' Go through the array of product styles within the array
' of stores to summarize information
        For ThisStyle = LBound(.Styles) To UBound(.Styles)
            With .Styles(ThisStyle)
                TotalDollarsSold = TotalDollarsSold + .UnitsSold * .Price
                TotalUnitsSold = TotalUnitsSold + .UnitsSold
                TotalDollarsOnHand = TotalDollarsOnHand + .UnitsOnHand * .Price
                TotalUnitsOnHand = TotalUnitsOnHand + .UnitsOnHand
            End With
        Next ThisStyle
```

20

```
            Range("A" & CurrRow & ":E" & CurrRow).Value = _
            Array(.Name, TotalUnitsSold, TotalDollarsSold, _
            TotalUnitsOnHand, TotalDollarsOnHand)
        End With
        CurrRow = CurrRow + 1
    Next ThisStore

End Sub
```

Figure 20.15

UDTs can make a potentially confusing multivariable program easier to write. (Note: The results of the program have been combined with the raw data for convenience.)

	A	B	C	D	E	F
1	Store	Style	Price	Units Sold	Units On Hand	
2	Store A	Style C	96.87	16	45	
3	Store A	Style A	38.43	7	94	
4	Store A	Style B	91.24	5	18	
5	Store A	Style E	19.89	0	96	
6	Store A	Style D	2.45	20	66	
7	Store B	Style B	92.59	4	83	
8	Store B	Style A	15.75	9	66	
9	Store B	Style F	13.12	2	35	
10	Store B	Style G	30.86	22	37	
11	Store B	Style H	37.38	21	77	
12						
13						
14						
15						
16						
17	Store Name	Units Sold	Dollars Sold	Units On Hand	Dollars On Hand	
18	Store A	48	$ 2,324.00	319	$ 11,684.00	
19	Store B	58	$ 2,002.00	298	$ 13,203.00	
20						

Next Steps

In Chapter 21, "Advanced UserForm Techniques," you'll learn about more controls and techniques you can use in building userforms.

20

Advanced UserForm Techniques

Chapter 9, "UserForms—An Introduction," covered the basics of adding controls to forms. This chapter continues on this topic by looking at more advanced controls and methods for making the most out of userforms.

Using the UserForm Toolbar in the Design of Controls on UserForms

In the Visual Basic Editor, hidden under View, Toolbars, are a few toolbars that don't appear unless the user intervenes. One of these is the Userform toolbar, shown in Figure 21.1:

- **Bring to Front**—Bring the selected control to the front of all other controls.
- **Send to Back**—Send the selected control to the back of all other controls.
- **Group**—Group the selected controls.
- **Ungroup**—Ungroup the selected grouping of controls.
- **Alignments**—The select controls are aligned according to their Lefts, Centers, Rights, Tops, Middles, Bottoms, To Grid.
- **Centering**—Center the selected control horizontally or vertically to the form.
- **Uniform Size**—Size the selected controls to be of uniform size according to Width, Height, Both.

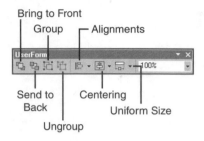

Figure 21.1
The Userform toolbar
has tools to organize the
controls on a userform.

> **TIP**   Use the Shift key to select multiple contiguous controls or the Ctrl key to select multiple non-contiguous controls.

Controls and Collections

In Chapter 20, "Creating Classes, Records, and Collections," several labels on a sheet were grouped together into a collection. With a little more code, these labels were turned into help screens for the users. Userform controls can be grouped into collections, too, and take advantage of class modules.

The following example checks or unchecks all the check boxes on the userform, depending on which label the user chooses.

Place the following code in the class module, clsFormEvents. It consists of one property, chb, and two methods, SelectAll and UnselectAll.

The SelectAll method places a check in a check box by setting its value to True:

```
Option Explicit
Public WithEvents chb As MSForms.CheckBox

Public Sub SelectAll()
chb.Value = True
End Sub
```

The UnselectAll method removes the check from the check box.

```
Public Sub UnselectAll()
chb.Value = False
End Sub
```

That sets up the class module. Next, the controls need to be placed in a collection. The following code, placed behind the form, frm_Movies, places the check boxes into a collection. The check boxes are part of a frame, f_Selection, which makes it easier to create the collection:

```
Option Explicit
Dim col_Selection As New Collection
```

```
Private Sub UserForm_Initialize()
Dim ctl As MSForms.CheckBox
Dim chb_ctl As clsFormEvents

' Go thru the members of the frame and add them to the collection
For Each ctl In f_Selection.Controls
    Set chb_ctl = New clsFormEvents
    Set chb_ctl.chb = ctl
    col_Selection.Add chb_ctl
Next ctl

End Sub
```

When the form is opened, the controls are placed into the collection. All that's left now is to add the code for labels to select and unselect the check boxes:

```
Private Sub lbl_SelectAll_Click()
Dim ctl As clsFormEvents

For Each ctl In col_Selection
    ctl.SelectAll
Next ctl

End Sub
```

The following code unselects the check boxes in the collection:

```
Private Sub lbl_unSelectAll_Click()
Dim ctl As clsFormEvents

For Each ctl In col_Selection
    ctl.Unselectall
Next ctl

End Sub
```

All the check boxes can be checked and unchecked with a single click of the mouse, as shown in Figure 21.2.

NOTE The check boxes can still be checked/unchecked on an individual basis.

Figure 21.2
Use frames, collections, and class modules together to create quick and efficient userforms.

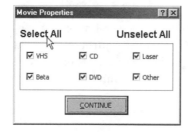

21

> **NOTE**
>
> A *tag* is a property that holds more information about a control. Its value is of type `string`, so it can hold any type of information. For example, it can be used to create an informal group of controls from different groupings.

More UserForm Controls

Chapter 9 began a review of some of the controls available on userforms. The review is continued here.

Option Buttons

Option buttons are similar to check boxes in that they can be used to select buttons. But, unlike check boxes, Option buttons can be easily configured to allow only one selection out of a group (see Figure 21.3).

A program can be used to allow only one item to be selected in a group, but Option buttons have a property, `Groupname`, that does this automatically. Option buttons with the same GroupName are automatically grouped together. Within this grouping, only one button can be toggled on at a time. Selecting an option button automatically deselects the other buttons in the same group or frame. To prevent this behavior, either leave the `GroupName` property blank, or enter another name.

Figure 21.3
Option buttons allow only one selection out of a group.

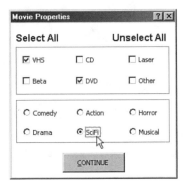

Tabstrip

The multipage control allows a userform to have several pages. Each page of the form can have its own set of controls, unrelated to any other control on the form. A tabstrip control also allows a userform to have many pages, but the controls on a tabstrip are identical; they are drawn only once. Yet, when the form is run, the information changes according to the strip that is active (see Figure 21.4).

Figure 21.4
A tabstrip allows a user-form with multiple pages to share controls, but not information.

→ To learn more about multipage controls, **see** "Using the Multipage Control to Combine Forms," **p. 176**, in Chapter 9.

By default, a tabstrip is thin, with two tabs at the top. Right-clicking on a tab enables you to add, remove, rename, or move a tab. The tabstrip should also be sized to hold all the controls.

> **NOTE** A button for closing the form should be drawn outside the tabstrip area.

The tabs can also be moved around the strip. This is done by changing the `TabOrientation` property. The tabs can be at the top, bottom, left, or right side of the userform:

The following lines of code were used to create the tabstrip form in Figure 21.4. The `Initialize` sub calls the sub, `SetValuestoTabStrip`, that sets the value for the first tab.

```
Private Sub UserForm_Initialize()
SetValuesToTabStrip 1 'As default
End Sub
```

These lines of code handle what happens when a new tab is selected.

```
Private Sub TabStrip1_Change()
Dim lngRow As Long

lngRow = TabStrip1.Value + 1
SetValuesToTabStrip lngRow

End Sub
```

This sub provides the data shown on each tab. A sheet was set up, with each row corresponding to a tab.

```
Private Sub SetValuesToTabStrip(ByVal lngRow As Long)
With frm_Staff
    .lbl_Name.Caption = Cells(lngRow, 2).Value
    .lbl_Phone.Caption = Cells(lngRow, 3).Value
    .lbl_Fax.Caption = Cells(lngRow, 4).Value
    .lbl_Email.Caption = Cells(lngRow, 5).Value
    .lbl_Website.Caption = Cells(lngRow, 6).Value
    .Show
End With
End Sub
```

21

The tabstrip's values are automatically filled in. They correspond to the tab's position in the strip; moving a tab changes its value.

> **TIP**
>
> If you wanted a single tab to have an extra control, the control could be added at runtime when the tab became active.

RefEdit

The RefEdit control allows the user to select a range on a sheet; the range is returned as the value of the control. It can be added to any form. Once activated by a click of the button on the right side of the field, the userform disappears and is replaced with the range selection form, used when selecting ranges with Excel's many wizard tools. Click the button on the right to show the userform once again.

The form in Figure 21.5 and following code allow the user to select a range, which is then made bold:

Figure 21.5
Use RefEdit to enable the user to select a range on a sheet.

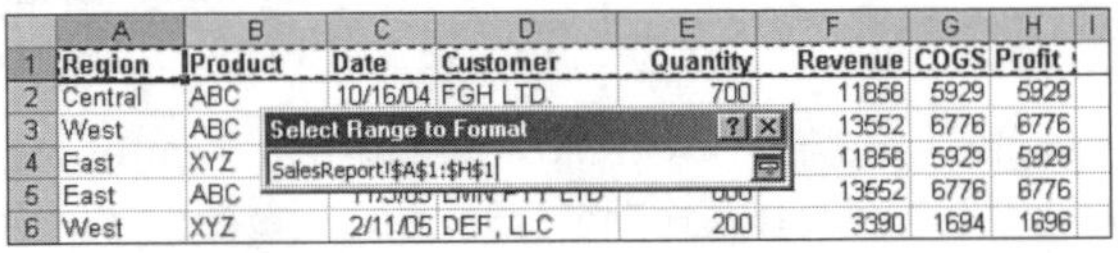

```
Private Sub cb1_Click()
Range(RefEdit1.Value).Font.Bold = True
End Sub
```

Modeless Userforms

Ever had a userform active but needed to look at something on a sheet? There was a time when the form had to be shut down before anything else in Excel could be done. No longer! Forms can now be *modeless*, which means they don't have to interfere with the functionality of Excel. The user can type in a cell, switch to another sheet, copy/paste data, use toolbars and menus—it is as if the userform were not there.

By default, a userform is modal, which means that there is no interaction with Excel other than the form. To make the form modeless, change the ShowModal property to False. After it is modeless, the user can select a cell on the sheet while the form is active, as shown in Figure 21.6

Figure 21.6
A modeless form enables the user to enter a cell while the form is still active.

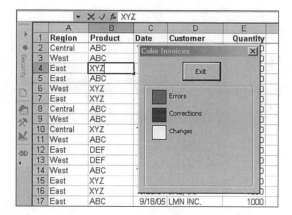

Hyperlinks in Userforms

In the userform example shown in Figure 21.4, there is a field for email and a Web site. Wouldn't it be nice to be able to click on these and have a blank email message or Web page automatically appear? You can! The following program creates a new message or opens a Web browser when the corresponding label is clicked:

The API declaration, and any other constants, go at the very top of the code.

```
Private Declare Function ShellExecute Lib "shell32.dll" Alias _
    "ShellExecuteA"(ByVal hWnd As Long, ByVal lpOperation As String, _
    ByVal lpFile As String, ByVal lpParameters As String, _
    ByVal lpDirectory As String, ByVal nShowCmd As Long) As Long

Const SWNormal = 1
```

This sub controls what happens when the email label is clicked, as shown in Figure 21.7.

```
Private Sub lbl_Email_Click()
Dim lngRow As Long

lngRow = TabStrip1.Value + 1
ShellExecute 0&, "open", "mailto:" & Cells(lngRow, 5).Value, _
    vbNullString, vbNullString, SWNormal

End Sub
```

This sub controls what happens when the Web site label is clicked.

```
Private Sub lbl_Website_Click()
Dim lngRow As Long

lngRow = TabStrip1.Value + 1
ShellExecute 0&, "open", Cells(lngRow, 6).Value, vbNullString, _
    vbNullString, SWNormal

End Sub
```

21

Figure 21.7
Turn email addresses and Web sites into clickable links.

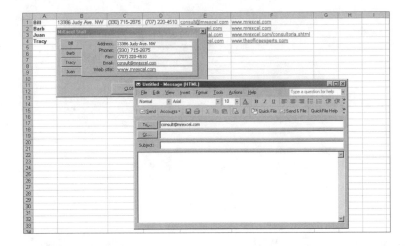

Adding Controls at Runtime

It is possible to add controls to a userform at runtime. This is very convenient if you are not sure how many items you will be adding to the form.

Figure 21.8 shows a very plain form. It has only one button. This plain form is used to display any number of pictures from a product catalog. The pictures and accompanying labels appear at runtime, as the form is being displayed.

Figure 21.8
Flexible forms can be created if you add most controls at runtime.

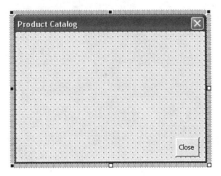

A sales rep making a sales presentation uses this form to display a product catalog. He can select any number of SKUs from an Excel worksheet and hit a hot key to display the form. If he selects 20 items on the worksheet, the form displays with each picture fairly small, as shown in Figure 21.9.

Figure 21.9
Here, the sales rep has asked to see photos of 20 SKUs. The UserForm_ Initialize procedure adds each picture and label on the fly.

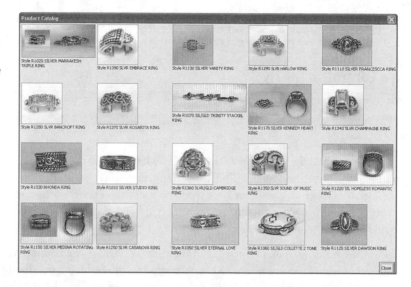

If the sales rep selects fewer items, then the images are displayed larger, as shown in Figure 21.10.

Figure 21.10
The logic in Userform_ Initialize decides how many pictures are being displayed and adds the appropriate size controls.

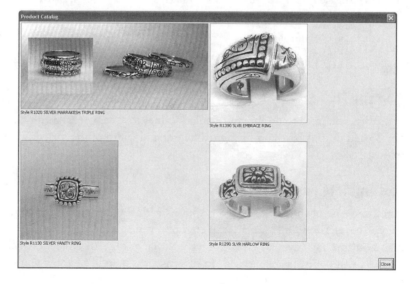

A number of techniques are used to create this userform on the fly. The initial form contains only one button, called cbClose. Everything else is added on the fly.

Resizing the Userform on the Fly

One goal is to give the best view of the images in the product catalog. This means having the form appear as large as possible. The following code uses the form's height and width properties to make sure the form fills almost the entire screen:

```
' resize the form
Me.Height = Int(0.98 * ActiveWindow.Height)
Me.Width = Int(0.98 * ActiveWindow.Width)
```

Adding a Control on the Fly

For a normal control added at design time, it is easy to refer to the control by using its name:

```
Me.cbSave.Left = 100
```

But, for a control that is added at runtime, you have to use the `Controls` collection to set any properties for the control. Thus, it is important to set up a variable to hold the name of the control. Controls are added with the `.Add` method. The important parameter is the `bstrProgId`. This code name dictates whether the added control is a label, text box, command button, or something else.

The following code adds a new label to the form. `PicCount` is a counter variable used to ensure that each label has a new name. After the form is added, you should specify a position for the control by setting the `Top` and `Left` properties. You should also set a `Height` and `Width` for the control:

```
LC = "LabelA" & PicCount
Me.Controls.Add bstrProgId:="forms.label.1", Name:=LC, Visible:=True
Me.Controls(LC).Top = 25
Me.Controls(LC).Left = 50
Me.Controls(LC).Height = 18
Me.Controls(LC).Width = 60
Me.Controls(LC).Caption = cell.value
```

Sizing on the Fly

In reality, you need to be able to calculate values for `Top`, `Left`, `Height`, and `Width` on the fly. You would do this based on the actual height and width of the form and on how many controls are needed.

No AutoComplete Funtionality

You lose some of the AutoComplete options with this method. Normally, if you would start to type **Me.cbClose.**, the AutoComplete options would present the valid choices for a command button. However, when you use the `Me.Controls(LC)` collection, VBA doesn't know what type of control is referenced. In this case it is helpful to know you need to set the `Caption` property instead of the `Value` property for a label.

Adding Other Controls

To add other types of controls, change the `ProgId` used with the `Add` method. Table 21.1 shows the `ProgIds` for various types of controls.

Table 21.1   UserForm Controls and Corresponding ProgIds

Control	ProgId
CheckBox	Forms.CheckBox.1
ComboBox	Forms.ComboBox.1
CommandButton	Forms.CommandButton.1
Frame	Forms.Frame.1
Image	Forms.Image.1
Label	Forms.Label.1
ListBox	Forms.ListBox.1
MultiPage	Forms.MultiPage.1
OptionButton	Forms.OptionButton.1
ScrollBar	Forms.ScrollBar.1
SpinButton	Forms.SpinButton.1
TabStrip	Forms.TabStrip.1
TextBox	Forms.TextBox.1
ToggleButton	Forms.ToggleButton.1

Adding an Image on the Fly

There is some unpredictability in adding images. Any given image might be shaped either landscape or portrait. The image might be small or huge. The strategy you might want to employ is to let the image load full size by setting the `.AutoSize` parameter to `True` before loading the image:

```
TC = "Image" & PicCount
Me.Controls.Add bstrProgId:="forms.image.1", Name:=TC, Visible:=True
Me.Controls(TC).Top = LastTop
Me.Controls(TC).Left = LastLeft
Me.Controls(TC).AutoSize = True
On Error Resume Next
Me.Controls(TC).Picture = LoadPicture(fname)
On Error GoTo 0
```

Then, after the image has loaded, you can read the control's `Height` and `Width` properties to determine whether the image is landscape or portrait and whether the image is constrained by available width or available height:

```
' The picture resized the control to full size
' determine the size of the picture
Wid = Me.Controls(TC).Width
Ht = Me.Controls(TC).Height
WidRedux = CellWid / Wid
HtRedux = CellHt / Ht
```

```
If WidRedux < HtRedux Then
    Redux = WidRedux
Else
    Redux = HtRedux
End If
NewHt = Int(Ht * Redux)
NewWid = Int(Wid * Redux)
```

After you find the proper size for the image to have it draw without distortion, you can set the AutoSize property to False and use the correct height and width to have the image not appear distorted:

```
' Now resize the control
Me.Controls(TC).AutoSize = False
Me.Controls(TC).Height = NewHt
Me.Controls(TC).Width = NewWid
Me.Controls(TC).PictureSizeMode = fmPictureSizeModeStretch
```

Putting It All Together

This is the complete code for the Picture Catalog userform:

```
Private Sub UserForm_Initialize()
    ' Display pictures of each SKU selected on the worksheet
    ' This may be anywhere from 1 to 36 pictures
    PicPath = "C:\qimage\qi"
    Dim Pics ()

    ' resize the form
    Me.Height = Int(0.98 * ActiveWindow.Height)
    Me.Width = Int(0.98 * ActiveWindow.Width)

    ' determine how many cells are selected
    ' We need one picture and label for each cell
    CellCount = Selection.Cells.Count
    ReDim Preserve Pics(1 To CellCount)

    ' Figure out the size of the resized form
    TempHt = Me.Height
    TempWid = Me.Width

    ' The number of columns is a roundup of SQRT(CellCount)
    ' This will ensure 4 rows of 5 pictures for 20, etc.
    NumCol = Int(0.99 + Sqr(CellCount))
    NumRow = Int(0.99 + CellCount / NumCol)

    ' Figure out the ht and wid of each square
    ' Each column will have 2 pts to left & right of pics
    CellWid = Application.WorksheetFunction.Max(Int(TempWid / NumCol) - 4, 1)
    ' each row needs to have 33 points below it for the label
    CellHt = Application.WorksheetFunction.Max(Int(TempHt / NumRow) - 33, 1)

    PicCount = 0 ' Counter variable
    LastTop = 2
    MaxBottom = 1
    ' Build each row on the form
    For x = 1 To NumRow
```

```
            LastLeft = 3
            ' Build each column in this row
            For Y = 1 To NumCol
                PicCount = PicCount + 1
                If PicCount > CellCount Then
                    ' There are not an even number of pictures to fill
                    ' out the last row
                    Me.Height = MaxBottom + 100
                    Me.cbClose.Top = MaxBottom + 25
                    Me.cbClose.Left = Me.Width - 50
                    Repaint
                    Exit Sub
                End If
                ThisStyle = Selection.Cells(PicCount).Value
                ThisDesc = Selection.Cells(PicCount).Offset(0, 1).Value
                fname = PicPath & ThisStyle & ".jpg"
                TC = "Image" & PicCount
                Me.Controls.Add bstrProgId:="forms.image.1", Name:=TC, Visible:=True
                Me.Controls(TC).Top = LastTop
                Me.Controls(TC).Left = LastLeft
                Me.Controls(TC).AutoSize = True
                On Error Resume Next
                Me.Controls(TC).Picture = LoadPicture(fname)
                On Error GoTo 0

                ' The picture resized the control to full size
                ' determine the size of the picture
                Wid = Me.Controls(TC).Width
                Ht = Me.Controls(TC).Height
                WidRedux = CellWid / Wid
                HtRedux = CellHt / Ht
                If WidRedux < HtRedux Then
                    Redux = WidRedux
                Else
                    Redux = HtRedux
                End If
                NewHt = Int(Ht * Redux)
                NewWid = Int(Wid * Redux)

                ' Now resize the control
                Me.Controls(TC).AutoSize = False
                Me.Controls(TC).Height = NewHt
                Me.Controls(TC).Width = NewWid
                Me.Controls(TC).PictureSizeMode = fmPictureSizeModeStretch
                Me.Controls(TC).ControlTipText = "Style " & _
        ThisStyle & " " & ThisDesc

                ' Keep track of the bottom-most & right-most picture
                ThisRight = Me.Controls(TC).Left + Me.Controls(TC).Width
                ThisBottom = Me.Controls(TC).Top + Me.Controls(TC).Height
                If ThisBottom > MaxBottom Then MaxBottom = ThisBottom

                ' Add a label below the picture
                LC = "LabelA" & PicCount
                Me.Controls.Add bstrProgId:="forms.label.1", Name:=LC, Visible:=True
                Me.Controls(LC).Top = ThisBottom + 1
                Me.Controls(LC).Left = LastLeft
                Me.Controls(LC).Height = 18
```

21

```
            Me.Controls(LC).Width = CellWid
            Me.Controls(LC).Caption = "Style " & ThisStyle & " " & ThisDesc

            ' Keep track of where the next picture should display
            LastLeft = LastLeft + CellWid + 4
        Next Y ' end of this row
        LastTop = MaxBottom + 21 + 16
    Next x

    Me.Height = MaxBottom + 100
    Me.cbClose.Top = MaxBottom + 25
    Me.cbClose.Left = Me.Width - 50
    Repaint
End Sub
```

Using a Scrollbar as a Slider to Select Values

Chapter 9 discussed using a spin button control to allow someone to choose a date. The spin button is good, but it allows clients to adjust up or down by only one unit at a time. An alternative method is to draw a horizontal scrollbar in the middle of the userform and use it as a slider. Clients can use arrows on the ends of the scrollbar like the spin button arrows, but they can also grab the scrollbar and instantly drag it to a certain value.

The userform shown in Figure 21.12 includes a label named Label1 and a scrollbar called ScrollBar1. The userform's Initialize button sets up the Min and Max values for the scrollbar. It initializes the scrollbar to a value from cell A1 and updates the Label1.Caption:

```
Private Sub UserForm_Initialize()
    Me.ScrollBar1.Min = 0
    Me.ScrollBar1.Max = 100
    Me.ScrollBar1.Value = Range("A1").Value
    Me.Label1.Caption = Me.ScrollBar1.Value
End Sub
```

Two event handlers are needed for the scrollbar. The _Change event handles if clients click on the arrows at the ends of the scrollbar. The _Scroll event handles if they drag the slider to a new value:

```
Private Sub ScrollBar1_Change()
    ' This event handles if they touch
    ' the arrows on the end of the scrollbar
    Me.Label1.Caption = Me.ScrollBar1.Value
End Sub

Private Sub ScrollBar1_Scroll()
    ' This event handles if they drag the slider
    Me.Label1.Caption = Me.ScrollBar1.Value
End Sub
```

Finally, the event attached to the button writes the scrollbar value out to the worksheet:

```
Private Sub CommandButton1_Click()
    Range("A1").Value = Me.ScrollBar1.Value
    Unload Me
End Sub
```

The scrollbar is shown in action in Figures 21.11 and 21.12.

Figure 21.11

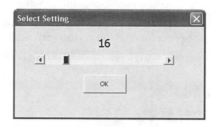

Figure 21.12
Using a scrollbar control as a control allows the user to quickly drag to a particular numeric or data value.

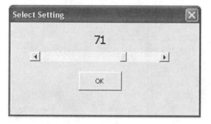

Adding Help Tips to Controls

Accelerator Keys

Built-in forms often have keyboard shortcuts that allow actions to be triggered or fields selected with a few keystrokes. These shortcuts are identified by an underlined letter on a button or label.

You can add this same capability to custom userforms by entering a value in the Accelerator property of the control. Alt + the accelerator key selects the control. For example, in Figure 21.13, Alt+H checks the VHS check box. Repeating the combination unchecks the box.

Figure 21.13
Use accelerator key combinations to give userforms the power of keyboard shortcuts.

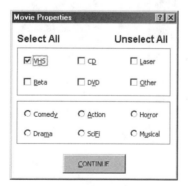

Control Tip Text

When a cursor is waved over a toolbar, tip text appears, hinting at what the control does. You can also add tip text to userforms by entering a value in the `ControlTipText` property of a control. In Figure 21.14, tip text has been added to the frame surrounding the various categories.

Figure 21.14
Add tips to controls to provide help to users.

Tab Order

Users can also tab from one field to another. This is an automatic feature in a form. To control which field the next tab brings a user to, you can set the `TapStop` property value for each control.

The first tab stop is zero, and the last tab stop is equal to the number of controls in a group. Remember, a group can be created with a frame. Excel does not allow multiple controls to have the same tab stop. After tabstops are set, the user can use the Tab key and spacebar to select/deselect various options, as shown in Figure 21.15.

Figure 21.15
The options in this form were selected with the tab key and space bar.

Coloring the Active Control

Another method for helping a user fill out a form is to color the active field. The following example changes the color of a text box or combobox when it is active, as shown in Figure 21.16.

Figure 21.16
Help users keep track of
which field they're filling
in by coloring the field
when it is active.

Place the following in a class module called clsCtlColor:

```
Public Event GetFocus()
Public Event LostFocus(ByVal strCtrl As String)
Private strPreCtr As String

Public Sub CheckActiveCtrl(objForm As MSForms.UserForm)

With objForm
    If TypeName(.ActiveControl) = "ComboBox" Or _
        TypeName(.ActiveControl) = "TextBox" Then
        strPreCtr = .ActiveControl.Name
        On Error GoTo Terminate
        Do
            DoEvents
            If .ActiveControl.Name <> strPreCtr Then
                If TypeName(.ActiveControl) = "ComboBox" Or _
                    TypeName(.ActiveControl) = "TextBox" Then
                    RaiseEvent LostFocus(strPreCtr)
                    strPreCtr = .ActiveControl.Name
                    RaiseEvent GetFocus
                End If
            End If
        Loop
    End If
End With

Terminate:
    Exit Sub

End Sub
```

Place the following behind the userform:

```
Private WithEvents objForm As clsCtlColor

Private Sub UserForm_Initialize()
Set objForm = New clsCtlColor
End Sub
```

This sub changes the BackColor of the active control when the form is activated.

```
Private Sub UserForm_Activate()
If TypeName(ActiveControl) = "ComboBox" Or _
    TypeName(ActiveControl) = "TextBox" Then
    ActiveControl.BackColor = &HC0E0FF
End If
objForm.CheckActiveCtrl Me
End Sub
```

21

This sub changes the `BackColor` of the active control when it gets the focus.

```
Private Sub objForm_GetFocus()
ActiveControl.BackColor = &HC0E0FF
End Sub
```

This sub changes the `BackColor` back to white when the control loses the focus.

```
Private Sub objForm_LostFocus(ByVal strCtrl As String)
Me.Controls(strCtrl).BackColor = &HFFFFFF
End Sub
```

This sub clears the `objForm` when the form is closed.

```
Private Sub UserForm_QueryClose(Cancel As Integer, CloseMode As Integer)
Set objForm = Nothing
End Sub
```

CASE STUDY

Multicolumn ListBox

You've created several spreadsheets containing store data. The primary key of each set is the store number. The workbook is used by several people, but not everyone memorizes stores by their store numbers. You need some way of letting a user select a store by its name, but at the same time, return the store number to be used in the code. You could use VLOOKUP or MATCH, but there's another way.

A ListBox can have more than one column, but not all the columns need to be visible to the user. Also, the user can select an item from the visible list, but the ListBox returns the corresponding value from another column.

Draw a ListBox and set the ColumnCount property to 2. Set the RowSource to a two-column range called Stores. The first column of the range is the store number; the second column is the store name. At this point, the ListBox is displaying both columns of data. To change this, set the column width to 0, 20—the text automatically updates to 0 pt;20 pt. The first column is now hidden. Figure 21.17 shows the ListBox properties as they need to be.

Figure 21.17
Setting the ListBox properties creates a two-column ListBox that appears to be a single column of data.

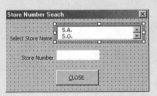 

The appearance of the ListBox has now been set. When the user activates the ListBox, she will see only the store names. To return the value of the first column, set the BoundColumn property to 1. This can be done through the Properties window or through code. This example uses code to maintain the flexibility of returning the store number (see Figure 21.18):

```
Private Sub lb_StoreName_Click()

lb_StoreName.BoundColumn = 2
lbl_StoreNum.Caption = lb_StoreName

End Sub
```

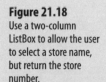

Figure 21.18
Use a two-column
ListBox to allow the user
to select a store name,
but return the store
number.

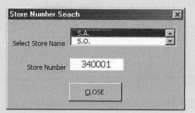

Transparent Forms

Ever had a form that you had to keep moving out of the way so you could see the data
behind it? The following code sets the userform at a 50% transparency (see Figure 21.19) so
that you can see the data behind without moving the form somewhere else on the screen
(and blocking more data).

Figure 21.19
Create a 50% transparent form to view the
data on the sheet
behind it.

Place the following in the declarations section of the userform:

```
Private Declare Function GetActiveWindow Lib "USER32" () As Long
Private Declare Function SetWindowLong Lib "USER32" Alias _
    "SetWindowLongA" (ByVal hWnd As Long, ByVal nIndex As Long, _
    ByVal dwNewLong As Long) As Long
Private Declare Function GetWindowLong Lib "USER32" Alias _
    "GetWindowLongA" (ByVal hWnd As Long, ByVal nIndex As Long) As Long
Private Declare Function SetLayeredWindowAttributes Lib "USER32" _
    (ByVal hWnd As Long, ByVal crKey As Integer, _
    ByVal bAlpha As Integer, ByVal dwFlags As Long) As Long
Private Const WS_EX_LAYERED = &H80000
Private Const LWA_COLORKEY = &H1
Private Const LWA_ALPHA = &H2
Private Const GWL_EXSTYLE = &HFFEC
Dim hWnd As Long
```

Place the following behind a userform. When the form is activated, the transparency will be
set:

```
Private Sub UserForm_Activate()
Dim nIndex As Long

hWnd = GetActiveWindow
nIndex = GetWindowLong(hWnd, GWL_EXSTYLE)
SetWindowLong hWnd, GWL_EXSTYLE, nIndex Or WS_EX_LAYERED
```

21

```
    '50% semitransparent
    SetLayeredWindowAttributes hWnd, 0, (255 * 50) / 100, LWA_ALPHA

    End Sub
```

Next Steps

In Chapter 22, "Windows Application Programming Interface (API)," you will learn how to access functions and procedures hidden in files on your computer.

Windows Application Programming Interface (API)

22

What Is the Windows API?

With all the wonderful things you can do in Excel VBA, there are some things that are out of its reach or just difficult to do—such as finding out what the user's screen resolution setting is. This is where the Windows Application Programming Interface, or API, can help.

If you look in the folder \Winnt\System32 (NT systems), you'll see a lot of files with the extension .dll. These files are *Dynamic Link Libraries*; they contain various functions and procedures that other programs, including VBA, can access. They give the user access to functionality used by the Windows operating system and many other programs. Keep in mind that Windows API declarations are accessible only on computers running the Microsoft Windows operating system.

This chapter doesn't teach you how to write API declarations, but it does teach you the basics of interpreting and using them. Several useful examples have also been included and you will be shown how to find more.

Understanding an API Declaration

The following line is an example of an API function:

```
Private Declare Function GetUserName _
   Lib "advapi32.dll" Alias "GetUserNameA" _
   (ByVal lpBuffer As String, nSize As Long) _
   As Long
```

There are two types of API declarations: *functions*, which return information, and *procedures*, which do something to the system. The declarations are structured similarly.

Basically, what this declaration is saying is

- It's Private, meaning it can only be used in the module in which it is declared. Declare it Public in a standard module if you want to share it among several modules.

> **CAUTION**
>
> API declarations in standard modules can be Public or Private. API declarations in class modules must be Private.

- It will be referred to as GetUserName in your program. This is the variable name assigned by you.
- The function being used is found in advapi32.dll.
- The alias, GetUserNameA, is what the function is referred to in the DLL. This name is case sensitive and cannot be changed; it is specific to the DLL. There are often two versions of each API function. One version uses the ANSI character set and has aliases that end with A. The other version uses the Unicode character set and has aliases that end with W. When specifying the alias, you are telling VBA which version of the function to use.
- There are two parameters, lpBuffer and nSize. These are two arguments that the DLL function accepts.

Using an API Declaration

Using an API is no different than calling a function or procedure you created in VBA. The following example uses the GetUserName declaration in a function to return the UserName in Excel:

```
Public Function UserName() As String
Dim sName As String * 256
Dim cChars As Long

cChars = 256
If GetUserName(sName, cChars) Then
    UserName = Left$(sName, cChars - 1)
End If
End Function

Sub ProgramRights()
Dim NameofUser As String

NameofUser = UserName

Select Case NameofUser
```

```
        Case Is = "Administrator"
            MsgBox "You have full rights to this computer"
        Case Else
            MsgBox "You have limited rights to this computer"
    End Select

    End Sub
```

22

Run the ProgramRights macro and you will learn whether you are currently signed on as the administrator or not. The result shown in Figure 22.1 indicates an administrator sign-on.

Figure 22.1

The GetUserName API function can be used to get a user's Windows login name—which is more difficult to edit than the Excel username.

API Examples

The following sections provide more examples of useful API declarations you can use in your Excel programs. Each example starts with a short description of what the example can do, followed by the actual declaration(s), and an example of its use.

GetComputerName

This API function returns the computer name. This is the name of the computer found under MyComputer, Network Identification:

```
Private Declare Function GetComputerName Lib "kernel32" Alias _
    "GetComputerNameA" (ByVal lpBuffer As String, ByRef nSize As Long) As Long

Private Function ComputerName() As String

Dim stBuff As String * 255, lAPIResult As Long
Dim lBuffLen As Long

lBuffLen = 255
lAPIResult = GetComputerName(stBuff, lBuffLen)
If lBuffLen > 0 Then ComputerName = Left(stBuff, lBuffLen)

End Function

Sub ComputerCheck()
Dim CompName As String

CompName = ComputerName

If CompName <> "BillJelenPC" Then
    MsgBox _
    "This application does not have the right to run on this computer."
        ActiveWorkbook.Close SaveChanges:=False
```

```
End If

End Sub
```

The ComputerCheck macro uses an API call to get the name of the computer. In Figure 22.2, the program refuses to run for any computer except the hard-coded computer name of the owner.

Figure 22.2
Use the computer name to verify that an application has the rights to run on the installed computer.

FileIsOpen

You can check whether you have a file open in Excel by trying to set the workbook to an object. If the object is Nothing (empty), then you know the file isn't opened. But what if you wanted to see whether someone else on a network has the file opened? The following API function returns that information:

```
Private Declare Function lOpen Lib "kernel32" Alias "_lopen" _
    (ByVal lpPathName As String, ByVal iReadWrite As Long) As Long

Private Declare Function lClose Lib "kernel32" _
    Alias "_lclose" (ByVal hFile As Long) As Long

Private Const OF_SHARE_EXCLUSIVE = &H10

Private Function FileIsOpen(strFullPath_FileName As String) As Boolean
Dim hdlFile As Long
Dim lastErr As Long

hdlFile = -1

hdlFile = lOpen(strFullPath_FileName, OF_SHARE_EXCLUSIVE)

If hdlFile = -1 Then
    lastErr = Err.LastDllError
Else
    lClose (hdlFile)
End If

FileIsOpen = (hdlFile = -1) And (lastErr = 32)

End Function

Sub CheckFileOpen()

If FileIsOpen("\\John\tracy's keepers\XYZ Corp.xls") Then
    MsgBox "File is open"
Else
    MsgBox "File is not open"
End If

End Sub
```

Calling the `FileIsOpen` function with a particular path and filename as the parameter will tell you whether someone has the file open. Figure 22.3 shows the message indicating the XYZ `Corp.xls` is open by someone on the network.

Figure 22.3
Verify whether another user on the network has the file open.

Retrieve Display Resolution Information

The following API function retrieves the computer's display size:

```
Declare Function DisplaySize Lib "user32" Alias _
    "GetSystemMetrics" (ByVal nIndex As Long) As Long

Public Const SM_CXSCREEN = 0
Public Const SM_CYSCREEN = 1

Function VideoRes() As String
Dim vidWidth
Dim vidHeight

vidWidth = DisplaySize(SM_CXSCREEN)
vidHeight = DisplaySize(SM_CYSCREEN)

Select Case (vidWidth * vidHeight)
    Case 307200
        VideoRes = "640 x 480"
    Case 480000
        VideoRes = "800 x 600"
    Case 786432
        VideoRes = "1024 x 768"
    Case Else
        VideoRes = "Something else"
End Select

End Function

Sub CheckDisplayRes()
Dim VideoInfo As String
Dim Msg1 As String, Msg2 As String, Msg3 As String

VideoInfo = VideoRes

Msg1 = "Current resolution is set at " & VideoInfo & Chr(10)
Msg2 = "Optimal resolution for this application is 1024 x 768" & Chr(10)
Msg3 = "Please adjust resolution"

Select Case VideoInfo
    Case Is = "640 x 480"
        MsgBox Msg1 & Msg2 & Msg3
    Case Is = "800 x 600"
        MsgBox Msg1 & Msg2
    Case Is = "1024 x 768"
```

```
            MsgBox Msg1
        Case Else
            MsgBox Msg2 & Msg3
    End Select

    End Sub
```

In Figure 22.4, the CheckDisplayRes macro warns the client that the display setting is not optimal for the application.

Figure 22.4

Check the display resolution and prompt the user to change the resolution to get the most out of your application.

Disable the Excel X for Closing the Application

In the upper-right corner of the Excel window, there is an X button that can be used to shut down the application. The following API declarations work together to disable that X, preventing the user from using that method of closing down Excel:

> **NOTE** Don't forget to reset `XButtonEnabled` `True` to re-enable the X button.

```
Public Declare Function FindWindow Lib "user32" Alias "FindWindowA" _
    (ByVal lpClassName As String, ByVal lpWindowName As String) As Long
Public Declare Function GetSystemMenu Lib "user32" _
    (ByVal hWnd As Long, ByVal bRevert As Long) As Long
Public Declare Function DeleteMenu Lib "user32" (ByVal hMenu As Long, _
    ByVal nPosition As Long, ByVal wFlags As Long) As Long
Private Const SC_CLOSE As Long = &HF060

Public Sub XButtonEnabled(ByVal bEnabled As Boolean)
Dim hWndForm As Long
Dim hMenu As Long

hWndForm = FindWindow("XLMAIN", Application.Caption)
hMenu = GetSystemMenu(hWndForm, bEnabled)
DeleteMenu hMenu, SC_CLOSE, 0&

End Sub

Public Sub ExcelXButton()

XButtonEnabled False

End Sub
```

If you look carefully at these API declarations, you'll notice that the first call uses an alias, but the next two don't. If you don't want to use an alias, then the function or procedure name must be the same name used in the DLL. In that case, the function name is automatically removed when the function is copied into a VBA module.

After using the ExcelXButton macro, the X button in the top corner of the Excel workbook is actually grayed out as shown in Figure 22.5.

Figure 22.5
Disable the Excel X button to prevent the user from using that method to shut down the application.

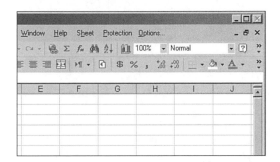

Disable the X for Closing a Userform

Just as the previous example disabled the X button of the Excel application, a slight modification disables the X button on a userform, forcing the user to use the Close button. When the form is initialized, the button is disabled. After the form is closed, the X button is reset to normal:

```
Private Declare Function FindWindow Lib "user32" Alias "FindWindowA" _
    (ByVal lpClassName As String, ByVal lpWindowName As String) As Long
Private Declare Function GetSystemMenu Lib "user32" (ByVal hWnd As Long, _
    ByVal bRevert As Long) As Long
Private Declare Function DeleteMenu Lib "user32" _
    (ByVal hMenu As Long, ByVal nPosition As Long, _
    ByVal wFlags As Long) As Long
Private Const SC_CLOSE As Long = &HF060

Private Sub UserForm_Initialize()
Dim hWndForm As Long
Dim hMenu As Long

hWndForm = FindWindow("ThunderDFrame", Me.Caption)   'XL2000
hMenu = GetSystemMenu(hWndForm, 0)
DeleteMenu hMenu, SC_CLOSE, 0&

End Sub
```

The DeleteMenu macro in the UserForm_Initialize procedure causes the X in the corner of the userform to be grayed out as shown in Figure 22.6. This forces the client to use your programmed Close button.

Figure 22.6
Disable the X button on a userform, forcing users to use the Close button to shut down the form properly and rendering them unable to bypass any code attached to the Close button.

Running Timer

You can use the NOW function to get the time, but what if you needed a running timer? A timer displaying the exact time as the seconds tick by? The following API declarations work together to provide that functionality. The timer is placed in cell A1 of Sheet1:

```
Public Declare Function SetTimer Lib "user32" _
    (ByVal hWnd As Long, ByVal nIDEvent As Long, _
    ByVal uElapse As Long, ByVal lpTimerFunc As Long) As Long
Public Declare Function KillTimer Lib "user32" _
    (ByVal hWnd As Long, ByVal nIDEvent As Long) As Long
Public Declare Function FindWindow Lib "user32" _
    Alias "FindWindowA" (ByVal lpClassName As String, _
    ByVal lpWindowName As String) As Long

Private lngTimerID As Long
Public datStartingTime As Date

Public Sub StartTimer()
lngTimerID = SetTimer(0, 1, 10, AddressOf RunTimer)
End Sub

Public Sub StopTimer()
Dim lRet As Long
lRet = KillTimer(0, lngTimerID)
End Sub

Private Sub RunTimer(ByVal hWnd As Long, _
    ByVal uint1 As Long, ByVal nEventId As Long, _
    ByVal dwParam As Long)
On Error Resume Next
Sheet1.Range("A1").Value = Now - datStartingTime
End Sub
```

Run the StartTimer macro to have the current date and time constantly updated in cell A1. In Figure 22.7, the cell has been formatted to show hours, minutes, and seconds.

Figure 22.7
A running timer can be added to the application to show the current time.

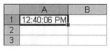

Clickable Links on Forms

The following API enables you to have clickable links on your userforms that will open up a new message or Web page:

```
Private Declare Function ShellExecute Lib "shell32.dll" _
    Alias "ShellExecuteA" (ByVal hWnd As Long, _
    ByVal lpOperation As String, ByVal lpFile As String, _
    ByVal lpParameters As String, ByVal lpDirectory As String, _
    ByVal nShowCmd As Long) As Long
Const SWNormal = 1

Private Sub lbl_Email_Click()
Dim lngRow As Long

ShellExecute 0&, "open", "mailto:" & lbl_Email.Caption, _
    vbNullString, vbNullString, SWNormal

End Sub

Private Sub lbl_Website_Click()
Dim lngRow As Long

ShellExecute 0&, "open", lbl_Website.Caption, _
    vbNullString, vbNullString, SWNormal

End Sub
```

The VBA code for `lbl_Email_Click` causes the client's default email program to open with an address filled in the To field as shown in Figure 22.8.

Figure 22.8
You can easily add the convenient functionality of clickable links on your userform with the right API declaration.

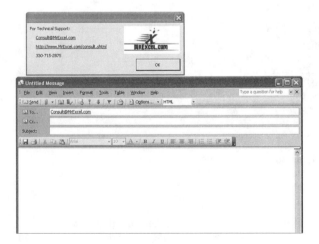

Playing Sounds

Ever wanted to play a sound to warn users or congratulate them? You could add a sound object to a sheet and call that, but it would be much easier just to use the following API declaration and specify the proper path to a sound file:

```
Public Declare Function PlayWavSound Lib "winmm.dll" _
    Alias "sndPlaySoundA" (ByVal LpszSoundName As String, _
    ByVal uFlags As Long) As Long

Public Sub PlaySound()
Dim SoundName As String

SoundName = "C:\WinNT\Media\Chimes.wav"
PlayWavSound SoundName, 0

End Sub
```

Retrieving a File Path

The following API enables you to create a custom file browser. The program example using the API customizes the function call to create a browser for a specific need—in this case, returning the file path of a user-selected file:

```
Type tagOPENFILENAME
    lStructSize As Long
    hwndOwner As Long
    hInstance As Long
    strFilter As String
    strCustomFilter As String
    nMaxCustFilter As Long
    nFilterIndex As Long
    strFile As String
    nMaxFile As Long
    strFileTitle As String
    nMaxFileTitle As Long
    strInitialDir As String
    strTitle As String
    Flags As Long
    nFileOffset As Integer
    nFileExtension As Integer
    strDefExt As String
    lCustData As Long
    lpfnHook As Long
    lpTemplateName As String
End Type

Declare Function aht_apiGetOpenFileName Lib "comdlg32.dll" _
    Alias "GetOpenFileNameA" (OFN As tagOPENFILENAME) As Boolean
Declare Function aht_apiGetSaveFileName Lib "comdlg32.dll" _
    Alias "GetSaveFileNameA" (OFN As tagOPENFILENAME) As Boolean
Declare Function CommDlgExtendedError Lib "comdlg32.dll" () As Long

Global Const ahtOFN_READONLY = &H1
Global Const ahtOFN_OVERWRITEPROMPT = &H2
Global Const ahtOFN_HIDEREADONLY = &H4
```

```
Global Const ahtOFN_NOCHANGEDIR = &H8
Global Const ahtOFN_SHOWHELP = &H10
Global Const ahtOFN_NOVALIDATE = &H100
Global Const ahtOFN_ALLOWMULTISELECT = &H200
Global Const ahtOFN_EXTENSIONDIFFERENT = &H400
Global Const ahtOFN_PATHMUSTEXIST = &H800
Global Const ahtOFN_FILEMUSTEXIST = &H1000
Global Const ahtOFN_CREATEPROMPT = &H2000
Global Const ahtOFN_SHAREAWARE = &H4000
Global Const ahtOFN_NOREADONLYRETURN = &H8000
Global Const ahtOFN_NOTESTFILECREATE = &H10000
Global Const ahtOFN_NONETWORKBUTTON = &H20000
Global Const ahtOFN_NOLONGNAMES = &H40000
Global Const ahtOFN_EXPLORER = &H80000
Global Const ahtOFN_NODEREFERENCELINKS = &H100000
Global Const ahtOFN_LONGNAMES = &H200000


Function ahtCommonFileOpenSave( _
            Optional ByRef Flags As Variant, _
            Optional ByVal InitialDir As Variant, _
            Optional ByVal Filter As Variant, _
            Optional ByVal FilterIndex As Variant, _
            Optional ByVal DefaultExt As Variant, _
            Optional ByVal FileName As Variant, _
            Optional ByVal DialogTitle As Variant, _
            Optional ByVal hwnd As Variant, _
            Optional ByVal OpenFile As Variant) As Variant

' This is the entry point you'll use to call the common
' file Open/Save As dialog. The parameters are listed
' below, and all are optional.
'
' In:
' Flags: one or more of the ahtOFN_* constants, OR'd together.
' InitialDir: the directory in which to first look
' Filter: a set of file filters
'    (Use AddFilterItem to set up Filters)
' FilterIndex: 1-based integer indicating which filter
' set to use, by default (1 if unspecified)
' DefaultExt: Extension to use if the user doesn't enter one.
' Only useful on file saves.
' FileName: Default value for the filename text box.
' DialogTitle: Title for the dialog.
' hWnd: parent window handle
' OpenFile: Boolean(True=Open File/False=Save As)
' Out:
' Return Value: Either Null or the selected filename

Dim OFN As tagOPENFILENAME
Dim strFileName As String
Dim strFileTitle As String
Dim fResult As Boolean

' Give the dialog a caption title.
If IsMissing(InitialDir) Then InitialDir = CurDir
If IsMissing(Filter) Then Filter = ""
```

```
If IsMissing(FilterIndex) Then FilterIndex = 1
If IsMissing(Flags) Then Flags = 0&
If IsMissing(DefaultExt) Then DefaultExt = ""
If IsMissing(FileName) Then FileName = ""
If IsMissing(DialogTitle) Then DialogTitle = ""
If IsMissing(OpenFile) Then OpenFile = True

' Allocate string space for the returned strings.
strFileName = Left(FileName & String(256, 0), 256)
strFileTitle = String(256, 0)

' Set up the data structure before you call the function
With OFN
    .lStructSize = Len(OFN)
    .strFilter = Filter
    .nFilterIndex = FilterIndex
    .strFile = strFileName
    .nMaxFile = Len(strFileName)
    .strFileTitle = strFileTitle
    .nMaxFileTitle = Len(strFileTitle)
    .strTitle = DialogTitle
    .Flags = Flags
    .strDefExt = DefaultExt
    .strInitialDir = InitialDir
    .hInstance = 0
    .lpfnHook = 0
    .strCustomFilter = String(255, 0)
    .nMaxCustFilter = 255
End With

' This passes the desired data structure to the
' Windows API, which will in turn displays
' the Open/Save As dialog.
If OpenFile Then
    fResult = aht_apiGetOpenFileName(OFN)
Else
    fResult = aht_apiGetSaveFileName(OFN)
End If

' The function call filled in the strFileTitle member
' of the structure. You have to write special code
' to retrieve that if you're interested.
If fResult Then
' You might care to check the Flags member of the
' structure to get information about the chosen file.
' In this example, if you bothered to pass a
' value for Flags, we'll fill it in with the outgoing
' Flags value.
    If Not IsMissing(Flags) Then Flags = OFN.Flags
        ahtCommonFileOpenSave = TrimNull(OFN.strFile)
```

```
        Else
            ahtCommonFileOpenSave = vbNullString
        End If

End Function

Function ahtAddFilterItem(strFilter As String, _
        strDescription As String, Optional varItem As Variant) As String
' Tack a new chunk onto the file filter.
' That is, take the old value, stick onto it the description,
' (like "Databases"), a null character, the skeleton
' (like "*.mdb;*.mda"), and a final null character.

If IsMissing(varItem) Then varItem = "*.*"
ahtAddFilterItem = strFilter & strDescription & _
    vbNullChar & varItem & vbNullChar

End Function

Private Function TrimNull(ByVal strItem As String) As String
Dim intPos As Integer

intPos = InStr(strItem, vbNullChar)

If intPos > 0 Then
    TrimNull = Left(strItem, intPos - 1)
Else
    TrimNull = strItem
End If

End Function
```

This is the actual program created to use this information:

```
Function GetFileName(strPath As String)
Dim strFilter As String
Dim lngFlags As Long

strFilter = ahtAddFilterItem(strFilter, "Excel Files (*.xls)")
GetFileName = ahtCommonFileOpenSave(InitialDir:=strPath, _
    Filter:=strFilter, FilterIndex:=3, Flags:=lngFlags, _
    DialogTitle:="Please select file to import")

End Function
```

Then create the userform. The following code is attached to the Browse button as shown in Figure 22.9. Note that the function specifies the starting directory.

```
Private Sub cmdBrowse_Click()

txtFile = GetFileName("c:\")

End Sub
```

22

Figure 22.9
Create a custom browse window to return the file path of a user-selected file. This can be used to ensure the user doesn't select the wrong file for import.

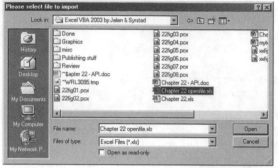

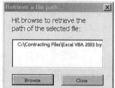

Finding More API Declarations

There are many more API declarations out there than the ones we have shown—we've barely scratched the surface of the wealth of procedures and functions available. Microsoft has many tools available to help you create your own APIs (search Platform SDK), but there are also many programmers who have developed declarations to share, such as Ivan F. Moala at `http://xcelfiles.homestead.com/APIIndex.html`. He has created a site full of not only examples, but instruction as well.

Next Steps

In Chapter 23, "Handling Errors," you will learn about error handling. In a perfect world, you want to be able to hand your applications off to a co-worker, leave for vacation, and not have to worry about an unhandled error appearing while you are on the beach. Chapter 23 discusses how to handle obvious and not-so-obvious errors.

Handling Errors

Errors are bound to happen. You can test and test your code, but after a report is put into daily production and used for hundreds of days, something unexpected will eventually happen. Your goal should be to try to head off obscure errors as you code. Always be thinking of what unexpected things could someday happen that would make your code not work.

What Happens When an Error Occurs

If VBA encounters an error and you have no error checking code in place, then the program stops and you (or your client) will be presented with the `Continue, End, Debug, Help` error message as shown in Figure 23.1.

When presented with the choice to End or Debug, you should click Debug. The Visual Basic Editor highlights the line that caused the error in yellow. You can hover the mouse pointer over any variable to see the current value of the variable. This provides a lot of information about what could have caused the error (see Figure 23.2).

Excel is notorious for returning errors that are not very meaningful. For example, dozens of situations can cause a 1004 error. Being able to see the offending line highlighted in yellow, plus being able to examine the current value of any variables, will help you to discover the real cause of an error.

After examining the line in error, click the Reset button to stop execution of the macro. The Reset button is the square button under the Run item in the main menu, as shown in Figure 23.3.

23

23

Figure 23.1
An unhandled error in an unprotected module presents you with a choice to End or Debug.

Figure 23.2
After clicking debug, the macro is in break mode. You can hover the mouse cursor over a variable and after a few seconds, the current value of the variable is shown.

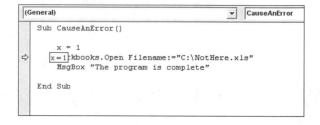

Figure 23.3
The Reset button looks like the Stop button in the set of three buttons that resemble a VCR control panel.

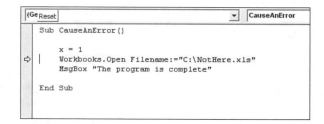

CAUTION

If you fail to click Reset to end the macro, and then attempt to run another macro, you are presented with the annoying error message shown in Figure 23.4. The message is annoying because you start in Excel, when this message window is displayed, the screen automatically switched to display the VB Editor. However, immediately after you click OK, you are returned to the Excel user interface instead of being left in the VB Editor. For as often as this message happens, it would be much more convenient if you could be returned to the VB Editor after clicking OK.

Debug Error Inside Userform Code Is Misleading

The line highlighted as the error after you click Debug can be misleading in one situation. Let's say that you call a macro. This macro then displays a userform. Somewhere in the userform code, an error occurs. When you click Debug, instead of showing the problem inside the userform code, Excel highlights the line in the original macro that displayed the userform. Follow these steps to find the real error.

Figure 23.4
This message appears if you forget to click Reset to end a debug session and then attempt to run another macro.

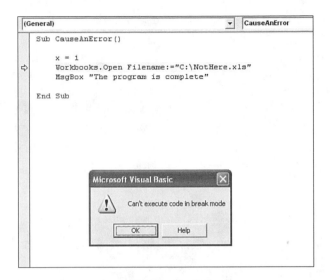

```
(General)                                    ▼   CauseAnError

    Sub CauseAnError()

        x = 1
⇨       Workbooks.Open Filename:="C:\NotHere.xls"
        MsgBox "The program is complete"

    End Sub
```

Microsoft Visual Basic

⚠ Can't execute code in break mode

OK   Help

1. After an error message box is shown as in Figure 23.5, press the Debug button.

Figure 23.5
Choose Debug in response to this error 13.

Microsoft Visual Basic

Run-time error '13':

Type mismatch

Continue   End   Debug   Help

2. You will see that the error allegedly occurred on a line that shows a userform, as shown in Figure 23.6. Because you've read this chapter, you will know that this is not the line in error.

Figure 23.6
`frmChoose.Show` is indicated as the line in error.

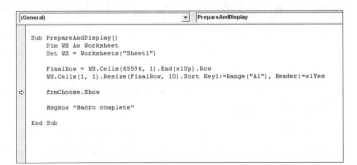

```
(General)                                    ▼   PrepareAndDisplay

    Sub PrepareAndDisplay()
        Dim WS As Worksheet
        Set WS = Worksheets("Sheet1")

        FinalRow = WS.Cells(65536, 1).End(xlUp).Row
        WS.Cells(1, 1).Resize(FinalRow, 10).Sort Key1:=Range("A1"), Header:=xlYes

⇨       frmChoose.Show

        MsgBox "Macro complete"

    End Sub
```

3. Press F8 to execute the Show method. Instead of getting an error, you are taken into the Userform_Initialize procedure.

4. Keep pressing F8 until you get the error message again. You must stay alert. As soon as you encounter the error, the error message box is displayed. Click Debug and you are returned to the userform.Show line. It is particularly difficult to follow the code when the error occurs on the other side of a long loop, as shown in Figure 23.7.

Figure 23.7
With 25 items to add to the list box, you must hit F8 51 times to get through this 3-line loop.

```
Private Sub UserForm_Initialize()
    Dim WS As Worksheet
    Set WS = Worksheets("Sheet1")
    FinalRow = WS.Cells(65536, 1).End(xlUp).Row
    For i = 2 To FinalRow
        Me.ListBox1.AddItem Cells(i, 1)
    Next i

    Me.ListBox1(0).Selected = True

    Me.Label1.Caption = "Select from " & FinalRow - 1 & " records."
End Sub
```

Imagine trying to step through the code in Figure 23.7. You carefully hit F8 five times with no problems through the first pass of the loop. Because the problem could be in future iterations through the loop, you continue to press F8. If there are 25 items to add to the list box, 48 more presses of F8 are required to get through the loop safely. Each time before pressing F8, you should mentally note that you are about to run some specific line.

At the point shown in Figure 23.7, the next press of the F8 key displays the error and returns you to the frmChoose.Show line back in Module1.

This is an annoying situation. When you click Debug and see that the line in error is a line that displays a userform, you need to start pressing the F8 key to step into the userform code until you get the error. Invariably, I get incredibly bored pressing F8 a million times and forget to pay attention to which line caused the error. As soon as the error happens, I am thrown back to the Debug message, which returns me to the frmChoose.Show line of code.

Basic Error Handling with the On Error GoTo Syntax

The basic error handling option is to tell VBA that in the case of an error, you want to have code branch to a specific area of the macro. In this area, you might have special code that alerts users of the problem and enables them to react.

A typical scenario is to add the error handling routine at the end of the macro. To set up an error handler, follow these steps:

1. After the last code line of the macro, insert the code line Exit Sub. This makes sure that the execution of the macro does not continue into the error handler.

2. After the Exit Sub line, add a label. A label is a name followed by a colon. For example, you might create a label called MyErrorHandler:.

3. Write the code to handle the error. If you want to return control of the macro to the line after the one that caused the error, use the statement `Resume Next`.

In your macro, just before the line that may likely cause the error, add a line reading `On Error GoTo MyErrorHandler`. Note that in this line, you do not include the colon after the label name.

Immediately after the line of code that you suspect will cause the error, add code to turn off the special error handler. This is very non-intuitive and tends to confuse people. The code to cancel any special error handling is `On Error Goto 0`. There is no label named zero. This line is a fictitious line that instructs Excel to go back to the normal state of displaying the End/Debug error message when an error is encountered. Do you see why it is important to cancel the error handling? In the following code, we've written a special error handler to handle the necessary action if the file has been moved or is missing. We definitely do not want this error handler invoked for another error later in the macro, such as a division by zero.

```
Sub HandleAnError()
    Dim MyFile as Variant
    ' Set up a special error handler
    On Error GoTo FileNotThere
    Workbooks.Open Filename:="C:\NotHere.xls"
    ' If we get here, cancel the special error handler
    On Error GoTo 0
    MsgBox "The program is complete"

    ' The macro is done. Use Exit sub, otherwise the macro
    ' execution WILL continue into the error handler
    Exit Sub

    ' Set up a name for the Error handler
FileNotThere:
    MyPrompt = "There was an error opening the file. It is possible the "
    MyPrompt = MyPrompt & " file has been moved. Click OK to browse for the "
    MyPrompt = MyPrompt & "file, or click Cancel to end the program"
    Ans = MsgBox(Prompt:=MyPrompt, VbMsgBoxStyle:=vbOKCancel)
    If Ans = vbCancel Then Exit Sub

    ' The client clicked OK. Let him browse for the file
    MyFile = Application.GetOpenFilename
    If MyFile = False Then Exit Sub

    ' What if the 2nd file is corrupt? We don't want to recursively throw
    ' the client back into this error handler. Just stop the program
    On Error GoTo 0
    Workbooks.Open MyFile
    ' If we get here, then return the macro execution back to the original
    ' section of the macro, to the line after the one that caused the error.
    Resume Next


End Sub
```

Multiple Error Handlers

It is possible to have more than one error handler at the end of a macro. Make sure that each error handler ends with either `Resume Next` or `Exit Sub` so that macro execution does not accidentally move into the next error handler.

Generic Error Handlers

Some developers like to direct any error to a generic error handler. They make use of the `Err` object. This object has properties for Error number and description. You can offer this information to the client and prevent them from getting a debug message:

```
On Error GoTo HandleAny
Sheets(9).Select

Exit Sub

HandleAny:
    Msg = "We encountered " & Err.Number & " - " & Err.Description
    MsgBox Msg
    Exit Sub
```

Handling Errors by Choosing to Ignore Them

Some errors can simply be ignored. Let's say that you are going to use the HTML Creator macro from Chapter 14, "Reading from and Writing to the Web." Your code erases any existing index.html file from a folder before writing out the next file.

The `Kill (FileName)` statement returns an error if `FileName` does not exist. Is this something you need to worry about? You are trying to delete the file. Who cares if someone already deleted it before running the macro? In this case, you should tell Excel to simply skip over the offending line and resume macro execution with the next line. The code to do this is `On Error Resume Next`:

```
Sub WriteHTML()
    MyFile = "C:\Index.html"
    On Error Resume Next
    Kill (MyFile)
    On Error Goto 0
    Open MyFile for Output as #1
    ' etc…
End Sub
```

You need to be careful with `On Error Resume Next`. It can be used selectively in situations where you know that the error can be ignored. You should immediately return error checking to normal after the line that might cause an error with `On Error GoTo 0`.

If you attempt to have `On Error Resume Next` skip an error that cannot be skipped, the macro immediately steps out of the current macro. If you have a situation where MacroA calls MacroB and MacroB encounters a non-skippable error, then the program jumps out of MacroB and continues with the next line in MacroA. This is rarely a good thing.

Page Setup Problems Can Often Be Ignored

Record a macro and perform a page setup. Even if you change only one item in the Page Setup dialog, the macro recorder records two dozen settings for you. These settings notoriously differ from printer to printer. For example, if you record the PageSetup on a system with a color printer, it may record a setting for `.BlackAndWhite = True`. This setting will fail on another system where the printer doesn't offer the choice. Your printer may offer a `.PrintQuality = 600` setting. If the client's printer offers only 300 resolution, then this code will fail. Surround the entire PageSetup with `On Error Resume Next` to ensure that most settings happen but the trivial ones that fail will not cause a runtime error:

```
On Error Resume Next
With ActiveSheet.PageSetup
    .PrintTitleRows = ""
    .PrintTitleColumns = ""
End With
ActiveSheet.PageSetup.PrintArea = "$A$1:$L$27"
With ActiveSheet.PageSetup
    .LeftHeader = ""
    .CenterHeader = ""
    .RightHeader = ""
    .LeftFooter = ""
    .CenterFooter = ""
    .RightFooter = ""
    .LeftMargin = Application.InchesToPoints(0.25)
    .RightMargin = Application.InchesToPoints(0.25)
    .TopMargin = Application.InchesToPoints(0.75)
    .BottomMargin = Application.InchesToPoints(0.5)
    .HeaderMargin = Application.InchesToPoints(0.5)
    .FooterMargin = Application.InchesToPoints(0.5)
    .PrintHeadings = False
    .PrintGridlines = False
    .PrintComments = xlPrintNoComments
    .PrintQuality = 300
    .CenterHorizontally = False
    .CenterVertically = False
    .Orientation = xlLandscape
    .Draft = False
    .PaperSize = xlPaperLetter
    .FirstPageNumber = xlAutomatic
    .Order = xlDownThenOver
    .BlackAndWhite = False
    .Zoom = False
    .FitToPagesWide = 1
    .FitToPagesTall = False
    .PrintErrors = xlPrintErrorsDisplayed
End With
On Error GoTo 0
```

Suppressing Excel Warnings

Some messages appear even if you have set Excel to ignore errors. Try to delete a worksheet using code, and you will still get the message `Data may exist in the sheet(s) selected for deletion. To permanently delete the data, click Delete`. This is annoying. We don't want our clients to have to answer this warning. It turns out that this is not an error, but an alert. To suppress all alerts and force Excel to take the default action, use `Application.DisplayAlerts = False`:

```
Sub DeleteSheet()
    Application.DisplayAlerts = False
    Worksheets("Sheet2").Delete
    Application.DisplayAlerts = True
End Sub
```

Encountering Errors on Purpose

Because programmers hate errors, this concept might seem counter-intuitive, but errors are not always bad. Sometimes it is faster to simply encounter an error.

Let's say you wanted to find out if the active workbook contains a worksheet named Data. To find this out without causing an error, you could code this:

```
DataFound = False
For each ws in ActiveWorkbook.Worksheets
    If ws.Name = "Data" then
    DataFound = True
    Exit For
    End if
Next ws
If not DataFound then Sheets.Add.Name = "Data"
```

This takes eight lines of code. If your workbook had 128 worksheets, the program would loop through 128 times before deciding that the data worksheet is missing.

The alternative is to simply try to reference the data worksheet. If you have error checking set to resume next, the code runs, and the `Err` object is assigned a number other than 0:

```
On Error Resume Next
X = Worksheets("Data").Name
If not Err.Number = 0 then Sheets.Add.Name = "Data"
On Error GoTo 0
```

This code runs much faster. Errors usually make me cringe, but in this case, and many other cases, they are perfectly acceptable.

Train Your Clients

You might be developing code for a client across the globe or for the administrative assistant so that he can run the code while you are on vacation. In either instance, you might find yourself remotely trying to debug code while you are on the telephone with the client.

It is important to train the clients about the difference between an error and a simple MsgBox. A MsgBox is a planned message. It still appears out of the blue with a beep. Teach your users that error messages are bad but not everything that pops up is an error message. I had a client keep reporting to her boss that she was getting an error from my program. In reality, she was getting an informational MsgBox. Both Debug errors and Msgbox messages beep at the user.

When clients get Debug errors, train them to call you while the Debug message is still on the screen. You can then get the error number and the description, and ask them to click Debug and tell you the module name, the procedure name, and the line in yellow. Armed with this information, you can usually figure out what is going on. Without this information, it is very unlikely that you'll be able to figure out the problem. Getting a call from a client saying that there was a 1004 error is of little help—1004 is a catchall error that can mean any number of things.

Errors While Developing Versus Errors Months Later

When you have just written code and are running it for the first time, you expect errors. In fact, you may decide to step through code line by line to watch the progress of the code the first time through.

It is another thing to have a program that has been running daily in production suddenly stop working with an error. This seems perplexing; the code has been working for months. Why did it suddenly stop working today?

It is easy to blame this on the client, but when you get right down to it, it is really the fault of developers for not considering the possibilities.

The following sections describe a couple of common problems that can strike an application months later.

Runtime Error 9: Subscript out of Range

You've set up an application for the client. You have provided a Menu worksheet where you store some settings. One day, the client reports the error message shown in Figure 23.8.

Figure 23.8
The Runtime Error 9 is often caused when you expect a worksheet to be there and it has been deleted or renamed by the client.

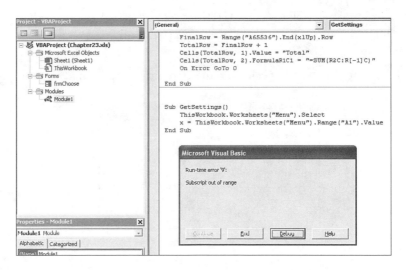

Your code expected there to be a worksheet named Menu. For some reason, the client either accidentally deleted the worksheet or renamed it. As soon as you tried to select the sheet, you received an error:

```
Sub GetSettings()
    ThisWorkbook.Worksheets("Menu").Select
    x = Range("A1").Value
End Sub
```

This is a classic situation where you can't believe the client would do something so crazy. After you've been burned by this one a few times, you might go to these lengths to prevent an unhandled Debug error:

```
Sub GetSettings()
    On Error Resume Next
    x = ThisWorkbook.Worksheets("Menu").Name
    If Not Err.Number = 0 Then
        MsgBox "Expected to find a Menu worksheet, but it is missing"
        Exit Sub
    End If
    On Error GoTo 0

    ThisWorkbook.Worksheets("Menu").Select
    x = Range("A1").Value
End Sub
```

RunTime Error 1004: Method 'Range' of Object '_Global' Failed

You have code that imports a text file each day. You expect the text file to end with a total row. After importing the text, you want to convert all the detail rows to italics.

The following code works fine for months:

```
Sub SetReportInItalics()
    TotalRow = Range("A65536").End(xlUp).Row
    FinalRow = TotalRow - 1
    Range("A1:A" & FinalRow).Font.Italic = True
End Sub
```

Then, one day the client calls with the error message shown in Figure 23.9.

Figure 23.9
The Runtime Error 1004 can be caused by a myriad of things.

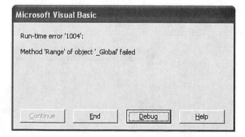

Upon examination of the code, you discover that something bizarre went wrong when the text file was FTP'ed to the client that day. The text file ended up as an empty file. Because the worksheet was empty, `TotalRow` was determined to be Row 1. When we assumed the last detail row was `TotalRow - 1`, this set our code up to attempt to format Row 0, which clearly does not exist.

After this episode, you will find yourself writing code that preemptively looks for this situation:

```
Sub SetReportInItalics()
    TotalRow = Range("A65536").End(xlUp).Row
    FinalRow = TotalRow - 1
    If FinalRow > 0 Then
        Range("A1:A" & FinalRow).Font.Italic = True
    Else
        MsgBox "It appears the file is empty today. Check the FTP process"
    End If
End Sub
```

23

The Ills of Protecting Code

It is possible to lock a VBA project so that it cannot be viewed. I do not recommend this at all. When code is protected and an error is encountered, your user is presented with an error message, but no opportunity to debug. The Debug button is there, but it is grayed out. This is useless in helping you discover the problem.

Further, the Excel VBA protection scheme is horribly easy to break. Programmers in Estonia offer $40 software that lets you unlock any project. So understand that office VBA code is not secure and get over it.

Case Study: Password Cracking

The password hacking schemes were very easy in Excel 97 and Excel 2000. The password cracking software could immediately locate the actual password in the VBA project and report it to the software user.

Then, in Excel 2002, Microsoft offered a brilliant protection scheme that temporarily appeared to foil the password cracking utilities. The password was tightly encrypted. For several months after the release of Excel 2002, password cracking programs would have to try brute force combinations. The software would be able to crack a password like "blue" in 10 minutes. But given a 24-character password like `*A6%kJJ542(9$GgU44#2drt8`, the program would take 20 hours to find the password. This was a fun annoyance to foist upon other VBA programmers who would potentially break into your code.

However, the next version of the password cracking software was able to break a 24-character password in Excel 2002 in about two seconds. When I tested my 24-character password-protected project, the password utility quickly told me that my password was XVII. I thought this was certainly wrong, but after testing, I found the project had a new password of

23

XVII. Yes, this latest version of the software resorted to another approach. Instead of using brute force to crack the password, it simply wrote a new random four-character password to the project and saved the file.

Now, this causes an embarrassing problem for whoever cracked the password. The developer has a sign on his wall reminding him the password is *A6%kJJ542(9$GgU44#2drt8. But, in the cracked version of the file, the password is now XVII. If there is a problem with the cracked file and it is sent back to the developer, the developer can't open the file anymore. The only person getting anything from this is the programmer in Estonia who wrote the cracking software.

There are not enough Excel VBA developers in the world. There are more projects than programmers right now. In my circle of developer friends, we all acknowledge that business prospects slip through the cracks because we are too busy with other customers.

So the situation of a newbie developer is not uncommon. He does an adequate job of writing code for a customer and then locks the VBA project.

The customer needs some changes. The original developer does the work. A few weeks later, some more changes and the developer delivers. A month later, the customer needs more work. Either the developer is busy with other projects or he has under-priced these maintenance jobs and has more lucrative work. The client tries to contact the programmer a few times, then, realizing he needs to get the project fixed, calls another developer—you!

You get the code. It is protected. You break the password and see who wrote the code. This is a tough call. You have no interest in stealing the guy's customer. You would prefer to do this one job and then have the customer return to the original developer. However, because of the password hacking, you've now created a situation where the two developers have a different password. Your only choice is to remove the password entirely.

More Problems with Passwords

The Excel 2002 password scheme is incompatible with Excel 97. If you protected code in Excel 2002, you cannot unlock the project in Excel 97. A lot of people are still using Excel 97 out there. As your application is given to more employees in a company, you invariably find one employee with Excel 97. Of course, that user comes up with some run time error. However, if you've locked the project in Excel 2002, you cannot unlock the project in Excel 97, and therefore cannot debug in Excel 97.

Bottom line: Locking code causes more trouble than it is worth.

Errors Caused by Different Versions

Microsoft does improve VBA in every version of Excel. Pivot table creation was drastically improved between Excel 97 and Excel 2000. Certain chart features were improved between Excel 97 and Excel 2000.

The TrailingMinusNumbers parameter is new in Excel 2002. If you write code in Excel 2002 or Excel 2003 and then send the code to a client with Excel 2000, that user gets a compile error as soon as she tries to run any code in the same module as the offending code. Consider this application with two modules.

Module1 has macros ProcA, ProcB, and ProcC. Module2 has macros ProcD and ProcE. It happens that ProcE has an `ImportText` method with the `TrailingMinusNumbers` parameter.

The client can run ProcA and ProcB on the Excel 2000 machine without problem. As soon as she tries to run ProcD, she will get a compile error reported in ProcD because Excel tries to compile all of Module2 as soon as she tries to run code in that module. This can be incredibly misleading: An error being reported when the client runs ProcD is actually caused by an error in ProcE.

One solution is to have access to every supported version of Excel, plus Excel 97, and test the code in all versions. Note that Excel 97 SR-2 was far more stable than the initial releases of Excel 97. A lot of clients are hanging on to Excel 97, but it is frustrating when you find someone who doesn't have the stable service release.

Macintosh users will believe that their version of Excel is the same as the Excel for Windows. Microsoft promised compatibility of files, but that promise ends in the Excel user interface. VBA code is *not* compatible between Windows and the Mac. It is close, but annoyingly different. Certainly, anything that you do with the Windows API is not going to work on a Mac.

Next Steps

This chapter discussed how to make your code more bullet-proof for your clients. In Chapter 24, "Using Custom Menus to Run Macros," you will learn how to design custom menus and toolbars to allow your clients to enjoy a professional user interface.

Using Custom Menus to Run Macros

24

So far, you've learned how to do just about everything with Excel VBA. You now need a way to allow your client to run your macros when they wish.

I definitely prefer giving the client a customized menu or a customized toolbar. There is nothing like having a user open his application and to see his name in the Excel menu bar. I will show you how to build fully customized menus or toolbars for your application.

There are other alternatives for running a macro. At the end of the chapter, you will learn how to use a keyboard shortcut, attach a macro to a command button, and attach a macro to an ActiveX control.

Creating a Custom Menu

A custom menu adds a professional look to your application. If you name the toolbar after the client's company, they will be always aware that their application has been custom designed for them. The custom menu becomes a convenient place for them to access all the routines you have provided. Figure 24.1 shows a custom menu for the XYZ company. The menu provides keyboard short-cuts and fly-out submenus.

Figure 24.1
A custom menu provides a convenient place for clients to find all their applications.

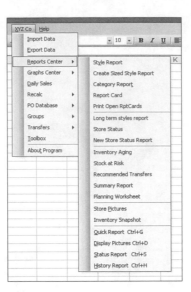

Deleting and Creating the Custom Menu

Excel's main menu bar is known in VBA as `Application.CommandBars(1)`. This menu bar typically has popup controls named File, Edit, View, and so on. Use the `Add` method to add a new popup menu item to the main menu. When adding the control, you need to specify the name of the menu item and its location.

The name of the menu item should be the text that you want to appear on the menu bar. If you specify that the name is "XYZ Co," then this appears on the menu bar. However, most of Excel's menu bars have a keyboard shortcut. For example, pressing Alt+V brings up the View menu. You can tell this because the V in View is underlined. It is easy to assign a keyboard shortcut to your custom menu. Simply put an ampersand before the letter you want to use as a keyboard shortcut. Entering **&XYZ Co** causes the X to be underlined on the Excel menu bar.

It is important to remember that the keyboard shortcuts for D, E, F, H, I, O, T, V, W are already taken by the regular Excel menu bar. You can assign two menu items the same shortcut without causing an error, but neither shortcut will work.

By default, Excel has 10 menu items: the XL icon, then File, Edit, View, Insert, Format, Tools, Data, Window, and Help. Indicating that the new menu item should appear before the tenth menu item puts the custom menu before the Help menu. In Windows, it is possible to put your custom menu item before the eleventh item, which puts the custom menu after Help. The Macintosh people feel so adamant that Help must be the last menu item that attempting to add a custom menu to the right of Help returns an error on the Macintosh.

You should always create two menu procedures. One menu procedure creates the menu bar. This can be called at `Workbook_Open`, `Workbook_Activate`, or `Worksheet_Activate`. You should also have a `DeleteToolbar` procedure that is called at `Workbook_BeforeClose`.

The CreateToolbar macro should call DeleteToolbar first to remove any stray copy of the menu that might still exist.

The following code shows the basic structure of the CreateToolbar and DeleteToolbar macros. The object variable `MenuObject` is defined as a `CommandBarPopup`. The code adds a control to the main Excel Menu bar, places it before the Help menu item, and gives it a label of XYZ Co:

```
Sub DeleteMenu()
    'This sub should be executed when the workbook is closed
    On Error Resume Next
    Application.CommandBars(1).Controls("&XYZ Co").Delete
    On Error GoTo 0
End Sub

Sub CreateMenu()
    Dim MenuObject As CommandBarPopup
    Dim MenuItem As Object

    ' Make sure the menus aren't duplicated
    Call DeleteMenu

    Set MenuObject = Application.CommandBars(1). _
        Controls.Add(Type:=msoControlPopup, _
        Before:=10, temporary:=True)
    MenuObject.Caption = "&XYZ Co"

    Set MenuItem = MenuObject.Controls.Add(Type:=msoControlButton)
    MenuItem.OnAction = "ImportData"
    MenuItem.Caption = "&Import Data"
End Sub
```

Adding a Single Menu Item

After the `MenuObject` is defined, you add items to the menu by using `MenuObject.Controls.Add` to add a command control of the type `msoControlButton`. The menu item needs to have a `Caption` that displays on the menu bar, and it has to have an `OnAction` property. The `OnAction` property specifies the name of the macro that is executed when the client selects this menu item.

To add several single menu items, repeatedly add new controls to the `MenuObject`. The following code creates an XYZ menu with four items, as shown in Figure 24.2:

```
Sub CreateSimpleMenu()
    Dim MenuObject As CommandBarPopup
    Dim MenuItem As Object

    ' Make sure the menus aren't duplicated
    Call DeleteMenu
```

```
        Set MenuObject = Application.CommandBars(1). _
            Controls.Add(Type:=msoControlPopup, _
            Before:=10, temporary:=True)
        MenuObject.Caption = "&XYZ Co"

        Set MenuItem = MenuObject.Controls.Add(Type:=msoControlButton)
        MenuItem.OnAction = "ImportData"
        MenuItem.Caption = "&Import Data"

        Set MenuItem = MenuObject.Controls.Add(Type:=msoControlButton)
        MenuItem.OnAction = "ExportData"
        MenuItem.Caption = "&Export Data"

        Set MenuItem = MenuObject.Controls.Add(Type:=msoControlButton)
        MenuItem.OnAction = "ProduceReport"
        MenuItem.Caption = "&Report"

        Set MenuItem = MenuObject.Controls.Add(Type:=msoControlButton)
        MenuItem.OnAction = "AboutMe"
        MenuItem.Caption = "Abou&t Program"
    End Sub
```

Figure 24.2
This simple menu has
four items.

Breaking Items into Groups

When you get a menu with several items, it may help to break them into logical groups. To
add a line between a set of menu items, you go to the first menu item below the line and
specify that the BeginGroup property for this item is True. The following code creates a
menu with a group line between the third and fourth menu item, as shown in Figure 24.3:

```
Sub CreateGroupedMenu()
    Dim MenuObject As CommandBarPopup
    Dim MenuItem As Object

  ' Make sure the menus aren't duplicated
    Call DeleteMenu

    Set MenuObject = Application.CommandBars(1). _
        Controls.Add(Type:=msoControlPopup, _
        Before:=10, temporary:=True)
    MenuObject.Caption = "&XYZ Co"

    Set MenuItem = MenuObject.Controls.Add(Type:=msoControlButton)
    MenuItem.OnAction = "ImportData"
    MenuItem.Caption = "&Import Data"

    Set MenuItem = MenuObject.Controls.Add(Type:=msoControlButton)
    MenuItem.OnAction = "ExportData"
    MenuItem.Caption = "&Export Data"
```

```
        Set MenuItem = MenuObject.Controls.Add(Type:=msoControlButton)
        MenuItem.OnAction = "ProduceReport"
        MenuItem.Caption = "&Report"

        Set MenuItem = MenuObject.Controls.Add(Type:=msoControlButton)
        MenuItem.OnAction = "AboutMe"
        MenuItem.Caption = "Abou&t Program"
        MenuItem.BeginGroup = True
    End Sub
```

Figure 24.3

Use the BeginGroup property to add horizontal bars between groups of menu items. The About item has its BeginGroup property set to True.

Adding a Fly-out Menu

You can reasonably fit 12 items on a typical menu. When you get beyond that number, it makes sense to group several menu items as subitems under a single menu heading. In Figure 24.1, the Reports Center menu item leads to a fly-out menu with many reports.

This is relatively simple to set up. The Reports Center menu item is a control of type msoControlPopup. After this is defined, then you can define many submenu items to the Reports Center menu item.

You define menu items in order, setting up the Report Center menu item, then the submenu items for Reports, then the Graph Center menu item, then the submenu items for Graphs, and so on. The following code produces the menu shown in Figure 24.4:

```
Sub CreateFullMenu()
    Dim MenuObject As CommandBarPopup
    Dim MenuItem As Object
    Dim SubMenuItem As Object

  ' Make sure the menus aren't duplicated
    Call DeleteMenu

    Set MenuObject = Application.CommandBars(1). _
        Controls.Add(Type:=msoControlPopup, _
        Before:=10, temporary:=True)
    MenuObject.Caption = "&XYZ Co"

    Set MenuItem = MenuObject.Controls.Add(Type:=msoControlButton)
    MenuItem.OnAction = "ImportData"
    MenuItem.Caption = "&Import Data"

    Set MenuItem = MenuObject.Controls.Add(Type:=msoControlButton)
    MenuItem.OnAction = "ExportData"
    MenuItem.Caption = "&Export Data"
```

```
    Set MenuItem = MenuObject.Controls.Add(Type:=msoControlPopup)
    MenuItem.Caption = "&Reports Center"
    MenuItem.BeginGroup = True

        Set SubMenuItem = MenuItem.Controls.Add(Type:=msoControlButton)
        SubMenuItem.OnAction = "StyleRptNew"
        SubMenuItem.Caption = "St&yle Report"

        Set SubMenuItem = MenuItem.Controls.Add(Type:=msoControlButton)
        SubMenuItem.OnAction = "CategoryRptNew"
        SubMenuItem.Caption = "Category Repor&t"

        Set SubMenuItem = MenuItem.Controls.Add(Type:=msoControlButton)
        SubMenuItem.OnAction = "ReportCard"
        SubMenuItem.Caption = "Report Card"

        Set SubMenuItem = MenuItem.Controls.Add(Type:=msoControlButton)
        SubMenuItem.OnAction = "OverRpt"
        SubMenuItem.Caption = "Long term styles report"
        SubMenuItem.BeginGroup = True

        Set SubMenuItem = MenuItem.Controls.Add(Type:=msoControlButton)
        SubMenuItem.OnAction = "CreateReportCard"
        SubMenuItem.Caption = "Store Status"

        Set SubMenuItem = MenuItem.Controls.Add(Type:=msoControlButton)
        SubMenuItem.OnAction = "InventoryAgingReportNew"
        SubMenuItem.Caption = "Inventory Aging"
        SubMenuItem.BeginGroup = True

        Set SubMenuItem = MenuItem.Controls.Add(Type:=msoControlButton)
        SubMenuItem.OnAction = "ShowStockReport"
        SubMenuItem.Caption = "Stock at Risk"

        Set SubMenuItem = MenuItem.Controls.Add(Type:=msoControlButton)
        SubMenuItem.OnAction = "ShowRecTransfer"
        SubMenuItem.Caption = "Recommended Transfers"

        Set SubMenuItem = MenuItem.Controls.Add(Type:=msoControlButton)
        SubMenuItem.OnAction = "ShowSummaryNew"
        SubMenuItem.Caption = "Summary Report"

    Set MenuItem = MenuObject.Controls.Add(Type:=msoControlPopup)
    MenuItem.Caption = "Graphs Center"

        Set SubMenuItem = MenuItem.Controls.Add(Type:=msoControlButton)
        SubMenuItem.OnAction = "GraphOne"
        SubMenuItem.Caption = "&Sales Graph"

        Set SubMenuItem = MenuItem.Controls.Add(Type:=msoControlButton)
        SubMenuItem.OnAction = "GraphTwo"
        SubMenuItem.Caption = "&Inventory Graph"

    Set MenuItem = MenuObject.Controls.Add(Type:=msoControlButton)
    MenuItem.OnAction = "AboutMe"
    MenuItem.Caption = "Abou&t Program"
    MenuItem.BeginGroup = True
End Sub
```

Figure 24.4
The Reports Center menu item is defined as a popup rather than a button. It leads to additional menu items. You can create several levels of popup menus.

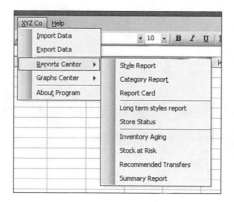

Creating a Custom Toolbar

Another professional touch is to add a custom toolbar to the application. The toolbar in Figure 24.5 has a variety of controls to allow the client to access features quickly.

Figure 24.5
This custom toolbar has four controls. A control can contain just a caption, an icon and a caption, or just an icon. Use `ToolTipText` to assist the client in understanding each control.

Deleting and Creating the Toolbar

As with a custom menu, you should have a routine to create the toolbar and to delete the toolbar. You always want to make sure that the toolbar is deleted when you close your application.

This method always creates a new toolbar on the fly. Older versions of Excel offered a method for permanently attaching a toolbar to a workbook. Avoid attaching menu bars to the application. It creates numerous headaches when you want to change the toolbar later.

To create the toolbar, add a `CommandBar`. You have to give the toolbar a name and a position:

```
Sub DeleteToolbar()
    On Error Resume Next
    CommandBars("XYZ").Delete
    On Error GoTo 0
End Sub

Sub CreateToolbar()
    Dim TBar As CommandBar
    Dim NewDD As CommandBarControl
    Dim NewBtn as CommandBarButton
```

```
    ' delete any old copy of the Toolbar
    DeleteToolbar

    ' Define the toolbar
    Set TBar = CommandBars.Add
    With TBar
        .Name = "XYZ"
        .Visible = True
        .Position = msoBarFloating
    End With

    Set NewBtn = TBar.Controls.Add(Type:=msoControlButton)
    With NewBtn
        .OnAction = "PrintCard"
        .Caption = "Print..."
        .TooltipText = "Select pages to print"
        .Style = msoButtonCaption
    End With
End Sub
```

Adding Buttons to the Toolbar

When you add a button to the toolbar, you need to specify the macro that should be run as the OnAction property for the button. You can also specify the Caption, a FaceID property to control the icon picture, and ToolTip text. When dealing with a toolbar that displays tiny icons, it is really important to include meaningful ToolTip text.

The .Style property controls whether you see just the caption, just the icon, or the icon and caption. In Figure 24.5, the Print button has a Type property set to msoButtonCaption. The Pictures control displays both the icon and the text by setting the Type property to msoButtonIconAndCaption. The Reports icon has a Type property of msoButtonIcon.

The following code creates a toolbar with the three types of command buttons:

```
Sub CreateToolbar()
    Dim TBar As CommandBar
    Dim NewDD As CommandBarControl
    Dim NewBtn as CommandBarButton

    ' delete any old copy of the toolbar
    DeleteToolbar

    ' Define the toolbar
    Set TBar = CommandBars.Add
    With TBar
        .Name = "XYZ"
        .Visible = True
        .Position = msoBarFloating
    End With

    Set NewBtn = TBar.Controls.Add(Type:=msoControlButton)
    With NewBtn
        .OnAction = "PrintCard"
        .Caption = "Print..."
        .TooltipText = "Select pages to print"
        .Style = msoButtonCaption
```

```
      End With

      Set NewBtn = TBar.Controls.Add(Type:=msoControlButton)
      With NewBtn
          .FaceId = 682
          .OnAction = "DispPictures"
          .Caption = "Pictures"
          .TooltipText = "Display pictures of selected group"
          .Style = msoButtonIconAndCaption
      End With

      Set NewBtn = TBar.Controls.Add(Type:=msoControlButton)
      With NewBtn
          .FaceId = 461
          .OnAction = "ProduceReport"
          .Caption = "Reports"
          .TooltipText = "Produce Reports"
          .Style = msoButtonIcon
      End With

  End Sub
```

Using `FaceID` Codes to Add Icons to the Toolbar

The picture that appears on an icon is controlled by the `FaceID` property. In theory, there are 4,096 possible images that can be added to a toolbar button, although many of these 4,096 are as yet undefined. Selecting the proper `FaceID` is critical to making a friendly toolbar, but it is difficult to randomly find the proper face ID. Several people offer freeware `FaceID` browsers that make this job much easier. One such browser is at

```
http://www.mvps.org/skp/faceid.htm
```

Adding Drop-downs to the Toolbar

In addition to having command buttons on the toolbar, you can have a drop-down control. This example adds a drop-down with the names of all visible worksheets in the workbook. When the client selects a worksheet from the drop-down, the GoToSheet macro navigates to that sheet. This concept can be extended to reporting certain regions or any such activity that involves grouping of objects or items. Add the following code to the existing CreateToolbar macro:

```
  Dim Sh as Worksheet
  Set NewDD = TBar.Controls.Add(Type:=msoControlDropdown)
  With NewDD
      .Caption = "Go To Sheet"
      .OnAction = "GoToSheet"
      .Style = msoButtonAutomatic
      For Each Sh In ActiveWorkbook.Worksheets
          If Sh.Visible = True Then
              .AddItem Sh.Name
          End If
      Next Sh
      .ListIndex = 1
      .Width = 110
  End With
```

```
Sub GoToSheet()
    Dim ThisItem as Integer
    Dim ThisName as String
    With CommandBars("XYZ").Controls("Go To Sheet")
        ThisItem = .ListIndex
        ThisName = .List(.ListIndex)
    End With
    'Activate this sheet
    Worksheets(ThisName).Activate
End Sub
```

Remembering a Toolbar's Position

If you have toolbars that are customized for each worksheet, you will want to delete and create the toolbar in each worksheet's `Worksheet_Activate` event procedure. You will find that as the toolbar is deleted and re-created, the toolbar moves down and to the right. It is very annoying to have the toolbar keep moving.

The nice feature about floating toolbars is that clients can customize where they want them to appear. The solution is to remember the location where the client most recently placed the toolbar before you delete it. You can store this on a hidden worksheet in the file:

```
Public Sub DeleteToolbar()
    Dim obj as CommandBar
    On Error Resume Next
    Set obj = CommandBars("XYZ")
    If Err.Number = 0 Then
    ' Remember the current location
        With ThisWorkbook.Sheets("Settings")
            .[I5].Value = obj.Top
            .[I6].Value = obj.Left
        End With
    End If
    obj.Delete
End Sub

Sub CreateToolbar()
    Dim nTop as Variant
    Dim nLeft as Variant
    Dim Tbar as Commandbar

    DeleteToolbar

    With ThisWorkbook.Sheets("Settings")
        nTop = .[I5].Value
        nLeft = .[I6].Value
    End With

    ' Define the toolbar
    Set TBar = CommandBars.Add
    With TBar
        .Name = "XYZ"
        .Visible = True
        .Position = msoBarFloating
        .Top = nTop
        .Left = nLeft
```

```
        End With
    End Sub
```

Other Ways to Run a Macro

As I mentioned, I think that custom menus and custom toolbars are the best ways to run a macro. However, if you have only a couple of macros to run, there are easier ways to invoke a macro without making the client choose Tools, Macro, Macros from the main menu, select the macro from the Macro dialog, and click the Run button.

Keyboard Shortcut

The easiest way to run a macro is to assign a keyboard shortcut to a macro. From the Macro dialog box (select Tools, Macro, Macros or press Alt+F8), select the macro and click Options. Assign a shortcut key to the macro. Figure 24.6 shows the shortcut Ctrl+j being assigned to the Jump macro. You can now conspicuously post a note on the worksheet reminding the client to hit Ctrl+j to Jump.

Figure 24.6
The simplest way to enable a client to run a macro is to assign a shortcut key to the macro. Ctrl+J now runs the Jump macro.

Attach a Menu to a Command Button

Two types of buttons can be embedded in your sheet. I really prefer the traditional Button shape that can be found on the Forms toolbar instead of the newer ActiveX Command Button.

To use a button, you first need to customize your toolbars to include the Button icon:

1. Right-click any toolbar and select Customize.

2. In the Categories list box on the Commands tab, click on Forms.

3. In the Commands list box, drag the button to an existing toolbar.

4. Click Close to close the Customize dialog.

5. Click on the Button icon in the toolbar.

6. Bring your mouse pointer to the place in the worksheet where you want to insert the button, then click and drag to create the shape of your new button.

7. When you release your left mouse button, the Assign Macro dialog displays. Select a macro to assign to the button and choose OK.

8. Highlight the text on the button and type new meaningful text.

9. To change the color, font, and other aspects of the button's appearance, right-click the button and choose Format Control from the popup menu.

CAUTION

There are two versions of the Format Control dialog box. One version offers seven tabs with settings for Font, Alignment, Size, Protection, Properties, Margins, and Web. The second version offers only one tab with settings for Font.

Which version you see is based on something very subtle. When you right-click the control, the look of the selection border can be either diagonal lines as shown in Figure 24.7 or dots as shown in Figure 24.8. The diagonal-lines selection border tends to appear immediately after editing the text on the button and leads to the Font-only Format Control dialog. The dots selection border leads to the full featured Format Control dialog.

If you right-click and diagonal lines appear as the selection border, you should first left-click the diagonal line selection border to change it to dots. You can then right-click again and choose Format Control.

---

10. To re-assign a new macro to the button, right-click the button and choose Assign Macro from the popup menu.

This method assigned a macro to an object that looks like a button. You can also assign a macro to any drawing object on the worksheet. To assign a macro to an Autoshape, right-click the shape and select Assign Macro, as shown in Figure 24.9.

Figure 24.7
The diagonal-lines selection border leads to a lesser Format Control dialog.

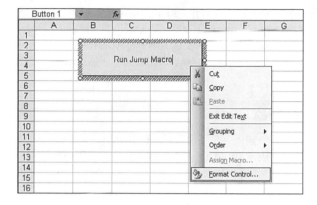

Figure 24.8
The dots selection border leads to the full version of the Format Control dialog.

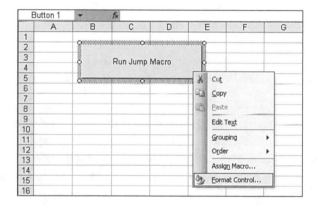

Figure 24.9
Macros can be assigned to any drawing object on the worksheet.

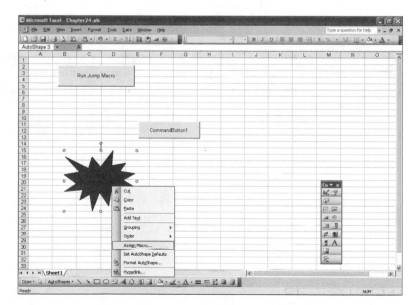

I prefer this method because I can easily add a drawing object with macro code and use the .OnAction property to assign a macro to the object. There is one big drawback to this method. If you assign a macro that exists in another workbook, and the other workbook is saved and closed, Excel changes the .OnAction for the object to be hard-coded to a specific folder.

Attach a Macro to an ActiveX Control

ActiveX Controls are newer and slightly more complicated to set up. Rather than simply assign a macro to the button, you will have a button_click procedure where you can either call another macro or have the macro code actually embedded in the button_click procedure. Follow these steps:

1. From the menu, select View, Toolbars, Control Toolbox.

2. Click the Command Button icon on the Control Toolbox toolbar. Draw a button shape on the worksheet as described in Step 6 for the Forms button.

3. To format the button, click the Properties icon in the toolbox. You can now adjust the button's caption and color in the Properties window, as shown in Figure 24.10.

> **NOTE** There is one annoying aspect of this Properties window. It is huge and covers a large portion of your worksheet. Eventually, if you want to use the worksheet, you are going to have to close this Properties window. When you close the Properties window, it also hides the Properties window in the Visual Basic Editor. You can see that this is missing in Figure 24.11. I would prefer that I could close this Properties window without affecting my VBE editor environment.

4. To assign a macro to the button, click the View Code button on the Control Toolbox (second row, left side). This creates a new procedure on the code pane for the current worksheet. Type the code that you want to have run, or the name of the macro you want to run in this procedure. Figure 24.11 shows the code for the button. This code appears on the code pane for the worksheet.

Figure 24.10
Clicking the Properties icon brings up the Properties window, where you can adjust many aspects of the ActiveX button.

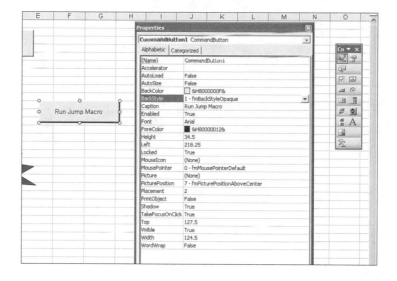

Figure 24.11
Click the View Code button in the Control Toolbox toolbar to open the macro for this button.

CASE STUDY

Case Study: Running a Macro from a Hyperlink

Using a trick, it is possible to run a macro from a hyperlink. Because many clients are used to touching a hyperlink to perform an action, this method may be more intuitive for your clients.

The trick is to set up placeholder hyperlinks that simply link back to themselves. Select a cell and select Insert, Hyperlink from the menu or press Ctrl+K. In the Insert Hyperlink dialog, click on Place In This Document. Figure 24.12 shows a worksheet with four hyperlinks. Each hyperlink points back to its own cell.

When a client clicks on a hyperlink, you can intercept this action and run any macro by using the `FollowHyperlink` event. Enter the following code on the code module for the worksheet:

```
Private Sub Worksheet_FollowHyperlink(ByVal Target As Hyperlink)
    Select Case Target.TextToDisplay
        Case "Widgets"
            RunWidgetReport
        Case "Gadgets"
            RunGadgetReport
        Case "Gizmos"
```

```
                 RunGizmoReport
            Case "Doodads"
                 RunDooDadReport
      End Select
End Sub
```

Figure 24.12

To run a macro from a hyperlink, you have to create placeholder hyperlinks that link back to their cells. Then, using an event handler macro on the worksheet's code pane, you can intercept the hyperlink and run any macro.

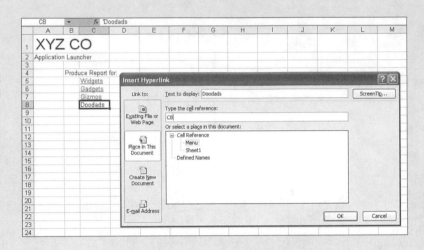

Next Steps

From custom menus and toolbars to simple buttons or hyperlinks, there are plenty of ways to ensure your clients never need to see the Macro dialog box. In Chapter 25, "Add-Ins," you will learn how to package your macros into add-ins that can be easily distributed to others.

Add-Ins

Using VBA, you can create standard add-in files for your clients to use. After the client installs the add-in on his PC, the program will be available to Excel and loads automatically every time he opens Excel.

This chapter discusses standard add-ins. Be aware that there are two other kinds of add-ins. There are COM add-ins and DLL add-ins. Neither of these can be created with VBA. To create these types of add-ins, you need either Visual Basic (such as VB6 or Visual Basic .NET) or Visual C++.

Characteristics of Standard Add-Ins

If you are going to distribute your applications, you may want to package the application as an add-in. Typically saved with an `.xla` extension, the add-in offers several advantages:

- Typically, clients can bypass your `Workbook_Open` code by holding down the shift key while opening the workbook. With an add-in, they cannot bypass the `Workbook_Open` code in this manner.

- After the Add-Ins dialog is used to install an add-in (select Tools, Add-Ins from the main menu in Excel), the add-in will always be loaded and available.

- Even if the macro security level is set to high, programs in an installed add-in can still run.

- Generally, custom functions work only in the workbook in which they are defined. A custom function added to an add-in is available to all open workbooks.

- The add-in does not show up in the list of open files in the Window menu item. The client cannot unhide the workbook by choosing Window, Unhide.

There is one strange rule you need to plan for. The add-in is a hidden workbook. Because the add-in can never be displayed, your code cannot select or activate any cells in the add-in workbook. You are allowed to save data in your add-in file, but you cannot select the file. Also, if you do write data to your add-in file that you wish to be available in the future, your add-in codes need to handle saving the file. Because your clients will not realize that the add-in is there, they will never be reminded or asked to save an unsaved add-in. You might add `ThisWorkbook.Save` to the add-in's `Workbook_BeforeClose` event.

CAUTION

It is possible to save add-in files only in versions starting with Excel 97.

Converting an Excel Workbook to an Add-In

Add-ins are typically managed by the Add-Ins dialog. This dialog presents an add-in name and description. You can control these by entering two particular properties for the file before you convert it to an add-in.

As shown in Figure 25.1, go to File, Properties and select the Summary tab. Fill in a name for the add-in in the Title field and fill in a short description in the Comments field.

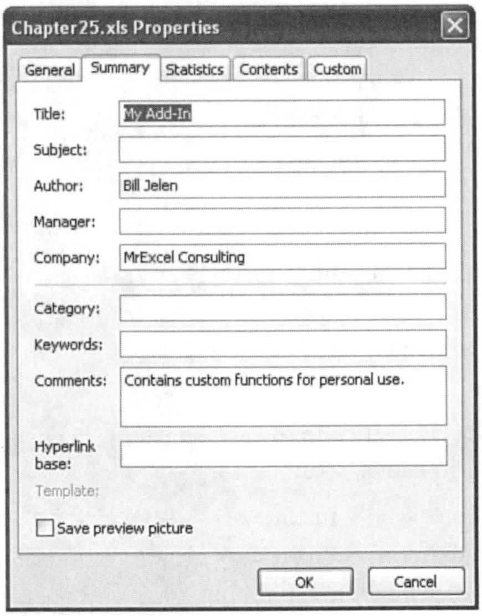

Figure 25.1
Fill in the Title and Comments fields before converting a workbook to an add-in.

There are now two ways to convert the file to an add-in. The first method is easier but has an annoying by-product. The second requires two steps, but gives you some extra control.

Using Save As to Convert a File to an Add-In

Select Save As from the File menu in Excel. In the Save as Type field, scroll all the way to the bottom and select Microsoft Office Excel Add-In (*.xla). As shown in Figure 25.2, the file name changes from `Something.xls` to `Something.xla`. Also note that the save location automatically changes to an AddIns folder. This folder location varies by operating system, but it will be something along the lines of `C:\Documents and Settings\Customer\Application Data\Microsoft\AddIns`. It is also confusing that, after saving the XLS file as an XLA type, the unsaved XLS file remains open. It is not necessary to keep an XLS version of the file, because it is easy to change an XLA back to an XLS for editing.

Figure 25.2
If you are creating an add-in for your own use, the Save As method changes the `IsAddIn` property, changes the name, and automatically saves the file in your AddIns folder.

> ___ CAUTION ___
>
> When using the Save As method to create an add-in, a worksheet must be the active sheet. The Add-In file type is not available if a Chart sheet is the active sheet.

Using the VB Editor to Convert a File to an Add-In

The former method is great if you are creating an add-in for your own use. However, if you are creating an add-in for a client, you probably want to keep the add-in stored in a folder with all the client's application files. It is fairly easy to bypass the Save As method and create an add-in using the Visual Basic Editor.

Open the workbook that you want to convert to an add-in. Switch to the Visual Basic Editor. In the project explorer, double-click on ThisWorkbook. In the Properties window, find the property called `IsAddIn` and change its value to `True`, as shown in Figure 25.3.

25

Figure 25.3
Creating an add-in is as
simple as changing the
IsAddIn property of
ThisWorkbook.

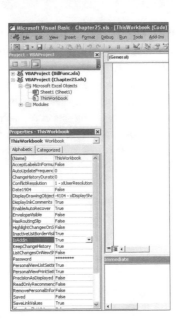

Press Ctrl+G to display the Immediate window. In the Immediate window, save the file,
using an .xla extension:

```
ThisWorkbook.SaveAs FileName:="C:\ClientFiles\Chap25.xla", FileFormat:=xlAddIn
```

You've now successfully created an add-in in the client folder that you can easily find and
email to your client.

Having Your Client Install the Add-In

After you email the add-in to your client, have her save it on her desktop or in another easy-
to-find folder. She should then follow these steps:

1. Open Excel. From the Tools menu, select Add-Ins.

2. In the Add-Ins dialog, click the Browse button (see Figure 25.4).

3. In the Browse dialog, select Desktop. Highlight your add-in and choose OK (see Figure
   25.5).

The add-in is now installed. Excel actually copies the file from the desktop to the proper
location of the AddIns folder. In the Add-Ins dialog, the title of the add-in and comments as
specified in the File Properties dialog are displayed (see Figure 25.6).

Figure 25.4
Your client selects
Browse from the Add-Ins
dialog.

Figure 25.5
Navigate to the desktop
and select your add-in.

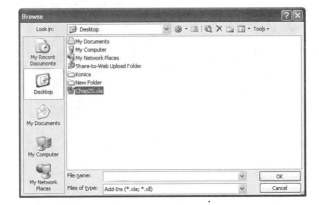

25

Figure 25.6
The add-in is now avail-
able for use.

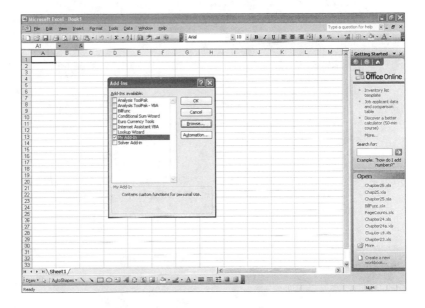

Standard Add-Ins Are Not Secure

Remember that anyone can go to the VBE, select your add-in, and change the `IsAddin` property to `False` to unhide the workbook. You can discourage this process by locking the XLA project for viewing and protecting it in the VBE, but be aware that plenty of vendors sell a password hacking utility for less than $40. To add a password to your add-in, follow these steps:

1. Go to the Visual Basic Editor.
2. From the Tools menu, select VBAProject Properties.
3. Select the Protection tab.
4. Check the Lock Project For Viewing box.
5. Enter the password twice for verification.

Closing Add-Ins

Add-ins can be closed in three ways:

1. Uncheck the add-in from the Add-Ins dialog found in the Tools menu. This closes the add-in for this session and ensures that it does not open during future sessions.
2. Use VBE to close the add-in. In the VBE's immediate pane, type this code to close the add-in:
   ```
   Workbooks("YourAddinName.xla").Close
   ```
3. Close Excel. All add-ins are closed when Excel is closed.

Removing Add-Ins

You may wish to remove an add-in from the list of available add-ins in the Add-In dialog box. There is no effective way to do this within Excel. Follow these steps:

1. Close all running instances of Excel.
2. Use Windows Explorer to locate the file. The file may be located in `C:\Documents and Settings\<user name>\Application Data\Microsoft\AddIns\`.
3. In Windows Explorer, rename the file or move it to a different folder.
4. Open Excel. You get a note warning you that the add-in could not be found. Click OK to dismiss this box.
5. Select Add-Ins from the Tools menu. In the Add-Ins dialog box, uncheck the name of the add-in you want to remove. Excel notifies you that the file cannot be found and asks whether you want to remove it from the list. Choose Yes.

Using a Hidden Workbook as an Alternative to an Add-In

One cool feature of an add-in is that the workbook is hidden. This keeps most novice users from poking around and changing formulas. However, it is possible to hide a workbook without creating an add-in.

It is easy enough to hide a workbook by selecting Hide from the Window menu in Excel. The trick is to then save the workbook as Hidden. Because the file is hidden, the normal File, Save choice does not work. This can be done from the VB Editor window. In the VB Editor, make sure that the workbook is selected in the Project Explorer. Then, in the Immediate window, type

```
ThisWorkbook.Save
```

Case Study: Using a Hidden Code Workbook to Hold All Macros and Forms

Access developers routinely use a second database to hold macros and forms. They place all forms and programs in one database and all data in a separate database. These database files are linked through the Link Tables function in Access.

For large projects in Excel, I recommend the same method. You use a little bit of VBA code in the Data workbook to open the Code workbook.

The advantage to this method is that when it is time to enhance the application, you can mail a new code file without affecting the client's data file.

I once encountered a single-file application rolled out by another developer that the client had sent the file out to 50 sales reps. The reps replicated the application for each of their 10 largest customers. Within a week, there were 500 copies of this file floating around the country. When they discovered a critical flaw in the program, patching 500 files was a nightmare.

We designed a replacement application that used two workbooks. The data workbook ended up with about 20 lines of code. This code was responsible for opening the code workbook and passing control to the code workbook. As the files were being closed, the data workbook would close the code workbook.

There were many advantages to this method. First, the customer data files were kept to a very small size. Each sales rep now has one workbook with program code and 10 or more data files for each customer. As enhancements are completed, we distribute new program code workbooks. The sales rep opens his or her existing customer data workbook, which automatically grabs the new code workbook.

Because the previous developer had been stuck with the job of trying to patch 500 workbooks, we were extremely careful to have as few lines of code in the customer workbook as possible. There are maybe 10 lines of code, and they were tested extremely thoroughly before being sent out. By contrast, the code workbook contains 3,000+ lines of code. So, if something goes wrong, I have a 99% chance that the bad code will be in the easy-to-replace code workbook.

25

In the customer data workbook, the `Workbook_Open` procedure has this code:

```
Private Sub Workbook_Open()
    On Error Resume Next
    X = Workbooks("Code.xls").Name
    If Not Err = 0 then
        On Error Goto 0
        Workbooks.Open Filename:= _
            ThisWorkbook.Path & Application.PathSeparator & "Code.xls"
    End If
    On Error Goto 0
    Application.Run "Code.xls!CustFileOpen"
End Sub
```

The `CustFileOpen` procedure in the code workbook handles adding a custom menu for the application. It also calls a macro named DeliverUpdates. If we ever have to change the 500 customer data files, the DeliverUpdates will handle this via code.

This dual-workbook solution works very well and allows updates to be seamlessly delivered to the client without touching any of the 500 customer files.

Next Steps

Chapter 26, "Case Study—Designing an Excel Application," is a bonus case study by Microsoft MVP Tushar Mehta. Tushar demonstrates the thought process required to code a fairly complex simulation.

Case Study: Designing an Excel Application

To conclude the book, we will turn the floor over to Excel consultant Tushar Mehta. Tushar has provided a case study in designing an Excel application from the ground up. His study involves numerous event handlers that present challenges when testing. Tushar discusses the design considerations as he walks through this case study.

About Tushar Mehta

Tushar Mehta, MPPM, Ph.D., an independent consultant based in Rochester, NY, specializes in developing solid business solutions that weave together technology, organizational architecture, marketing, and operations. The financial and economic impact of these solutions is measurable along the dimensions of increased productivity, efficient marketing, revenue growth, lower operating costs, and improved value for the client's customers.

Tushar has received the Most Valuable Professional (MVP) award from the Microsoft Corporation every year since 2000. This makes him one of about 65 people worldwide so recognized for the Excel software. Some of his productivity-enhancing products are available from www.tushar-mehta.com.

In addition to a doctorate in business administration from the University of Rochester, Tushar has a masters in management (MPPM) from the Yale University School of Organization and Management, and a bachelor of technology (B.Tech.) degree in electrical engineering, with a special emphasis on computer science from the Indian Institute of Technology in Bombay, India.

Using Excel for More Than Number Crunching

In this case study, Excel serves as the platform to document the customized configuration of an electrical control system that consists of up to 6,000 contact points. Each contact point can be connected to one other point by a wire. Although it is unlikely that all 6,000 points will be used at any given time, the solution must cater to the possibility.

Further, the method used to identify these contact points is industry specific. The points are labeled by a combination of two numbers separated by a slash, as in *m/nnn*, where *m* goes from 1 to 10 horizontally, and *nnn* goes from 101 to 700 vertically.

Each of the 6,000 contact points is represented by one Excel cell. When one contact point is connected to another, the respective cells contain the identifier of the *other* contact.

Of course, if the intended connection uses a point that is already in use, the connection cannot be allowed. Finally, in addition to making connections, there is also a need to undo connections and to change them. Clearly, to maintain this system by hand, whether in Excel or in some other format, would be a laborious and extremely error-prone task.

To create this you will have to

- Map application (that is, client) terminology to/from Excel terminology.
- Create the initial visual effects.
- Design the functional procedures needed for the desired application capability.
- Develop VBA event procedures to implement the functional procedures.

The immediate question that comes to mind is whether it is possible to automate this system, and if so, how. Would it be possible to simply write in the cell corresponding to some contact point A the code corresponding to contact point B, and have Excel automatically update the cell corresponding to contact point B with the location of contact point A? And, of course, the system should disallow the connection if contact point B is already in use.

To undo an existing connection, the user would simply delete the entry in one of the cells associated with that connection. For example, to remove the link established between 1/101 and 10/700, the user would simply delete the contents of the cell corresponding to one of the contacts, 1/101 or 10/700. The system would restore the original "unconnected" values and formats to both those cells.

Changing a connection would require a two-step process. In the first, the system must delete the existing connection and in the second step, establish a new one.

The Solution

The grid corresponding to the electrical contacts contains 100 elements left to right and 60 elements going down. Because Excel supports 256 columns and 65,536 rows, both those requirements are well within Excel's capabilities.

The idea is to create the grid by entering the *m/nnn* numbering scheme in cells starting with cell A1. An unused connection is visually identified by a light gray font, as shown in Figure 26.1.

Figure 26.1
Unused connections are identified by a light gray font.

	A	B	C	D	E	F
1	1/101	1/102	1/103	1/104	1/105	1/106
2	1/111	1/112	1/113	1/114	1/115	1/116
3	1/121	1/122	1/123	1/124	1/125	1/126
4	1/131	1/132	1/133	1/134	1/135	1/136
5	1/141	1/142	1/143	1/144	1/145	1/146
6	1/151	1/152	1/153	1/154	1/155	1/156
7	1/161	1/162	1/163	1/164	1/165	1/166
8	1/171	1/172	1/173	1/174	1/175	1/176
9	1/181	1/182	1/183	1/184	1/185	1/186

As connections are entered, the old state of the cell and the new value is tracked. If the old state indicates "no connection" (light gray), then the new connection needs to be validated. If it is accepted, the contents of both that cell and the complementary cell (the other end of the connection) are updated and the font color changed to, say, blue. Figure 26.2 shows the result of connecting point 1/101 to point 1/175.

Figure 26.2
Connecting 1/101 to 1/175 changes the font color of the connections.

	A	B	C	D	E	F
1	1/175	1/102	1/103	1/104	1/105	1/106
2	1/111	1/112	1/113	1/114	1/115	1/116
3	1/121	1/122	1/123	1/124	1/125	1/126
4	1/131	1/132	1/133	1/134	1/135	1/136
5	1/141	1/142	1/143	1/144	1/145	1/146
6	1/151	1/152	1/153	1/154	1/155	1/156
7	1/161	1/162	1/163	1/164	1/165	1/166
8	1/171	1/172	1/173	1/174	1/101	1/176
9	1/181	1/182	1/183	1/184	1/185	1/186

Any software solution must make editing existing connections just as easy. It should be possible to delete a connection with the same ease with which one deletes the content of any cell in Excel, that is, with the Delete or the Backspace key. Similarly, changing a connection to point somewhere else should be just as easy as entering the *m/nnn* ID of the new point in a cell. The software should delete the existing connection and make the new connection— assuming it meets the conditions for a legitimate connection.

The solution does not attempt to block the user from intentionally damaging the wiring grid. For example, if the user copies a range of cells in some other worksheet and pastes that range into the wiring grid, the result is a corrupt system. Similarly, if the user selects a single cell, then right-clicks and selects Delete, the result is a corrupt system. The implementation of a system that protects the user from herself or himself is beyond the scope of this case study.

Implementing the Solution in Excel and VBA

One aspect of this case study to keep in mind is that the solution requires extensive use of event procedures. The more event procedures, the more difficult it is to test the code. In this case, it is probably easier to take the time to write correct code than to try and correct bad code through testing!

Adopting a structured approach involves approaching the solution in two parallel and related tracks. On the one hand, you flesh out the code in a top-down fashion. This is done in such a fashion that at any step, the code at that point can be used for prototyping purposes. Concurrent to this top-down development, add key components that act as "bridges" between application-specific and Excel-specific components and terminology. As you complete these components, they become support functions that mesh perfectly with the overall code being developed top-down.

With each "pass" through the code, flesh out the code some more, until you get to a fully functional system.

Pass 1—Top-Down Concepts

Before going too far, you need to decide the level at which to locate the event procedures that you will need. Whatever event procedures you choose to develop, it is likely that they could be at the worksheet level, the workbook level, or the application level. Use workbook procedures because they add the flexibility of maintaining multiple diagrams, one in each worksheet of the workbook, and are slightly easier to implement than application-level events. The major downside, of course, is that the code and the data will reside in the same workbook. Of course, now that the event procedures will be at the workbook level, they will be triggered for every worksheet in the workbook, whether that sheet contains a wiring diagram or not. Hence, you need to ensure that the event procedures operate on only those worksheets that contain a wiring diagram, and leave untouched any worksheets used for other purposes. So, you need to somehow *tag* each worksheet that contains a wiring diagram.

It would appear that you need just one event procedure, `Workbook_SheetChange`, which goes into the Workbook's code module:

```
Private Sub Workbook_SheetChange( _
      ByVal sh As Object, ByVal Target As Range)
    If Not TypeOf sh Is Worksheet Then Exit Sub
    If Not (sh.Range(cWSWiringTagAddr).Value = cWSWiringTagID) Then _
      Exit Sub                    '<<<<<
End Sub
```

Note that as of now, you haven't figured out how the change in a cell will translate into an action, and if so, whether it is adding a new connection, deleting an existing connection, or changing an existing connection. However, there's no need to address this quite yet. You'll do it later.

The major non-event procedure seems to be just the one that will create the initial setup. This requires filling in all the wiring codes in the *m/nnn* format in the correct locations and setting the font color to light gray. This procedure should also warn the client if the worksheet is not empty. Finally, it should add the tag to identify this worksheet as containing a wiring diagram. The following code goes into a standard module:

```
Sub createWiringData(aWS As Worksheet)
End Sub

Sub addWiringWSTag(aWS As Worksheet)
End Sub

Sub initializeSystem()
    If Not TypeOf ActiveSheet Is Worksheet Then
        MsgBox "The active sheet must be a worksheet"
        Exit Sub                         '<<<<<
    End If
    If Not (ActiveSheet.UsedRange.Address = "$A$1" And _
        IsEmpty(Range("a1"))) Then
        If MsgBox("This worksheet contains data.  " _
                & "OK to delete existing content", vbOKCancel) _
                = vbCancel Then _
            Exit Sub                      '<<<<<
    End If
    createWiringData ActiveSheet
    addWiringWSTag ActiveSheet
End Sub
```

Once again, you haven't figured out what goes into each of the procedures createWiringData and addWiringWSTag. The time to do that is later.

Pass 1—Key Components Defined

Clearly, an important support capability is the translation between the industry-specific *m/nnn* codes and the address of the associated Excel cell. An Excel cell is identified by two values, the row and the column. For that, you need a User Defined Type, or UDT. Next, because you plan to start with cell A1 containing 1/101, you can write the two translation functions and put them in the standard module used for the initializeSystem code in the previous section:

```
Public Type ExcelCoords
    Row As Long
    Col As Long
    End Type

Function XLtoWiringCoords(aRow As Long, aCol As Long)
    XLtoWiringCoords = CStr((aCol - 1) \ 10 + 1) & "/" _
        & CStr(100 + (aRow - 1) * 10 + (aCol - 1) Mod 10 + 1)
End Function

Function WiringToExcelCoords(WiringCode As String) As ExcelCoords
    Dim FirstPart As Long, SecondPart As Long, SlashLoc As Long
    SlashLoc = InStr(1, WiringCode, "/")
    If SlashLoc = 0 Then Exit Function
    On Error Resume Next
    FirstPart = CLng(Left(WiringCode, SlashLoc - 1))
    SecondPart = CLng(Right(WiringCode, Len(WiringCode) - SlashLoc))
    On Error GoTo 0
    If FirstPart < 1 Or FirstPart > 10 Then Exit Function   '<<<<<
    If SecondPart < 101 Or SecondPart > 700 Then Exit Function  '<<<<<
    WiringToExcelCoords.Row = (SecondPart - 101) \ 10 + 1
```

26

```
        WiringToExcelCoords.Col = (FirstPart - 1) * 10 + _
            (SecondPart - 101) Mod 10 + 1
    End Function
```

Finally, you need some global constants. The color choices of light gray (unused wiring contact) and blue (in-use contact) correspond to the index values 15 and 5, respectively, in Excel's default color palette. And the way to tag a worksheet as containing a wiring diagram is to add a specific constant to a specific cell in the worksheet. These constants are declared `Public` because they will be used in multiple modules. The following code goes at the top of the same standard module used for the previous example:

```
Public Const _
    cUnusedColorIdx As Integer = 15, cInUseColorIdx As Integer = 5, _
    cWSWiringTagID As String = "TM Wiring", _
    cWSWiringTagAddr As String = "A61"
```

This concludes the first pass at building the code for the system. The code not only compiles but will even execute. It doesn't do much, but some of the safety checks in the event procedure can be tested.

Pass 2—Top-Down Code

The skeleton code of pass 1 needs to be fleshed out. The easiest routine to complete is the `addWiringWSTag`:

```
Sub addWiringWSTag(aWS As Worksheet)
    Application.EnableEvents = False
    On Error GoTo ErrHandler
    aWS.Range(cWSWiringTagAddr).Value = cWSWiringTagID
    Application.EnableEvents = True
    Exit Sub
ErrHandler:
    MsgBox "Unexpected error in addWiringWSTag:" & vbNewLine _
        & "Error=" & Err.Description & " (" & Err.Number & ")"
    Application.EnableEvents = True
End Sub
```

Next, address `createWiringData`. This creates the grid of *m/nnn* values ranging from 1/101 in A1 to 10/700 in CV60. These consist of 10 blocks of values m/101 to m/700 (m=1,2,..,10) with each block containing 60 rows by 10 columns. This is basically how the code creates the grid. It creates one block of *nnn* values, duplicates it 9 times (for a total of 10 blocks), and then adds the correct *m/* part to each block:

```
Sub createWiringData(aWS As Worksheet)
    Dim Dest As Range, i As Long
    'This creates the block of m/nnn values ranging from _
     1/101 in A1 to 10/700 in CV60.  These consist of 10 _
     blocks of values m/101 to m/700 (m=1,2,..,10) with each _
     block containing 60 rows by 10 columns.  This is basically _
     how the code creates the grid.  It creates one block of _
     nnn values, duplicates it 9 times (for a total of 10 blocks), _
     and then adds the correct m/ part to each block.  While _
     creating the nnn blocks, the cells must be formatted to _
     recognize numbers, whereasile for the latter phase, the cells must _
```

```
            be formatted as text, otherwise m/nnn will be interepreted as _
            a division of the number m by the number nnn — and that is not _
            what is intended

        Application.EnableEvents = False
        On Error GoTo ErrHandler
        resetFormatting aWS
        createOneDataBlock aWS
        cloneDataBlocks aWS
        addMSlash aWS
        Application.EnableEvents = True
        Exit Sub
ErrHandler:
    MsgBox "Unexpected error in createWiringData:" & vbNewLine _
        & "Error=" & Err.Description & " (" & Err.Number & ")"
    Application.EnableEvents = True
End Sub
```

The one procedure from pass 1 that remains is the Workbook_SheetChange procedure. Excel calls this procedure whenever a cell value changes. If the value is different from the old value, you need to decide whether this is a new connection, a deletion of an existing connection, or a change to an existing connection.

To detect a new connection, you rely on the cell format. If it is that of an unused contact, you know this change establishes a new connection.

To detect a deletion, you rely on the cell being empty (the user has used either the Delete or Backspace key).

Anything else is a change in an existing connection.

Also, remember that if the client's action violates a wiring rule, you need to warn the client and restore the previous value.

Obviously, you need to store the previous value somewhere. The Workbook_SheetSelectionChange procedure provides the perfect method. Excel runs that code whenever the user selects a cell. In it you can save the value of the cell.

Pass 2—Key Components

Acknowledging the need to store the old value in a cell, the client is about to update leads to the addition of the Workbook_SheetSelectionChange procedure to the Workbook code module. Of course, it is possible for the client to select multiple cells at one time. From the perspective of the application, the only time it might make sense is when the user wants to delete multiple connections. Although it might be a useful capability to have, you will leave it out of this version of the software. You therefore need to ensure that the user is not allowed to select multiple cells at the same time. The code for both the Workbook_SheetChange and the Workbook_SheetSelectionChange procedures follows this paragraph. It also contains the skeleton code to add and delete a connection (addAConnection and deleteAConnection, respectively), as well as the complete code for changing a connection (changeAConnection). The last one turns out to be easy because all it

does is validate the change, protects the new value entered by the user, calls
`deleteAConnection`, restores the protected new value, and calls `addAConnection`! Remember
that all the following code goes into the `ThisWorkbook` code module:

```
Dim OldVal As String

Function addAConnection(Sh As Worksheet, Target As Range)
End Function

Sub deleteAConnection(Sh As Worksheet, Target As Range, OldVal As String)
End Sub

Sub changeAConnection(Sh As Worksheet, Target As Range, OldVal As String)
    Dim Conn2 As ExcelCoords
    Dim SavedVal As String
    Conn2 = WiringToExcelCoords(Target.Value)
    If Conn2.Row = 0 Then
        MsgBox Target.Value & " is not an acceptable value"
        Application.EnableEvents = False
        Target.Value = OldVal
        Application.EnableEvents = True
        Exit Sub      '<<<<<
    End If
    SavedVal = Target.Value
    deleteAConnection Sh, Target, OldVal
    Application.EnableEvents = False
    Target.Value = SavedVal
    Application.EnableEvents = True
    addAConnection Sh, Target
End Sub


Private Sub Workbook_SheetChange( _
        ByVal Sh As Object, ByVal Target As Range)
    If Not TypeOf Sh Is Worksheet Then Exit Sub
    If Not (Sh.Range(cWSWiringTagAddr).Value = cWSWiringTagID) Then _
        Exit Sub                    '<<<<<
    If Target.Cells.Count > 1 Then
        MsgBox "Version 1 of the software doesn't support" & vbNewLine _
            & "concurrent changes to multiple connections" & vbNewLine _
            & "This change should not have happened." & vbNewLine _
            & "The worksheet is probably corrupt!  " & vbNewLine _
            & "No automatic (complementary) changes have been made"
        Exit Sub
    End If
    If OldVal = Target.Value Then Exit Sub  '<<<<<
    If Target.Font.ColorIndex = cUnusedColorIdx Then
        addAConnection Sh, Target
    ElseIf IsEmpty(Target) Then
        deleteAConnection Sh, Target, OldVal
    Else
        changeAConnection Sh, Target, OldVal
    End If
End Sub


Private Sub Workbook_SheetSelectionChange( _
    ByVal Sh As Object, ByVal Target As Range)
    If Not TypeOf Sh Is Worksheet Then Exit Sub
```

```
        If Not (Sh.Range(cWSWiringTagAddr).Value = cWSWiringTagID) Then _
            Exit Sub                    '<<<<<
        If Target.Cells.Count > 1 Then
            MsgBox "Version 1 of the software doesn't support" & vbNewLine _
                & "concurrent changes to multiple connections" & vbNewLine _
                & "Please select only one cell at a time"
            Target.Cells(1).Select   'forces an intentional recursive call!
            Exit Sub
        End If
        OldVal = Target.Value
    End Sub
```

Pass 3—Top-Down Code Completed

You are almost finished. All that's left to do is fill in the gaps in the procedures associated with the creation of the initial system, and complete the two procedures `addAConnection` and `deleteAConnection`.

Each of the remaining four procedures associated with initializing the system is pretty straightforward:

- `resetFormatting` simply clears all the cells in the worksheet, sets the number format to General, and sets the color index to light gray (strictly speaking, to the constant used to indicate an unused cell).

```
Sub resetFormatting(aWS As Worksheet)
    With aWS.Cells
        .ClearContents
        .NumberFormat = "General"
        .Font.ColorIndex = cUnusedColorIdx
    End With
End Sub
```

- `createOneDataBlock` uses the equivalent of the GUI command Edit, File, Series to create one block 60 rows by 10 columns filled with *nnn* values from 101 to 700. The first data series creates a single row containing the values 101 to 110. The second fills 60 rows with the appropriate numbers.

```
Sub createOneDataBlock(aWS As Worksheet)
    With aWS.Range("A1")
        .FormulaR1C1 = "101"
        .DataSeries Rowcol:=xlRows, Type:=xlLinear, _
            Date:=xlDay, _
            Step:=1, Stop:=110, Trend:=False
        .Resize(1, 10).DataSeries Rowcol:=xlColumns, _
            Type:=xlLinear, Date:=xlDay, _
            Step:=10, Stop:=700, Trend:=False
    End With
End Sub
```

- `cloneDataBlocks` identifies the starting locations of each of the nine remaining blocks and then copies the first block in one step. The result consists of 10 blocks of the *nnn* numbers in a single range 60 rows by 100 columns.

```
Sub cloneDataBlocks(aWS As Worksheet)
    Dim Dest As Range, i As Integer
```

26

```
      With aWS.Range("A1")
          Set Dest = .Offset(, 10)
          For i = 2 To 9
              Set Dest = Union(Dest, .Offset(, i * 10))
          Next i
          .CurrentRegion.Copy Dest
      End With
  End Sub
```

- Finally, addMSlash uses a single Excel formula entered into a range 60 rows by 100 columns located below the existing data. The formula maps the *nnn* values already present to the corresponding *m/nnn* results. Then the procedure replaces the existing *nnn* values with the result in this new range. Finally, it deletes the range with the now unneeded formulas.

```
Sub addMSlash(aWS As Worksheet)
    With aWS.Range("A1").Offset(60, 0).Resize(60, 100)
        .FormulaR1C1 = _
            "=TRUNC((COLUMN()-1)/10,0)+1 &""/""&R[-60]C"
        aWS.Cells.NumberFormat = "@"
        .Copy
        aWS.Range("a1").PasteSpecial xlPasteValues
        .EntireRow.Delete
    End With
End Sub
```

The last two procedures are addAConnection and deleteAConnection. addAConnection first checks that the other end of the connection is acceptable and then ensures that that contact is available. If no error is found, both ends of the connection are updated with the other's ID. Note that in the case of an error, the cell contents are returned to the previous value through the resetValue procedure. This makes it easy to reset a cell to its unused state without respect to where it happens.

```
Function addAConnection(Sh As Worksheet, Target As Range)
    Dim Conn2 As ExcelCoords
    Conn2 = WiringToExcelCoords(Target.Value)
    If Conn2.Row = 0 Then
        MsgBox Target.Value & " is not an acceptable value"
        addAConnection = True
        resetValue Target
        Exit Function    '<<<<<
        End If
    With Sh.Cells(Conn2.Row, Conn2.Col)
    If .Font.ColorIndex <> cUnusedColorIdx Then
        MsgBox Target.Value & " is already in use!" & vbNewLine _
            & "It is connected to " & Cells(Conn2.Row, Conn2.Col).Value
        resetValue Target
        addAConnection = True
        Exit Function '<<<<<
        End If
    Application.EnableEvents = False
    On Error GoTo ErrHandler
    .Value = XLtoWiringCoords(Target.Row, Target.Column)
    .Font.ColorIndex = cInUseColorIdx
        End With
```

```
        Target.Font.ColorIndex = cInUseColorIdx
        Application.EnableEvents = True
        Exit Function
ErrHandler:
    MsgBox "Unexpected error in addAConnection: Target=" & _
        Target.Address & vbNewLine _
        & "Error=" & Err.Description & " (" & Err.Number & ")"
    Application.EnableEvents = True
End Function
```

Finally, in `deleteAConnection` each of the cells involved in the connection is reset to the unused state through the use of the `resetValue` procedure.

```
Sub deleteAConnection(Sh As Worksheet, Target As Range, OldVal As String)
    Dim Conn2 As ExcelCoords
    Conn2 = WiringToExcelCoords(OldVal)
    Application.EnableEvents = False
    On Error GoTo ErrHandler
    With Conn2
    resetValue Sh.Cells(.Row, .Col)
        End With
    resetValue Target
    Application.EnableEvents = True
    Exit Sub
ErrHandler:
    MsgBox "Unexpected error in deleteAConnection: Target=" & _
        Target.Address & vbNewLine _
        & "Error=" & Err.Description & " (" & Err.Number & ")"
    Application.EnableEvents = True
End Sub
```

Pass 3—Key Components Completed

There is the one final support function to code: the one used by `addAConnection` and `deleteAConnection` to reset a cell to an unused state: `resetValue` restores the default wiring code and the color index for a given cell.

```
Sub resetValue(Target As Range)
    Application.EnableEvents = False
    On Error GoTo ErrHandler
    With Target
        .Value = XLtoWiringCoords(.Row, .Column)
        .Font.ColorIndex = cUnusedColorIdx
    End With
    Application.EnableEvents = True
    Exit Sub
ErrHandler:
    MsgBox "Unexpected error in resetValue: Target=" _
        & Target.Address & vbNewLine _
        & "Error=" & Err.Description & " (" & Err.Number & ")"
    Application.EnableEvents = True
End Sub
```

26

Summary

This case study stepped through the development of a software module to address a real problem. It demonstrated the use of structured analysis coupled with the parallel development of support routines to build a solution that is easy to prototype at any stage of its development life. Its code was broken up into functional routines, each of which performed just one task. Comments provided a description of the intent when a particular routine used a methodology that was somewhat off the beaten path.

Next Steps

If as authors we've done our job correctly, you now have the tools you need to design your own VBA applications in Excel. You understand the shortcomings of the macro recorder, yet know how to use it as an aid in learning how to do something. You know how to use Excel's power tools in VBA to produce workhorse routines that can save you hours of time per week. You've also learned how to have your application interact with others so that you can create applications to be used by others in your organization or other organizations.

If you have found any sections of the book that you thought were confusing or could have been spelled out better, we welcome your comments and they will be given consideration as we prepare the second edition of this book. Write to us—bill@MrExcel.com and Tracy@MrExcel.com.

Whether your goal was to automate some of your own tasks or to become a paid Excel consultant, we hope that we've helped you on your way. Both are rewarding goals. With 400 million potential customers, we find that being Excel consultants is a friendly business. If you are interested in joining our ranks, this book is your training manual. Master the topics and you will be qualified to join the team of Excel consultants.

INDEX

AppEvent_SheetFollow
Hyperlink(), 164
AppEvent_Window
Activate(), 164
AppEvent_Window
Deactivate(), 165
AppEvent_WindowResize(),
165
AppEvent_Workbook
Activate(), 165
AppEvent_WorkbookAddin
Install(), 165
AppEvent_WorkbookAddIn
Uninstall(), 165
AppEvent_Workbook
BeforeClose(), 165
AppEvent_Workbook
BeforePrint(), 166
AppEvent_WorkbookNew
Sheet(), 166
AppEvent_Workbook
Open(), 166
trapping, 422-424

**ApplySpecialFormattingAll
function, 133**

area charts, 202

Areas collection, 74

array formulas, 135

arrays
advantages of, 389-390
array formulas, 135
declaring, 385-386
defined, 385
dynamic arrays, 391
emptying, 388-389
filling, 386-388
multidimensional arrays,
386
names, 142
one-dimensional arrays, 386
passing, 392
transposing, 390

Assign Macro dialog box, 18

assigning
keyboard shortcuts, 497
macros
to form controls, 17-18
to toolbar buttons, 16-17

AssignMacro() function, 330

audio, 468

**Auto List members option
(charts), 188-189**

**AutoFilterCustom()
function, 240**

**AutoFilters, 239-240,
298-299**

automatic subtotals, 260

automation. *See also* **charts;
pivot tables; Web queries**
Advanced Filter, 213-214
case study, 236-239
criteria ranges, 221-224
Filter In Place option,
231-232
formula-based
conditions, 225-230
no matching records,
handling, 230
unique list of values,
extracting, 214-221
xlFilterCopy, 232-235
AutoFilters, 239-240,
298-299
case, changing, 328-329
cells
highlighting, 314-315
non-contiguous cells,
selecting/deselecting,
317-319
progress indicator,
325-326
selecting with
SpecialCells, 330-331
conditional formatting
AutoFilter with more
than two conditions,
298-299
cell highlighting, 314

conditional formatting
with more than three
conditions, 297-298
custom data transposition,
316-317
custom delete event,
329-330
custom sort order, 324-325
cut/copy/paste, disabling,
322-324
files
closing and deleting,
301-303
CSV files, importing,
303-304
CSV files, reading and
parsing, 304-305
exporting to Word,
308-309
listing, 299-301
formula bar, hiding, 332
page setup, 319-321
protected password box,
326-328
rows, deleting with
conditions, 331-332
time to execute code,
calculating, 321-322
Word automation
bookmarks, 377-379
compile errors, 367
Document objects,
371-372
early binding, 365-367
filtered reports, 379-382
late binding, 368
object creation, 369-370
object model, 370-371
object references,
369-370
Range objects, 374-376
Selection objects, 373
workbooks
combining, 306-307
deleting after specific
date, 301
separating worksheets
into, 305-306

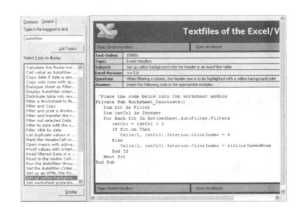